Readings in Juvenile Delinquency and Juvenile Justice

Readings in Juvenile Delinquency and Juvenile Justice

Edited by

Thomas C. Calhoun
Southern Illinois University, Carbondale

Constance L. Chapple
University of Nebraska, Lincoln

Prentice
Hall

Upper Saddle River, New Jersey 07458

Library of Congress Cataloging-in-Publication Data

Readings in juvenile delinquency and juvenile justice/Thomas C. Calhoun, Constance L. Chapple.
    p. cm.
Includes bibliographical references.
ISBN 0-13-028171-9
1. Juvenile delinquent—United States. 2. Juvenile delinquency—Research—United States.
3. Juvenile justice, Administration of—United States I. Calhoun, Thomas C.
II. Chapple, Constance L.

HV9104. R35 2003
364.36 0973—dc21   2002192682

Publisher: Nancy Roberts
Senior Acquisitions Editor: Chris DeJohn
Editorial Assistant: Veronica D'Amico
Production Liaison: Joanne Hakim
Project Manager: Marty Sopher/Lithokraft II
Prepress and Manufacturing Buyer: Mary Ann Gloriande
Cover Art Director: Jayne Conte
Cover Designer: Bruce Kenselaar
Senior Marketing Manager: Amy Speckman
Marketing Assistant: Adam Laitman

This book was set in 10/12 Palatino by Lithokraft II
and was printed and bound by Hamilton Printing Company.
The cover was printed by Coral Graphics.

© 2003 by Pearson Education, Inc.
Upper Saddle River, New Jersey 07458

Printed in the United States of America

10 9 8 7 6 5 4 3 2 1

ISBN: 0-13-028171-9

Pearson Education Ltd., *London*
Pearson Education Australia, PTY. Limited, *Sydney*
Pearson Education Singapore, Pte. Ltd
Pearson Education North Asia Ltd, *Hong Kong*
Pearson Education Canada, Ltd., *Toronto*
Pearson Educación de Mexico, S.A. de C.V.
Pearson Education—Japan, *Tokyo*
Pearson Education Malaysia, Pte. Ltd
Pearson Education, *Upper Saddle River, New Jersey*

Dedication

We are indebted to several people who assisted us in completing this project. First, this project could not have been completed without the support of our families, who listened to our gripes and frustrations thoughout the entire process. To them we are extremely thankful. Additionally, we are grateful to the individuals who contributed essays and articles that comprise this work, for without their scholarly productivity the finished product would not be of the caliber that we sought.

Contents

Chapter 3
Methods

Chapter 4
Family

Chapter 5
Schools, Media, and Crime

Chapter 6
Drugs and Delinquency

Chapter 9
Policy and Crime

Preface

We are extremely excited about having written this book and we hope that you will enjoy reading it as much as we did in developing it. The study of juvenile delinquency is one of the most invigorating areas within sociology. All of us can remember times when we were younger and some of the things we did but really didn't know exactly why we did them. One of the many things that you will learn as you read and study this book is how to place your prior behavior in sociological context. In other words, you will learn about social, cultural, and environmental factors that influence our behavior in one fashion or another. Our experience with previous readers similar to this one is that they often are not exciting and fail to stimulate interesting discussions. We have put together a set of readings that are both exciting and challenging.

In *Readings in Juvenile Delinquency and Juvenile Justice* we assembled articles that we believe cover broadly some of the most important aspects of the subject under discussion. An introduction to each chapter is presented because it is our belief that students prefer having an overview of what is to follow prior to their reading of the article. These introductory comments provide a thumb nail view of the main focus of the article.

This collection includes classic and contemporary articles, as well as articles written specifically for this reader. In all cases we have included the entire article so that you, the reader, can see exactly what was studied, why it was studied, and what the findings mean. We have included such classic pieces as Anthony Platt's "The Rise of the Child-Saving Movement" and Travis Hirschi's "Attachment to Parents." The contemporary articles include such pieces as Whitbeck et al's "Families of Homeless and Runaway Adolescents: A Comparison of Parent/Caretaker and Adolescent Perspective on Parenting, Family Violence and Adolescent Conduct" and Thompson et al's "Representing Gangs in the News: Media Constructions of Criminal Gangs." Finally, we have included pieces that were written specifically for this reader and do not appear anywhere else in print such as Connie Freng's "Chicago Women's Contribution to Delinquency" and Trina Hope's "Do Families Matter?: The Relative Effects of Family Characteristics, Self-Control, and Delinquency on Gang Membership." By including classical, contemporary, and original works we hope that the study of delinquency will be both exciting and challenging to a wide range of undergraduate and graduate students.

The articles we selected use a variety of theoretical perspectives. We believe the study of delinquency, due to its complexity, defies the use of one single theoretical frame but encompasses multiple explanations. In this vein it is also important to recognize that we have not devoted individual sections to specific theories as is done in other anthologies on this subject. Rather, we included articles that provide students with different theoretical frameworks. This approach gives the instructor the opportunity to expand on the theoretical perspectives included in the article as well as the opportunity to offer alternative explanations. This integrated approach is exciting and will provide for lively classroom discussion.

Our sincere appreciation goes to our colleagues whose works appear in this anthology but particularly to those who contributed original manuscripts. There is an abundance of materials that could have been included but we chose these because we felt they best represent the diversity and complexity of issues surrounding the study of delinquency and juvenile justice. Finally we would like to thank Addrain Conyers for locating some of the articles included here and his meticulous attention to the nuts and bolts associated with publishing a reader. A special thank you also goes to John Boulahanis who assisted with the introductions to each chapter. Lastly, this project could not have been completed without the assistance of Chris DeJohn and others at Prentice-Hall.

Thomas C. Calhoun
Constance L. Chapple

Readings in Juvenile Delinquency and Juvenile Justice

Chapter 1

Problem Areas
in Delinquency

INTRODUCTION

Although empirical evidence clearly indicates that juvenile crime has recently declined, the popular perception shared by the public and criminal justice policy makers alike is that juvenile crime is "out of control." This perception has led to a "get tough" approach in dealing with violent youth. Juvenile curfew mandates against youth are popular strategies in dealing with juvenile crime. Hemmens and Bennett examine the constitutionality of juvenile curfews by focusing on decisions rendered in lower courts. In analyzing various recent court rulings, Hemmens and Bennett conclude that courts are split on whether or not juvenile curfews are constitutional. Although the Supreme Court has ruled that "children are different" and the "law must somehow reflect this," it has yet to provide any type of framework for states to follow. Until the Supreme Court provides a clear framework, confusion will reign in the lower courts.

Research on gang activity has a long and storied past from Thrasher's analysis of gangs in Chicago in the twenties to Cloward and Ohlin's theoretical analysis of gang development to modern surveys and field research on gangs and gang members. Modern research on gangs and gang members focuses primarily on ethnographic field research in which the motivations and identities of gang members are chronicled. Hagedorn critiques much of the contemporary research on gangs that rely on incomplete sampling and interviewing of gang members. Hagedorn suggests that the hallmarks of good research—multiple methods and multiple researchers—must be used in gang research if it is to transcend the anecdotes of individual gangs and gang members.

Esbensen, Winfree, Jr., and Taylor highlight the importance of consistent definitions for gang-affiliation and gang-related activity in gang research. In this study, they pose the following questions: "When is a gang a gang, and why does it matter?" To answer these questions, Esbensen, et al. surveyed approximately 6,000 eighth-grade students from 11 cities in the United States. Students were asked various questions pertaining to gang activity and membership using five different definitions of gang membership. Definitions ranged from youth claiming gang membership at one point in time, to those who are current core members in some type of organizational structure and are involved in some illegal activities. The findings indicated significant differences in attitudes and behaviors among those who reported prior gang membership when compared to those who reported no involvement in gangs. As the definition of a gang shifted to a more restrictive classification, reported attitudes and behaviors became more antisocial. In other words, hard-core members tended to report the "most extreme responses." The findings have broader political and theoretical implications. Examining the shifting definitions of gang behavior and membership provides a stepping-stone for understanding broader theoretical and political responses to this behavior.

Juvenile Curfews and the Courts:

Judicial Response to a Not-So-New Crime Control Strategy

Craig Hemmens
Katherine Bennett

A perception that juvenile crime is out of control is shared by the public, legislatures, and many criminal justice policy makers. Although the empirical evidence indicates that this perception is incorrect (Howell 1997), it has led to the adoption of a get tough approach to juvenile offenders. Legislatures and other government agencies are implementing a number of measures intended to reduce juvenile crime, including more liberal provisions for waiver to adult court (Fritsch and Hemmens 1995), increased use of incarceration as a sanction for serious juvenile offenders (Jeffs and Smith 1996), and modification of the goals of the juvenile justice system to align it more closely with the criminal justice system (Hemmens, Fritsch, and Caeti 1997).

Juvenile curfews are another currently popular approach to the problem of juvenile crime and delinquency. Although it is unclear whether they are effective in reducing crime, it is clear that they are being embraced by communities across the country (Conference of Mayors 1997). This article examines the constitutional ramifications and current status of juvenile curfew laws in the United States. The history, purpose, and form of juvenile curfews are first presented, followed by a discussion of the appropriate standard of constitutional review for cases involving curfews. Finally, the major state and federal cases addressing juvenile curfew constitutionality are examined and categorized.

A BRIEF HISTORY OF JUVENILE CURFEWS

Curfews, or laws requiring people to vacate public areas and streets, have existed for centuries. Early curfews were aimed at all inhabitants of a town, not just juveniles, and were used as a means of social control of the citizenry (Hall 1957; Ward 1956). In this country, curfews were used in the antebellum South to control when slaves and free Blacks could be on the streets (Federle 1995). Curfews have also been used during times of local or national emergency, such as during World War II (Freitas 1996). Curfews have occasionally been used to proscribe a particular activity during certain time periods. For instance, at least 18 states have a night-driving curfew for young drivers and permit holders (Williams and Lund 1986).

Craig Hemmens and Katherine Bennett, CRIME & DELINQUENCY, Vol. 45 No. 1, January 1999 99–121 © 1999 Sage Publications, Inc. Reprinted by permission of Sage Publications, Inc.

Juveniles have been the most common curfew target in this country. Juvenile curfews began to gain popularity during the latter part of the nineteenth century. The first juvenile curfew ordinance was enacted in Omaha, Nebraska, in 1880 (Schwartz 1985). In 1884, juvenile curfews were endorsed as a panacea by President Harrison (Note 1958). By 1900, there were more than 3,000 juvenile curfew ordinances in this country (Mooney 1977). Progressive era reformers, largely responsible for the creation of a separate juvenile justice system, saw curfews as a means to control as well as to protect unsupervised and neglected children, an increasingly common phenomena in the new urbanized, industrial society (Platt 1969).

Although many cities have had curfew ordinances on the books for the better part of a century, enforcement has been sporadic. Police departments have frequently asserted that they were too busy investigating "serious" crimes to be bothered with enforcing a curfew or that they lacked the resources to enforce the curfew (Scherr 1992). Enforcement of juvenile curfews increased in this country during World War II, when juvenile delinquency again became a national concern. After the war, America experienced a population boom, leading to a tremendous increase in the number of teenagers by the late 1950s. Cities responded by enacting juvenile curfews. As of 1957, a little more than half of the 109 cities with populations in excess of 100,000 had juvenile curfew ordinances (Note 1958).

The 1970s saw the discarding of the rehabilitative ideal and adoption of the "justice" or "just deserts" model in criminal justice. Juvenile crime was perceived as spiraling out of control. One result was the get tough on juvenile crime movement and increased sanctions for youthful offenders (Boland and Wilson 1978; Fritsch, Caeti, and Hemmens 1998; Fritsch and Hemmens 1995). These sanctions include juvenile curfews, which seem to some practitioners and legislators to be an ideal means of dealing with new problems such as juvenile street gangs and violent juvenile crime. Indeed, some commentators assert that the recent spate of curfew adoptions is directly attributable to gun violence committed by (and on) urban juveniles (Ruefle and Reynolds 1995).

A recent study reveals that 59 of the 77 (77 percent) American cities with a population in excess of 200,000 have juvenile curfew ordinances (Ruefle and Reynolds 1995). It has been estimated that approximately 1,000 local juvenile curfew ordinances have been adopted since 1990 (Sheperd 1996). President Clinton has endorsed juvenile curfews, and the 1996 Anti-Gang and Youth Violence Act provides $75 million for support of local initiatives such as curfews and antitruancy ordinances (Department of Justice 1996). Cities with curfew ordinances already on the books are suddenly enforcing them, while other cities are enacting curfew laws (Feldmann 1996; Sharp 1996; Smith 1994).

PURPOSE, FORM, EFFECTIVENESS, AND OPINION OF JUVENILE CURFEWS

Proponents of juvenile curfews provide four major justifications for such ordinances: protecting juveniles from crime, reducing juvenile crime, protecting society, and reinforcing parental authority (Carmen, Parker, and Reddington 1997). Curfew laws are a manifestation of the twin goals of the juvenile justice system of the Progressive era—seeing to the best interests of the child while, at the same time, imposing stricter social controls on unruly youth (Platt 1969; Rothman 1980).

The vast majority of juvenile curfews are acts of local municipal legislation. Municipalities are free to enact regulatory ordinances in the exercise of their police powers as long as those ordinances do not unduly restrict or impair a constitutional right. The terms of juvenile curfews vary by city (see, e.g., Bilchik 1996). Many ordinances require that juveniles be off of the streets late at night, whereas others focus on preventing truancy by limiting their access to the streets or certain businesses during school hours. Most curfews are set at later hours on weekends and during the summer. Most of them also provide a number of exceptions to the general rule, allowing juveniles out past curfew for emergencies or to go to work or to a legitimate social function.

Different police responses to curfew violators are also permitted: Some cities require police officers to arrest juvenile curfew violators and bring them to a detention center; others permit them to take the child home; still others allow them to simply issue a ticket to the juvenile. Sanctions also vary by city. For example, many cities divert first offenders, whereas others permit the imposition on them of fines and/or community service (Bilchik 1996). Parents may also be held responsible in more egregious cases (Kalvig 1996).

There is strong support for juvenile curfews. Law enforcement and city officials applaud them as an effective tool for crime prevention (Conference of Mayors 1997; Trollinger 1996). A number of city residents also favor curfews. For example, a 1994 survey found that 92 percent of Cincinnati residents supported that city's curfew, whereas a survey of juveniles in the District of Columbia found that 77 percent of them supported the citywide curfew enacted in 1995 (Crowell 1996).

Although curfew opponents sometimes raise the specter of racist motivation for such laws, support for curfews is not limited to White citizens. Of Black residents living in Mobile, Alabama, 75 percent who were surveyed in 1994 supported a proposed curfew ordinance (Crowell 1996). Blacks comprise a majority of the District of Columbia city council, which enacted a juvenile curfew in 1995. The New Orleans juvenile curfew was proposed by a Black mayor, enacted by a majority Black city council, and enforced by a police department headed by a Black chief (Ruefle and Reynolds 1996).

From the beginning, there has been opposition to curfews. An 1896 critic voiced concerns echoed today: Juvenile crime occurs mainly during the day rather than at night when the curfew is in force, and there are a number of legitimate reasons for juveniles to be afoot at odd hours (Buck 1896). Other critics have argued that curfews do not foster family harmony and parental authority; rather, they damage family relations by interposing the authority of the state between parent and child (Chen 1997).

Another criticism is that law enforcement does not always enforce the curfew equitably (National Council on Crime and Delinquency 1972; Ruefle and Reynolds 1995). A belief held by some is that police officers target minority youth and use the curfew as an excuse to harass those youth. In jurisdictions in which juvenile curfews were enforced in the past, citizen complaints and claims of arbitrary and discriminatory enforcement were not uncommon.

There is remarkably little empirical research on the impact of curfews on either juvenile crime or the overall crime rate; thus, it is unclear how effective they are at reducing crime. Several cities that have begun vigorously enforcing curfew ordinances insist that doing so has resulted in a marked reduction in juvenile crime; juvenile victimization; and, in some instances, the overall crime rate (Bilchik 1996; Sharp 1996). Although these studies are incomplete, it is apparent that vigorous curfew enforcement has certainly had an impact on the lives of juveniles—almost 6,000 children have been arrested in New Orleans since the city began enforcing a curfew ordinance in June 1994 (Sheperd 1996).

Other studies suggest that curfews may simply cause temporal or geographic crime displacement. A study of the effects of a juvenile curfew that was adopted by Detroit in 1976 in response to a rash of crimes involving juveniles found that although juvenile crime dropped 6 percent during curfew hours, it actually increased by 13 percent in the midafternoon hours (Hunt and Weiner 1977). Nationally, violent crimes committed by juveniles are most frequent between the hours of 3 p.m. and 4 p.m., and approximately 33 percent of all juvenile violent crime takes place between 3 p.m. and 7 p.m. Less than 20 percent of violent juvenile crime occurs during normal curfew hours (Snyder, Sickmund, and Poe-Yamagatta 1996). Although most juvenile curfews proscribe the presence of juveniles in public areas during the late night and early morning hours, less than 8 percent of all violent juvenile crime occurs between 11 p.m. and 1 a.m. (Fox and Newman 1997). These statistics suggest that reliance on curfews to substantially reduce juvenile crime may be misplaced, at best.

CONSTITUTIONAL RIGHTS AND JUDICIAL STANDARDS OF REVIEW

Juvenile curfews have been challenged as violating several different provisions of the constitution, including the First and Fourteenth Amendments. First Amendment freedoms restricted by juvenile curfews include those of association and assembly. Fourteenth Amendment rights affected by juvenile curfews include equal protection and due process. Claims involving violations of enumerated constitutional rights are often coupled with challenges based on overbreadth or vagueness (Toth 1995).

Although most challenges to juvenile curfews have centered on impairment of the rights of juveniles, from the beginning there have been challenges based on the infringement of the parents' rights to raise their children. The Supreme Court has historically accorded parents the authority to raise their children as they see fit, without state interference. In addition, most states have statutes expressly holding parents responsible for their children.

The Supreme Court has repeatedly asserted that the constitution and the protections found in the Bill of Rights apply to juveniles. It has also held on numerous occasions that states and municipalities may place restrictions on the constitutional rights of juveniles, which would be per se unconstitutional if applied to adults. This section discusses the differing standards of constitutional review that are applied to juvenile curfews.

JUDICIAL STANDARDS OF REVIEW

Often in constitutional law, the outcome of a case is determined as much by the standard of review that the court employs as by the facts of the case. Not all of the individual protections set forth in the Bill of Rights are accorded the same respect—rather, there is a hierarchy of rights. The court employs either strict scrutiny or rational basis review, depending on whether a fundamental right is implicated or a suspect classification is affected (Tribe 1988).

Fundamental rights are those freedoms that are essential to the concept of ordered liberty; they are rights without which neither liberty nor justice would exist. Examples include virtually all of the various provisions of the Bill of Rights. Fourteenth Amendment guarantees of due process and equal protection are also included in the list of fundamental rights. Such rights are fundamental for adults, but juveniles have traditionally been accorded fewer rights based on their youthful status; therefore, rights deemed fundamental for adults may not be seen as fundamental for juveniles.

To date, the Supreme Court has held that only race and religion are suspect classifications in all circumstances, although gender, illegitimacy, and poverty have occasionally been treated as suspect classifications by the high court (Tribe 1988). Although discrimination on the basis of a suspect classification is considered presumptively irrational and constitutionally invalid, age is not a suspect classification (Chen 1997). The Equal Protection Clause of the Fourteenth Amendment prohibits states from treating citizens in an arbitrary and discriminatory manner, but this does not mean that all disparate treatment is unconstitutional, only that the state may not treat people differently without a valid reason.

STRICT SCRUTINY REVIEW

Under strict scrutiny review, the state may not enact legislation that abridges a fundamental right unless (1) it has a compelling interest that justifies restricting a fundamental right and (2) the legislation is narrowly tailored so that the fundamental right is not abridged any more than absolutely necessary to effectuate the state's compelling interest. In addition, the Supreme Court requires that for legislation to be narrowly tailored, there must exist a sufficient nexus between the legislative body's stated interest and either the classification drawn or the means chosen to advance the state's compelling interest. This standard of review is referred to as the strict scrutiny test because the court looks closely at the purpose and the effect of the legislation rather than merely accepting the claims of the legislature that the legislation is needed or accepting the legislation as presumptively valid. The reason for employing a higher standard of review when legislation affects a fundamental right or suspect classification is that closer analysis is required when individual liberties are threatened.

RATIONAL BASIS REVIEW

If neither a fundamental right nor a suspect classification is implicated, a state may enact legislation abridging that right or affecting that class so long as there is a rational basis for the legislation. This standard of review is generally referred to as the rational basis test because under it, the court will not strike down legislation that appears to have some rational basis. The court does not look closely at the effects of the legislation, unlike the strict scrutiny test. Under this standard of review, state actions are presumptively valid (Tribe 1988). This standard of review is obviously a much easier one to pass. The legislature need not choose the best possible means; it must merely appear that it has chosen means that are not wholly unrelated to achievement of the legislative purpose.

The determination of whether a right is fundamental is the key to the outcome of many cases. The question for juvenile curfews, then, is do curfews impinge on any fundamental rights? If so, courts must apply strict scrutiny review and the curfew ordinance is likely to be invalidated. If, on the other hand, courts determine that juvenile curfews do not abridge any fundamental rights, the ordinance need pass only rational basis review and, consequently, it is likely to be upheld.

SUPREME COURT CASES AFFECTING THE CONSTITUTIONAL RIGHTS OF JUVENILES

Early Supreme Court cases involving regulation of juveniles treated the issue as a conflict between the interests of the state and the authority of the parents rather than as a conflict between the child and the state. In 1923, the court struck down a state law that prohibited the use of any language other than English in schools; in so doing, the court held that such a law infringed on the parents' "right of control" over their children by limiting who they could hire as a teacher (*Meyer v. Nebraska* 1923). Two years later, in *Pierce v. Society of Sisters* (1925), the court struck down an Oregon state law requiring children younger than age 17 to attend public, rather than private, schools. The court determined that such a law constituted an unreasonable interference with the authority of parents to determine the path of their child's education. The language of these cases suggested that children did not possess rights independent of their parents.

The Supreme Court continued to follow the approaches of *Meyer v. Nebraska* (1923) and *Pierce v. Society of Sisters* (1925) to juvenile rights for several decades. In *Wisconsin v. Yoder*, decided in 1972, the court struck down a state compulsory education statute as applied to members of the Amish religious order. The court focused not on how the law restricted children's

religious freedoms but rather on how it limited parents' First Amendment rights.

The idea that juveniles were second-class citizens, subordinate to their parents, began to lose favor, however, during the 1960s. In *Tinker v. Des Moines Independent Community School District* (1969), the court determined that a school policy banning the wearing of black armbands to protest the Vietnam conflict violated the minor's fundamental right to freedom of speech. In doing so, it made no distinction between the rights of children (students) and adults (teachers and/or parents).

During the 1960s, the Supreme Court decided on a series of cases extending specific due process rights to juveniles involved in juvenile court proceedings. These rights included the right to counsel at a juvenile hearing, the right to notice of the charges, the privilege against self-incrimination, the right to a waiver hearing, and the requirement that guilt be proved beyond a reasonable doubt (Manfredi 1998). Although the court's extension of a number of rights is notable, also notable is its refusal to treat juveniles the same as adults. The Supreme Court has long recognized that the state has greater authority over children than it has over adults. In *Ginsberg v. New York* (1968), the Supreme Court held that juveniles do not have the same First Amendment rights as do adults; thus, the state could prohibit the sale of sexually explicit magazines to juveniles. In *McKeiver v. Pennsylvania* (1971), the Supreme Court declined to provide the right to a jury trial in juvenile proceedings. The rights accorded to juveniles by the court during this period were largely procedural in nature—states were required to process juveniles in the juvenile justice system in much the same manner as they processed adults in the criminal justice system. However, these decisions did not prevent states from enforcing laws that

affected juveniles differently than they affected adults.

THE *BELLOTTI V. BAIRD* TEST

In *Bellotti v. Baird* (1979), the Supreme
Court clearly illuminated its rationale for
denying juveniles the protection of some
fundamental rights while extending the
protection of others to the same degree as
enjoyed by adults. In striking down a
Massachusetts statute requiring pregnant
women younger than age 18 to obtain the
consent of both parents before undergoing
an abortion, the Supreme Court first noted
that children are not without some constitutional protections. The court also acknowledged that children are different
than adults and that the state has a special
duty to protect children. Consequently,
although juveniles generally possess the
same constitutional rights as do adults,
the state may adjust its legal system to take
into account the special vulnerability of
children. From this, the court enunciated
three considerations that provided states
with the authority to infringe on the rights
of a juvenile to a greater degree than on an
adult's rights: (1) the "peculiar vulnerability of children"; (2) the inability of children
to make important decisions in a mature,
intelligent manner; and (3) the importance
of the parent in child rearing.

This three-part test has been applied
by federal and state courts to determine
when the state may restrict fundamental
rights of juveniles in contexts other than
the decision whether to have an abortion.
A number of courts faced with challenges
to juvenile curfew ordinances have used
the *Bellotti* test to determine the validity
of the curfew, although the Supreme Court
has yet to rule on the applicability of the
Bellotti test to such curfews. Commentators
have suggested that reliance on *Bellotti* by
the lower courts is misplaced because that
case dealt with the extremely sensitive and
complex issue of abortion and the concerns
expressed in that case may not extend to
curfews (Toth 1995).

CASES INVOLVING JUVENILE CURFEWS

Although juvenile curfews have existed
since the latter part of the nineteenth century, there are relatively few cases involving challenges to these ordinances. All of
the early cases are state court decisions because no federal court considered a juvenile curfew case until 1975. This section
reviews the leading state and federal cases
dealing with juvenile curfews.

EARLY JUVENILE CURFEW CASES

Courts deciding early challenges to juvenile curfews did not look to the Fourteenth
Amendment or the provisions of the Bill of
Rights for guidance because the Supreme
Court had not yet begun the process of incorporating the Bill of Rights into the Fourteenth Amendment's guarantee of due
process. Instead, courts relied on general
legal principles, such as vagueness and
over-breadth.

The first case involving a juvenile
curfew was decided in 1898. In *Ex parte
McCarver* (1898), a Texas state court held
unconstitutional a curfew ordinance that
prohibited persons younger than the age of
21 from being on the public streets after 9
p.m. unless accompanied by a parent or
seeking medical attention. The court criticized the curfew as "paternalistic," "an invasion of the personal liberty of the
citizen," and an "attempt to usurp the
parental functions."

In *Baker v. Borough of Steelton* (1912), a
Pennsylvania court upheld as a lawful exercise of police power a municipal ordinance prohibiting those persons younger

than age 16 from being on the streets after 9 p.m. unless accompanied by a parent or guardian or unless in possession of a note indicating that there was an emergency. The court noted that the city had a legitimate interest in protecting children from possible harm, determining that the curfew was related to this legitimate end and employing what is today referred to as the rational basis test.

In *People v. Walton* (1945), a California appellate court upheld a Los Angeles curfew prohibiting juveniles younger than age 16 from "remaining" or "loitering" on the street after 9 p.m. unless approval was obtained from the police. The court distinguished *McCarver* by noting that the Texas ordinance prohibited being on the streets altogether, whereas the Los Angeles ordinance prohibited the more narrow activities of "remaining" and "loitering." The court went on to say that juveniles are not accorded the same rights as adults, precisely because of their status as juveniles. As in *Baker*, the court used a rational basis standard of review.

RECENT JUVENILE CURFEW CASES

Although the Supreme Court has not dealt directly with the issue of juvenile curfews, an increasing number of lower federal courts and state courts have done so in recent years. These courts have focused on the constitutionality of juvenile curfews and whether a fundamental right is implicated or a suspect classification exists. The crucial factor in these recent cases is whether the court applies rational basis or strict scrutiny review.

Many courts apply the rational basis standard of review. They do this (1) because they believe that the state has a heightened interest in the regulation of children's behavior, (2) because they believe that children possess lesser rights

than adults and that no fundamental right is implicated, or (3) because children may be treated differently and are not a suspect classification.

Other courts have applied strict scrutiny analysis. Those doing so have generally found that the higher level of review is required because curfews implicate rights of minors similar to those of adults and, hence, are fundamental. Although strict scrutiny analysis often results in state legislation being invalidated, such is not always the case. Courts applying strict scrutiny analysis to juvenile curfews have struck down some curfews while upholding others. Courts striking down the curfews have done so because the state failed to establish a compelling state interest or because the means of achieving the state interest were not sufficiently narrowly tailored. Courts upholding juvenile curfews while applying strict scrutiny analysis have done so because the state established both a compelling state interest and the curfew ordinance appears to be sufficiently narrowly tailored.

State cases involving juvenile curfews. There have been a number of recent state court decisions involving juvenile curfews. These are presented in Table 1 and discussed below.

Several state courts have upheld juvenile curfews. In *People v. Chambers* (1976), the Illinois statewide curfew law was upheld by the state supreme court. The curfew was unusual in that it was enacted by the state legislature and covered the entire state, including rural and urban areas. The bulk of curfew laws are enacted at the local level in response to local problems. In upholding the law, the court acknowledged both the state's legitimate interest in reducing juvenile crime, which was increasing at the time, and the state's traditional authority to protect children. These interests

---

TABLE 1:   Significant State Cases Challenging Juvenile Curfews

Case	Alleged Violation	Basis for Review	Violation Found
People v. Chambers, 360 N.E. 2d 55 (Illinois, 1976)	First, Fourteenth Amendments	Real and substantial relation to government interests	No
In re J. M., 768 P.2d 219 (Colorado, 1989)	Freedom of movement, overbroad	Rational basis	No
Panora v. Simmons, 445 N.W.2d 363 (Iowa, 1989)	Vagueness, right to travel	Rational basis	No
City of Maquoketa v. Russell, 484 N.W.2d achieve 179 (Iowa, 1992)	First Amendment, overbroad	Strict scrutiny state interests	Yes, not narrowly tailored to
In re Mariciopa County, 887 P.2d 599 (Arizona, 1994)	First Amendment	Rational basis	No

---

permitted the state to infringe on the juvenile's rights. The fact that the law extended statewide was not a problem but rather a benefit because it indicated that the law did not discriminate in its application, at least in regard to geography.

In *In re J. M.* (1989), the Colorado Supreme Court upheld a local ordinance that made it unlawful for a person younger than age 18 to loiter in any public or private area between the hours of 10 p.m. and 6 a.m. unless accompanied by an adult. The court determined that the ordinance was a legitimate means by which the state could reinforce parental authority and that the curfew actually encouraged parents to take an active role in supervising their children. The court saw curfews as a necessary support mechanism for parents who were unable to adequately supervise and to be responsible for their children. In addition, the court determined that the city ordi-

nance was narrowly drawn, thus achieving its goals without unduly infringing on the liberty interests of juveniles.

In *Panora v. Simmons* (1989), the Iowa Supreme Court upheld a juvenile curfew ordinance that prohibited juveniles younger than age 18 from being in a public place between the hours of 10 p.m. and 5 a.m. The state court determined that no fundamental rights or suspect classifications were implicated by the ordinance and therefore applied a rational basis standard of review. Under this level of analysis, the city met its burden of demonstrating that the juvenile curfew ordinance was rationally related to the legitimate state interest in protecting society.

The Arizona Court of Appeals, in *In re Maricopa County* (1994), upheld a 10 p.m. juvenile curfew enacted in 1993 by the city of Phoenix. The curfew provided an exception for juveniles "on reasonable, legitimate and specific business or activity directed or permitted by his parent." The court held that the juvenile curfew was a valid means by which the state could support parents and aid in supervising children in the "many cases [where] the traditional family unit . . . has dissolved." Using the three part *Bellotti* test in its analysis, the court determined that the peculiar circumstances of childhood dictated a heightened interest held by the state in protecting children, thus justifying the limitation on a fundamental right.

Few state courts have struck down juvenile curfews. Just three years after the decision in *Panora v. Simmons* (1989) to uphold a curfew, the Iowa Supreme Court in *City of Maquoketa v. Russell* (1992) struck down an ordinance modeled after the one upheld in *Panora*. The city ordinance prohibited juveniles from being outside after 10 p.m., unless accompanied by a parent or going directly to or from work or a "parentally approved supervised activity." Justice Lavorato, who dissented in *Panora*, wrote the majority opinion. He asserted that juvenile curfew laws implicated fundamental rights of juveniles, including First Amendment freedoms of religion, speech, and association. Therefore, strict scrutiny, rather than rational basis, was the proper standard of review. Under this level of analysis, the juvenile curfew fell for not being narrowly tailored to achieve the state interests.

Federal cases involving juvenile curfews. Prior to 1975, no federal court had decided a case involving a juvenile curfew ordinance. Since the first decision in *Bykofsky v. Borough of Middletown* (1975), at least six cases have been decided in federal courts. These are presented in Table 2.

Several federal courts have upheld juvenile curfews, either under rational basis review or strict scrutiny. The juvenile

curfew ordinance at issue in *Bykofsky v. Borough of Middletown* (1975) prohibited minors younger than age 18 from being on the street between the hours of 10 p.m. (younger than age 12), 10:30 p.m. (age 12 or 13), or 11 p.m. (age 14 to 17) and 6 a.m. unless one or more of several stated exceptions applied. Exceptions included being accompanied by a parent, in the case of an emergency, or if returning home from a legitimate social activity such as a school or church event.

The ordinance was challenged by the plaintiff mother on behalf of her 12-year-old son. No curfew violation had occurred; rather, the plaintiff sought an injunction and declaratory relief. The plaintiff contended that phrases in the ordinance were impermissibly vague, violated First Amendment rights of minors, violated minors' right to travel, infringed on parents' right to control the upbringing of their children, and denied minors equal protection.

The district court determined that portions of the ordinance that gave virtually unfettered discretion to the mayor were too vague, but the court held that with the deletions of the impermissibly vague words and phrases, the ordinance as an entity was not unconstitutionally vague. The court also held that juveniles' constitutional rights may be regulated to a greater extent than adults without violating the Constitution. The court determined that although the curfew restricted freedom of movement, such freedom was personal rather than absolute and was subject to "reasonable regulations." The court thus ruled that freedom of movement was neither a fundamental right nor a First Amendment right. The court further concluded that there was a rational relationship between the ordinance and the interests of the city. Governmental interests in advancing and protecting the general

TABLE 2:   Significant Federal Cases Challenging Juvenile Curfews

Case	Alleged Violation	Basis for Review	Violation Found
Bykofsky v. Borough of Middletown, 401 F. Supp. 1242 (1975)	First, Fourteenth Amendments, Right to travel, parental rights of child rearing, vagueness	Rational basis	Yes to vagueness; no to all other allegations
Naprstek v. City of Norwich, 545 F.2d 815 (Second Circuit, 1976)	First, Fourteenth Amendments, vagueness	Rational basis	Yes, voided curfew for vagueness
Johnson v. City of Opelousas, 658 F.2d 1065 (Fifth Circuit, 1981)	First, Fourteenth Amendments, right to travel, vagueness, overbroad	Strict scrutiny	Yes, unconstitutionally overbroad
McCollester v. City of Keene, 586 F. Supp. 1381 (D.N.H., 1984)	First, Fourteenth Amendments, overbroad	Strict scrutiny	Yes, facially overbroad
Waters v. Barry, 711 F. Supp. 1125 (D.D.C., 1989)	First, Fourth, Fifth Amendments, overbroad	Strict scrutiny	Yes to First, Fifth Amendments and overbreadth
Qutb v. Strauss, 11 F.3d 488 (Fifth Circuit, 1993)	First, Fourteenth, Fifth, Fourteenth Amendments, vagueness, overbroad	Strict scrutiny	No
Hutchins v. District of Columbia, 942 F. Supp. 665 (D.D.C., 1996)	First, Fourth, Fifth Amendments, vagueness, overbroad	Strict scrutiny	Yes to Fifth Amendment violation of equal protection and due process
Nunez v. City of San Diego, 1997 WL304747 (Ninth Circuit, 1997)	First Amendment, vagueness, parental rights of child rearing	Strict scrutiny	Yes to vagueness, First Amendment, and parental rights

community's welfare and safety outweighed the minor's freedom of movement interest.

The court did agree with plaintiffs that the minor's First Amendment right to freedom of association for social purposes was infringed. It held, however, that this right was outweighed by legitimate government interests furthered by the ordinance. The First Amendment right to free speech was not violated at all because the ordinance did not regulate speech, only "noncommunicative conduct."

Courts and commentators have argued that the *Bykofsky* court misapplied the process by which it is determined whether a fundamental right is implicated (Chen 1997; Tribe 1988). The proper method is to first determine the nature of the right that was restricted and then to select the appropriate standard of review. The *Bykofsky* court, however, reversed the process, first determining that the state had a heightened interest in the welfare of children and then concluding that minors' freedom of movement was not a fundamental right.

In 1994, a court for the first time upheld a juvenile curfew while applying strict scrutiny review. In *Qutb v. Strauss* (1993), the Fifth Circuit Court of Appeals upheld a Dallas curfew that prohibited persons younger than age 17 "from remaining in a public place or establishment from 11 p.m. until 6 a.m. on week nights and from 12 midnight until 6 a.m. on weekends." The curfew provided several exceptions, including being accompanied by a parent or guardian; running an errand for a parent or guardian or an emergency errand; traveling in a motor vehicle to or from work; being involved in employment-related activities; or engaging in interstate travel. Minors affected by the curfew could still "attend school, religious, or civic organization functions, or gen-

erally exercise First Amendment speech and association rights." The curfew also permitted minors to remain on sidewalks in front of their homes or in front of neighbors' homes.

The Fifth Circuit noted that because the ordinance differentiated classes of individuals based on age, the curfew must be analyzed under the equal protection clause. The plaintiffs charged that the curfew impinged on the fundamental right "to move about freely in public." Assuming that the right to move about freely is a fundamental right and that it is impinged on by the curfew ordinance, the court accordingly subjected the ordinance to strict scrutiny review and asked whether it was sufficiently narrowly drawn to accomplish the state's compelling interest.

Dallas presented statistical data establishing the amount of juvenile crime and the time of day that violent crime was likely to occur. Even though the city could not provide data regarding juvenile crime committed during curfew hours or juvenile victimization occurring during those hours, the circuit court held that the city did provide adequate data to establish that the age classification of the curfew fit the state's compelling interest. The court further stated that the ordinance, particularly in light of the numerous exceptions, employed the least restrictive means of accomplishing its stated goals. The Fifth Circuit was unimpressed with the district court's examples of activities that would be curtailed by the curfew, such as "concerts, movies, plays, study groups, or church activities that may extend past curfew hours" or even "an innocent stroll or gazing at stars from a public park." The court noted that minors could engage in those activities if accompanied by a parent or guardian. The court then stated that "innocent strolls" could still be taken until 11 p.m. on weeknights and 12 a.m. on weekends; "indeed, a juvenile may stare at the stars all night long from the front sidewalk of his or her home or the home of a neighbor."

Several federal courts have struck down juvenile curfews, generally after employing a strict scrutiny analysis. In 1976, the Second Circuit in *Naprstek v. City of Norwich* invalidated a curfew ordinance, ruling it void for vagueness. The curfew had been in existence for 56 years. Constitutional issues raised by the plaintiffs were similar to those raised in *Bykofsky*, including violations of freedom of speech, assembly, association, and parents' rights to due process and family privacy. The appellate court ruled that by failing to provide a termination time for the curfew, the ordinance was "void for vagueness" and unconstitutional in its application. In *Johnson v. City of Opelousas* (1981), the Fifth Circuit found the Opelousas ordinance to be unconstitutionally vague and facially overbroad, in violation of the First and Fourteenth Amendments, and in violation of the minor's right of interstate and intrastate travel. The curfew in Opelousas prohibited minors younger than age 17 from being on the street or in a public place between 11 p.m. and 4 a.m. between Sunday and Thursday and 1 a.m. and 4 a.m. on Friday and Saturday, unless accompanied by an adult or in response to an emergency. The Fifth Circuit recognized that restrictions on minors that would be unconstitutionally invalid if applied to adults may be justified, but only if they serve significant state interests. The court then held that the curfew was unconstitutionally overbroad because it unnecessarily prohibited minors from engaging in First Amendment activities, such as association and interstate travel. By including innocent activities in its list of prohibited activities, the curfew was not sufficiently narrowly drawn. The fault with the curfew in this case was that it al-

lowed too few exceptions. The court decided that the nighttime activities prohibited by the curfew, such as religious or school meetings, burdened minors' fundamental rights. The ordinance at issue prevented minors from engaging in legitimate employment, being on the sidewalk in front of their own houses, and interstate travel.

In 1984, a federal district court struck down a New Hampshire city curfew ordinance in *McCollester v. City of Keene* (1984). The curfew applied to juveniles younger than age 16 and was in effect from 10 p.m. until 5 a.m. The ordinance contained several exceptions, including minors who were passengers in a motor vehicle and minors traveling before midnight to or from participation in a public assembly. The plaintiffs contended that the ordinance was still overly broad and violated due process guarantees against unreasonable governmental interference with citizens' liberty and privacy rights. The defendants claimed that the ordinance was narrowly drawn, given the exceptions provided for legitimate activity. Furthermore, the city argued that restrictions on the minors' or the minors' parents' liberty and privacy interests were justified by the "significant and legitimate public purposes" that were served by the ordinance.

The district court sided with the plaintiffs and found the ordinance to be overbroad and to impermissibly curtail liberty and privacy rights of both juveniles and their parents; the court also found it in violation of the three-pronged *Bellotti* test. The city's interests in suppression of crime, promotion of juvenile morality, and support of parental authority did not justify infringing on individual rights of travel and privacy. The court acknowledged that the state had a great interest in regulating the activities of children and a legitimate interest in controlling crime and promoting public welfare. Regardless, the court found the curfew to be too broad and in violation of the due process clause of the Fourteenth Amendment. The state's objectives were not sufficient enough to justify the juvenile curfew. The curfew provided no exemption for emergencies and the existing exceptions were limited to employment travel or being with a chaperone approved by the ordinance.

In *Waters v. Barry* (1989), the district court for the District of Columbia struck down a curfew ordinance that prohibited juveniles from being on the street or in public places between the hours of 11 p.m. and 6 a.m. Exceptions included minors traveling with their parents in a car, those returning from a job, and those on an emergency errand. The District of Columbia patterned its curfew exceptions after Middletown's curfew exemptions, which had withstood constitutional challenge. The District of Columbia district court held, however, that the District of Columbia's ordinance was more limiting than the Middletown ordinance. It also noted that it could not agree with the *Bykofsky* court that the constitutional rights of minors are less deserving of protection than are those of adults.

In reaching this decision, the district court applied the three *Bellotti* criteria in an in-depth analysis. Addressing the first criterion, the court noted that the District of Columbia posed just as much danger to adults as to children; therefore, there was no reason to place a "peculiar burden" on juveniles' constitutional rights. The second criterion, "juveniles' inability to make critical decisions in an informed mature manner," was not supported by the ordinance because a minor's "decision to either stay inside or roam at night does not present the type of profound decision which *Bellotti* would leave to the state." Likewise, the court viewed the ordinance as impermissibly encroaching on the third criterion:

the importance of the parents' role in directing the upbringing of their children.

Thus, the court found no justification for according juveniles lesser rights. Because the curfew affected rights that the court determined fundamental and because there was no *Bellotti* justification for treating juveniles differently in this instance, the court applied strict scrutiny analysis. The court then determined that although the statute's purpose, to protect juveniles from harm, was legitimate and indeed a compelling state interest, the curfew ordinance was not narrowly tailored to effectuate that purpose. The court noted that the curfew was enacted without credible statistical evidence that juveniles either commit more crimes or are more frequently victims of crime during the hours of the curfew. Although violence was widespread, there was no evidence that juveniles were more likely to be involved in it than adults.

After the curfew ordinance was invalidated in *Waters*, the District of Columbia enacted a new ordinance. The curfew affected persons younger than age 17 and contained eight exceptions, which were copied verbatim after Dallas' juvenile curfew upheld in *Qutb*. In 1996, the district court addressed the constitutionality of this curfew in *Hutchins v. District of Columbia* (1996). Acknowledging that minors' fundamental rights may not always be treated in the same fashion as adults' fundamental rights, the court applied the three *Bellotti* factors to determine whether legitimate grounds existed for treating minors' right to free movement differently from adults' right to free movement. The court followed *Waters* in applying the first two factors. It noted an absence of necessary evidence showing that most parents in the District of Columbia were unable to control or protect their children to circumvent the third *Bellotti* factor, the importance of parental control in child rearing. The court concluded that there were no legitimate grounds for treating the minors' fundamental rights differently from adults; thus, the curfew was subject to strict scrutiny analysis.

The District of Columbia offered statistical information to substantiate its compelling state interest in reducing juvenile crime and victimization. Furthermore, it pointed to the exceptions as establishing that the curfew was narrowly drawn and the least intrusive means necessary to achieve its stated goals, but it failed to convince the court. The court was particularly unmoved by the statistical information and described the information as a "hodgepodge of national, as opposed to local, statistics, other cities' statistics, unverifiable charts, and statistics for people over the age of seventeen." Juvenile crime data included all persons younger than age 18; the curfew, however, targeted minors younger than age 17. Therefore, the statistics were overinclusive and, hence, unreliable. Furthermore, other crime statistics were not broken down by the time of day or night when the incident occurred or by the ages of perpetrators and victims. The court observed that the District of Columbia ignored "available statistics that show that more than ninety percent of all juveniles committed no crimes at all and were not arrested at night or any other time."

The District of Columbia acknowledged that it had adopted the Dallas juvenile ordinance that withstood strict scrutiny analysis in *Qutb*. The *Hutchins* court noted, however, that the District of Columbia "did not—and could not—also adopt wholesale the evidentiary statistics that allowed the Dallas ordinance in *Qutb* to withstand constitutional scrutiny." The court also stated that many of the exceptions were "vague and undefined." The district court held that the ordinance was not narrowly tailored to further the compelling interests of the District of Columbia and declared it unconstitutional.

San Diego enacted a juvenile curfew ordinance in 1947 and began enforcing it in 1993. Applying strict scrutiny analysis in *Nunez v. City of San Diego* (1997), the Ninth Circuit struck down the ordinance. The Ninth Circuit rejected the curfew for three reasons. First, it determined that the language in the ordinance was too vague. Juveniles could not be expected to be able to discern what kind of behavior was illegal. In addition, the loose language afforded law enforcement too much discretion in deciding how to enforce the ordinance. Second, the court held that the curfew unfairly limited juveniles' First Amendment rights of free speech, religion, and travel. Third, it found that the curfew unconstitutionally burdened parents, usurping their rights as guardians. The court said that the "ordinance [is] an exercise in sweeping state control irrespective of parents' wishes. Without proper justification, it violated the fundamental right to rear children without undue interference." The court did go on to make clear that a less restrictive curfew ordinance might withstand constitutional scrutiny. The 1947 statute contained dated language and requirements that were rarely found in newer ordinances.

CONCLUSION

Juvenile curfews are the latest fad in juvenile justice, a field strewn with the remnants of quick fixes to a serious problem (see, e.g., Bernard 1992; Hemmens et al. 1997). There is little evidence that curfews work, yet they have been adopted wholesale—the public wants action of some kind, any kind—a "just do something" mentality. This demand is related to feelings of loss of control over our youth, a feeling that appears periodically in American culture (Bernard 1992). Juvenile curfews are an attempt both to protect children and to prevent juvenile crime, thereby protecting society. Although these are laudable goals, it is less clear whether a curfew is the most appropriate means of achieving these ends.

Curfews are not going away—less than two weeks after the San Diego curfew ordinance was struck down in *Nunez*, the San Diego City Council approved a new ordinance modeled after the Dallas ordinance upheld in *Qutb* (Jones 1996). A recent study by the United States Conference of Mayors indicates that more than three quarters of American cities have some form of nighttime curfew, and more than 90 percent of these cities believe nighttime curfews are useful tools for law enforcement (Conference of Mayors 1997). These figures suggest that curfews are widely viewed as appropriate.

The question that enactment and enforcement of juvenile curfews begs is whether these laws are constitutional. The answer, according to the courts, is mixed. The Supreme Court has acknowledged that children are different and that the law must somehow reflect this fact. Yet, the Supreme Court has failed to establish a structured framework for minors' rights. The *Bellotti* test may not apply outside of the abortion context because the greater need to protect children considering an abortion may justify state action in instances in which it would otherwise be impermissible. Other cases involving juvenile rights are split. Whether juveniles have the same rights as adults is still in question until the Supreme Court issues a definitive pronouncement.

The consequence of an absence of a definitive pronouncement by the Supreme Court is confusion among the lower courts. There is disagreement about whether juveniles possess the same fundamental rights as adults. If not, then rational basis review applies and the curfew is likely to stand. If so, then strict scrutiny review applies and the curfew is likely to fall. Courts that uphold curfews while purporting to apply strict scrutiny have done so only by either misapplying the test or by accepting at face value crime statistics. This is not true strict scrutiny review. The Supreme Court should address the constitutionality of juvenile curfews and, in doing so, set forth a clear framework for consideration of the (sometimes) competing interests of the child, parent, and state. Until the high court provides clear guidance, lower federal courts and state courts are likely to continue to issue conflicting rulings. The curfew ordinance upheld in *Qutb* and struck down in *Hutchins* is a prime example of the differing results that lower courts may reach when they work without sufficient guidance from the Supreme Court.

Curfews clearly threaten the exercise of a number of rights. The district court in *Waters v. Barry* (1989) likened the District of Columbia's curfew to "a bull in a china shop of constitutional values." Historically, juveniles have been treated as second-class citizens under the rationale that they needed more protection than adults. The question that blanket juvenile curfews raise is, When does protection become impairment?

The current trend is for courts to uphold juvenile curfews so long as the ordinance provides exceptions for legitimate activities and the city is able to make a showing of a serious juvenile crime problem. Lack of empirical evidence on curfew effectiveness works in a city's favor in two ways—it is easy to convince a court in these times that there is a juvenile crime problem and, without statistics, it is difficult to determine whether a curfew actually has any effect on juvenile crime. Courts are often reluctant to disagree with the conclusions of the elected representatives without explicit empirical evidence to the contrary.

"History teaches that grave threats to liberty often come in times of urgency, when constitutional rights seem too extravagant to ignore" (Justice Marshall dissenting in *Skinner v. Railway Labor Executives Association* 1989). The recent surge in the popularity of curfew enactment and enforcement and the urgency with which some cities have turned to them, almost as a panacea, suggest that juvenile curfews are a sign of public hysteria rather than a reasoned response to juvenile crime and delinquency. Surely, criminalizing another activity instead of addressing the underlying social problems is unwise, unproductive, and doomed for failure.

References

Baker v. Borough of Steelton, 17 Dauphin 17 (Pennsylvania, 1912).

Bellotti v. Baird, 443 U.S. 622 (1979).

Bernard, Thomas J. 1992. *The Cycle of Juvenile Justice.* New York: Oxford University Press.

Bilchik, Shay. 1996. "Curfew: An Answer to Juvenile Delinquency and Victimization?" *Juvenile Justice Bulletin* (April):1–11.

Boland, Barbara and James Q. Wilson. 1978. "Age, Crime, and Punishment." *The Public Interest* 51:22–34.

Buck, Winifred. 1896. "Objections to a Children's Curfew." *North American Review* 164:381–4.

Bykofsky v. Borough of Middletown, 401 F. Supp. 1242 (1975).

Carmen, Rolando V., del, Mary Parker, and Francis Reddington, 1997. *Briefs of Leading Cases in Juvenile Justice.* Cincinnati, OH: Anderson.

Chen, Gregory Z. 1997. "Youth Curfews and the Trilogy of Parent, Child, and State Relations." *New York University Law Review* 72:131–74.

City of Maquoketa v. Russell, 484 N.W.2d 179 (Iowa, 1992).

Conference of Mayors. 1997. *A Status Report on Youth Curfews in America's Cities.* Washington, DC: United States Conference of Mayors.

Crowell, Anthony. 1996. "Minor Restrictions: The Challenge of Juvenile Curfews." *Public Management* (August):4–12.

Department of Justice. 1996. *Anti-Gang and Youth Violence Act.* Washington, DC: Department of Justice.

Ex parte McCarver, 46 S.W. 936 (Texas, 1898).

Federle, Katherine H. 1995. "Children, Curfews, and the Constitution." *Washington University Law Quarterly* 73:1315–68.

Feldmann, Linda. 1996. "Cities Adopt Curfews. But Impact on Crime is Debated." *Christian Science Monitor*, January 4, p. A1.

Fox, James A. and Sanford A. Newman. 1997. "Juvenile Crime Rate Spikes When School Lets Out, Study Indicates." *Criminal Justice Newsletter* 28:5–6.

Freitas, Susan L. 1996. "After Midnight: The Constitutional Status of Juvenile Ordinances in California." *Hastings Constitutional Law Quarterly* 24:219–46.

Fritsch, Eric J., Tory J. Caeti, and Craig Hemmens. Forthcoming. "Juvenile Justice in Texas: An Analysis of Changing Policy Assumptions." *Law and Policy*.

Fritsch, Eric J. and Craig Hemmens. 1995. "Juvenile Waiver in the United States 1977–1995: A Comparison and Analysis of Waiver Statutes." *Juvenile and Family Court Journal* 46:17–35.

Ginsberg v. New York, 390 U.S. 629 (1968).

Hall, Donald M. 1957. "Note: Locomotion Ordinances as Abridgment of Personal Liberty." *Tulane Law Review* 32(1):117–9.

Hemmens, Craig, Eric J. Fritsch, and Tory J. Caeti. 1997. "Juvenile Justice Code Purpose Clauses: The Power of Words." *Criminal Justice Policy Review* 8:221–46.

Howell, James C. 1997. *Juvenile Justice and Youth Violence.* Thousand Oaks, CA: Sage.

Hunt, A. Lee and Ken Weiner. 1977. "The Impact of A Juvenile Curfew: Suppression and Displacement Patterns of Juvenile Offenses." *Journal of Police Science and Administration* 5:407–12.

Hutchins v. District of Columbia, 942 F. Supp. 665 (D.D.C., 1996).

In re J. M., 768 P.2d 219 (Colorado, 1989).

In re Maricopa County, 887 P.2d 599 (Arizona, 1994).

Jeffs, Tony and Mark K. Smith. 1996. "Getting the Dirtbags Off the Streets: Curfews and Other Solutions to Juvenile Crime." *Youth and Policy* 53:1–14.

Johnson v. City of Opelousas, 358 F.2d 1065 (Fifth Circuit, 1981).

Jones, Charisse. 1996. "Cities Give Curfew Laws a Closer Look." *USA Today*, June 21, p. A1.

Kalvig, Kenneth A. 1996. "Oregon's New Parental Responsibility Acts: Should Other States Follow Oregon's Trail?" *Oregon Law Review* 75:829–901.

Manfredi, Christopher P. 1998. *The Supreme Court and Juvenile Justice.* Lawrence: University of Kansas Press.

McCollester v. City of Keene, 586 F. Supp. 1381 (D.N.H., 1984).

McKeiver v. Pennsylvania, 403 U.S. 528 (1971).

Meyer v. Nebraska, 262 U.S. 390 (1923).

Mooney, Martin E. 1977. "Note: Assessing the Constitutional Validity of Juvenile Curfew Statutes." *Notre Dame Lawyer* 52:858–81.

Naprstek v. City of Norwich, 545 F.2d 815 (Second Circuit, 1976).

National Council on Crime and Delinquency. 1972. "Juvenile Curfews: A Policy Statement." *Crime & Delinquency* 18:132–3.

Note. 1958. "Curfew Ordinances and the Control of Nocturnal Juvenile Crime." *University of Pennsylvania Law Review* 107:66–101.

Nunez v. City of San Diego, 1997 WL 304747 (Ninth Circuit, 1997).

Panora v. Simmons, 445 N.W.2d 363 (Iowa, 1989).

People v. Chambers, 360 N.E.2d 55 (Illinois, 1976).

People v. Walton, 161 P.2d 498 (California, 1945).

Pierce v. Society of Sisters, 268 U.S. 510 (1925).

Platt, Anthony. 1969. *The Childsavers*. Chicago: University of Chicago Press.

Qutb v. Strauss, 11 F.3d 488 (Fifth Circuit, 1993).

Rothman, David J. 1980. *Conscience and Convenience*. New York: HarperCollins.

Ruefle, William and Kenneth M. Reynolds. 1995. "Curfew and Delinquency in Major American Cities." *Crime & Delinquency* 41:347–63.

———. 1996. "Keep Them at Home: Juvenile Curfew Ordinances in 200 American Cities." *American Journal of Police* 15:63–84.

Scherr, Peter L. 1992. "The Juvenile Curfew Ordinance: In Search of A New Standard of Review." *Washington University Journal of Urban And Contemporary Law* 41:163–92.

Schwartz, Robert. 1985. "Rights Issue Teen-Age Curfews—A Revival." *The Los Angeles Times*, August 10, p. D1.

Sharp, Deborah. 1996. "New Orleans Puts its Curfew in Good Light." *USA Today*, October 4, p. A4.

Sheperd, Robert E. 1996. "The Proliferation of Juvenile Curfews." *American Bar Association Criminal Justice Section Newsletter* (September):1–3.

Skinner v. Railway Labor Executives Association, 489 U.S. 602 (1989).

Smith, Wesley R. 1994. "Don't Stand So Close to Me." *Policy Review* (Fall):48–54.

Snyder, Howard, Melissa Sickmund, and Eileen Poe-Yamagatta. 1996. *Juvenile Offenders and Victims: 1996 Update on Violence*. Washington, DC: Department of Justice.

Tinker v. Des Moines Independent School District, 393 U.S. 503 (1969).

Toth, Jeremy. 1995. "Juvenile Curfew: Legal Perspectives and Beyond." *In the Public Interest* 14:39–82.

Tribe, Laurence H. 1988. *American Constitutional Law*. Minneapolis, MN: West.

Trollinger, Tona. 1996. "The Juvenile Curfew: Unconstitutional Imprisonment." *William and Mary Bill of Rights Journal* 4:949–1003.

Ward, Regina M. 1956. "Comment: Constitutional Law—Police Power—Municipal Ordinance—Philadelphia Curfew Law." *Villanova Law Review* 1:51–63.

Waters v. Barry, 711 F. Supp. 1125 (D.D.C., 1989).

Williams, Allan F. and Adrian K. Lund. 1986. "Adults' Views of Laws That Limit Teenagers' Driving and Access to Alcohol." *Journal of Public Health Policy* 7:190–7.

Wisconsin v. Yoder, 406 U.S. 205 (1972).

The Emperor's New Clothes:
Theory and Method in Gang Field Research

John M. Hagedorn,

INTRODUCTION

In the last few years there has been a resurgence of field research on gangs. In New York, Los Angeles, San Francisco, Detroit, St. Louis, and elsewhere social scientists have gone "back to the field" to study gangs, drugs, and violence. This has been a welcome development. However, the recent profusion of field research has also brought to light a few problems.

This paper intends to initiate an academic discussion about the representativeness and validity of data in modern gang studies.[1] I think we need to ask two rudimentary questions of every study: 1) how representative are their samples? and 2) how have the researchers separated lies and "hype" from more valid and reliable data? Let me briefly explain how our research in Milwaukee has prompted me to ask these questions.

In my early research (1988) I learned what Thrasher (1963) meant in saying "no two gangs are just alike." Milwaukee's gangs vary by neighborhood, ethnicity, age, and gender and are quite different from gangs in other cities (Moore 1988). But while each gang may be different, my current research (1994a) has taught me

Free Inquiry in Creative Sociology, Special Issue: Gangs, Drugs & Violence, Volume 24, No. 2, November 1996, 111–121.

there also are differences *within* each gang. Some studies I've read interview only one or two members of a gang, and we're not told why the researchers think their respondents are representative of all or most gang members. If there is substantial variation within a gang, selectivity in sampling may strongly influence the findings and distort any theoretical conclusions based on those findings.

Further, even if a sample is representative, gang members simply don't always tell the truth. Yablonsky (1966) warned long ago that to gang members "every researcher could be a 'cop.'" I've learned that gang members, like everyone else, present "accounts" of themselves which project an image they wish to maintain in the eyes of outsiders (Campbell 1984). Gang members manage their appearances to researchers and few of us have reported on how we have seen through such "presentational" data (Goffman 1959).

These methodological problems have theoretical consequences. Could some studies which conclude that gang members are strongly committed either to deviant or to conventional norms be based on interviews with unrepresentative outliers? Might some proponents of cultural deviance theories have interviewed or observed only atypical gang members who were "loco," violence-prone, or drug-crazed? Might some strain theorists have taken at face value self-serving comments from gang members or "wannabes" who were just trying to "look good?"

These issues are also crucial if the new nineties gang research is to be used for humane policy ends. I am particularly concerned with research that paints gang members as "hopelessly deviant" and thus provides a justification for right wing policies of increased incarceration. But I also cannot neglect critiquing studies, like my own, which see gang members as basically conventional, and may be incorrectly minimizing the gang problem.

Many of the nineties gang field studies are important contributions to the literature. However, until we examine the methodology of these studies we cannot be convinced of the validity of their findings or theoretical conclusions. Without such a methodological critique, our appreciation of any these studies may be no more than sociologists admiring the emperor's new clothes. This article examines how the findings and theoretical conclusions of contemporary gang research—including my own—have been influenced by selectivity and how gang members distort information. In conclusion, I discuss some political and ethical consequences of our research.

SELECTIVITY IN SAMPLING

The truism that "gangs vary" is as old as gang research itself. Variation between gangs in different cities and between gangs within a city have long been acknowledged (Cloward, Ohlin 1960; Moore's introduction to Hagedorn 1988; Spergel 1964). Gangs also vary by ethnic group (Spergel 1989) and by gender (Campbell 1990).[2] Specific gangs may also become more or less violent over time (Moore 1993). Klein (1995) has forcefully reminded

both the social science and law enforcement communities that not all gangs deal drugs or are violent.

There are only a few studies which have overlooked variation between gangs. However, I think researchers today who find no between-gang variation have a sociological burden of proof. Attentiveness to variation becomes even more theoretically relevant when we look at differences within a gang.

The "gang" in research is often seen as a monolithic entity. Observations or Interviews with one or a few gang members are sometimes assumed to be descriptive of the gang as a whole. Since accessing street gangs is quite difficult, often studies only interview those gang members who are willing to be interviewed and ignore the implications of such selectivity (Moore 1978; Whyte 1943). Our study (Hagedorn 1994a) has demonstrated that even among core members of gangs, there are both conventional and deviant life-styles as well as different orientations toward the future (Vigil 1988). We found most adult gang members ("homeboys," "legits," and most "dope fiends") had a conventional orientation with a varied work history, while only a minority of the gang, some "dope fiends" and the "new jacks," eschewed work and glorified violence.

I suspect some studies which portray gang members as adhering to deviant or violent norms may have sampled only new jacks or other outliers. Other studies which have downplayed organization or violent behavior may have interviewed only legits or less involved "wannabes." Ignoring variation within the gang can distort our understanding of the extent to which gang members are committed to gang norms or whether they aspire to mainstream American cultural goals, as suggested by strain theory (Cloward, Ohlin 1960).

For example, Martin Sanchez Jankowski (1991) bases his cultural deviance model on his conclusion that gang members as a whole are "hard nuts" with "defiant individual" personality traits quite different from other residents in their neighborhoods. His respondents appear to have similar hard-nosed outlooks and lifestyles. They appear unlike the complicated and conflicted people usually found in field work (Becker 1970) as well as the respondents in our Milwaukee study. While admittedly Jankowski's interest was in analyzing the gang as a unit, he virtually ignores within-gang variation. This may have led Jankowski to mistakenly attribute the personal characteristics of some gang members to the entire gang.

Sanders (1994) also neglects variation within the core membership of the gang and finds core gang members are *defined* by their adherence to violent subcultural norms. Sanders spent ten years riding with police gang squads investigating drive-by shootings. His interviews with gang members involved with Homicides gives a chilling, but perhaps not representative, picture of amorality. For example, he reports that "gang members"—apparently as a whole—"lack remorse" for the accidental killing of babies in drive-by shootings (Sanders 1994). Surely this finding would shock most veteran field researchers. In our own study, the vast majority of gang members we interviewed reacted with deep remorse to incidents of tragedy and death within their communities. Sanders does not quote anyone who felt remorse, and we don't know if the gang amorality he found is typical of San Diego gang members. Might Sanders' method of access and homicide-based sample have influenced his findings?[3]

Finally, in a much quoted study, Skolnick (1990) interviewed 39 inmates in a one-shot, one hour interview. He con-cluded from this study that northern California African American gang members were part of "instrumental" gangs, similar to organized crime, while southern California Latino gangs were more "cultural," or neighborhood based. Were Skolnick's respondents representative of gang drug dealers of each ethnic group? Skolnick interviewed only those members of a gang who had been arrested, convicted, and sentenced to prison for committing crimes and then were picked out for an interview by correctional officials. Might his prison-based, prison-guard-selected sample have contributed to his rather sweeping findings?[4]

The problem with all of these studies, as well as many more from contemporary gang research,[5] is selectivity. We don't know how the respondents who were interviewed or quoted differ from others within their gang or how prevalent the cited views are within their gang. Could the methods of selection in these studies have led these researchers to mistakenly conclude that gang members are deeply committed to criminal or violent norms? Might more attention to sampling within gangs have led these researchers to different conclusions?

SAMPLING STRATEGIES

One well respected and often used sampling strategy in gang field research is the "snowball sample" (Biemacki, Waldorf 1981). A snowball sample can be constructed by asking one respondent to refer a second, and so on. This is normally done when "there are no known lists or populations from which respondents could reasonably be selected" (Lauderback, Hansen, Waldorf 1992). However, while gangs may be "hidden populations" like drug users, burglars, or the homeless, they do have a definite, if diffuse, social organization with loosely definable populations which can be sampled. This makes snowball sampling a strategy of second choice, and a choice that presents its own problems in selection.

Decker and Van Winkle's (1994, 1996) study is a good example. Through a snowball sample they interviewed 99 active gang members from 29 gangs with respondents varying in age from 13 to 29 years. Unfortunately we do not know how responses differed by age, a reasonable question for a sample with such a wide age range. Decker and Van Winkle do not tell us why they believed those interviewed were representative of all gang members, or members of any specific gang. They did corroborate gang membership by field observation, but that still begs the question of representativeness.

A snowball sample is also only as good as the gatekeeper or the key link on the chain (Whyte 1943). If the chain referral begins with non-gang members, like Decker and Van Winkle's (1996), or with community agencies, like Fagan's (1990), we may have problems with selectivity. This problem then compounds itself as initial respondents refer researchers along "chains" which may also be unrepresentative.

How can a researcher be sure those contacted by snowball are active gang members and not "wannabes" who might puff themselves up, ex-members with an axe to grind, or non-gang hustlers out for a buck? In Biernacki and Waldorf's (1981) snowball method, theoretically the researcher exercises increasing control over the referrals, deliberately searching for representativeness. Respondents also could be asked if they could refer to the researcher someone else within the gang who is "different" than the respondent in some key aspect (Guba, Lincoln 1989). I have not read many instances, however,

where gang researchers utilized these techniques. Our Milwaukee research has found that referrals from non-gang sources tend to produce a disproportionate number of respondents who are on the fringes, not the core of the gang (Medico 1995).

SAMPLING FROM ROSTERS

Another method of sampling is based on constructing rosters of gang members. Whyte's (1943) study was with a known population of a single Cornerville gang as was Padilla's (1992) in Chicago. Short and Strodtbeck's (1965) classic test of cultural deviance and strain theories worked from rosters of Chicago gangs. Joan Moore (1978) randomly sampled from age-graded rosters of multiple "klikas" from gangs in East Los Angeles. Both our Milwaukee studies were based on sampling from gang rosters. All of these studies, it should be pointed out, have found variation within the gang and shifting membership rosters. Each of them also found conventional success goals were important to gang members and questioned the validity of cultural deviance theories. So how is a roster compiled and maintained?

Few gangs issue membership cards or keep written rosters and police lists of members of a gang are notoriously inaccurate (Klein 1971). In our 1988 research we simply asked those interviewed to list the street names of all those people who were present when the gang took a name. We wanted only those "core" members who hung out everyday, not hangers-on who came and went. The first respondents were gang members who I had either hired or had worked with me for several years in my capacity as a gang intervention program director. I knew from years of work with these respondents that they were original or founding members. The rosters they compiled were then checked with each successive respondent, who was asked whether there was anyone left off the list or anyone listed who wasn't really a member. The respondent was asked whether each of the members was working, had been to prison, and how involved each member still was with the gang.

In our initial study we interviewed only two or three people from each gang, mainly leaders. We developed an accurate roster from the gang my collaborator, Perry Macon, belonged to, and from a few others. However, some of the other rosters proved to be incomplete. In the current follow-up research, all our staff were founding members of their gangs and they interviewed all or nearly all of the members on their own gang's roster.[6]

PROBLEMS OF SAMPLING FROM ROSTERS

Unfortunately, drawing up a roster does not, in itself, guarantee representativeness. For one thing, gang members vary by age-group. Moore (1978, 1981) solved this problem by randomly sampling all known "klikas" or age-groups of East Los Angeles gangs. In Milwaukee, where gangs formed in 1980s, we interviewed only members from the *founding* group of Milwaukee gangs, those men and women of roughly the same age who were present when the gang first took a name. Therefore we can't be sure the Milwaukee founding group is representative of succeeding groups of gang members. For example, the founders may be more enterprising or daring than gang members who later joined an established gang. Core members, like our founders, also differ from peripheral members or wannabes (Vigil 1988). On the other hand, our strategy was to learn as much as possible about one age-group of gang

members over time in order to develop "working hypotheses" about gang drug selling (Lincoln, Guba 1985). For this purpose, our sample worked well.[7]

I have spent quite some time criticizing how others have sampled, and it would only be fair to subject our own work to the same scrutiny. While most of our rosters were confirmed by each of our respondents, some gang members never did agree on who was properly a member, though the disputed list was quite small. Sometimes "gang members" were improperly included on the roster so our community researcher could interview them and pay them the $50 fee. We weren't always successful in developing satisfactory rosters for gangs from which we had not hired staff.

Once a roster was drawn up, even more problems ensued. While in three of the gangs we interviewed at least 90 percent of the original founding gang members, in two other gangs, we were able to interview only about a third (15 of 35 founding members and 11 of 36). Anyone who does gang research knows that getting interviews is not always easy. We didn't always succeed either and that means we had to be alert for problems of selectivity.

In one of these two gangs where we didn't interview everyone, we limited the number of interviews ourselves due to constraints of time and after getting a detailed picture of the gang drug business, our main objective. While we can't be sure our sample was representative, no one refused to be interviewed. But in the other gang we did run into problems of some members refusing to be interviewed. Refusals may introduce systematic bias, perhaps hiding involvement in drug use, violent behavior, or gang members who have gone "legit" and do not want to dig up their past.

Refusals in this one case turned out to be a staff related problem. The staff person for the gang where we had many refusals was a "legit" (Hagedorn 1994a) someone who had been a member of the gang about the time of its founding, but had moved away, held a job as a security guard for a while, and had gone on to college. He and his family were well known and had been well respected among the gang, but his upward mobility led to tensions with the gang. We generally had the most success getting good interviews when our homeboy interviewers had been to prison or had once been a "newjack" themselves. These interviewers were more trusted by their home-boys than legits or someone who had never done time.

Our legit was not trusted by some within the gang and his first interviews were with more deviant "dope fiends" who mainly wanted the interview fee. Those interviews contained little information and lots of lying. Further interviews came slowly. Our staff member felt discouraged and panic set in that maybe we weren't going to be able to get the interviews we needed. At that point the gang looked to us like an anomic association of cocaine addicted dead beats.

We solved this problem by continuing to interview. We did get several more interviews of high quality over the next few months, but still we had not located most members of the gang. The gang, however, then began to look more like other gangs we were researching. We looked back over those we interviewed and made sure we had interviewed some who were involved with drug sales and some who were not, as well as some who had actively sold dope and some who had quit the dope game. We ended up interviewing about a third of the entire roster, and fortunately we discovered we had interviewed "homeboys," "dope fiends,"

"legits," as well as "new jacks." Had we generalized about the entire gang from our initial interviews, we would have received a much different picture of the gang than the one we patched together after all the interviews were done. Still, we can't say that our interviews in this gang were "representative."

To summarize: gang research needs to avoid the convenience sample, where gang members are interviewed and observed not because of representativeness, but because of their availability or their uniqueness. *Our research suggests that interviewing everyone on the roster, or sampling rosters on theoretical grounds, would, in most cases, find gang members who resemble middle class Americans more than underclass demons.* But we have too few studies of the entire membership of individual gangs to confidently generalize. I suspect many findings of extreme deviance of gang members are tied up with issues of selectivity which interact with a researcher's prior theoretical assumptions.

THE PRESENTATIONAL ACCOUNTS OF GANG MEMBERS

Representativeness is not the only problem in gang research. We also have the problem of validity. What kind of information are we getting when we interview a gang member? Campbell points out there are many "realities" from which gang members, like all of us, "present" to others.

Social interaction is a creative process in which we select to present ourselves as a particular type of person and then offer accounts of our actions which support that view of ourselves. . . So the accounts the girls give are likely to be a function of their conceptions of themselves and the persons they wanted to present to me. In that sense, everything they say is true. Sometimes however, the facts may have been altered. (Campbell 1984)

An important issue for research is to understand when "the facts have been altered" and when they are reported accurately. Otherwise we report whatever our respondents have to tell us without any context or regard to validity or reliability. Their "accounts" may tell us something about the individual respondents, but little about the social reality in which those individuals are embedded. This is an important consideration in all research, but particularly today when the media has discovered the new and scary role of "gang member" (Ice-T 1994). The violent, drug-selling "gangsta" has attained "a special place in the commercially organized fantasies of the nation" (Goffman 1959).

I question whether cultural deviance theories of gangs may be based on data drawn from gang members' hyped-up "presentational" accounts of their lives as "gangstas" (Shakur 1993). But the rigors of social science also compel me to explore the opposite possibility: could strain theories of gangs, which stress the adherence of gang members' to common American cultural goals, be based on "accounts" which emphasize gang members' conventional side and minimize deviance? How can we methodologically differentiate "presentational" from "operational" data (Van Maanen 1979) and untangle its effects on our research?

"Interviewees," Oakley (1981) reminds us, "are people with a considerable potential for sabotaging the attempt to research them." Use of "hype" is a common strategy for gang members, particularly younger kids, who want to build themselves up to an outsider. Taylor (1989) reports that members of "scavenger" gangs were "very talkative and some were

great braggarts." The problem is made worse when interviews are done in a group where such braggadocio can be contagious as gang members seek to impress one another as well as the interviewer. Younger people also tend to brag more than older ones (Waldorf 1993).[8]

The less familiar the interviewer is with the respondent, the greater opportunity exists for the respondent to exaggerate or to produce an "account" which creates a role of "gang member" to match the "background expectancies" of the researcher (Hyman 1954; Scott, Lyman 1968). Thus studies which seek out an interview with a gang member and then never see him or her again are particularly susceptible to "hype." Conclusions drawn from such interviews could mistakenly find gang members are firmly committed to deviant gang norms and paint an exaggerated picture of a gang.

For example, is this respondent interviewed by Carf Taylor (1989) giving his real feelings, or playing a role for the interview?

> I likes to bust heads. Violence? What's that? [laughing] You got to dog everybody or they gonna dog you. Doggin' is my speciality. . . I'll just see someone and start doggin' them in the street.

On the other hand, why should we believe Jankowski's (1991) class conscious respondents, like this one, who uniformly claim their gang "helps the community:"

> Me and the guys in our group we try to help the community because that's the only way that all of us can protect ourselves from those rich bastards!

It is extremely difficult for outsiders to cut through hype or lies in gang interviews. Even sincerity is a poor test. As Goffman (1959) points out, an actor's performance must be sincere to be successful. In most one-shot gang interviews the respondent has an "account" to present which he can freely develop at the time of the interview, unconstrained from past experience with the interviewer or the anticipation of future contact. How can any sensible theoretical conclusions be drawn from such presentational data?

In our study, through peer interviewers, we tried to capture the individual perspective of gang members looking back over their lives reflectively. The accounts we wanted were not those which might be given to outsiders, but rather "insider" information, "operational data" concerning how the drug game worked and how it affected the life of the respondent. We wanted to go "back stage," to listen to how friends talk with one another privately, where "suppressed facts make an appearance" (Goffman 1959). While such data are themselves accounts, and not some objective reality, we believed these insider accounts would yield an insightful picture of the drug game minus the hype often given to outsiders.

Hype was a minor problem in our interviews mainly because we knew the people we were interviewing. When the respondents tried to play a "gangsta role" to their homeboy interviewer, it was considered crass and was confronted. We did our interviews privately, one on one, with the express purpose of allowing the respondent to talk about his/her life and reflect upon it. Vigil and Long (1990) explain that in certain situations gang members drop their "cholo" front, and this was our expressed intention. The interview situation was not set up to be a chance to brag about exploits as a gang member but, as much as possible, as a talk between friends.

Sometimes hype is the result of a strong belief in the mythology of the gang.

There are certain norms that some gang members hold that they may not want to admit are broken and may even deny to themselves. They want their "account" of the gang to reflect the myths they firmly believe. Consider the question of snitching. While most of our respondents discussed instances of snitching, some denied any such thing ever took place within the gang. In discussing a practice which strongly violates gang norms, some respondents would suddenly switch their identity from "friend" of the interviewer to the stereotypical role of "gangsta":

> *Q:*   Have any of your gang ever snitched on you or anyone else in the gang?
> *#44:*   No! That was against the rules.

What is remarkable about this answer is that the interviewer and respondent were from the same gang. Several years back the interviewer himself had been snitched on by a fellow gang member and went to prison. This incident was well known by everyone in the gang and it caused serious repercussions within the gang, a tightly knit group of friends. The respondent was well aware of the incident but allegiance to mythical gang norms forced him to deny it even to a friend of his—the interviewer—who was the one who had been snitched on! How would an outsider have figured out that this respondent was lying?

On the other extreme, respondents may also lie or give socially acceptable answers to outsiders on some questions on difficult topics. Hyman (1954) pointed out that questions of extreme sensitivity like those asked about communist sympathies in a "period of public fear" like the McCarthy era were most likely to be distorted to researchers. Getting valid data on drug use and gang activities in today's "period of public fear" about gangs and drugs is a rather good analogy to doing research during the 1950s red scare. Denial of involvement in drug dealing is a common response in gang research today (Taylor 1989; Waldorf 1993).

It happened to us too. While we got detailed descriptions of drug sales by the gangs of our staff, we were often lied to by respondents from other gangs. We interviewed two members of one gang which had come to dominate one area's drug business in the last few years. The first interview, with the leader, was a disaster. Although we knew he ran the gang, which was no more than a drug business, he steadfastly denied any involvement with drugs:

> *Q:* How has selling dope changed from when the gang started selling it?
>
> *#22:* What gang? Far as gangs, period? Oh, you know, they got the money, bigger guns, more cars, posse members trying to get deeper, you know how that goes. Like I said, I just say no to drugs.

We knew this was nonsense. When our interviewer was selling drugs several years before in the same neighborhood, he had become friends with this respondent, who was a major dealer in the area. Still, this respondent did not want to admit on tape of his involvement with drug selling. We then followed up that interview with another member of the same gang who gave us detailed information on the gang's lucrative drug trade.

The issue here is that reporting information from this respondent or the one who said snitching was "against the rules" tells us something about the individual gang member, but gives a false picture of reality on those issues. We used Whyte and Deans's (1969) first check in detecting

distortion—"implausibility." Our community researchers, by virtue of their prior gang status, simply *knew* what was a plausible story and what was not. Then, by interviewing others within the gang, they could get beneath the "presentational" account and reconstruct the "real story"—or at least the "real story" as it is presented among intimates.

PROBLEMS OF PEER INTERVIEWS

Hype may be the main threat to validity in most gang research, but minimizing deviant behavior was the main problem in our study. While cultural deviance theorists need to look at how their methods may have led to their conclusions, those of us who see gang members as more conventional than deviant also need to look at how we capture data.

Other research has shown that minority populations in general have less trust in research than whites. Researchers must be concerned that "respondents will provide socially desirable responses or will not be able to provide accurate retrospective reports of behavior" (Collins 1992). While we thought interviewing by persons very familiar with the respondent would counter the tendency to provide socially desirable responses, the strategy at times backfired. While almost 90 percent of the interviews were scored by our community researchers as "truthful" or "mostly truthful" there were several problems.

First were three concerns about the nature of the interaction between the interviewers and the interviewed. Our community researchers interviewed all the members of their own gang, meaning any interviewer effects would be constant across each gang (Hyman 1954). For example, one interviewer was involved in acts of gang violence and consistently failed to question his homeboys about those acts.

Another community researcher was discharged when his interviews were few and poor in quality. His homeboys didn't trust him enough to do an interview and we never did get a good picture of that gang.

A second problem was that our community researchers had a certain status within their gangs, and had a long history with each of the respondents. Where relationships were strained, the interview suffered. More significantly, the respondents reacted to the gang status of the community researcher, and perhaps did not share details that might compromise that relationship. In one extreme case, a community researcher's current husband had been previously married to another homegirl. This created some rather touchy problems in the interview.

Third, the "community researcher" role adopted by our interviewers led to some jealously from peer respondents, who would have loved to have the job themselves. The community researcher's "advocacy" role also may have led some respondents to want to give their "advocate" what he or she wanted, rather than give out the unvarnished truth. For example, one of our interviewers was very active in finding jobs for respondents and some people may have sought out an interview in the expectation of getting work. They would not have wanted to offend or disappoint their link to a job.

It is important to understand the "accounts" our homeboys and homegirls received as the voices of gang members talking to their friends, as opposed to talking to outsiders. This tight relationship between interviewer and interviewed gives our study its uniqueness. But just as you, the reader, are unlikely to be perfectly frank about all aspects of your lives to every friend, that's also the case for gang members. Accounts varied among gang members and even within an interview.

Gang research needs to learn the lessons of feminist methodology which has been exploring variation in accounts by reporting "polyphonically" (Cancian 1992) all the voices they hear, not just the ones that agree with the researcher. In anthropology as well there are increasing concerns with how research may report stereotypes or average frequencies, rather than a more complex reality. Hopper (1995) examines several ways that respondents distort information to ethnographers, even when the ethnographer is well aware of a different reality.

In some cases, outsiders might actually get more information than insiders. For example, many of the gang members I interviewed revealed differences within the gang and criticisms of leaders that might not have come out in peer interviews (1994b). Some respondents confessed beliefs and actions to me they might not have shared with homeboys. I also knew what I was looking for theoretically, and could probe on certain questions where peer interviewers might not. On the other hand, my interviews were not shared reminiscences between friends, and certainly lost important detail. Having a variety of interviewers would probably improve validity.

MINIMIZING DEVIANCE

Overall, both in interviews by peers and by myself, respondents clearly stressed conventional aspirations. It is not clear if those same sentiments would have emerged in interviews given to strangers. The conventional orientation we uncovered cannot be entirely ruled out as an effect of the collaborative method.

For example, respondents consistently minimized or even denied cocaine use. I discovered this as I interviewed the members of one gang, all of whom I had known for ten years. As I did each interview, the respondent claimed his own drug use was minimal, but others were heavy users. This bothered me and concerned me even more when I interviewed a celebrated "dope fiend" of the gang and asked him about the prior respondent.

> Q: Was Bob using heavily that year too?
> #33: Yeah, we all was smoking . . . heavy.

Perhaps since I was a non-gang outsider, some respondents did not want to admit heavy use to me. A few other respondents from other gangs had claimed light or moderate usage when I knew they were crackheads and they knew I knew. But surprisingly, community researchers also reported their own homeboys minimized cocaine use in their interviews. Why?

Several explanations were explored by staff. Among Latinos, who were still heavy into the gang, drug use, if known, could get them "violated." Respondents may have been unsure whether our staff, some of whom once had "rank" within their gangs, might report them to the current "chiefs." Cocaine use, unlike heroin use in Moore's study of East Los Angeles, was relatively new in Milwaukee. Norms did not exist which recognized and legitimized its use.

The order of the interview questions also contributed to some respondents downplaying their drug use. The first hour of the interview concerned the operation of the drug business and the reflections of the respondents over what happened to them and the gang over the last five years. By the time we got to the section where respondents report their drug use, the interview was already two hours old. Even our interviewers complained by then they were "tired out."

The basic problem, however, was how the interview situation itself led to gang members minimizing drug use. Our two to three hour taped interview focused on the adult gang experience and respondents were asked to detail their involvement in drug dealing. In most cases they were looking back at a life they had left or wanted to leave. They often spoke deprecatingly of the dope fiends who had bought their drugs. To their minds, the role of "heavy drug user" was inconsistent with their more "manly" role of "drug dealer." To be seen, even by their homeboys, as a heavy drug user was considered "shameful." Gang members saw their drug use as demonstrating weakness, as this African-American respondent explains:

> #90: As I see it it's a mind game, and if you ain't a strong person it's (cocaine) the wrong thing to mess with.

Their reports consistently minimized drug use, even when the interviewer knew better. Our male respondents simply did not want to admit to their homeboy interviewers or to me that they were not "strong." This pattern was repeated by female respondents, who similarly did not want to be stigmatized as "dope fiends" by their homegirls or those listening to the tape.

There is some confirmation in the literature that familiarity with an interviewer may contribute to under-reporting drug use. In the 1984 National Longitudinal Survey of Youth, Mensch and Kandel (1988) found that when follow-up interviews were conducted by the same interviewer, respondents under-reported drug use as opposed to those who were reinterviewed by a different interviewer. They concluded:

We speculate that interviewer familiarity increases salience of normative standards and that participants respond not only in terms of their past familiarity but also in terms of their subjective expectations regarding the probability of a future encounter with the interviewer. (Mensch, Kandel 1988)

If we ask ourselves whether our collaborative method may have influenced our findings, we have to answer "yes." Our research prompted gang members to reflect on their lives and that process itself may have encouraged more conventional judgments. Some deviance, particularly if it cast the respondent in a poor light, was minimized to peer interviewers.

On the other hand, our conclusions concerning the conventional orientation of gang members were based on many questions in the interview and on harder data like work and family histories (Hagedorn 1994a). In fact it was our collaborative method which allowed us to detect distortion and report it to you along with the rest of our findings. Adherents of cultural deviance models need to similarly examine how their methods may have contributed to the nature of their findings.

DISCUSSION

The use of multiple methods (Webb, Campbell, Schwartz, Sechrest 1966) is still the best way to "triangulate" and verify data. Our own study utilized official statistics, interviews with gang members, surveys of a probability sample of neighborhood residents, interviews with "old heads" from those neighborhoods, the life experiences of our staff, and participant observation by the author in various drug selling locales. All these methods have contributed to our emerging interest in strain theory.

Some researchers who have found deviance where we've found convention-

ality may be working from biased samples or unsuspectingly reporting "hype" as data. When researchers sample from rosters and understand some of their data as "presentational," I believe they will find that most gang members are not sociopaths, but a lot like the rest of us. Confronting selectivity and the presentational aspects of our own data has been a rewarding and healthy process. Today's gang researchers must more seriously examine how their methods have influenced their findings and report it to us. Otherwise, we are in danger of engaging in theoretical debates which are little more than fashion writing about the emperor's new clothes.

I am convinced of the overall utility of our collaborative methods, despite a tendency of our respondents to minimize some types of deviance. Collaborative research is designed to describe the reality of the streets from a back stage perspective which is seldom attained by outsiders, even if they may live among the "natives" for a spell. By involving gang members in every facet of the research, and using representative sampling, the entire gang can be described, including conventional and deviant aspects. Thus while our study argues that most gang members have a conventional orientation, we avoid romanticizing gang life.

These issues are not abstract and significant only for theory—they also have public policy implications. There are at least two mainstream political agendas on gangs which have their own distorted "official definitions" (Mills 1959) of the reality of gang life. Politicians pick and chose from research to buttress their own agendas.

The main policy thrust toward gangs, the law enforcement agenda, wants justification for its war on drugs and build-up of the criminal justice system. It supports and encourages research which presents gang members as especially violent, imperialistic drug dealers, or as purely evil underclass villains (Reeves, Campbell 1994). Law enforcement officials embrace field research whose findings can lend credibility to their self-interested notions of the "threat" posed by gangs. Cultural deviance theory is especially suited to be used by politicians to demonize gang members and make it seem that the only solution is more police and more prisons.

On the other hand, some researchers who are looking to counter this law enforcement juggernaut tend to underplay the organization of drug-dealing, violence, and other ugliness of gang life. William Julius Wilson (1987) pointed out that liberal sociology has suffered a "confused and defensive" reaction to the pathology of the ghetto. One such reaction may be to selectively look for field data which dispute talk-show stereotypes and to report such findings, even though the data may be questionable. I believe such presentational data, like the gang leader in our interviews who "said no to drugs," are not ultimately convincing and their use will backfire.[9]

While this discussion of our research methods has theoretical and political aspects, there are also ethical reasons for paying attention to representativeness and selectivity. Susan Sontag (1973) has said that "to photograph is to appropriate the thing photographed." This is also true of academic descriptions of gang members. As one of our community researchers put it, distorted studies "do violence" to the lives of our respondents. They stigmatize and label gang members and impose on them an outside definition of their lives. Improper labels, like "sociopath," are not only used by authorities, but may be destructively embraced by some of the labeled (Lemert 1967). Portraying gang members as helpless victims is similarly demeaning, takes away agency, and paints

a false and unbelievable picture of gangs in poor communities.

We should never forget that what we as sociologists write has consequences. We must exercise extreme care that the new theoretical realities we construct do not contribute to the dehumanization of a segment of the American people.

End Notes

1. Reliability and validity are old problems in gang research. Here is Spergel's candid admission on his classic research thirty years ago:

> It should be clearly understood that the research was neither rigorously designed nor executed. While much care was exercised in the collection and processing of data, there were no systematic checks on validity or reliability. (Spergel 1964)

There are few current discussions of gang member veracity in the literature. Waldorf (1993) raises the issue briefly in the Final Report of his San Francisco gang study. Also see Vigil and Long (1990) on emic and etic perspectives in anthropological research.

2. Some still forget female gangs. For example Jankowski claims to be studying the "gang problem in general" but he omits any discussion of female gangs (Chesney-Lind 1993). Jankowski's overall methodology has also come under severe attack (Fagan 1993; Klein 1992; Sullivan 1994).

3. Sanders' study is informed by Goffman's work, but he apparently neglected Goffman's rather categorical advice to field researchers:

> There's no way in which, if you're dealing with a lower group, you can start from a higher group. . . You can't move down a social system. You can only move up a social system. So, if you've got to be with a range of people, be with the lowest people first. (Goffman 1989)

4. Skolnick's defense that his interviews with both inmates and correctional officials were consistent confounds reliability with validity. That everyone gave roughly the same story should raise suspicion or at the least prompt a negative case analysis or use of multiple methods (Lincoln, Guba 1985; Webb et al 1966). For other problems of gang interviews in prison, see Moore 1993, Hagedorn 1990, and Decker and Van Winkle 1994.

5. For example Daniel Monti (1994) conducted interviews with "approximately 400" students in a suburban school district. Many—but we don't know how many—of these were selected by the principal of each

school and interviews took place in the school office. In at least one school, administrators were present during the interview. Monti simply abandoned any notion of scientific sampling and confidentiality, for that matter.

6. Our original 1988 rosters were revised by staff and cross-checked with each person interviewed until we were confident of their accuracy. In the first study, N= 19 gangs and 260 members. For the second study we were not satisfied with updated rosters for three gangs and we added rosters from two other gangs which were not included in the 1987 study but had special characteristics which made them important to include. We thus tracked 18 gangs with 296 founding members.

7. Some studies regrettably do not report the age of those interviewed (Lauderback et al 1992) and this can have distorting effects. For example, a sixteen-year-old may report his/her activities in the gang quite differently than a twenty-five-year old. If samples are to be drawn across age groups, each age-graded group should be sampled (Moore 1978, 1991) or else the gang should be sampled by developmental age (Waldorf 1993).

8. Our interviews were done individually, not in groups, to minimize gang members saying things to please friends, leaders, or influential members. Subordinates may play more exaggerated roles to impress leaders or on the other hand, do little more than second what leaders say as a way to hide divisions from outsiders. Group interviews tend to mask variation (Short, Strodbeck 1965). They are particularly susceptible to what Goffman (1959) calls "team performance." A group will typically cooperate "to maintain a particular definition of the situation" toward the audience, i.e. the researcher. A key aspect of any team, according to Goffman, is it "must be able to keep its secrets and have its secrets kept." Gang members with intense group solidarity may also demonize the researcher in the same way as they have been demonized by the media and some research. Group interviews are more useful as a means to triangulate with other data than as a sole source of information (Fontana, Frey 1994).

9. Researchers might not confront a respondent who is giving "politically correct" information minimizing deviance. Goffman explains that such a researcher may be:

> motivated to act tactfully because of an immediate identification with the performers, or because of a desire to avoid a scene, or to ingratiate themselves with the performers for purposes of exploitation. (1959)

References

Becker HS 1970 *Sociological Work: Method and Substance* Chicago: Aldine

Biernacki P, D Waldorf 1981 Snowball sampling: problems and techniques of chain referral sampling *Sociological Methods and Research*. 10 141–163

Campbell A 1984 *The Girls in the Gang*. Oxford: Basil Blackwell Publisher Ltd.

_____ 1990 Female participation in gangs. 163–182 In RC Huf ed *Gangs in America*. Newbury Park, CA: Sage

Cancian FM 1992 Feminist science: methodologies that challenge inequality.?? 6 623–642

Chesney-Lind M 1993 Girls, gangs and violence: anatomy of a backlash *Humanity & Society* 17 321–344

Cloward R, L Ohlin 1960 *Delinquency and Opportunity* Glencoe, IL: Free Press

Collins RL 1992 Methodological issues in conducting substance abuse research on ethnic minority populations. In JE Trimble, CS Bolek, SJ Niemcryk eds *Ethnic and Multicultural Drug Abuse* NY: Haworth Press

Decker S, B Van Winkle 1994 Slinging dope *Justice Quarterly* 11 4 583–604

_____ 1996 *Life in the Gang: Family Friends and Violence* Cambridge, MA:

Fagan J 1990 Social processes of delinquency and drug use among urban gangs. In CR Huffed *Gangs in America* Newbury Park, CA: Sage

_____ 1993 Promises and Lies: The False Criminology of "Islands in the Street." Paper presented at Annual Meeting of the American Society of Criminology. Phoenix (November)

Fontana A, JH Frey 1994 Interviewing: The Art of Science." In NK Denzin, YS Lincoln eds *Handbook of Qualitative Research* Thousand Oaks: Sage

Goffman E 1959 *The Presentation of Self in Everyday Life*. NY: Anchor Books.

_____ 1989 On fieldwork *J Contemporary Ethnography* 18 123–132

Guba EG, YS Lincoln *1989 Fourth Generation Evaluation*. Newbury Park, CA: Sage

Hagedorn JM 1988 *People and Folks: Gangs, Crime, and the Underclass in a Rustbelt City*. Chicago: Lakeview Press

_____ 1990 Back in the field again: gang research in the nineties. In R Huff ed *Gangs in America* Beverly Hills: Sage

_____ 1994 Homeboys, dope fiends, legits, and new Jacks: adult gang members, drugs, and work *Criminology* 32 197–219

_____ 1994 Neighborhoods, markets, and gang drug organization 32 197–219

Hooper K 1995 Society for urban anthropology *Anthropology Newsletter* 3

Hyman HH 1954 *Interviewing in Social Research*. Chicago: U Chicago

Ice- T 1994 To live & die in L.A. *Playboy*.??

Jankowski MS 1991 *Islands in the Street: Gangs and American Urban Society*. Berkeley: U California

Klein M 1971 *Street Gangs and Street Workers*. Englewood Cliffs, NJ: Prentice Hall.

_____ 1992 The new street gang . . . or is it? *Contemporary Sociology.* 21:80–82

_____ 1995 Attempting Gang Control by Suppression: The Misuse of Deterrence Principles. 304–313 In MW Klein, CL Maxsom, J Miller eds *The Modern Gang Reader* Los Angeles: Roxbury

Lauderback D, J Hansen, D Waldorf 1992 'Sisters are doin' it for themselves'; a black female gang in San Francisco. *Gang J* 1 57–70

Lemert EM 1967 *Human Deviance, Social Problems, and Social Control.* Englewood Cliffs, NJ: Prentice-Hall

Lincoln YS, EG Guba 1985 *Naturalistic Inquiry.* Beverly Hills: Sage

Medico R 1995 Puerto Rican and Mexican American teenage girls involved with gangs. Unpublished Masters of Arts. University of Wisconsin-Milwaukee.

Mensch B, DB Kandel 1988 Underreporting of substance use in a national longitudinal youth cohort *Public Opinion Qrtly* 52 100–124

Mills CW 1959 *The Sociological Imagination.* London: Oxford U Press

Monti DJ 1994 *Wannabe: Gang in Suburbs and Schools.* Cambridge, MA: Blackwell

Moore JW 1978 *Homeboys: Gangs, Drugs, and Prison in the Barrios of Los Angeles.* Philadelphia: Temple U Press.

_____ 1988 Gangs and the Underclass: A Comparative Perspective." In JM Hagedorn ed *People and Folks: Gangs, Crime, and the Underclass in a Rustbelt City* Chicago: Lake View Press

_____ 1991 *Going Down to the Barrio: Homeboys and Homegirls in Change.* Philadelphia: Temple U Press

_____ 1993 Gangs, drugs, and violence. 27–48 In S Cummings, DJ Monti eds *Gangs* Albany: SUNY

Oakley A 1981 Interviewing women: a contradiction in terms. In H Roberts ed *Doing Feminist Research* London: Routledge & Keegan Paul

Padilla F 1992 *The Gang as an American Enterprise.* New Brunswick: Rutgers U Press

Reeves JL, R Campbell 1994 *Cracked Coverage: Television News, the Anti-Cocaine Crusade, and the Reagan Legacy.* Durham and London: Duke U Press

Sanders WB 1994 *Gangbangs and Drivebys* NY: Aldine de Gruyter

Scott MB, SM Lyman 1968 Accounts *Amer Sociolog Rev* February 46–62

Shakur S 1993 *Monster: The Autobiography of an L.A. Gang Member* NY: Penguin Books

Short JF, FL Strodtbeck 1965 *Group Process and Gang Delinquency.* Chicago: U Chicago

Skolnick JH 1990 The social structure of street drug dealing *Amer J Police* 9: 1–41

Sontag S 1973 *On Photography* NY: Farrar, Straus and Giroux

Spergel IA 1964 *Racketville Slumtown Haulberg* Chicago: U Chicago.

_____ 1989 Youth gangs: Problem and Response. A Review of the Literature." National Youth Gang Suppression and Intervention Project. University of Chicago School of Social Science Administration.

Sullivan ML 1994 *Islands of the Street* (review) 99 1640–1642

Taylor C 1989 *Dangerous Society.* East Lansing, MI: Michigan State U Press

Thrasher F 1963 *The Gang.* Chicago: U Chicago

Van Maanen J 1979 The fact of fiction in organizational ethnography *Administrative Sci Qrtly* 24 539–550

Vigil D 1988 *Barrio Gangs* Austin: U Texas

Vigil JD, JM Long 1990 Emic and etic perspectives on gang culture: the Chicano case. In 71–102 CR Huff ed *Gangs In America* Beverly Hills: Sage

Waldorf D 1993 Final Report of the Crack Sales, Gangs, and Violence Study: NIDA Grant 5#R01DA06486." Institute for Scientific Analysis. Alameda, CA

Webb EJ, DT Campbell, RD Schwartz, L Sechrest 1966 *Unobtrusive Measures: Nonreactive Research in the Social Sciences.* Chicago: Rand McNally College Publishing

Whyte WF 1943 *Street Corner Society.* Chicago: U Chicago

Whyte WF, JP Dean 1969 How do You Know if the Informant is Telling the Truth." In GJ McCall, JL Simmons eds *Issues in Participant Observations* Reading, MA: Addison-Wesley

Wilson WJ 1987 *The Truly Disadvantaged* Chicago: U Chicago

Yablonsky L 1966 *The Violent Gang* NY: MacMillian

Acknowledgments

The research reported on in this article was funded by NIDA Grant RO107128.

Youth Gangs and Definitional Issues:

When Is a Gang a Gang, and Why Does It Matter?

Finn-Aage Esbensen
L. Thomas Winfree, Jr.
Ni He
Terrance J. Taylor

Social science research is predicated on the practice of employing definitions that allow for replication and independent assessment of any set of research findings. As a general observation, gang research in the United States suffers from definitional shortcomings and calls into question its ability to inform policy makers and expand criminological knowledge. There is little, if any, consensus as to what consti-

Earlier versions of this article were presented at the 1997 American Society of Criminology meeting in Miami, Florida, and the 1998 Western Society of Criminology meeting in Newport Beach, California. This research was supported under Award 94-IJ-CX-0058 from the National Institute of Justice, Office of Justice Programs, U.S. Department of Justice. Points of view in this document are those of the authors and do not necessarily represent the official position of the U.S. Department of Justice. We would like to thank our colleagues Fran Bernat, Libby Deschenes, Wayne Osgood, Chris Sellers, Ron Taylor, and Ron Vogel for their contributions to the research enterprise. We also acknowledge the excellent work of our many research assistants who were responsible for much of the data collection.

Finn-Aage Esbensen, L. Thomas Winfree, Jr., Ni He, and Terrance J. Taylor, CRIME & DELINQUENCY, Vol. 47 No. 1, January 2001 105–130 ©2001 Sage Publications, Inc. Reprinted by permission of Sage Publications, Inc.

tutes a gang and who is a gang member, let alone what gangs do, either inside or outside the law (Ball & Curry, 1995; Decker & Kempf-Leonard, 1991; Gardner, 1993; Klein, 1969; Miller, 1975, 1980; Needle & Stapleton, 1983). When describing their conceptual and operational definitions, many contemporary gang researchers note the absence of definitional consensus. They subsequently identify two widely used benchmarks for assessing whether a given social group is a gang: (1) youth status, defined as an age classification ranging between 10 and the early 20s or even older, and (2) the engagement by group members in law-violating behavior or, at a minimum, "imprudent" behavior. What follows this declaration often takes the following rather vague form: "The definition of gangs used here relies on the work of the leading experts in the field" (see, for example, Howell, 1998, p. 1). The irony, of course, is that even the "experts" cannot agree on what constitutes a gang or gang behavior, and many experts find fault with nearly every definition.

Failure to employ universal definitions of youth gangs and gang membership has numerous implications for gang research and gang-related public policy. For example, research on the extent and nature of the gang problem faces three possible outcomes: (1) accurately stating the gang problem with the best definition for the research question, (2) underestimating it with a far too narrow definition, or (3) overestimating it if the definition is too broad, capturing individuals, groups, and behavior that are of little interest to the intended audience. Of importance, then, is the question guiding the research reported in this article: When is a gang a gang and why does it matter?

The possibility of under- or overestimating gang membership is far from a trivial matter. Resource allocation and public concern (i.e., fear of gang crime) are largely shaped by reports of the magnitude of the problem. Estimates of gang members in the United States in the mid-1990s ranged from about 660,000 to perhaps as many as 1.5 million (Office of Juvenile Justice and Delinquency Prevention, 1997; Curry, Ball, & Decker, 1996; Knox, 1996), numbers that at least one gang expert characterized as "probably conservative because many jurisdictions deny, often for political and image reasons, that there is a problem, especially in the early stages of youth gang development in a community" (Huff, 1998, p. 1). Public policies, particularly law enforcement practices, respond in very direct ways to these numbers, whether the estimates are for the nation or a single community. Hence, how gang is defined impacts the numerator in any per capita rate, let alone the gross number of gangs or gang members.

In addition to the issue of accurately estimating the size of the gang problem is the concern of accurately assessing the epidemiology of gang members. Quite disparate estimates exist with regard to the demographic composition of youth gangs (Esbensen & Winfree, 1998). Law enforcement data paint a picture of inner-city, minority males (generally from single-parent households) (National Youth Gang Center, 1999). Ethnographic studies of older and more homogeneous samples tend to confirm this picture. Surveys, however, call into question the extent to which these stereotypes accurately depict youth gang members.

In this article, we attempt to disentangle some of the definitional questions that arise. Do gang definitions used in community or school-based surveys, for example, produce overestimates of gang youths? That is, do surveys include youths who would not be considered gang members by law enforcement? Or, alternatively, are law enforcement estimates too narrow in scope, excluding individuals who should be included as gang members? Will more restrictive definitions in survey research produce lower prevalence estimates? Will these more restrictive definitions change the demographic depiction of gang members? More specifically, does the application of a more restrictive definition of gang membership in survey data produce estimates of gang membership and depictions of gang members that are more similar to those derived from law enforcement data?

Clearly, the definitions of gang and gang membership used by researchers and policy makers have important implications for both research results and the ways in which policy makers employ those findings. The present study, then, provides multiple answers to a single compound research question: When is a gang a gang, and why does it matter? We propose that by shifting from a less restrictive definition through increasingly more restrictive ones, the analysis should yield valuable insights into the overall gang phenomenon.

DEFINING THE GANG

Nearly from the onset of 20th-century gang research, a popular strategy for defining gangs was to let the youths do it themselves (i.e., those who claimed membership). Thrasher (1927/1963), recognizing the scientific need "to discover what is typical rather than what is unique," centered his definition of a gang on its natural history, those characteristics that made it unique and distinct from other "types of collectives" (p. 37). His list of definitional characteristics included (a) a spontaneous and unplanned origin, (b) intimate face-to-face relations, (c) a sense of organization, solidarity, and morale that is superior to that exhibited by the mob, (d) a tendency to move through space and meet a hostile element, which can precipitate cooperative, planned conflict, a morale-boosting activity in itself, (e) the creation of a shared esprit de corps and a common tradition or "heritage of memories," and (f) a propensity for some geographic area or territory, which it will defend through force if necessary (Thrasher, 1927/1963, pp. 36–46). Nowhere in his definition, however, does Thrasher mention delinquent or law-violating behavior as a criterion for a gang. Certainly, he acknowledged that the criminal gang was one type, but he also stressed that among his 1,313 gangs were some that were good and some that were bad (Thrasher, 1927/1963, pp. 47–62; see also Bursik & Grasmick, 1993).

Almost 50 years after Thrasher, Klein (1971) argued persuasively for the self-definition of gang members: a gang is "any denotable adolescent group of youngsters who (a) are generally perceived as a dis-

tinct aggregation by others in their neighborhood, (b) recognize themselves as a denotable group (almost invariably with a group name), and (c) have been involved in a sufficient number of delinquent incidents to call forth a consistent negative response from neighborhood residents and/or law enforcement agencies" (p. 428). As Bursik and Grasmick (1993) have further noted, the first two criteria are easily met by a number of social groups, including Greek fraternities and, we might add, Greek sororities, the Boy and Girl Scouts, and Police Athletic League members, among others. Even if the fraternities identified by Bursik and Grasmick exhibited the third quality and enjoyed a "dangerous" reputation on campus, they would not, in all likelihood, come to the attention of the law enforcement community's groups that target gangs. The qualitative differences between how fraternities compared to street gangs fulfill the first two criteria tend to neutralize much of the behavioral element and lead to it being reclassified as "college pranks," unless, as has happened, someone is seriously injured or dies.

Ball and Curry (1995) have provided perhaps the most cogent and erudite treatment of definitional alternatives and issues surrounding the term *gang*. After engaging in a lengthy linguistic analysis of various ways to define *gang*, they proposed that "gang definitions would do better to focus on the abstract, formal characteristics of the phenomenon rather than connotative, normative content" (Ball & Curry, 1995, p. 240). In this regard, they mirrored the much earlier concerns of Short (1968), who stated, "It is clear . . . that in most cases gangs and subcultures are not coterminous and that among gang boys most delinquencies do not involve the total group . . . and the behavior of gang members is a function not only of participation in the subculture of the gang, but of other subcultures as well, e.g., social class and ethnicity associates with neighborhood residence" (p. 11).

This caveat—its early and recent versions—has generally fallen on deaf ears. Largely conceptual treatments of gangs, such as those offered by Curry and Decker (1998), include a merger of Thrasher's (1927/1963) and Klein's (1971) elements, including being a social group, using symbols, engaging in verbal and nonverbal communications to declare their "gangness," a sense of permanence, gang identified territory or turf, and, lastly, crime (pp. 2–6). Maxson (1998) emphasizes that not only are adjectives often necessary to make sense of gangs, as in drug gangs and street gangs, but gangs also exhibit a remarkably fluid social structure (p. 2).[1] Moreover, "the terms 'wannabe,' 'core,' 'fringe,' 'associate,' 'hardcore,' and 'O.G.' (original gangster) reflect the changing levels of involvement and the fact that the boundaries of gang membership are penetrable" (Maxson, 1998, p. 2).

Quantitative data-based gang researchers continue to employ crime, and thereby Ball and Curry's (1995) connotative behavioral content, as a defining criterion. For example, Battin, Hill, Abbott, Catalano, and Hawkins (1998) disposed of the gang question with the following: "Gang membership at ages 14 and 15 was measured by the question, 'Do you belong to a gang?' To validate gang membership, follow-up questions about the gang's name and characteristics were asked" (p. 97) (see Battin-Pearson, Thornberry, Hawkins, & Krohn, 1998).

Winfree, Fuller, Bäckström, and Mays (1992) explored the empirical utility of both parts of this procedure for defining gang membership. That is, they employed two definitions of gang membership in answering the following two-part question: What is the effect of changing the definition of gang membership on (a) the level of gang involvement and (b) the prediction of self-reported group-context offending? They reported that the self-designation method alone yielded nearly equal numbers of wannabes (i.e., youths indicating that they had been interested in joining a gang), former gang members (i.e., youths indicating that they had been involved with gangs in the past but not now), and currently active gang members (i.e., youths indicating a continuing involvement in gangs); however, a restrictive definition, such as that employed by Battin and associates (1998), revealed that most of the sample, more than 70%, were wannabes, with active gang members outnumbering former gang members two to one (Winfree et al., 1992, p. 33). They also found that the same set of predictors revealed more about self-nomination gang membership than the restrictive definition (Winfree et al., 1992, p. 35). Winfree and associates (1992) suggested three reasons for this anomaly: first, youths in "near-gangs" may feel considerable motivation to demonstrate their "gang-worthiness" by participating in group-context offending; second, the sample of "true" gang members may not include the most criminally active ones as they may not be in school; and third, those criminally active youths still in school may have absented themselves from the survey (pp. 35–36) (see Winfree, Bäckström, & Mays, 1994). In essence, changing the definition of what constitutes a gang and membership in that gang can alter the findings even within the same sample.

DELINQUENCY THEORY, GANGS, AND CRITERION-RELATED VALIDATION

The current research question comports well with a criterion-related validity check. We elected to include in the analyses variables drawn from the key constructs associated with Akers's (1985, 1994) variant of social learning theory and Gottfredson and Hirschi's (1990) self-control theory. As Kerlinger (1973) has noted, "in criterion-related validation, which is often practical and applied research, the basic interest is usually more in the criterion, some practical outcome, than in the predictors. . . . A test high in criterion-related validity is one that helps investigators make successful decisions in assigning people to treatments, conceiving treatments broadly" (pp. 459–460). In this case, we are interested in what happens to the relationships between the theoretical variables and gang membership when we change the definition of what constitutes a *gang*. The goal, then, would be to look at the utility of such variable labels as gang for theorists and practitioners.

Social learning theory has logical links to gang behavior, especially given the social nature of much gang-related offending (Bjerregard & Smith, 1993; Hill, Howell, Hawkins, & Battin-Pearson, 1999; Maxson, Whitlock, & Klein, 1998; Winfree et al., 1994). In particular, many social learning variables have demonstrated predictive efficacy for gang membership and gang-related delinquency, including differential associations, or the extent to which one's peers are involved in delinquent versus pro-social activities; positive and negative social reinforcers, here measured as commitment to negative peers and positive peers; and differential definitions, defined as neutralizations and perceived level of guilt for misbehavior (Esbensen & Deschenes, 1998; Winfree, Bernat, & Esbensen, in press). Similarly, gang membership and gang-related misbehavior fit closely with Gottfredson and Hirschi's (1990) concept of analogous behaviors, ones commonly observed in low self-

control individuals (Decker & Van Winkle, 1996; Deschenes & Esbensen, 1999; Fleisher, 1998; Lynskey, Winfree, Esbensen, & Clason, 2000). Key among the self-control variables, and ones included in this analysis, are the level of parental monitoring, or the extent to which parents are aware of their children's location, activities, and friends; impulsivity, or a propensity to engage in actions without thinking through all of the consequences; and risk-seeking, a tendency to engage in actions that entail more than a modicum of danger to the participants (Arneklev, Grasmick, Tittle, & Bursik, 1993; Gibbs & Giever, 1995; Gibbs, Giever, & Martin, 1998; Gottfredson & Hirschi, 1990).

We are not, strictly speaking, testing either of these theories or even the specific variables included in this analysis. Rather, based on our research question, we posit tests of five different definitions of self-declared gang membership and their links to theoretical constructs. That is, we are predicting gang membership, variably defined as an either/or condition, from social learning and self-control variables. Our objectives in this research are two-fold: (a) to what extent are the prevalence and characteristics of gang members altered by varying the operational definition of youth gang membership? and (b) to what extent are theoretical concepts derived from social learning theory and self-control theory capable of distinguishing gang from non-gang youth under five increasingly restrictive definitions of gang membership?

THEORETICAL AND POLICY IMPLICATIONS

The two questions posed above are of significance for both theoretical and policy relevant reasons. First, what we know about delinquency in urban areas is largely based on youth gang research; many advances in delinquency research and theory have taken gangs as their focal point (Esbensen & Winfree, 1998). Consequently, it is not surprising that theory-based gang studies often employ gang membership and other group-context criminality as dependent variables. For example, Cloward and Ohlin's (1960) *Delinquency and Opportunity*, a work that introduced differential opportunity theory as an expansion of both anomie and differential association theories, was subtitled *A Theory of Delinquent Gangs*.[2] Citing Thrasher's work on urban gangs, Cloward and Ohlin noted that collective alternative solutions to the commonly felt problems of urban youth do not create a gang until a group of youth "becomes a conflict group." As a general rule, then, theory-based youth gang studies have begun with the assumption that for a given social group to be a gang, it must engage in some negativistic, law-violating behavior, among other things. The delinquent gang is subsequently viewed as a likely venue in which to test or develop a delinquency theory. To what extent has this definitional decision by researchers and theorists impacted the variance found in the dependent variable and, in some cases, its ties to explanatory variables?

For policy makers, the perceived need to control gangs and gang behavior has led to the passage of antigang laws and codes. Although many of these legal actions have been challenged, most have withstood the legal scrutiny of the appellate courts. For example, persons convicted of violating the federal Criminal Street Gangs Statute (1999) can receive an additional sentence enhancement of up to 10 years. Some states, like California, have adopted sentence enhancements for persons found to have committed a felony "for the benefit of, at the direction of, or in association with any criminal street gang, with the specific intent to promote, further, or assist in any criminal conduct by gang members" (California Penal Code, 1999, section 186.22 [b][1]). In fact, "actively participating in any criminal street gang" can, by itself, result in a jail or prison sentence in California (California Penal Code, 1999, section 186.22[a]). As a further example of legislation intended to control gang members, Illinois statutorily denies probation to persons convicted of forcible felonies if the offenses were related to the activities of organized gangs.[3] Given the lack of consensus about what constitutes gang membership, is it viable to implement policies that subject individuals to criminal justice processing due to their alleged gang status?

RESEARCH DESIGN

SITE SELECTION AND SAMPLE

During Spring 1995, eighth-grade students in 11 cities—Las Cruces (NM), Omaha (NE), Phoenix (AZ), Philadelphia (PA), Kansas City (MO), Milwaukee (WI), Orlando (FL), Will County (IL), Providence (RI), Pocatello (ID), and Torrance (CA)—completed self-administered questionnaires as part of the National Evaluation of the Gang Resistance Education and Training (GREAT) program (Esbensen & Osgood, 1999). The final sample consisted of 5,935 eighth-grade public-school students, representing 42 schools and 315 classrooms. Passive parental consent, in which excluded students were those whose parents did not want their children participating, was used at all sites except one. Torrance relied on active consent, in which parents had to return signed permission forms for their children. Participation rates, or the percentage of children providing answers to the questionnaires, varied between 98% and 100% at the passive consent sites. At the four active consent schools, the participation rates varied from a low of 53% to a high of 75% (Esbensen et al., 1997). Comparison of school district data indicates that the study sample is representative of eighth-grade students enrolled in public schools in these 11 communities.

This public school-based sample has the standard limitations associated with school-based surveys, such as exclusion of private school students, exclusion of truants, sick, and/or tardy students, and the potential underrepresentation of high-risk youth. With this caveat in mind, the current sample is composed of nearly all eighth-grade students in attendance on the days questionnaires were administered in these 11 jurisdictions. The sample includes primarily 13- to 15-year-old students attending public schools in a broad cross-section of communities across the continental United States. This is not a random sample and strong generalizations cannot be made to the adolescent population as a whole. However, students from these 11 jurisdictions do represent the following types of communities: large urban areas with a majority of students belonging to a racial or ethnic minority (Philadelphia, Phoenix, Milwaukee, and Kansas City), medium-sized cities (population ranges between 100,000 and 500,000) with considerable racial and/or ethnic heterogeneity (Providence and Orlando), medium-sized cities with a majority of White students but a substantial minority enrollment (Omaha and Torrance), a small city (fewer than 100,000 inhabitants) with an ethnically diverse student population (Las Cruces), a small, racially homogeneous (i.e., White) city (Pocatello), and a

rural community in which more than 80% of the student population is White (Will County). Such a sample is appropriate to the prototypical prevention approach exemplified by GREAT, which addresses a social problem through a simple intervention delivered to the broadest possible population, rather than concentrating a more intensive program on a smaller high-risk population. Furthermore, Maxson and Klein (1994) and Curry et al. (1996) document that gangs are not exclusively an urban phenomenon, as is often suggested. They report that gangs also exist in communities with populations of less than 25,000. According to the 1995 National Youth Gang Survey, law enforcement agencies in nine of the sites represented in this study reported active youth gangs in their jurisdictions during 1995 (National Youth Gang Center, 1997).

MEASURES

Gang Definition

Our primary purpose in this article is to examine the criterion-related validity of the self-nomination technique of gang membership. We explore this issue by assessing the effect of five different definitions on attitudes and behaviors. Self-report studies rely on respondent self-identification of gang membership, similar to police reliance on gang members "claiming" affiliation. Just as the police often require additional criteria to be met (i.e., using gang signs, wearing colors, and associating with known gang members), self-report surveys often include follow-up questions that provide confirmation of gang affiliation. In the current study, respondents were asked two filter questions: "Have you ever been a gang member?" and "Are you now in a gang?" These two questions provide our first two levels of gang membership.

Three increasingly more restrictive definitions of gang membership were then created. Although there is some disagreement concerning inclusion of illegal activity as a requisite for gang membership (Ball & Curry, 1995; Bursik & Grasmick, 1993; Short, 1968), it is our position that participation in criminal activity is a key element that distinguishes youth gangs from other youth groups. As such, aside from self-nomination, our first criterion for designation as a delinquent gang member was for the respondent to indicate that their gang was involved in at least one of the following illegal activities: getting in fights with other gangs, stealing things, robbing other people, stealing cars, selling marijuana, selling other illegal drugs, or damaging property.

The next criterion required gang members to indicate that their gang had some level of organization. Specifically, the survey respondents were asked if the following described their gang: "there are initiation rites, the gang has established leaders, the gang has symbols or colors." An affirmative response to all three of these descriptors led to designation as an "organized gang" member.

The last criterion used to determine gang membership was an indicator of whether individuals considered themselves a core member or a peripheral member. This classification was determined by their response to the following instructions. A five-ringed concentric circle (i.e., a target) was drawn on the chalkboard and students were asked to think of the circle as their gang and to indicate "how far from the center of the gang are you?" Those students indicating they were in the inner two circles were classified as "core," whereas those indicating they were in circles 3 through 5 were classified as "peripheral" members (see Appendix A for a listing of the five definitions).

Demographic, Attitudinal, and Behavioral Measures

Demographic, attitudinal, and behavioral measures were obtained from students completing the self-administered questionnaires. Responses to five questions describe the demographic composition of our sample and allow for comparisons of gang and nongang youth. Students provided the following background information:

- their sex;
- family structure (i.e., do they live with both their mother and father [including stepparents], with only their mother, with only their father, or some other situation);
- their race (White, African American, Hispanic, Asian, or other);
- their age; and
- the highest level of schooling completed by their mother and father.

Attitudinal measures used in these analyses are representative of social learning theory and self-control theory. Due to the cross-sectional nature of this sample, we do not attempt to conduct theory testing, but we do use theoretical concepts to explore the relationship between gang membership and indicators of these two theoretical perspectives. Indicators of self-control theory include the following: parental monitoring, impulsivity, and risk-seeking. Social learning theory is represented by the following measures: delinquent peers, prosocial peers, commitment to negative peers, commitment to positive peers, neutralization (tolerance of fighting under specified situations), and perceived guilt. Unless otherwise indicated, the scales (which are described in more detail in Appendix B) were adapted from the National Youth Survey (Elliott, Ageton, & Huizinga, 1985) or the Denver Youth Survey (Huizinga, Esbensen, & Weiher, 1991).

We also obtained measures of self-reported delinquency and drug use. Students were provided a list of 17 behaviors and 5 different drugs and then asked to indicate if they had ever committed the act or used the drug. If the students answered yes, they were asked to indicate how many times they had engaged in the behavior during the past 12 months. In addition to a general delinquency measure, we created five subscales of behavior: status offenses, minor offenses, property offenses, crimes against person, and drug sales (items included in these subscales are listed in Appendix B).

RESULTS

BIVARIATE ANALYSES

The demographic composition of gangs using the five different definitions of gang affiliation is reported in Table 1. A total of 4,773 (82.6%) respondents indicated that they had never been in a gang, whereas 994 (16.8% of the sample) answered yes to the question of ever having been a gang member. In columns 3 and 4 (identified as Gang 1 and Gang 2), we distinguish between those youth who reported ever being in a gang from those who reported current gang membership (522 or 8.8% of the sample). Likewise, under the remaining three columns, we include those youth who no longer fit the increasingly restrictive criteria as nongang members. Of primary importance is to highlight the degree to which prevalence estimates of gang membership are an artifact of measurement. In this sample, the prevalence of gang membership could be said to be any one of the following: 17% based on the "ever" gang member question; 9% according to the "current" gang member question; 8% are "delinquent" gang members;

slightly less than 5% are "organized" gang members; and only 2% are "core" gang members.

The second column in Table 1 reveals that 45% of those youth who had never been in a gang were male, 44% were White, 30% lived in single parent homes, and 68% reported that at least one of their parents had more than a high school education (i.e., attended some college or more). Compared to the "never in gang" youth, all five definitions of gang member status indicate that gang members are more likely to be male (ranging from 54% male in the most restrictive definition to 63% male under the less restrictive gang definitions). Gang members are also more likely to be a racial or ethnic minority, to live in single parent homes, and to have parents who have not graduated from high school. Contrary to what we had expected, the most restrictive definition did not produce a picture of gang members that was more consistent with law enforcement data than was the least restrictive definition. That is, the core gang members, relative to the "ever" gang members, were not more likely to be male or members of racial and ethnic minorities, a finding inconsistent with law enforcement-based surveys.

In Table 2, we report the mean scores for both gang and nongang youths on the self-control and social learning measures. Here we see that the gang members reported increasingly lower levels of parental monitoring with each new restriction to gang membership. And, in each instance, the gang members' perceptions of parental monitoring were statistically significantly different from the nongang members. The same pattern holds for each theoretical construct. As the definition of gang membership becomes increasingly more restrictive, the expressed attitudes of the gang members become increasingly more antisocial. That is, gang members are more

TABLE 1: Demographic Characteristics of Gang Members

	Total Sample	GANG 1	GANG 1	GANG 2	GANG 2	GANG 3	GANG 3	GANG 4	GANG 4	GANG 5
		Never in Gang	Ever in Gang	Now in Gang	Non-Gang	Delinquent Gang	Non-Gang	Organized Delinquent	Non-Gang	Core Gang
	n = 5935	n = 4773	n = 483	n = 522	n = 502	n = 467	n = 692	n = 275	n = 827	n = 137
Age (M)	13.8	13.8	14	14.1	14	14.1	14	14.1	14.1	14
Gender (%)*										
Male	48	45	59	63	59	63	61	60	62	54
Female	52	55	41	37	41	37	39	40	38	46
Race (%)*										
White	41	44	26	24	25	24	24	27	24	30
Black	27	25	30	31	30	31	32	28	32	23
Hispanic	19	17	30	25	30	25	29	25	28	22
Other	14	14	15	19	15	20	16	20	16	25
Family structure (%)*										
Single	31	30	35	41	35	41	36	41	37	40
Intact	62	64	56	47	55	46	53	46	52	46
Other	7	6	10	13	10	13	11	13	11	15
Parents' education (%)*										
<high school	10	9	13	16	13	17	14	15	14	18
High school	24	24	27	27	28	27	28	26	28	24
>high school	66	68	60	57	60	57	58	59	58	57

* $p < .01$. All chi-square tests comparing gang youth with those never in a gang are statistically significant.

TABLE 2: Tests of Attitudinal Variables by Gang Membership

	Total Sample	Never in Gang	GANG 1	GANG 2	GANG 3		GANG 4		GANG 5	
			Ever in Gang	Now in Gang	Non-Gang	Delinquent Gang	Non-Gang	Organized Delinquent	Non-Gang	Core Gang
Self-control theory										
Parental monitoring	3.72	3.82	3.49	3.16	3.49	3.12	3.39	3.13	3.36	3.01
Impulsivity	2.85	2.78	3.05	3.25	3.05	3.25	3.1	3.3	3.12	3.39
Risk-seeking	3.06	2.95	3.41	3.7	3.4	3.74	3.47	3.79	3.5	3.92
Social learning theory										
Guilt	2.31	2.42	2.03	1.66	2.03	1.63	1.93	1.6	1.89	1.54
Commitment to negative peers	2.4	2.23	2.71	3.5	2.71	3.54	2.94	3.52	3.01	3.7
Commitment to positive peers	3.8	3.93	3.54	3.04	3.53	2.99	3.38	3.01	3.34	2.95
Neutralization, fight	3.98	3.85	4.36	4.66	4.36	4.7	4.46	4.72	4.49	4.75
Pro-social peers	2.97	3.08	2.68	2.36	2.68	2.34	2.6	2.3	2.57	2.23
Delinquent peers	2	1.82	2.43	3.1	2.43	3.19	2.59	3.27	2.68	3.4

NOTE: All *t* tests of the attitudinal variables by gang membership are statistically significant at the .01 level: never in gang/nongang in each gang definition, never in gang/gang in each gang definition, nongang/gang in each gang definition.

impulsive, engage in more risk-seeking behavior, have more delinquent friends, have fewer pro-social peers, report less perceived guilt, have a greater tendency to view fighting as appropriate behavior, are more committed to delinquent peers, and are less committed to positive peers. In short, as the definition of gang membership takes on more characteristics of the media image of an organized, delinquent street gang, the members express more antisocial attitudes.

The same pattern evidenced with respect to attitudes is reflected in behavioral self-reports. With each increasingly restrictive definition, the gang members reported greater participation in illegal activity. For example, whereas the mean number of crimes committed against persons for the youth who were never in a gang was 0.60, those youth who were currently core members of a delinquent youth gang reported committing an average of 3.69 (six times as many) crimes against persons. For each of these self-report subscales, the ratio of offending for core gang members and never gang members ranged from 4:1 for status offenses to 22:1 for drug sales (see Table 3).

MULTIVARIATE ANALYSES

To examine the extent to which demographic characteristics and attitudes can predict gang membership, we conducted a series of logistic regression analyses. Step-wise forward inclusion procedures were used to identify the relative predictive power of demographic variables and the indicators of social learning and self-control theories. For parsimony, we report only the final models for each gang definition in Table 4. One notable observation is that the effect of demographic variables becomes less important with each increasingly restrictive definition. Whereas all but the family structure variable were significant in the ever gang member definition, none of the demographic characteristics was statistically significant in the full model predicting core gang membership.

These summary models highlight the importance of peers (both having delinquent peers and expressing a commitment to negative peers) and of attitudes about right and wrong (perceptions of guilt and tolerance of fighting). Importantly, it is exposure to delinquent peers that is vital, not association with pro-social peers. In each model, the delinquent activity of the peer group was predictive of gang membership. Battin et al. (1998), in an examination of the simultaneous effects of gang membership and delinquent peers on both self-reported and court-reported delinquency, noted that gang membership "contributed directly to delinquency and substance use above and beyond association with delinquent peers" (p. 106). Thus, it is not simply a case that the variable representations for delinquent peers and gangs are measuring the same thing. Having delinquent peers and belonging to a gang are two different states; however, the former would appear to be predictive of the latter. As noted by Esbensen and Huizinga (1993), among others (Cairns & Cairns, 1991; Hill et al., 1999; Thornberry, Krohn, Lizotte, & Chard-Wierschem, 1993), aggressive and delinquent youth and youth who have shown a propensity to enjoy the company of like-minded youth, are more likely to become gang youth.

In addition to peer variables, the variables that are most predictive of gang membership are the respondents' perceptions of guilt and the degree to which they indicate that fighting is an appropriate response in specific situations. To measure guilt, respondents were asked to indicate how guilty they would feel if they engaged in one of 16 different delinquent acts (corresponding to those included in

TABLE 3: Tests of Behavioral Variables by Gang Membership

	Total Sample M	Never in Gang M	GANG 1 Ever in Gang M	GANG 2 Now in Gang M	Non Gang M	GANG 3 Delinquent Gang M	Non Gang M	GANG 4 Organized Delinquent M	Non Gang M	GANG 5 Core Gang M
Status offenses	1.92	1.47	3.21	5.14	3.22	5.42	3.75	5.56	3.95	5.94
Minor offenses	1.31	0.92	2.25	4.08	2.22	4.32	2.8	4.2	3.01	4.37
Property offenses	0.83	0.57	1.29	2.93	1.27	3.09	1.72	3.14	1.9	3.37
Personal offenses	0.82	0.6	1.21	2.65	1.2	2.85	1.52	3.13	1.67	3.69
Drug sale	0.5	0.21	0.86	3.16	0.83	3.52	1.36	3.89	1.6	4.79
Drug use	1.29	0.92	2.23	4.07	2.23	4.24	2.69	4.41	2.86	5.06
Delinquency, total	0.99	0.67	1.67	3.52	1.66	3.76	2.14	3.92	2.32	4.41

NOTE: All three-way *t* tests of the behavioral variables by gang membership are statistically significant at the .01 level: never in gang/nongang in each gang definition, never in gang/gang in each gang definition, nongang/gang in each gang definition.

TABLE 4: Predicting Gang Membership: Logistic Regression Analysis

	EVER IN GANG			NOW IN GANG			DELINQUENT GANG			ORGANIZED DELINQUENT			CORE GANG		
	B	SE	Exp(B)	B	SE	Exp(B)	B	SE	Exp(B)	B	SE	Exp(B)	B	SE	Exp(B)
Demographics															
Age	0.26*	0.06	1.3	0.26*	0.08	1.29	0.26*	0.09	1.31	0.1	0.09	1.1	-0.08	0.1	0.92
Female	-0.29*	0.09	0.75	-0.24	0.12	0.78	-0.17	0.13	0.84	0.07	0.15	1.08	0.34	0.2	1.4
Race															
Black	0.68*	0.12	1.98	0.64*	0.16	1.9	0.65*	0.17	1.91	0.16	0.21	1.18	-0.03	0.28	0.98
Hispanic	0.93*	0.12	2.54	0.65*	0.16	1.92	0.64*	0.17	1.89	0.35	0.2	1.41	0.13	0.26	1.13
Other	0.88*	0.13	2.42	0.93*	0.18	2.53	0.86*	0.19	2.35	0.60*	0.22	1.82	0.63	0.27	1.88
Family															
Single parent	0.09	0.1	1.1	0.33*	0.13	1.4	0.33*	0.13	1.4	0.39	0.16	1.47	0.32	0.21	1.37
Other	0.34	0.16	1.41	0.46	0.2	1.58	0.48	0.21	1.62	0.52	0.25	1.68	0.65	0.31	1.92
Social learning															
Neutral fight	0.42*	0.06	1.52	0.60*	0.1	1.35	0.61*	0.11	1.85	0.61*	0.14	1.84	0.65*	0.2	1.91
Delinquent peers	0.58*	0.06	1.79	0.71*	0.08	2.03	0.80*	0.08	2.24	0.80*	0.1	2.22	0.79*	0.13	2.21
Pro-social peers	-0.04	0.07	0.94	-0.03	0.09	0.97	0.01	0.1	1.01	0.01	0.12	1.01	0.01	0.15	1.01
Commitment to negative peers	0.15*	0.04	1.16	0.33*	0.06	1.39	0.33*	0.06	1.38	0.18*	0.07	1.19	0.16	0.1	1.18
Commitment to postitive peers	-0.02	0.04	0.98	-0.05	0.05	0.95	-0.06	0.06	0.94	0.01	0.07	1.01	0.02	0.09	1.02
Guilt	-0.77*	0.1	0.46	-0.91*	0.14	0.4	-0.93*	0.15	0.39	-1.03*	0.19	0.36	-1.03*	0.27	0.36
Self-control															
Impulsivity	0.06	0.07	1.06	0.09	0.09	1.1	0.03	0.09	1.03	0.14	0.11	1.15	0.14	0.14	1.15
Parental monitoring	-0.04	0.06	0.96	-0.04	0.07	0.96	-0.08	0.08	0.92	-0.03	0.09	0.97	-0.02	0.12	0.98
Risk-seeking	0.04	0.06	1.05	-0.09	0.08	0.92	-0.06	0.09	0.95	-0.04	0.1	0.96	0.06	0.14	1.06
Model X^2	1227.08*			1057.42*			1040.29*			617.71*			350.11*		
Degree of freedom	16			16			16			16			16		
Nagelkerke R^2	0.344			0.397			0.414			0.341			0.306		

$* p < .01.$

the self-report inventory). Acceptance of physical violence as a suitable response to conflict was measured by three questions tapping the appropriateness of getting in a physical fight if, for example, someone was threatening to hurt friends or family. As seen in the bivariate analyses (Table 2), the core gang members had a mean of 1.54 on the 3-point guilt scale (with 1 indicating *not at all guilty* and 3 representing *very guilty*) compared to a mean of 2.42 for those never in a gang. For the neutralization to fighting measure, the core gang members averaged a score of 4.75 on a 5-point scale (5 indicates *strongly agree*), whereas those youth who reported never being in a gang averaged 3.85. These latter two findings comport well with the general discussion of normative saliency for social deviance (Krohn, Akers, Radosevich, & Lanza-Kaduce, 1982; Sellers, Winfree, & Griffiths, 1993), and that concept's link to social learning theory's differential definitions (Akers, 1985). As we report, gang members, youth who have been shown by other researchers to be more violent and delinquency-engaged than other comparable youth, even delinquents (Howell, 1998, pp. 8–11; Huff, 1998; Thornberry & Burch, 1997), exhibit lower perceptions of guilt and greater tolerance for physical violence.

DISCUSSION

So what have we learned? When is a gang a gang, and why does it matter? These questions result in somewhat different answers for researchers, theorists, and policy makers. For researchers, it is important to refine measurement: to assess the validity and reliability of the measures being used. For theorists, it is important to better understand factors associated with gang membership and associated behaviors,

whether testing or constructing theory. For policy makers, it is important to know the extent and nature of the gang problem to allow for development of appropriate policies and programs. Clearly, the primary domains of interest for theorists, researchers, and policy makers are not mutually exclusive and, in fact, are closely intertwined.

Considerable debate has centered around the attributes that constitute a gang and the criteria necessary to classify someone a gang member. Miller (1980), Klein (1995), Short (1996), Spergel (1995), and others have been engaged in this debate for three decades with little success in resolving their differences. Of particular concern in this debate have been the following questions: Is involvement in delinquent activity a prerequisite for classifying a youth group a gang? Must a youth group possess some level of organizational structure to be classified as a gang? Are self-nomination techniques valid measures of gang membership? and Are core members more antisocial than peripheral gang members? We are not presumptuous enough to suggest that we can accomplish what has eluded others. However, with the data at hand, we have been able to undertake analyses of a large, although limited, sample of young adolescents that contribute new insights to this debate. We turn first to a discussion of the gang member issues prior to consideration of the gang definition concerns.

In one way or another, gang research, as well as law enforcement classification of gang activity, has relied on self-nomination (i.e., "claiming") of gang members. That is, if a person has claimed to be a gang member, that has been adequate grounds for inclusion in a study of gangs or for special prosecution by the justice system. To what extent is such a crude measure a valid predictor of gang membership? Our findings lend credence to the continued reliance on this technique that is often summarized by the following colloquialism: "If it walks like a duck and talks like a duck, it is a duck." The largest observed differences in attitudes and behaviors are those found in comparing youths who reported never having been gang members and those who reported prior gang involvement. Whatever it is that this one question captures, the respondents clearly reacted to the stimulus and the gang members reported substantially more antisocial attitudes and behaviors than the nongang youths. As additional restrictions were placed on the criteria necessary for classification as a gang member, the attitudes and behaviors of the gang members became increasingly more antisocial, with the relatively small sample of core gang members manifesting the most extreme responses.

So, if a person claims gang affiliation, what does this mean? What is a gang? Our methodological approach does not allow a direct response to this question. However, we can address this question indirectly by filtering respondents out of the gang based on the conceptual criteria identified by researchers and theorists as requisites for gang status. As discussed above, the simple question "Have you ever been a gang member?" was understood by the respondents in such a manner that one can surmise that there exists a shared understanding of what this term means, not only by former and current gang members, but also by nongang youth. Does the imposition of conceptually determined criteria alter the size, composition, or characteristics of the gang? Exclusion of current gang youth who did indicate their gang was involved in delinquent activity resulted in elimination of 55 (11%) of the 522 current gang members and only minimal change in the reported attitudes and behaviors.

Further reduction in the size of the gang sample and expression of more negative attitudes and behaviors were produced with the additional criterion that the gang possess organizational components. Clearly, conceptually based definitions of gang membership have significant ramifications for estimates about the size of the gang problem and for descriptions of the attitudes and behaviors of gang members. However, personal characteristics (i.e., sex, age, race) remain relatively stable, regardless of definition.

From a research perspective, we can conclude that the self-nomination technique is a particularly robust measure of gang membership capable of distinguishing gang from nongang youth. The magnitude of the gang problem, as measured by prevalence rates of gang membership, varies substantially (from a high of 16.8% when using the ever gang member question to 2.3% for delinquent, organized core gang members), but the demographic characteristics of the gang members remain relatively stable across definitions. Likewise, whereas the filtering (i.e., exclusion of respondents not meeting the restricted definition) process results in an increasingly more anti-social gang member, as reflected in reported attitudes and behaviors, the largest difference is between the never gang and the ever gang youth.

From a theoretical perspective, what is the relevance of our findings? With a broad definition of gangs and gang membership, we are left with the impression that demographic characteristics are significant predictors (older, male, and minority youth) of gang membership. However, as we invoke conceptual restrictions on those youth claiming gang status, the theoretical predictors from social learning theory (especially association with delinquent peers, perceptions of guilt, and neutralizations for fighting) supersede the importance of demographic characteristics.

The varying prevalence estimates of gang membership and the changes in attitudes and behavior have distinct policy relevance. Obviously, the definition used greatly affects the perceived magnitude of the gang problem. By restricting gang membership status to gangs that are involved in delinquent activity and have some level of organization, we reduce the size of the gang problem substantially. A similar finding was recently discovered in the law-enforcement estimates provided to the National Youth Gang Center (NYGC). In its 1998 survey, the NYGC included a restricted definition for the survey respondents to use. Analyses incorporating this restricted definition indicate that earlier NYGC estimates may have overestimated the number of youth gangs in the United States by 35% and the number of youth gang members by 43% (Klein, personal correspondence). In terms of resource allocation, not to mention public hysteria, such definitional issues assume considerable importance.

From a policy perspective, the validity of the self-nomination method lends credence to the police practice of targeting youth who claim gang affiliation. However, caution needs to be exercised. Although it is the case that the largest distinction in this study is that between those youths who claim to never have been a gang member and those who claim gang affiliation at some time, it is vital to note that those gang members who no longer claim gang status are substantially more pro-social in both attitudes and behavior than are those persisting in their membership, a finding consistent with longitudinal results from the Denver and Rochester studies (e.g., Esbensen & Huizinga, 1993; Thornberry et al., 1993). Law enforcement,

therefore, should be encouraged to remove former members from their gang lists.

Additional policy issues surround responses to youth gangs. Civil injunctions, antiloitering statutes, and sentence enhancements aimed at gang members may be too encompassing of their targeted audience. Whereas some of these approaches have received legal support (e.g., sentencing enhancements), others have failed to receive judicial backing (e.g., Chicago's Gang Congregation Ordinance). Given the permeability of gang membership, policies linking legal action to an individual's perceived status may erroneously criminalize that individual. As such, we suggest that legislation targeting gang status should be discouraged in favor of legislation focused on actual behavior.

APPENDIX A:
Gang Definitions

GANG 1: Have you ever been a gang member?

GANG 2: Are you now a gang member?

GANG 3: Are you now a gang member? and

Does your gang do any of the following things? (Yes to at least one)

• get in fights with other gangs?
• steal things?
• rob other people?
• steal cars?
• sell marijuana?
• sell other illegal drugs?
• damage or destroy property?

GANG 4: Current gang member and gang is delinquent

Do the following describe your gang? (Yes to all three)

• there are initiation rites

- the gang has established leader
- the gang has symbols and colors

GANG 5: Current gang member, gang is delinquent, and has organizational aspects Self-identification as a "core" member.

APPENDIX B:
Attitudinal Measures and Summary Scale Characteristics

Unless otherwise indicated, these measures were adopted from the National Youth Survey (Elliott et al., 1985) or the Denver Youth Survey (Huizinga et al., 1991).

Parental Monitoring: Four items measuring communication with parents about activities, e.g., "My parents know who I am with if I am not at home."
Scale Mean = 3.72
Scale Standard Deviation = .81
Alpha = .74

Risk Seeking (Grasmick, Tittle, Bursik, & Arneklev, 1993): Four items about risk-taking behavior, e.g., "Sometimes I will take a risk just for the fun of it."
Scale Mean = 3.06
Scale Standard Deviation = .94
Alpha = .82

Impulsivity (Grasmick et al., 1993): Four items measuring impulsive behavior, e.g., "I often act on the spur of the moment without stopping to think."
Scale Mean = 2.85
Scale Standard Deviation = .74
Alpha = .63

Commitment to Negative Peers: Three questions such as "If your friends were getting you in trouble at home, how likely is it that you would still hang out with them?
Scale Mean = 2.40
Scale Standard Deviation = 1.14
Alpha = .84

Commitment to Positive Peers: Two questions such as "If your friends told you not to do something because it was against the law, how likely is it that you would listen to them?
Scale Mean = 3.80
Scale Standard Deviation = 1.12
Alpha = .77

Neutralization: Three items tapping the respondent's belief that it is okay to get in physical fights if extenuating factors are present. For instance, "It's okay to get in a physical fight with someone if they hit you first."
Scale Mean = 3.98
Scale Standard Deviation = .97
Alpha = .83

Guilt: 16 questions asking how guilty the youth would feel if they did such things as "hit someone with the idea of hurting them" or "using alcohol."
Scale Mean = 2.31
Scale Standard Deviation = .56
Alpha = .94

Positive Peer Behavior: Eight items about the kinds of pro-social things in which friends are involved.
Scale Mean = 2.97
Scale Standard Deviation = .80
Alpha = .84

Negative Peer Behavior: 16 items about illegal activities in which the friends are involved.
Scale Mean = 1.99
Scale Standard Deviation = .86
Alpha = .94

Status Offenses: Skipped classes without an excuse. Lied about your age to get into someplace or to buy something.

Minor Offenses: Avoided paying for things such as movies, bus, or subway rides. Purposely damaged or destroyed property that did not belong to you.

Property Offenses: Stole or tried to steal something worth less than $50. Stole or tried to steal something worth more than $50. Went into or tried to go into a building to steal something. Stole or tried to steal a motor vehicle.

Crimes Against Person: Hit someone with the idea of hurting them. Attacked someone with a weapon. Used a weapon or force to get money or things from people. Shot at someone because you were told to by someone else.

Drug Sales: Sold marijuana. Sold other illegal drugs such as heroin, cocaine, crack, or LSD.

Drug Use: Used tobacco products. Used alcohol. Used marijuana. Used paint, glue, or other things you inhale to get high. Other illegal drugs.

Total Delinquency: A summary index consisting of the preceding 14 items and 3 additional items: Have been involved in gang fights; avoided paying for things such as movies, bus, or subway rides; lied about your age to get into someplace or to buy something.

Notes

1. Also, as previously observed, Howell (1998), in his overview of the American gang scene, notes that most researchers use the terms *youth gangs* and *gangs* interchangeably, although the latter term has many other uses in which youth are only tangentially involved.

2. Cohen's (1955) *Delinquent Boys: The Culture of the Gang* introduced his reaction formation theory, another gang-based exploration of general juvenile delinquency from a more social psychological perspective. It is interesting that Cohen defines the behavior of gangs—delinquent subcultures—as nonutilitarian, malicious, and negativistic (pp. 27–29). In so doing, Cohen also relies on Thrasher's earlier work and the research of Shaw and McKay (1942), the latter work

playing an important role in explaining gang delinquency's versatility, or gang members's willingness to get involved in a wide variety of antisocial and illegal activities. Unlike Cloward and Ohlin's (1960) *Delinquency and Opportunity, Delinquent Boys* is long on theory and short on empirical proof.

3. Before July 1, 1994, an organized gang was defined as "an association of 5 or more persons, with an established hierarchy, that encourages members of the association to perpetrate crimes or provides support to the members of the association who do commit crimes" (Illinois Compiled Statutes Annotated, 1999, Chapter 730, Section 5-5-3[c][2][JJ]). After July 1, 1994, "'Streetgang' or 'gang' or 'organized gang' or 'criminal street gang' means any combination, confederation, alliance, network, conspiracy, understanding, or other similar conjoining, in law or in fact, of 3 or more persons with an established hierarchy that, through its membership or through the agency of any member engages in a course or pattern of criminal activity" (Illinois Compiled Statutes Annotated, 1999, Chapter 730, Section 5-5-3[c][2][JJ]).

References

Akers, R. L. (1985). *Deviant behavior: A social learning approach* (3rd ed.). Belmont, CA: Wadsworth.

Akers, R. L. (1994). *Criminological theory: Introduction and evaluation*. Los Angeles: Roxbury.

Arneklev, B. J., Grasmick, H. G., Tittle, C. R., & Bursik, R. J. (1993). Low self-control and imprudent behavior. *Journal of Quantitative Criminology, 9*, 225–247.

Ball, R. A., & Curry, G. D. (1995). The logic of definition in criminology: Purposes and methods for defining gangs. *Criminology, 33*, 225–245.

Battin, S. R., Hill, K. G., Abbott, R. D., Catalano, R., & Hawkins, J. D. (1998). The contributions of gang membership to delinquency beyond delinquent friends. *Criminology, 36*, 67–92.

Battin-Pearson, S. R., Thornberry, T. P., Hawkins, J. D., & Krohn, M. D. (1998). *Gang membership, delinquent peers, and delinquent behavior*. OJJDP Juvenile Justice Bulletin. Washington, DC: Department of Justice.

Bjerregard, B., & Smith, C. (1993). Gender differences in gang participation, delinquency, and substance use. *Journal of Quantitative Criminology, 4*, 329–355.

Bursik, R. J., Jr., & Grasmick, H. G. (1993). *Neighborhoods and crime: The dimensions of effective community control*. New York: Lexington Books.

Cairns, R. B., & Cairns, B. D. (1991). Social cognition and social networks: A developmental perspective. In D. J. Pepler & K. H. Rubin (Eds.), *The development and treatment of childhood aggression*. Hillsdale, NJ: Erlbaum.

California Penal Code. Part 1, Title 7, Chapter 11, 186.22 (1999).

City of Chicago v. Morales, et al., 524 U.S. 975. (Ill. 1998).

Cloward, R. A., & Ohlin, L. E. (1960). *Delinquency and opportunity: A theory of delinquent gangs*. New York: Free Press.

Cohen, A. K. (1955). *Delinquent boys: The culture of the gang*. New York: Free Press.

Criminal Street Gangs Statute, 18 U.S.C.A. § 521 (1999).

Curry, G. D., Ball, R. A., & Decker, S. H. (1996). *Estimating the national scope of gang crime from law enforcement data*. Research in Brief. Washington, DC: U.S. Department of Justice, Office of Justice Programs, National Institute of Justice.

Curry, G. D., & Decker, S. H. (1998). *Confronting gangs: Crime and community*. Los Angeles, CA: Roxbury.

Decker, S., & Van Winkle, B. (1996). *Life in the gang: Family, friends, and violence*. New York: Cambridge University Press.

Decker, S. H., & Kempf-Leonard, K. (1991). Constructing gangs: Social definition and youth activities. *Criminal Justice Policy Review, 5*, 271–291.

Deschenes, E. P., & Esbensen, F-A. (1999). Violence and gangs: Gender differences in perceptions and behaviors. *Journal of Quantitative Criminology, 15*, 53–96.

Elliott, D. S., Ageton, S. S., & Huizinga, D. (1985). *Explaining delinquency and substance use*. Beverly Hills, CA: Sage.

Esbensen, F.-A., & Deschenes, E. P. (1998). A multisite examination of youth gang membership: Does gender matter? *Criminology, 36*, 799–827.

Esbensen, F.-A., Deschenes, E. P., Vogel, R. E., West, J., Arboit, K., & Harris, L. (1997). Active parental consent in school-based research: An examination of ethical and methodological issues. *Evaluation Review, 20*, 737–753.

Esbensen, F.-A., & Huizinga, D. (1993). Gangs, drugs and delinquency in a survey of urban youth. *Criminology, 31*, 565–589.

Esbensen, F.-A., & Osgood, D. W. (1999). Gang Resistance Education and Training (G.R.E.A.T.): Results from the national evaluation. *Journal of Research in Crime and Delinquency, 36*, 194–225.

Esbensen, F.-A., & Winfree, L. T., Jr. (1998). Race and gender differences between gang and nongang youths: Results from a multisite survey. *Justice Quarterly, 15*, 505–526.

Fleisher, M. (1998). *Dead end kids*. Madison: University of Wisconsin Press.

Gardner, S. (1993). *Street gangs*. New York: Franklin Watts.

Gibbs, J. J., & Giever, D. M. (1995). Self-control and its manifestations among university students: An empirical test of Gottfredson and Hirschi's general theory. *Justice Quarterly, 12*, 231–255.

Gibbs, J. J., Giever, D. M., & Martin, J. S. (1998). Parental management and self-control: An empirical test of Gottfredson and Hirschi's general theory. *Journal of Research in Crime and Delinquency, 35*, 40–70.

Gottfredson, M. R., & Hirschi, T. (1990). *A general theory of crime*. Stanford, CA: Stanford University Press.

Grasmick, H. G., Tittle, C. R., Bursik, R. J., Jr., & Arneklev, B. J. (1993). Testing the core assumptions of Gottfredson and Hirschi's general theory of crime. *Journal of Research in Crime and Delinquency, 30*, 5–29.

Hill, K. G., Howell, J. C., Hawkins, J. D., & Battin-Pearson, S. R. (1999). Childhood risk factors for adolescent gang membership: Results from the Seattle Social Development Project. *Journal of Research in Crime and Delinquency, 36*, 300–322.

Howell, J. C. (1998). *Youth gangs: An overview*. Juvenile Justice Bulletin. Washington, DC: Office of Juvenile Justice and Delinquency Prevention.

Huff, C. R. (1998). *Comparing the criminal behavior of youth gangs and at-risk youths*. Research in brief. Washington, DC: National Institute of Justice.

Huizinga, D., Esbensen, F.-A., & Weiher, A. W. (1991). Are there multiple paths to delinquency? *Journal of Criminal Law and Criminology, 82*, 83–118.

Illinois Compiled Statutes Annotated. 730. Chapter V. Article 5 (1999).

Kerlinger, F. N. (1973). *Foundations of behavioral research* (2nd ed.). New York: Holt, Rinehart and Winston.

Klein, M. W. (1969). Violence in American juvenile gangs. In D. J. Mulvihill, M. M. Tumin, & L. A. Curtis (Eds.), *Crime of violence, volume 13, a staff report to the National Commission on the Causes and Prevention of Violence*. Washington, DC: Government Printing Office.

Klein, M. W. (1971). *Street gangs and street workers*. Englewood Cliffs, NJ: Prentice Hall.

Klein, M. W. (1995). *The American street gang: Its nature, prevalence, and control*. New York: Oxford University Press.

Knox, G. W. (1996). The 1996 national law enforcement gang analysis survey. *Journal of Gang Research, 3*, 41–55.

Krohn, M. D., Akers, R. L., Radosevich, M. J., & Lanza-Kaduce, L. (1982). Norm qualities and adolescent drinking and drug behavior. *Journal of Drug Issues, 12*, 343–359.

Lynskey, D. P., Winfree, L. T., Jr., Esbensen, F.-A., & Clason, D. L. (2000). Linking gender, minority group status, and family matters to self-control theory: A multivariate analysis of key self-control concepts in a youth-gang context. *Juvenile and Family Court Journal, 1* (3), 1–20.

Maxson, C. L. (1998). *Gang members on the move*. OJJDP Juvenile Justice Bulletin. Washington, DC: Department of Justice.

Maxson, C. L., & Klein, M. W. (1994). *Gang structures and crime patterns in U.S. cities*. Paper presented at the annual meeting of the American Society of Criminology, November, Miami, FL.

Maxson, C. L., Whitlock, M. L., & Klein, M. W. (1998). Vulnerability to street gang membership: Implications for practice. *Social Service Review, 72*, 70–91.

Miller, W. B. (1975). *Violence by youth gangs and youth groups as a crime problem in major American cities*. Washington, DC: National Institute for Juvenile Justice and Delinquency Prevention.

Miller, W. B. (1980). Gangs, groups and serious youth crime. In D. Schichor & D. H. Kelly (Eds.), *Critical issues in juvenile delinquency.* Lexington, MA: D.C. Heath and Co.

National Youth Gang Center. (1997). *1995 national youth gang survey.* Washington, DC: U.S. Department of Justice, Office of Justice Programs, Office of Juvenile Justice and Delinquency Prevention.

National Youth Gang Center. (1999). *1996 national youth gang survey.* Washington, DC: U.S. Department of Justice, Office of Justice Programs, Office of Juvenile Justice and Delinquency Prevention.

Needle, J. A., & Stapleton, W. V. (1983). *Reports of the national juvenile justice assessment centers: Police handling of youth gangs.* Washington, DC: Office of Juvenile Justice and Delinquency Prevention.

Office of Juvenile Justice and Delinquency Prevention. (1997). *Highlights of the 1995 national youth gang survey.* OJJDP Fact Sheet. Washington, DC: Department of Justice.

Sellers, C. S., Winfree, L. T., Jr., & Griffiths, C. T. (1993). Legal attitudes, permissive norm qualities, and substance abuse: A comparison of American Indians and non-Indian youths. *Journal of Drug Issues, 23,* 493–513.

Shaw, C. R., & McKay, H. D. (1942). *Juvenile delinquency and urban areas.* Chicago: University of Chicago Press.

Short, J. F. (1968). Introduction: On gang delinquency and the nature of subcultures. In J. F. Short (Ed.), *Gang delinquency and delinquent subcultures.* New York: Harper and Row.

Short, J. F. (1996). Foreword: Diversity and change in U.S. gangs. In C. R. Huff (Ed.), *Gangs in America* (2nd ed.). Thousand Oaks, CA: Sage Publications.

Spergel, I. A. (1995). *The youth gang problem: A community approach.* New York: Oxford University Press.

Thornberry, T. P., & Burch, J. H., III (1997). *Gang members and delinquent behavior.* OJJDP Juvenile Justice Bulletin. Washington, DC: Department of Justice.

Thornberry, T. P., Krohn, M. D., Lizotte, A. J., & Chard-Wierschem, D. (1993). The role of juvenile gangs in facilitating delinquent behavior. *Journal of Research in Crime and Delinquency, 30,* 55–87.

Thrasher, F. M. (1963). *The gang: A study of one thousand three hundred thirteen gangs in Chicago.* Chicago: University of Chicago Press. A bridged with a new introduction by James F. Short, Jr. (Original work published 1927).

Winfree, L. T., Jr., Bäckström, T. V., & Mays, G. L. (1994). Social learning theory, self-reported delinquency, and youth gangs: A new twist on a general theory of crime and delinquency. *Youth & Society, 26,* 147–177.

Winfree, L. T., Jr., Bernat, F. P., & Esbensen, F-A. (in press). Hispanic and Anglo gang membership in two southwestern cities. *The Social Science Journal.*

Winfree, L. T., Jr., Fuller, K., Bäckström, T. V., & Mays, G. L. (1992). The definition and measurement of "gang status": Policy implications for juvenile justice. *Juvenile and Family Court Journal, 43,* 20–37.

Chapter 2

Historical Foundations

INTRODUCTION

In the first selection, Tuthill explains the first juvenile court laws, which went into effect July 1, 1899, in Cook County, Illinois. These laws were created in part because of the states' failure to adequately deal with children who were without proper parental care. Conditions revealed that children were being held in county jails and being exposed to the "evil association" of older, more experienced criminals. The law mandated that the state act as the parent of the delinquent youth (in loco parentis). Judges in the circuit court in Cook County were responsible for appointing a judge to preside in the juvenile court. The law differentiated between three classes of children: the "dependent child," the "neglected child," and "the delinquent child." Each of which was to be dealt with in the juvenile court. The court, in rendering its decision, is to consider the "welfare and interests of the child," "the welfare of the community," and "the interests and feeling of the parents and relatives."

In 1889, Jane Adams and Ellen Gates Star opened Hull-House, and three years later the University of Chicago was founded. According to Frey, for the next 30 years, these two organizations played a major role in defining sociology and criminology in the United States. In this article, Frey describes the characteristics of Chicago at the turn of the century in an attempt to "set the stage," and examines the contributions of various key members who had an influential role in the Chicago school of thought. These include Jane Adams, Walter Reckless, William I. Thomas, Ernest

Burgess, Frederic M. Thrasher, Clifford Shaw, Henry McKay, and Edwin Sutherland. Frey argues that although individual perspectives varied, all recognized the effect macro-social forces had on individual behavior, only some (predominately women) acknowledge the interplay between the individual and the community. She further contends that this variation makes it difficult to place the school into the classical or positivist paradigm.

Critics of the juvenile court have argued that children are not granted the same constitutional safeguards accorded to adults accused of crimes, whereas supporters of the juvenile court believe that the primary function is a parental one, thus under the parens patriae principal, the state operates with the best interests of the child in mind, and the need to define constitutional rights is lessened. In providing a historical account of the origins of the juvenile court, Mennel argues that the juvenile court controversy can be traced back beyond the creation of the juvenile court. For example, houses of refuge and reform schools were created to "secure the parental authority of the state over destitute and delinquent children." These institutions were to resemble schools more than prisons; they were to prevent delinquent children from cruel punishment and insure that they were punished correctly. However, after the Civil War, it was discovered that life in these reform schools was characterized as brutal, thus a growing sentiment to keep children out of these institutions emerged. The creation of the juvenile court is due to a distrust in custodial institutions (reform schools, etc.) and as an "attempt to recast the parental authority of the state in a different mold."

Platt examines the rise of the "child-saving" movement. Child-savers called for reform in the treatment of youthful offenders at the end of the nineteenth century. The movement, which was guided largely by middle-class feminist reformers, helped create judicial and correctional institutions geared at labeling, processing, and managing "troublesome" youth. Platt argues that the analysis of child-savers affords us the opportunity to examine other correctional issues. Various questions pertaining to the problems caused by "agency-determined" research, political and policy oriented implications on politically sensitive institutions, and understanding the relationship between correctional reforms and changes in the administration of criminal justice, as well as the motives of those who generate such reform are addressed in this article.

The Juvenile Court Law in Cook County, Illinois, 1899

Hon. R. S. Tuthill

Illinois has claimed and in many respects has justly claimed the right to be classed with the advanced states of the Union. Yet a deplorable condition with respect to the treatment of children has existed in the state from its organization up almost to the present time. This condition in Cook County is stated in moderate language in the official reports of grand juries, month after month, in substantially these words:

> There is at present in this county no proper place for the detention or final commitment of youthful offenders. We have no institution where friendless children of tender age, who have been arrested for offenses against the law, can be sent, educated, and possibly saved from a criminal career. A commitment to the Glenwood School under sentence for crimes committed is not allowed, as that institution is simply for incorrigible children. We call attention to the fact that there are at present confined in our county jail, children of eleven, twelve, thirteen, and fourteen years of age, where they are exposed to the evil association of older criminals.

Indeed, in the county jail, we found children of nine years of age, who had been bound over to the grand jury by incompetent or corrupt justices of the peace, in disregard of the fact that the laws of Illinois recognize no capacity for criminality in a child of that age.

This condition, especially in Cook County, grew worse from year to year, until at length the people of the state awakened to the fact that the state by the inadequacy of its laws and failure to care for these children who were without proper parental care was creating—breeding as it were—an army of criminals who in a short time would be its open and avowed enemies. An appeal was made to the General Assembly at its last session for relief. A law was prepared as a result of extended consideration of the subject by men and women of all creeds and political affiliations and was submitted for enactment. It was, in the form originally agreed upon, probably as well considered, as wise, and humane a measure as was ever presented to the lawmaking body of the state. The Bar Association of Chicago composed of the ablest and best members of our metropolitan bar was active in the preparation of the bill and gave its powerful influence toward its enactment. The good women of the state, always quick and earnest in everything which tends to the proper care of children, were leaders in the movement, laboring in season and out of season to induce the representatives of the people by the passage of this bill to place Illinois

Joseph G. Weis, Robert D. Crutchfield, and George Bridges, Juvenile Delinquency: Readings, pp. 13–16, copyright © 2001, by Pine Forge Press, Reprinted by Permission of Sage Publications, Inc.

primus inter pares in respect to provisions made for the exercise of this highest duty of a state—a civilized state—to stand *in loco parentis*, to be a parent to all the neglected and delinquent children of the state. It is to be regretted that various antagonistic interests made themselves manifest and opposed the bill with such mistaken pertinacity as that some of the most essential features in it were per force dropped.

Yet, what is known as the Juvenile Court Law became the law of Illinois, going into effect July 1, 1899.

The law made it the duty of the judges of the circuit court in Cook County to designate one of their number to preside in this new branch, which for convenience was designated as the Juvenile Court. This designation was promptly made. The duty of inaugurating the work was placed upon me.

There are three classes of children mentioned in the law as coming within its purview. First is the "dependent child" and second, the "neglected child," which classes are defined to mean

any child who for any reason is destitute or homeless or abandoned; or dependent upon the public for support; or has not proper parental care or guardianship; or who habitually begs or receives alms; or who is found living in any house of ill-fame or with any vicious or disreputable persons; or whose home by reason of neglect or depravity on the part of its parents, guardian, or other person in whose care it may be, is an unfit place for such child; and any child under the age of eight years who is found peddling or selling any article or singing or playing any musical instrument upon the street or giving any public entertainment.

Third is the "delinquent child," which it is declared "shall include any child under the age of sixteen years who violates any law of this State, or city or village ordinance" and "who is not now or hereafter an inmate of a state institution or any training school for boys or industrial school for girls." Section 5 of the law has this provision: "Pending the final disposition of any case, a child may be retained in the possession of the person having the charge of the same or may be kept in *some suitable place* provided by the city or county authorities."

Section 11 provides: "No court or magistrate shall commit a child under the age of twelve years to a jail or police station."

Here was an immediate difficulty inasmuch as neither city nor county had a place of detention such as the law contemplated for the children brought under this operation.

The county had prior to the enactment of the law cared for the dependent and neglected children in a building at the county hospital used for the temporary detention of insane persons. A more serious difficulty was to secure a place other than the jail or police station of the city for the detention, pending the hearing of the delinquent. The generous action of the Board of Directors of the Illinois Industrial Association gave the use of their cottage for this purpose. This has since served as a detention home.

The law makes provision for the appointment by the court of probation officers. It declares that "it shall be the duty of the said probation officer to make such investigation as may be required by the Court; to be present in Court in order to represent the interest of the child when the case is heard; to furnish to the Court such information and assistance as the judge may require; and to take such charge of any child before and after trial as may be directed by the Court."

Printed instructions are given to each probation officer when appointed.

INSTRUCTION TO PROBATION OFFICERS

In appointing probation officers, the court places a special reliance upon the faithfulness and wisdom of the persons so designated. There is no more important work than that of saving children, and much will depend upon your faithfulness.

This appointment is made under the provision of the law, enacted by the Legislature of 1899. Your attention is particularly called to the last section of that act, which declares the purpose of the law as follows:

> This act shall be liberally construed to the purpose that its end may be carried out to wit: That the care, custody, and discipline of a child shall approximate as nearly as may be that which should be given by its parents, and in all cases where it can be properly done, the child be placed in an approved family home and become a member of the family by legal adoption or otherwise.

It will be the endeavor of the court to carry out both the letter and the spirit of this act, and to this end the court will have in mind the following considerations in order named:

1. *The welfare and interests of the child.* It is the desire of the court to save the child from neglect and cruelty, also to save it from the danger of becoming a criminal or a dependent.
2. *The welfare of the community.* The most practical way of lessening the burdens of taxations and the loss of property through the ravages of the crime class is by the prevention of pauperism and crime. Experience proves that the easiest and most effective way of doing this is by taking hold of the children while they are young—the younger the better.
3. *The interests and feelings of parents and relatives.* It is right and necessary that parental affection should be respected, as far as this can be done without sacrificing the best interests of the child and without exposing the community to unnecessary damage.

DEPENDENTS AND DELINQUENTS

The law divides the children into two classes, dependents and delinquents. Cases of both classes will be referred to you (a) for investigation pending action of the court, (b) for temporary supervision pending action of the court, and (c) for supervision after action by the court.

Investigation

When cases are referred for investigation, you will be expected to make personal inquiry into the facts of the case, with the view to assist the court in deciding what ought to be done. To this end, it will be necessary to record the history and the circumstances of the child as fully as possible, and blanks will be provided for this purpose. The court will desire to ascertain the character, disposition, and tendencies and school record of the child; also, the character of the parents and their capability for governing and supporting the child, together with the character of the home as to comforts, surroundings, inmates, and so on.

This information will be obtained in your own way, from the child, from the parents, neighbors, teachers, clergymen, police officers, and from the records of the poor department, the police department, and the various charitable agencies.

The court will wish to determine, from these inquiries, whether the child should be separated from the parents, guardian, or custodian, and if so, whether it should be committed to the care and guardianship of some individual or to some suitable institution. The court will not ordinarily separate children from their parents unless (a) the parents are criminals, (b) the parents are vicious or grossly cruel, (c) the parents are entirely unable to support the children, or (d) the home is in such condition as to make it extremely probable that the child will grow up to be vicious or dependent.

Temporary Care

The law forbids the keeping of any child in any jail or police station. A place of detention for children under the care of the court will be provided, but it is the desire of the court to avoid congregating children even in this temporary home. Whenever practicable, therefore, the child will be left in the care of the parents or of some suitable family, under the supervision of the probation officer, pending the final action of the court. In your investigations, you will have in mind the question whether the child can be suitably cared for in his own home, and, if not, whether a suitable temporary home can be secured without expense.

Supervision After Action of the Court

The law makes it the duty of the court, as far as possible, to locate its young wards, both dependents and delinquents, in family homes. When practicable, the child will be remanded to its parents, or will be placed directly in the family of some suitable citizen. In such cases, the probation officer will be expected to maintain a special oversight of the child, either by personal visits at frequent intervals or by written report from parents or custodian. All visits to wards of the court will be reported on blanks provided for that purpose.

The probation officer feature is in my judgment the keystone which supports the arch of this law, an arch which shall be as a rainbow of hope to all who love children and who desire that all children shall be properly cared for.

Early Chicago Contributions

Connie Frey

INTRODUCTION

In 1889, Jane Addams and Ellen Gates Starr opened Hull-House. Three years later, the University of Chicago was founded. For the next 30 years or so, both of these organizations would define what sociology and criminology in the United States were to become.

Both the men at the University of Chicago and the women at Hull-House recognized the effect macro-social forces had on individual behavior. However, many also acknowledged the interplay between the individual and the community. It was largely the women who emphasized this interaction. For this reason, it is difficult to place the school as a whole into the classical or positivist paradigm. While there are many theories and theorists that might fall into one or the other, when taken as a whole, it is difficult at best to place the entire school into one camp. One thing that can be said about the school's perspective is that it was the birthplace of and, therefore, heavily influenced by symbolic interactionism. William I. Thomas along with George H. Mead were founders of the Chicago School of Symbolic Interactionism.

THE STAGE

Chicago was experiencing tremendous changes during the late nineteenth and early twentieth centuries. In 1860, Chicago was "at the center of a web of [railroad] lines, the jumping off point for the western part of the country, and the commercial and business center of the Middle West" (Bulmer 1984:13). Its population in general was growing by leaps and bounds. In 1890, Chicago was the second largest city behind New York City (Bulmer 1984). Deegan (1988) notes that "between 1880 and 1890 it [Chicago] had doubled its size from one half a million to over a million" (p. 290). Furthermore, "by 1900 over a million and a half people lived in Chicago and by 1910, two million" (Deegan 1988:291). Within these same time periods, 1880 and 1910, the foreign-born population in Cook Country, Illinois, grew from almost 205,000 to more than 780,000—a 280 percent increase (U.S. Bureau of the Census 1999). Across the United States, people were moving from rural areas to urban ones such as Chicago to find jobs created by the industrial revolution. In 1900, 60 percent of the United States population were living in a rural area whereas almost 11 percent were living in cities with 500,000 or more people. By 1930, only 43.8 percent were living in a rural area and 17 percent were in cities with a population greater than 500,000. Rapid technological advances included improved communications, mass transit, and the automobile. In 1900, there were 1,355,911 telephones in the United States. By 1930, there were over 20 million. There was also a rapid increase in the middle class and tremendous growth in the number of children in elementary schools due to passage of child labor laws.

This was also a time when family size was decreasing, more and more poor and foreign-born women were entering the paid workforce, and the women's movement was actively campaigning for the right to vote, to be educated, and to work. There were an increasing number of divorces and a reduction of the number of hours in a work week which resulted in an increase in leisure time and with it an emergence of mass recreation.

Chicago was not ready for this kind of rapid change. Great extremes of poverty and wealth, privilege and oppression, and defenses and critiques of capitalism characterized Chicago. It was a place of dirt, disease, exhaustion, crowding, confusion, hopelessness, and pain. Upton Sinclair's *The Jungle* (1906) paints a grim picture of Chicago during this time.

During the years between 1880 and 1910, women were seen as ideally suited to studying social change and improving society (Deegan 1988). Women flocked to Chicago to study sociology at the university because of its receptiveness to women. For example, the university was coeducational when few schools were. As time passed, however, the male faculty became more conservative and began to reject their former radical ideas and feminist perspectives. In effect, this left women unable to obtain academic positions once they earned their degrees. Thus, a dual system of sex-segregated labor was created (Deegan 1988). Male sociologists were aligned with academics and theory whereas female sociologists were associated with social settlements, the practical and applied research. Even so, many women who earned their degrees at Chicago were

recognized in the discipline as knowledgeable colleagues and scholars.

The founding Chicago criminologists were a prolific group. I draw, therefore, only a brief sketch of their work here. They are presented in chronological order.

JANE ADDAMS

Like her colleagues at the University of Chicago, Addams's work countered Lombroso's (1911) theory that criminal behavior was the result of defective biology. Rather than seeing crime as inherent in the individual, Addams believed that "illegal acts were a symptom of social maladjustment; a sign of a lack of accounting for and response to the human impulses to idealize, to strive for greatness and challenge" (Deegan 1988:298). Furthermore, Deegan (1988) states "Addams saw delinquency as a product of social malfunction and maladaptation to the spirit of youth, and not as a result of the evil nature or pathology of the young" (p. 296). Although Addams clearly saw individuals as having agency, she understood how structure shaped and constrained their choices, a characteristic of the Neoclassical perspective that would not be defined for approximately 60 more years. In particular, she argued that patriarchy and capitalism impacted interaction between males and females and fashioned the options from which they had to choose.

In *The Spirit of Youth and the City Streets* (1909). Addams addresses the relationship of the modern city, the family, play, the nickel theater, and work with juvenile delinquency. Each individual center of activity and the sum of all said centers can either serve to prevent or cause delinquency. Her holistic perspective is what makes her theory strong.

Addams finds two major faults with the modern city. First, she argues that the city's failure to address the needs of youth in terms of play and outdoor physical activity leads to an increase in juvenile delinquency rates. Furthermore, it is the clash between the modern city structure and the "spirit of youth" that results in increased juvenile delinquency. The "spirit of youth" is a concept that Addams uses to refer to children's nature, which is comprised of a passionate desire for play, an innate goodness, keenly sharp senses, low self-control, inability to discriminate, and a yearning for order and beauty.

Addams saw evidence that the city youth of her day found adventure, or play, at the railroad. With little or no opportunity for play, many children turned to crime. Using court records, Addams documented the types of charges brought against youth and observed that "the deeds were doubtless inspired much more by the adventurous impulse than by a desire for the loot itself" (1909:56). Moreover, she (1912b) later found that "the number of arrests among juvenile delinquents falls off surprisingly in a neighborhood where such a park has been established" (p. 619). It should not be surprising, then, that Addams was a founder of the social movement to create public parks and playgrounds (see Mead 1999).

A second and related characteristic of the modern city that contributes to increasing delinquency rates is sensory overload. In fact. Addams (1909) argues that it is "nothing short of cruelty to over-stimulate his senses as does the modern city" (p. 27). This contention is illustrative of how Addams does not separate the physical body from the social self. Instead, she draws a direct link between the rapidly changing bodies of youth, their immediate social environments, and their levels of maturity. Addams (1909) suggests that youth engage in delinquent behavior because their spirit is unable to adequately manage the responsibilities and stimulation of living in the modern city.

A New Conscience and an Ancient Evil (Addams 1912a) is an analogy between prostitution and American slavery. Addams (1912a) uses the term "ancient evil" "to designate the sexual commerce permitted to exist in every large city, usually in a segregated district, wherein the chastity of women is bought and sold"—namely, prostitution and female sexual slavery (p. 9). What is important to note here is that, like Addams's discussion of juvenile delinquency, she finds the primary cause of and solution to prostitution in the modern city. Two of those causes are rapid urbanization and an explosion in the immigrant population.

Addams (1912a) felt that language barriers along with a new culture allowed prostitution and delinquency to flourish, in part, because parents were unable to issue effective controls, as they were confused about their new environments as well (p. 26). Newly arrived immigrants as well as former rural Americans had not yet adjusted to the culture of the modern city. Concurrently, the new city was not equipped to handle the needs of its new residents. Shaw and McKay later referred to this phenomenon as social disorganization.

Addams (1912a) argued that, before the modern city, the community dealt with prostitution and delinquency in a much more effective way because social controls were more stringent. Two conditions brought about changes in the effectiveness of social control: "first and second, when the individual felt that he was above social control and when the individual has had an opportunity to hide his daily living" (Addams 1912a:209). The modern city brought with it anonymity. The village gossip was no longer an agent of social control, for as Addams (1912a) states

> The village gossip with her vituperative tongue after all performs a valuable function both of castigation and retribution: but her fellow-townsman, although quite unconscious of her restraint, coming into a city hotel often experiences a great sense of relief which easily rises to a mood of exhilaration. (P. 199)

Addams's theory of prostitution begins with gender. For women and girls, she argues that prostitution is attractive in comparison to the low wages they receive in the labor force. Although wages were low for all workers of the time, they were particularly low for females due to the convergence of patriarchal ideology, which holds that girls and women do not need to be paid livable wages because they are, or should be, economically provided for by men and capitalism, which emphasizes profits over humanity. Prostitution is made more attractive when the family claim is exerted on females. The family claim is the demand exerted on females "to put the family and their needs before other considerations" (Deegan 1988:231). For girls in the modern city, there is constant and great pressure to bring wages home to help support their families. When women and girls were unable to live up to the family claim, they often secretly turned to prostitution. Addams (1912a) concluded that it is, in part, the "desire to fulfill family obligations such as would be accepted by any conscientious girl" that leads some girls to prostitution (p. 61).

WALTER RECKLESS

Walter Reckless ([1933] 1969), a Chicago criminologist, offers a competing, more individualistic explanation for the existence of prostitution. He suggests "criminolo-gists agree that most girls who enter prostitution have been delinquent and have had previous experience prior to entering the life" (p. 45). While both Addams and Reckless recognize the impact of social structure on the individual, Addams emphasizes the interplay between structure and the individual. Furthermore, Addams saw prostitution and crime in general as a social issue—not an individual problem. Despite the fact that prostitution is typically understood as a female crime, Addams saw it as a crime of the community. Daniel Levine (1971) suggests that Addams thought "sometimes a girl would become a prostitute through much the same spirit that drove boys' gangs to crime" (p. 117). Constraints of city life and repression of the spirit of youth affected boys and girls in essentially the same manner.

Whereas Reckless ([1933] 1969) sees a distinct difference between prostitution and female sexual slavery, both Addams (1912a) and Barry (1979) understand prostitution as only one particular type of sexual slavery. Females may enter prostitution and sexual slavery under different circumstances; nevertheless, the impact on the individuals and the community are the same. Barry (1979), Reckless ([1933] 1969), and Addams (1912a) all agree with one basic idea, and that is that the patriarchal structure allows and even encourages forced and nonforced prostitution.

WILLIAM I. THOMAS

William I. Thomas was a friend and supportive colleague of Addams's. Both Thomas and Addams observed that the community often used gossip as a tool in defining and reinforcing the moral code. Addams influenced Thomas's ideas on prostitution. Deegan (1988) states that "prostitution and other forms of women's deviance were analyzed by Thomas as an indicator of social control over women and changing social structures" (p. 207). Thomas was also aware of the importance of community and social organization. In 1923, he wrote *The Unadjusted Girl* and noted that "when crime and prostitution appear as professions they are the last and most radical expressions of loss of family and community organization" (p. 69). Thomas ([1923] 1969) maintained that when changes, either structural or cultural, occur in a community or a particular setting, the individual or the community as a whole is likely to change the definition of the situation. It is these changes that have the potential to result in social disorganization. More importantly, it is the competing definitions that lead to vagueness and confusion about the norms.

The Unadjusted Girl ([1923] 1969) is best known for its explanation of the four wishes. Wishes, according to Thomas ([1923] 1969), are "the forces which impel action" (p. 4). The first wish is for new experience. Actions associated with it include adventure, instability, and responsibility (p. 4). The second wish is for security and is diametrically opposed to the first wish. It is "based on fear" and is associated with caution, conservatism, and apprehensiveness (p. 12). The third wish is for response. This wish is "the most social of the wishes" and involves the need for love, connection, appreciation, and sexuality (p. 31). The last wish is for recognition. Thomas contended that for boys and men, this wish is expressed through fame, bragging, bullying, cruelty, and ambition (p. 32). For girls and women, the wish is expressed through being frail and ill (p. 32). Moreover, Thomas stated that girls use dress and fashion as "the favorite means of securing distinction and showing class" (p. 31).

Crime and deviance are the consequences of unmet wishes according to Thomas. He argued that girls have to learn that they have value for things other than their sexuality. Otherwise, they will use sex as a means to satisfy the four wishes. For example, when girls and women cannot satisfy their wish for response (love and intimacy), they can either enter into prostitution or develop an intimate relationship with a pimp (Thomas [1923] 1969:142).

ERNEST W. BURGESS

Ernest W. Burgess came to the department as an assistant professor in 1916. In his work with Robert E. Park, he developed the concentric zone theory (Burgess 1925). This theory states that a city will grow and develop radiating outward from a city's central business district, which Burgess referred to as Zone I. The next zone is Zone II, the zone of transition where light manufacturing and businesses are. Here is where the city's slums, a high concentration of poverty, first generation immigrants, vice, disease, and crime are found. Zone III is the zone of "workingmen's homes." This is the area that one is more likely to find second-generation immigrants living. Zone IV is the residential area with high-class apartment buildings and restricted single family dwellings. Zone V is the commuter's zone or the suburbs. Burgess described the city in terms of its extension, succession, and concentration. Extension has to do with the actual physical space that a city occupies. Succession is the process by which city residents move from one zone to another. In other words, those living in Zone II after some time will eventually "work their way up" to Zone III. Concentration has to do with the concentration of services and people in one area. This model is an illustration of what Burgess believed to be a "natural" growth of the city.

Like Addams and Shaw and McKay, who will be discussed later, Burgess contributed much of the city's problems on increased mobility of the population. He defined mobility as "movement in response to a new stimulus or situation" (Burgess 1925:58). In his discussion on mobility in the city, Burgess argued that humans needed stimulation to grow. Furthermore, he felt that "where mobility is the greatest, and where in consequence primary controls break down completely, as in the zone of deterioration in the modern city, there develop areas of demoralization, or promiscuity, and of vice" (p. 59).

FREDERIC M. THRASHER

In 1927, Frederic M. Thrasher published *The Gang: A Study of 1,313 Gangs in Chicago*. Typical of the Chicago School of Criminology at the time, Thrasher argued that gangs are a naturally occurring group. Gangs, furthermore, are a natural product of their environment, specifically the interstitial area just outside the central business district of Chicago. Most gangs develop out of spontaneous play groups and are opposed to conventional society. It "is a symptom of disorganization in the larger social framework" (Thrasher [1927] 1963:33). The community is disorganized in that it cannot meet the needs or, to use Thomas's term, wishes of its members. Young males, then, satisfy their wish for thrills, excitement, physical activity, and status in the gang.

Thrasher found that gangs are characterized by face-to-face interactions, an attachment to a specific territory, and an "*espirit [sic] de corps*" ([1927] 1963:40). Gang members spend most of their time just hanging out, smoking cigarettes, and drinking alcohol. Gang members respond to their natural environment, for example, those who inhabit a territory near railroad tracks typically engage in "junking." Thrasher maintained that gangs did not *cause* crime; they only make crime easier.

Thrasher also found that most gang members were poor immigrant males. He argued that middle-class boys did not join gangs because "their lives are organized and stabilized for them by American traditions, customs, and institutions to which the children of immigrants do not have adequate access" (Thrasher [1927] 1963: 152). Girls did not join gangs, according to Thrasher, in part because they were more closely supervised than boys. Consequently, they were more integrated into conventional institutions than boys.

Thrasher identified three types of gang members—those in the inner circle, the rank and file, and the fringers. Inner circle members include the leader and his "lieutenants" (Thrasher [1927] 1963:229). Those in the rank and file are members in good standing but with less power and status than inner circle members. Fringers have the least power and status within the gang and "are more or less hangers-on and are not considered regular members" (p. 229).

CLIFFORD R. SHAW
AND HENRY D. MCKAY

Shaw and McKay (1931, 1942) responded to the changes they witnessed in Chicago by developing a theory of social disorganization. Social disorganization is defined "as the *inability of a community structure to realize the common values of its residents and maintain effective social controls*" (Sampson 1995:198; italics in original). It is important to note that social disorganization is not about anomie or normlessness. It is about conflicting norms—old norms conflicting with new norms. Social disorganization in Chicago was the product of rural norms clashing with urban norms, and "old world" norms clashing with "new world" norms. It was Shaw and McKay's contention that neighborhoods, because they were socially disorganized, could not effectively manage resident's behaviors, specifically adolescent residents. Social control of community members was especially difficult because of the factors mentioned above. Rapid urbanization left the city unprepared to deal with the needs of the residents.

The similarities between Addams's discussion of the anonymous nature of modern city life and Shaw and McKay's (1942) assertion regarding the same are remarkable. Taylor, Walton, and Young (1973) call Shaw and McKay "the most prolific writers in the school on the subject of crime and deviance" (p. 11). Shaw and McKay (1942), both Chicago criminologists, contend that "because of the anonymity in urban life, the individual is freed from much of the scrutiny and control which characterize life in primary-group situations in small towns and rural communities" (p. 66). Likewise, Roncek and Maier (1991) wrote that "the presence of more people can increase the anonymity of an area and result in people ignoring or less effectively performing the guardianship activities that they might undertake in less busy areas" (p. 726). Anonymity is an important concept in the contemporary theory of routine activities. What Shaw and McKay and Addams are all describing is a socially disorganized community. Others have written on the concept of social disorganization as well (Bursik 1999, Park, Burgess, and McKenzie 1925; Sampson 1995). Simultaneously, critics such as William F. Whyte (1943) have argued that instead of being socially disorganized, "slum life often is highly organized, although the values around which the organization of behavior occurs may seem immoral, unjust, or incredible to observers" (Gusfield 1963:70–71).

In addition to the theory of social disorganization, Shaw and McKay (1942) formulated the theory of cultural transmission. This theory "focuses on the development in some urban neighborhoods of a criminal tradition that persists from one generation to another despite constant changes in population" (Cloward and Ohlin 1960:146). Cultural transmission theory is often seen as an unnecessary extension of social disorganization. In a sense, there is a feedback loop that occurs between the two theories. Shaw and McKay (1942) start by arguing the social disorganization leads to a particular set of values and norms which work to maintain the socially disorganized area. With its emphasis on culture, tradition, meanings, and values, cultural transmission theory clearly is a product of the strong influence of symbolic interactionism in the Chicago School of sociology and criminology.

EDWIN H. SUTHERLAND

Edwin H. Sutherland, another Chicago criminologist, was heavily influenced by Thomas and Shaw and McKay and "drew on three major theories from the Chicago School: ecological and cultural transmission theory, symbolic interactionism, and culture conflict theory" to develop his theory of differential association (Williams and McShane 1999:78). By 1947, Sutherland had refined his theory and developed nine specific points. Sutherland began his theory by claiming that criminal behavior is learned through interaction with other individuals in intimate groups, just as any other behavior is learned. Learning criminal behavior includes acquiring techniques and *"the specific direction of motives, drives, rationalizations, and attitudes"* associated with the behavior (Sutherland and Cressey 1978: 80–82). A person engages in crime and delinquency when there are more definitions favorable to law violation than definitions unfavorable to law violation. Moreover, when definitions favorable to law violations are more frequent, longer lasting, learned from individuals held in high esteem, and more intense than those unfavorable to law violations, individuals are more likely to engage in criminal or delinquent behavior. The emphasis on definitions is reflective of the influences of symbolic interactionism and Thomas on Sutherland's work.

THE CONSEQUENCES

Throughout the Chicago School of Criminology and the Hull-House School of Criminology, there was an emphasis on social reform and social action. The Juvenile Protective Association (JPA) was founded and ran by Hull-House women. It later became the Institute for Juvenile Research (IJR). The data Shaw used for his ethnographies titled *The Jack-Roller: A Delinquent Boy's Own Story* (1930) and *Brothers in Crime* (1938) came from the IJR. Other works produced as a result of the IJR include *Delinquency Areas* (Shaw, Zorbaugh, McKay, and Cottrell 1929), *Organized Crime in Chicago* (Landesco 1929), *The Natural History of a Delinquent Career* (Shaw and Moore 1931), and *Social Factors in Juvenile Delinquency* (Shaw and McKay 1931), the latter having been written for the Wickersham Commission.

The Chicago Vice Commission included the JPA. This group was formed to examine the scope of vice crimes and to make policy recommendations. Reckless ([1933] 1969) published a book on the Commission's activities. The women of Hull-House were instrumental in writing and passing the Juvenile Court Act (1899), which established the first juvenile court in the United States.

Thrasher ([1927] 1963) suggested that crime prevention could only be effective if programs and policies were based in the community. Like the IJR's Chicago Area Project (CAP), Thrasher contended that research should inform crime prevention programs, that programs should be open to all children in the area, and that responsibility for crime prevention should be located in the area in question. The CAP, started by the IJR in 1932, was an urban delinquency prevention program. The objectives of CAP were "to mobilize local informal social organization and social control among the law-abiding residents" and "to overcome the influence of delinquent peers and criminal adults in the neighborhoods by providing more opportunities for association with conventional adults and peers" (Akers 2000:155). Shaw and McKay (1942) outlined the major characteristics of CAP as:

1. the "neighborhood is the unit of operation" (p. 322);
2. "activities are planned and carried on by a committee composed of representative local citizens" (p. 323);
3. the CAP staff should be locals;
4. local CAP units should cooperate with local community agencies and groups;
5. activities include such things as "recreation, summer camping, scouting, handicraft, forums, and interest trips" as well as sanitation projects, parent teacher organizations, employment opportunities, meeting basic needs; and
6. credit for CAP work should be given to local residents.

The theories and theorists that were a part of the Chicago School of Criminology still hold a prominent place in U.S.

criminology today. Many of our more contemporary theories, policies, and crime prevention programs can be traced back to the Chicago School.

CITED

Addams, J. 1909. *The Spirit of Youth and the City Streets*. NY: Macmillan Co.

_. 1912a. *A New Conscience and an Ancient Evil*. NY: Macmillan Co.

_. 1912b. "Recreation as a Public Function in Urban Communities." *American Journal of Sociology* 17: 615–619.

Akers, RL. 2000. *Criminological Theories: Introduction, Evaluation and Application*. 3rd ed. Los Angeles, CA: Roxbury Publishing Co.

Barry, K. 1979. *Female Sexual Slavery*. Englewood Cliffs, NJ: Prentice-Hall.

Bulmer, M. 1984. *The Chicago School of Sociology: Institutionalization, Diversity, and the Rise of Sociological Research*. Chicago: University of Chicago Press.

Burgess, EW. 1925. "The Growth of the City: An Introduction to a Research Project." In *The City*, ed. Robert E. Park, Ernest W. Burgess, and Roderick D. McKenzie. Chicago: University of Chicago Press.

Bursik Jr., R. 1999. "The Informal Control of Crime Through Neighborhood Networks." *Sociological Focus* 32: 85–97.

Cloward, Richard A., and Lloyd E. Ohlin. 1960. *Delinquency and Opportunity: A Theory of Delinquent Gangs*. New York: Free Press.

Deegan, Mary Jo. 1988. *Jane Addams and the Men of the Chicago School, 1892–1918*. New Brunswick, NJ: Transaction Press.

Gusfield, Joseph R. 1963. *Symbolic Crusade: Status Politics and the American Temperance Movement*. Urbana, IL: University of Illinois Press.

Landesco, John. 1929. *Organized Crime in Chicago*. Chicago: University of Chicago Press.

Levine, Daniel. 1971. *Jane Addams and the Liberal Tradition*. Madison, WI: The State Historical Society of Wisconsin.

Lombroso, Cesare. 1911. *Criminal Man According to the Classification of Cesare Lombroso*. Edited by Gina Lombroso-Ferrero. New York: Putnam.

Mead, George H. 1999. *Play, School, and Society*. Edited and introduction by Mary Jo Deegan. New York: Peter Lang.

Park, Robert E., Ernest W. Burgess, and Roderick D. McKenzie, eds. 1925. *The City*, Chicago: University of Chicago Press.

Reckless, Walter C. [1933] 1969. *Vice in Chicago*. Montclair, NJ: Patterson Smith.

Roncek, Dennis W., and Pamela A. Maier. 1991. "Bars, Blocks, and Crimes Revisited: Linking the Theory of Routine Activities to the Empiricism of 'Hot Spots.'" *Criminology* 29: 725–753.

Sampson, Robert J. 1995. "The Community." P. 193–216 In *Crime*, ed. J. Wilson and J. Petersilia. San Francisco, CA: ICS.

_. 1930. *The Jack-Roller, A Delinquent Boy's Own Story*. Chicago: University of Chicago Press.

Shaw, Clifford R. 1938. *Brothers in Crime*. Chicago: University of Chicago Press.

Shaw, Clifford R., and Henry D. McKay. 1931. *Report on the Causes of Crime*. Vol. 2: *Social Factors in Juvenile Delinquency*. National Commission on Law Observance and Enforcement, Report No. 13. Washington, DC: U.S. Government Printing Office.

_. 1942. *Juvenile Delinquency in Urban Areas*. Chicago: University of Chicago Press.

Shaw, Clifford R., and Maurice E. Moore. 1931. *The Natural History of a Delinquent Career*. Philadelphia: A. Saifer.

Shaw, Clifford R., Frederick Zorbaugh, Henry McKay, and Leonard Cottrell. 1929. *Delinquent Areas: A Study of the Geographic Distribution of School Truants, Juvenile Delinquents, and Adult Offenders in Chicago*. Chicago: University of Chicago Press.

Sinclair, Upton. 1906. *The Jungle*. New York: Viking Press.

Sutherland, Edwin H., and Donald R. Cressey. 1978. Pp. 237–243 in *Theories of Deviance*, 5th ed., edited by Stuart H. Traub and Craig B. Little. Itasca, IL: F. E. Peacock Publishers, Inc.

Taylor, Ian, Paul Walton, and Jock Young. 1973. *The New Criminology: For A Social Theory of Deviance*. Boston: Routledge.

Thomas, William I. [1923] 1969. *The Unadjusted Girl: With Cases and Standpoint for Behavioral Analysis*. Montclair, NJ: Patterson Smith.

Thrasher, Frederic M. [1927] 1963. *The Gang: A Study of 1,313 Gangs in Chicago*. Chicago: University of Chicago Press.

U.S. Bureau of the Census. 1999. Tech Paper 29: Table 22. "Nativity of the Population for Urban Places Ever Among the 50 Largest Urban Places Since 1870: 1850 to 1990." Retrieved November 6, 1999 (http://www.census.gov/population/www/documentation/twps0029/tab22.html).

Whyte, William F. 1943. *Street Corner Society: The Social Structure of an Italian Slum*. Chicago: University of Chicago Press.

Williams, Frank P., and Marilyn D. McShane. 1999. *Criminological Theory*. 3rd ed. Upper Saddle River, NJ: Prentice Hall.

Origins of the Juvenile Court:

Changing Perspectives on the Legal Rights of Juvenile Delinquents

Robert M. Mennel

The widespread establishment of juvenile courts in the early years of this century represented one of the proudest achievements of progressive reformers. Grace Abbott, chief of the U.S. Children's Bureau, 1921–34, believed that these special tribunals had effected a historic breakthrough in public policy toward youthful crime. In her words, the child offender was no longer regarded "as a *criminal* but as a *delinquent*."[1] Jane Addams, equally enthusiastic, recalled:

> There was almost a change in *mores* when the Juvenile Court was established. The child was brought before the judge with no one to prosecute him and with no one to defend him—the judge and all concerned were merely trying to find out what could be done on his behalf. The element of conflict was absolutely eliminated and with it, all notions of punishment as such with its curiously belated connotation.[2]

Juvenile courts supposedly resembled the English High Court of Chancery

which, under the principles of equity, exercised the Crown's prerogative to serve as *parens patriae* for children whose welfare was in jeopardy. Since the juvenile court purported to act in the best interest of the state's wards, it was exempt from the obligation to provide defendants with guarantees of due process which the Constitution insured adult persons accused of crimes.

The juvenile court has always had its critics, but not until recent years have its theoretically benevolent purposes come under sustained attack. Recent decisions of the Supreme Court have questioned whether the court treats children humanely enough to justify its immunity from the safeguards of criminal law. Thus in the *Kent* case (1966), Justice Fortas, while praising the "laudable purposes" of the court, asked "whether actual performance measures well enough against theoretical purpose to make tolerable the immunity of the process from the reach of constitutional guarantees applicable to adults." He concluded. "There is evidence, in fact, that there may be grounds for concern that the child receives the worst of both worlds: that he gets neither the protection accorded to adults nor the solicitous care and regenerate treatment postulated for children."[3]

Robert M. Mennel, CRIME & DELINQUENCY, Vol. 18, 1972, pp. 68–78, © Sage Publications, Inc. Reprinted by Permission of Sage Publications, Inc.

[1]Quoted in Sophonisba P. Breckinridge and Edith Abbott. *The Delinquent Child and the Home* (New York: Charities Publication Committee, 1912), p. 247.

[2]Jane Addams, *My Friend Julia Lathrop* (New York: Macmillan, 1935), p. 137.

---

[3]*Kent v. United States*, 383 U.S. 541, 545 (1966).

The *Kent* decision warned juvenile courts against "procedural arbitrariness." The following year the *Gault* decision went beyond *Kent* in guaranteeing juveniles such specific rights as notification, cross-examination of complainants and other witnesses, and warning of the privilege against self-incrimination. "Under our Constitution." said Justice Fortas, "the condition of being a boy does not justify a kangaroo court."[4]

Recent studies of the juvenile court have examined and questioned what Justice Fortas termed its "original laudable purposes." As early as 1923. Roscoe Pound pointed out that the juvenile court actually originated in criminal law rather than in chancery court proceedings, which traditionally considered cases involving neglected and dependent children.[5] In 1949 Paul Tappan characterized the *parens patriae* doctrine as an *ex post facto* justification for practices that in fact originated with the statutory creation of the juvenile court.[6] In *The Child Savers*, a study of the citizens who founded the original juvenile court in Illinois in 1899. Anthony Platt concludes that the reformers "implicitly assumed the 'natural' dependence of adolescents and created a special court to impose sanctions on premature independence and behavior unbecoming to youth." The juvenile court, according to Platt, did not herald a new system of justice but rather reinforced policies developed during the nineteenth century.[7]

Platt's work delineates the reform outlook toward juvenile delinquency in the late nineteenth century but does not probe the history underlying that outlook. A few observations, therefore, on the origins of the *parens patriae* doctrine as applied to delinquent children and on the nature of efforts to prevent juvenile delinquency in the nineteenth century may advance understanding of the exaggerated hopes of the "child savers."

EARLY PUNISHMENT

Before 1825, special institutions for delinquent children did not exist in the United States. Public authority sanctioned the power of parents and masters to punish youthful lawbreakers. Under the common law in England and America, the child under seven years of age was considered incapable of mischief, and the child between seven and fourteen was assumed to be incapable of felony but, according to Blackstone, "if it appear to the court and jury, that he could discern between good and evil, he may be convicted and suffer death."[8]

Both common law and customary practice assumed that children accused of misbehavior and crimes were guilty as charged. Possiblé innocence was not considered: the jury's responsibility was to determine whether children understood their offenses. Juries were reluctant to condemn children to jail and often acquitted them after a nominal trial, finding "lack of knowledge" the reason for the crime.[9]

---

[4]*In re Gault*, 387 U.S. 28 (1967).
[5]Roscoe Pound. *Interpretations of Legal History* (New York: Macmillan, 1923), pp. 134–35.
[6]Paul Tappan, *Juvenile Delinquency* (New York: McGraw-Hill, 1949), p. 169.
[7]Anthony Platt, *The Child Savers* (Chicago: University of Chicago Press, 1969), p. 176.

[8]William Blackstone, *Commentaries on the Laws of England* (London: A. Strahan and W. Woodfall, 1795), vol. 4. p. 23.
[9]In a study of fourteen cases on the criminal responsibility of children, Platt concluded that guilty findings were seldom returned despite evidence indicating that the defendant understood that he had committed a crime. See Platt, *op. cit. supra* note 7, p. 202.

By the early nineteenth century, this method of handling delinquent children had become unsatisfactory on two counts. First, it did not work all the time: despite courtroom partiality toward youths, increasing numbers were being convicted and sent to jails where, it was commonly believed, they were schooled by adult inmates for future crime. Second, and more important, some children gained acquittal by appealing to the jury's sympathy—an equally unsatisfactory disposition because it allowed them to escape the consequences of their actions.

These shortcomings in the criminal justice system prompted concerned citizens in New York, Boston, and Philadelphia to establish special institutions for delinquent children. The first was the New York House of Refuge, which was founded in 1824 by members of the Society for the Reformation of Juvenile Delinquents. In 1826, following the recommendation of Mayor Josiah Quincy, the Boston City Council founded the House of Reformation for juvenile offenders. At the same time, a group of prominent Philadelphians received a charter to form a House of Refuge, which they opened in 1828. The New York and Philadelphia refuges were privately managed, though they received public sanction and aid; the Boston House of Reformation was a municipal institution. These three institutions were the only organized efforts to reform juvenile delinquents until 1847, when state institutions were opened in Massachusetts and New York.

Illustrative of the initial concern with juvenile delinquency is this comment by founders of the New York House of Refuge about the legal disposition of delinquent children in the early 1820's:

If acquitted, they returned destitute, to the same haunts of vice from which they had been taken, more emboldened to the commission of crime by their escape from present punishment. If convicted, they were cast into a common prison with older culprits to mingle in conversation and intercourse with them, acquire their habits, and by their instruction to be made acquainted with the most artful methods of perpetrating crime.[10]

Although the task of the refuge was to prevent delinquent children from being punished cruelly, it was also to insure that they were punished correctly. The necessity of providing accused delinquents with the legal safeguards of due process was not an issue.

To implement their plan, founders of the New York Refuge drew upon an 1822 study of American penitentiaries conducted by the Society for the Prevention of Pauperism. This report called for "the erection of new prisons for juvenile offenders," concluding:

These prisons should be rather schools for instruction, than places of punishment. . . . The youth confined there should be placed under a course of discipline, severe and unchanging, but alike calculated to subdue and conciliate. A system should be adopted that would prove a mental and moral regimen.[11]

Faithful to the words of the study, the managers of the New York Refuge—and the other refuge leaders too—established "a mental and moral regimen" to instill the habits of piety, honesty, sobriety, and hard work in their children. In 1835, a typical day in the New York Refuge featured two hours of school before breakfast, an

---

[10]New York Society for the Reformation of Juvenile Delinquents, *Annual Report, 1826*, New York, 1827, pp. 3–4. (Hereinafter cited as S.R.J.D.)

[11]New York Society for the Prevention of Pauperism. *Report on the Penitentiary System in the United States*, New York, 1822, pp. 59–60.

eight-hour workday, and then 2-1/2 more hours of school after which, the institution's journal informs us, "children are conducted to their dormitories . . . and are locked up for the night, when perfect silence reigns throughout the establishment."[12]

Under the terms of their incorporation, refuges received children who were destitute and orphaned as well as those who were actually convicted of felonies in state and local courts. Some of the "convicted" children were guilty of no greater crimes than vagrancy, idleness, or stubbornness—those familiar catchalls for mild youthful misbehavior. By training both destitute and delinquent children and by separating them from their natural parents and adult criminals, refuge managers believed that they were preventing poverty *and* crime.

THE REFUGE AS PARENT

Because these early child savers regarded convicted criminals and parents of delinquent children as one and the same, they sought to counter their influence by establishing the parental powers of the refuges. To do so, the institutions had to rebut claims that they were illegally depriving inmates of their liberty. In this instance, the significant legal challenge was *Ex parte Crouse*. In 1838, Mary Ann Crouse's father attempted to free her from the Philadelphia House of Refuge on a writ of habeas corpus. The Pennsylvania Supreme Court denied his claim, saying, "The right of parental control is a natural, but not an unalienable one"; and it continued:

The object of the charity is reformation, by training its inmates to industry; by imbuing

their minds with principles of morality and religion; by furnishing them with means to earn a living; and, above all, by separating them from the corrupting influence of improper associates. To this end, may not the natural parents, when unequal to the task of education, or unworthy of it, be superseded by the *parens patriae*, or common guardian of the community?. . . The infant has been snatched from a course which must have ended in confirmed depravity; and, not only is the restraint of her person lawful, but it would be an act of extreme cruelty to release her from it.[13]

Alexis de Tocqueville and Gustave de Beaumont had reached a similar conclusion on the rights of refuge children during their tour of American penal institutions in 1831. "The children," they wrote, "were not the victims of persecution, but merely deprived of a fatal liberty."[14]

The New York legislature showed its sympathy for refuge aims by channeling revenue from several taxes to the institution. This money was derived in part—or, so it was thought—from the pernicious habits of the parents of refuge children. Stephen Allen, president of the Refuge corporation, lobbied successfully to gain a portion of the state's revenue from a tax on theater licenses. The legislature also taxed the taverns of New York City to support the refuge.[15]

The origins of these parents were as suspect as their habits. As early as 1801, Thomas Eddy, a founder of the New York Refuge, warned that West Indian and lower-class European immigration would

---

[12]S.R.J.D. *Annual Report, 1835*, pp. 6–7.

[13]*Ex parte Crouse*, 4 Whart. 9 (Pa. 1838).

[14]Gustave de Beaumont and Alexis de Tocqueville, *On the Penitentiary System in the United States*, Francis Lieber, transl. (Philadelphia: Carey, Lea and Blanchard, 1833), p. 115.

[15]Stephen Allen to Walter Bowne, March 17, 1824, and Stephen Allen to John Morss, April 1, 1824. The Papers of Stephen Allen, New York Historical Society.

result in an uncontrollable younger generation.[16] The New York legislature agreed by allotting part of the state's emigrant head tax to the refuge. By the mid-1830's, refuges were publishing the birthplaces of both inmates and their parents; the preponderance of Irish children reflected the beginning of the Irish migration to America.[17] Refuge managers did not view these poor peasants and their children sympathetically. Stephen Allen summarized the attitude when he said:

> The tide of emigration . . . while it enriches our country, leaves much of its refuse in our city. Pauper families, and even felons, are not infrequently sent over to us as a cheap way of disposing of them . . . thus swelling the number of houseless, friendless and lawless youth, drifting loose upon society.[18]

The doctrine of *parens patriae* gave refuge managers the best of two worlds, familial and legal: it separated delinquent children from their natural parents, and it circumvented the rigor of criminal law by allowing courts to commit children, under loosely worded statutes, to specially created "schools" instead of jails. Once the child was received by the refuge, procedures of criminal law no longer applied.

The *parens patriae* argument provided criminal courts with a convenient rationale for disposing of dependent and delinquent children. It conferred parental powers upon institutions to prevent natural parents, who were usually impoverished or foreign or both, from gaining or regaining custody of their children. Refuges received state sanction to exercise parental power over inmates throughout the period of their minority, and thus these institutions could and did apprentice delinquents to whaling captains and farmers without informing the natural parents. In remote farming and nautical districts. the state's purposes were further promoted since the parent-child ties were often severed permanently.[19]

In this manner, houses of refuge gained a self-proclaimed "victory" over juvenile delinquency—one which depended on their control, though perhaps not their reform, of delinquent children. Annual reports of the institutions were notoriously self-promoting, reflecting until 1850 a serene pride in their accomplishments. Refuge managers boasted regularly that both juvenile crime in the city and juvenile incarceration in penitentiaries and jails had decreased dramatically as a result of refuge work. They claimed a high percentage of "saved" apprentices, citing as proof the number of favorable letters from farmers and the absence of detrimental reports.[20] Refractory inmates, though not yet considered a serious challenge to the institutions' authority or prestige, were severely handled. Although the punishment was usually corporal, some children were sent to the penitentiary. In the words of Nathaniel Hart, superintendent of the New York Refuge, "We will be fathers to them if they obey the rules."[21]

---

[16]Thomas Eddy, *An Account of the State Prison or Penitentiary House in the City of New York* (New York: Isaac Collins, 1801).

[17]*S.R.J.D.*, *Annual Report, 1834*, p. 61; Philadelphia House of Refuge, *Tenth Annual Report, 1838*, p. 4; Boston Common Council, *City Doc.* 19 (1846), pp. 10–11.

[18]*S.R.J.D. Annual Report, 1849*, p. 11.

[19]See, for example, Philadelphia House of Refuge. *Third Annual Report, 1831*, pp. 5–6.

[20]Boston Prison Discipline Society. *Second Annual Report*. This society, founded in 1826 by Louis Dwight, of Boston, collected annual reports from all types of penal institutions.

[21]Quoted in Robert S. Pickett, *House of Refuge: Origins of Juvenile Reform in New York State, 1815–1857* (Syracuse: Syracuse University Press, 1969), p. 144. For an early criticism of the disciplinary methods of the New York House of Refuge see Elijah Devoe. *The Refuge System, or Prison Discipline Applied to juvenile Delinquents* (New York: J. R. M'Gown, 1848).

If imitation really is the sincerest form of flattery, by 1850 managers of the first refuges could brush aside criticism and reflect upon the exemplary nature of their institutions, because by this time a number of other municipal and state institutions either were in the planning stage or had been opened.[22] Invariably, inaugural ceremonies of the new reform schools were marked by tributes to the first institutions. Familiar sentiments were expressed—the need to remove children from jail and the even greater need to separate them from their parents or other adults in order to teach them values of thrift, honesty, and individual responsibility.[23]

THE FAILURE OF REFUGES

Although early refuge leaders took pride in their creations, the very proliferation of reform schools bespoke not only their failure to put a stop to juvenile delinquency but also their inability to prevent its growth. The increasingly violent activities of street gangs in the larger municipal centers both during and after the Civil War are matters of common knowledge. The major point is not that reform schools, both old and new, were unable to hold all the youthful law violators (although, of course, they could not and many delinquents either were sent to jail or were simply left to roam). Rather, the notable characteristic of reform schools in the later nineteenth century was their inability to cope with the relatively few children who *did* come under their charge.

This failure resulted from the increasingly harsh nature of institutional life. Faced with large numbers of children and only limited public financial support, reform school managers were forced to rely upon the contract system. This system had been part of refuge life from the beginning, but it now assumed a more exploitative character. Clothing and shoe manufacturers, whose piecework was once welcomed because it was thought to encourage good habits, were now viewed with greater skepticism because they often insisted upon replacing institution officials with company supervisors in order to squeeze maximum productivity out of the children's working hours. Officials at the Philadelphia Refuge complained of this practice in 1866:

> Those immediately entrusted with the government of the boys are generally but illy qualified for so responsible a position. . . . If the work be well done and a responsible amount of it, they are satisfied. These seven and a half hours of labor are spent without one moral lesson taught the boys, at least so far as the workmen of the shops are concerned.[24]

In 1871, the New York Commission on Prison Labor, headed by Enoch Wines, investigated the contract system and uncovered many instances of exploitation and brutality. The commissioners received this picture of shop life from former New York

---

[22]The following reformatory and child-saving institutions were opened around mid-century: House of Refuge, New Orleans (1847); State Reform School (boys), Massachusetts (1847): Western House of Refuge. New York (1849): Colored House of Refuge, Philadelphia (1850): House of Refuge, Cincinnati (1850); New York Juvenile Asylum (1853); Children's Aid Society, New York (1853); Western House of Refuge, Pittsburgh (1854): State Industrial School (girls). Massachusetts (1856); Ohio Reform School (1857).

[23]See, for example, Michael Katz. *The Irony of Early School Reform: Educational Opinion in Mid-nineteenth Century Massachusetts* (Cambridge, Mass.: Harvard University Press. 1969), pp 167–70, an analysis of opinion favoring the establishment of a state reform school.

[24]Enoch C. Wines and Theodore W. Dwight, *Report on the Prisons and Reformatories of the United States and Canada* (Albany, N.Y.: Van Benthuysen, 1867), p.431.

Refuge employees Thomas Crowne and Valentine Feldman:

Q. Have you ever known instructors employed by the contractors to strike the boys? **A.** (Crowne) I have seen them do it, though it is forbidden. I have also seen them, when a keeper was around, and they did not dare to strike tread on the boys' bare toes . . . so as to cause them to squirm all around. . . .

Q. Have you ever seen any of the boys abused by the contractors' employees? **A.** (Feldman) Often and often. They do not call it abusing a boy to give him a kick, or a blow on the head. . . .

Q. Please describe the way in which they are punished. **A.** I have seen boys punished for not completing their tasks, so that blood ran down into their boots.[25]

The new cottage reform schools, founded in the 1850's and 1860's to discipline and care for children in small family units and to teach them the benefits of farm life, also fell victim to demands for economy. Rev. Marcus Ames, superintendent of the girls' cottage reformatory at Lancaster, Mass., resigned in 1874 rather than accept the installation of workshops.[26] At the New Jersey State Reform School at Jamesburg, farming and maintenance work gave way to shirt-making in 1875 and a factory appeared among the cottages. Legislative investigators found life in the institution "hard, routine and monotonous." James Leiby concludes in his comprehensive study of New Jersey institutions. "Jamesburg was not a family, nor a reformatory, but a boys prison."[27]

Not surprisingly, incendiarism, rioting, and even murder marked the history of nearly every reform school. In 1859 Daniel Credan and five of his friends put the torch to the Massachusetts Reform School at Westborough.[28] On May 17, 1872, Justus Dunn stabbed to death Saul Calvert, an overseer in the North Shop of the New York Refuge.[29] Five years later, the superintendent of the Massachusetts girls' reformatory reported. "House No. 3, an old building . . . replete with interesting associations, was burned to the ground, having been set on fire by two of our inmates."[30]

These events posed serious questions for reformatory institutions whose custodial power depended upon the *parens patriae* doctrine. If reform schools did not improve—indeed, if they abused delinquent children—how could they then justify their parental role? How could they avoid being labeled prisons? How could they pretend that the scope of their custodial power extended to vagrant and semidelinquent children, as well as to youths convicted of felonies?

CHANGING LEGAL DECISIONS

Soon after the Civil War, legal decisions interpreting *parens patriae* began to reflect increasing distrust of the intentions and performance of reform schools and, conversely, new appreciation for natural parents. In 1870 the Illinois Supreme Court reversed the vagrancy sentence of Daniel O'Connell to the Chicago Reform School on the grounds that he had not committed

[25]New York State Assembly, *Documents, 1871*, IV, Doc. 18, "Report of the Commission on Prison Labor." Albany, 1871. pp. 164, 181.

[26]Massachusetts State Industrial School for Girls. *Annual Report, 1875*, Boston, 1875. pp. 8–9.

[27]James Leiby, *Charities and Correction in New Jersey* (New Brunswick, N.J.: Rutgers University Press, 1967), p. 82.

[28]Massachusetts, State Reform School at Westborough. *Thirteenth Annual Report, 1859*, Boston, 1959, pp. 3–4.

[29]S.R.J.D. *Annual Report 1872*, pp. 45–47.

[30]Massachusetts, State Industrial School for Girls. *Annual Report, 1878*, Boston, 1878, p. 16.

a crime and had been imprisoned without due process of law. "Why should minors be imprisoned for misfortune?" asked the court. "Destitution of proper parental care, ignorance, idleness and vice, are misfortunes, not crimes. . . . This boy is deprived of a father's care; bereft of home influences; has no freedom of action; is committed for an uncertain time; is branded as a prisoner; made subject to the will of others, and thus feels that he is a slave."[31] In 1897 an appellate court freed Jonie Becknell from the Whittier State School in California on the grounds that he had been committed solely on the basis of a grand jury hearing and "cannot be imprisoned as a criminal without a trial by jury."[32]

It is true, of course, that other decisions supported the state's traditional exercise of parental power. The case of a Chinese youth named Ah Peen, "minor child, of the age of sixteen, leading an idle and dissolute life," is representative. Ah Peen's commitment to an industrial school without a jury trial was a justifiable exercise of *parens patriae*, said the California Supreme Court, and therefore not subject to the safeguards of criminal law. The decision concluded, "The purpose in view is not punishment for offenses done, but reformation and training of the child to habits of industry, with a view to his future usefulness when he shall have been reclaimed to society."[33]

Nevertheless, the animus against reform schools was strong enough to find other means of expression. Beginning in the 1850's the New York Children's Aid Society shipped Manhattan Street urchins to western farms in wholesale lots to prevent philanthropists and local authorities from committing them to the Refuge. Charles Loring Brace, the society's founder, asked: "If enough families can be found to serve as reformatory institutions, is it not the best and most practical and economical method of reforming these children?"[34]

"Placing-out" remained a popular alternative to institutionalization, even after the demand for youthful workers subsided in the agrarian West. In 1890 the Children's Aid Society of Pennsylvania, with the cooperation of local courts, offered to place in foster homes delinquents who would otherwise be committed to reform schools. This probation experiment was not undertaken without misgiving. "We have sometimes left our wards . . . and returned half expecting the next mail to announce their evildoing and disappearance," recalled Homer Folks, secretary of the Society. "But we have been happily surprised as weeks passed by and all the reports were hopeful."[35] The New York Society for the Prevention of Cruelty to Children established a similar program after influencing passage of state legislation which enabled it to receive children from the courts. Massachusetts continued to increase the size of its state visiting agency, which had been established in 1869 to serve as a probation and parole office for delinquents.

The idea of a juvenile court had, therefore, several roots. In many locales, children were still being detained in or sentenced to jail. Their plight was much lamented at philanthropic meetings and at state and national charity conferences. The creation of a probate tribunal, it was reasoned, would minimize and perhaps even

---

[31]*People v. Turner*, 55 Ill. 280 (1870).
[32]*Ex parte Becknell*, 51 P. 692 (Calif. 1897).
[33]*Ex parte Ah Peen*, 51 California 280 (1876).

[34]Second Convention of Managers and Superintendents of Houses of Refuge and Schools of Reform, *Proceedings, 1859*, New York, 1860, p. 48.
[35]Homer Folks, "The Care of Delinquent Children," *Proceedings*, National Conference of Charities and Corrections, 1891, pp. 137–39.

eliminate this perennial problem. More important, however, in the origin of the juvenile court was the widespread belief that reform schools were no longer equal to the task of providing parental guidance for delinquent children. The reality of institutional life—the riots, the exploitation, the cruel punishments—mocked the ideal. In 1891, Homer Folks listed "the contaminating influence of association" and "the enduring stigma . . . of having been committed" as reasons to avoid sending children to reform school.[36]

The popularity of nineteenth-century probation plans—the forerunners of the juvenile court—can be traced directly to this distrust. The Illinois juvenile court act (1899) combined the Massachusetts and New York systems of probation with several New York laws providing delinquents with special court sessions and separate detention facilities.[37] Juvenile courts developed their own probation staffs, detention homes, and auxiliary services, thus relegating reform schools to places of *"dernier resort,"* in the words of one superintendent.[38] By relieving institutions of their parental power, juvenile courts were declaring that their own exercise of *parens patriae* would seek, above all, to reform delinquents without institutionalizing them. In this context, it is easy to understand why Jane Addams believed that the new tribunal "absolutely eliminated . . . all notions of punishment."[39]

---

[36]*Id.*, pp. 137–40.

[37]For the New York laws, see "An Act for the Protection of Children, and to Prevent and Punish Certain Wrongs to Children," ch. 428, *Laws of the State of New York*, Albany, N.Y., 1877, p. 486, and "An Act . . . Relative to Criminal Charges against Children," ch. 217, *Laws of the State of New York, 1892*, Vol. I, Albany, N.Y., 1892, pp. 459–60.

[38]H. W. Charles, "The Problem of the Reform School," *Proceedings*, Vol. II, Child Conference for Research and Welfare, 1910, p. 86.

[39]Addams, *op. cit. supra* note 2, p. 137.

THE EARLY JUVENILE COURT

The purpose of this paper is not to examine the many ways in which the juvenile court failed to live up to its promise. It is appropriate, however, to make observations about the court and the expectations with which it commenced. First, the brightness of the promise came in large measure from the preceding darkness: judges enhanced the reputation of their courts merely by refusing to send children to jail or commit them to reform school. Such dispositions made the juvenile court seem to be more of a miracle worker than it actually was. Second, and as a corollary, enthusiasm over the novelty of the institution encouraged its widespread adoption in one form or another throughout the United States. The sheer amount of organizational and promotional activity disguised for a long while the court's quite traditional attitudes and policies toward the legal rights of delinquent children and their parents. Far from limiting the parental power of the state, advocates of the juvenile court sought to increase it. A 1905 decision upholding the legality of a juvenile court in Pennsylvania is representative:

> To save a child from becoming a criminal, or from continuing in a career of crime, to end in maturer years in public punishment and disgrace, the legislatures surely may provide for the salvation of such a child, if its parents or guardians be unable or unwilling to do so, by bringing it into one of the courts of the state without any process at all, for the purpose of subjecting it to the state's guardianship and protection.[40]

Parents of delinquent children could not expect much sympathy from Ben

---

[40]*Commonwealth v. Fisher*, 62 A. 198 (Pa. 1905); see also *Mill v. Brown*, 88 p. 609 (Utah 1905).

Lindsey, the famous "children's judge," who regularly berated "the careless father, unworthy as a man, dangerous as a citizen."[41] On a more sophisticated level, psychologist Augusta Bronner urged that juvenile courts be allowed to remove children from "unworthy or stupid" parents who did not understand the principles of child psychology.[42] Homer Folks, without a trace of irony, concluded that the new court provided "a new kind of reformatory, without walls and without much coercion."[43]

The spirit of these comments would have seemed familiar to the father of Mary Ann Crouse. The juvenile court, like the early reform school, exercised parental power to punish parents for their children's delinquencies and to deny children legal rights on the pretext that they were being protected, not punished. In 1972 as in 1872, interest in providing delinquent children with legal safeguards is based upon belief that the state has not fulfilled its parental duties. Current legal interpretations protecting accused delinquents in the juvenile court resemble earlier decisions restricting the parental power of the reform school. The *Gault* case, like the *O'Connell* case nearly a century before, protects children against unfair loss of liberty; both of these decisions prefer the guardianship of natural parents to that of the state. Today, as then, we can no longer disqualify parents from caring for their children simply because they are poor of unfamiliar with the principles of child psychology. Parents may indeed abuse or fail to exercise their disciplinary authority. There is, however, little historical evidence to indicate that public authorities in the United States have provided viable and humane alternatives.

---

[41]Benjamin B. Lindsey, "The Child, the Parent and the Law," *Juvenile Court Record*, May 1904, pp. 9–10.

[42]Augusta F. Bronner, "The Contribution of Science to a Program for Treatment of Juvenile Delinquency," in Julia Lathrop *et al.*, *The Child, the Clinic and the Court* (New York: New Republic, 1925), p. 84.

[43]Homer Folks, "Juvenile Probation," *Proceedings*, National Conference of Charities and Corrections, 1906, pp. 117–22.

The Rise of the Child-Saving Movement:

A Study in Social Policy and Correctional Reform*

By Anthony Platt

Studies of crime and delinquency have, for the most part, focused on their psychological and environmental origins. Correctional research has traditionally encompassed the relationship between prisoners and prison-management, the operation of penal programs, the implementation of the "rehabilitative ideal" and, in recent years, the effectiveness of community-based corrections. On the other hand, we know very little about the social processes by which certain types of behavior come to be defined as "criminal" or about the origins of penal reforms.[1] If we intend rationally to assess the nature and purposes of correctional policies, it is of considerable importance to understand how laws and legislation are passed, how changes in penal practices are implemented, and what interests are served by such reforms.

This paper analyzes the nature and origins of the reform movement in juvenile justice and juvenile corrections at the end of the nineteenth century. Delinquency raises fundamental questions about the objects of social control, and it was through the child-saving movement that the

modern system of delinquency-control emerged in the United States. The child-savers were responsible for creating a new legal institution for penalizing children (juvenile court) and a new correctional institution to accommodate the needs of youth (reformatory). The origins of "delinquency" are to be found in the programs and ideas of these reformers, who recognized the existence and carriers of delinquent norms.

IMAGES OF DELINQUENCY

The child-saving movement, like most moral crusades, was characterized by a "rhetoric of legitimization,"[2] built on traditional values and imagery. From the medical profession, the child-savers borrowed the imagery of pathology, infection, and treatment; from the tenets of Social Darwinism, they derived their pessimistic views about the intractability of human nature and the innate moral defects of the working class; finally, their ideas about the biological and environmental origins of crime may be attributed to the positivist

Annals of The American Academy of Political and Social Science, 381, 1969, pp. 21–38

[1] This perspective is influenced by Howard S. Becker, *Outsiders: Studies in the Sociology of Deviance* (New York: Free Press, 1966).

[2] This term is used by Donald W. Ball, "An Abortion Clinic Ethnography," 14 *Social Problems*, 1967, pp. 293–301.

tradition in European criminology and to anti-urban sentiments associated with the rural, Protestant ethic.

American criminology in the last century was essentially a practical affair. Theoretical concepts of crime were imported from Europe, and an indiscriminating eclecticism dominated the literature. Lombrosian positivism and Social Darwinism were the major sources of intellectual justification for crime workers. The pessimism of Darwinism, however, was counterbalanced by notions of charity, religious optimism, and the dignity of suffering which were implicit components of the Protestant ethic.

Before 1870, there were only a few American textbooks on crime, and the various penal organizations lacked specialized journals. Departments of law and sociology in the universities were rarely concerned with more than the description and classification of crimes. The first American writers on crime were physicians, like Benjamin Rush and Isaac Ray, who were trained according to European methods. The social sciences were similarly imported from Europe, and American criminologists fitted their data to the theoretical framework of criminal anthropology. Herbert Spencer's writings had an enormous impact on American intellectuals, and Cesare Lombroso, perhaps the most significant figure in nineteenth-century criminology, looked for recognition in the United States when he felt that his experiments had been neglected in Europe.[3]

Although Lombroso's theoretical and experimental studies were not translated into English until 1911, his findings were known by American academics in the early 1890's, and their popularity, like that of Spencer's works, was based on the fact that they confirmed popular assumptions about the character and existence of a "criminal class." Lombroso's original theory suggested the existence of a criminal type distinguishable from noncriminals by observable physical anomalies of a degenerative or atavistic nature. He proposed that the criminal was a morally inferior human species, characterized by physical traits reminiscent of apes, lower primates, and savage tribes. The criminal was thought to be morally retarded and, like a small child, instinctively aggressive and precocious unless restrained.[4] It is not difficult to see the connection between biological determinism in criminological literature and the principles of "natural selection"; both of these theoretical positions automatically justified the "eradication of elements that constituted a permanent and serious danger."[5]

NATURE VERSUS NURTURE

Before 1900, American writers were familiar with Lombroso's general propositions but had only the briefest knowledge of his research techniques.[6] Although the emerging doctrines of preventive criminology implied human malleability, most American penologists were preoccupied with the intractability of the "criminal classes." Hamilton Wey, an influential physician at Elmira Reformatory, argued before the

[3]See Lombroso's Introduction to Arthur MacDonald, *Criminology* (New York: Funk and Wagnalls, 1893).

[4]Marvin E. Wolfgang, "Cesare Lombroso," in Hermann Mannheim (ed.), *Pioneers in Criminology* (London: Stevens and Sons, 1960), pp. 168–227.

[5]Leon Radzinowicz, *Ideology and Crime* (London: Heinemann Educational Books, 1966), p. 55.

[6]See, for example, Arthur MacDonald, *Abnormal Man* (Washington, D.C.: U.S. Government Printing Office, 1893); and Robert Fletcher, *The New School of Criminal Anthropology* (Washington, D.C.: Judd and Detwiler, 1891).

National Prison Association in 1881 that criminals were "a distinct type of human species," characterized by flat-footedness, asymmetrical bodies, and "degenerative physiognomy."[7]

Literature on "social degradation" was extremely popular during the 1870's and 1880's, though most such "studies" were little more than crude polemics, padded with moralistic epithets and pre-conceived value judgments. Richard Dugdale's series of papers on the Jukes family, which became a model for the case-study approach to social problems, was distorted almost beyond recognition by anti-intellectual supporters of hereditary theories of crime.[8] Confronted by the evidence of Darwin, Galton, Dugdale, Caldwell, and many other disciples of the biological image of man, correctional professionals were compelled to admit that "a large proportion of the unfortunate children that go to make up the great army of criminals are not born right."[9] Reformers adopted the rhetoric of Darwinism in order to emphasize the urgent need for confronting the "crime problem" before it got completely out of hand. A popular proposal was the "methodized registration and training" of potential criminals, "or these failing, their early and entire withdrawal from the community."[10]

The organization of correctional workers through national representatives and their identification with the professions of law and medicine operated to discredit the tenets of Darwinism and Lombrosian theory. Correctional workers did not think of themselves merely as the custodians of a pariah class. The self-image of penal reformers as doctors rather than guards and the domination of criminological research in the United States by physicians helped to encourage the acceptance of "therapeutic" strategies in prisons and reformatories. As Arthur Fink has observed:

> The role of the physician in this ferment is unmistakable. Indeed, he was the dynamic agent. . . . Not only did he preserve and add to existing knowledge—for his field touched all borders of science—but he helped to maintain and extend the methodology of science.[11]

Perhaps what is more significant is that physicians furnished the official rhetoric of penal reform. Admittedly, the criminal was "pathological" and "diseased," but medical science offered the possibility of miraculous cures. Although there was a popular belief in the existence of a "criminal class" separated from the rest of mankind by a "vague boundary line," there was no good reason why this class could not be identified, diagnosed, segregated, changed, and controlled.[12]

By the late 1890's, most correctional administrators agreed that hereditary theories of crime were overfatalistic. The

---

[7]Hamilton D. Wey, "A Plea for Physical Training of Youthful Criminals," in National Prison Association, *Proceedings of the Annual Congress* (Boston, 1888), pp. 181–193.

[8]Richard L. Dugdale, "Hereditary Pauperism, as Illustrated in the 'Jukes' Family," in Annual Conference of Charities. *Proceedings* (Saratoga, 1877), pp. 81–99; *The Jukes: A Study in Crime, Pauperism, Disease, and Heredity* (New York: G. P. Putnam's Sons, 1877).

[9]Sarah B. Cooper, "The Kindergarten as Child-Saving Work," in National Conference of Charities and Correction, *Proceedings* (Madison, 1883), pp. 130–138.

[10]I. N. Kerlin, "The Moral Imbecile," in National Conference of Charities and Correction, *Proceedings* (Baltimore, 1890), pp. 244–250.

[11]Arthur E. Fink, *Causes of Crime: Biological Theories in the United States, 1800–1915* (New York: A. S. Barnes, 1962), p. 247.

[12]See, for example, Illinois, Board of State Commissioners of Public Charities, *Second Biennial Report* (Springfield: State Journal Steam Print, 1873), pp. 195–196.

superintendent of the Kentucky Industrial School of Reform told delegates to a national conference on corrections that heredity is "unjustifiably made a bugaboo to discourage efforts at rescue. We know that physical heredity tendencies can be neutralized and often nullified by proper counteracting precautions."[13] E.R.L. Gould, a sociologist at the University of Chicago, similarly criticized biological theories of crime for being unconvincing and sentimental. "Is it not better," he said, "to postulate freedom of choice than to preach the doctrine of the unfettered will, and so elevate criminality into a propitiary sacrifice?"[14]

Charles Cooley was one of the first sociologists to observe that criminal behavior depended as much upon social and economic circumstances as it did upon the inheritance of biological traits. "The criminal class," he said, "is largely the result of society's bad workmanship upon fairly good material." In support of this argument, he noted that there was a "large and fairly trustworthy body of evidence" to suggest that many "degenerates" could be converted into "useful citizens by rational treatment."[15]

URBAN DISENCHANTMENT

Another important influence on nineteenth-century criminology was a disenchantment with urban life—an attitude which is still prevalent in much "social problems" research. Immigrants were regarded as "unsocialized," and the city's impersonality compounded their isolation and degradation. "By some cruel alchemy," wrote Julia Lathrop, "we take the sturdiest of European peasantry and at once destroy in a large measure its power to rear to decent livelihood the first generation of offspring upon our soil."[16] The city symbolically embodied all the worst features of industrial life. A member of the Massachusetts Board of Charities observed:

Children acquire a perverted taste for city life and crowded streets; but if introduced when young to country life, care of animals and plants, and rural pleasures, they are likely . . . to be healthier in mind and body for such associations.[17]

Programs which promoted rural and primary group concepts were encouraged because slum life was regarded as unregulated, vicious, and lacking social rules. Its inhabitants were depicted as abnormal and maladjusted, living their lives in chaos and conflict.[18] It was consequently the task of social reformers to make city life more wholesome, honest, and free from depravity. Beverley Warner told the National Prison Association in 1898 that philanthropic organizations all over the country were making efforts to get the children out of the slums, even if only once a week, into the radiance of better lives. . . . It is only by

---

[13]Peter Caldwell, "The Duty of the State to Delinquent Children," National Conference of Charities and Correction, *Proceedings* (New Haven, 1895), pp. 134–143.

[14]E. R. L. Gould. "The Statistical Study of Hereditary Criminality," National Conference of Charities and Correction, *Proceedings* (New Haven, 1895), pp. 134–143.

[15]Charles H. Cooley, " 'Nature v. Nurture' in the Making of Social Careers," National Conference of Charities and Correction, *Proceedings* (Grand Rapids, Michigan, 1896), pp. 399–405.

[16]Julia Lathrop, "The Development of the Probation System in a Large City," 13 *Charities* (January 1905), p. 348.

[17]Clara T. Leonard, "Family Homes for Pauper and Dependent Children," Annual Conference of Charities, *Proceedings* (Chicago, 1879), p. 174.

[18]William Foote Whyte, "Social Disorganization in the Slums," 8 *American Sociological Review* (1943), pp. 34–39.

leading the child out of sin and debauch-ery, in which it has lived, into the circle of life that is a repudiation of things that it sees in its daily life, that it can be influenced.[19]

Although there was a wide difference of opinion among experts as to the precipi-tating causes of crime, it was generally agreed that criminals were abnormally conditioned by a multitude of biological and environmental forces, some of which were permanent and irreversible. Biologi-cal theories of crime were modified to in-corporate a developmental view of human behavior. If, as it was believed, criminals are conditioned by biological heritage and brutish living conditions, then prophylac-tic measures must be taken early in life. Criminals of the future generations must be reached. "They are born to crime," wrote the penologist Enoch Wines in 1880, "brought up for it. They must be saved."[20]

MATERNAL JUSTICE

The 1880's and 1890's represented for many middle-class intellectuals and pro-fessionals a period of discovery of the "dim attics and damp cellars in poverty-stricken sections of populous towns" and of "innumerable haunts of misery throughout the land."[21] The city was sud-denly discovered to be a place of scarcity, disease, neglect, ignorance, and "danger-ous influences." Its slums were the "last re-sorts of the penniless and the criminal": here humanity reached its lowest level of degradation and despair.[22]

The discovery of problems posed by "delinquent" youth was greatly influenced by the role of feminist reformers in the child-saving movement. It was widely agreed that it was a woman's business to be involved in regulating the welfare of children, for women were considered the "natural caretakers" of wayward children. Women's claim to the public care of chil-dren had some historical justification dur-ing the nineteenth century, and their role in child-rearing was considered paramount. Women were regarded as better teachers than men and were also more influential in child-training at home. The fact that public education also came more under the direc-tion of women teachers in the schools in-creased the predominance of women in the raising of children.[23]

Child-saving was a predominantly feminist movement, and it was regarded even by antifeminists as female domain. The social circumstances behind this ap-preciation of maternalism were women's emancipation and the accompanying changes in the character of traditional fam-ily life. Educated middle-class women now had more leisure time but a limited choice of careers. Child-saving was a reputable task for women who were allowed to ex-tend their house-keeping functions into

[19]Beverley Warner, "Child-Saving," in National Prison Association, *Proceedings of the Annual Congress* (Indianapolis, 1893), pp. 377–378.

[20]Enoch C. Wines, *The State of Prisons and of Child-Saving Institutions in the Civilized World* (Cambridge, Mass.: Harvard University Press, 1880), p. 132.

[21]William P. Letchworth, "Children of the State," National Conference of Charities and Correction, *Proceedings* (St. Paul, Minn., 1886), p. 138. The idea that intellectuals *discovered* poverty as a result of their own alienation from the centers of power has been fully treated by Richard Hofstadter, *The Age of Reform* (New York: Vintage Books, 1955); and Christopher Lasch, *The New Radicalism in America, 1889–1963; The Intellectual as a Social Type* (New York: Alfred A. Knopf, 1965).

[22]R. W. Hill, "The Children of Shinbone Alley," Na-tional Conference of Charities and Correction, *Proc-eedings* (Omaha, 1887), p. 231.

[23]Robert Sunley, "Early Nineteenth Century Amer-ican Literature on Child-Rearing," in Margaret Mead and Martha Wolfenstein (eds.), *Childhood in Contempo-rary Cultures* (Chicago: University of Chicago Press, 1955), p. 152; see also Orville G. Brim, *Education for Child-Rearing* (New York: Free Press, 1965), pp. 321–349.

the community without denying antifeminist stereotypes of woman's nature and place. "It is an added irony," writes Christopher Lasch in his study of American intellectualism,

that the ideas about woman's nature to which some feminists still clung, in spite of their opposition to the enslavement of woman in the home, were these very clichés which had so long been used to keep her there. The assumption that women were morally purer than men, better capable of altruism and self-sacrifice, was the core of the myth of domesticity against which the feminists were in revolt. . . . [F]eminist and antifeminist assumptions seemed curiously to coincide.[24]

Child-saving may be understood as a crusade which served symbolic and status functions for native, middle-class Americans, particularly feminist groups. Middle-class women at the turn of the century experienced a complex and far-reaching status revolution. Their traditional functions were dramatically threatened by the weakening of domestic roles and the specialized rearrangement of family life.[25] One of the main forces behind the child-saving movement was a concern for the structure of family life and the proper socialization of young persons, since it was these concerns that had traditionally given purpose to a woman's life. Professional organizations—such as Settlement Houses, Women's Clubs, Bar Associations, and penal organizations—regarded child-saving as a problem of women's rights, whereas their opponents seized upon it as an opportunity to keep women in their proper place. Child-saving organizations had little or nothing to do with militant supporters of the suffragette movement. In fact, the new role of social worker was created by deference to antifeminist stereotypes of a "woman's place."

A WOMAN'S PLACE

Feminist involvement in child-saving was endorsed by a variety of penal and professional organizations. Their participation was usually justified as an extension of their housekeeping functions so that they did not view themselves, nor were they regarded by others, as competitors for jobs usually performed by men. Proponents of the "new penology" insisted that reformatories should resemble home life, for institutions without women were likely to do more harm than good to inmates. According to G. E. Howe, the reformatory system provided "the most ample opportunities for woman's transcendant influence."[26]

Female delegates to philanthropic and correctional conferences also realized that correctional work suggested the possibility of useful careers. Mrs. W. P. Lynde told the National Conference of Charities and Correction in 1879 that children's institutions offered the "truest and noblest scope for the public activities of women in the time which they can spare from their primary domestic duties."[27] Women were exhorted by other delegates to make their lives meaningful by participating in welfare programs, volunteering their time and services, and getting acquainted with less privileged groups. They were told to seek jobs in institutions where "the

---

[24]Lasch, *op. cit.*, pp. 53–54.

[25]Talcott Parsons and Robert F. Bales, *Family, Socialization and Interaction Process* (Glencoe, Ill.: Free Press, 1955), pp. 3–33.

[26]G. E. Howe, "The Family System," National Conference of Charities and Correction, *Proceedings* (Cleveland, 1880), pp. 212–213.

[27]W. P. Lynde, "Prevention in Some of Its Aspects," Annual Conference of Charities, *Proceedings* (Chicago, 1879), p. 167.

woman-element shall pervade . . . and soften its social atmosphere with motherly tenderness."[28]

Although the child-savers were responsible for some minor reforms in jails and reformatories, they were more particularly concerned with extending governmental control over a whole range of youthful activities that had previously been handled on an informal basis. The main aim of the child-savers was to impose sanctions on conduct unbecoming youth and to disqualify youth from enjoying adult privileges. As Bennett Berger has commented, "adolescents are not made by nature but by being excluded from responsible participation in adult affairs, by being rewarded for dependency, and penalized for precocity."[29]

The child-saving movement was not so much a break with the past as an affirmation of faith in traditional institutions. Parental authority, education at home, and the virtues of rural life were emphasized because they were in decline at this time. The child-saving movement was, in part, a crusade which, through emphasizing the dependence of the social order on the proper socialization of children, implicitly elevated the nuclear family and, more especially, the role of women as stalwarts of the family. The child-savers were prohibitionists, in a general sense, who believed that social progress depended on efficient law enforcement, strict supervision of children's leisure and recreation, and the regulation of illicit pleasures. What seemingly began as a movement to humanize the lives of adolescents soon developed into a program of moral absolutism through which youth was to be saved from movies, pornography, cigarettes, alcohol, and anything else which might possibly rob them of their innocence.

Although child-saving had important symbolic functions for preserving the social prestige of a declining elite, it also had considerable practical significance for legitimizing new career openings for women. The new role of social worker combined elements of an old and partly fictitious role—defenders of family life— and elements of a new role—social servant. Social work was thus both an affirmation of cherished American values and an instrumentality for women's emancipation.

JUVENILE COURT

The essential preoccupation of the child-saving movement was the recognition and control of youthful deviance. It brought attention to, and thus "invented," new categories of youthful misbehavior which had been hitherto unappreciated. The efforts of the childsavers were institutionally expressed in the juvenile court, which, despite recent legislative and constitutional reforms, is generally acknowledged as their most significant contribution to progressive penology.

The juvenile-court system was part of a general movement directed towards removing adolescents from the criminal-law process and creating special programs for delinquent, dependent, and neglected children. Regarded widely as "one of the greatest advances in child welfare that has ever occurred," the juvenile court was considered "an integral part of total welfare

[28]Clara T. Leonard, "Family Homes for Pauper and Dependent Children," in Annual Conference of Charities, *Proceedings*, 1879, *loc. cit.*, p. 175.

[29]Bennett Berger, Review of Frank Musgrove, *Youth and the Social Order, 32 American Sociological Review*, 1927, p. 1021.

[30]Charles L. Chute, "The Juvenile Court in Retrospect," 13 *Federal Probation* (September 1949), p. 7; Harrison A. Dobbs, "In Defense of Juvenile Courts," 13 *Federal Probation* (September 1949), p. 29.

planning."[30] Charles Chute, an enthusiastic supporter of the child-saving movement, claimed:

No single event has contributed more to the welfare of children and their families. It revolutionized the treatment of delinquent and neglected children and led to the passage of similar laws throughout the world.[31]

The juvenile court was a special tribunal created by statute to determine the legal status of children and adolescents. Underlying the juvenile-court movement was the concept of *parens patriac* by which the courts were authorized to handle with wide discretion the problems of "its least fortunate junior citizens."[32] The administration of juvenile justice differed in many important respects from the criminal-court processes. A child was not accused of a crime but offered assistance and guidance; intervention in his life was not supposed to carry the stigma of criminal guilt. Judicial records were not generally available to the press or public, and juvenile-court hearings were conducted in relative privacy. Juvenile-court procedures were typically informal and inquisitorial. Specific criminal safeguards of due process were not applicable because juvenile proceedings were defined by statute as civil in character.[33]

The original statues enabled the courts to investigate a wide variety of youthful needs and misbehavior. As Joel Handler has observed, "the critical philosophical position of the reform movement was that no formal, legal distinctions should be made between the delinquent and the dependent or neglected."[34] Statutory definitions of "delinquency" encompassed (1) acts that would be criminal if committed by adults; (2) acts that violated county, town, or municipal ordinances; and (3) violations of vaguely defined catch-alis—such as "vicious or immoral behavior," "incorrigibility," and "truancy" —which "seem to express the notion that the adolescent, if allowed to continue, will engage in more serious conduct."[35]

The juvenile-court movement went far beyond a concern for special treatment of adolescent offenders. It brought within the ambit of governmental control a set of youthful activities that had been previously ignored or dealt with on an informal basis. It was not by accident that the behavior selected for penalizing by the child-savers—sexual license, drinking, roaming the streets, begging, frequenting dance halls and movies, fighting, and being seen in public late at night—was most directly relevant to the children of lower-class migrant and immigrant families.

The juvenile court was not perceived by its supporters as a revolutionary experiment, but rather as a culmination of traditionally valued practices.[36] The child-saving movement was "antilegal," in the

---

[31]Charles L. Chute, "Fifty Years of the Juvenile Court," *1949 National Probation and Parole Association Yearbook* (1949), p. 1.

[32]Gustav L. Schramm. "The Juvenile Court Idea," 13 *Federal Probation* (September 1949), p. 21.

[33]Monrad G. Paulsen, "Fairness to the Juvenile Offender," 41 *Minnesota Law Review*, 1957, pp. 547–567. Note: "Rights and Rehabilitation in the Juvenile Courts," 67 *Columbia Law Review*, 1967, pp. 281–341.

[34]Joel F. Handler, "The Juvenile Court and The Adversary System: Problems of Function and Form," *1965 Wisconsin Law Review*, 1965, p. 9.

[35]Joel F. Handler and Margaret K. Rosenheim, "Privacy and Welfare: Public Assistance and Juvenile Justice," 31 *Law and Contemporary Problems*, 1966, pp. 377–412.

[36]A reform movement, according to Herbert Blumer, is differentiated from a revolution by its inherent respectability and acceptance of an existing social order. "The primary function of the reform movement is probably not so much the bringing about of social change, as it is to reaffirm the ideal values in a given society."—Herbert Blumer, "Collective Behavior," in Alfred McClung Lee (ed.), *Principles of Sociology* (New York: Barnes and Noble, 1963), pp. 212–213.

sense that it derogated civil rights and procedural formalities, while relying heavily
on extra-legal techniques. The judges of
the new court were empowered to investigate the character and social life of predelinquent as well as delinquent children;
they examined motivation rather than
intent, seeking to identify the moral reputation of problematic children. The requirements of preventive penology and
child-saving further justified the court's intervention in cases where no offense had
actually been committed, but where, for
example, a child was posing problems for
some person in authority such as a parent
or teacher or social worker.

THE PERSONAL TOUCH

Judges were expected to show the same
professional competence as doctors and
therapists. The sociologist Charles Henderson wrote:

> A careful study of individuals is an essential
> element in wise procedure. The study must
> include the physical, mental and moral pe-
> culiarities and defects of the children who
> come under the notice of the courts. Indeed
> we are likely to follow the lead of those cities
> which provide for a careful examination of
> all school children whose physical or psychi-
> cal condition is in any way or degree abnor-
> mal, in order to prevent disease, correct
> deformity and vice, and select the proper
> course of study and discipline demanded by
> the individual need.[37]

Juvenile court judges had to be carefully selected for their skills as expert diag-
nosticians and for their appreciation of the
"helping" professions. Miriam Van Waters,

for example, regarded the juvenile court as
a "laboratory of human behavior" and its
judges as "experts with scientific training
and specialists in the art of human relations." It was the judge's task to "get the
whole truth about a child" in the same way
that a "physician searches for every detail
that bears on the condition of a patient."[38]

The child-savers' interest in preventive strategies and treatment programs
was based on the premise that delinquents possess innate or acquired characteristics which predispose them to crime
and distinguish them from law-abiding
youths. Delinquents were regarded as constrained by a variety of biological and environmental forces, so that their proper
treatment involved discovery of the "cause
of the aberration" and application of "the
appropriate corrective or antidote.[39] "What
the trouble is with the offender," noted
William Healy, "making him what he is,
socially undesirable, can only be known by
getting at his mental life, as it is an affair of
reactive mechanisms."[40]

The use of terms like "unsocialized,"
"maladjusted," and "pathological" to describe the behavior of delinquents implied
that "socialized" and "adjusted" children
conform to middle-class morality and participate in respectable institutions.[41] The

---

[37]Charles R. Henderson, "Theory and Practice of
Juvenile Courts," National Conference of Charities
and Correction, *Proceedings* (Portland, 1904), pp.
358–359.

[38]Miriam Van Waters, "The Socialization of Juvenile Court Procedure," 12 *Journal of Criminal Law and
Criminology*, 1922, pp. 61, 69.

[39]Illinois, Board of State Commissioners of Public
Charities, *First Biennial Report* (Springfield: Illinois
Journal Printing Office, 1871), p. 180.

[40]William Healy, "The Psychology of the Situation:
A Fundamental for Understanding and Treatment of
Delinquency and Crime," in Jane Addams (ed.), *The
Child, The Clinic and The Court* (New York: New Re-
public Inc., 1925), p. 40.

[41]C. Wright Mills, "The Professional Ideology of
Social Pathologists," in Bernard Rosenberg, Israel
Gerver, and F. William Howton (eds.), *Mass Society in
Crisis* (New York: The Macmillan Company, 1964), pp.
92–111.

failure empirically to demonstrate psychological differences between delinquents and nondelinquents did not discourage the child-savers from believing that rural and middle-class values constitute "normality." The unique character of the child-saving movement was its concern for predelinquent offenders—"children who occupy the debatable ground between criminality and innocence"—and its claim that it could transform potential criminals into respectable citizens by training them in "habits of industry, self-control and obedience to law."[42] This policy justified the diminishing of traditional procedures in juvenile court. If children were to be rescued, it was important that the rescuers be free to provide their services without legal hindrance. Delinquents had to be saved, transformed, and reconstituted. "There is no essential difference," said Frederick Wines, "between a criminal and any other sinner. The means and methods of restoration are the same for both."[43]

THE REFORMATORY SYSTEM

It was through the reformatory system that the child-savers hoped to demonstrate that delinquents were capable of being converted into law-abiding citizens. The reformatory was initially developed in the United States during the middle of the nineteenth century as a special form of prison discipline for adolescents and young adults. Its underlying principles were formulated in Britain by Matthew Davenport Hill, Alexander Maconochie,

Walter Crofton, and Mary Carpenter. If the United States did not have any great penal theorists, it at least had energetic penal administrators who were prepared to experiment with new programs. The most notable advocates of the reformatory plan in the United States were Enoch Wines, Secretary of the New York Prison Association; Theodore Dwight, the first Dean of Columbia Law School; Zebulon Brockway, Superintendent of Elmira Reformatory in New York: and Frank Sanborn, Secretary of the Massachusetts State Board of Charities.

The reformatory was distinguished from the traditional penitentiary by its policy of indeterminate sentencing, the "mark" system, and "organized persuasion" rather than "coercive restraint." Its administrators assumed that abnormal and troublesome individuals could become useful and productive citizens. Wines and Dwight, in a report to the New York legislature in 1867, proposed that the ultimate aim of penal policy was reformation of the criminal, which could only be achieved

by placing the prisoner's fate, as far as possible, in his own hand, by enabling him, through industry and good conduct to raise himself, step by step, to a position of less restraint; while idleness and bad conduct, on the other hand, keep him in a state of coercion and restraint.[44]

But, as Brockway observed at the first meeting of the National Prison Congress in 1870, the "new penology" was tough-minded and devoid of "sickly sentimentalism. . . . Criminals shall either be cured, or

---

[42]Illinois, Board of State Commissioners of Public Charities, *Sixth Biennial Report* (Springfield: H. W. Rokker, 1880), p. 104.

[43]Frederick H. Wines, "Reformation as an End in Prison Discipline," National Conference of Charities and Correction, *Proceedings* (Buffalo, 1888), p. 198.

[44]Max Grünhut, *Penal Reform* (Oxford, England: Clarendon Press, 1948), p. 90.

kept under such continued restraint as gives guarantee of safety from further depredations."[45]

Reformatories, unlike penitentiaries and jails, theoretically repudiated punishments based on intimidation and repression. They took into account the fact that delinquents were "either physically or mentally below the average." The reformatory system was based on the assumption that proper training can counteract the impositions of poor family life, a corrupt environment, and poverty, while at the same time toughening and preparing delinquents for the struggle ahead. "The principle at the root of the educational method of dealing with juvenile crime," wrote William Douglas Morrison, "is an absolutely sound one. It is a principle which recognizes the fact that the juvenile delinquent is in the main, a product of adverse individual and social conditions.[46]

The reformatory movement spread rapidly through the United States, and European visitors crossed the Atlantic to inspect and admire the achievements of their pragmatic colleagues. Mary Carpenter, who visited the United States in 1873, was generally satisfied with the "generous and lavish expenditures freely incurred to promote the welfare of the inmates, and with the love of religion." Most correctional problems with regard to juvenile delinquents, she advised, could be remedied if reformatories were built like farm schools or "true homes." At the Massachusetts Reform School, in Westborough, she found an "entire want of family spirit," and, in New York, she complained that there was no "natural life" in the reformatory. "All the arrangements are artificial," she said; "instead of the cultivation of the land, which would prepare the youth to seek a sphere far from the dangers of large cities, the boys and young men were being taught trades which will confine them to the great centers of an over-crowded population." She found similar conditions in Philadelphia where "hundreds of youth were there congregated under lock and key," but praised the Connecticut Reform School for its "admirable system of agricultural training."[47] If she had visited the Illinois State Reformatory at Pontiac, she would have found a seriously overcrowded "minor penitentiary" where the inmates were forced to work ten hours a day manufacturing shoes, brushes, and chairs.

TO COTTAGE AND COUNTRY

Granted the assumption that "nurture" could usually overcome most of nature's defects, reformatory-administrators set about the task of establishing programs consistent with the aim of retraining delinquents for law-abiding careers. It was noted at the Fifth International Prison Congress, held in Paris in 1895, that reformatories were capable of obliterating hereditary and environmental taints. In a new and special section devoted to delinquency, the Congress proposed that children under twelve years

> should always be sent to institutions of preservation and unworthy parents must be deprived of the right to rear children. . . . The preponderant place in rational physical

---

[45]This speech is reprinted in Zebulon Reed Brockway, *Fifty Years of Prison Service* (New York: Charities Publication Committee, 1912), pp. 389–408.

[46]William Douglas Morrison, *Juvenile Offenders* (New York: D. Appleton, 1897), pp. 274–275.

[47]Mary Carpenter, "Suggestions on Reformatory Schools and Prison Discipline, Founded on Observations Made During a Visit to the United States," National Prison Reform Congress, *Proceedings* (St. Louis, 1874), pp. 157–173.

training should be given to manual labor, and particularly to agricultural labor in the open air, for both sexes.[48]

The heritage of biological imagery and Social Darwinism had a lasting influence on American criminology, and penal reformers continued to regard delinquency as a problem of individual adjustment to the demands of industrial and urban life. Delinquents had to be removed from contaminating situations, segregated from their "miserable surroundings," instructed, and "put as far as possible on a footing of equality with the rest of the population."[49]

The trend from congregate housing in the city to group living in the country represented a significant change in the organization of penal institutions for young offenders. The family or cottage plan differed in several important respects from the congregate style of traditional prisons and jails. According to William Letchworth, in an address delivered before the National Conference of Charities and Correction in 1886:

A fault in some of our reform schools is their great size. In the congregating of large numbers, individuality is lost. . . . These excessive aggregations are overcome to a great extent in the cottage plan. . . . The internal system of the reformatory school should be as nearly as practicable as that of the family, with its refining and elevating influences; while the awakening of the conscience and the inculcation of religious principles should be primary aims.[50]

The new penology emphasized the corruptness and artificiality of the city; from progressive education, it inherited a concern for naturalism, purity, and innocence. It is not surprising, therefore, that the cottage plan also entailed a movement to a rural location. The aim of penal reformers was not merely to use the countryside for teaching agricultural skills. The confrontation between corrupt delinquents and unspoiled nature was intended to have a spiritual and regenerative effect. The romantic attachment to rural values was quite divorced from social and agricultural realities. It was based on a sentimental and nostalgic repudiation of city life. Advocates of the reformatory system generally ignored the economic attractiveness of city work and the redundancy of farming skills. As one economist cautioned reformers in 1902:

Whatever may be said about the advantages of farm life for the youth of our land, and however much it may be regretted that young men and women are leaving the farm and flocking to the cities, there can be no doubt that the movement city-ward will continue. . . . There is great danger that many who had left the home [that is, reformatory], unable to find employment in agricultural callings, would drift back to the city and not finding there an opportunity to make use of the technical training secured in the institution, would become discouraged and resume their old criminal associations and occupations.[51]

The "new" reformatory suffered, like all its predecessors, from overcrowding,

---

[48]Negley K. Teeters, *Deliberations of the International Penal and Penitentiary Congresses, 1872–1935* (Philadelphia: Temple University Book Store, 1949), pp. 97–102.

[49]Morrison, *op. cit.*, pp. 60, 276.

[50]William P. Letchworth, "Children of the State," National Conference of Charities and Correction, *Proceedings* (St. Paul, Minnesota, 1886), pp. 151, 156.

[51]M. B. Hammond's comments at the Illinois Conference of Charities (1901), reported in Illinois, Board of State Commissioners of Public Charities, *Seventeenth Biennial Report* (Springfield: Phillips Brothers, 1902), pp. 232–233.

mismanagement, "boodleism," under-staffing, and inadequate facilities. Its distinctive features were the indeterminate sentence, the movement to cottage and country, and agricultural training. Although there was a decline in the use of brutal punishments, inmates were subjected to severe personal and physical controls: military exercises, "training of the will," and long hours of tedious labor constituted the main program of reform.

SUMMARY AND CONCLUSIONS

The child-saving movement was responsible for reforms in the ideological and institutional control of "delinquent" youth. The concept of the born delinquent was modified with the rise of a professional class of penal administrators and social servants who promoted a developmental view of human behavior and regarded most delinquent youth as salvageable. The child-savers helped to create special judicial and correctional institutions for the processing and management of "troublesome" youth.

There has been a shift during the last fifty years or so in official policies concerning delinquency. The emphasis has shifted from one emphasizing the criminal nature of delinquency to the "new humanism" which speaks of disease, illness, contagion, and the like. It is essentially a shift from a legal to a medical emphasis. The emergence of a medical emphasis is of considerable significance, since it is a powerful rationale for organizing social action in the most diverse behavioral aspects of our society. For example, the child-savers were not concerned merely with "humanizing" conditions under which children were treated by the criminal law. It was rather their aim to extend the scope of governmental control over a wide variety of personal misdeeds and to regulate potentially disruptive persons.[52] The child-savers' reforms were politically aimed at lower-class behavior and were instrumental in intimidating and controlling the poor.

The child-savers made a fact out of the norm of adolescent dependence. "Every child is dependent," wrote the Illinois Board of Charities in 1899, "even the children of the wealthy. To receive his support at the hands of another does not strike him as unnatural, but quite the reverse."[53] The juvenile court reached into the private lives of youth and disguised basically punitive policies in the rhetoric of "rehabilitation."[54] The child-savers were prohibitionists, in a general sense, who believed that adolescents needed protection from even their own inclinations.

The basic conservatism of the child-saving movement is apparent in the reformatory system which proved to be as tough-minded as traditional forms of punishment. Reformatory programs were unilateral, coercive, and an invasion of human dignity. What most appealed to correctional workers were the paternalistic assumptions of the "new penology," its belief in social progress through individual reform, and its nostalgic preoccupation with the "naturalness" and intimacy of a preindustrial way of life.

The child-saving movement was heavily influenced by middle-class women who extended their housewifely roles into public service. Their contribution may also be seen as a "symbolic crusade" in defense

---

[52]This thesis is supported by a European study of family life, Phillipe Aries, *Centuries of Childhood* (New York: Vintage Books, 1965).

[53]Illinois, Board of State Commissioners of Public Charities, *Fifteenth Biennial Report* (Springfield: Phillips Brothers, 1899), pp. 62–72.

[54]Francis A. Allen, *The Borderland of Criminal Justice* (Chicago: University of Chicago Press, 1964), *passim*.

of the nuclear family and their positions within it. They regarded themselves as moral custodians and supported programs and institutions dedicated to eliminating youthful immorality. Social service was an instrumentality for female emancipation, and it is not too unreasonable to suggest that women advanced their own fortune at the expense of the dependency of youth.

This analysis of the child-saving movement suggests the importance of (1) understanding the relationship between correctional reforms and related changes in the administration of criminal justice, (2) accounting for the motives and purposes of those enterprising groups who generate such reforms, (3) investigating the methods by which communities establish the formal machinery for regulating crime, and (4) distinguishing between idealized goals and enforced conditions in the implementation of correctional reforms.

IMPLICATIONS FOR CORRECTIONS AND RESEARCH

The child-saving movement illustrates a number of important problems with the quality and purposes of correctional research and knowledge. The following discussion will draw largely upon the child-saving movement in order to examine its relevance for contemporary issues.

POSITIVISM AND PROGRESSIVISM

It is widely implied in the literature that the juvenile court and parallel reforms in penology represented a progressive effort by concerned reformers to alleviate the miseries of urban life and to solve social problems by rational, enlightened, and scientific methods. With few exceptions, studies of delinquency have been parochial and inadequately descriptive, and

they show little appreciation of underlying political and cultural conditions. Historical studies, particularly of the juvenile court, are, for the most part, self-confirming and support an evolutionary view of human progress.[55]

The positivist heritage in the study of social problems has directed attention to (1) the primacy of the criminal actor rather than the criminal law as the major point of departure in the construction of etiological theory, (2) a rigidly deterministic view of human behavior, and (3) only the abnormal features of deviant behavior.[56] The "rehabilitative ideal" has so dominated American criminology that there have been only sporadic efforts to undertake sociolegal research related to governmental invasion of personal liberties. But, as Francis Allen has suggested:

Even if one's interests lie primarily in the problems of treatment of offenders, it should be recognized that the existence of the criminal presupposes a crime and that the problems of treatment are derivative in the sense that they depend upon the determination by law-giving agencies that certain sorts of behavior are crimes:[57]

The conservatism and "diluted liberalism"[58] of much research on delinquency

---

[55]See, for example, Herbert H. Lou, *Juvenile Courts in the United States* (Chapel Hill: University of North Carolina, 1927); Negley K. Teeters and John Otto Reinemann, *The Challenge of Delinquency* (New York: Prentice-Hall, 1950); Katherine L. Boole, "The Juvenile Court: Its Origin, History, and Procedure" (Unpublished doctoral dissertation, University of California, Berkeley, 1928). One notable exception is Paul W. Tappan, *Delinquent Girls in Court* (New York: Columbia University Press, 1947).

[56]David Matza, *Delinquency and Drift* (New York: John Wiley, 1964).

[57]Allen, *op. cit.*, p. 125.

[58]This phrase and its perspective are taken from C. Wright Mills (ed.), *Images of Man* (New York: George Braziller, 1960), p. 5.

results from the fact that researchers are generally prepared to accept prevailing definitions of crime, to work within the premises of the criminal law, and to concur at least implicitly with those who make laws as to the nature and distribution of a "criminal" population. Thus, most theories of delinquency are based on studies of convicted or imprisoned delinquents. As John Seeley has observed in another context, professional caution requires us "to *take* our problems rather than *make* our problems, to accept as constitutive of our 'intake' what is held to be 'deviant' in a way that concerns enough people in that society enough to give us primary protection."[59] Money, encouragement, co-operation from established institutions, and a market for publications are more easily acquired for studies of the socialization or treatment of delinquents than for studies of how laws, law-makers, and law-enforcers contribute to the "registration" of delinquency.

Law and its implementation have been largely dismissed as irrelevant topics for inquiry into the "causes" of delinquency. According to Herbert Packer, it is typical that the National Crime Commission ignored the fundamental question of: "What is the criminal sanction good for?"[60] Further research is needed to understand the dynamics of the legislative and popular drive to "criminalize."[61] Delinquency legislation for example, as has been noted earlier, was not aimed merely at reducing crime or liberating youth. The reform movement also served important symbolic and instrumental interests for groups who made hobbies and careers out of saving children.

POLICY RESEARCH

Correctional research in this country has been dominated by persons who are intimately concerned with crime and its control. The scholar-technician tradition in corrections, especially with regard to delinquency, has resulted in the proliferation of "agency-determined" research whereby scholarship is catered to institutional interests.[62] Much of what passes under the label of "research" takes the form of "methods engineering," produced in the interest of responsible officials and management.[63] It is only rarely, as in Erving Goffman's study of "total institutions," that sympathetic consideration is given to the perceptions and concerns of subordinates in the correctional hierarchy.[64]

There are many historical and practical reasons why corrections has been such a narrow and specialized field of academic interest. First, corrections has been intellectually influenced by the problematic perspective of scholar-technicians, which limits the scope of "research" to local, policy issues. In the last century especially, penology was the exclusive domain of philanthropists, muckrakers, reformers, and missionaries. Secondly, the rise of the "multiversity" and of federal-grant research has given further respectability to

[59]John R. Seeley, "The Making and Taking of Problems: Toward an Ethical Stance." 14 *Social Problems*, 1967, pp. 384–385.

[60]Herbert L. Packer, "A Patchy Look at Crime," *New York Review of Books*, Vol. 17, October 12, 1967.

[61]Sanford H. Kadish, "The Crisis of Over-criminalization," THE ANNALS, Vol. 374, November 1967), pp. 157–170.

[62]Herbert Blumer, "Threats from Agency-determined Researching: The Case of Camelot," in Irvin Louis Horowitz (ed.), *The Rise and Fall of Project Camelot* (Cambridge, Mass.; M.I.T. Press, 1967), pp. 153–174.

[63]See, for example, Daniel Glaser, *The Effectiveness of a Prison and Parole System* (New York: Bobbs-Merrill, 1964).

[64]Erving Goffman, *Asylums* (New York: Anchor Books, 1961).

applied research in corrections, to the extent that social science and public policy are inextricably linked.[65] Nevertheless, such research is minimal when compared, for example, with that done under the auspices of the Defense Department.[66] It is quite true, as the National Crime Commission reports, that research in corrections has been unsystematic, sporadic, and guided primarily by "intuitive opportunism."[67] Thirdly, it should be remembered that correctional institutions are politically sensitive communities which resist instrusions from academic outsiders unless the proposed research is likely to serve their best interests.[68] Research which undermines policy is generally viewed as insensitive and subversive, aside from the fact that it helps to justify and harden administrators' suspicions of "intellectuals." The lack of critical research is, no doubt, also due to "the reluctance of scholars to address the specific problems faced by those charged with the perplexing task of controlling and rehabilitating offenders."[69]

---

[65]Clark Kerr, *The Uses of the University* (New York: Anchor Books, 1961).

[66]"Approximately 15 per cent of the Defense Department's annual budget is allocated for research, compared with one per cent of the total federal expenditure for crime control."—U.S., President's Commission on Law Enforcement and Administration of Justice (National Crime Commission), *The Challenge of Crime in a Free Society* (the General Report) (Washington, D.C.: U.S. Government Printing Office, 1967), p. 273.

[67]U.S., President's Commission on Law Enforcement and Administration of Justice (National Crime Commission), *Task Force Report: Corrections* (Washington, D.C.: U.S. Government Printing Office, 1967), p. 13.

[68]Controversial studies of official institutions run the risk of hampering further academic investigations, as was apparently the case with Jerome Skolnick's study of a California police department, *Justice without Trial* (New York: John Wiley & Sons, 1966).

[69]*The Challenge of Crime in a Free Society, op. cit.*, p. 183.

POLITICS AND CORRECTIONS

Correctional institutions have been generally regarded as distinct, insulated social organizations. Their relationship to the wider society is viewed in a bureaucratic, civil-service context, and their population is defined in welfare terms. Prisons and their constituency are stripped of political implications, seemingly existing in an apolitical vacuum. Corrections as an academic specialization has focused on the prison community to the neglect of classical interest in the relationship between political decision-making and social policies. As Hans Mattick has observed:

> There is very little appreciation . . . that this "contest between good and evil," and the whole "drama of crime," is taking place within the larger arena of our political system and this, in part, helps to determine public opinion about the nature of crime, criminals and how they are dealt with.[70]

As the gap between social deviance and political marginality narrows, it becomes increasingly necessary to examine how penal administrators are recruited, how "new" programs are selected and implemented, and how local and national legislatures determine correctional budgets. The crisis caused by white racism in this country also requires us to appreciate in what sense prisons and jails may be used as instrumentalities of political control in the "pacification" of black Americans. Similarly, it furthers our understanding of "delinquency" if we appreciate the motives and political interests of those reformers and professionals who perceive youth as threatening and troublesome.

---

[70]Hans W. Mattick (ed.), "The Future of Imprisonment in a Free Society," 2 *Key Issues*, 1965, p. 5.

FAITH IN REFORM

The child-saving movement further illustrates that corrections may be understood historically as a succession of reforms. Academics have demonstrated a remarkably persistent optimism about reform, and operate on the premise that they can have a humanitarian influence on correctional administration. As Irving Louis Horowitz has observed, to the extent that social scientists become involved with policymaking agencies, they are committed to an elitist ideology:

> They come to accept as basic the idea that men who really change things are at the top. Thus, the closer to the top one can get direct access, the more likely will intended changes be brought about.[71]

There is little evidence to support this faith in the ultimate wisdom of policymakers in corrections. The reformatory was not so much an improvement on the prison as a means of extending control over a new constituency: probation and parole became instruments of supervivision rather than treatment: halfway houses have become a means of extending prisons into communities rather than democratically administered sanctuaries; group therapy in prisons has justified invasion of privacy and coercive treatment on the dubious grounds that prisoners are psychologically unfit; community-based narcotics programs, such as the nalline clinic, disguise medical authoritarianism in the guise of rehabilitation. Nevertheless, the optimism continues, and this is nowhere more apparent than in the National Crime Commission's

Task Force Report on Corrections, which reveals that, in Robert Martinson's words, correctional policy consists of "a redoubling of efforts in the face of persistent failure."[72]

Finally, we have neglected to study and appreciate those who work in corrections. Like the police and, to an increasing extent, teachers and social workers, correctional staffs are constrained by the ethic of bureaucratic responsibility. They are society's "dirty-workers," technicians working on people. As Lee Rainwater has observed:

> The dirty-workers are increasingly caught between the silent middle class, which wants them to do the dirty work and keep quiet about it, and the objects of that dirty work, who refuse to continue to take it lying down. . . . These civilian colonial armies find their right to respect from their charges challenged at every turn, and often they must carry out their daily duties with fear for their physical safety.[73]

Correctional workers are required to accommodate current definitions of criminality and to manage victims of political expediency and popular fashion—drug users, drunks, homosexuals, vagrants, delinquents, and "looters." They have minimal influence on law-makers and rarely more than ideological rapport with law enforcers. They have no clear mandate as to the purpose of corrections, other than to reduce recidivism and reform criminals. They have to live with the proven failure of

---

[71]Horowitz (ed.), *loc. cit.*, p. 353.

[72]Robert Martinson. "The Age of Treatment: Some Implications of the Custody-Treatment Dimension," 2 *Issues in Criminology* (Fall 1966), p. 291.

[73]Lee Rainwater, "The Revolt of the Dirty-Workers," 5 *Trans-action* (November 1967), p. 2.

this enterprise and to justify their role as pacifiers, guards, warehouse-keepers, and restrainers.[74]

___

[74]Henry McKay's "Report on the Criminal Careers of Male Delinquents in Chicago" concludes that "the behavior of significant numbers of boys who become involved in illegal activity is not redirected toward conventional activity by the institutions created for that purpose."—U.S., President's Commission on Law Enforcement and Administration of Justice (National Crime Commission), *Task Force Report: Juvenile Delinquency and Youth Crime* (Washington, D.C.: U.S. Government Printing Office, 1967), p. 113.

They are linked to a professional system that relegates them to the lowest status in the political hierarchy but uses them as a pawn in electoral battles. They are doomed to annual investigations, blue-ribbon commissions, ephemeral research studies, and endless volumes of propaganda and muckraking. They live with the inevitability of professional mediocrity, poor salaries, uncomfortable living conditions, ungrateful "clients," and tenuous links with established institutions. It is understandable that they protect their fragile domain from intrusive research which is not supportive of their policies.

Chapter 3

Methods

INTRODUCTION

In this seminal work on the validity of the self-report method, Hindelang, Hirschi, and Weis detail how they conducted their research. The authors varied both the method and the administration of questionnaires administered to juveniles regarding their involvement in delinquency. In doing, they are able to discern differences in responses that may or may not be attributed to different methods of data collection. Since the advent of self-report data in the early fifties, respondents' truthfulness has long been questioned, especially within delinquent and criminal populations. Hindelang, Hirschi, and Weis discuss the methodological strengths and weaknesses of self-report data and conclude on the veracity of self-report responses.

Hannon and Dufour's content analysis of articles from four major criminological journals investigates the potential androcentric bias of researchers in criminology. They find that although research on women has increased since the 1970s it is still a "man's world" in criminology research. This is a criticism long supported by feminist researchers in criminology and delinquency. Although boys and men commit the overwhelming majority of serious offenses, when compared to women's rate of offending, crime by women and girls has rarely been the focus of research.

Whitbeck, Hoyt, and Ackley's piece addresses an important facet of self-report research: the validity of children's report of home conditions. Their sample of runaway adolescents and their caretakers report different levels of parental warmth, support, abuse, and juvenile behavior. Although the youths and caretakers report different levels of these behaviors and attitudes, their reports are in the same direction. Because of this validation, Whitbeck et al. suggest that juveniles' self-reports of their family background, even among seriously troubled youths, are valid and accurately reflect the juveniles' "troubled" family background.

Designing The Research

Hindelang, Michael J., Hirschi, Travis and Joseph G. Weis

The data upon which this study is based were collected in Seattle. Washington, during the 1978–1979 academic year. All interviews and questionnaires were administered by project staff in a field office adjacent to downtown Seattle. This section describes procedures for obtaining respondents, transporting them to the field site, and assigning them to the various experimental conditions. It also describes these experimental conditions and the logic underlying them. Finally, it assesses the adequacy of the samples obtained for the purposes of the research.

THE RESEARCH SITE

The city of Seattle had a population of slightly greater than 500,000 in 1975, down about 10% from its 1960 population. Racially, Seattle's population is made up mostly of whites (85%), with blacks constituting an additional 9% of the population. Asians are the next largest minority population in Seattle (5%). Our study limits itself to a consideration of delinquency among black and white adolescents. In the

Michael J. Hindelang, Travis Hirschi, and Joseph G. Weis, Sage Library of Social Research, Vol. 123, pp. 27–41, copyright © 1981 by Sage Publications, Inc. Reprinted by permission of by Sage Publications, Inc.

public high school population of Seattle, blacks constituted 20% of the total black and white population enrolled, as of December 1, 1978. The percent black in the Seattle public school population was increasing dramatically at the end of the 1970s. reflecting a decline in the white school population from 47,000 in 1975–1976 to 30,000 in 1979–1980. This decline in the white population apparently resulted from movement to the suburbs rather than from more general migration from the area.

DESIGN OF THE RESEARCH

The comparisons in this research were intended to allow examination of the effects of anonymity and method of administration (questionnaire or interview) on the amount of delinquency reported by respondents and on the reliability and validity of such reports. The methods conditions were as follows:

Condition A.
   (1) Anonymous questionnaire (AQ)
   (2) Deep probe of a subset of all positive delinquency responses to elicit information on
      (a) the nature of the event
      (b) the basis for the subject's frequency estimate

(3) Randomized response technique with 8 delinquency items

Condition B.
  (1) Anonymous interview (AI)
  (2) Repeat of subset of questionnaire items to assess reliability of 22 of the delinquency and 4 of the nondelinquency items
  (3) Randomized response technique with 8 delinquency items

Condition C.
  (1) Nonanonymous questionnaire (NQ)
  (2) Repeat of subset of questionnaire items to assess reliability of 22 of the delinquency and 4 of the nondelinquency items
  (3) Randomized response technique with 8 delinquency items

Condition D.
  (1) Nonanonymous interview (NI)
  (2) Reinterview using the Psychological Stress Evaluator obtrusively
  (3) Randomized response technique with 8 delinquency items.

In addition to the methods conditions specified above, respondent characteristics for study as part of the design were race, socioeconomic status (SES), and sex. All of these characteristics are associated with either self-reported or official delinquency and all have been the basis of dispute about the relative merits of these two measurement procedures. Given the centrality of the validity question, respondents were also stratified by official delinquency status, permitting a reverse record check. These various dimensions produced the design presented in Table 1.

To produce the numbers in the cells of this table, the population was first stratified by age, sex, race, SES of census tract (white males only), and official delinquency status. Sampling was inversely proportional to the size of the subcell

population such that the numbers of the cells would be equal, except that official nondelinquents were oversampled by 50% because they were expected to report less delinquency than their officially delinquent counterparts. Once these samples had been identified, subjects were randomly assigned to the four methods conditions. Stratification by age was intended to control a possibly important source of variation. The age range of subjects in the sample was designed to be limited to 15- and 16-year-olds but had to be expanded as the study progressed. The final effective age range among males was 15 to 18 with a mean of 16.5.

It was anticipated that at least some of the design variables could be collapsed if found unrelated to the delinquency measures being investigated. SES as a *design* variable was particularly problematic from the beginning (we were, a priori, limited to a census tract indicator) and was included because of its historical and theoretical importance.

Within each method condition, we attempted to approximate standard research practice. No effort was made to maximize differences beyond those ordinarily present in delinquency research. It is well-established that research results can be markedly affected by extreme conditions of administration. We were not interested in exploring these extremes. Rather, we were interested in assessing the effects of interviews as opposed to questionnaires and of having the subject sign his or her name rather than relying upon a numerical code for identification. In all conditions, subjects were assured that the information they supplied would be treated confidentially, that even if their names were initially provided, they would be removed in subsequent processing of the data.

In the anonymous conditions, the person picking up the respondent gave

TABLE 1: Design of the Seattle Study, with Cell Ns Indicated

	BLACK MALES				WHITE MALES								BLACK FEMALES		WHITE FEMALES			
	Method[a]				Lower Class Method[a]				Higher Class Method[a]				Lower Class Method[a]		Lower Class Method[a]		Higher Class Method[a]	
	A	B	C	D	A	B	C	D	A	B	C	D	A	D	A	D	A	D
No Police or Court Record	31	40	39	40	44	43	54	38	55	56	52	57	24	18	27	24	37	32
Police Record	27	26	22	22	30	24	28	31	32	28	28	28	22	24	29	21	22	20
Court Record	30	28	29	34	27	30	24	29	28	26	27	27	17	19	21	17	13	9

[a] A = Anonymous Questionnaire

  B = Anonymous Interview

  C = Nonanonymous Questionnaire

  D = Nonanonymous Interview

him or her a number used for room assignment and identification. In the anonymous interview, face-to-face contact between interviewer and interviewee was prevented by a screen. (Another member of the staff escorted the subject to the interview room, and the subject at no time saw the interviewer and, in fact, the subject's name was never used after the driver made contact with the respondent.)

The nonanonymous conditions were of course face to face and involved asking the subject to put his or her name on the questionnaire or to give it to the interviewer. Otherwise, no attempt was made to emphasize the different conditions under which the data were collected. In order to explore other important methodological questions, different procedures were attached to each of the four basic conditions. For example, under the nonanonymous questionnaire condition, a subset of questionnaire items was repeated to assess the test-retest reliability of delinquent and nondelinquent items. In addition, under this condition, the Warner randomized response technique (Warner, 1965; Greenberg et al., 1971) was applied to a subset of delinquency items some of which had been asked earlier. (This technique, designed to maximize assurances of anonymity, was in fact used in all conditions.)

Under the anonymous questionnaire conditions, a probe of a subset of positive responses to delinquency items was introduced in order to explore the nature of the event (Gold, 1966) and the basis of the subject's frequency estimate.

In the nonanonymous interview condition, subjects were reinterviewed on a subset of delinquency items and "neutral" items using the Psychological Stress Evaluator (PSE). Subjects were told that this device, like a lie detector, allowed assessment of the truth of their responses and were shown paper tape graphs illustrating "truthful" and "untruthful" responses. As indicated, our use of the PSE assumed either or both of the following: (1) that it could motivate the respondents to provide more accurate responses or (2) that it could be used subsequently as a "lie detector" to assess the validity of their responses. Because we had available independent data on the official police and court records of the respondents, we could also evaluate the validity of the PSE itself.

The anonymous interview condition is identical to the nonanonymous questionnaire condition with respect to the ancillary conditions (test/retest and randomized response), allowing examination of the behavior of the ancillary procedures under maximally different main conditions.

The interviewers, including both black and white males and females, were randomly assigned to conditions and respondents.

SAMPLING

The sampling procedure was designed to accomplish two aims: to maximize variance on delinquency and to represent the general adolescent population of Seattle. To accomplish this efficiently, three populations were sampled.

The first was a sample of students enrolled in Seattle public schools for the 1977–1978 academic year who met the age requirements of the design. Among the males, the parents of all students enrolled were contacted by the Seattle School District to inform them of the study and to request that if they did *not* want their son's name to appear on the list from which study participants would be randomly selected, to return and so indicate on a form provided. As a result, 18% of the parents so indicated. Of the students remaining, those with known records of police or court contact were excluded to produce an official nondelinquent population. The race of members of this population was provisionally determined by inspection of year-book pictures and school attended. Since the blacks in the nondelinquent population were, as expected, predominantly low SES, we decided not to stratify them further; the whites were sufficiently numerous that an SES distinction on the basis of median income of census tract of residence could be made.

Female nondelinquents, like male nondelinquents, were drawn from lists of students enrolled in the Seattle School District. The female population differed from the male population in two ways. The population list was for the 1978–1979 academic year, rather than 1977–1978. With the females, rather than starting with the complete population list, sampling began with a random sample of 1,000 females meeting the sampling criteria. This sample was reduced by about 14% due to parental refusal to release their child's name to the researchers and by discovery of a police or court record. Thus, 859 females remained on the "population" list from which the sample was drawn. Of these, 700 were white and 159 were black. As with white males, white females were further stratified by median income of census tract before samples were actually drawn or subjects assigned to conditions.

The middle stratum on delinquency was made up of those with a record of contact with the Seattle Police, but with no King County (Seattle) Juvenile Court record. As noted, persons with a police record were excluded from the official nondelinquent population. Criteria for inclusion in the police record population were the same with respect to age, race, and residence as in the high school population, and in addition the offense had to be a nondependency and nontraffic offense.

Males and females were selected using the same criteria.

The third source of study participants was the population of adolescents referred to the King County Division of Youth Services—the juvenile court serving Seattle. The population included those who met the selection criteria with respect to age, race, residence in the city of Seattle, offense (excluding dependency and traffic offenses), and who had not been disposed of by diversion to another social agency.

To recapitulate: Respondents from three separate Seattle populations were sampled—official nondelinquents, police record only delinquents, and court delinquents. These strata were "unduplicated" using the rule that the populations were to be mutually exclusive and subjects with any record of delinquency were to be assigned to the most delinquent stratum for which they qualified (i.e., a boy or girl with a record of both police and court contact would be assigned to the court stratum). Within these strata, subjects were further stratified by race, sex, and median income of census tract (whites only), to form the 18 subject pools required by the design (Table 1). From each of these 18 subject pools, subjects were selected randomly and were assigned at random to one of the four method conditions. (Because of limited funds and their lower rates of delinquency, only two of the method conditions were used for females.)

Before this last step could be undertaken, however, it was necessary to obtain *positive* consent from each participant and from his or her parents or guardian. This was accomplished by mail, follow-up mail, telephone calls, and follow-up telephone calls. The information necessary to contact potential participants was provided in the first instance by the School District, police files, or court files. We had expected much of this information to be out of date, and our expectations were fulfilled. Tracking down study participants turned out to be an enormous—and often unsuccessful—task. The information provided by the School District, police files, or court was often simply incorrect or out of date. Many of those in all strata who were selected to be contacted turned out to be quite mobile. And among those contacted, we had some difficulty getting the respondents or their parents to consent to participation even though we paid respondents $10 and gave them a choice of a currently popular record album for two hours of participation.

The participation rates in Table 2 indicate the percentages of those potential respondents who could not be located and the percent of those located who agreed to participate in the study. As would be expected, contact rates are higher for the

TABLE 2: Percent of Original Sample Not Located and Percent of those Located Agreeing to Participate in the Seattle Study

	Percent of original sample not located		Percent of those located agreeing to participate	
		MALES		
BLACK				
Court Delinquents	29.6	(287)	66.8	(202)
Police Delinquents	44.0	(273)	68.6	(153)
Nondelinquents	22.4	(326)	66.4	(253)
WHITE-HIGH SES				
Court Delinquents	19.3	(274)	57.9	(221)
Police Delinquents	14.7	(254)	78.5	(214)
Nondelinquents	9.7	(373)	70.9	(337)
WHITE-LOW SES				
Court Delinquents	29.0	(335)	57.1	(238)
Police Delinquents	21.5	(339)	78.2	(266)
Nondelinquents	13.2	(334)	65.5	(290)
		FEMALES		
BLACK				
Court Delinquents	48.5	(136)	55.7	(70)
Police Delinquents	45.0	(180)	83.8	(99)
Nondelinquents	17.3	(75)	77.4	(62)
WHITE-HIGH SES				
Court Delinquents	41.7	(96)	41.1	(56)
Police Delinquents	40.5	(163)	59.8	(97)
Nondelinquents	1.3	(151)	60.4	(149)
WHITE-LOW SES				
Court Delinquents	42.9	(140)	61.2	(80)
Police Delinquents	33.5	(242)	77.0	(161)
Nondelinquents	6.5	(123)	65.2	(115)

nondelinquent strata. Rates of participation, however, suggest that while in most cases court delinquents were least likely to agree to participate, police delinquents on the whole were the most likely to agree to participate in the study. The relatively high participation rates among police delinquents as compared to nondelinquents are not consistent with standard results for research in this area. This anomaly is apparently produced by unexpectedly low participation rates among located nondelinquents. Since the nondelinquent population was in all subgroups more likely to be located (Table 2), there is no reason to believe that the nondelinquent population is more poorly represented than is the population of police delinquents.

Our sampling procedure may be seen as a form of stratified, disproportionate, random sampling where the strata initially overlap one another. With such a design, the major task is to assign weights in such a way as to permit unbiased estimates of population parameters. When the population is fully defined in advance of sample selection and strata are mutually exclusive, the assignment of such weights is straightforward. In the present case the problem is complicated by possible overlap among our three populations. As mentioned, a good deal of the time of the field staff was spent attempting to enumerate these populations and eliminate overlap. Once separate populations had been identified, it seemed a simple matter to reproduce the Seattle adolescent population in terms of rates of delinquency by race, sex, and class. Unfortunately, estimates of these parameter values produced by our searches of school, police, and court records did not always match those available from independent sources, and neither was necessarily consistent with reasonably well-established findings of

previous research. The question was then which of these estimates to use in reconstituting the Seattle population of interest (we do not believe in so-called theoretical sampling or that inferences to hypothetical populations are the goal of empirical research). When all was said and done, we decided it would be best to approximate census and general juvenile justice statistics for the city as a whole, rather than to rely solely on counts generated internally. This decision was made only after carefully comparing the results of several weighting schemes based on rather different assumptions. Although a good many of our findings would be essentially the same whichever of these schemes was used, the weighting scheme adopted describes the population that to us conforms most closely to the greatest number of known features of the population of the city of Seattle. The delinquency rates of the Seattle population are shown in Table 3. These rates describe a population whose prevalence rates for police contacts are roughly similar to those reported by Gordon (1976) and Wolfgang et al. (1972).

Prior to the question of external validity is, of course, the question of internal validity. Because of the nature of our study, the administrative tasks—from selecting and contacting subjects, obtaining consent, picking up subjects at home, paying subjects, managing the interviewing of subjects, and returning the subjects to their homes—are so overwhelming during the data collection stage that threats to internal validity may occur as a result of error or oversight. As far as we can determine, however, there was only one brief period where some subjects may not have been randomly assigned to conditions. Internal checks designed to determine whether within a given subsample (e.g., nondelinquent, black, male) subjects differ system-

TABLE 3: Rates of Official Delinquency in Seattle by Sex, Race, and Median Income of Census Tract.[a] (Percent with police or court records.)

	MALE	FEMALE	
WHITE			
Low Income	32	12	
	(2884)	(2834)	
High Income	25	7	
	(2652)	(2773)	
TOTAL WHITE	28	9	
	(5536)	(5607)	
TOTAL BLACK	47	26	
	(1560)	(1575)	
TOTAL POPULATION	33	13	23
	(7096)	(7182)	(14.278)

[a] Estimated from sample and population data.

atically on characteristics unlikely to be affected by the method condition (e.g., age) reveal no obvious nonrandom patterns.

The only other threat to internal validity that we see (and this is really a mixed internal/external issue) relates to design variables for which random allocation was absent, namely, the variables that make ours a "quasi-experiment" rather than a true experiment—all variables except method condition. This is not problematic *within* a given subpopulation (e.g., white, male, high SES, court delinquent), but comparisons across these 18 subpopulations may be problematic. That is, if for some reason one or more of the subpopulations self-selects such that only the most truthful members participate, that group would not be representative of its population and comparisons with other populations would not be appropriate. Therefore, this *possibility* reduces to the problems associated with subgroup bias and questions of external validity.

Throughout the remainder of this volume, we summarize the relevant re-

search literature regarding methodological issues in self-reported delinquency. In parallel fashion, we begin a preliminary analysis and presentation of our methodological and related data from the Seattle Youth Study. Since the Seattle data were collected with resolution of important methodological issues in mind, these aspects of the Seattle data will be given primary attention.

THE SELF-REPORT INSTRUMENT AND SELF-REPORT DELINQUENCY IN THE SEATTLE SAMPLE

Our basic self-report instrument contained 69 items, grouped into five categories: contacts with the criminal justice system (official contacts); serious crimes; general delinquency; drug offenses; and school and family offenses.

Comparison of these distributions with comparable items in previous self-report research tells us something about the Seattle sample, about trends in delinquent behavior, and about the difficulties of self-report research.

DRUG USE

The Seattle sample is much more heavily involved in the use of alcohol and marijuana than self-report samples studied at earlier periods. For example, the Institute for Juvenile Research (1972, cited by Empey. 1978) reported in 1972 that within an only slightly younger sample of Illinois juveniles. 22% had used marijuana. In the Seattle sample, this figure exceeds 70% in all race-sex subgroups. The Seattle figures are, however, consistent with current research, which typically shows a *prevalence* of marijuana use among 12th graders of about 70% (New York State Division of Substance Abuse Services, 1978). (The Seattle data show a similar pattern with respect to alcohol. Although reported levels of use are higher than those found in earlier self-report research, they are consistent with figures currently being reported, New York State Division of Substance Abuse Services, 1978.)

In contrast, the 1% figure for heroin use in the Seattle sample shows little change from previous results, a finding also consistent with current research.

STATUS OFFENSES

The level of "truancy" (item 64) is generally higher in the Seattle sample than in previous self-report research, even though our truancy item is considerably more restrictive than the truancy item typically employed. The relatively high level of truancy apparently stems from the nature of our sample, which includes a full contingent of out-of-school delinquents, who would be expected to have histories of high levels of truancy. (Interestingly, while the truancy item does not discriminate between blacks and whites or between males and females,

it is a good predictor of official delinquency among white males and a weak predictor of official delinquency among black males. Apparently, the qualifier "when your parents thought you were there" differentially conditions the item for blacks and whites. In any event, it is clear that truancy without parental knowledge does not have the same delinquency implications for black and white males.)

Another standard self-report status offense is runaway. Once again we attempted to make the item more serious than the standard Short-Nye item by adding the qualifier "and stayed overnight." Even so, our sample has a higher rate of runaway than the typical self-report sample (see Empey, 1978: 146) and the item we use is a good predictor of official delinquency in all subgroups (the delinquent to nondelinquent ratios for runaway are 3.69 and 3.24 for white and black males, respectively).

THEFT

The three Short-Nye theft items have been widely used in subsequent self-report research with no (or apparently trivial) wording changes. Since we intended to replicate the six-item Richmond Youth Project self-report scale, which contains these items, we felt free to modify the wording of the Short-Nye theft items for our 69-item instrument. This modification in all cases involved adding "from a store" to the basic theft items, thus converting them to the more specific "shoplifting" category.

Comparison of the Seattle results on the general theft items with those produced by previous research shows higher rates in Seattle (see Empey, 1978: 148). Direct comparison with the Richmond sample (Table 4) shows that this difference maintains in all race-sex subgroups. Only for theft of items of large value (worth

TABLE 4: Richmond Items, Seattle (1978) and Richmond (1965). Percent Admitting Ever Involvement, by Race and Sex. Weighted

	WHITE MALES		BLACK MALES		WHITE FEMALES		BLACK FEMALES	
	Seattle	Richmond	Seattle	Richmond	Seattle	Richmond	Seattle	Richmond
Little things (worth less than $2)	75.9	53.1	66.8	47.4	62.5	31.0	47.9	24.3
Things of some value (between $2 and $50)	39.8	19.2	44.0	23.6	26.2	7.7	29.1	5.5
Things of large value (worth over $50)	16.5	6.5	17.3	12.0	1.7	1.7	6.6	1.8
Taken a car without owner's permission (wording change)	9.7	11.0	7.3	12.8	0.8	3.6	1.7	4.0
Banged up something that did not belong to you on purpose	43.1	25.5	36.4	32.0	19.2	8.3	28.5	15.4
Beaten up or hurt anyone on purpose	50.9	41.9	47.3	45.9	24.4	15.2	36.7	28.7

more than $50) among white females are the Seattle and Richmond results similar.

Although the precise sources of these sometimes marked differences are beyond the scope of our research, we can say that age differences and differences in the distribution of official delinquency between the Richmond and Seattle samples cannot account for more than a small portion of the difference in levels of self-reported theft. The *shoplifting* rate for items of small value among official *nondelinquents* in the Seattle sample is higher than the *general theft rate* (for items of comparable value) in the Richmond sample among both black and white males. At the same time, no age group in the Richmond sample has theft rates as high as the overall theft rates in Seattle.

Addition of "from a store" to the theft items results in a decline in rates (a logical but not empirical necessity, see below) and produces sharp reductions in sex ratios. Among black males, petty shoplifting (less than $2) is reported *less* frequently by official delinquents than by official nondelinquents, and among white males it is among the weakest predictors of official delinquency in the entire set of self-report items.

This "wording" effect is clearly illustrated by comparing the remaining Short-Nye items from Richmond with their Seattle equivalents.

The Richmond auto theft item followed the trend in self-report research toward making the description of this "offense" more closely approximate a criminal act than the description provided by the original Short-Nye item. We continued this trend by requiring that the car belong "to someone you didn't know". (The nearest approximation to our item is provided by Bachman, 1970, who excluded cars belonging to "someone in your family.")

The change in wording is undoubtedly responsible for the fact that this item shows a lower rather than a greater rate of delinquency in the Seattle than in the Richmond sample. In fact, the prevalence of auto theft in the Seattle sample is, with minor exceptions, lower than the prevalence typically reported in the literature (Empey, 1978: 148), even though the Seattle sample is on most counts considerably more delinquent than the typical self-report sample.[1]

VANDALISM

The vandalism or malicious mischief rates from previous self-report research are highly variable. The prevalence rates for "destroying property" among boys reported by Empey (1978: 148) range from 27% to 66%. This puts the Seattle and Richmond samples, judged by the Richmond item (Table 4), toward the low end of the distribution. But some three dozen more or less distinct property destruction items have been used in self-report research since Short and Nye first wrote their item 19, and the results are apparently highly contingent on item wording. Among males, particularly black males, the prevalence rates for the specific vandalism item are higher than the rates for the general vandalism item. Obviously, the specific item does better at triggering recall or the general item is not seen by respondents as including the specific act of window breaking. In any event, the prevalence of vandalism obtained by an accumulation of the several specific types of vandalism described in our 69-item scale would greatly exceed the prevalence estimate obtained by a single general item, and the volatility of both estimates should make us nervous about efforts to estimate the prevalence or incidence of such offenses from self-report data.

It is apparent that the magnitude and even the direction of race and sex differences in delinquency are often contingent on item content or wording. For now it is sufficient to note that while the Seattle sample has on the whole a higher level of self-report delinquency than previous self report samples, its features are not inconsistent with recent, comparable data. Candor requires that we also note that the *level* of self-report delinquency within a sample appears to fluctuate broadly as a function of apparently minor changes in item content. Such instability of course at least partially justifies our interest in the effect of method of administration on the psychometric properties of self-report instruments.

Note

1. The follow-up probe of the auto theft item under the anonymous questionnaire condition revealed that in some cases respondents did not attend to the requirement that the car belong to someone they did not know and reported taking cars belonging to friends or relatives.

Still Just the Study of Men and Crime?
A Content Analysis[1]

Lance Hannon[2] and Lynn Resnick Dufour

It is often quietly argued that because serious crime is much less frequent among females, studying female crime is much less serious. Combined with the reality of a largely male-dominated academic area, this line of thinking has contributed to the underrepresentation of women as subjects in studies of crime and delinquency. Feminist critics have contended that the knowledge of significant gender differences in participation in crime should produce *more* emphasis on studying women and crime (Daly & Chesney-Lind, 1988; Heidensohn, 1987; Smart, 1976). Understanding why people *do not* commit certain crimes is as important as understanding why they do, yet it is still common for researchers to legitimate their selection of an all male sample with such comments as, "crime is still overwhelmingly a man's vice" (Herrnstein & Murray, 1994, p. 245). Of course, there is nothing wrong with focusing on a limited population as long as the researcher recognizes this as a limitation, not a necessity.

Reprinted from Sex Roles, Vol. 38, No. 1–2, pp. 63–71, Lance Hannon and Lynn Resnick Dufour, "Still Just the Study of Men and Crime?", 1998, with permission from Plenum Publishing Corporation.
[1]We would like to thank Myra Marx Ferree, Kathleen Shannon, and the anonymous reviewers for their very helpful comments.
[2]To whom correspondence should be addressed at Department of Sociology—U68, University of Connecticut, Storrs, CT 06269-2068.

Studies that sample only men but claim to capture the general concepts of crime and delinquency reinforce the marginalization of gender in theories of crime.

ANDROCENTRICITY AND OVERGENERALIZATION

We used Eichler's (1988) specific conceptualizations of androcentricity and overgeneralization as tools for assessing the degree to which "male is the norm" within criminological research. According to Eichler, androcentricity refers to the disproportionate presence of research focusing solely on men. Overgeneralization refers to research that focuses only on one sex, but presents itself as applicable to both sexes.

Androcentricity has been a key concept in the feminist critique of the sciences in general, and sociology in particular (Stacey & Thorne, 1985; Acker, 1989). In reviewing key areas of sociology such as occupations (Feldberg & Glenn, 1979; Acker, 1990) and economic stratification (Smith, 1987; Acker, 1989), feminist theorists have noted the ways in which androcentricity distorts our understanding of gendered social processes by making male patterns seem normative and thus ungendered.

Androcentricity in criminology leads us to believe that while men are committing the most serious of crimes, women are nonexistent—neither conforming nor deviating. As Daly & Chesney-Lind (1988, p. 527) have noted, "Gender differences in crime suggest that *crime* may not be so normal after all." When researchers sample only men because men commit more crime, they are often sampling around the dependent variable by excluding a group known to be disproportionately located on one side of the mean.

Criminologists are just recently beginning to understand the ramifications of sampling around the dependent variable. For example, within criminology there has been a long history of bias toward urban samples. This bias is currently the focus of controversy (Kpowsowa, Breault, & Harrison, 1995). Believing that crime is more prevalent in the cities, criminologists have focused their efforts on explaining urban crime rates. But as many new studies have pointed out, there is serious crime in rural areas—it is just not as prevalent as in the cities. Thus many researchers have begun to ask questions like, "If poverty is an important determinant of violent crime, why do rural areas, which are often substantially poorer than urban areas, have low violent crime rates?" The same types of questions can be asked of criminologists who do not acknowledge the importance of studying women and crime. "If delinquency results from feelings of alienation and social strain, why do women (who generally have comparable levels of alienation and social strain) refrain from committing certain crimes?"

A related problem of androcentric research is that the exclusion of the majority of the population puts extreme limits on the generalizability of findings. Studies of men cannot (and should not) be generalized to the population as a whole. While this does not mean that limiting a sample to men is unacceptable, it does mean that such limits should be acknowledged as a constraint on the generality of the processes examined.

Overgeneralization, a less recognized tendency in research, also has profound effects on criminology. When researchers only studying men title their articles to give the impression that their findings are generalizable to all people, the discipline looks less androcentric than it really is. It appears that we have a vast knowledge of crime and delinquency when in fact we have a vast knowledge of male crime and male delinquency.

Overgeneralization affects the questions researchers and theorists ask. Criminologists commonly develop research questions by surveying the landscape of the discipline for gaps. These gaps would be much more apparent if titles of articles based on male samples did not claim to be about "the effects of self-esteem on delinquency" but more accurately "the effects of self-esteem on male delinquency." The first title conceals the fact that women have been excluded, thus glossing over the unstudied relationship between gender, self-esteem, and behavior for both sexes.

Moreover, if many researchers overgeneralize their findings, studies that do *not* overgeneralize (or that attempt to fill in the gaps) may be viewed as out of the mainstream, specialized, and less important. As Renzetti (1993) has argued, despite a growing body of research on women and crime, women continue to be "on the margins of the malestream."

PREVIOUS STUDIES

Several authors have argued that criminology and criminal justice are androcentric disciplines (Baro & Eigenberg, 1993; Eigenberg & Baro, 1992; Morris & Gelsthorpe, 1991; Chesney-Lind, 1989; Daly &

Chesney-Lind, 1988; Heidensohn, 1987). In an early critique Smart (1976, p. 185) wrote,

> Criminology and the sociology of deviance must become more than the study of men and crime if they are to play any significant part in the development of our understanding of crime, law and the criminal process and play any role in the transformation of existing social practices.

Along these lines, some have attempted to document the frequent exclusion of women as subjects of inquiry (Garrison, McClelland, Dambrot, & Casey, 1992; Dorworth & Henry, 1992; Mahan & Anthony, 1992; Moyer, 1985).

In separate content analyses of introductory criminology and criminal justice texts, Baro and Eigenberg (1993) and Wright (1992) concluded that women are repeatedly "rendered invisible" and that when women are portrayed, they are often depicted in stereotypical ways. Baro and Eigenberg (1993, p. 28) called for further research in the social construction of knowledge in criminology and noted that increased documentation in this area can be used "to demand change." Wright's (1987) content analysis of subject headings in *Sociological Abstracts* provides the most thorough investigation of the coverage of women and crime in journals. His data showed that despite a substantial increase in the publication of journal articles on women and crime between 1956 and 1980, the coverage of women and crime in textbooks remained constant.

We hope to add to the existing literature on the representation of women in criminology by examining criminological research sampling individuals. Previous research has been focused solely on articles categorized as about "women and crime." But criminological studies that are *not* necessarily focused on women and crime should include women in their samples.

Our broad sampling frame reflects the belief that gender is an important concept for studying men and crime as well.

THE RESEARCH DESIGN

We analyzed articles from four major criminology journals: *Criminology, The British Journal of Criminology, The Journal of Research in Crime and Delinquency*, and *The Journal of Criminal Law and Criminology* (the criminology section). The selection of these journals was guided in part by Cohn and Farrington's (1994) analysis of the central sources of criminological information. While all of these journals present findings related to criminal justice issues, their main focus seems to be the etiology of law breaking and the social construction of crime. Still, these journals cover a broad range of specific topics—from the psychological correlates of child abuse to the impact of welfare reform on violent crime. We examined all articles published in the periods 1974–1978 and 1992–1996. These intervals contain a decent sample size ($n = 376$) and are reasonably separated (a gap of 13 years).

In order to assess the degrees of androcentricity and overgeneralization in our samples, we coded articles by sex composition of the sample, specification of generality in the title, and space devoted to the discussion of gender differences. Articles that did not appear to sample individual people were excluded from the samples; these included aggregate level studies of cities, theoretical pieces, methodological commentaries, and literature reviews. Sex composition of the sample consisted of three categories: (1) only males were sampled, (2) only females were sampled, and (3) both males and females were sampled. Specification of generality in the title meant whether or not an article's title specifically noted the selection of an all male or all female sample. For those articles sampling both sexes, we examined the proportion that included separate analyses for males and females or gender-based interaction terms, *or* devoted at least half of a page to the discussion of gender differences. (Almost all of the articles with separate analyses for males and females also had at least half a page of discussion of gender differences in the text.) This measure represents an attempt to distinguish between studies that examined gender as a central axis of variability and those that included respondent's sex merely as a statistical control.

We found a few articles for which we could not determine the sex composition of the sample even by close reading of the entire manuscript. These articles were excluded from our analyses.

RESULTS

Focusing only on articles sampling individuals, we found some significant differences between the two time periods (Table 1). The percentage of articles sampling both men and women has increased dramatically (from 34% in the 1970s to 68% in the 1990s). Meanwhile, the percentage of articles sampling men has substantially decreased (from 60% in the 1970s to 26% in the 1990s). The percentage of articles sampling only women has remained stable (6% in both periods). However, this figure does not take into account the apparent general decline in single-sex samples overall. The proportional share of women only articles of all single-sex articles has increased from 8% in the 1970s period to 18% in the 1990s.

Among those articles sampling both sexes, our analysis indicated that attention to gender differences was greater in the 1970s than in the 1990s. While 41% of 1970s articles sampling both sexes devoted at least half a page to gender differences or included separate analyses for males and females, only 28% of 1990s articles did so. Thus the finding of a significant increase in the proportion of all articles that sampled both sexes is qualified by the finding that gender variation seems to receive less attention in more recent studies. There appears to be a greater use of dummy variables indicating respondent's sex simply as a statistical control.

Looking at those articles only sampling one sex, we see that men continue to be the norm in that titles for male only samples are typically over-generalized (Table 2). In both periods about 90% of the

TABLE 1: Type of Sample and Attention to Gender by Period			
Type of Sample	Attention to Gender	1974–1978	1992–1996
Only males	Specifies sex in title	6% (*n* = 12)	3% (*n* = 6)
	Does not specify sex in title	54% (*n* = 110)	23% (*n* = 40)
Only females	Specifies sex in title	5% (*n* = 10)	6% (*n* = 10)
	Does not specify sex in title	1% (*n* = 1)	0% (*n* = 0)
Both males and females	Gender is more than a control variable	14% (*n* = 28)	19% (*n* = 33)
	Gender is just a control variable	20% (*n* = 41)	49% (*n* = 85)
		100% (*n* = 202)	100% (*n* = 174)

TABLE 2: Sex Composition of Sample and Period by Explicitness of Title

Sex of Sample	Period	Specifies Sample Sex	Does not Specify Sample Sex
Only males	1974–1978	10% ($n = 12$)	90% ($n = 110$)
	1992–1996	13% ($n = 6$)	87% ($n = 40$)
Only females	1974–1978	91% ($n = 10$)	9% ($n = 1$)
	1992–1996	100% ($n = 10$)	0% ($n = 0$)

articles that only sample males did *not* specify their sample composition in the title. For those researchers who sample only women ($n = 21$), such lack of specificity is extremely rare—only one article in the 1970s period and none in the 1990s. Moreover, the one female only article that did not specify sample composition in the title (Jensen, 1977) included an important caveat that was not present in the data/methods sections of the overgeneralized male only studies. Jensen (1977, p. 558) cautioned,

> The analysis to follow is based on data gathered from female felons and misdemeanants imprisoned in a correctional center in the South Eastern United States. Since most arguments about age, crime, and adjustment to prison have been based on data for males, the nature of the population studied should be kept in mind.

Separate analyses of the articles dealing with crime and articles dealing with delinquency revealed similar findings. The changes in sample composition between the two time periods were similar for crime articles and delinquency articles. Likewise, period differences for overgeneralization and attention to gender were roughly equivalent for crime and delinquency studies.

A supplemental analysis of articles listed in *Sociofile* for two time periods also revealed very similar results ($n = 152$ for 1974–1978 and $n = 293$ for 1990–1994).

Sociofile contains article citations and abstracts for all of the top criminology journals *and* includes a variety of journals from other areas. We selected articles from the *Sociofile* database by searching for all entries that had the word *delinquency, delinquent*(s), *crime*(s), *criminality*, or *criminal*(s) in the title of the article. We chose *crime* and *delinquency* as key words because they are frequently used to imply a broader significance to the article. The search was limited further by excluding dissertation abstracts, articles published outside the United States, and articles published in languages other than English.

The results of this alterative analysis supported the general findings of our examination of criminology journals: (1) there was a substantial increase in the proportion of articles sampling both sexes, (2) there was a significant decrease in the percentage of articles sampling males only, (3) there was no increase in the percentage of articles sampling women only, (4) male only studies typically overgeneralized their titles, and (5) almost all female only studies specified the limits of generalizability in their titles.

DISCUSSION

The findings of this analysis are mixed. There has been a significant increase in the percentage of crime and delinquency research that includes both men and women.

This is consistent with Wright's (1987) analysis. However, this finding is qualified by the result that recent articles sampling both sexes appear to pay less attention to gender differences than in the past. Moreover, despite the growth in samples that contain both males and females, "male" appears to still be the norm within criminological research. It is still an accepted practice for researchers to sample only males, yet not specify this when they write their titles. The following titles are recent examples of overgeneralization from male only samples: "Adapting to Strain: an Examination of Delinquent Coping Mechanisms" (Brezina, 1996), "The Stability of Criminal Potential from Childhood to Adulthood" (Nagin & Farrington, 1992), and "Age, Differential Expectations, and Crime Desistance" (Shover & Thompson, 1992). In contrast, researchers who just sample women almost always note the limits of generalizability in their titles. Examples of these more explicit titles include "Women, Race and Crime" (Hill & Crawford, 1990) and "Race, Father-Absence, and Female Delinquency" (Austin, 1978). These findings emphasize the need for editorial policy mandating truth in labeling.

Criminology may be expanding to include women as subjects of inquiry, but this response only touches a part of the feminist critique. It is equally important to challenge the equation of male experiences with that of all of humanity and to develop a gendered understanding of crime and delinquency. Men are also affected by gender socialization; they are not ungendered abstract people. The continuing failure to acknowledge the omission of women legitimizes the marginalization of gender in criminological theory and inhibits new research initiatives. Furthermore there may be adverse effects associated with the blind application of androcentric research to populations that include women and programs that specifically focus on female offenders.

Our investigation leaves many questions unanswered. For instance, how would our analyses apply to criminal justice research? In particular, to what degree is criminal justice research focused on women as victims of crime (particularly of male offenders) and how has criminal justice research changed with the increase in female personnel in the criminal justice system? Future studies might also examine the connections between gender, authorship, and use and presentation of sample composition. In sum, further research is needed to clarify the subtle and not so subtle processes through which research on women and crime becomes both underrepresented and overlooked.

References

Acker, J. (1989). Making gender visible. In R. Wallace (Ed.), *Feminism and sociological theory*. Newbury Park, CA: Sage.

Acker, J. (1990). Hierarchies, jobs, bodies: A theory of gendered organizations. *Gender and Society, 4,* 139–158.

Austin, R. L. (1978). Race, father-absence, and female delinquency. *Criminology, 15,* 478–504.

Baro, A., & Eigenberg, H. (1993). Images of gender: A content analysis of photographs in introductory criminology and criminal justice textbooks. *Women and Criminal Justice, 5,* 3–36.

Brezina, T. (1996). Adapting to strain: an examination of delinquent coping mechanisms. *Criminology, 34,* 39–60.

Chesney-Lind, M. (1989). Girls' crime and woman's place: Toward a feminist model of female delinquency. *Crime and Delinquency, 35,* 5–29.

Cohn, E. G., & Farrington, D. P. (1994). Who are the most influential criminologists in the English-speaking world. *British Journal of Criminology, 34,* 204–225.

Daly, K., & Chesney-Lind, M. (1988). Feminism and criminology. *Justice Quarterly, 5,* 497–535.

Dorworth, V. E., & Henry, M. (1992). Optical illusions: The visual representation of blacks and women in introductory criminal justice textbooks. *Journal of Criminal Justice Education, 3,* 293–314.

Eichler, M. (1988). *Nonsexist research methods*. Boston: Allen and Unwin.

Eigenberg, H., & Baro, A. (1992). Women and publication patterns in criminal justice journals: A content analysis. *Journal of Criminal Justice Education, 3,* 293–314.

Feldberg, R. L., & Glenn, E. N. (1979). Male and female: Job versus gender models in the sociology of work. *Social Problems, 26,* 525–536.

Garrison, C. G., McClelland, A., Dambrot, F., and Casey, K. A. (1992). Gender balancing the criminal justice curriculum and classroom. *Journal of Criminal Justice Education, 3,* 203–222.

Heidensohn, F. (1987). Women and crime: Questions for criminology. In P. Carlen & A. Worral (Eds), *Gender, crime and justice.* London: Milton Keynes—Open University Press.

Herrnstein, R. J., & Murray, C. (1994). *The bell curve.* New York: The Free Press.

Hill, G. D., & Crawford, E. M. (1990). Women, race, and crime. *Criminology, 28,* 601–626.

Jensen, G. F. (1977). Age and rule breaking in prison: a test of sociocultural interpretations. *Criminology, 14,* 555–568.

Kpowsowa, A. J., Breault, K. D., & Harrison, B. M. (1995). Reassessing the structural co-variates of violent and property crimes in the U.S.A.: A county level analysis. *British Journal of Sociology, 46,* 79–105.

Mahan, S., & Anthony, A. M. (1992). Including women in corrections texts. *Journal of Criminal Justice Education, 3,* 261–275.

Morris, A., & Gelsthorpe, L. (1991). Feminist perspectives in criminology: transforming and transgressing. *Women and Criminal Justice, 2,* 3–26.

Moyer, I. (1985). Academic criminology: A need for change. *American Journal of Criminal Justice, 9,* 197–212.

Nagin, D., & Farrington, D. P. (1992). The stability of criminal potential from childhood to adulthood. *Criminology, 30,* 235–260.

Renzetti, C. (1993). On the margins of the malestream (or, They still don't get it, do they?): feminist analyses in criminal justice education. *Journal of Criminal Justice Education, 4,* 219–234.

Shover, N., & Thompson, C. Y. (1992). Age, differential expectations and crime desistance. *Criminology, 30,* 89–104.

Smart, C. (1976). *Women, crime and criminology.* London: Routledge and Kegan Paul.

Smith, D. (1987). *The everyday world as problematic.* Boston: Northeastern University Press.

Stacey, J., & Thorne, B. (1985). The missing feminist revolution in sociology. *Social Problems, 32,* 301–316.

Wright, R. (1987). Are sisters in crime finally being booked? The coverage of women and crime in journals and textbooks. *Teaching Sociology, 15,* 418–422.

Wright, R. (1992). From vamps and tramps to teases and flirts: Stereotypes of women in criminology textbooks, 1956 to 1965 and 1981 to 1990. *Journal of Criminal Justice Education, 3,* 223–236.

Families of Homeless and Runaway Adolescents:

A Comparison of Parent/Caretaker and Adolescent Perspectives on Parenting, Family Violence, and Adolescent Conduct

Les B. Whitbeck, Danny R. Hoyt, and Kevin A. Ackley

INTRODUCTION

Although there is a growing literature on homeless and runaway adolescents, we know very little about their parents and families. Studies that address the parent-child relationship have relied exclusively on the runaway adolescents reports of their parents behaviors and child-rearing practices. The results of these reports recently have come under scrutiny. Parent advocacy groups and some policy makers have questioned the validity of adolescent self-reports about family backgrounds, asserting that they often are exaggerated self-serving fabrications of out-of-control

young people. Some state legislatures are revisiting juvenile statutes relating to runaways and are considering criminalization and/or mandatory return of runaways to parental custody by police (e.g. Washington State's Becca Bill). To our knowledge there have been no systematic studies that have included parent reports regarding the family backgrounds of runaway and homeless adolescents.

There are numerous practical reasons for this gap in the literature. Homeless and runaway adolescents are difficult to study systematically. Access to their parents or caretakers is even more difficult. When runaways are contacted on the streets or in shelters, they are often reluctant to talk at all, let alone provide names and addresses of their parents. When they do provide such information, they may give false names and addresses to interviewers and shelter operators for fear of being returned to abusive or dysfunctional family situations. For their part, parents may be hard to locate and when contacted, they may be

Reprinted from Child Abuse and Neglect, Vol. 21, No. 6, pp. 517–528, Les B. Whitbeck, Danny R. Hoyt, and Kevin A. Ackley, "Families of Homeless and Runaway Adolescents", 1997, with permission from Elsevier Science.

Key Words—Runaways, Families of runaways, Homeless adolescents.

reluctant to talk about their runaway adolescents due to frustration, feelings of inadequacy, or abdication of the parent role.

In this paper we report findings from telephone interviews and mailed questionnaires from 120 parents of homeless and runaway young people contacted as part of an ongoing four-state study of runaway and homeless youth. Homeless and runaway adolescents were interviewed by agency outreach workers directly on the street, in shelters, and in drop-in centers in Missouri, Iowa, Nebraska, and Kansas. At the end of their interviews, the adolescents were asked for permission to contact the person they had designated as their primary caretaker while growing up. When permission to contact was granted, the primary caretaker was contacted and interviewed.

The focus of this report is to investigate parent-child relationships of runaway and homeless adolescents using both adolescent and parent/caretaker reports. First, we compared the responses of runaway adolescents and their parents/caretakers on measures of parental monitoring, parental warmth and supportiveness, parental rejection, and abuse. Reports on the parenting measures were then contrasted to those of similarly aged nonrunaway adolescents and their parents from two-parent and single-parent households from the Midwest. Second, responses to problem behavior measures were compared using reports of parents of runaways and parents of nonrunaways. Finally, parent and runaway adolescents reports of externalizing behaviors were compared.

FAMILIES OF HOMELESS AND RUNAWAY ADOLESCENTS

When runaway and homeless adolescents are asked about their families, they typically describe them as dysfunctional and often physically and/or sexually abusive. Although rates of adolescent reports of abusive family backgrounds vary widely across studies, they all indicate severe risk for physical and sexual abuse. Janus, Burgess, and McCormack (1987) found that 71.5% of the male runaways they interviewed reported physical abuse, and 38.2% reported sexual abuse. Silbert and Pines' (1981) study of juvenile and adult street prostitutes indicated that 60% had been sexually abused. In the Kurtz, Kurtz and Jarvis (1991) report based on shelter intake records of 2,019 runaways from eight southeastern states, 28% of the runaways identified themselves as having been sexually or physically abused. About 30% of Kufeldt and Nimmo's (1987) sample of 474 runaways reported physical abuse. Bridge, Inc. in Boston (Saltonstall, 1984) has reported a 65% physical abuse rate. Only 5% of their sample clearly stated there was no abuse in their homes (Saltonstall, 1984, p. 78). A Los Angeles County shelter/drop-in center study (Pennbridge, Yates, David, & MacKenzie, 1990) reported a 47% abuse/neglect rate. Using the Conflict Tactics Scale (Straus & Gelles, 1990). Whitbeck and Simons (1993) found adolescents reported physical abuse rates ranging from 80% for slapping to 48% for being beat up for a sample of 150 street youth in Des Moines. Thirty-seven percent of the young women reported forced sexual activity by an adult caretaker.

Besides high rates of adolescent reported abuse, homeless and runaway adolescents typically rate their families as more dysfunctional than do nonrunaways. Schweitzer and colleagues (1994) found that homeless adolescents scored higher than housed children on measures of deprivation based on the Parental Bonding Inventory (Parker, Tupling, & Brown, 1979) and the Family Environment Scale (Moos & Moos, 1981). Stefanidis and colleagues

(1992) reported homeless adolescents who were nonresponsive to stabilization efforts scored significantly lower on measures of attachment than those who were responsive to agency stabilization efforts. Controlled studies also indicate that homeless adolescents report higher levels of parent marital discord and lower levels of parental care and acceptance than adolescents remaining at home (Daddis, Braddock, Cuers, Elliott, & Kelly, 1993).

Although these adolescent self-reports of family backgrounds correlate systematically with related behavioral and victimization variables (Whitbeck & Simons, 1990; Whitbeck, Hoyt, & Ackley, in press), an important dimension has been missing in the literature. We have yet to hear the parents' stories. Small but very vocal groups of parent advocates along with frustrated law enforcement officials are urging a crackdown on street youth, focusing on their delinquent behavior and the sense that they are beyond the control of both parents and law enforcement agencies. Systematic information on family risk factors is sorely needed to contribute to this debate.

The importance of multiple reporters of family processes.   It is not unusual for family members to rate relationship quality and each other's behaviors, particularly negative behaviors, differently. There is evidence for such discrepant evaluations throughout the family literature, ranging from spouse reports on marital quality, to parent and child reports on relationship quality from adolescence (Conger & Elder, 1994) to later in life (Hagested, 1984). However, regardless of some reporter discrepancy, the general stories family members tell about family processes are usually moderately correlated and in the same direction. Differences tend to be in degree rather than content. Indeed, using multiple

reporters in modeling family processes allows researchers to triangulate measures to reduce measurement error inherent in self-reports across multiple measures (Lorenz & Melby, 1994; Lorenz, Conger, Simons, Whitbeck, & Elder, 1991; Patterson, 1982).

In the case of reports of homeless and runaway adolescents and their parents/caretakers, we predicted that although they will differ statistically (as will parent-adolescent reports in nonrunaway families), the reports will be in the same general direction. That is, both parents/caretakers and their runaway adolescents will report troubled family relationships and adolescent behavioral problems. Moreover, we predicted both runaway adolescents and their parent/caretakers will score lower on measures of parental support and parental monitoring, and higher on the measure of parental rejection than a comparison group of two-parent and single-parent nonrunaway families from the same region of the United States. On measures of physical and sexual abuse, runaway adolescent reports and parent/caretaker reports were hypothesized to be similar on measures of less severe abuse and diverge with increase in severity with adolescents reporting greater severity. Similarly, parents/caretakers of runaway adolescents were expected to report higher levels of adolescent problem behaviors then their adolescents themselves, and the two-parent and single-parent nonrunaway family comparison group.

METHOD

SAMPLE

This analysis is a based on 120 matched parent/caretaker-runaway adolescent interviews from an ongoing study of runaway and homeless adolescents in four

Midwestern states Adolescents were interviewed on the streets, in shelters, and in drop-in centers by outreach workers affiliated with youth services agencies serving runaway and homeless youth in Missouri, Iowa, Nebraska, and Kansas. The youth interview lasted about 1 and 1/2 half hours. Adolescents were provided a break and a snack about half-way through the interview and were reimbursed $15 for participating. Referral and support services were offered young people on the streets and provided to them in shelters as part of the participating agencies regular outreach program. Agreeing to be interviewed was not a precondition for any of the services the agencies provided. The study complied with mandatory child abuse reporting statutes.

During the initial informed consent prior to beginning the interview the young people were told that they would be asked if the project researchers could contact a parent or caretaker at the end of the interview. Following the interview and after reimbursement was given, adolescents were asked for consent for parental contact. They were assured of confidentiality of interview content and that the parent/caretaker would only be given the date of interview and the agency name and address where the contact occurred. (Agencies welcomed contact from parents as part of their mission to reunite runaways with their families.) The adolescents were told that a separate interviewer from the Center for Family Research on Rural Mental Health, Iowa State University would contact their parents by telephone in about 2 weeks. This interviewer would have no information regarding the young person except for that on the consent form.

Parent/caretakers were sent a letter letting them know they would be receiving a call from a project interviewer. About 1 week after receiving the letter they were asked to participate in a 25–minute Computer Assisted Telephone Interview. At the end of the interview they were asked if they would agree to complete a mailed questionnaire and offered $25 reimbursement for return of a usable questionnaire.

Response rates for adolescents have varied by agency ranging from a low of 82% to a high of 100% with an average rate across all agencies of 94%. The adolescent respondents ranged in age from 12–21 years with an average age of 16.4 years for the young men and 16.0 years for the young women. The ages are almost normally distributed. Seventy-eight percent of the adolescents were European American and 12.5% were African American with the remainder Latino/Latina, American Indian, or Asian. Most of the young people were from larger metropolitan areas. Fifty-one percent reported that they were originally from a city or suburb of a city of 100,000 or more people. Eighteen percent said that they lived in cities from 50 to 100 thousand people. Only 13% were from very small towns (2,500 people or less) or from the country.

For the parents/caretakers of the adolescents, there are two refusal points in this type of research design. The first involves the adolescents' willingness to give permission to contact and to provide a usable address for parents/caretakers. The second is the actual refusal rate from the parents/caretakers themselves. Adolescent consent for contact has been about 50% for the project. The parent/caretaker response rate is about 70%, well above our initial projections. Adolescent males were slightly more apt to refuse permission to contact parents/caretakers than were females. Forty-seven percent of the young men and 50% of the young women gave permission. European American young people were more likely to give consent to contact than African American or Latino/Latina young people. Adolescents from less educated and lower SES families were also somewhat less apt to give permission to contact. A comparison of means indicated no differences in refusal of parent/caretaker contact based on history of abuse, street victimization, or adolescent drug and alcohol use. Adolescents who identified themselves as gay, lesbian, or bisexual were less apt to give permission to contact parents than youth who identified themselves as heterosexual. Young men who were involved in deviant subsistence strategies were also somewhat less likely to give permission to contact.

Our analysis of parent/caretaker refusal rates indicated that parents/caretakers of girls were more likely to participate in the interview than parents/caretakers of boys. Race and ethnicity, income, and education of parents/caretakers had no effects on refusal rates. An opposite trend from that of adolescent permission to contact emerged for adolescent characteristics. Parents/Caretakers of adolescents involved in dangerous and deviant subsistence strategies on the streets were somewhat more likely to agree to be interviewed than parents of adolescents who were not involved in such behaviors. Adolescent reports of parental abuse had no effects on parent's willingness to respond. Similarly, age of adolescent had no effect on parents refusal rates.

In summary, older, somewhat more deviant young people were less likely to give consent for parental contact or provide accurate information for making such contacts. Once contacted, however, parents of moderately deviant adolescents were those who were most willing to participate. Most of the differences between adolescents who granted permission to contact and those who did not and between par-

ents who refused participation and those we interviewed were very slight. Although differences were apparent when frequencies were compared, they seldom achieved statistical significance.

Seventy percent of the designated caretakers were mothers or step-mothers of the runaway or homeless adolescent, 17% were fathers or step-fathers, and 8% were grandparents. The remaining caretakers consisted primarily of other relatives, foster parents or guardians. Twenty-five percent rated their occupation as managerial or professional, 32% as technical, sales or administrative support, 27% as service workers, and 16% as mechanics, construction, or laborers.

At the time of the interview the adolescents had spent an average of 42 days on the street and had been an average of 138 days on their own (includes street time and unsupervised time when housed, e.g., living with friends). The amount of movement by adolescents and families was striking. Adolescents had experienced an average of 16 changes in residence and/or living situation and three changes in family configuration (e.g., parents divorce, remarried, etc.).

Comparison two-parent and single-parent nonrunaway families were taken from the Iowa Youth and Families Project (IYFP), a 4–year panel study of 450 Iowa families (Conger & Elder, 1994) and the Iowa Single Parent Project (ISPP) (Simons, 1996), a related 3–year panel study of 200 divorced, mother-headed families. Families were selected from waves of the panels where the target adolescent was aged 16 years to correspond to the average ages of the homeless and runaway sample. These comparison families had responded to the same parenting measures and conduct measures as the parents/caretakers in our sample.

MEASURES

Parental monitoring was measured with five items that asked parents and adolescents to indicate how often the parent knew where the adolescent was, who they were with, whether they had a set time to be home on weekend nights, how often the parent knew if the adolescent was in on time, and the extent that parents and child talked about what was going on in the young person's life. Response categories ranged from 1 = always and 4 = never. Cronbach's alphas for the scale was .70 for the adolescents and .67 for their parents and caretakers. For the two-parent comparison group, alphas were .60 for mothers and .70 for adolescents. Among the single-parent comparison group, alphas were .62 for mothers and .72 for adolescents.

Parental warmth and supportiveness was assessed with an 7–item scale that asked the degree to which parents and adolescents worked together to solve problems, whether the parent asked the adolescent's opinions regarding decisions that affected him or her, and the extent that the parent let the child know that he/she was trusted and cared about. Response categories ranged from 1 = always to 4 = never. Reliabilities for the measure were .89 for runaway adolescents and .61 for their parents or caretakers. For the two-parent comparison group, alphas were .82 for mothers and .87 for adolescents. For the single-parent comparison group, the coefficients were .86 for adolescents and .80 for parents.

Elliott's *parental rejection scale* (Brennen, 1974) was used to assess the quality of the parent-child relationship. The measure is a 5–item scale that assesses the amount the parent is perceived to care and trust the adolescent, and the extent the parent blames the adolescent for things. Response categories ranged 1 = always to 4 = never.

Alphas for the measure were .73 for runaway adolescents and .56 for their parents or caretakers. For the two-parent comparison group it was .80 for mothers and .81 for adolescents. For the single-parent comparison group, alphas were .78 for mothers and .85 for adolescents.

Quay and Peterson's *conduct disorder scale* (Quay & Peterson, 1983) was completed by the parents and caretakers of the runaway and homeless adolescents. This 22–item measure assesses aggressive behaviors, temper problems, and other behavioral problems of the adolescent. Response categories ranged from 1 = not a problem to 4 = a severe problem. Cronbach's alpha for the measure was .93 for the caretakers and parents of runaway adolescents. .93 for mothers in two-parent families and .95 for mothers in single-parent families.

The *externalization scale* of the YSR (Achenbach, 1991) was completed by adolescents and by parents through the Child Behavior Checklist (Achenbach, 1991). Cronbach's alpha for the externalization scale from the Child Behavior Checklist was .94 for parents/caretakers. Youth self-report on the externalization items of the YSR had an alpha of .88.

RESULTS

PARENTING MEASURES

Table 1 presents means for parent and adolescent responses to measures of parental monitoring, parental warmth and supportiveness, and parental rejection for runaway, two-parent (IYFP), and single-parent families (ISSP) on the same measures. This table includes a summary of *t*-test comparisons of means for parents and their adolescents within samples and respectively for parents and adolescents across

TABLE 1:   Comparisons of Parent and Adolescent Reports on Parenting Behaviors

	SAMPLES		
	Two-Parent	**Single-Parent**	**Runaway**
Monitoring			
Parent	4.27[a]	4.11[a,d]	3.89[a,c,d]
Adolescent	3.87	3.68[b]	3.58[c,d]
Warmth and Supportiveness			
Parent	3.87[a]	3.82[a]	3.61[a,d]
Adolescent	3.56	3.53	2.75[c,d]
Rejection			
Parent	1.85[a]	2.18[b]	3.29[a,c,d]
Adolescent	1.78	2.13[b]	2.86[c,d]

[a] *T*-Test indicates significant difference between parent and adolescent reports ($p \leq .05$).

[b] *T*-Test indicates significant difference between two-parent and single-parent sample ($p \leq .05$).

[c] *T*-Test indicates significant difference between runaway and single-parent sample ($p \leq .05$).

[d] *T*-Test indicates significant difference between runaway and two-parent sample ($p \leq .05$).

samples. For all of the parent-adolescent comparisons but one (single mothers and their adolescent children on the measure of parental rejection), the differences in average responses between parent and child respondents were statistically significant. Regardless of runaway or nonrunaway family status, parent and children reports differed with the parents consistently giving themselves higher scores on monitoring and warmth/supportiveness. Although magnitude of differences are small, it is noteworthy that the parents from runaway and two-parent families gave themselves higher scores on parental rejection than their adolescent child's ratings.

T-Test comparisons of parent reports from runaway and nonrunaway families indicate that all three adult caretaker groups differed significantly on reports of parental monitoring and parental rejection (Table 1, footnotes b, c, and d). Parents/ Caretakers of runaways differed significantly from nonrunaway two-parent families on reports of parental warmth and supportiveness, but did not differ significantly from divorced mother-headed families. For two of these measures a pattern emerges. Parents/caretakers of runaway adolescents report less monitoring, and greater rejection scores than either single-mothers or mothers from two-parent households. They report lower warmth and supportiveness than mothers in two-parent families. Among two-parent and single-parent households, single-mothers scored significantly lower than mothers in two-parent households on measures of monitoring, and higher on measures of rejection. Clearly, the parents/caretakers of runaway and homeless adolescents are reporting more parenting problems than their counterparts in nonrunaway families.

A similar pattern emerges for adolescent reports (Table 1, footnotes b, c, and d). Runaway and homeless adolescents report lower monitoring, less warmth and supportiveness, and higher levels of rejection from their parents than do nonrunaway adolescents in two-parent and single-parent households. Adolescents in single-parent households report less monitoring and higher rejection scores than parents in two-parent households, but do not differ from two-parent families on the measure of parental warmth and supportiveness.

In summary, although teenagers reports on measures may differ in magnitude from those of their parents on measures of parenting, parent/caretakers and their runaway offspring are telling the same story regarding parenting practices and the parent-child relationship. Both indicate that there is less monitoring, less warmth and supportiveness, and higher levels of rejection in their families then parents and adolescents in the nonrunaway comparison groups.

PHYSICAL AND SEXUAL ABUSE

A more complicated picture emerges when parent/caretaker responses to measures of physical and sexual abuse are compared to those of the runaway adolescents (Table 2). Parents/Caretakers and adolescent reports do not differ on measures of pushed or shoved in anger or slapping face or head. However, as the severity of the abusive behavior increases, the reports begin to differ significantly. It is important to note that

although the levels of severely abusive behaviors reported by parent/caretakers are lower than the adolescents assert, they remain very high. (Endorsement of an item does not indicate that the reporting parent was the perpetrator. The questions referred to a parent, a foster parent, an adult relative, or any adult that was supposed to be taking care of the child.) According to parents/caretakers, 33% of the adolescent boys and 30% of the girls had been hit with an object, 16% of the boys and 10% of the girls had been beaten with fists. Moreover, they reported that 18% of the adolescent girls had been approached sexually by an adult caretaker and 15% had been sexually abused. Even using the parent/caretaker reports of abusive backgrounds as a conservative estimate, the levels of violent and sexually exploitive family relationships are remarkable. Although life-time estimates of abuse rates based on the Straus & Gelles (1990) Conflict Tactics Scale are not available, national data indicate that only 7% of adolescents 15–17 years of age experienced severe violence (i.e. slapped, spanked, hit with an object) by an adult caretaker in the

TABLE 2:   Parents/Caretakers and Male and Female Adolescent Reports of Adolescent Physical and Sexual Abuse

| | MALE | | FEMALE | |
| | Caretaker Proportion | Adolescent Proportion | Caretaker Proportion | Adolescent Proportion |
Variable				
Thrown Something in Anger	.37	.65*	.24	.70*
Pushed or Shoved in Anger	.81	.88	.82	.86
Slapped	.67	.79	.67	.71
Hit	.33	.65*	.30	.70*
Beat Up	.16	.40*	.10	.39*
Threatened With a Weapon	0	.23*	.03	.19*
Assaulted With a Weapon	0	.12*	.01	.05
Attempted to Touch Sexually	.05	.09	.18	.30
Forced Sex	.05	.09	.15	.35*

*Significant difference between parent and adolescent reports (p ≤ .05)

past year and only 2.1% experienced very severe violence (e.g. hit with fist, beaten up) (Straus & Gelles, 1990, p. 106)

The often violent nature of family interactions in families of runaways is further supported by parent/caretaker reports of violence directed toward them by the adolescent (Table 3). Twenty-five percent of parents/caretakers report having been slapped by their adolescent, 13% beaten with fists, and 14% threatened with a weapon. Compare these to the adolescent reports that 23% of boys and 19% of girls had been threatened with a weapon, and 12% of boys and 5% of girls actually assaulted with a weapon by a parent or caretaker. The Straus and Gelles (1990) national data indicate that about 10% of parents reported any level of violence directed towards them by adolescents aged 15–17 years during the past year and only 3.5% reported severe violence (e.g. hit with object or fist). Regardless of reporter, the picture that emerges is of mutually coercive family interactions that spiral into very serious violence.

PARENT/CARETAKER AND RUNAWAY ADOLESCENT REPORTS OF ADOLESCENT CONDUCT PROBLEMS

We have two separate measures of adolescent conduct problems to which the parents/caretakers responded. The first, Quay and Peterson's (1983) Conduct Disorder Scale, allows comparison with IYFP mothers from intact, two-parent families and the divorced single mothers from ISPP who have adolescent children of the same average age as those in our runaway families (Table 4). As one would expect, the parent/caretakers of runaway adolescents rate their children's conduct problems significantly higher than mothers from intact and single-parent nonrunaway families. Single mothers rate their adolescents as

TABLE 3: Adolescent Aggression Towards Parents/Caretakers

Have Any of the Following Ever Occurred?	Caretaker Report Percent (N = 120)
Thrown Something in Anger	36.7
Pushed or Shoved in Anger	52.5
Slapped	25.0
Hit	15.0
Beat Up	13.3
Threatened With a Weapon	14.2
Assaulted With a Weapon	0.8

TABLE 4: Parent/Caretaker and Adolescent Reports of Adolescent Conduct Problems

	Mean
Conduct Disorder[a]	
Mothers, two-parent family	1.35
Mother, single-parent family	1.50[b]
Caretaker, runaway family	2.72[c,d]
Externalization Scale[e]	
Males	
Caretaker	32.11
Adolescent	26.11[f]
Females	
Caretaker	25.02
Adolescent	22.31

[a]Only caretakers and mothers reported on Adolescent Conduct Disorder.

[b]*T*-test comparison of means indicates a significant difference between two-parent and single-parent mother's reports.

[c]*T*-test comparison between caretaker of runaway and single-parent mother reports.

[d]*T*-test comparison between caretaker of runaway and two-parent mother report.

[e]Only administered in the runaway sample.

[ff]*T*-test comparison of means indicates a significant difference between caretaker and runaway adolescent.

having more conduct problems than mothers from intact two-parent households.

We also had parents/caretakers and runaway adolescents complete the externalization scale for adolescents from the Child Behavior Checklist and YSR (Achenbach, 1991). As Table 4 indicates, both adolescents and parents/caretakers scored the young people at or above the borderline clinical cutoff ranges (17 for boys: 22 for girls). Adolescent boys scored themselves well above the clinical range for the externalization scale as did their parent/caretakers. Parents/caretaker scores were higher than their adolescent boys, and average scores differed significantly. However, adolescent girls and their parents/caretakers scored the girls within the borderline clinical range (parents/caretakers at the top of the range, adolescent girls at the bottom of the range) and the means did not differ statistically.

In summary, parents/caretakers of adolescents rate their children as having more conduct problems than the mothers in the nonrunaway comparison groups. Parents/Caretakers and runaway adolescents both report clinical (boys) or borderline clinical (girls) levels of externalizing behaviors. Again, parents and their runaway adolescents are telling essentially the same story.

DISCUSSION AND CONCLUSIONS

Because we have almost no systematic information from the parents and caretakers of runaway and homeless youth, this research has important implications for current policy debates about runaway and homeless adolescents. The most important finding is that regardless of who is providing the information, adult caretakers or the runaways themselves, the depictions of family processes are essentially the same. Parents/Caretakers and adolescents alike report problematic parent-child relationships characterized by low levels of parental monitoring, parental warmth and supportiveness, and high levels of parental rejection. Both adult caretakers and runaway adolescents report high levels of family violence, virtually concurring on levels of less severe violence. And, where reports diverge, even the more conservative adult reports indicate critical levels of physical and sexual abuse. The addition of parents/caretaker reports makes it difficult to dismiss these findings regarding the families of runaways as the exaggerations of defiant, out of control adolescents.

Family members also concur on behavior problems of the adolescents. Both adult caretakers and runaways indicate serious conduct problems on the part of the adolescents. As one would expect, parents/caretakers of runaways rate their children significantly more troubled than their nonrunaway counterparts.

The family portraits that emerge from multiple reporters involve troubled family relationships often characterized by sexual exploitation, mutual aggression, and violence. These family characteristics have long been associated with externalizing behaviors among adolescents (Jessor & Jessor, 1977; Patterson, 1982; Widom, 1994). Our findings are particularly compelling in that the most troubled of the homeless and runaway adolescents refused us access to their families. It is important to note, however, that the results of this study do not lay the blame on the reporting parents/caretakers alone. Often these adult caretakers are struggling to repair early developmental damage caused by another adult caretaker or cope with disruptive and difficult family situations past and present.

Many are looking for answers and assistance.

Frustrated policy makers responding to vocal parent advocacy groups and anecdotal information risk an oversimplification of the problem of homeless and runaway adolescents that could result in potentially dangerous solutions. Our adult caretakers are clearly indicating that, on average, they are not simply beleaguered parents attempting to cope with delinquent, defiant children. Rather, they have serious, often dangerous, family problems that need attention. Simple policy solutions such as the mandatory return of the runaway to parental custody ignore these potentially dangerous family problems and may place both parent and child in jeopardy. The parents that we interviewed clearly knew the extent and seriousness of their family troubles. Indeed, over 60% of the parent/caretakers in our sample reported that they would only accept the runaway back into their homes if he or she met certain behavioral conditions. Eighteen percent said that the adolescent was not welcome home under any conditions.

Policy makers must realize that there are no easy solutions when families have reached the point where the child chooses the risks of street life over living at home. Forced return to parents almost certainly will mean continued conflict and may put both child and parent at risk for serious harm. Criminalization often means punishing the victim of sexual exploitation and physical abuse for attempting to escape it. Early intervention, shelter, and outreach are needed immediately when adolescents run to reduce the odds of further, even more serious victimization (Whitbeck & Simons. 1990; Whitbeck, Hoyt, & Ackley, in press). Our parent/caretaker data indicate that a comprehensive family evaluation is crucial before adolescents are returned home.

References

Achenbach, T. M. (1991). *Manual for the Youth Self-Report and 1991 Profile*. Burlington, VT: University of VT.

Brennon, T. (1974). *Evaluation and validation regarding the national strategy for youth development*. Boulder, CO: Behavioral Research Evaluation Program.

Conger, R., & Elder. G. (1994). *Families in troubled times: Adapting to change in rural America*. New York: Aldyne de Gruyter.

Daddis, M., Braddock, D., Cuers, S., Elliott, A., & Kelly, A. (1993). Personal and family distress in homeless adolescents. *Community Mental Health Journal.* **29**, 413–422.

Hagestad, G. (1984). The continuous bond: A dynamic, multigenerational perspective on parent-child relations between adults. In M. Perlmutter (Ed.). *Minnesota symposia on child psychology* (Vol 17, pp. 129–158). Hillside, NJ: Earlbaum.

Janus, M., Burgess, A., & McCormack, A. (1987). Histories of sexual abuse in adolescent male runaways. *Adolescence.* **22**, 405–417.

Jessor, S., & Jessor, R. (1977). *Problem behavior and psychosocial adjustment*. New York: Academic Press.

Kufeldt, K., & Nimmo, M. (1987). Youth on the street: Abuse and neglect in the eighties. *Child Abuse & Neglect.* **11**, 531–543.

Kurtz, P., Kurtz, G., & Jarvis, S. (1991). Problems of maltreated runaway youth. *Adolescene.* **26**, 544–555.

Lorenz, F., & Melby, J. (1994). Analyzing family stress and adaptation: Methods of study. In R. Conger & G. Elder (Eds.). *Families in troubled times: Adaptime to change in rural America* (pp. 21–56) New York. Aldine de Gruyter.

Lorenz, F., Conger, R., Simons, R., Whitbeck, I., & Elder, G. (1991). Economic pressure and marital quality: An illustration of the method variance problem in the causal modeling of family processes. *Journal of Marriage and the Family.* **53**, 357–379.

Moos, R., & Moos, B. (1981). *Family Environmental Scale manual*. Palo Alto. CA: Consulting Psychologists Press.

Parker, G., Tupling, H., & Brown, I. (1979). A parental bonding instrument. *British Journal of Medical Psychology.* **53**, 1–10.

Patterson, G. R. (1982). *Coercive family processes*. Eugene. OR: Castilia.

Pennbridge, J., Yate, G., David, T., & Mackenzic, R. (1990). Runaway and homeless youth in Los Angeles Country. California. *Journal of Adolescent Health Care.* **11**, 159–165.

Quay, H. C., & Peterson, D. R. (1983). *Interun manual for the Revised Behavior Problem Checklist* (1st ed.). Coral Cables. FL: University of Miami.

Saltonstall, M. (1984). *Street youth and runaways on the streets of Boston: One agency's response* Boston, MA: The Bridge Press.

Schweitzer, R., Hier, S., & Terry, D. (1994). Parental bonding, family systems, and environmental predictors of adolescent homelessness. *Journal of Emotional and Behavioral Disorders*. **2**, 39–45.

Silbert, M., & Pines, A. (1981). Sexual child abuse as an antecedent to prostitution. *Child Abuse & Neglect*. **5**, 407–411.

Simons, R. (1996). *Understanding differences between divorced and intact families: Stress, interaction, and child outcomes*. Beverly Hills, CA: Sage.

Stefanidis, N., Pennbridge, J., MacKenzie, R., & Pottharst, K. (1992). Runaway and homeless youth: The effects of attachment history on stabilization. *American Journal of Orthopsychiatry*. **62**, 442–446.

Straus, M., & Gelles, R. (1990). *Physical violence in American families*. Brunswick, NJ: Transaction Books.

Whitbeck, L. B., Hoyt, D. R., & Ackley, K. A. (in press). Abusive family backgrounds and later victimization among runaway and homeless youth. *Journal of Adolescent Research*.

Whitbeck, L. R., & Simons, R. L., (1990). Life on the streets: The victimization of runaway and homeless adolescents. *Youth & Society*. **22**, 108–125.

Whitbeck, L. B., & Simons, R. L. (1993). A comparison of adaptive strategies and patterns of victimization among homeless adolescents and adults. *Violence and Victims*. **8**, 135–152.

Widom, C. (1994). Childhood victimization and adolescent problem behaviors. In R. Ketterllinus & M. Lamb (Eds.). *Adolescent problem behaviors* (pp. 127–164). Hillsdale, NJ: Lawrence Erlbaum.

Chapter 4

Family

INTRODUCTION

Hirschi's classic Social Control Theory in delinquency research rests on the importance of parenting behavior. According to Hirschi, strong bonds to conventional others deter youth from delinquency. Hirschi investigates youth's attachment to parents as a major element in conventional socialization. In this influential chapter Hirschi details the nature of the parental attachment bond and suggests its importance in deterring delinquency.

Simons, Lin, and Gordon examine the connection between young men's early socialization experience and family environment and their subsequent involvement in dating violence. Because family violence, either between parents or between parent and child, is often associated with children's later use of intimate violence, researchers have long assumed that children are modeling the violent behavior of their parents in later intimate situations. Simons et al. suggest an alternate explanation in which dating violence is part of a general antisocial behavior pattern.

Trina Hope examines the familial influence on youth's gang membership. Gang membership previously has been found to be associated with prior delinquency (see the Esbensen and Huizinga piece in the Peers and Delinquency chapter) and with disrupted family situations. Using self-report data on junior high and high school students, Hope examines the relative impact of family characteristics on the respondents' level of self-control, delinquency, and gang membership. Trina Hope's article offers important insight into the family's effect on one's self-control, delinquency, and gang membership.

Attachment to Parents

Travis Hirschi

Control theory assumes that the bond of affection for conventional persons is a major deterrent to crime. The stronger this bond, the more likely the person is to take it into account when and if he contemplates a criminal act. The ability to take something into account, however, suggests the corollary ability to do something about it, and crimes are of course committed in the face of strong attachments to conventional others. Yet the attached person, by his greater efforts to avoid detection and by his unwillingness to take the risks the unattached freely takes, proves the potency of his attachment even as he commits the crime. In fact, when detection is certain, the attached person may hit upon unusual means for preventing those whose opinion he values from gaining knowledge of his act: "I intend to kill my wife after I pick her up from work. I don't want her to have to face the embarrassment that my actions will surely cause her."[1]

A persistent image in delinquency theory is that of a child *already* without a family—at least without a family whose unhappiness is of concern to him. Like most such images, this one contains much that is true. Since most delinquent acts are committed outside the home, since few delinquencies are committed at parental urging, and since most detected acts cause parents embarrassment and/or inconvenience, it is not surprising that an image of the delinquent as not only physically but emotionally free of his parents has developed.

But a social vacuum is abhorrent to theories based on the assumption that the delinquent act is "positively" motivated.[2] If behavior is normatively oriented, if man requires social support for his actions, then there must be others who are willing to praise and reward that which parents condemn. As a consequence, in most sociological theories of delinquency the gang rushes in to fill the void created by estrangement from parents. The incontestable fact that most delinquent acts are committed with companions is taken as evidence supporting this view. Walter C. Reckless goes so far as to say: "There is almost every reason to admit that companionship is one of the most important, universal causes of crime and delinquency among males."[3] But the link between "companionship" and delinquency is still

[1]Charles Joseph Whitman, quoted by *Newsweek*, August 15, 1966.

[2]Muzafer Sherif and Carolyn W. Sherif, *Reference Groups: Explorations into Conformity and Deviation of Adolescents* (New York: Harper and Row, 1964), especially pp. 271–273.

[3]Walter C. Reckless, *The Crime Problem*, 3rd ed. (New York: Appleton-Century-Crofts, 1961) p. 311.

a matter of dispute, and the Gluecks, unimpressed by a mountain of sociological theory and research, and by their own data which shows a strong relation between delinquency and the delinquency of companions, could still argue that boys become delinquents *before* they choose their companions.[4]

And, indeed, studies of neglected children, of the psychopathic personality, appear to support the Gluecks' view. They suggest that the capacity to form attachments to others may be generally impaired so that the child who feels nothing for his parents is less likely to feel anything for anyone else. They suggest that the freedom that severance of the bonds to family creates is *not* immediately lost by being swallowed up in a new group, that there are those outside the "web of group affiliations" who have in some sense lost the capacity to belong. Delinquents may be with other boys when they commit their delinquent deeds, but this does not necessarily mean that these acts are a response to pressures emanating from a moral community.

For that matter, no good evidence has been produced to show that attachment to peers is actually conducive to delinquency. Unless delinquent behavior is valued among adolescents, there is no reason to believe that attachments to other adolescents should produce results different from those obtaining from attachments to conventional *adults*. Predictions about the effects of peer attachments thus hinge on the assumed conventionality or nonconventionality of peers. If the peer "culture" requires delinquent behavior, then presumably attachment would foster conformity—that is, delinquency. However, if the peer culture is identical to the conventional culture, then attachment to persons within this culture should foster conformity to conventional standards.

No such ambiguity adheres in predictions about the effect of attachments to teachers and the school. Teachers, by inclination and law, espouse conventional standards. Here, again, however, the question of the extent of carry-over from attitudes toward parents to attitudes toward teachers is of interest, as is the question of the relative importance of attachments to persons variously located in conventional society.

In this and following chapters, I examine attachments to parents, teachers, and peers. Although I shall devote much of the analysis to factors affecting attachment (and some to the effects of attachment on other elements of the bond to conventional society), the burden of the argument rests on the relations between the various attachments and delinquency. I shall begin by assuming that all "others" are conventional and only later investigate the effects of attachment to persons not conforming to the conventional model.

ATTACHMENT TO CONVENTIONAL PARENTS

Although denied in some theories and ignored in others, the fact that delinquents are less likely than nondelinquents to be closely tied to their parents is one of the best documented findings of delinquency research.[5] As is true with most well-established relations in the field of delinquency, there are many ways of accounting for this relation.

[4]Sheldon and Eleanor Glueck *Unraveling Juvenile Delinquency* (Cambridge, Mass.: Harvard University Press, 1950), p. 164.

[5]*Ibid.*, especially Chapter 11; F. Ivan Nye, *Family Relationships and Delinquent Behavior* (New York: Wiley, 1958), Chapter 8.

In the light of the cultural deviance perspective, the child unattached to his parents is simply more likely to be exposed to "criminogenic influences." He is, in other words, more likely to be free to take up with a gang. His lack of attachment to his parents is, in itself, of no moral significance.[6]

Strain theory appears to have particular difficulty with the relation between attachment to parents and delinquency, and it is therefore largely ignored by strain theorists.[7] (If, for example, there are systematic differences in the adequacy of socialization between social classes, then no differences in pressures to deviate are required to explain the differential rates of deviation.)

It is in control theory, then, that attachment to parents becomes a central variable, and many of the variations in explanations of this relation may be found within the control theory tradition. Perhaps the major focus of attention has been on the link between attachment and the adequacy of socialization, the internalization of norms. As is well known, the emotional bond between the parent and the child presumably provides the bridge across which pass parental ideals and expectations.[8] If the child is alienated from the parent, he will not learn or will have no feeling for moral rules, he will not develop an adequate conscience or superego.[9] Among those with a more psychoanalytic orientation, actual separation from the parent, especially the mother, is held to be more serious than lack of attachment to a physically present mother.[10] In fact, the maternal deprivation hypothesis has received endorsement reminiscent of that granted feeble-mindedness hypotheses in the early years of the twentieth century: ". . . on the basis of this varied evidence it appears that there is a very strong case indeed for believing that prolonged separation of a child from his mother (or mother-substitute) during the first five years of life stands foremost among the causes of delinquent character development and persistent misbehaviour."[11]

Like the feeble-mindedness hypothesis, this form of the maternal deprivation hypothesis can take little comfort from quantitative research based on reasonably large samples of noninstitutional popula-

---

[6]Edwin H. Sutherland and Donald R. Cressey, *Principles of Criminology*, 7th ed. (Philadelphia: Lippincott, 1966), especially pp. 225–228.

[7]Robert K. Merton suggests that persons in the social class with the highest rate of crime tend to be inadequately socialized. However, Cloward and Ohlin are more consistent in this regard and explicitly deny variations in the adequacy of socialization as a cause of delinquency. For Merton's position, see *Social Theory and Social Structure* (New York: The Free Press, 1957), p. 141. One of the clearest statements in the literature with respect to the varying assumptions of the strain, cultural deviance, and control theories on this point may be found in Richard A. Cloward and Lloyd E. Ohlin, *Delinquency and Opportunity* (New York: The Free Press, 1960), p. 106.

[8]David G. McKinley, *Social Class and Family Life* (New York: The Free Press, 1964), p. 57. McKinley argues that the higher the status of the parent, the stronger the emotional bond between the parent and the child.

[9]Nye, *Family Relationships*, p. 71; William McCord and Joan McCord, *Origins of Crime* (New York: Columbia University Press, 1959), pp. 198–199.

[10]Kate Friedlander, *The Psycho-Analytical Approach to Juvenile Delinquency* (New York: International Universities Press, 1947), p. 70.

[11]John Bowlby, *Forty-Four Juvenile Thieves* (London: Bailliero, Tindall and Cox, 1946), p. 41, quoted by Barbara Wootton in *Social Science and Social Pathology* (New York: Macmillan, 1959), p. 137. Wootton's treatment of the maternal separation studies is clearly "devastating"—but it is difficult to imagine any kind of social research that would satisfy the criteria of evaluation she uses. If the results are consistent and reasonably conclusive, Wootton does not hesitate to conclude that "homely truths" are lurking behind a "pretentious scientific facade."

tions. McCord and McCord[12] and Nye[13] both report no difference in delinquent behavior between those whose homes were broken before five years of age and those whose homes were broken later. And in the present data those living with both parents prior to age five are just as likely to have committed delinquent acts as children separated from one or both parents during this period.[14]

Explanation of the effects of attachment to the parents on delinquent behavior by reference to the internalization of norms (or, as is common in social control theories, by reference to "internal" or "personal" control)[15] creates difficulties in explaining variations in delinquent activity over time. If the conscience is a relative constant built into the child at an early age, how do we explain the increase in delinquent activity in early adolescence and the decline in late adolescence? It is also easy to slip into mere tautology when the locus of control is placed inside the person. Reiss, for example, defines personal control as "the ability of the individual to refrain from meeting needs in ways which conflict with the norms and rules of the community." After relating psychiatric classifications to rates of recidivism, Reiss concludes that his *observations* show "that delinquent recidivists are less often persons with mature ego ideals or nondelinquent social roles and appropriate

and flexible rational controls which permit the individual to guide action in accord with non-delinquent group expectations."[16] Given commonly accepted meanings of the terms in this statement, it could never be shown to be false. In fact, explanation of the recidivism of those delinquents with mature ego ideals and nondelinquent social roles is virtually ruled out. The only way their recidivism can be explained is to admit error in the psychiatric classifications. In other words, the explanation is beyond the reach of empirical observation.

These difficulties are avoided if we ignore internalization and assume that the moral element in attachment to parents resides directly in the attachment itself. If the bond to the parent is weakened, the probability of delinquent behavior increases; if this bond is strengthened, the probability of delinquent behavior declines. Attachment may easily be seen as *variable* over persons and over time for the same person.

There are many elements of the bond to the parent, all of which may not be equally important in the control of delinquent behavior. Let us therefore look more closely at the process through which attachment to the parent presumably works against the commission of delinquent acts.

The child attached to his parents may be less likely to get into situations in which delinquent acts are possible, simply because he spends more of his time in their presence. However, since most delinquent acts require little time, and since most adolescents are frequently exposed to situations potentially definable as opportunities for delinquency, the amount of time spent with parents would probably be only a minor factor in delinquency prevention. So-called "direct control" is not, except as a

---

[12]McCord and McCord, *Origins of Crime*, p. 83.

[13]Nye, *Family Relationships*, p. 47.

[14]In a book first published in 1953, Bowlby states that there is "no room for doubt" about the proposition that "prolonged maternal deprivation" causes severe psychiatric disturbance (John Bowlby, *Child Care and the Growth of Love* [Baltimore: Penguin Books, 1963], p. 50).

[15]Nye, *Family Relationships*, pp. 5–6; Albert J. Reiss, Jr., "Delinquency as the Failure of Personal and Social Controls," *American Sociological Review*, XVI (1951), 196–207.

[16]*Ibid.*, pp. 196 and 204.

limiting case, of much substantive or theoretical importance.[17] The important consideration is whether the parent is psychologically present when temptation to commit a crime appears. If, in the situation of temptation, no thought is given to parental reaction, the child is to this extent free to commit the act.

Which children are most likely to ask themselves, "What will my parents think?" Those who think their parents know where they are and what they are doing. Two items on the questionnaire bear directly on such virtual supervision: "Does your mother (father) know where you are when you are away from home?" And, "Does your mother (father) know whom you are with when you are away from home?" The response categories were: "Usually," "Sometimes," and "Never." The two mother items, which correlated .59, were combined, equally weighted, so that the mothers of boys obtaining a score of 4 "usually" know where they are and whom they are with. The relation between this index of supervision and self-reported delinquency is shown in Table 1.

The skewness of the distribution evident in the bottom row of Table 1, together with hindsight, suggests that the boys should have been allowed to report that their mothers "almost always" know where they are and whom they are with, since the majority of boys in the sample are, according to this measure, well and equally supervised. Even so, the range of virtual supervision present in the table is sufficient to produce marked variation in delinquent activity: children who perceive their parents as unaware of their whereabouts

TABLE 1:	Self-Reported Delinquency by Mother's Virtual Supervision (in percent)				
	MOTHER'S SUPERVISION				
Self-Reported Acts	Low 0	1	2	3	High 4
None	0	28	45	59	63
One	45	31	26	21	26
Two or more	55	41	29	20	12
Totals	100	100	100	100	101
	(11)	(29)	(236)	(252)	(698)

abouts are highly likely to have committed delinquent acts. Although only 11 boys say their mothers never know where they are and whom they are with, all 11 have committed delinquent acts in the year prior to administration of the questionnaire. The majority of the sample who in this sense usually have their mothers with them are much less likely to have committed delinquent acts than those who, at least sometimes, feel they have moved beyond the range of parental knowledge or interest.

We assume that the supervision illustrated in Table 1 is indirect, that the child is less likely to commit delinquent acts not because his parents actually restrict his activities, but because he shares his activities with them; not because his parents actually know where he is, but because he perceives them as aware of his location. Following this line of reasoning, we can say that the more the child is accustomed to sharing his mental life with his parents, the more he is accustomed to seeking or getting their opinion about his activities, the more likely he is to perceive them as part of his social and psychological field, and the less likely he would be to neglect their

----

[17]Items measuring the amount of time spent talking with parents, working around the house, and the like, are related to the commission of delinquent acts in the expected direction, but these relations are uniformly weak.

opinion when considering an act contrary to law—which is, after all, a potential source of embarrassment and/or inconvenience to them.

Several items on the questionnaire are appropriate as measures of the intimacy of communication between parent and child. The boys were asked: "Do you share your thoughts and feelings with your mother (father)?" And, "How often have you talked over your future plans with your mother (father)?" Independent analysis reveals that these items are sufficiently correlated to justify combining them on empirical as well as conceptual grounds. They were combined, equally weighted, such that boys with highest scores often share their thoughts and talk over their plans with their parents, while the boys with the lowest scores never have such communication with their parents. This index, which I shall call an index of intimacy of communication (A), is correlated .25 with mother's virtual supervision, and .26 with father's virtual supervision.[18]

A second index of intimacy of communication (B), distinguished from the first by the fact that the flow of communication is from the parent to the child rather than from the child to the parent, was constructed from the following items: "When you don't know why your mother (father) makes a rule, will she explain the reason?" "When you come across things you don't understand, does your mother (father) help you with them?" And, "Does your mother (father) ever explain why she feels the way she does?"

As would be expected, the two indexes of intimacy of communication are strongly correlated (for mothers, the corre-

lation is .42; for fathers, .52). The second index is even more strongly correlated with virtual supervision than the first (for mothers, $r = .35$; for fathers, $r = .40$). Both indexes appear in subsequent analysis.

As Table 2 illustrates, the intimacy of communication between child and parent is strongly related to the commission of delinquent acts. Only 5 percent of the boys who often discuss their future plans and often share their thoughts and feelings with their fathers have committed two or more delinquent acts in the year prior to administration of the questionnaire, while 43 percent of those never communicating with their fathers about these matters have committed as many delinquent acts. As reported earlier, however, those who spend much time talking with their parents are only slightly less likely than those who spend little time talking with their parents to have committed delinquent acts. All of which suggests that it is not simply the fact of communication with the parents but the focus of this communication that is crucial in affecting the likelihood that the child will recall his parents when and if a situation of potential delinquency arises.

If we assume that the child considers the reaction of his parents, he must then ask himself a further question: "Do I care what my parents will think?" Most studies of the effects of parent-child relations concentrate on this second question. Thus affectional identification, love, or respect is taken as the crucial element of the bond to the parent. Even if the child does in effect consider the opinion of his parents, he may conclude that parental reaction is not sufficiently important to deter him from the act (given, of course, a certain risk of detection). This conclusion is presumably more likely the less the child cares for his parents.

Since most items measuring aspects of parent-child relations reflect to some extent the favorability of the child's attitudes

---

[18]Each index is constructed separately for each parent. The correlations are thus between, for example, intimacy of communication with mother and mother's virtual supervision.

TABLE 2:   Self-Reported Delinquency by Intimacy of Communication (A) with Father[a] (in percent)

Self-Reported Acts	LITTLE INTIMATE COMMUNICATION			MUCH INTIMATE COMMUNICATION	
	0	1	2	3	4
None	39	55	55	63	73
One	18	25	28	23	22
Two or more	43	20	17	15	5
Totals	100	100	100	101	100
	(97)	(182)	(436)	(287)	(121)

[a]The comparable index of intimacy of communication with the mother is more badly skewed (boys are more likely to report intimate communication with the mother) and is slightly less strongly related to delinquency.

toward his parents, this dimension is both easy and difficult to measure. (The ubiquity of the favorability-unfavorability dimension may well be the reason that many analyses seem to suggest that everything the parent does "matters" with respect to delinquency.) Perhaps the best single item in the present data is: "Would you like to be the kind of person your mother (father) is?"

As affectional identification with the parents increases, the likelihood of delinquency declines (Table 3). On the basis of measures available,[19] it appears reasonable

---

[19]Indexes of emotional attachment to the father and to the mother produce relations only slightly stronger than that shown in Table 20. The items available for measuring attachment to the parents on the original questionnaire are a source of some uneasiness, since they are uniformly indirect. For example, the most direct items on the questionnaire are: "Does your father seem to understand you." "Have you ever felt unwanted by your father." And, "Would your father stick by you if you got into really bad trouble." (An index composed of these items, equally weighted, is used in subsequent analysis. It is called an index of attachment.) Nevertheless, in a separate study of a subsample of the students used here, Irving Piliavin asked a series of direct questions about the child's emotional attachment to his parents (for example, "Are you interested in what your father thinks of you?"). The relations between Piliavin's items and delinquency appear to be no stronger than those reported here.

to suggest that the extent and nature of communication between the parent and the child are as important as feelings of affection for the parent. We have had some indications already, however, that distinctions between the dimensions of attachment to the parent may be artificial. Let us therefore examine the joint effects of intimacy of communication and identification with the father (Table 4).

As would be expected, those who identify with their fathers tend to discuss their personal problems with them, and vice versa, with few students reporting no desire to emulate the father on the one hand and extensive intimate communication with him on the other. Even so, each of these dimensions appears to have an independent effect on the likelihood that the child will commit delinquent acts. With few exceptions, as the intimacy of communication increases, the less likely the child is to have committed delinquent acts, regardless of his identification with his father. The only boys for whom the relations do not hold quite as expected are those reporting a very high level of identification with the father. Given prevailing cultural prescriptions about the kinds of attitudes one should express toward one's parents,

TABLE 3:   Self-Reported Delinquency by Affectional Identification with the Father[a]
(in percent)

Self-Reported Acts	"WOULD YOU LIKE TO BE THE KIND OF PERSON YOUR FATHER IS?"				
	In Every Way	In Most Ways	In Some Ways	In Just a Few Ways	Not at All
None	64	65	58	48	41
One	21	24	25	30	22
Two or more	16	11	17	22	38
Totals	101	100	100	100	101
	(121)	(404)	(387)	(172)	(138)

[a]The relation between identification with the mother and delinquency is somewhat stronger than the relation shown in the table. I do not combine the items for the two parents because such a combination has little, if any, additional effect. As discussed below, part of the reason for the lack of additive effect is that the boys in the sample tend very strongly to have similar attitudes toward both parents.

TABLE 4:   Percent Committing Two or More Delinquent Acts by Index of Intimacy of Communication with Father and Identification with Father

"Like to be like father?"	INTIMACY OF COMMUNICATION				
	Low 0	1	2	3	High 4
In every way	—[a]	—	10	19	10
	(3)	(8)	(31)	(42)	(21)
In most ways	—	16	13	9	3
	(10)	(31)	(153)	(117)	(61)
In some ways	36	19	15	18	3
	(25)	(59)	(141)	(102)	(31)
In just a few ways	—	20	23	—	—
	(15)	(44)	(70)	(19)	(4)
Not at all	59	24	28	—	—
	(41)	(33)	(32)	(4)	(2)

[a]Too few cases for stable percentages.

we would expect a lower level of validity at this end of an attachment scale.

Without misevaluating the significance of the feeling of affection of the child for the parent, we can say that the psychological presence of the parent depends very much on the extent to which the child interacts with the parent on a personal basis. The idea that those committing criminal acts as often do not think of the consequences of their acts for those whose opinion they value as they do not care about the consequences of their acts is supported by these data.

Consistent with much previous research, then, the present data indicate that the closer the child's relations with his parents, the more he is attached to and identifies with them, the lower his chances of delinquency. It is argued here that the moral significance of this attachment resides directly in the attachment itself. The more strongly a child is attached to his parents, the more strongly he is bound to their expectations, and therefore the more strongly he is bound to conformity with the legal norms of the larger system.

ATTACHMENT TO UNCONVENTIONAL PARENTS

The major alternative to this explanation is found in theories of cultural deviance. According to one variant of cultural deviance theory, the values of many parents (largely in the lower class), while not explicitly criminal, are at least conducive to criminality.[20] According to a second variant of this perspective, there are areas of society in which crime is openly encouraged: "Stealing in the neighborhood was a common practice among the children and approved of by the parents."[21]

If either view is accurate, alienation from parents should not work to produce delinquency in all segments of the sample. If some parents in the sample hold criminal values, lack of attachment to them may have effects opposite to the effects of lack of attachment to conventional parents, and the effects of attachment on delinquency for the sample as a whole may be attenuated.[22] Are some children in this sample likely to be delinquent *because* they are attached to their parents?

There are several ways to approach this question.[23] We have previously identified one group of parents whose sons have relatively high rates of delinquency. This group, those who have been unemployed and/or on welfare, should also be the group in the sample most likely to be members of the "lower-class culture." Does attachment to parents in this group have less effect on—or is it actually conducive to—delinquency? Table 5 provides an ambiguous answer to the question.

Table 5 suggests that boys strongly attached to a lower-class father are as likely to be delinquent as boys weakly attached to a lower-class father, with boys moderately attached to a lower-class father somewhat less likely to commit delinquent acts. It thus appears to support both the lower-class culture thesis and the view that lack of attachment to a lower-class father is conducive to delinquency. Attachment to a father who in effect encourages delinquency is conducive to delinquency; on the other hand, alienation from such a father need not be expressed in adherence to conventional forms of conduct. In fact, the child unattached to a nonconventional father is, like the child unattached to a

---

[20]Walter B. Miller, "Lower Class Culture as a Generating Milieu of Gang Delinquency," *Journal of Social Issues*, XXIV (1958), 5–19.

[21]Cloward and Ohlin, *Delinquency and Opportunity*, p. 153, quoting C. R. Shaw, *The Jack-Roller* (Chicago: University of Chicago Press, 1930), p. 54.

[22]Nye (*Family Relationships*, p. 72) recognizes this problem but does not pursue it further. See also Martin Gold, *Status Forces in Delinquent Boys* (Ann Arbor: Institute for Social Research, 1963), pp. 40–41.

---

[23]Not the least important of which is examination of previous research on delinquency. Although they do not directly address this question, the McCords' data on type of discipline, criminality of father, and conviction for crimes may be taken to suggest that attachment to a criminal father reduces one's chances of crime (McCord and McCord, Origins of Crime, especially p. 94). The families of the Gluecks' delinquents were lower class and highly likely to have members with criminal records (67 percent of the fathers and 45 percent of the mothers), yet the Gluecks' data show strong negative relations between attachment to parents and delinquency (Glueck and Glueck, *Unraveling*, pp. 93–134). On the other hand, Hamblin, Abrahamson, and Burgess conclude that attachment to parents *fosters* delinquency among most slum youth (Robert L. Hamblin, Mark J. Abrahamson, and Robert L. Burgess, "Diagnosing Delinquency," *Trans-Action*, I [1964], 10–15).

TABLE 5: **Percent Committing Two or More Delinquent Acts[a] by Intimacy of Communication with Father and Father's Employment History/Welfare Status**

Intimacy of Communication	No History of Welfare or Unemployment	History of Welfare and/or Unemployment
High	10 (325)	25 (60)
Medium	17 (331)	17 (76)
Low	29 (193)	27 (64)

[a]The trends observable in the table hold true regardless of the point at which delinquency is dichotomized.

conventional father, free to commit delinquent acts without too much concern for the consequences.

This interpretation of Table 5 entails acceptance of the view that there is a substantial number of fathers in the sample who either approve of or are neutral to delinquency. Without denying the existence of fathers who encourage delinquency, we may still assume they are too rare to account for the results in the right-hand column of the table. By questioning one of the theories with which we interpret the data, we call the data themselves into question. Let us assume that only one cell in Table 5 is out of line. If it is the upper right-hand cell, the cultural deviance theory is disconfirmed; if it is the middle right-hand or the lower right-hand cell, the cultural deviance theory is confirmed. Since such a minor fluctuation in the data would lead to drastically different conclusions, the matter is worth pursuing further.

Let us take the lower-class culture thesis at its word. The number of persons sharing in or influenced by this culture is very large, from 40 to 60 percent of the population. Parents within this culture are not likely to be too disturbed by the delinquencies of their children because the rules being violated are those of a class to which they do not belong. In fact, since delinquency "derives from a positive effort to achieve what is valued within [the lower-class] tradition, and to conform to its ex-

plicit and implicit norms,"[24] attachment to members of the lower-class culture should foster delinquency, and lack of attachment might even foster conformity to middle-class norms, that is, nondelinquency.

Our first attempt to test this hypothesis was inconclusive, presumably because of the small number of cases in the lower-class group. Given the estimates of the size of the lower class provided by advocates of the lower-class culture thesis, however, many families in the sample in addition to the unemployed and those on welfare should be firmly lower class. We therefore returned to father's occupation as a measure of class status and reintroduced Negro boys to assure that we were dealing with a group sufficiently low in class status to provide a reasonable test of the hypothesis (Table 6).

The message in Table 6 is clear: regardless of the class or racial status of the parent, the closer the boy's ties to him, the less likely he is to commit delinquent acts. We may infer, then, that those lower-class boys committing delinquent acts are not finding support for their actions from their parents or from their "class culture." If alienation from lower-class parents is conducive to delinquency, as the table clearly shows it is, then Sykes and Matza's argument against the view that delinquency

---

[24]Miller, "Lower Class Culture," p. 19.

TABLE 6:   Percent Committing Two or More Delinquent Acts by Intimacy of Communication with Father, Race, and Father's Occupation—Boys Living with Real Father

FATHER'S OCCUPATION	INTIMACY OF COMMUNICATION	RACE			
		Negro		White	
Unskilled labor	High	12	(43)	10	(48)
	Medium	20	(66)	14	(68)
	Low	28	(57)	25	(41)
Semi- and skilled labor	High	15	(63)	11	(164)
	Medium	15	(39)	19	(179)
	Low	21	(35)	31	(100)
White collar	High	—[a]	(15)	19	(58)
	Medium	—	(16)	16	(77)
	Low	—	(9)	39	(28)
Professional	High	—	(16)	8	(109)
	Medium	—	(7)	13	(94)
	Low	—	(6)	22	(58)

[a]Too few cases for stable percentages.

springs from deviant class values is supported: "There is a strong likelihood that the family of the delinquent will agree with respectable society that delinquency is wrong, even though the family may be engaged in a variety of illegal activities."[25]

ATTACHMENT AND EXPOSURE TO CRIMINAL INFLUENCES

A second approach to the cultural deviance perspective on the effects of attachment involves a choice between intervening variables. In control theory, lack of attachment to the parents is directly conducive to delinquency because the unattached child does not have to consider the consequences of his actions for his relations with his parents. In cultural deviance theory, in contrast, lack of attachment to the parents merely increases the probability that the child will be exposed to criminal influences, that he will learn the attitudes, values, and skills conducive to delinquency. Being free of parental control is not enough to produce delinquency; a learning process must intervene: "If the family is in a community in which there is no pattern of theft, the children do not steal, no matter how much neglected or how unhappy they may be at home."[26]

It would perhaps be difficult to find a community in which there was no pattern of theft, and therefore difficult directly to falsify this proposition. However, this proposition assumes that certain experiences must intervene if attachment to the family is to influence delinquent conduct. If we can measure some of these experiences, we can determine whether they

[25]Gresham M. Sykes and David Matza, "Techniques of Neutralization: A Theory of Delinquency," *American Sociological Review*, XXII (1957), 665.

[26]Sutherland and Cressey, *Principles of Criminology*, p. 227.

affect the influence of attachment to parents on the likelihood the child will *steal*.[27]

If it is true that lack of attachment to parents has no direct effect on delinquency, then among those whose exposure to "criminal influences" is identical, the effects of attachment to parents should be considerably reduced, if not eliminated. In Chapter VIII the influence of peers on delinquent conduct is examined in some detail. Suffice it to show here that, as cultural deviance theory predicts (and as control theory also predicts), the delinquency of one's friends is strongly related to one's own record of delinquent conduct.

Table 7 indicates that three-fourths of those boys with four or more close friends who have been picked up by the police have themselves committed delinquent acts in the previous year, while only slightly more than one-fourth of those with no delinquent friends have committed delinquent acts during the same period. Percentaged in the other direction, the table would show that of those boys committing two or more delinquent offenses 82 percent have had at least one close friend picked up by the police, while only 34 percent of

those committing no delinquent acts have delinquent friends.[28]

The magnitude of this relation adds plausibility to the thesis that exposure to criminal influences must intervene if lack of attachment to the parent is to result in delinquency. However, a direct test of this hypothesis requires that we examine the effects of attachment to parents and "criminal influences" simultaneously, as in Table 8.

With respect to the issue at hand, Table 8 supports control theory. Regardless of the delinquency of his friends, the child attached to his father is less likely to commit delinquent acts. Among those with no delinquent friends and among those with several delinquent friends, the weaker the attachment to the father, the greater the likelihood of delinquency.[29]

We should not allow selective emphasis to take us too far from the data,

---

[27]Four of the six items in the self-report index involve theft.

[28]In calculating these percentages, I have excluded the boys who had no knowledge of their friends' contacts with the police.

[29]Gary Jensen has examined the relation between attachment to parents and delinquency with much more extensive controls for "criminal influences" and "definitions favorable to violation of law" than those used here—with the same result: attachment to parents has an independent effect on the commission of delinquent acts.

TABLE 7: Self-Reported Delinquency by Friends' Contacts with the Police (in percent)

Self-Reported Acts	"HAVE ANY OF YOUR CLOSE FRIENDS EVER BEEN PICKED UP BY THE POLICE?"					
	No	One	Two	Three	Four or More	Don't Know
None	73	51	41	32	25	61
One	20	27	37	24	30	24
Two or more	7	21	21	44	45	15
Totals	100	99	99	100	100	100
	(520)	(164)	(99)	(62)	(208)	(227)

TABLE 8:   Percent Committing Two or More Delinquent Acts by Intimacy of Communication with Father and Delinquency of Friends

Intimacy of Communication	NUMBER OF FRIENDS PICKED UP BY POLICE		
	None	One-Two	Three or More
High	4 (190)	16 (85)	30 (63)
Medium	9 (184)	22 (88)	39 (77)
Low	11 (87)	23 (53)	53 (83)

however, since in all other respects Table 8 offers impressive evidence in favor of a cultural deviance interpretation. Children unattached to their parents are much more likely to have delinquent friends (this fact is of course expectable also from a social control perspective), and delinquency of companions is strongly related to delinquency regardless of the level of attachment to the father. It is the latter fact that poses problems for control theory. It will therefore be discussed in some detail in Chapter VIII.

FATHER OR MOTHER?

The empirical evidence that the father is more important than the mother in the causation of delinquency is matched on the whole by evidence that he is less important.[30] The theoretical literature also offers us a choice.[31] As a general orientation to such problems, control theory offers little in the way of preconceptions or solutions:

although akin to psychoanalytic theory in many respects, it has not tended to develop beyond common sense (or, perhaps better, it has not gotten away from common sense) in describing the mechanisms through which relations with parents affect the morality of the child. As a consequence, research from within the control tradition on the relative importance of the father and the mother in the causation of delinquency has been radically empirical. The general strategy is to compare the effects on delinquency of attitudes toward the father with the effects of attitudes toward the mother, to compare the effects of the father's "role model" with the effects of the mother's "role model," and so on. The result is often a long list of complicated, ostensibly empirical conclusions. For example: "Maternal and paternal passivity differ in their relationships to criminality. Maternal passivity is similar in effect to maternal neglect. Paternal passivity resembles paternal warmth in its relation to crime."[32]

Since almost all items used in the present study were repeated for both parents, it would be easy to address again the question of the relative importance of

---

[30]McCord and McCord, *Origins of Crime*, p. 116; Nye, *Family Relationships*, p. 156; Robert G. Andry, "Parental Affection and Delinquency," *The Sociology of Crime and Delinquency*, ed. Marvin E. Wolfgang et al. (New York: Wiley, 1962), pp. 342–352.

[31]Gold, *Status Forces*, pp. 39–41; Talcott Parsons, "Age and Sex in the Social Structure of the United States," in *Essays in Sociological Theory* (New York: The Free Press, 1954), pp. 89–103.

---

[32]McCord and McCord, *Origins of Crime*, p. 116.

parents using procedures widely used in the past. However, the ultimate complication and ambiguity of the conclusions of these studies suggest the need for a modified approach.

Nye concludes that "the father's behavior is more often significantly related to delinquent behavior than is the behavior of mothers," but he suggests that this is a consequence of greater variation in paternal behavior and thus does not reflect greater intrinsic importance of the paternal role.[33] Given the interrelations among Nye's independent variables, it is possible that he simply measured items relevant to the father more often than he measured items relevant to the mother. For that matter, one strong mother item would swamp numerous father items and make attitudes toward the mother easily more important than attitudes toward the father. The hypothesis Nye offers to explain the greater apparent importance of fathers, that the greater homogeneity of mothers' role definitions accounts for the relative absence of significant relations between their behavior and delinquency, is not supported by his own data, since on most items the variation for mothers is as great as that for fathers.[34]

One way to avoid counting the number of significant relations, many of which may duplicate each other, is to compare the overall effects of a variety of mother items with the overall effects of the same father items. If we select the items important for both the father and the mother, this comparison should be meaningful, at least within the context of the data at hand. We have previously seen that supervision by the mother and the intimacy of communication with and attachment to the father are importantly related to delinquency. An index of disciplinary techniques used by the parents should also be included, since discipline has "obvious" connections to delinquency, and analysis not reported has shown that it is weakly but tenaciously related to delinquency.[35] When these items are simultaneously related to delinquency separately for the father and mother, the results are those shown in Tables 9 and 10.[36]

For present purposes, the important statistic in Tables 9 and 10 is the coefficient of multiple correlation, R. For the mother items, it is .35, for the father items, .33. For all practical and theoretical purposes, the

---

[33]Nye, *Family Relationships*, p. 156.

[34]Gold (*Status Forces*, pp. 129–137) also argues that relations with the father are more important than those with the mother in the control of delinquency. I think it fair to say that Gold's data offer, at best, very weak evidence in favor of this position.

[35]Items included in the index are: "Do your parents ever punish you by slapping or hitting you?" "By not letting you do things you want to do?" "By calling you bad names?" And, "By nagging or scolding you?"

As is now expected, the use of any disciplinary technique is *positively* related to delinquent behavior. Since the application of "negative sanctions," from slapping by the mother to imprisonment by the state, generates an empirical relation which suggests that the effort at control has the effect opposite of that intended, some recent writers have reached the conclusion that the "real" purpose of punishment is to generate that which it is ostensibly designed to prevent. See, for example, Kai T. Erikson, "Notes on the Sociology of Deviance," *The Other Side*, ed. Howard S. Becker (New York: The Free Press, 1964), pp. 9–21.

[36]The analytic technique producing Tables 9 and 10, which I use occasionally throughout the study, is discussed in Appendix B. The partial regression coefficients show the linear effect of an independent variable on delinquency when the effects of the other variables included in the table have been removed. Thus, for example, in Table 9, a change in age of one year produces an average increase of .05 in the number of delinquent acts, regardless of intimacy of communication with mother, attachment to mother, and so on.

TABLE 9:   **Self-Reported Delinquency and Selected Mother Items—Boys Living
with Real Father and Real Mother**

| | | PARTIAL REGRESSION COEFFICIENTS | |
VARIABLE	ZERO-ORDER CORRELATIONS	Raw	Normalized
Intimacy of communication (A)	−.17	−.06	−.06
Intimacy of communication (B)	−.22	−.04	−.05
Attachment	−.22	−.08	−.11
Supervision	−.27	−.24	−.20
Disciplinary techniques used	+.11	+.05	+.07
Age	+.09	+.05	+.08
Number of siblings	+.11	+.06	+.09

(R = .35) Number of cases = 955

conclusion that attitudes toward and relations with the mother and the father are equally important in the causation of delinquency appears justified. It is of course true that we can reach no final answer to this question, since it is possible that some item not included may differentiate markedly between the parents. However, since the items included are those upon which theory has traditionally focused, and since experience shows that the point of diminishing returns is reached very rapidly in this kind of analysis,[37] the conclusion of no difference would seem adequate.

---

[37] ". . . in general, the increase in the multiple correlation which results from adding variables beyond the first five or six is very small" (Quinn McNemar, *Psychological Statistics* [New York: Wiley, 1949], p. 163). In the present case, we have already reached the point of rapidly diminishing returns, since the second index of intimacy of communication contributes very little. Of course, as McNemar adds, if we were to add variables that were much more highly correlated with delinquency and/or variables having small relations with those already used, this statement would not apply. There are no parental items in the present data more highly correlated with delinquency than those used, and we would not expect to find important parental items having small relations with those already included in the analysis.

A more important question, especially with respect to control theory, is whether attachment to *a* parent is as efficacious as attachment to both parents in preventing delinquent conduct. It may be, for example, that the boy strongly attached to his mother is unlikely to be delinquent regardless of his feelings toward his father; it may be that strong attachment to both parents adds little in the way of control. If true, this would help explain the fact that the one-parent family is virtually as efficient a delinquency controlling institution as the two-parent family, contrary to expectations deriving from "direct control" hypotheses. The solution to this problem would appear to be straightforward: we examine the combined effects of attachments to the father and the mother to determine whether there is an increment over the effects of attachment to a single parent.

The multiple correlation of all of the items in Tables 9 and 10 with delinquency is .36. Since we began with a multiple correlation between the mother items and delinquency of .35, the conclusion that knowing attitudes toward both parents adds *nothing* to our ability to predict delinquency is inescapable. (The multiple

TABLE 10: Self-Reported Delinquency and Selected Father Items—Boys Living with Real Father and Real Mother

VARIABLE	ZERO-ORDER CORRELATIONS	PARTIAL REGRESSION COEFFICIENTS	
		Raw	Normalized
Intimacy of communication (A)	−.20	−.09	−.09
Intimacy of communication (B)	−.23	−.02	−.02
Attachment	−.24	−.08	−.11
Supervision	−.24	−.17	−.16
Disciplinary techniques used	+.12	+.04	+.07
Age	+.09	+.05	+.08
Number of siblings	+.12	+.06	+.08

(R = .33) Number of Cases = 940

correlation cannot decline when additional variables are added. Thus some increment is eventually a logical necessity.) This conclusion, despite its statistical correctness, appears to be in direct conflict with common sense. Suppose, for example, a boy loves his mother and hates his father; suppose his relations with one parent are warm and intimate while his relations with the other are cold and distant. Surely it seems reasonable to think that it would help to know these facts—they would, after all, lead to opposite predictions. Although this argument sounds plausible, it contains errors of assumption and fact.

TABLE 11: Correlations Between Father and Mother Items[a]

Index	Correlation
Intimacy of communication (A)	.75
Intimacy of communication (B)	.77
Attachment	.74
Disciplinary techniques used	.68
Supervision	.80

[a]The correlations in this table are based on 909 white boys living with their real fathers and mothers.

The argument is, after all, based on a confusion of statements of existence with statements of frequency. There are, no doubt, adolescents who love one parent and hate the other, but, however true this may be, it tells us virtually nothing about the frequency of such discrepancies. In fact, adolescents whose attitudes toward and relations with one parent differ markedly from those with the other parent are very rare (Table 11). The correlations in Table 11 show why, on statistical grounds, knowledge of attitudes toward both parents adds little to our ability to predict delinquency. In most cases, to know attitudes toward one parent is to know attitudes toward the other, at least with respect to those attitudes relevant to delinquency.[38]

---

[38]I have attempted by several methods to determine whether attitudes toward the father and the mother interact in their effects on delinquency. The results have been consistently negative. (On the basis of previous research, it is plausible to guess that the weaker the attachment to one parent, the more important is attachment to the other. The differences I have found point in this direction, but they are too small to merit attention.)

These correlations, and the corollary finding that the multiple correlation based on both parents is for all intents and purposes equal to the multiple correlation based on a single parent, suggest that research systematically comparing the effects of attitudes toward the mother with those of attitudes toward the father without ever asking how these attitudes are related to each other may be seriously misleading.[39] It is not surprising that such analysis can produce differences between the father and the mother that "make sense" with respect to delinquency. We could do the same by comparing Tables 9 and 10: these tables show that supervision by the mother is "more important" than supervision by the father; that intimacy of communication with the father is more important than intimacy of communication with the mother; and so on. Although in these cases the differences may not be statistically significant, eventually such differences would of necessity appear.

Since we assume that in considering a delinquent act the child takes into account the reactions of his parents, we naturally assume that he takes into account the reaction of each parent. But the latter requires a calculus of pleasure beyond the grasp of man. Compare the potential delinquent's situation with that of the professor assigning grades in a course. The grade assigned (the delinquent act) will normally be correlated with each of the measures of performance gathered during the term. However, as the diminishing returns problem in multiple correlation suggests, given

enough measures of performance (all more or less highly correlated with each other), it is conceivable that some will add nothing to the explained variance in final grades. It would then be correct to say that these particular measures of performance did not "count." Given the fixed and limited values of his final grades, and given the limitations on his capacities to consider simultaneously the various bits of information available to him, there was simply more information available to the professor than he could use. If the professor, in the quiet of his study, with time to consider and weigh alternatives, and with several options open to him, cannot assure us that he will "count" the first midterm, why should we expect the adolescent, who has vague fears in place of concrete scores, who has to decide in a matter of moments which course of action to take, who may experience pressures against his better judgment, and the like, to "count" his father?

We should not expect this. And, in the control theory, we do not have to expect it. Relations with and attitudes toward the parents are in some sense equivalent to the professor's answer to the question, "How good a student is he, really?" Answers to this question will presumably be correlated with final grades; but if we were to break the question into component questions, we would undoubtedly quickly find components that contribute nothing additional to the final result.

The alternative is to argue that relations with parents are somehow built into the child, that crime satisfies special psychological or social needs stemming from relations with the parents. If the child has needs stemming from his relations with each parent, and if these needs must somehow be satisfied, then the personality of

[39]Although Nye does not report the relations between the mother and father items he examines, the marginal distributions in his study frequently suggest that the relations could be as strong as those reported here (see *Family Relationships*, especially pp. 74–76).

each parent will show in the actions of the child, as in these findings reported by the McCords: "Passive mothers produced high proportions of sexual criminals and traffic offenders, yet their sons did not commit crimes of violence; . . . overprotective mothers had high proportions of 'violent criminals' and traffic offenders among their sons but a very low proportion of sexual criminals."[40] Although we cannot prove that the McCords' statistically significant findings will never again appear in the literature of crime and delinquency, we can ask: Why, if A (sex crimes) is psychologically compatible with B (traffic offenses), and B is psychologically compatible with C (crimes of violence), should we not expect in the next study to find A, B, and C or A and C turning up together for both types of parents? And, we can also ask: Why, if specific crimes satisfy specific psychological needs, are persons committing any given crime much more likely than "noncriminals" to commit every other type of offense?[41]

CONCLUSION

It is thought that one reason lower-class children have high rates of delinquency is that they have little respect for and do not establish intimate ties with their parents.[42] Related to this is the view that even if the lower-class parent does command the respect and affection of his children, such ties are not as conducive to conformity as

is true for the middle-class parent simply because the "model" is himself less likely to exhibit conventional behavior.

Data bearing on the argument that lower-class children have less respect for and establish less intimate ties with their parents have been incidentally presented in this chapter. Tables 5 and 6 show a very small relation in the predicted direction: for example, in Table 5, 38 percent of the sons of those having no history of welfare or unemployment are high on intimacy of communication compared to 30 percent of the sons of those who have been on welfare or have been unemployed. These differences are about the same as those revealed by previous research.[43]

If the view that the lower-class parent is less likely to command the respect and affection of his children finds very weak support in these data, the view that even if he does command their respect and affection such ties will not be conducive to conformity receives no support at all. The child attached to a low-status parent is no more likely to be delinquent than the child attached to a high-status parent.

It seems clear, then, that the lower-class parent, even if he is himself committing criminal acts, does not publicize this fact to his children. Since he is as likely to express allegiance to the substantive norms of conventional society as is the middle-class parent,[44] he operates to foster obedience to a system of norms to which he himself may not conform.

---

[40]McCord and McCord, Origins of Crime, p. 151.

[41]For evidence of the versatility of delinquents, see Albert K. Cohen, *Delinquent Boys* (New York: The Free Press, 1955), pp. 29–30. There is, to be sure, much evidence of versatility in the present data.

[42]Gold, *Status Forces*, pp. 124, 136; McKinley, *Social Class and Family Life*, p. 57.

---

[43]*Gold, Status Forces*, pp. 136–137.

[44]"A growing body of research has documented the higher degree of intolerance for deviant behavior among those of low education and socioeconomic position" (Stanton Wheeler, "Sex Offenses: A Sociological Critique," *Sexual Deviance*, ed. John Gagnon and William Simon [New York: Harper and Row, 1967], p. 90).

If the child does not care or think about the reaction of his parents, their control over him is seriously reduced. While we have emphasized that the child may not care about the reaction of his parents, the data appear to emphasize that he may not think about their reaction. In the ideal control situation, parents are the center of a communication network that is staffed by adult authorities, relatives, neighbors, other children, and the child himself. A traditional explanation of the ineffectiveness of disorganized areas in controlling deviant behavior emphasizes their anonymity, the failure of adult authorities, relatives (who are back in the old country or back on the farm), and neighbors to communicate relevant information to the parents. This factor is undoubtedly important in determining the overall rate of delinquency in an area. Within the context of the present data, however, the decisive links in this communication network are those between parent and child. If the child does not communicate with his parents, if he does not tell them of his activities, then he does not have to concern himself with their imagined reactions to his behavior. If, by the same token, they do not tell him how they feel about his behavior, this too frees him from an important source of potential concern. He can act in the present without

worrying about reenacting the scene at some later date before a possibly disapproving audience; today's play, in other words, will at no time in the future be reviewed.[45]

In the next Chapter I look at the effects on delinquency of performance in and attitudes toward the school. For now, it is worth mentioning that the child doing poorly in school is less likely to report close communication with his parents. We could explain this relation by noting that some families are less intellectual or, at least, less verbal than others. While there may be something to this argument, it is also a fact that we are all more willing to pass on to others our successes as opposed to our failures. Success in the wider world may thus serve to raise the level of intimate, personal communication within the family; failure may serve to retard it. Thus the power of the family as a controlling agency may at least partially depend on the school performance of the child.

---

[45]For a study of communication between delinquents and adults outside the family that suggests similar conclusions, see James F. Short, Jr., Harvey Marshall, and Ramon J. Rivera, "Significant Adults and Adolescent Adjustment: An Exploratory Study," *Journal of Research in Crime and Delinquency*, IV (1967).

Socialization in the Family of Origin and Male Dating Violence:

A Prospective Study

Ronald L. Simons, Kuei-Hsiu Lin, and Leslie C. Gordon

Evidence from a variety of studies indicates that physical violence occurs in at least 20% of all dating relationships (Arias, Samios, & O'Leary, 1987; Riggs, O'Leary, & Breslin, 1990; Sigelman, Berry, & Wiles, 1984; White & Koss, 1991). Although most of this aggression consists of pushing, grabbing, or slapping, from 1% to 3% of participants in college samples report that they have experienced severe forms of aggression such as beatings or assaults with an object (Arias et al., 1987; Makepeace, 1981, 1986; Riggs, 1993; Riggs et al., 1990; Sigelman et al., 1984). Research indicates that males and females are equally likely to engage in dating violence. However, women are at much greater risk than men for sustaining injuries from dating aggression (Arias et al., 1987; Bookwala, Frieze, Smith, & Ryan, 1992; Makepeace, 1986; Riggs, 1993; Stets & Pirog-Good, 1987; Sugarman & Hotaling, 1989).

The study of dating violence is important for two reasons. First, such behavior often results in physical and emotional

injury. Makepeace (1986), for example, found that 50% of female college students who experienced dating aggression sustained physical injuries as a result of the assault. Second, there is reason to believe that dating violence is often a precursor to spousal abuse. Many battered women report that they were first assaulted by their husband during courtship (Kelly & Loesch, 1983; Roscoe & Benaske, 1985). Thus research on dating violence may further our understanding of the etiology of marital violence.

The most popular explanation for dating violence is that it is a learned behavior acquired in the family of origin. Witnessing parents' marital aggression or being the victim of harsh corporal punishment may greatly increase the chances that a child will grow up to use violence in dating relationships. Although this idea is widely accepted, investigations of the hypothesis have provided mixed results. Such inconsistent findings may be a consequence of methodological deficiencies inherent in much of the prior research. In the study presented here, we specify three avenues whereby parental behavior might increase an adolescent's risk for dating violence. In an effort to avoid the limitations

Journal of Marriage and the Family, 60 (May 1998): 467–478. Copyrighted 1998 by the National Council on Family Relations, 3989 Central Ave. NE, Suite 550, Minneapolis, MN 55421. Reprinted by permission.

associated with previous studies, we use parent and child reports and a prospective design to evaluate the adequacy of these three hypotheses regarding experiences in the family of origin and dating aggression.

PARENTAL BEHAVIOR AND DATING VIOLENCE

Researchers usually specify observational learning as the process whereby parents influence the probability that their children will be violent in intimate relationships. Some describe the learning process as one of imitation; others emphasize lessons about the legitimacy of violence in intimate relationships. The imitation explanation asserts that children learn about romantic relationships by observing interactions between their parents. Children exposed to violent parental interaction learn that aggression is a normal part of romantic relationships, and as adults they are likely to engage in such behavior when interacting with a dating partner. Although some studies have reported that childhood exposure to violence between parents increases the probability of dating aggression (Foo & Margolin, 1995; O'Keefe, Brockopp, & Chew, 1986). others have failed to find an association (Bernard & Bernard, 1983; Follete & Alexander, 1992; Riggs & O'Leary, 1996; Sigelman et al., 1984).

Although some researchers have advanced the imitation idea that adolescents who witnessed their parents hit each other are apt to engage in dating violence, others have proposed a broader modeling perspective. Childhood exposure to family violence, whether marital violence or harsh parenting, is seen as providing lessons that facilitate aggression toward romantic partners (O'Leary, 1988; Strauss, Gelles, & Steinmetz, 1980; Strauss & Smith, 1990). Strauss et al., for example, argued that

both harsh physical discipline and marital violence teach children that it is legitimate, indeed often necessary, to hit those you love. Thus, exposure to any form of family violence is seen as promoting attitudes that increase the probability that children will grow up to behave aggressively toward a romantic partner This legitimation perspective suggests that young adults who were exposed to corporal punishment (and not simply those who witnessed interparental violence) are at risk for engaging in dating violence. Consistent with this viewpoint, there is some evidence that childhood exposure to harsh corporal punishment increases the probability of dating violence (Sigelman et al., 1984). The majority of studies, however, have failed to find this association (Foo & Margolin, 1995; O'Keefe et al, 1986; Riggs & O'Leary, 1996).

Although the imitation and legitimation perspectives are assumed to be rooted in social learning principles, both views fail to incorporate an important principle of the theory. Social learning theory maintains that individuals observe the contingencies that follow people's actions in a particular situation and then use this information to design a plan of behavior when they encounter a similar situation (Bandura, 1973, 1977). According to the theory, individuals do not simply copy or imitate the behavior of others. Rather, they emulate actions that lead to positive consequences and eschew behaviors that produce undesirable results. Even if a behavior is viewed as legitimate, it is unlikely that a person will engage in the action unless he or she perceives that it will have a positive effect.

We expect that children usually observe few, if any, positive consequences when their parents engage in violence toward each other. Persons who are slapped or shoved by their spouse are apt to respond with an emotional outburst, a threat, or violence. It seems unlikely that such exchanges would teach a child that physical violence is an effective way to get a family member to do something you want them to do. On the other hand, children often modify their behavior when faced with the threat of corporal punishment. Corporal punishment may produce residual feelings of anger or rejection, but it often produces at least a temporary change in behavior. Given this fact, children who experience corporal punishment may conclude that physical violence is sometimes a necessary and effective strategy for achieving behavioral change in family and intimate relationships.

We have seen that the imitation argument proposes that dating violence is a learned response to witnessing interparental violence and that the legitimation perspective posits that dating violence is legitimized either by witnessing interparental violence or by exposure to corporal punishment. In contrast, observational learning, as it is described in social learning theory, seems to suggest that corporal punishment increases the chances of dating violence, but witnessing interparental violence has little, if any, impact on the probability of dating violence.

Most research on the etiology of dating violence has emphasized modeling processes. However, the criminological literature suggests an alternative avenue whereby parents might increase the probability that their children will engage in aggression toward romantic partners. Studies by criminologists have shown that deviant acts tend to be correlated—individuals who engage in one type of deviant behavior tend to participate in other types, as well (e.g., Donovan & Jessor, 1985; Farrington, 1990; Jessor & Jessor, 1977; Osgood, Johnston, O'Malley, & Bachman, 1988). There is also evidence that antisocial behavior is stable over the life course (Caspi

& Moffitt, 1992; Loeber, 1982; Loeber & Le Blanc, 1990; Sampson & Laub, 1993). Those who manifest high levels of antisocial behavior at an early age are at risk for chronic delinquency during adolescence and continued reckless and irresponsible behavior during adulthood (Farrington, 1991; Loeber & Le Blanc, 1990; Patterson & Yoeger, 1993). In other words, antisocial behavior shows the characteristics of a behavior trait, a pattern of behavior that is expressed across time and situations (Allport, 1937). This body of research suggests that dating violence is likely to be an expression of a more general antisocial pattern of behavior. It indicates that persons who engage in persistent aggression toward dating partners are likely to have a history of involvement in a variety of other antisocial behaviors, as well.

If dating violence is an expression of a general antisocial orientation, how does such an orientation develop? Criminological research suggests that antisocial tendencies tend to emerge in childhood. A number of studies indicate that children are at risk for developing an antisocial pattern of behavior when they are exposed to ineffective parenting practices such as low supervision, rejection, and inconsistent discipline (Patterson, Reid, & Dishion, 1992; Sampson & Laub, 1993; Simons, Wu, Conger, & Lorenz, 1994).

Further, this research indicates that there is an increased probability that parents will engage in ineffective parenting if they have antisocial tendencies like excessive drinking, erratic work records, altercations with peers (Capaldi & Patterson, 1991; Patterson et al., 1992; Simons, Beaman, Conger, & Chao, 1993). These antisocial tendencies often include domestic violence (Fagan, Steward, & Hansen, 1983; Hotaling, Straus, & Lincoln, 1990; Simons, Wu, Johnson, & Conger, 1995; Walker, 1979). Thus antisocial parents are likely to hit each other and their children and to engage in ineffective parenting. This ineffective parenting, in turn, increases the probability that their children will grow up to engage in antisocial behavior of all sorts, including violence toward dating partners. In other words, it is a general pattern of antisocial behavior, not specific lessons regarding dating or family violence, that is transmitted across generations in violent families (Simons & Johnson, in press; Simons et al., 1995).

This criminological perspective suggests a set of hypotheses that contrasts with the modeling viewpoint that has guided most research on dating violence. First, the framework posits that it is the absence of involved and supportive parenting practices (e.g., warmth, inductive reasoning about rules, monitoring, consistent discipline), rather than either interparental aggression or corporal punishment, that places a child at risk for dating violence. The theory grants that both aggression between parents and harsh corporal punishment are likely to be inversely correlated with involved and supportive parenting, but it contends that the absence of involved and supportive parenting practices, not these other family processes, increases the probability that a child will engage in violence toward romantic partners. To the extent that this is true, neither interparental aggression nor harsh corporal punishment should be related to dating violence once the influence of involved and supportive parenting is taken into account.

Second, this theoretical perspective asserts that ineffective parenting increases the chances of dating violence because it fosters a general antisocial orientation. It suggests that adolescents who hit their dating partners are likely to be individuals with a history of conduct problems. If this

is true, delinquent behavior during early adolescence should predict subsequent dating violence, and the effect of ineffective parenting on dating violence should be indirect through its association with delinquent behavior.

Unfortunately, there has been little effort to apply this criminological perspective to the phenomenon of dating violence. There are some studies, however, that provide at least indirect support for the approach. Riggs and O'Leary (1996), for example, found that growing up in a violent family indirectly increased the probability of dating violence by promoting a generally aggressive orientation toward people. Similarly, Simons and his colleagues (1995; Simons & Johnson, in press) reported findings that indicate that marital violence tends to be an expression of a more general antisocial lifestyle and that childhood exposure to harsh parenting increases the chances that a person will engage in marital violence because individuals who experience such parenting often develop an antisocial orientation to life. This pattern of results supports the criminological perspective on dating violence if one assumes that dating and marital violence stem from the same faulty process of family socialization.

METHODOLOGICAL LIMITATIONS OF PAST RESEARCH

Past studies of the link between experiences in the family of origin and dating violence have produced contradictory findings. We believe that these inconsistent findings are explained, at least in part, by methodological problems that have plagued prior research on this topic. First, many of the studies have utilized volunteer samples. The backgrounds, attitudes, and motivations of the participants in these studies may be biased in some respects. It likely to be the case, for example, that such samples would contain few antisocial individuals. Second, and perhaps more important, most prior studies have used retrospective reports to measure family-of-origin variables. Evidence suggests that the recall of childhood events often is inaccurate (Bean, Leeper, Wallace, Sherman, & Jagger, 1979; Brewin, Andrews, & Gotlib, 1993; Cannell, 1977; Pelligrini-Hill & Ross, 1982; Robins et al., 1985). People are especially likely to have difficulty with questions that ask them to recall "how frequently" they experienced various incidents. Although reports of whether they were ever exposed to events such as corporal punishment or interparental violence may be valid, the accuracy of recollections about how often these events occurred is questionable. Unfortunately, errors in recall tend to be colored by the current attitudes and emotional state of the respondent (Baucom, Sayers, & Duhe, 1989; Lorenz, Conger, Simons, Whitbeck, & Elder, 1991; Watson & Clark, 1984). Thus angry, pugnacious people are likely to recall violent events that occurred while they were growing up, whereas cheerful, amicable individuals are apt to remember events that were happy and congenial.

This raises the possibility that correlations reported in previous studies between experiences in the family of origin and dating violence may simply be methodological artifacts produced by biases in the measurement of constructs. In an effort to avoid this problem, the study presented here employs a prospective design. Annual reports of the use of corporal punishment and marital violence were obtained from parents while their sons were in early adolescence. These parent self-reports are used to predict the boys' dating violence during late adolescence.

Prior research on the association between parental behavior and dating violence also has been compromised by the failure to include parental support and involvement (e.g., warmth and support, supervision, consistent discipline) as an explanatory variable. Some studies measure only interparental violence, others assess only harsh corporal punishment, and a few incorporate both of these constructs. None of these studies, however, has included involved and supportive parenting as a construct. This is a potentially important omission because the criminological perspective argues that, although the quality of parental involvement is correlated with interparental violence and the use of harsh corporal punishment, it is actually the level of involved and supportive parenting that is the primary determinant of child deviant behavior. Consistent with this idea, studies have reported that the association between harsh corporal punishment and child adjustment is significantly reduced or eliminated once the effect of involved and supportive parenting is taken into account (Baumrind, 1994; Rohner, Kean, & Cournoyer, 1991; Rohner, Bourque, & Elordi, 1996; Simons, Johnson, & Conger, 1994). Our study uses involved and supportive parenting, as well as harsh corporal punishment and interparental violence, to predict dating aggression.

METHODS AND PROCEDURES

Longitudinal data from 113 adolescent boys and their parents were used to test the competing hypotheses. Structural equation modeling (SEM) with a dichotomous outcome was used to examine the effect of the three parenting constructs—corporal punishment, interparental aggression, and quality of control and involvement—on dating violence. In an effort to avoid the problem of shared method variance (Bank, Dishion, Skinner, & Patterson, 1989), self-report data from the boys were used to assess dating violence, and parent self-reports were used to construct measures of the explanatory variables.

Data collected at Years 1.2, and 3 of the study were utilized as indicators for the three parental constructs. Using data collected across 3 years increased the probability that the parenting constructs represented stable patterns of conduct. The corporal punishment construct, for example, represented the persistent use of physical punishment over a 3-year period. Thus adolescent boys with high scores on this construct were not merely persons who had experienced an occasional spanking; they were individuals who had been hit, pushed, or shoved with some regularity during the 3-year period.

Information collected at Waves 4 and 5 was employed to construct a measure of dating violence. Hence the SEM analyses used measures of parental behavior collected during the first three waves of the study to predict fourth and fifth wave assessments of adolescent adjustment. This prospective approach provided a stronger test of the causal priorities assumed by the hypotheses than is afforded by cross-sectional designs.

SAMPLE

As part of study of family stress and coping, a sample of two-parent families was recruited through the cohort of all seventh-grade students in eight counties in North Central Iowa who were enrolled in public or private schools during spring, 1989.

Seventy-eight percent of eligible families agreed to participate in the study. This is comparable with the response rates reported by other studies that attempt to recruit multiple family members (Capaldi & Patterson, 1987). Substantial remuneration appears to be a requisite for obtaining the participation of multiple family members in studies involving intensive assessment procedures and multiple waves of data collection (Capaldi & Patterson, 1987). Families in our project received $250 per year for their effort, which translated into about $10 per hour for each family member's time. At Wave 1, data were obtained from 205 boys and their parents. One hundred and sixty-three of these boys and parents participated in all five waves of data collection. Because it is not possible to engage in dating violence unless one is dating, only boys who indicated that they had gone on a date were included in the analyses. This provided a sample of 113 boys.

The families in the sample lived on farms (about one third) or in small towns. All of the families were White, and their annual income ranged from zero to $135,000, with a mean of $29,642. The fathers' education ranged from 8 to 20 years, with a mean of 13.5 years. For mothers, the range was from 8 to 18 years, with a mean of 13.4 years. The fathers ranged in age from 31 to 68 years, with a median of 40 years; mothers' ages ranged from 29 to 53 years, with a median of 38 years.

PROCEDURES

Data were collected annually from families when the target child was in seventh, eighth, ninth, 10th, and 12th grades. Essentially, the same procedures and instruments were used at all five data collection points. Each wave of data collection involved two visits to each of the study families. During the first visit, each of the four family members completed a set of questionnaires focusing on family processes, individual characteristics, and socioeconomic circumstances. On average, it took approximately 2 hours to complete the first visit. Between the first and second visits, family members completed questionnaires left with them by the first interviewer. These questionnaires dealt with information concerning the extended family, the parents' developmental history, and plans for the future. Each family member was instructed to place his or her completed questionnaire in an envelope, seal it, and give it to the interviewer at the time of the second visit. During the second visit, which normally occurred within 2 weeks of the first visit, the family was videotaped while engaging in several structured interaction tasks. The videotaped data were not used in this article.

MEASURES

Corporal punishment. At Waves 1, 2, and 3, both fathers and mothers used two items adapted from the Conflict Tactics Scale (Straus et al., 1980) to self-report the extent to which they used corporal punishment when disciplining the target child. The two items were: "How often do you spank or slap [target child] when he does something wrong? When punishing [target child], how often do you hit him with a belt, paddle, or something else?" Response categories ranged along a 5-point continuum (1 = never, 3 = about half the time, and 5 = always). For both mothers and fathers, the correlation between these two items was above .45 in all three waves. The items were summed across waves to form a six-item measure of corporal punishment for each parent. Coefficient alpha was .84 for mothers and .82

for fathers. The correlation between fathers' and mothers' scores was .60. Finally, the scores for mothers and fathers were summed to form a composite measure of the extent to which the target child was exposed to corporal punishment during early adolescence.

This construct should not be interpreted as analogous to abusive parenting. This self-report measure does not allow one to assess the extent to which parental behavior meets the criteria for abuse. Presumably, in the majority of cases, the behavior of the parents would not be considered abusive. The construct should, however, be considered an indicator of a harsh, aggressive approach to discipline. Although spanking or slapping is normative during early childhood, it is less typical and more indicative of severe discipline if it continues during adolescence (Straus, 1983). The adolescents in the study were in the seventh, eighth, and ninth grades when the assessments of corporal punishment were collected. Although one of the items in the measure focused on how often the child had been "spanked or slapped," it is unlikely that the punishment merely consisted of a swat on the buttocks, as is often the case with young children. This would be an age-inappropriate and innocuous punishment for a teenager.

Marital violence. At Waves 1, 2 and 3, both husbands and wives were asked to think about times during the preceding month when they had spent time talking or doing things together and then to respond to the following question: "During the past month, how often did your spouse hit, push, grab, or shove you?" The response format ranged from 1 (*never*) to 7 (*always*), with the middle category of 4 defined as *about half the time*. The wife's report of her spouse's assaultive behavior was summed across waves to construct a measure of husband marital violence, and the husband's reports of his spouse's aggressive actions were summed to obtain a measure of wife marital violence. Coefficient alpha was .70 for violence by the husband and .89 for violence by the wife. The correlation between the two measures was .39. Husband and wife scores were summed to form a composite measure of the extent to which the target child was exposed to interparental violence during early adolescence.

Involved/supportive parenting. Involved, supportive parents show warmth and affection, demonstrate consistent discipline, engage in monitoring and supervision, and use inductive reasoning to explain rules and expectations (Amato, 1990: Maccoby & Martin, 1983; Rollins & Thomas, 1979). At Waves 1, 2, and 3, parents self-reported the extent to which they engage in these behaviors.

Parents reported on their warmth and acceptance using an eight-item scale (e.g., "I really trust my child: I experience strong feelings of love for him"). The response format for these items ranged from 1 (*strongly disagree*) to 5 (*strongly agree*). Coefficient alphas ranged from .73 to .81 across the three waves.

Parents reported on their monitoring using a four-item scale (e.g., "How often do you know who your seventh grader is with when he is away from home?"). The response format ranged from 1 (*never*) to 5 (*always*). Coefficient alpha was approximately .60 at each wave.

Parents were asked to rate their consistency of discipline using a six-item scale (e.g., "How often do you punish your ninth grader for something at one time and then at other times not punish him for the same thing?"). The response format ranged

from 1 (*never*) to 5 (*always*). Coefficient alphas ranged from .60 to .73 across the three waves.

Finally, a five-item scale was used to obtain parents' ratings of the extent to which they used inductive reasoning in the course of setting rules or disciplining their children (e.g., "How often do you discipline your child by reasoning, explaining, or talking to him?"). The response format ranged from 1 (*never*) to 5 (*always*). Coefficient alphas ranged from .75 to .81 across the three waves.

These four scales were standardized and summed across waves for both mothers and fathers. Scores for mothers correlated .78 with scores for fathers. The scores for mothers and fathers were summed to form a composite measure of involved/ supportive parenting. This total served as an indicator of the extent to which, during early adolescence, the target child experienced parenting that combined love and control.

Delinquent behavior. At Waves 1, 2, and 3, two measures were used to assess the target child's general involvement in antisocial behavior. First, the respondents completed a delinquency inventory adapted from the National Youth Survey (Elliott, Huizinga, & Ageton, 1985; Elliott, Huizinga, & Menard, 1989). This instrument asked respondents to indicate how often (0 = *never*, 5 = *five or more times*) during the preceding year they had engaged in each of 24 delinquent acts. Acts varied from relatively minor offenses such as skipping school to more serious offenses such as attacking someone with a weapon or stealing something worth more than $25. Coefficient alpha for this instrument was approximately .80 at each wave.

The second measure of antisocial behavior consisted of a substance use or abuse instrument adapted from the National Youth Survey (Elliott et al., 1985, 1989). This 24-item instrument asked respondents to report how often in the last year that they had used each of the substances (e.g., alcohol, marijuana) and the extent to which they had experienced difficulties as a result (e.g., got sick, got into a fight). The response format for the items ranged from 0 (*never*) to 5 (*six or more times*). Coefficient alpha was above .80 at each wave.

The delinquency and substance use scales were standardized and summed across waves. Scores on this composite measure indicated the extent to which the target child engaged in a variety of antisocial behaviors during early adolescence.

Dating violence. An item adapted from the Conflict Tactics Scale (Straus et al., 1980) was used to assess aggression toward a dating partner. At Waves 4 and 5, the adolescent boys were asked to think about times during the past year that they had spent talking or doing things with a girlfriend and then to respond to the following question: "When you had a disagreement with your girlfriend, how often do you hit, push, grab, or shove her?" The response format for the item ranged from 1 (*never*) to 7 (*always*), with the middle category of 4 defined as "about half the time."

RESULTS

A majority of the parents at each wave reported that they sometimes used corporal punishment to discipline the target child. Approximately 30% reported at all three waves that they had used corporal punishment during the previous year. A much smaller proportion admitted to engaging in violence toward their spouse. At each

wave, approximately 11% of the husbands said they had been hit by their wife during the preceding month; roughly 8% of wives at each wave said they had been hit by their husband during the previous month. Approximately 5% of the husbands and 3% of the wives reported that they had been hit in the preceding month at all three waves. There were not enough cases in the sample to estimate a structural equation model that treated the annual assessments of each variable as indicators of a latent construct. Therefore, we summed the three assessments for each variable to form a composite measure.

Twelve percent of the adolescent boys indicated that they had engaged in dating violence at least once. Two percent of the boys indicated that they had resorted to violence at least half of the time when they experienced a disagreement with their girlfriend. Given the skewed distribution of this construct, it was recoded to be a dichotomous variable for purposes of the correlational analyses and structural equational modeling. However, the same pattern of findings was obtained when log transformations of dating violence, rather than the dichotomous recodes, were used for the analyses.

Table 1 presents the bivariate correlations between the study constructs. There is a small but significant association between corporal punishment and marital violence, and both of these variables are negatively related to involved/supportive parenting. Both involved/supportive parenting and corporal punishment show significant correlations with delinquent behavior, which in turn, is related to dating violence. None of the parenting variables shows a significant association with dating violence, although the correlation for corporal punishment approaches significance at the .10 level. This pattern of

TABLE 1: Correlation Matrix for Study Variables

Construct	1	2	3	4	5	X̄	SD
1. Involved/supportive parenting	1.0	−.67*	−.20*	−.31*	−.06	.56	6.13
2. Corporal punishment		1.0	.14*	.25*	.12	15.50	4.32
3. Marital violence			1.0	.05	−.01	.48	1.19
4. Delinquent behavior				1.0	.28*	.26	2.35
5. Dating violence					1.0	.12	.33

Note: *n* = 113.

*$p \leq .05$.

relationships suggests that much of the impact of the parenting variables on dating violence may be indirect through delinquent behavior. Any direct influence of parental behavior on dating violence appears to be limited to the effect of corporal punishment.

Structural equation modeling (LISREL VIII; Jöreskog & Sörbom, 1989) with a dichotomous criterion variable was used to test these ideas. The families in the sample were largely working class and, therefore, represented a restricted range of socioeconomic status. Analysis showed that neither family income nor parents' level of education was related to delinquent behavior or dating violence. Hence, in an effort to save degrees of freedom, these variables were not included in the structural equation modeling. Also, the models were originally run separately by the gender of parent, and the results were virtually identical whether mother's or father's behavior was used as a predictor of adolescent behavior. Therefore, father's and mother's scores were combined to form composite measures for each of the parent constructs.

We began the structural equation modeling by running the fully recursive model. Many of the paths were near zero and had low *t* values. In an effort to obtain a more parsimonious model, paths with a *t*

of 1.0 or below were deleted, and the model was reestimated. The results for the reduced model are presented in Figure 1. The chi-square, adjusted-goodness-of-fit index, and critical *N* all indicate that the model provides a good fit to the data. The difference in chi-square (1.14, *df* = 4) between the reduced and fully recursive model does not approach statistical significance. Thus the reduced model appears to provide a more parsimonious fit of the data. Importantly, the model trimming did not modify the relative strength of the remaining paths in the model. The magnitude and significance levels for the paths shown in Figure 1 are comparable with those obtained in the fully recursive model.

Figure 1 shows mixed support for a modeling explanation of the effect of parental behavior on dating violence. Corporal punishment is significantly related to dating violence (= .20), but marital violence is not. Consistent with the criminological perspective, there is a path of .28 from delinquent behavior to dating violence. This is consonant with the contention that adolescent males who engage in dating violence tend to be persons who are antisocial in a variety of ways. Further, involved/supportive parenting is negatively related to delinquent behavior (= −.19). This is in keeping with the

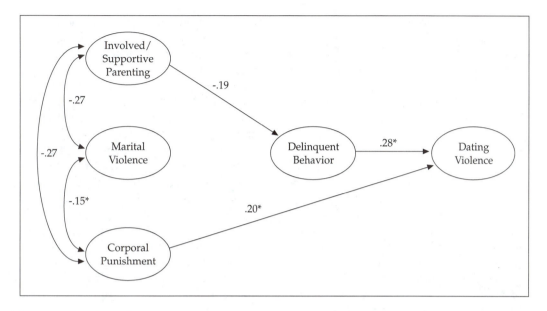

Figure 1. Results of Structural Equation Modeling
*p ≤ .05.

hypothesis that the quality of parental involvement indirectly influences the probability of dating violence by reducing the chances that a child will adopt an antisocial lifestyle.

Although corporal punishment was related to delinquent behavior at the bivariate level (see Table 1), Figure 1 shows that there is no significant relationship between these variables once the effect of involved/supportive parenting is taken into account. This is consistent with the contention that it is the quality of parental involvement, rather than corporal punishment, that places a child at risk for antisocial behavior.

DISCUSSION

Past research regarding the link between experiences in the family of origin and dating violence has been limited by

convenience samples, retrospective reports of parental behavior, and a single source of data to measure study constructs (i.e., the problem of shared method variance). We were able to avoid these problems in the present study. The sample consisted of all adolescents and their families in a several counties who met study criteria. A prospective design was employed whereby parental behavior over a 3-year period was used to predict the dating violence of adolescent males. Parent self-reports were used to assess marital violence, corporal punishment, and parental involvement. Adolescent self-reports were used to measure dating violence.

The results provided rather strong support for the criminological perspective. Low support and involvement by parents was associated with adolescent delinquency and drug use. Delinquency and drug use, in turn, predicted involvement in dating violence. This is consistent with past studies that have found that men who engage in spousal abuse often have participated in a variety of other criminal activities (Fagan et al., 1983; Stacy & Shupe, 1983; Simons et al., 1995, 1997; Walker, 1979). Thus it appears that both dating violence and spousal abuse are frequently components of a more general antisocial orientation.

The results failed to support the imitation hypothesis that children who observe their parents hit each other grow up to hit their dating partners. There was no association between parents' aggression toward one another and their adolescent child's involvement in dating violence. Perhaps this should not be surprising because the notion of imitation is actually a distortion of social learning theory. Research on observational learning (Bandura, 1977) does not indicate that people copy the behaviors they see displayed by others. Rather, they adopt only actions that appear to produce positive consequences. It is our guess that the violent exchanges that children sometimes witness between their parents rarely result in positive consequences. Aggression toward a marital partner is apt to be followed by counter-aggression, verbal threats, crying, or hysteria. We think it unlikely that children who observe such contingencies would conclude that violence is an effective strategy for influencing a romantic partner.

Although we found no evidence that interparental aggression fosters dating violence, there was a significant relationship between exposure to corporal punishment and subsequent dating violence. This suggests that corporal punishment provides a type of training that increases the probability of violence toward dating partners. But what is the lesson that is taught? Some (e.g., Straus, 1991) have argued that corporal punishment is an ineffective punish-

ment that promotes aggressive and antisocial behaviors. Our results showed, however, that corporal punishment does not predict delinquency and substance use. And in prior analyses based on this sample (Simons et al., 1994), we demonstrated that controlling for involved and supportive parenting eliminates any association between corporal punishment and aggressiveness toward peers. Thus it appears that the lessons taught by corporal punishment may be specific to intimate relationships.

Straus and his colleagues (1980; Straus & Smith, 1990) have argued that childhood exposure to family violence, whether spousal abuse or corporal punishment, teaches children that it is legitimate to hit those you love. Although both corporal punishment and marital violence may promote the idea that it is legitimate to hit those you love, we argue that it is unlikely that children who witness interparental violence will conclude that it is an effective interpersonal strategy. Children who experience corporal punishment, however, learn firsthand that violence changes behavior. Whatever the long-term consequences of corporal punishment, its short-term effect almost always produces behavior change. Thus corporal punishment teaches that it is both legitimate and effective to hit those you love. If this is the case, the deleterious consequences of corporal punishment are not limited to dating relationships. Corporal punishment would be expected to increase the probability of aggression in other intimate relationships as well. Consonant with this idea, past research has provided evidence that childhood exposure to corporal punishment increases the probability that adults will hit either their children (Egeland, Jacobvitz, & Papatola, 1987; Herrenkohl, Herrenkohl, & Toedter, 1983; Simons, Whitbeck, Conger, & Wu, 1991; Straus et al., 1980) or their spouse (Rosenbaum & O'Leary, 1981; Straus et al., 1980).

Although our study design reduced or eliminated many of the problems inherent in past research, it also presented some limitations that need to be acknowledged. First, the sample consisted of White families living in rural areas. Such a sample is not representative of the country as a whole, but we believe there is little reason to think that our findings are specific to families with these characteristics. It is clearly the case, however, that the study needs to be replicated with a more diverse and urban sample. Second, one might question the validity of using self-reports to assess corporal punishment, interparental aggression, and dating violence. People might be expected to underreport such behaviors, given their social undesirability. Although this is a weakness inherent in self-report measures, past research has shown a rather strong correlation between parent and child reports of corporal punishment (Simons et al., 1991) and between spousal reports of marital aggression (Straus, 1990).

There is, however, another potential problem associated with using parent reports to measure interparental aggression. Although the use of parent self-reports to assess marital violence eliminated shared methods variance between our measures of interparental aggression and dating violence, the parents may have reported events that their children did not witness. This is an important issue because children cannot imitate aggressive acts that they did not witness. Although this may have been the case for some of the marital violence reported by the parents, our measure focused on frequency of violence over a 3-year period. It seems reasonable to assume that children are most likely to observe interparental violence when it is persistent over a long time. Therefore, although the study children may not have witnessed all of the marital aggression reported by their parents, the amount of violence that they observed should be highly correlated with the level reported by their parents. However, in order to ensure that children have witnessed their parents' marital violence and in order to avoid the problem of shared methods variance, future research would do well to use adolescent reports of interparental violence with victim (i.e., girlfriend) reports of dating violence.

Note

During the past several years, support for this research has come from multiple sources, including the National Institute of Mental Health (MH00567, MH19734, MH43270, MH48165, MH51361). National Institute on Drug Abuse (DA05347), the Bureau of Maternal and Child Health (MCJ109572), the MacArthur Foundation Research Network on Successful Adolescent Development Among Youth in High-Risk Settings, and the Iowa Agriculture and Home Economics Experiment Station (Project No. 3320).

References

Allport, G. W. (1937). *Personality: A psychological interpretation.* New York: Holt, Rinehart & Winston.

Amato, P. R. (1990). Family environment as perceived by children. *Journal of Marriage and the Family, 52.* 613–620.

Arias, I., Samios, M., & O'Leary, K. D. (1987). Prevalence and correlates of physical aggression during courtship. *Journal of Interpersonal Violence, 2,* 82–90.

Bandura, A. (1973). *Aggression: A social learning analysis.* Englewood Cliffs, NJ: Prentice-Hall.

Bandura, A. (1977). *Social learning theory.* Englewood Cliffs, NJ: Prentice-Hall.

Bank, L., Dishion, T. J., Skinner, M., & Patterson, G. R. (1989). The glop problem in structural equation modeling. In G. R. Patterson (Ed.), *Family social interaction* (pp. 247–280). Hillsdale, NJ: Erlbaum.

Baucom, D. H., Sayers, S. L., & Duhe, A. (1989). Attributional style and attributional patterns among married couples. *Journal of Personality and Social Psychology, 56,* 596–607.

Bean, J. A., Leeper, J. D., Wallace, R. B., Sherman, B. M., & Jagger, H. (1979). Variations in the reporting of menstrual histories. *American Journal of Epidemiology, 109,* 181–185.

Bernard, M. L., & Bernard, J. L. (1983). Violent intimacy: The family as a model for love relationships. *Family Relations, 32,* 283–286.

Bookwala, J., Frieze, I. H., Smith, C., & Ryan, K. (1992). Predictors of dating violence: A multivariate analysis. *Violence and Victims, 7,* 297–311.

Brewin, C. R., Andrews, B., & Gotlib, I. H. (1993). Psychopathology and early experience: A reappraisal of retrospective reports. *Psychological Bulletin, 113,* 82–98.

Cannell, C. F. (1977). A summary of studies of interviewing methodology. *Vital and Health Statistics, 2,* 69.

Capaldi, D., & Patterson, G. R. (1987). An approach to the problem of recruitment and retention rates for longitudinal research. *Behavioral Assessment, 9,* 169–177.

Capaldi, D. M., & Patterson, G. R. (1991) Relation of parental transitions to boys' adjustment problems. *Developmental Psychology, 27,* 489–504.

Caspi, A., & Moffitt, T. E. (1992). The continuity of maladaptive behavior: From description to understanding in the study of antisocial behavior. In D. Cicchetti & D. Cohen (Eds.), *Manual of developmental psychopathology,* New York: Wiley.

Donovan, J. E., & Jessor, R. (1985). Structure of problem behavior in adolescence and young adulthood. *Journal of Consulting and Clinical Psychology, 53,* 890–904.

Egeland, B., Jacobvitz, D., & Papatola, K. (1987). Intergenerational continuity of abuse. In R. J. Gelles & J. B. Lancaster (Eds.), *Child abuse and neglect: Biosocial dimensions* (pp. 255–276). New York: Aldine.

Elliott, D. S., Huizinga, D., & Ageton, S. S. (1985). *Explaining delinquency and drug use.* Beverly Hills. CA: Sage.

Elliott, D. S., Huizinga, D., & Menard, S. (1989). *Multiple problem youth: Delinquency, substance use, and mental health problems.* New York: Springer.

Fagan J. A., Stewart, D. K., & Hansen, K. V. (1983). Violent men or violent husbands? Background factors and situational correlates. In D. Finkelhor, R. J. Gelles, G. T. Hotaling, & M. A. Straus (Eds.), *The dark side of families: Current family violence research* (pp. 49–67). Beverly Hills, CA: Sage.

Farrington, D. P. (1991). Childhood aggression and adult violence: Early precursors and later life outcomes. In D. J. Pepler & K. H. Rubin (Eds.), *The development and treatment of childhood aggression* (pp. 5–30). Hillsdale, NJ: Erlbaum.

Follette, V., & Alexander, P. C. (1992). Dating violence: Current and historic correlates. *Behavioral Assessment, 14,* 39–52.

Foo, L., & Margolin, G. (1995). A multivariate investigation of dating aggression. *Journal of Family Violence, 4,* 351–377.

Herrenkohl, E. C., Herrenkohl, R. C., & Toedter, L. J. (1983). Perspectives on the intergenerational transmission of abuse. In D. Finkelhor, R. J. Gelles, G. T. Hotaling, & M. A. Straus (Eds.), *The dark side of families: Current family violence research* (pp. 305–316). Beverly Hills, CA: Sage.

Hotaling, G. T., Straus, M. A., & Lincoln, A. J. (1990). Intrafamily violence and crime and violence outside the family. In M. A. Straus & R. J. Gelles (Eds.), *Physical violence in American families* (pp. 431–470). New Brunswick, NJ: Transaction.

Jessor, R. L., & Jessor, S. L. (1977). *Problem behavior and psycho-social development.* New York: Academic Press.

Jöreskog, K. G., & Sörbom, D. (1989). *LISREL VII: Analysis of linear structural relationships by maximum likelihood, instrumental variables, and least squares.* Uppsala, Sweden: University of Uppsala.

Kelly, E. M., & Loesch, L. C. (1983). Abused wives: Perceptions during crisis counseling. *American Mental Health Counseling Association Journal, 5,* 132–140.

Loeber, R. (1982). The stability of child antisocial behavior: A review. *Child Development, 53,* 1431–1446.

Loeber, R., & LeBlanc, M. (1990). Toward a developmental criminology. In M. Tonry & N. Morris (Eds.), *Crime and justice: A review of research* (Vol. 12, pp. 375–473). Chicago: University of Chicago Press.

Lorenz, F. O., Conger, R. D., Simons, R. L., Whitbeck, L. B., Elder, G. L., Jr. (1991). Economic pressure and marital quality: An illustration of the method variance problem in the causal modeling of family processes. *Journal of Marriage and the Family, 53,* 375–389.

Maccoby, E. E., & Martin, J. A., (1983). Socialization in the context of the family: Parent-child interaction. In P. Mussen (Ed.), *Handbook of child psychology* (pp. 1–101). New York: John Wiley.

Makepeace, J. M. (1981). Courtship violence among college students. *Family Relations, 30,* 97–102.

Makepeace, J. M. (1986). Gender differences in courtship violence victimization. *Family Relations, 35,* 383–388.

O'Keefe, N. K., Brockopp, K., & Chew, E. (1986). Teen dating violence. *Social Work, 31,* 465–468.

Osgood, D. W., Johnston, L. D., O'Malley, P. M., & Bachman, J. G. (1988). The generality of deviance in late adolescence and early adulthood. *American Sociological Review, 53,* 81–93.

O'Leary, K. D. (1988). Physical aggression between spouses: A social learning theory perspective. In V. B. Van Hasselt, R. L. Morrison, A. S. Bellack, & M. Hersen (Eds.), *Handbook of family violence,* New York: Plenum.

Patterson, G. R., Reid, J. B., & Dishion, T. J. (1992). *Antisocial boys.* Eugene, OR: Castalia.

Patterson, G. R., & Yoerger, K. (1993). Development models for delinquent behavior. In S. Hodgins (Ed.), *Mental disorder and crime* (pp. 140–172). Newbury Park, CA: Sage.

Pellegrini-Hill, A., & Ross, A. K. (1982). Reliability of recall of drug use and other health-related information. *American Journal of Epidemiology, 116,* 114–122.

Riggs, D. S. (1993). Relationship problems and dating aggression: A potential treatment target. *Journal of Interpersonal Violence, 8,* 18–35.

Riggs, D. S., & O'Leary, K. D. (1996). Aggression between heterosexual dating partners: An examination of a causal model of courtship aggression. *Journal of Interpersonal Violence, 11,* 519–540.

Riggs, D. S., O'Leary, K. D., & Breslin, F. C. (1990). Multiple correlates of physical aggression in dating couples. *Journal of Interpersonal Violence, 5,* 61–73.

Robins, L. N., Schoenberg, S. P., Holmes, S. J., Ratcliff, K. S., Behham, A., & Works, J. (1985). Early home environment and retrospective recall: A test of concordance between siblings with and without psychiatric disorders. *American Journal of Orthopsychiatry, 55,* 27–41.

Rohner, R. P., Bourque, S. L., & Elordi, C. A. (1996). Children's perceptions of corporal punishment, caretaker acceptance, and psychological adjustment in a poor, biracial Southern community. *Journal of Marriage and the Family, 58,* 842–852.

Rollins, B. C., & Thomas, D. L., (1979). Parental support, power, and control techniques in the socialization of children. In W. R. Burr, R. Hill, F. I. Nye, & I. L. Reiss (Eds.), *Contemporary theories about the family* (pp. 317–364). New York: Free Press.

Roscoe, B., & Benaske, N. (1985). Courtship violence experienced by abused wives: Similarities in patterns of abuse. *Family Relations, 34,* 419–424.

Rosenbaum, A., & O'Leary K. D., (1981). Marital violence: Characteristics of abusive couples. *Journal of Consult. Clinical Psychology, 49,* 63–71.

Sampson, R. J., & Laub, J. H. (1993). *Crime in the making: Pathways and turning points through life.* Cambridge, MA: Harvard University Press.

Sigelman, C. K., Berry, C. J., & Wiles, K. A. (1984). Violence in college students dating relationships. *Journal of Applied Social Psychology, 5,* 530–548.

Simons, R. L., Beaman, J., Conger, R. D., & Chao, W. (1993). Stress, support, and antisocial behavior trait as determinants of emotional well-being and parenting practices among single mothers. *Journal of Marriage and the Family, 55,* 385–398.

Simons, R. L., & Johnson, C. (in press). An examination of competing explanations for the intergenerational transmission of domestic violence. In Y. Danieli (Ed.), *Multigenerational legacies of trauma: An international handbook.* New York: Plenum.

Simons, R. L., Johnson, C., & Conger, R. D. (1994). Harsh corporal punishment versus quality of parental involvement as an explanation of adolescent maladjustment. *Journal of Marriage and the Family, 56,* 591–607.

Simons, R. L., Wu, C., Conger, R. D., & Lorenz, F. O. (1994). Two routes to delinquency: Differences between early and late starters in the impact of parenting and deviant peers. *Criminology, 32,* 247–276.

Simons, R. L., Wu, C., Johnson, C., & Conger, R. D. (1995). A test of various perspectives on the intergenerational transmission of domestic violence. *Criminology, 33,* 141–172.

Simons, R. L., Whitbeck, L. B., Conger, R. D., & Wu, C. (1991). Intergenerational transmission of harsh parenting. *Developmental Psychology, 27,* 159–171.

Stacy, W. A., & Shupe, A. (1983). *The family secret: Domestic violence in America.* Boston: Beacon Press.

Stets, J. E., & Pirog-Good, M. A. (1987). Violence in dating relationships. *Social Psychology Quarterly, 50,* 237–246.

Straus, M. A. (1983). Ordinary violence, child abuse, and wife-beating: What do they have in common? In D. Finkelhor, R. J. Gelles, G. T. Hotaling, & M. A. Straus (Eds.), *The dark side of families: Current family violence research* (pp. 213–234). Beverly Hills, CA: Sage.

Straus, M. A. (1990). The Conflict Tactics Scale and its critics: An evaluation and new data on validity and reliability. In M. A. Straus & R. J. Gelles (Eds.), *Physical violence in American families* (pp. 49–73). New Brunswick, NJ: Transaction.

Straus, M. A. (1991). Discipline and deviance: Physical punishment of children and violence and other crime in adulthood. *Social Problems, 38,* 133–154.

Straus, M. A., Gelles, R. J., & Steinmetz, S. K. (1980). *Behind closed doors: Violence in the American family.* Beverly Hills, CA: Sage.

Straus, M. A., & Smith, C. (1990). Family patterns and primary prevention of family violence. In M. A. Straus & R. J. Gelles (Eds.), *Physical violence in American families* (pp. 507–528). New Brunswick, NJ: Transaction.

Sugarman, D. B., & Hotaling, G. T. (1989). Dating violence: Prevalence, context, and risk markers. In M. A. Pirog-Good & J. E. Stets (Eds.), *Violence in dating relationships: Emerging social issues* (pp. 3–32). New York: Praeger.

Walker, L. E. (1979). *The battered woman.* New York: Harper & Row.

Watson, D., & Clark, L. A. (1984). Negative affectivity: The disposition to experience aversive emotional states. *Psychological Bulletin, 96,* 465–490.

White, J. W., & Koss, M. P. (1991). Courtship violence: Incidence in a national sample of higher education students. *Violence and Victims, 6,* 247–256.

Do Families Matter?

The Relative Effects of Family Characteristics, Self-Control, and Delinquency on Gang Membership

Trina L. Hope

The first institution with which children have contact is of course, the family. Some of the family's primary long-term functions are to maintain and socialize children—to teach them to avoid the temptations of crime, think of the future, and take their place in the world as responsible adults. The way families successfully socialize children is relatively simple. As Patterson (1980) has shown, the parents of nondelinquents are more likely than the parents of delinquents to monitor their children's behavior, recognize deviant behavior when it occurs, and punish the behavior. When it comes to encouraging law-abiding behavior, the role of the gang is in stark contrast to the role of the family. It does not maintain children, does not help them to avoid the temptations of illegal behavior, and certainly does not prepare them for success in the adult world. The association of gang membership with delinquency leads to the logical conclusion that the weakness of the family (which is important for the prediction of crime) contributes to the power of the gang.

Using self-report data from 1,049 middle and high school students in Fayetteville, Arkansas—a mostly white, semi-rural university town—this research explores the characteristics of gang members among a population not usually studied by gang researchers. It also explores the role of family characteristics in the prediction of gang membership—that is, do family variables such as attachment, supervision, and parental deviance predict gang membership? If so, is the relationship between these family characteristics and gang membership mediated by the self-control and/or delinquency of the respondents? According to Gottfredson and Hirschi (1990), the behavior of parents, especially those relating to attachment, discipline, and supervision, are important predictors of self-control. Low self-control in turn increases the likelihood of delinquency (Pratt and Cullen 2000), and delinquency is strongly related to gang membership (Thornberry 1998). Although self-control has been applied to a host of criminal and analogous behaviors (Pratt and Cullen 2000), with few exceptions (Chapple and Hope 2001; Hope and Damphousse 2001; Le Blanc and Lanctot 1998; Lynskey et al. 1999), it has not been applied to the study of gang members.

THE FAMILY IN GANG RESEARCH

When studying the predictors of gang membership, many researchers do not focus much attention on family characteristics—probably because many come from cultural deviance and/or strain perspectives, which do not give the family an important role in delinquency or gang membership. Researchers who do include the family in discussions of gang membership generally describe poor family relationships as precursors to gang membership or as one characteristic distinguishing gang from nongang youth.

Compared to nongang youth, gang members are more likely to live in homes characterized by family problems. Gang members report stressful relationships with parents, including family conflict, poor parent-child attachment, and low parental support (see Esbensen, Huizinga, and Weiher 1993; Friedman, Mann, and Friedman 1975; Hill et al. 1999; Johnstone 1983; Maxson, Whitlock, and Klein 1998; Moore 1991; Thornberry 1998; Vigil 1988b).

Gang members are more likely to live in single-parent homes (Bowker and Klein 1983; Ianni 1989; Johnstone 1983; Klein 1971; Moore 1991; Vigil 1998a) and to be poorly supervised (Le Blanc and Lanctot 1998; Thornberry 1998). Compared to their nongang peers, youth who report gang membership are more likely to have parents with criminal histories and siblings who are gang members (see Cohen et al. 1994; Curry and Spergel 1992; Decker and Van Winkle 1996; Hill et al. 1999; Klein 1971; Maxson, Whitlock, and Klein 1998). Finally, gang youth are more likely to report parental maltreatment/abuse. "When youth are beaten physically and molested sexually, their odds of gang involvement are four times higher than those who do not experience maltreatment" (Thompson and Braaten-Antrim 1998:328).

Not all researchers in search of the relationship between family variables and gang membership find it, however. Bjerregaard and Smith (1993), for instance, found that attachment to parents and family supervision did not predict later gang membership. Additionally, Hill et al. (1999) found that although family form, parental attitudes towards violence, siblings' antisocial behavior, and poor family management practices (all at ages 10–12) were significant predictors of gang membership at ages 13–18, parental drinking and attachment to parents were not.

After reviewing the literature on the relationship between family characteristics and gang membership, it does appear that compared to nongang youth, gang members experience more family hardships. Not surprisingly, the research on the relationship between family characteristics and crime/delinquency is consistent as well.

THE FAMILY, SELF-CONTROL, AND CRIME

Gottfredson and Hirschi's general theory of crime suggests that the tendency to engage in crime is explained by the concept of self-control, which they define as ". . . the differential tendency of people to avoid criminal acts whatever the circumstances in which they find themselves" (1990:87). Self-control is a measure of an individual's tendency to engage in crime. Whether or not an individual criminal event will occur, however, is a combination of the propensity of the individual and the opportunity that the situation presents. As the following discussion will illustrate, family characteristics are important for both self-control and opportunity.

According to Gottfredson and Hirschi, those with low self-control are likely to behave in ways that bring quick, easy, and simple rewards. They are more likely to weigh the costs and benefits of potential lines of action with an eye toward the present than they are to weigh costs and benefits with an eye toward the future—even if the future is measured in minutes. This tendency toward impulsivity can be seen and measured among children long before we label their behavior "delinquent" (Sampson and Laub 1993). This tendency is stable over time (Farrington 1992; White et al. 1990), and when children are big enough and unsupervised enough, the tendency that used to manifest itself in tantrums, grabbing toys, and hitting other children now manifests itself in delinquency—incorrigibility, stealing, and assaults.

There is much research confirming both the fact that "antisocial" (low self-control) children are at greater risk for delinquency/crime as they age (Caspi, Dem, and Elder 1989; Fergusson and Lynskey 1998) and that parental behaviors are important predictors of such early childhood behaviors (Gottfredson and Hirschi 1990; Junger 1994; Sampson and Laub 1993). This process of socialization includes a variety of parental attitudes and behaviors—and these attitudes and behaviors are not only important for a child's level of self-control, but are also key for a child's level of delinquent behavior (Lamb 1995).

THE FAMILY AND CRIME: INDIVIDUAL TENDENCIES

Research exploring how family characteristics influence crime shows consistent results. Effective parental socialization generally requires strongly attached parents who supervise their children, emotionally support them, and consistently and fairly discipline them. Such parents are more likely to have children who think about the future and who weigh costs and benefits based on future, rather than immediate, rewards. One important predictor of parents' likelihood to monitor, recognize, and punish is the degree of attachment between parent(s) and child(ren).

Nondelinquent youth are more strongly attached to their parents than are delinquent youth. In their study of 500 delinquent and 500 matched nondelinquent boys, the Gluecks (1950) found that affection of the mother and father for their boy was one of the strongest predictors of delinquency (see also Sampson and Laub 1993). One of the central elements of Hirschi's (1969) social control theory is the concept of attachment. Children who care about the opinions/feelings of their parents are less likely to engage in acts that disappoint, hurt, or inconvenience them: ". . . the more strongly a child is attached to his parents, the more strongly he is bound to their expectations, and therefore the more strongly he is bound to conformity with the legal norms of the larger society" (1969:94). On the one hand, children who respect their parents, share thoughts and feelings with their parents, and feel loved and wanted by them are less likely to be delinquent. On the other hand, delinquent youth are more likely to live in homes where communication and support is low (Hindelang 1973; Rankin and Wells 1990), and where they feel unwanted by their parents (Marcus and Gray 1998; Pulkkinen 1982). Delinquency is also more prevalent among youth who live in homes characterized by family tensions and parental discord (Rutter 1977), as well as quarrels and negligence (Loeber and Stouthamer-Loeber 1986; Mak 1996). Overall, strong emotional bonds between parent and child reduce the risk of delinquency (Smith et al. 1995).

Another characteristic of families is discipline, how parents react to their children's antisocial behavior. As Gottfredson and Hirschi (1990) point out, ". . . the person who cares for the child will watch his behavior, see him doing things he should not do, and correct him" (p. 97). Characteristics that are more likely to produce delinquency include lax and erratic discipline (Glueck and Glueck 1950; Peiser and Heaven 1996) and overall inept parenting, including neglect, cruelty, and conflict (Patterson 1980; Simons et al. 1995). Poor parenting not only predicts more delinquency, but predicts negative outcomes for children generally:

> Authoritarian, permissive, and neglectful parenting have been associated with adolescents who are less competent socially, have lower self-esteem, and are more likely to exhibit negative behavior; conversely, parents who are authoritative and democratic tend to have adolescents who are more socially competent, responsible, mature, and independent (Resnick and Burt 1996:176) (see also Straus et al. 1991).

Parents who do not recognize and respond to such behavior as tantrum throwing, talking back, and fighting are more likely to have children who grow up to steal from and assault others. And, such behavior is likely to continue. Lattimore et al. studied the predictors of rearrest among serious youthful offenders, and found that "even among a relatively homogeneous group of youthful offenders, the majority of whom had substantial criminal records, evidence of family violence, parental criminality, and parental neglect or poor supervision significantly increased parolees' risk of rearrest for violent crimes" (1995:76).

As this discussion illustrates, family variables play a key role in the generation of self-control and crime. Additionally, the variables discussed above are closely related to one another—attachment and discipline tend to predict one another as well as predicting crime. These characteristics influence the opportunity to engage in crime as well as the individual tendency—through the main family variable that predicts opportunity, supervision.

THE FAMILY AND CRIME: SUPERVISION AND OPPORTUNITY

One of the main family variables that influences the opportunity to engage in crime is supervision. Delinquents are more likely than nondelinquents to live in homes characterized by neglect and lax discipline, so we should not be surprised that supervision plays such an important role. As Hirschi (1995) points out: "The family may reduce the likelihood of delinquency by restricting its children's activity, by maintaining actual physical surveillance of them, and by knowing their whereabouts when they are out of sight" (p. 128). This conclusion is backed up by a large body of empirical research (Glueck and Glueck 1950; Hirschi 1969; Junger and Marshall 1997). Children are less likely to engage in delinquent behavior when they are under the watchful eyes of parents, or when they are aware that their parents know where they are, who they are with, and what they are doing.

Family characteristics such as attachment and discipline predict individual propensity toward crime. They can also influence opportunities for crime, however, if they affect supervision. Parents who are less attached to their children are less likely to supervise them. Lax discipline by definition involves a lack of supervision. Within families, the supervision and socialization of children are intertwined. There are situations that make these important socialization functions more difficult to achieve. Single parents find it harder to monitor and discipline their children, and are less attached (Hirschi 1995). The proportion of single-parent households in a community is a very strong predictor of crime (Sampson 1987), and even accounts for the relationship between community poverty level and crime (Smith and Jarjoura 1988). Additionally, parents who are themselves criminal are generally less effective at socializing their children to refrain from crime. As Gottfredson and Hirschi note, "If criminal behavior is oriented toward short-term rewards, and if child-rearing is oriented toward long-term rewards, there is little reason to expect parents themselves lacking in self-control to be adept at instilling self-control in their children" (1990:101).

This discussion of the family's effect on self-control and crime has illustrated that effective socialization of children appears to be the best protection against low self-control. A breakdown in socialization can occur in many ways—through broken homes, where one parent cannot monitor, recognize, and punish as well as two; in large families where more children make this process more difficult; in homes where parents do not care about their children, do not recognize deviant behavior when it occurs, or do recognize it but engage in short-term responses such as slapping or beating.

RESEARCH QUESTIONS

This research seeks to address two questions regarding gang membership among Fayetteville's youth. First, do characteristics of families—especially those relating to Gottfredson and Hirschi's descriptions of effective parenting—predict gang membership? Second, are the effects of the family on gang membership direct or indirect through self-control and/or delinquency?

METHODS

SAMPLE DESCRIPTION AND CHARACTERISTICS

Data for this study were collected in the spring of 1997 in Fayetteville, Arkansas, a medium-sized, suburban/rural city that houses a major southern university. Students in Fayetteville's two public school districts in grades 9 through 11 present on the day of data collection were included in the sample. The students present were asked to complete a 200-question self-report survey. Given policies in this school district, only passive consent from the participating parents was required to survey minor children. Parents not wishing their children to be involved in the survey were given the right to refuse participation. No parents disallowed their child's participation. The students were assured of anonymity and were advised to refrain from either answering questions that made them feel uncomfortable or to refrain from data collection completely. No students refused to fill out the survey although approximately 5 percent of surveys contained such incomplete data that they were unusable. Fayetteville has two high schools and two junior high schools; one district serves mostly middle and upper class families and the other serves mostly working class families in Fayetteville.

The resulting survey instrument contains data on delinquency, victimization, and etiological variables thought to influence crime for 1,139 junior high and high school students. These data are the result of a cross-sectional, self-report sample that encompasses the majority of all enrolled students in grades 9 through 11 in Fayetteville. According to Spring 1997 enrollment figures provided by the Fayetteville school district, the sample captures 69 percent of 9th graders, 62 percent of 10th graders, and 58 percent of 11th graders enrolled in Fayetteville's public school system. The sample contains a good representation of boys, girls, and racial minorities and reflects the demographics of Fayetteville's youth as a whole.[1]

The primary aim of this sample was to collect data tenable for testing the General Theory of Crime rather than to produce nationally or locally representative estimates of delinquency. Cross-sectional data is particularly useful for exploratory studies of associations between crime and etiological variables. Since no data tenable for testing the General Theory of Crime had been collected on juvenile populations at the time the surveys were administered, this was the preliminary first step on the path to more representative and longitudinal data. A study of high school students is particularly attractive as it captures potential offenders in their prime years of offending. High school samples, although not as criminal as incarcerated samples (particularly with respect to serious delinquency), do report significant levels of involvement in various criminal activities (Hindelang et al. 1981). We have certainly missed some serious offenders who were not enrolled in school, or if enrolled, are unlikely to be present, yet have also captured a number of students who report high levels of delinquency and involvement in serious crimes.[2]

MEASURES

Predictor Variables

Control Variables

The independent variables to be used in the analyses include demographic variables (such as age, sex, race, and socioeconomic status), family characteristics, self-control, and delinquency. Age is a categorical variable (14 or younger = 1; 15 = 2; 16 = 3; 17 = 4; 18 or older = 5), along with sex (male = 1, female = 0), and race (1 = nonwhite, 0 = white). The survey contains two questions that can be used to measure socioeconomic status. One question simply asks respondents to choose their family income from five categories, and the other asks about family welfare receipt. Because children may not know their family incomes, I use receipt of welfare benefits to measure social class (84.4 percent of the respondents indicated that they had never received benefits, 12.2 percent indicated they were not now, but used to receive benefits, and 3.4 percent reported that they were currently receiving benefits).

Family Characteristics

The items relating to family characteristics are divided into two categories. The first are structural and include family form (coded 1 if child lives with both biological parents, 0 if any other family form),

---

[1]Compared to the Fayetteville city population, our respondents are more likely to be ages 15 and 16. The sample and the population are similarly distributed in terms of sex. In terms of race, our sample is slightly more representative of minority students than the population of Fayetteville itself. Fayetteville's population of 14–17 year olds are 90% white, 4.7% black, 1.5% Native American, 1.3% Asian, and 5.4% Hispanic. Our sample is 86.4% white, 5.2% black, 2.7% Native American, 2.2% Asian, and 3.5% Hispanic. Overall, our sample has more blacks, Native Americans, and Asians, but fewer Hispanics than the Fayetteville population.

[2]46% of our sample report at least one act of "Used force to get something you wanted from another person," and 5.5% report having done it "many times," 42% have "Beaten up on someone (not a brother or sister) or hurt anyone on purpose" at least once, and 5.9% report having done it "many times." 25% of the sample has been picked up by the police and 3.2% report being picked up "many times."

mother and father's education (coded 1 = some high school or less, 2 = graduated from high school, 3 = trade or business school, 4 = some college or junior college, 5 = graduated from a four-year college), and family size.

The second set of family characteristics attempts to tap the underlying concept of effective parenting described by Gottfredson and Hirschi. Items representing attachment, supervision, and parental deviance were entered into an oblique principal components analysis and rotated. The PCA (Principle Components Analysis) produced four factors with eigenvalues greater than one, two representing attachment, one supervision, and one parental deviance (see Appendix A for factor loading scores and Appendix B for items making up all four effective parenting scales).

The first attachment scale (Factor 1) measures the respondent's attachment to his or her parents and includes five questions. Reliability analysis showed the Cronbach's alpha for the scale to be 0.78. The second attachment scale (Factor 2) attempts to tap parental attachment to the respondent with two questions ("Would your mother/father stick by you if you got into really bad trouble?"). Cronbach's alpha for this scale is 0.67.

The supervision scale (Factor 3) was first composed of three questions asking about parental knowledge of the respondent's whereabouts. Reliability analysis showed an intial alpha of .61. However, the alpha improved to .65 with the deletion of the question "Have you ever gone out looking for someone to hang around with at night?" So the supervision scale used in the analyses consists of the first two supervision questions from Appendix B and has a Cronbach's alpha of .65. For both the attachment and supervision scales, a high value represents high attachment/

supervision, and a low value represents low attachment/supervision.

The parental deviance scale (Factor 4) consists of three items asking if the respondent has ever "Been hit by either parent?", "Seen your father hit your mother?", and "Seen your mother hit your father?" Cronbach's alpha for this scale is .67. A high score on the parental deviance scale represents high levels of parental deviance; a low score represents low levels.

Attitudinal and Behavioral Self-Control

Although most previous research has used only attitudinal measures of self-control, Gottfredson and Hirschi suggest that self-control can also be measured by noncriminal, but imprudent behavior (e.g, accidents). To create the measures of self-control, I began with a number of items representing concepts of both social and self-control. A principal components analysis with rotation revealed three factors with eigenvalues over 1, substantively corresponding to attitudinal self-control, behavioral self-control/accidents, and social control. The attitudinal self-control factor contains 12 items tapping a number of the elements of self-control as described by Gottfredson and Hirschi. The questions represent various aspects of self-control, such as easy or simple gratification of desires (e.g., "I see no need for hard work." "An easy life is a happy life"), risk-taking (e.g., "I am usually pretty cautious," "Sometimes, I take a risk just for the fun of it"), little interest in the future (e.g., "I live for today, and let tomorrow take care of itself"), and indifference/insensitivity towards others (e.g., "I try to get things I want even when I know that it's causing problems for other people"). Reliability analysis of the scale showed that dropping any of the items would decrease rather than increase its reliability (Cronbach's alpha for the scale is .70—see Appendix C for the items making up the scale).

For the attitudinal self-control measure, the analyses do not use the scale created by the PCA, nor do they use an additive scale from scores on the individual questions. Both of these methods produce a composite score that gives more weight to some items than others. Following the logic of Grasmick et al. (1993), who argue that nothing in the general theory suggests that various items should be unequally weighted, z-score transformations are used in order to give equal weight to each item's variance in the variance of the composite score. High scores on the attitudinal self-control scale reflect high self-control; low scores reflect low self-control.

As mentioned above, the original PCA produced three factors, and one of them consisted of four questions measuring incidents of broken bones, motorcycle, car, or bike accidents, and being taken to the emergency room because of injuries. This scale is referred to as behavioral self-control/accidents. Reliability analyses of these four questions show that the scale is actually most reliable when pared down to two questions (these two items were reverse-coded so that high scores on the scale represent high self-control). The specific items comprising the behavioral self-control/accident scale are listed in Appendix B. The attitudinal and behavioral self-control scales are significantly correlated at .188, which illustrates that the higher one's level of attitudinal self-control, the higher their level of behavioral self-control (and the fewer accidents they report).

Delinquency

The final independent variable used in the multivariate analyses is a self-reported delinquency scale. The relationship between gang membership and delinquency is well established in the literature (Thornberry 1998). Gang members are more delinquent than nongang youth before, during, and after their time in the gang (Esbensen and Huizinga 1993). For these analyses, I use delinquency as a control variable to further explore the relationship between family variables and gang membership.

To create the delinquency scale, 18 delinquency items were entered into an oblique principal components analysis (see Appendix D for a list of the specific questions). The PCA produced four components with eigenvalues greater than 1 although most loaded on the first factor (which had an eigenvalue of 6.52, followed by the second factor's value of 1.81). Because of this large break in the eigenvalues, and the fact that research supports the versatility of offending (among both offenders in general [Britt 1994] as well as gang members [Klein 1995]), one overall delinquency scale (Cronbach's alpha = .89) will be used in the analysis.

None of the independent variables in the analyses are correlated highly enough to warrant concern about multicollinearity (Tabachnick and Fidell [1996] suggest avoiding inclusion of two variables with a correlation above .70 in the same analysis). The highest correlations among the independent variables are father and mother's education at .58, and the delinquency scale and attitudinal self-control at − .53.

Outcome Variable

The main outcome variable for the analyses is current gang membership and is measured by the question "Are you currently in a gang?" This self-report method of identifying gang members has been used in other research and is an accepted measure in the gang literature (Bjerregaard and Smith 1993; Curry and Decker 1998; Klein 1995; Sampson 1986). *Yes* is coded as 1, *no* as 0. Forty-two respondents (or 3.7 percent of the total sample) indicated they were current gang members. Because the number of gang members in the sample is so low, to validate the measure, I spoke with local police concerning the level of juvenile crime and gang membership in Fayetteville. A sergeant in the Juvenile Crime Division indicated that gang-related crimes in Fayetteville were rare, and that 3.7 percent of the sample reporting gang membership seemed reasonable.

As an additional check of the validity of the gang membership measure, I ran comparisons similar to those by Thornberry (1998), who presents data culled from four projects showing the percentage of delinquent acts committed by gang members in the Three City Gang Study (Fagan 1990), the Rochester Youth Development Study (Thornberry 1996), the Denver Youth Study (Huizinga 1997), and the Seattle Social Development Project (Battin et al. 1996). Data from these four projects show that gang members are responsible for a disproportionate amount of crime relative to their numbers in the sample. In Fagan's Three City Gang Study, for instance, the proportion of crimes committed by gang members is anywhere from 2.3 to 3 times their proportion of the sample. I present similar analysis for the Fayetteville sample in Table 1[3]. Similar to the data summarized by Thornberry, those respondents reporting gang membership in the Fayetteville data are responsible for a

---

[3]All of the delinquency items have response categories of "never," "once or twice," "several times," and "many times." To replicate Thornberry's analyses, I assigned values of 0 to "never," 1 to "once or twice," 4 to "several times," and 7 to "many times."

TABLE 1:   Percentage of Delinquent Acts Committed by Gang Members

	%
Prevalence of Gang Membership	3.7
Percentage of Offenses	
Drug use (other than marijuana)	6
Minor theft (> $2)	7
Marijuana use	7
Strong-arm	8
Medium theft ($2–$50)	9
Vandalism	10
Assault	11
Hit a parent	13
Joyride	14
Hit a dating partner	15
DUI	15
Arrests	16
Serious theft (< $50)	17

disproportionate number of offenses—anywhere from 1.4 times their proportion of the sample for drug use to 3 times their proportion for assault to 4.6 times their proportion for serious theft. Although the Fayetteville sample contains fewer gang members than those collected at more traditional sites, it appears that the measure of gang membership is valid.

One caveat concerning the data must be mentioned. Given the cross-sectional nature of the data and the prevalence measures, the causal order of such phenomena as gang membership, delinquency, and parental attachment cannot be determined. However, given the low to moderate amount of offending reported by the majority of the sample, their relative youth, and the general age/crime relationship for most offenders, I assume that the respondents are reporting relatively recent events, suggesting that "past" behavior and "current" attitudes/relationships are proximal. Additionally, Hirschi and

Gottfredson (2001) recognize the stability of offending and predictors of offending over the life-course. The effects of parental attachment, monitoring and discipline, as well as the development of self-control, regardless of when they are measured, are believed to precede gang membership and therefore are assumed to be temporally prior.

ANALYSIS

Two analytic techniques are used in this research. First, to establish the differences between gang and nongang youth, bivariate relationships between gang membership and the demographic variables are presented. Gang and nongang respondents are compared by sex, age, race, and social class. Next, the results of a path analysis are presented to establish the relative impact of the demographic variables, the family, self-control, and delinquency on gang membership.

Before turning to the analyses, a note about the data. As with most self-report surveys, I was faced with the challenge of missing data, especially on the scales (since they are comprised of multiple items). Rather than exclude all cases with missing data, or replace them with overall mean scores, for some of the variables correlations were used to replace missing data. Following the logic of Tabachnick and Fidell's (1996:63) description of inserting group means for missing values, for each of the scale variables with missing data, another highly correlated item from the questionnaire was used to generate replacement values that would more accurately represent the respondent. For instance, missing data on the attitudinal self-control scale were replaced with mean scores by responses to a question asking how often the respondent talks over future plans with his/her parents. The only cases

excluded from the analyses were those with missing data on the categorical variables where mean replacement was not appropriate. So all of the subsequent analyses use a subsample of 1,049 respondents. Table 2 presents descriptive statistics for all the variables in the analyses.

RESULTS

BIVARIATE ANALYSIS

Table 3 compares gang to nongang youth by sex, age, race, and welfare benefits. Among nongang youth, 46.8 percent are male, compared to 72.5 percent of gang youth. When looking at the relationship between age and gang membership, those indicating gang membership are more likely to be 14 or younger, and to be 18 or older compared to nongang respondents. Turning to race and gang membership we see that African Americans, Hispanics, and Native Americans are overrepresented among gang members, whites are

TABLE 2: Descriptive Statistics for Variables in the Analyses

Variable	Mean	SD
Gang Membership	.038	.190
Male	.480	.500
Nonwhite	.125	.331
Intact Family	.455	.497
Welfare Benefits	1.200	.480
Father's Education	3.720	1.470
Mother's Education	3.680	1.440
Family Size	2.366	1.749
Attachment to Parents	16.152	4.598
Parental Attachment to Child	6.358	1.661
Parental Supervision	6.967	2.146
Parental Deviance	4.143	1.738
Attitudinal Self-Control	.312	5.547
Behavioral Self-Control	8.698	1.414
Delinquency	29.603	9.722

Note: *n* = 1,049

TABLE 3:	Percent Reporting Gang Membership by Sex, Age, Race, and Welfare Benefits	
	Yes	**No**
Sex		
Male, N	29	472
Column %	72.5%	46.8%
Female, N	11	537
Column %	27.5%	53.2%
Total N	40	1,009
Age		
14 or younger, N	5	93
Column %	12.5%	9.2%
15, N	11	343
Column %	27.5%	34.0%
16, N	11	336
Column %	27.5%	33.9%
17, N	11	211
Column %	27.5%	20.9%
18 or older, N	2	26
Column %	5.0%	2.6%
Total N	40	1,009
Race		
African American, N	5	44
Column %	12.2%	4.3%
Asian, N	1	23
Column %	2.4%	2.3%
Hispanic, N	4	28
Column %	9.8%	2.8%
Native American, N	4	26
Column %	9.8%	2.6%
White, N	27	891
Column %	65.8%	88.0%
Total N[5]	41	1,012
Welfare Benefits		
No, never	27	848
Column %	67.5%	84.0%
Not now, but used to	11	125
Column %	27.5%	12.4%
Yes, now	2	36
Column %	5.0%	3.6%
Total N	40	1,009

[5]One respondent who answered "yes" and three respondents who answered "no" indicated that they were more than one race (which explains the Ns of 41 and 1,012, respectively).

underrepresented, and Asians are similarly distributed among gang and nongang youth. Finally, Table 3 shows the relationship between welfare benefits and gang membership. Those reporting gang membership come from families more likely to have experienced financial hardships—they are less likely than non-gang youth to report "never" receiving benefits, and are more likely to report past or current receipt of benefits.

MULTIVARIATE ANALYSES

The bivariate analysis presented in Table 3 showed that among the youth population of Fayetteville, those who report gang membership are more likely to be male, nonwhite, and past or current recipients of welfare benefits. In the multivariate analysis, I turn to the questions posed earlier—what effects do family variables have on gang membership, especially controlling for self-control and delinquency? Previous research with the Fayetteville data found that both self-control and delinquency are significant predictors of gang membership (Hope and Damphousse 2001). Do family characteristics, especially those relating to control theory's concept of effective parenting, predict gang membership, and if so, are the effects direct or indirect? To answer this question, a statistical technique capable of analyzing both direct and indirect effects is needed.

Table 4 presents the results of a path analysis (using Mplus[4]), and examines the direct and indirect effects of parental attachment, parental supervision, and parental deviance on gang membership. For ease of presentation, the significant coefficients for the other independent variables in the model are shown on Table 5.

[4]Unlike other statistical software programs, Mplus can estimate path analysis models with both continuous and categorical dependent variables.

TABLE 4: Direct and Indirect Effects of Effective Parenting Variables, Self-Control, and Delinquency on Gang Membership (Significant Standardized Coefficients Only)

	Attitudinal Self-Control	Behavioral Self-Control	Delinquency	Gang Membership
Attachment to Parents	13***	—	—	—
Parental Supervision	.28***	—	−.38***	—
Parental Deviance	−.12***	−.12**	.20***	.15*
Attitudinal Self-Control	—	—	—	−.33***
Behavioral Self-Control	—	—	—	−.16**
Delinquency	—	—	—	.25***
R2	.25	.05	.29	.45

*$p < .05$

**$p < .01$

***$p < .001$

TABLE 5: Significant Standardized Coefficients Showing Effects of Exogenous Variables on Endogenous Variables in Table 4

	EXOGENOUS VARIABLES					
Endogenous Variables	Male	Non-white	Welfare Receipt	Father's Education	Mother's Education	Intact Home
Attitudinal Self-Control	−.19**	—	—	.09*	—	—
Behavioral Self-Control	−.13**	—	—	.09*	−.07*	—
Delinquency	.13***	.05*	.05*	−.07*	—	−.09**
Gang Membership	.18*	.11*	—	—	—	—

*$p < .05$

**$p < .01$

***$p < .001$

Beginning with the independent variables that directly predict gang membership (see Table 4), we see that parental deviance is the only family variable that directly predicts gang membership. Respondents who live in homes with high levels of violence are more likely to report gang membership. Parental deviance also directly predicts self-control and delinquency. Respondents who report high levels of parental deviance score lower on both measures of self-control and are more delinquent. Both attitudinal and behavioral self-control, along with delinquency, are significant direct predictors of gang membership. Self-control is negatively associated with gang membership, and delinquency is positively associated. The other two variables that directly predict gang membership are sex and race. Males and nonwhites are more likely to be gang members than are females and whites (see Table 5).

Attachment to parents and parental supervision are not direct predictors of gang membership (the parental attachment to child scale was not a significant predictor of any of the endogenous variables), but are indirectly related to gang membership. Those with higher parental attachment and supervision also score higher on the attitudinal self-control scale. Self-control, in turn, is negatively related to gang membership. Parental supervision is also a significant predictor of delinquency—those with less supervision are more delinquent. Delinquency, in turn, is positively related to gang membership. Among the other exogenous family variables, father's education predicts gang membership through both measures of self-control and delinquency, mother's education predicts through behavioral self-control (although in an unexpected direction), and family form predicts through delinquency.

Overall, the results of the path analysis present a picture of gang members that is consistent with prior research utilizing more urban samples. Those who report gang membership in Fayetteville are more likely to be male and nonwhite, with low levels of self-control and high levels of delinquency. Parental deviance is both a direct and indirect predictor of gang membership, whereas attachment to parents and supervision indirectly predict gang membership through self-control and delinquency. Together, the independent variables explain 45 percent of the variance in gang membership.

DISCUSSION AND CONCLUSIONS

The main question this research sought to address was the relationship between family variables and gang membership, especially in light of self-control and delinquency. Previous research has found that gang membership is predicted by a variety of family variables. The question this research especially sought to explore is the nature of this relationship—do gang members uniquely experience family problems or are their lower levels of self-control and/or delinquency accounting for the relationship? There are a number of variables predictive of gang membership that this research did not address, but my purpose was to specifically explore the family-gang membership connection. Among the scales tapping Gottfredson and Hirschi's concept of effective parenting, only parental deviance has a direct effect on gang membership. Consistent with other research (Thompson and Braaten-Antrim 1998), those who live in violent homes are at greater risk for gang membership. Attachment and supervision are both related to gang membership indirectly— through self-control and/or delinquency. So, with the exception of parental deviance, it does not appear that gang members uniquely experience family problems. Controlling for self-control and delinquency, they are no more likely than non-gang youth to be weakly attached to their parents, or to be poorly supervised.

So what are we to take away from the results of this research? Because of its strong association with delinquency, gang membership poses a challenge to law enforcement, policy makers, communities, and individual families. It seems that there are a few important policy implications of this research. Because gang membership is predicted by self-control and delinquency, policies aimed at early intervention— especially those with the explicit goals of increasing self-control—would seem appropriate. And, because both self-control and delinquency are predicted by family variables, programs aimed at strengthening families and communities are also in order. Programs like G.R.E.A.T. seek to educate students about the dangers of gang life and provide them with the skills to re-sist peer pressure to join gangs (Esbensen and Osgood 1999). In addition to such pro-grams, others aimed at either at-risk or general populations of children (and their families) with the intention of increas-ing self-control and/or effective parenting would also seem to be appropriate long-term responses to the gang problem.

References

Battin, Sara R., Karl G. Hill, J. David Hawkins, Richard F. Catalano, and Robert Abbott. 1996. "Testing Gang Membership and Association with Antisocial Peers as Independent Predictors of Anti-social Behavior: Gang Members Compared to Non-Gang Members of Law-Violating Youth Groups." Paper presented at the annual meetings of the American Society of Criminology, Chicago.

Bjerregaard, Beth, and Carolyn Smith. 1993. "Gender Differences in Gang Participation, Delinquency, and Substance Use." *Journal of Quantitative Crimi-nology* 9: 329–355.

Bowker, Lee H., and Malcolm W. Klein. 1983. "The Etiology of Female Juvenile Delinquency and Gang Membership: A Test of Psychological and Social Structural Explanations." *Adolescence* 18: 739–751.

Britt, Chester L. 1994. "Versatility." in *The Generality of Deviance*, edited by Travis Hirschi and Michael R. Gottfredson. New Brunswick, NJ: Transaction.

Caspi, Avshalom, Daryl J. Dem, and Glen H. Elder Jr. 1989. "Continuities and Consequences of Interac-tional Styles Across the Lifecourse." *Journal of Per-sonality* 57: 375–406.

Chapple, Constance L., and Trina L. Hope. 2001. "Birds of a Feather? An Analysis of the Self-Control and Criminal Versatility of Gang and Dating Vio-lence Offenders." Unpublished manuscript.

Cohen, M. I., K. Williams, A. M. Bekelman, and S. Crosse. 1994. "Evaluation of the National Youth Gang Drug Prevention Program." in *The Modern Gang Reader*, edited by Malcolm W. Klein, Cheryl Maxson, and Jody Miller. Los Angeles: Roxbury Publishing Company.

Curry, G. David, and Scott H. Decker. 1998. *Confronting Gangs: Crime and Community*. Los Ange-les: Roxbury Publishing Company.

Curry, G. David, and Irving A. Spergel. 1992. "Gang Involvement and Delinquency Among Hispanic and African-American Adolescent Males." *Journal of Research in Crime and Delinquency* 29: 273–291.

Decker, Scott H., and Barrik Van Winkle. 1996. *Life in the Gang: Family, Friends, and Violence*. New York: Cambridge University Press.

Esbensen, Finn-Aage, and David Huizinga. 1993. "Gangs, Drugs, and Delinquency in a Survey of Urban Youth." *Criminology* 31: 565–587.

Esbensen, Finn-Aage, David Huizinga, and Anne W. Weiher. 1993. "Gang and Non-Gang Youth: Differ-ences in Explanatory Variables." *Journal of Contem-porary Criminal Justice* 9: 94–116.

Esbensen, Finn-Aage, and D. Wayne Osgood. 1999. "Gang Resistance and Education Training (GREAT): Results from the National Evaluation." *Journal of Research in Crime and Delinquency* 36: 194–225.

Fagan, Jeffrey. 1990. "Social Processes of Delinquency and Drug Use Among Urban Gangs." In *Gangs in America*, edited by C. Ronald Huff. Newbury Park, CA: Sage Publications.

Farrington, David P. 1992. "Explaining the Beginning, Progress, and Ending of Antisocial Behavior from Birth to Adulthood." in *Facts, Frameworks, and Fore-casts*, edited by Joan McCord. Vol. 3 in *Advances in Criminological Theory*, series editors Freda Adler and William Laufer. New Brunswick: Transaction Publishers.

Fergusson, David M., and Michael T. Lynskey. 1998. "Conduct Problems in Childhood and Psychosocial Outcomes in Young Adulthood: A Prospective Study." *Journal of Emotional and Behavioral Disorders* 6: 2–18.

Friedman, C. Jack, Fredrica Mann, and Alfred S. Friedman. 1975. "A Profile of Juvenile Street Gang Members." *Adolescence* X: 563–606.

Glueck, Sheldon, and Eleanor Glueck. 1950. *Unraveling Juvenile Delinquency*. New York: The Commonwealth Fund.

Gottfredson, Michael R., and Travis Hirschi. 1990. *A General Theory of Crime*. Stanford, CA: Stanford Uni-versity Press.

Grasmick, Harold G., Charles R. Tittle Jr., Robert J. Bursik, and Bruce J. Arneklev. 1993. "Testing the Core Implications of Gottfredson and Hirschi's General Theory of Crime." *Journal of Research in Crime and Delinquency* 30: 5–29.

Hill, Karl G., James C. Howell, J. David Hawkins, and Sara R. Battin-Pearson. 1999. "Childhood Risk Fac-tors for Adolescent Gang Membership: Results from the Seattle Social Development Project." *Journal of Research in Crime and Delinquency* 36: 300–322.

Hindelang, Michael J. 1973. "Causes of Delinquency: A Partial Replication and Extension." *Social Prob-lems* 20: 471–487.

Hindelang, Michael J., Travis Hirschi, and Joseph G. Weis. 1981. *Measuring Delinquency*. Beverly Hills: Sage Publications.

Hirschi, Travis. 1969. *Causes of Delinquency*. Berkeley: University of California Press.

Hirschi, Travis. 1995. "The Family." in *Crime*, edited by James Q. Wilson and Joan Petersilia. San Fran-cisco: ICS Press.

Hirschi, Travis, and Michael R. Gottfredson. 2001. "Control Theory and the Life-Course Perspective", pp. 229–241 in *Life-Course Criminology: Contempo-rary and Classic Readings*, edited by Alex Piquero and Paul Mazerolle. Belmont, CA: Wadsworth.

Hope, Trina L., and Kelly R. Damphousse. 2001. "Applying Self-Control Theory to Gang Membership in a Non-Urban Setting." Unpublished Manuscript.

Huizinga, David H. 1997. "Gangs and the Volume of Crime." Paper presented at the annual meeting of the Western Society of Criminology, Honolulu, Hawaii.

Ianni, Francis. 1989. *The Search for Structure: A Report on American Youth Today*. New York: Free Press.

Johnstone, John W. C. 1983. "Recruitment to a Youth Gang." *Youth and Society* 14: 281–300.

Junger, Marianne. 1994. "Accidents." in *The Generality of Deviance*, edited by Travis Hirschi and Michael R. Gottfredson. New Brunswick, NJ: Transaction Publishers.

Junger, Marianne, and Ineke Haen Marshall. 1997. "The Interethnic Generalizability of Social Control Theory: An Empirical Test." *Journal of Research in Crime and Delinquency* 34: 79–112.

Klein, Malcolm W. 1971. *Street Gangs and Street Workers*. Englewood Cliffs, NJ: Prentice-Hall.

Klein, Malcolm W. 1995. *The American Street Gang: Its Nature, Prevalence, and Control*. New York: Oxford University Press.

Lamb, Kevin. 1995. "The Causal Factors of Crime: Understanding the Sub-Culture of Violence." *The Mankind Quarterly* 36: 105–116.

Lattimore, Pamela K., Christy A. Visher, and Richard L. Linster. 1995. "Predicting Rearrest for Violence Among Serious Youthful Offenders." *Journal of Research in Crime and Delinquency* 32: 54–83.

Le Blanc, Marc, and Nadine Lanctot. 1998. "Social and Psychological Characteristics of Gang Members According to the Gang Structure and Its Subcultural and Ethnic Make Up." *Journal of Gang Research* 5: 15–28.

Loeber, Rolf, and Magda Stouthamer-Loeber. 1986. "Family Factors as Correlates and Predictors of Juvenile Conduct Problems and Delinquency." Pp. 29–149 in *Crime and Justice: An Annual Review of Research*, Vol. 7, edited by Michael Tonry and Norval Morris. Chicago: University of Chicago Press.

Lynskey, Dana Peterson, L. Thomas Winfree Jr., Finn-Aage Esbensen, and Dennis L. Clason. 1999. "Linking Gender, Minority Group Status, and Family Matters to Self-Control Theory: An Analysis of Key Self-Control Concepts in a Youth-Gang Context." Paper presented at the meetings of the *American Sociological Association*.

Mak, Anita S. 1996. "Adolescent Delinquency and Perceptions of Parental Care and Protection: A Case Control Study." *Journal of Family Studies* 2: 29–39.

Marcus, Robert F, and Lewis Gray Jr. 1998. "Close Relationships of Violent and Nonviolent African American Delinquents." *Violence and Victims* 13: 31–46.

Maxson, Cheryl L., Monica L. Whitlock, and Malcolm W. Klein. 1998. "Vulnerability to Street Gang Membership: Implications for Practice." *The Social Service Review* 72: 70–91.

Moore, Joan W. 1991. *Going Down to the Barrio*. Philadelphia: Temple University Press.

Patterson, Gerald R. 1980. "Children Who Steal." In *Understanding Crime: Current Theory and Research*, edited by Travis Hirschi and Michael Gottfredson. Beverly Hills: Sage.

Peiser, Nadine C, and Patrick C. L. Heaven. 1996. "Family Influences on Self-Reported Delinquency Among High School Students." *Journal of Adolescence* 19: 557–568.

Pratt, Travis C, and Francis T. Cullen. 2000. "The Empirical Status of Gottfredson and Hirschi's General Theory of Crime: A Meta-Analysis." *Criminology* 38: 931–964.

Pulkkinen, Lea. 1982. "Self-control and Continuity from Childhood to Late Adolescence." in *Life-Span Development*, vol. 4, edited by Paul B. Baltes and Orville. G. Brim. New York: Academic Press.

Rankin, Joseph H, and L. Edward Wells. 1990. "The Effect of Parental Attachments and Direct Controls on Delinquency." *Journal of Research in Crime and Delinquency* 27: 140–165.

Resnick, Gary, and Martha R. Burt. 1996. "Youth at Risk: Definitions and Implications for Service Delivery." *American Journal of Orthopsychiatry* 66: 172–188.

Rutter, Michael. 1977. "Separation, Loss, and Family Relations." In *Child Psychiatry: Modern Approaches*, edited by M. Rutter and L. Herson. Oxford: Blackwell.

Sampson, Robert J., 1986. "Effects of Socioeconomic Context on Official Reaction to Juvenile Delinquency." *American Sociological Review* 5: 876–885.

Sampson, Robert J. 1987. "Urban Black Violence: The Effect of Male Joblessness and Family Disruption." *American Journal of Sociology* 93: 348–382.

Sampson, Robert J, and John H. Laub. 1993. *Crime in the Making: Pathways and Turning Points Through Life*. Cambridge, MA: Harvard University Press.

Simons, Ronald L., Chyi-In Wu, Christine Johnson, and Rand D. Conger. 1995. "A Test of Various Perspectives on the Intergenerational Transmission of Domestic Violence." *Criminology* 33: 141–172.

Smith, Carolyn, Alan J. Lizotte, Terence P. Thornberry, and Marvin D. Krohn. 1995. "Resilient Youth: Identifying Factors that Prevent High-Risk Youth from Engaging in Delinquency and Drug Use." *Current Perspectives on Aging and the Life Cycles* 4: 217–247.

Smith, Douglas A, and Roger Jarjoura. 1988. "Social Structure and Criminal Victimization." *Journal of Research in Crime and Delinquency* 25: 27–52.

Straus, Murray A., Demie Kurz, Donileen R. Loseke, and Joan McCord. 1991. "Discipline and Deviance: Physical Punishment of Children and Violence and Other Crime in Adulthood." *Social Problems* 38: 133–154.

Tabachnick, Barbara G, and Linda S. Fidell. 1996. *Using Multivariate Statistics*. New York: HarperCollins College Publishers Inc.

Thompson, Kevin M, and Rhonda Braaten-Antrim. 1998. "Youth Maltreatment and Gang Involvement." *Journal of Interpersonal Violence* 13: 328–345.

Thornberry, Terence P. 1996. *The Contribution of Gang Members to the Volume of Delinquency.* Fact sheet prepared for the U.S. Department of Justice, Office of Juvenile Justice and Delinquency Prevention.

Thornberry, Terence P. 1998. "Membership in Youth Gangs and Involvement in Serious and Violent Offending." Pp. 147–166 in *Serious and Violent Juvenile Offenders* edited by Rolf Loeber and David P. Farrington. Thousand Oaks, CA: Sage Publications, Inc.

Vigil, James Diego. 1988a. *Barrio Gangs: Street Life and Identity in Southern California.* Austin: University of Texas Press.

Vigil, James Diego. 1988b. "Group Processes and Street Identity: Adolescent Chicano Gang Members." *Ethos* 16: 421–445.

White, Jennifer L., Terrie E. Moffitt, Felton Earls, Lee Robins, and Phil A. Silva. 1990. "How Early Can We Tell? Predictors of Childhood Conduct Disorder and Adolescent Delinquency." *Criminology* 28: 507–528.

APPENDIX A: FACTOR LOADING SCORES OF PARENTAL EFFECTIVENESS VARIABLES

Item Description	Factor Number and Loading Scores			
	F1	F2	F3	F4
I share my thoughts and feelings with my mother.	.807			
I would like to be the kind of person my mother is.	.774			
I would like to be the kind of person my father is.	.364			
My mother seems to understand me.	.817			
I talk over future plans with my parents.	.591			
Would your mother stick by you if you got into really bad trouble?		.817		
Would your father stick by you if you got into really bad trouble?		.893		
Have you ever gone looking for someone to hang around with at night?			.776	
My parents know where I am when I am away from home.			−.608	
My parents always know who I am dating.			−.533	
Have you ever seen your father hit your mother?				.851
Have you ever seen your mother hit your father?				.828
Have you ever been hit by either parent?				.620

**APPENDIX B: ITEM DESCRIPTION: FAMILY AND BEHAVIORAL
SELF-CONTROL SCALES**

Child's Attachment to Parents Scale Items (Cronbach's alpha = .78; range = 5 to 25):

I share my thoughts and feelings with my mother.[a]
I would like to be the kind of person my mother is.[a]
I would like to be the kind of person my father is.[a]
My mother seems to understand me.[a]
I talk over future plans with my parents.[a]

Parental Attachment to Child Scale Items (Cronbach's alpha = .67; range = 2 to 8):

Would your mother stick by you if you got into really bad trouble?[b]
Would your father stick by you if you got into really bad trouble?[b]

Supervision Items (final scale includes first two items only: alpha = .64; range = 2 to 10):

My parents know where I am when I am away from home.[a]
My parents always know who I am dating.[a]
Have you ever gone looking for someone to hang around with at night?[c]

Behavioral Self-Control/Accidents Items (final scale includes first two items only:
   alpha = .58; range = 2 to 10):

Have you ever been to the emergency room of a hospital because of injuries due to an
   accident?[c]
Have you ever broken one of your bones?[c]
Have you ever been in a car, truck, or motorcycle accident?[c]
Have you ever been hurt riding your bike, skateboard, or rollerblades?[c]

Response Categories:

a)	b)	c)
1 = strongly disagree	1 = I doubt it	1 = never
2 = disagree	2 = maybe	2 = once or twice
3 = undecided	3 = probably	3 = several times
4 = agree	4 = certainly	4 = many times
5 = strongly agree		

APPENDIX C: ATTITUDINAL SELF-CONTROL SCALE ITEMS

Item	Mean	SD	Factor Loading
*I see no need for hard work.	4.09	1.07	.657
*I try to get things I want even when I know it's causing problems for other people.	3.37	1.07	.606
*I don't devote much thought and effort to preparing for the future.	3.67	1.23	.561
*An easy life is a happy life.	2.85	1.26	.548
*Most things people call delinquency don't really hurt anyone.	3.15	1.01	.517
*I live for today and let tomorrow take care of itself.	2.70	1.25	.494
*I lose my temper easily.	2.99	1.29	.465
*Sometimes, I take a risk just for the fun of it.	2.39	.98	.428
I am usually pretty cautious	3.92	1.26	.402
Whatever I do, I try hard.	3.84	.95	.400
Hitchhiking is too dangerous for me.	3.73	1.30	.364
*Fools and suckers deserve what they get.	2.62	1.15	.334

mean = 312; SD = 5.547; = 70; range = −20.23 to 14.55

*items recoded for consistency

APPENDIX D: ITEM DESCRIPTION: DELINQUENCY SCALE

Have you ever. . .

Stayed away from school because you had better things you wanted to do?
Taken little things (worth less than $2) that did not belong to you?
Taken things of medium value (between $2 and $50) that did not belong to you?
Taken things of large value (worth over $50) that did not belong to you?
Taken a car for a ride without the owner's permission?
Banged up something, on purpose, that did not belong to you?
Beaten up on someone (not a brother or sister) or hurt anyone on purpose?
Driven a car when you had been drinking?
Used force to get something you wanted from another person?
Hit one of your parents?
Hit someone you were dating?
Shot dice for money?
Bet money on sporting events?
Played cards for money?
Drank alcohol?
Smoked cigarettes?
Smoked marijuana?
Used other drugs (cocaine, ecstasy, heroin, LSD, steroids)?

Chapter 5

Schools, Media, and Crime

INTRODUCTION

With so much recent attention paid to crime in schools, researchers have renewed their interest in the relationship between school factors and juvenile crime at school. Past research on firearm carrying and use has ignored an important population: juveniles in school. May's important contribution to the delinquency literature fills a void in our understanding of firearms and delinquency. May investigates whether youths carry firearms because of social pressures, general involvement in delinquency, or out of fear of victimization. According to May's research, firearm carrying is reflective of youth's social bonds, involvement in delinquency, and their fear of crime.

In their article, Thompson, Young, and Burns examine the images of criminal gangs and society's responses to gangs by conducting a content analysis of 4,445 articles printed in the *Dallas Morning News* from 1991 to 1996. In doing so, eight recurrent themes were identified. These included stories devoted to "gang crime," "gang busting," "gang accounts," "gang resisting," "gang references," "foreign gangs," "gang research," and "gang rape." The findings indicate that stories devoted to the reporting of gang crime were outnumbered by stories dealing with community responses to gangs. Stories devoted to research on gangs received the least amount of media attention. Using a social constructionist approach, the researchers argue the importance of examining the discourse presented by the media as it plays a role in the construction of gangs as a social problem and the maintenance of symbolic power and social control.

Boulahanis and Heltlsey take a social constructionist approach in examining the reporting patterns of juvenile homicide by the news media. In doing so, they argue that the news media tend to overreport "atypical" types of homicide cases. To examine this, they compare Chicago homicide cases reported in the *Chicago Sun-Times* and the *Chicago Tribune* to cases receiving no attention by the papers from 1992 to 1998. The findings suggest that significant differences between reported and unreported cases were present. The newspapers tended to overreport cases involving Caucasian victims and offenders, while underreporting cases involving Latinos. Additional findings revealed increased attention devoted to female victims and young victims and offenders (under 14). In examining the type of weapon used to carry out the homicide, Boulahanis and Heltsley observed that although most homicides involved guns as the weapon of choice, the newspapers tended to favor cases that involved "other" weapons. These cases tended to involve some type of dramatic element and tended to be extremely violent. No significant differences were noted in the spatial distribution of the reporting patterns of homicide in Chicago. Taken together, these findings suggest that atypical features of crime are overrepresented, and may possibly assist in constructing a distorted image of the juvenile offender, victim, and circumstances surrounding the case.

Scared Kids, Unattached Kids, or Peer Pressure

Why Do Students Carry Firearms to School?

David C. May

Firearm homicides are the second leading cause of death for youngsters 15 to 19 years old and are the leading cause of death for Black males aged 10 to 34 years (Fingerhut, 1993). Between 1980 and 1990, there was a 79% rise in the number of juveniles committing murder with guns (Senate Hearings, 1993) and in 1990, 82% of all murder victims aged 15 to 19 years and 76% of victims aged 20 to 24 years were killed by firearms (Roth, 1994).

AUTHOR'S NOTE: I would like to thank Crime and Justice Research Unit and Dr. Arthur Cosby, Director, at the Social Science Research Center, Mississippi State University for access to the data used in this study. These data were collected under a grant to the Social Science Research Center by the Division of Public Safety Planning, Mississippi Department of Public Safety. Principal investigators for the project were Drs. Melvin Ray and Phyllis Gray-Ray. I also would like to thank Barbara Costello of Mississippi State University, Brian Fife, William Ludwin, and T. Neil Moore of Indiana University-Purdue University Fort Wayne, and two anonymous reviewers for their helpful comments on the composition of this article. Correspondence concerning this article should be addressed to David C. May at the School of Public and Environmental Affairs, Indiana University—Purdue University Fort Wayne, Neff Hall, 2101 Coliseum Blvd. East, Fort Wayne, Indiana 46805: E-mail: mayd@ipfw.edu; phone: 219-481-6531 (office), or 219-481-6346 (fax).

David C. May, YOUTH & SOCIETY, Vol. 31 No. 1, pp. 100–127. Copyright © 1999 by Sage Publications, Inc. Reprinted by permission of Sage Publications, Inc.

The problem of violent crime among adolescents is particularly acute in places where youth spend much of their time. Arguably, there is no single place where youth consistently congregate more than at school. Although deaths at school as a result of violence are rare events (76 violent student deaths in the 1992–1994 academic years), the general perception is that school-associated violence is on the increase (Kachur et al., 1996). Although Kachur et al. indicate that this does not appear to be the case, school violence, and particularly gun violence at school, is a problem that is not easily ignored. Some have argued that approximately 100,000 students take guns to school every day (Senate Hearings, 1993; Wilson & Zirkel, 1994). Estimates of the percentage of students who take guns to school vary widely, however; the percentage has been determined to be anywhere from .5% (Chandler, Chapman, Rand, & Taylor, 1998) to approximately 9% who carry a gun to school at least "now and then" (Sheley & Wright, 1993, p. 5). Furthermore, a majority of students say it would be little or no trouble to get a gun if they wanted one (Sheley & Wright, 1993). It is obvious that firearms in our schools are a problem.

Although numerous studies have examined prevalence of firearms possession among school-aged adolescents (Callahan & Rivara, 1992; Center to Prevent Handgun Violence, 1993; Chandler et al. 1998; Hechinger, 1992; Roth, 1994; Wilson & Zirkel, 1994), the study of causes of firearm possession at school has all but been neglected. Of those researchers who have attempted to examine determinants of adolescent firearm possession, many argue that protection is an often cited reason for weapon possession and provide various explanations for this finding (Asmussen, 1992; Bergstein, Hemenway, Kennedy, Quaday, & Ander, 1996; Blumstein, 1995; Hemenway, Prothrow-Stith, Bergstein, Ander, & Kennedy, 1996; Sheley, 1994; Sheley & Wright, 1993); in fact, Sheley and Wright (1995) determined that 89% of the gun carriers in their sample of youth in correctional facilities and inner-city youth felt that self-protection was a *very important* reason for owning a handgun. Only one study (Sheley & Brewer, 1995), however, examines the association between fear and firearm possession at school (see below for detailed discussion).

There have been many studies that have attempted to determine characteristics of adult firearms owners as well as research that seeks to determine individuals' motivation for owning guns. One explanation that has surfaced to account for why adults own firearms is the "fear and loathing hypothesis" (Wright, Rossi, & Daly, 1983, p. 49). The fear and loathing hypothesis suggests that people buy guns in response to their fear of crime and other incivilities present in our society. According to the fear and loathing hypothesis, individuals, fearful of elements of the larger society (e.g., crime and violence), go through a mental process in which they begin to deplore crime, criminals, and the like and purchase firearms for protection. Recently, many researchers have diminished the loathing aspect of the hypothesis

and have examined what would more accurately be called the fear of criminal victimization hypothesis.

Several studies have attempted to test this hypothesis, with mixed results (Arthur, 1992; Lizotte, Bordua, & White, 1981; Smith & Uchida, 1988; Wright & Marston, 1975). These studies, however, are limited in that they use only adult populations; excluding the study conducted by Sheley and Brewer (1995), the fear of criminal victimization hypothesis has never been tested using a sample of adolescents.

Sheley and Brewer (1995), in an examination of suburban high school students in Louisiana, were the first to specifically test the fear of criminal victimization hypothesis among adolescents by investigating the effect of fear on adolescent gun possession at school. They determined that fear had a nonsignificant association with carrying firearms to school, particularly for males. Their study was limited, however, by the fact that they used a single-item indicator of fear of criminal victimization, a method often criticized in the fear of crime literature (see Ferraro, 1995, for a review).

Although there may be no reason to treat gun ownership among adults as a deviant behavior, gun possession among juveniles should be treated as such. Despite the fact that legislation allows adults to carry firearms in many areas, it is illegal in all areas for juveniles to carry firearms to school. This act is not only a violation of the law, it also undermines the authority of schoolteachers and other officials. For these reasons, this act must be considered delinquent.

Furthermore, it is expected that the correlates of delinquency should be the same as the correlates of juvenile gun ownership. Although many of the aforementioned evaluations offer various explanations as to why youth possess firearms, often arguing that the possession is due to structural or personality factors, none attempt to test the effects of fear of criminal victimization on adolescent firearm possession, while controlling for competing explanations of delinquent behavior. These studies, although accepting that carrying a weapon for protection may be due to fear of criminal victimization, fail to examine the specific relationship between fear of criminal victimization and firearm possession. This study attempts to fill that void.

The study makes two major contributions to the literature concerning adolescent firearm possession. First, I test the effect of the fear of criminal victimization hypothesis on juvenile firearm possession at school using a cumulative index to represent fear of criminal victimization, an effort heretofore unexplored. Second, this analysis enhances the relevant scholarship by controlling for variables in Hirschi's (1969) social control theory and a derivative of Sutherland's (1939/1947) differential association theory, a much-needed improvement in this area (see Benda & Whiteside, 1995, for a discussion).

Following social control theory, youth whose bond to society is weakest will be more likely to carry guns to school; advocates of differential association would argue that delinquent tendencies of a juvenile's associates would induce the adolescent to carry firearms to school. On the other hand, following the fear of criminal victimization hypothesis, those youth who are most fearful would be most likely to carry guns to school. Thus, this study seeks to determine if fear of criminal victimization is associated with juvenile gun possession at school, controlling for two acknowledged explanations of delinquency.

SOCIAL CONTROL THEORY

Social control theory is most often associated with Travis Hirschi's (1969) *Causes of Delinquency*. He explains the desire for delinquency by positing that we are all capable of committing criminal acts. Hirschi stated that individuals who have strong social bonds and attachments to society and social institutions (such as the family and school) are less likely to commit delinquent acts.

According to Hirschi (1969), there are four elements of the social bond: attachment, commitment, involvement, and belief. Hirschi argues that the stronger the attachment between the adolescent and the society, and the more committed that adolescent is to the rules of society, the smaller the chance that the juvenile will become delinquent. Hirschi further states that those youth involved in conventional activities (jobs, extracurricular activities at school, etc.) and those adolescents who believe in the conventions of society and the restrictions of behavior placed on them by society will be less likely to commit delinquent acts. A number of more recent studies have confirmed Hirschi's ideas (Cernkovich, 1978; Cernkovich & Giordano, 1987, 1992; Fagan & Wexler, 1987; Rankin & Kern, 1994; Wiatrowski, Griswold, & Roberts, 1981). Following Hirschi's theory, those who exhibit a weaker social bond with society will be more likely to carry guns to school.

DIFFERENTIAL ASSOCIATION THEORY

Differential association theory was begun by Edwin Sutherland (1939/1947) in his classic work *Principles of Criminology*. Sutherland argued that people engage in deviant activity because of "an excess of definitions favorable to violation of law over definitions unfavorable to violation of law" (p. 6). Sutherland posited that individuals learn these definitions from intimate personal groups; thus, according to Sutherland, individuals learn to engage in criminal behavior through interactions with others who have values and beliefs that encourage breaking the law.

Although differential association theory has been one of the major theoretical explanations of engagement in crime for more than 50 years (see Akers, 1996, for a thorough review of history and present state of differential association), recently Akers (1985, 1992) has merged differential association theory with operant conditioning. Like Sutherland (1939/1947), Akers argues that delinquent conduct is more likely to develop when the peers of an adolescent define delinquent behavior as appropriate and reward that individual for delinquent behavior (see Winfree, Backstrom, & Mays, 1994, for a review of process). Williams and McShane (1999) review numerous works that test differential association theory and surmise that most research testing differential association has established that association with peers who are criminal or delinquent is one of the strongest predictors of involvement in delinquency. Following Akers's and Sutherland's theories, then, those whose friends have values and beliefs that encourage breaking the law will be most likely to carry guns to school.

FEAR OF CRIMINAL VICTIMIZATION HYPOTHESIS

The fear of criminal victimization hypothesis argues that firearm ownership and possession among some people has been motivated by fear of criminal victimization (Newton & Zimring, 1969). Consequently, according to the fear of criminal victimization hypothesis, a group of gun owners

purchase guns for protection from crime and criminals; consequently, those who are most fearful of criminal victimization will be those most likely to own a firearm.

According to the fear of crime literature, females, the elderly, those with lower income and education, urban residents, and African Americans are more fearful than their counterparts (Baumer, 1985; Belyea & Zingraff, 1988; Box, Hale, & Andrews, 1988; Braungart, Braungart, & Hoyer, 1980; Clemente & Kleiman, 1976, 1977; Garofalo, 1979; Kennedy & Krahn, 1984; Kennedy & Silverman, 1984; Larson, 1982; Lawton & Yaffee, 1980; Parker, 1988; Sharp & Dodder, 1985). It follows that these groups would also be the most likely to purchase and carry guns.

As alluded to earlier, tests of this hypothesis have produced inconclusive results. Some authors find that those who are most fearful are most likely to own guns for protection (Lizotte et al., 1981; Smith & Uchida, 1988); other researchers have found little evidence that fear of crime influences carrying a gun for protection (Adams, 1996; Arthur, 1992; Bankston & Thompson, 1989; Bankston, Thompson, Jenkins, & Forsyth, 1990; Williams & McGrath, 1976; Wright et al., 1983).

Although a tremendous volume of research has been produced in the area of fear of criminal victimization and its effect on adult gun ownership and use, two glaring inadequacies remain. The fear of criminal victimization hypothesis has not been tested on adolescents; by the same token, it has not been tested either against, or along with, any other theory of juvenile delinquency or as an explanation for delinquent behavior. The purpose of this study is to fill this void within the literature. This study will attempt to determine the impact of the fear of criminal victimization on juvenile firearms possession. This relationship then will be tested against the relationship between the control that social institutions (such as family and school) have and the influence that peers have on adolescents' firearm possession, to determine the association that these factors have on adolescent gun possession.

The fear of criminal victimization hypothesis, social control theory, and differential association all offer explanations for juvenile firearm possession; the substance of each theory's explanation, however, varies greatly. According to the fear of criminal victimization hypothesis, adolescents who are more fearful would be more likely to carry guns; advocates of control theory would argue that adolescents with weaker bonds to society would be more likely to carry guns; and finally, proponents of differential association theory would argue that youth whose peers were most approving of engagement in delinquency would be most likely to carry guns. Thus, if, after controlling for two known explanations of deviance, the relationship between fear of criminal victimization and adolescent firearm possession still persists, support for the fear of criminal victimization hypothesis will increase.

METHOD

SAMPLE

Data for this study were obtained from a study of Mississippi high school students conducted in the spring of 1992. As the South has the highest rate of gun ownership by region (Kleck, 1997), and Mississippi was the site of the first of several highly publicized schoolyard shootings in the academic year of 1997–1998, gun-carrying behavior of Mississippi adolescents is of particular interest in this field of inquiry. A two-stage sampling process was used to ensure selection of urban, semiurban, and

rural counties in Mississippi. Census data were used to determine the four (urban) metropolitan counties in Mississippi. The rest of the counties then were divided into semiurban and rural groups, based on population, and a sample was chosen from each (Ray, Gray-Ray, Robertson, & Turner, 1994).

Letters encouraging participation in the study then were sent to all of the superintendents in each school district. As anticipated, some of the selected school superintendents refused to participate in the study. The 10th, 11th, and 12th graders in each school in the districts that agreed to participate then were surveyed via a closed-ended questionnaire. The sample is composed of a total of 8,338 respondents.

As some of the district superintendents refused to participate in the study, the sampling process cannot be viewed as "strict probability methodology" (Ray et al., 1994, p. 15). However, the data were acquired both from rural and urban areas in the state (Ray et al., 1994) and ensures an adequate representation of the state's high school population. The sample also is representative of the high school population in terms of race and gender.[1]

DEPENDENT VARIABLE

The dependent variable is juvenile firearm possession at school and was operationalized through the question, "How many times have you carried a gun to school?" Responses were collapsed into two categories, with those who answered *never* coded (0) and those who responded *one or more* times coded as (1). Only 637 students (8.1%) indicated that they had carried a firearm to school one or more times.

INDEPENDENT VARIABLES

The independent variables include an index representing fear of criminal victimization, an index representing the strength of the adolescent's bond to society (social control), and a similar index representing deviant attitudes of the adolescent's peers (differential association). Due to their significant associations with delinquent behavior found in the literature, race, gender, residence, number of parental figures in the household, socioeconomic status, and gang membership are used as control variables. Finally, as neighborhood incivility has been determined to be a strong predictor of fear of crime among adults (Bursik & Grasmik, 1993; Will & McGrath, 1995), an index of perceived neighborhood incivility is included as a control variable as well. The questions used to measure the independent variables are in the appendix.

PERCEIVED NEIGHBORHOOD INCIVILITY INDEX

The exogenous variable, perceived neighborhood incivility, was obtained by constructing an index using responses to statements concerning how the respondent viewed his or her neighborhood, such as "There are drug dealers in my neighborhood." The indicators used to construct the perceived neighborhood incivility scale are in the appendix. Item analysis was conducted on the index and Cronbach's alpha was used to determine its reliability. The construct demonstrated an internal reliability of .753, indicating that the index is a reliable measure of perceived neighborhood incivility.

FEAR OF CRIMINAL VICTIMIZATION INDEX

The fear of criminal victimization hypothesis states that those who are more fearful will be more likely to carry guns (Wright et al., 1983). This hypothesis does not postulate that excessive fear leads to crime commission. In contrast, its premise is that the fearful will carry fire-arms to protect themselves from crime.

Fear of crime among the adolescents was measured through construction of a fear of criminal victimization index composed of nine items. The items used to measure the respondent's fear are also in the appendix. The Cronbach's alpha for the scale was .896. It is hypothesized that those respondents scoring higher on the fear scale will be more likely to have carried a gun to school.

SOCIAL CONTROL INDEX

The research reviewed earlier suggests that those adolescents with stronger bonds between themselves and family and school institutions will be less likely to commit delinquent acts (Hirschi, 1969; Jensen, 1972; Reiss, 1951; Wiatrowski et al., 1981). The adolescent's involvement with social institutions was measured by creating a social control index. The index consists of 11 questions or statements, which are included in the appendix. The Cronbach's alpha for the scale was .734. It is hypothesized that those adolescents scoring at the lower end of the scale will be more likely to carry a firearm to school than those on the higher end of the scale.

DIFFERENTIAL ASSOCIATION INDEX

As noted from the research reviewed earlier, those adolescents whose peers have the greatest amount of definitions favorable to violation of the law and engage in the most deviant acts are more likely to engage in delinquent acts (see Williams & McShane, 1999, for a review). Following differential association theory, an index was created to represent the deviant definitions and activities of one's peers.

Cronbach's alpha was used to measure the reliability of the index. The for the scale was .614. It is hypothesized that those adolescents scoring at the higher end of the scale will be more likely to carry a firearm to school than those on the lower end of the scale.

DEMOGRAPHIC CHARACTERISTICS

It is feasible to suggest that as adolescents age and become more familiar with their school surroundings and peers, they will be more able and thus more likely to obtain a firearm if they desire. Thus, it is hypothesized that older youth will be more likely to bring firearms to school than their younger counterparts.

Race will also be used as a control variable. As the overwhelming majority of Mississippi residents fall into one of two racial categories (White and African American), responses to the race question were dichotomized into two categories: White and Black. Several researchers have determined that Whites are less delinquent than Blacks (Cernkovich & Giordano, 1987; Rosen, 1985) and Whites are less fearful than non-Whites; subsequently, Blacks will be more likely to carry guns to school.

Regardless of the theory employed when predicting delinquency, males are more likely than females to be delinquent (Cernkovich & Giordano, 1987, 1992; Hirschi & Gottfredson, 1994). However, the fear of criminal victimization hypothesis would predict that females, the more fearful group, would be more likely to carry firearms. Sheley and Wright (1995) further determined that protective gun possession was more common among females than males in their sample. The question used to assess firearm possession in this study, however, does not allow the researcher to gauge reasons for possession. Thus, even though females may be more likely to possess firearms for protection, it is hypothesized that males will be much more likely to carry guns to school than will their female counterparts, a finding confirmed in numerous studies (e.g. Arria, Wood, & Anthony, 1995; Sheley & Wright, 1995).

Several researchers have identified an inverse relationship between socioeconomic status and delinquency (Reiss, 1951; Rosen, 1985; Wiatrowski et al., 1981). People with lower incomes also are more fearful. Thus, those youth from households with lower household income will be more likely to carry firearms to school.

Although some have argued that family structure does not affect delinquency, particularly violent delinquency (Salts, Linholm, Goddard, & Duncan, 1995), many have indicated that juveniles from disrupted households (those with one parent) will be more likely than those from intact households (two or more adults in the household) to commit delinquent acts (Gove & Crutchfield, 1982; Hirschi & Gottfredson, 1994; Matsueda & Heimer, 1987; Reiss, 1951). Such findings support Hirschi's control theory. According to Hirschi (1969), two parents will have more control over the juvenile and his or her whereabouts than will one, especially if one of the two parents is not employed. It is reasonable to assume that the relationship will be the same for firearm possession at school as well. Following control theory, it is expected that those juveniles from disrupted family settings will be more likely to carry a gun to school than will their counterparts from households with two parents.

Finally, gang members have been demonstrated to engage in disproportionate amounts of delinquency, including carrying guns (Block & Block, 1993; Blumstein, 1995; Dukes, Martinez, & Stein, 1997; Knox, 1991; Spergel, 1990). Thus, it is hypothesized that gang members will be more likely to carry guns as well.

As the dependent variable is dichotomous, logistic regression will be used in the analysis. Logistic regression uses maximum likelihood of estimation (MLE) to estimate parameter values in the regression equation. For large samples, MLE estimates are unbiased and normally distributed (Bohrnstedt & Knoke, 1994).

RESULTS

Characteristics of the sample are presented in **Table 1**. Table 1 classifies the sample into gun carriers and nongun carriers. There were several statistically significant differences between the two groups. First, the mean score was significantly higher for the gun carriers than for the nongun carriers on the fear scale (17.101 vs. 14.271, $p < .001$) and the perceived incivility scale (7.139 vs. 5.842, $p < .001$). Gun carriers also scored significantly lower on the social control index (27.250) than did the nongun carriers (30.568, $p < .001$) and significantly higher on the differential association index (6.932 vs. 5.394, $p < .001$).

The percentage distributions in Table 1 also reveal important differences between gun and nongun carriers. As expected, the percentage of gun carriers who were male (83.7%) is much larger than the percentage of nongun carriers who were male (41.5%), as was the percentage of gun carriers who were gang members (61.5% vs. 4.6%). The percentage of gun carriers who were Black (55.4%) was also larger than the percentage of nongun carriers who were Black (46.2%). A lower proportion of the gun carriers came from two-parent households (50.7%) than did nongun carriers (58.0%). Furthermore, a larger percentage of youth from the 17 to 18 years and 19 to 20 years age groups (61.1% and 11.8%, respectively) were found among the gun carriers than among the nongun carriers (54.6% and 5.2%, respectively). Finally, there was little difference between gun

carriers and nongun carriers across household income or place of residence.

The results presented in Table 1 indicate that significant associations exist between adolescent firearm possession and the independent variables included in this study. To determine the effect of the factors reflected in the perceived incivility index, the fear index, the social control index, and the differential association index on adolescent firearm possession, controlling for the demographic variables, logistic regression will be used.

The results of regressing gun possession at school on the variables in this study are presented in Table 2. The first logistic regression model presented in Table 2 regresses adolescent gun possession on those demographic variables that have been determined to have statistically significant associations with firearm ownership among adults, namely, gender, race, age, household income, place of residence, and gang membership. In addition, due to the adolescent nature of the sample, a variable representing parental presence in the household is included as well. In the second model, perceived neighborhood incivility and the index representing fear of crime are added and adolescent firearm possession is regressed on these variables and the set of demographic variables. The final model includes the index representing social control and differential association, with the previous demographic variables, the fear of crime index, and the index representing perceived neighborhood incivility. As there was an inordinate amount of missing data for the variables included in the social control, differential association, and perceived neighborhood incivility indices (which, analysis reveals, was due to respondent attrition because of their placement at the end of the questionnaire), race-sex subgroup mean substitution is used throughout the analysis.

TABLE 1:   Characteristics of Gun Carriers and Nongun Carriers

Variable	GUN CARRIERS		NONGUN CARRIERS	
	M	**SD**	**M**	**SD**
Social control scale	27.250***	4.915	30.568	4.599
Differential association scale	6.932***	1.946	5.394	1.598
Fear scale	17.101***	6.215	14.271	4.812
Perceived incivility	7.139***	2.302	5.842	2.048
	n	**%**	**n**	**%**
Gender				
Male	533	83.7	3,011	41.5
Female	104	16.3	4,238	58.5
Total *n*	637		7,249	
Race				
White	284	44.6	3,901	53.8
Black	353	55.4	3,348	46.2
Total *n*	637		7,249	
Age (years)				
13–14	6	0.9	50	0.7
15–16	166	26.1	2,866	39.6
17–18	389	61.1	3,954	54.6
19–20	75	11.8	376	5.2
Total *n*	636		7,246	
Parental arrangement				
2 or more parents (intact) household	323	50.7	4,205	58.0
Single-parent (disrupted) household	313	49.1	3,036	41.9
Total *n*	636		7,241	
Family income				
Less than $10,000	88	13.8	922	12.7
$10,000–$19,999	101	15.9	1,368	18.9
$20,000–$29,999	140	22.0	1,546	21.3
$30,000–$39,999	120	18.8	1,503	20.7
More than $40,000	159	25.0	1,652	22.8
Total *n*	608		6,991	
Gang membership				
Yes	286	61.5	315	4.6
No	179	38.5	6,523	95.4
Total *n*	465		6,838	
Place of residence				
Rural farm	72	11.3	579	8.0
Rural nonfarm	101	15.9	1,580	21.8
Outside suburbs	90	14.1	1,020	14.1
In suburbs	169	26.5	1,831	25.3
Near center of city	202	31.7	2,212	30.5
Total *n*	634		7,222	

***$p < .001$

TABLE 2: Logistic Regression Results of Adolescent Gun Carrying on Demographic Variables, Incivility, Fear of Criminal Victimization, Social Control Index, and Differential Association Index

Variable	MODEL 1 β/SE	Exp (B)	Wald	MODEL 2 β/SE	Exp (B)	Wald	MODEL 3 β/SE	Exp (B)	Wald
Male	1.815/.132***	6.142	189.404	1.804/.133***	6.073	173.511	1.482/.137***	4.402	116.693
Black	.353/.117**	1.423	9.157	.208/.122	1.232	2.925	.487/.128***	1.627	14.503
Age	.460/.086***	1.585	28.715	.470/.087***	1.601	29.481	.524/.089***	1.689	34.497
Two-parent home	-.301/.110**	.740	7.445	-.291/.112**	.748	6.696	-.264/.115*	.768	5.238
Family income	.084/.043*	1.088	3.879	.133/.044**	1.142	9.239	.120/.045**	1.128	7.214
Urban	-.028/.040	.973	.485	-.051/.041	.950	1.598	-.051/.042	.950	1.494
Gang member	2.198/.119***	9.003	338.761	2.004/.124***	7.415	262.080	1.665/.130***	5.283	165.247
Perceived incivility				.162/.023***	1.176	48.024	.105/.025***	1.111	18.186
Fear index				.069/.009***	1.072	59.212	.070/.009***	1.072	55.702
Social control index							-.079/.012***	.924	43.573
Differential assoc. index							.277/.031***	1.319	78.687
Constant	-5.044/.287***		264.682	-7.759/.346***		358.552	-6.737/.593***		129.117
Listwise *n*	7,303			7,303			7,303		
-2 Log Likelihood	2,855.631			2,740.868			2,574.519		
Goodness of Fit	6,619.220			6,608.242			6,074.746		
Model chi-square	759.356***			874.119***			1,040.468***		

*p < .05. **p < .01. ***p < .001.

The results obtained from regressing adolescent firearm possession on the demographic variables are presented in the first model in Table 2. The results indicate that, as expected, gender, race, age, parental structure, income, and gang membership had statistically significant associations with adolescent firearm possession. The regression coefficients indicate that males ($\beta = 1.815, p < .001$) were six times as likely as females to possess a firearm at school whereas Blacks ($\beta = .353, p < .01$) were 1.4 times as likely as Whites to carry a firearm to school. Older adolescents ($\beta = .460, p < .001$) were also more likely to carry guns to school than were their younger counterparts. The association between parental structure and adolescent firearm possession was also significant, as those youth from households with other than two adults were significantly more likely ($\beta = -.301, p < .01$) than their counterparts from two-parent homes to carry a firearm to school. Those students from families with higher incomes were more likely than students from families with lower incomes ($\beta = .084, p < .05$) to carry guns to school. Finally, gang members were nine times as likely to carry firearms to school as adolescents who were not in gangs ($\beta = 2.198, p < .001$). Place of residence had no statistically significant effect on adolescent firearm possession at school.

The second model in Table 2 presents the results of regressing adolescent firearm possession on the variables included in the first model with the addition of the perceived neighborhood incivility index and the fear of criminal victimization index. Males ($\beta = 1.804, p < .001$) were again six times as likely as females to indicate that they had carried a firearm to school. Interestingly, however, with the addition of perceived neighborhood incivility and the fear of crime index, the effect of race became nonsignificant.[2] Youth from two-parent

homes ($\beta = -.291, p < .01$) were again significantly less likely than youth from other than two-parent homes to carry a firearm to school, whereas older youth continued to be significantly more likely than younger youth to carry a firearm to school ($\beta = .470, p < .001$). Gang members remained significantly more likely to carry a firearm to school than youth who were not in gangs ($\beta = 2.004, p < .001$). The association between household income and adolescent firearm possession remained statistically significant, with those youth from households with greater income again significantly more likely to carry a gun to school than their counterparts from households with lower incomes ($\beta = .133, p < .01$). The perceived incivility index and the fear of criminal victimization index had statistically significant effects on adolescent firearm possession at school, indicating that those youth who perceived their neighborhood to be most disorderly ($\beta = .162, p < .001$) and those youth who were most fearful of criminal victimization ($\beta = .069, p < .001$) were significantly more likely to carry a gun to school than their counterparts, who perceived their neighborhood to be less disorderly and who were less fearful, respectively. Thus, following the fear of criminal victimization hypothesis, those youth who are most fearful and who perceive their neighborhoods as most disorderly are most likely to carry a gun to school.

The third model in Table 2 presents the results of regressing adolescent firearm possession on the variables included in the second model with the addition of the social control index and the differential association index. Males ($\beta = 1.482, p < .001$), Blacks ($\beta = .487, p < .001$), older respondents ($\beta = .524, p < .001$), youth from other than two-parent homes ($\beta = -.264, p < .05$), gang members ($\beta = 1.665, p < .001$), and respondents with higher levels of household income (β = .120, $p < .01$) continued to be significantly more likely than their counterparts to carry a firearm to school, whereas those adolescents who perceived their neighborhoods as disorderly (β = .105, $p < .001$) and those adolescents who were most fearful (β = .070, $p < .001$) were again significantly more likely than their counterparts to indicate that they had carried a firearm to school. Moreover, those who scored lower on the social control index and those who scored higher on the differential association index (β = −.079, $p < .001$ and β = .277, $p < .001$, respectively) were significantly more likely to indicate that they had carried a firearm to school. Thus, as expected, those youth with weaker bonds to society and those youth with more deviant friends were more likely to carry a firearm to school.

DISCUSSION

The results of this study generally support the findings of previous studies dealing with social control, differential association, and delinquent acts. Those children who scored lower on the social control scale, exhibiting lower parental and familial attachment, were significantly more likely to possess firearms at school, as were those youth who scored higher on the index measuring differential association. Both of these findings are consistent with the literature reviewed earlier.

The findings concerning family structure also conform with those from other studies; namely, those children from single-parent homes parents were significantly more likely to carry guns to school. The evaluation also is consistent with previous studies in demonstrating that males, Blacks, and gang members were more likely to commit the delinquent act in question.

As expected, age was positively associated with gun carrying; the older youth were more likely to carry guns to school than were their younger counterparts.

Household income also had a statistically significant positive association with carrying firearms to school; those youth who were from families with higher household income were more likely to carry firearms to school. As this finding is contrary to the literature concerning social control, differential association, and the fear of criminal victimization hypothesis, this finding deserves some explanation. There are two divergent explanations for this finding. It could be that those youth from homes with higher household income had greater financial resources to purchase firearms, thus allowing them to carry a gun to school, whereas other youth might choose some less expensive weapon. This study is limited in that it is unable to examine that relationship.

A second, and perhaps more likely, explanation is that the relationship between household income and adolescent firearm possession may be due to the methodology of the study. Adolescents were asked to estimate their household income; it is quite probable that many of the youth did not have this knowledge and may have exaggerated their household income. Finally, the size of the sample also leads one to question the substantive value of this finding. In a sample this large, associations may achieve statistical significance ($p < .05$) but not substantive significance. Whatever the explanation, this finding should be viewed with extreme caution.

Place of residence had no statistically significant association with adolescent firearm possession. This contradicted the hypothesis concerning the relationship between these variables. One explanation for this might be that the adolescents are unaware of the actual size of their residence;

furthermore, inasmuch as the sample consists of adolescents from Mississippi, a primarily rural state, even those who classified themselves as living at the center of the city probably live in areas that could not be characterized as traditional, urban residents.

The most interesting finding from this study concerns the relationship between perceived neighborhood incivility, fear of criminal victimization, and adolescent firearm possession. Adolescents who perceived their neighborhoods as most disorderly and who were most fearful were significantly more likely to carry a gun to school. These findings support the fear of criminal victimization hypothesis: at least in part, students carry guns to school because of the fear of classmates and the perceived criminogenic conditions of their neighborhoods that they experience. It is evident that fear of criminal victimization in juveniles creates similar reactions to fear of criminal victimization in adults.

On further review, the association might not be as peculiar as it sounds. With the prevalence of guns in our society, guns are readily available for juveniles. As mentioned earlier, a majority of students know where to get a gun if they desire. Those students who are most fearful might take action to get a gun and take that gun to school for protection. Another plausible explanation might be that those juveniles who are most delinquent are also most fearful of other delinquents with whom they may interact. If this is the case, their fear might be a result instead of a cause of delinquency. It could be that the delinquents develop their fear after they have committed delinquent acts.

It also could be that adolescents' fear might be explained by the lifestyles approach, which states that those individuals who put themselves in situations in which crimes will occur are more likely to commit

crimes and to be victimized by them (Cohen & Felson, 1979; Hindelang, Gottfredson, & Garofalo, 1978). These adolescents could very well develop the fear because they see so many delinquent acts being committed by their peers (as this study shows, those adolescents whose peers were most delinquent, as well as those youth who were gang members, were also more likely to carry firearms) and thus become fearful that one day their delinquent friends, or adversaries of their friends, might harm them. It is beyond the nature of this study to test this temporal relationship. However, further research in this area would be beneficial. A longitudinal study might be used to determine which occurs first; the fear or the firearm-related delinquency.

IMPLICATIONS

The purpose of this study was to examine the association between the fear of criminal victimization hypothesis and adolescent firearm possession, while controlling for more traditional explanations of delinquency—namely, differential association and social control theory. Analysis of the results indicate that the fear of criminal victimization hypothesis, social control theory, and differential association are all statistically significant indicators of adolescent firearm possession.

The implications of this study are twofold. First, social control theory, differential association theory, and the fear of criminal victimization hypothesis have a significant association with firearms possession. Second, the fear of criminal victimization hypothesis seems to apply to gun ownership and possession at least as well among juveniles as among adults.

This knowledge may aid policy makers who, due to the perceived rash of school shootings in 1998, are concerned with preventing school violence, particularly serious violence. As the findings from this study indicate, at least part of the reason that youth carry firearms to school is because of a fear of criminal victimization at school and a perception that their neighborhoods are dens of criminal activity. The findings from this study explicate a phenomenon known to social science researchers for quite some time but only recently identified and prioritized by policy makers. To reduce the number of firearms in school, the circumstances that cause youth to bring firearms to school must be reduced. Although taking steps to alleviate the problem of fear on the school grounds is important, it is equally important that these steps be taken in the neighborhoods where these youth live as well. It is imperative that we find measures to reduce the fear of crime of students at school, as well as their fear of crime in their neighborhoods.

There are a number of steps that could be implemented in this regard that are already in place with adult populations. First, as Kenney and Watson (1998) suggest, adolescents should be empowered to make use of school and police resources to reduce fear and disorder problems at school and at home. By implementing problem-solving methods widely used by police and Neighborhood Watch programs throughout the country, adolescents can be empowered to identify sources of fear of crime in their environment and identify and implement steps aimed at alleviating those conditions.

Second, it is well demonstrated that much of the public perception of crime in the United States is strongly influenced by the media. Thus, it is imperative that more accurate information about the problem of guns and violence in schools be presented. Universities throughout the country regularly publish reports identifying the crime

that goes on at their campus. It is quite possible that if junior high and high schools throughout the country were to implement a similar reporting system, the perception that crime, particularly crime with guns, is rampant at schools could be alleviated and thus reduced.

Finally, an important step in this effort to curb violence and fear of violence among adolescents might be to ensure that adolescents do not carry firearms to school. Although various measures have been implemented in an attempt to curb this activity (e.g., metal detectors, banning book bags, increased use of locker searches), each needs to be evaluated to determine its effectiveness in combating crime at school. Those measures that are most effective subsequently can be implemented in schools throughout the country. When these measures are institutionalized, the first step will be taken in reducing firearm possession at school and concomitantly reducing school violence.

Getting into trouble in my group is a way of earning respect. The kinds in my group often get into trouble.

The remaining item was coded as (1) for *strongly agree* and (4) for *strongly disagree*.

The members of my group feel that laws should be obeyed.

Responses were combined into a summated index with high scores representing those youth whose associates had an excess of definitions favorable to deviance. The Cronbach's alpha for the idex was .614.

Notes

1. According to the U.S. Bureau of the Census (1990), the school-age population (ages 6–18 years) in Mississippi was as follows: 154,608 Black females

(28.4%), 144,010 White females (26.4%). 121,215 Black males (22.4%), and 125,293 White males (23.0%). The estimates for those same groups in this sample were as follows: 2,195 Black females (27.2%), 2,208 White females (27.2%), 1,627 Black males (20.2%), and 2,042 White males (25.3%)

2. Separate analyses were run for Blacks and Whites to determine if an interaction existed with either perceived incivility or fear of victimization. The analyses revealed no such interaction; the effect of each of the variables included in the model was similar for both Blacks and Whites.

References

Adams, K. (1996). Guns and gun control. In T.J. Flanagan & D.R. Longtime (Eds.), *Americans view crime and justice: A national public opinion survey* (pp. 109–123). Thousand Oaks, CA: Sage.

Akers, R. L. (1985). *Deviant behavior: A social learning approach* (3rd ed.). Belmont, CA: Wadsworth.

Akers, R. L. (1992). *Drugs, alcohol, and society: Social structure, process, and policy.* Belmont, CA: Wadsworth.

Akers, R. L. (1996). Is differential association/social learning cultural deviance theory? *Criminology, 34*(2), 229–247.

Arria, A. M., Wood, N. P., & Anthony, J. (1995). Prevalence of carrying a weapon and related behaviors in urban schoolchildren, 1989 to 1993. *Archives of Pediatric and Adolescent Medicine, 149*, 1345–1350.

Arthur, J. A. (1992). Criminal victimization, fear of crime, and handgun ownership among Blacks: Evidence from national survey data. *American Journal of Criminal Justice, 16*(2), 121–141.

Asmussen, K. J. (1992). Weapon possession in public high schools. *School Safety, 28*, 28–30.

Bankston, W., & Thompson, C. (1989). Carrying firearms for protection: A causal model. *Sociological Inquiry, 59*(1), 75–87.

Bankston, W., Thompson, C., Jenkins, Q., & Forsyth, C. (1990). The influence of fear of crime, gender, and Southern culture on carrying firearms for protection. *Sociological Quarterly, 31*(2), 287–305.

Baumer, T. (1985). Testing a general model of fear of crime: Data from a national sample. *Journal of Research in Crime and Delinquency, 22*(3), 239–255.

Belyea, M. J., & Zingraff, M. T. (1988). Fear of crime and residential location. *Rural Sociology, 53*(4), 473–486.

Benda, B. B., & Whiteside, L. (1995). Testing an integrated model of delinquency using LISREL. *Journal of Social Service Research, 21*(2), 1–32.

Bergstein, J. M., Hemenway, D., Kennedy, B., Quaday, S., & Ander, R. (1996). Guns in young hands: A survey of urban teenagers' attitudes and behaviors related to handgun violence. *Journal of Trauma, Injury, Infection, and Critical Care, 41*(5), 794–798.

Block, C. R., & Block, R. (1993). *Street gang crime in Chicago.* Washington, DC: National Institute of Justice.

Blumstein, A. (1995). *Violence by young people: Why the deadly nexus?* Washington, DC: National Institute of Justice.

Bohrnstedt, G. W., & Knoke, D. (1994). *Statistics for social data analysis.* Itasca, IL: F.E. Peacock.

Box, S., Hale, C., & Andrews, G. (1988). Explaining fear of crime. *British Journal of Criminology, 28*(3), 340–356.

Braungart, M., Braungart, R., & Hoyer, W. (1980). Age, sex, and social factors in fear of crime. *Sociological Focus, 13*(1), 55–66.

Bursik, R. J., Jr., & Grasmick, H. G. (1993). *Neighborhoods and crime: The dimensions of effective community control.* Lexington, MA: Lexington Books.

Callahan, C. M., & Rivara, F. P. (1992). Urban high school youth and handguns: A school-based survey. *Journal of the American Medical Association, 267*(22), 3038–3042.

Center to Prevent Handgun Violence. (1993). *Kids carrying guns.* Washington, DC: Government Printing Office.

Cernkovich, S. A. (1978). Evaluating two models of delinquency causation. *Criminology, 16*(3), 335–354.

Cernkovich, S. A., & Giordano, P. C. (1987). Family relationships and delinquency. *Criminology, 25*(2), 295–321.

Cernkovich, S. A., & Giordano, P.C. (1992). School bonding, race, and delinquency. *Criminology, 30*(2), 261–289.

Chandler, K. A., Chapman, C. D., Rand, M. R., & Taylor, B. M. (1998). *Students' reports of school crime: 1989 and 1995.* Washington, DC: Departments of Education and Justice.

Clemente, F., & Kleiman, M. (1976). Fear of crime among the aged. *The Gerontologist, 16*(3), 207–210.

Clemente, F., & Kleiman, M. (1977, December). Fear of crime in the United States: A multivariate analysis. *Social Forces, 56*, 519–531.

Cohen, L. E., & Felson, M. (1979). Social change and crime rate trends: A routine activities approach. *American Sociological Review, 44*, 588–608.

Dukes, R. L., Martinez, R. O., & Stein, J. A. (1997). Precursors and consequences of membership in youth gangs. *Youth and Society, 29*(2), 139–165.

Fagan, J., & Wexler, S. (1987). Family origins of violent delinquents. *Criminology, 25*(3), 643–669.

Ferraro, K. F. (1995). *Fear of crime: Interpreting victimization risk.* Albany: State University of New York Press.

Fingerhut, L. (1993, March 23). *Firearm mortality among children, youth, and young adults 1–34 years of age, trends and current status: United States, 1985–90: Advance Data.* Hyattsville, MD: National Center for Health Statistics.

Garofalo, J. (1979). Victimization and the fear of crime. *Journal of Research on Crime and Delinquency, 16*, 80–97.

Gove, W. R., & Crutchfield, R. D. (1982). The family and juvenile delinquency. *Sociological Quarterly, 23*(3), 301–319.

Hechinger, F. M. (1992). *Fateful choices: Healthy youth for the 21st century.* New York: Hill and Wang.

Hemenway, D., Prothrow-Stith, D., Bergstein, J. M., Ander, R., & Kennedy, B. P. (1996). Gun carrying among adolescents. *Law and Contemporary Problems, 59*(1), 39–53.

Hindelang, M., Gottfredson, M., & Garofalo, J. (1978). *Victims of personal crime: An empirical foundation for a theory of personal victimization.* Cambridge, MA: Ballinger.

Hirschi, T. (1969). *Causes of delinquency.* Berkeley: University of California Press.

Hirschi, T, & Gottfredson, M. (1994). *The generality of deviance.* New Brunswick, NJ: Transaction Publishers.

Jensen, G. F. (1972). Parents, peers, and delinquent action: A test of the differential association perspective. *American Journal of Sociology, 78*(3), 562–575.

Kachur, S. P., Stennies, G. M., Powell, K. E., Modzeleski, W., Stephens, R., Murphy, R., Kresnow, M., Sleet, D., & Lowry, R. (1996). School-associated violent deaths in the United States, 1992 to 1994. *Journal of the American Medical Association, 275*(22), 1729–1733.

Kennedy, L. W., & Krahn, H. (1984). Rural-urban origin and fear of crime: The case for rural baggage. *Rural Sociology, 49*(2), 247–260.

Kennedy, L. W., & Silverman, R. A. (1984). Significant others and fear of crime among the elderly. *International Journal of Aging and Human Development, 20*(4), 241–256.

Kenney, D. J., & Watson, T. S. (1998). *Crime in the schools: Reducing fear and disorder with student problem solving.* Washington, DC: Police Executive Research Forum.

Kleck, G. (1997). *Targeting guns: Firearms and their control.* Hawthorne, NY: Aldine.

Knox, G. W. (1991). *An introduction to gangs.* Berrien Springs, MI: Vande Vere.

Larson, C. J. (1982). City size, fear, and victimization. *Free Inquiry in Creative Sociology, 10*(1), 13–22.

Lawton, M. P., & Yaffee, S. (1980). Victimization and fear of crime in elderly housing tenants. *Journal of Gerontology, 35*, 768–79.

Lizotte, A. J., Bordua, D. J., & White, C. S. (1981). Firearms ownership for sport and protection: Two not so divergent models. *American Sociological Review, 46*, 499–503.

Matsueda, R. L., & Heimer, K. (1987). Race, family structure, and delinquency: A test of differential association and social control theories. *American Sociological Review, 52*(6), 826–840.

Newton, G. D., & Zimring, F. E. (1969). *Firearms and violence in American life: A staff report to the national commission on the causes and prevention of violence.* Washington, DC: Government Printing Office.

Parker, K. D. (1988). Black-White differences in perceptions of fear of crime. *Journal of Social Psychology, 128*(4), 487–494.

Rankin, J. H., & Kern, R. (1994). Parental attachments and delinquency. *Criminology, 32*(4), 495–515.

Ray, M., Gray-Ray, P., Robertson, C., & Turner, S. (1994). Determinants of weapons carrying in Mississippi schools. In J. Bledinger & N. B. Lovell (Eds.), *Coping with violence in the schools* (pp. 9–31). Mississippi State: Mississippi State University College of Education.

Reiss, A. J., Jr. (1951). Delinquency as the failure of personal and social controls. *American sociological Review, 16*(2), 196–206.

Rosen, L. (1985). Family and delinquency: Structure or function? *Criminology, 23*(3), 553–573.

Roth, J. A. (1994). *Firearms and violence.* Washington, DC: National Institute of Justice.

Salts, C. J., Lindholm, B. W., Goddard, H. W., & Duncan, S. (1995). Predictive variables of violent behavior in adolescent males. *Youth and Society, 26*(3), 377–399.

Senate Hearings. (1993). *Children and gun violence.* Washington, DC: Government Printing Office.

Sharp, P. M., & Dodder, R. A., (1985). Victimization and the fear of crime: Some consequences by age and sex. *International Journal of Contemporary Sociology, 22*(1, 2), 149–161.

Sheley, J. F. (1994). Drug activity and firearms possession and use by juveniles. *The Journal of Drug Issue, 24*(3), 363–382.

Sheley, J. F., & Brewer, V. E. (1995). Possession and carrying of firearms among suburban youth. *Public Health Reports, 110*, 18–26.

Sheley, J. F., & Wright, J. D. (1993). *Gun acquisition and possession in selected juvenile samples.* Washington, DC: National Institute of Justice.

Sheley, J. F., & Wright, J. D. (1995). *In the line of fire: Youth, guns, and violence in urban America.* Hawthorne, NY: Aldine.

Smith, D. A., & Uchida, C. D. (1988). The social organization of self-help: A study of defensive weapon ownership. *American Sociological Review, 53*, 94–102.

Spergel, I. A. (1990). Youth gangs: Continuity and change. In M. Tonry & N. Morris (Eds.), *Crime and justice: A review of research* (Vol. 12, pp. 171–275). Chicago: University of Chicago Press.

Sutherland, E. H. (1947). *Principles of criminology* (4th ed.). Philadelphia: J. B. Lippincott. (Original work published in 1939).

U.S. Bureau of the Census. (1990). *1990 Census of population, social, and economic characteristics, United States.* Washington, DC: Author.

Wiatrowski, M. D., Griswold, D. B., & Roberts, M. K. (1981). Social control theory and delinquency. *American Sociological Review, 46*, 525–541.

Will, J. A., & McGrath, J. H. (1995). Crime, neighborhood perceptions, and the underclass: The relationship between fear of crime and class position. *Journal of Criminal Justice, 23*(2), 163–176.

Williams, F. P., III, & McShane, M. D. (1999). *Criminological theory* (3d ed.). Englewood Cliffs, NJ: Prentice Hall.

Williams, J. S., & McGrath, J. H., III. (1976). Why people own guns. *Journal of Communication, 26*, 22–30.

Wilson, J. M., & Zirkel, P. A. (1994). When guns come to school. *American School Board Journal, 181*, 32–34.

Winfree, L. T., Backstrom, T. V., & Mays, G. L. (1994). Social learning theory, self-reported delinquency, and youth gangs: A new twist on a general theory of crime and delinquency. *Youth and Society, 26*(2), 147–177.

Wright, J. D., & Marston, L. (1975). The ownership of the means of destruction: Weapons in the United States. *Social Problems, 23*, 92–107.

Wright, J. D., Rossi, P., & Daly, K. (1983). *Under the gun: Weapons, crime, and violence in America.* Hawthorne, NY: Aldine.

APPENDIX

Size of Residence

Which of the following responses best matches where you live?

1. In a neighborhood near the center of the city
2. In the suburbs but still inside the city/town limits
3. Outside the suburbs of my city/town
4. A rural nonfarm residence
5. A rural farm residence

Recoded: 1 = (5), 2 = (4), 3 = (3), 4 = (2), 5 = (1).

Age

How old are you?

1. Between 13 and 14 years old
2. Between 15 and 16 years old
3. Between 17 and 18 years old
4. Between 19 and 20 years old

Race

Which of the following best describes your racial or ethnic group?

1. White
2. African American/Black
3. Mexican/Spanish American
4. American Indian
5. Asian

Recoded: 1 = (0), 2 = (1), all other cases were deleted.

Gender

What is your gender?

1. Male
2. Female

Recoded: 1 = (1), 2 = (0).

Income

Please tell us what you think your family's total income was last year.

1. Less than $9,999
2. Between $10,000 and $19,999
3. Between $20,000 and $29,999
4. Between $30,000 and $39,999
5. More than $40,000

Family Composition

Whom are you living with?

1. Both parents
2. One parent
3. Both parents and grandparents
4. One parent and grandparents
5. Other

Recoded: 1 = (1, 3); 0 = (2, 4, 5).

Gang Membership

Are you a member of a youth gang?

1. Yes
2. No

Recoded: 1 = (1), 2 = (0).

Perceived Neighborhood Incivility Index

Respondents were asked to indicate how common each of the following items were in their neighborhood.

Broken cars on the street
Trash on the streets
Gang graffiti
Houses looking like they need repairing

Responses were coded as follows:

1. Not common at all
2. Somewhat common
3. Very common

Responses were combined into a summated index with high scores representing those youth who perceived their neighborhoods as most criminogenic.

Cronbach's alpha = .753

Fear of Criminal Victimization Index

Responses to the following nine items were scored in a four-item Likert scale ranging from *strongly agree* to *strongly disagree*. *Strongly agree* was coded as 4 and *strongly disagree* was coded as 1.

I am afraid to come to school sometimes

I am afraid to go to the school restroom at school sometimes.

I am afraid to go to the school lunchroom sometimes.

I am afraid of getting beaten up.

I am afraid of other kids taking my money/property.

I am afraid of being in study hall.

I am afraid when I walk to school.

I am afraid to attend athletic events because of fights.

I am afraid to go out at night with friends because of kids who like to make trouble.

Responses were combined into a summated index with high scores representing those youth who were most fearful of criminal victimization. The Cronbach's alpha for the index was .896.

Social Control Index

The index representing the strength of the individual's bond to society (social control) consists of 11 items. The items were as follows:

On average, how many hours do you spend studying each day?

1. None
2. 1 to 2 hours
3. 3 to 4 hours
4. 5 to 6 hours

The remaining 10 responses were scored in a four-item Likert scale ranging from *strongly agree* (coded as 4) to *strongly disagree* (coded as 1).

I enjoy school.

I try hard to do well in school.

I am involved in extracurricular activities.

I am proud of my school.

I spend time each day working on my homework.

My parents or parent know who I'm with when I'm away from home.

My parents or parent know where I am when I'm away from home.

I spend a lot of time interacting with my parents.

I spend a lot of time interacting with my sisters and brothers.

My family is important to me.

Responses were combined into a summated index with high scores representing those youth who had the strongest societal bond. The Cronbach's alpha for the index was .738.

Differential Association Index

The index representing the definitions favorable to deviance of the adolescent's peers (differential association) consists of three items. Responses to the following two items were scored in a four-item Likert scale ranging from *strongly agree* to *strongly disagree*. *Strongly agree* was coded as (4) and *strongly disagree* was coded as (1):

Representing Gangs in the News:

Media Constructions of Criminal Gangs

Carol Y. Thompson, Robert L. Young, and Ronald Burns

What people believe about crime and criminals influences Supreme Court decisions, criminal justice policies, the election of public leaders, and the routine activities of the public. Many attitudes and beliefs about crime and criminals are shaped and influenced by media representations of crime. In fact, it has been suggested that the media penetrate every aspect of social life and are as important to American culture as family, church, or economic institutions (Croteau and Hoynes 1997; Gergen 1991; McLuhan 1964). Most people spend several hours per day reading, watching, or listening to the mass media. Indeed, some spend more time in "mass-mediated" interaction than in actual human interaction (Erikson, Baranek, and Chan 1991; Gergen 1991). From CNN to the local newspaper, people look to the media for entertainment, information, assistance, and knowledge. As many researchers of crime and the media have suggested, crime news has long been and continues to be an information priority for the media (Altheide and Snow 1979; Barak 1994; Chermak 1995a; Media Monitor 1997;

Pritchard and Hughes 1997; Surette 1992) and constitutes a large percentage of news stories (Chermak 1995a:97; Chermak 1995b:47; Media Monitor 1997:2). Concentration on crime news not only influences public attitudes and opinions toward crime and criminals, it also helps to maintain crime as a salient political issue (Surette 1992).

One of the most prevalent crime news topics of the past two decades has been gang crime. The activities of violent criminal gangs have become a focal point of crime news, and fear of gangs has seriously eroded the quality of life among American urban dwellers. News stories that focus on gangs have influenced attitudes and opinions by providing vivid public images of gang crime and criminals. Gang news not only presents information, it also articulates ideological messages concerning the meaning and definition of gangs. Moreover, news stories influence community responses to gang activities, which in turn become part of the story to be reported. Despite the importance of gangs and gang activity as a social problem, and despite the frequently expressed conviction that news reporting gives shape and sometimes life to such problems, a comprehensive and systematic analysis of newspaper coverage of gangs and society's war on gangs has not been undertaken. Therefore, in this research we examined the images of criminal gangs and society's responses to them that emerge from newspaper reports. We also analyzed the role of the gang concept as a theme in social problems discourse. Through this analysis, we hope to understand the nature of these images and the meaning this discourse has for American culture.

THE SOCIAL CONSTRUCTION OF CRIME

Our analysis of the importance of media representations on the formation of social reality is informed by a social constructionist perspective. Our analysis fits most closely what Best (1993) has called *contextual constructionism*, inasmuch as we aim to study social problems discourse "within its context of culture and social structure" (p. 119). Generally, the information individuals use to construct a sense of reality comes from four sources: personal experience, other individuals, social groups and institutions, and the mass media (Altheide 1985; Surette 1992). Individuals in complex postindustrial societies have become especially dependent on the mass media as a resource in the formation of a sense of social reality (Altheide 1985; Cohen and Young 1981; Gergen 1991). This is especially true of beliefs and attitudes related to crime and criminal justice because most individuals have limited personal contact and experience with crime (Graber 1980; Surette 1992).

Inasmuch as most of the larger organizations that constitute the media are for-profit businesses, economic factors influence the content of broadcasts and publications. Newspapers produce news stories on the basis of what they think the public wants to read about. Because crime news is attention grabbing, it sells. Thus, the economic interests of the media are a major factor in the shaping of public attitudes about crime and its social context (Potter and Kappeler 1998).

In addition to their choices of what to cover, newspapers also contribute to the social construction of reality by participating in what Ibarra and Kitsuse (1993) called a rhetoric of social problems discourse. That is, the repetitive rhetorical tools used by reporters and the claims makers to whom they give voice help define and shape perceptions of the problems they discuss. One such device is the *motif* (cf. Best 1996). "Motifs are recurrent thematic elements and figures of speech that encapsulate or highlight some aspect of a social problem" and include such elements as "morally imbued metaphors and phrases" that are used in claims making (Ibarra and Kitsuse 1993:43). Also found in such discourse are a variety of rhetorical idioms, which call forth or draw on clusters of images (Ibarra and Kitsuse 1993:30). Indeed, the influence of the news media, even the print media, and the success of individual reporters rest on their ability to create powerful graphic images in the minds of consumers. In the world of social problems discourse, such images are as central a feature as the rhetoric through which they are created.

It is important, however, to recognize that the news media and the consumers of news are coparticipants in the social construction of reality (McLuhan 1964). For their part, readers select newspapers (at least in large multipaper markets) on the basis of their entertainment value as well as the perceived news-worthiness of what they report. News consumers also participate in the newsmaking process by formulating actions on the basis of the news they consume, thus playing a part in the creation of subsequent events, some of which will be deemed newsworthy. To varying degrees, therefore, newspapers and their consumers are part of a dynamic interaction through which the news is reflexively produced (Erikson et al. 1991).

Thus, our research sought to illuminate the socially constructed images of gangs and those individuals, groups, and institutions that, in one way or another, respond to gangs. By examining these images, we hope to highlight the repetitive themes and messages consumed by the public and to identify certain rhetorical devices through which the news shapes the ideological meaning of gangs in public discourse.

METHOD

Our data were derived from 4,445 articles from a major metropolitan newspaper, the *Dallas Morning News*. We selected all articles that included the words *gang* or *gangs* from the years 1991 through 1996. A content analysis of the articles was performed with the intention of identifying major discourse themes, trends, and changes in the socially constructed image of gangs and their activities over time. Specifically, our analysis used the constant comparative method as outlined by Glaser and Strauss (1967) and explicated by Charmaz (1988). We analyzed the data through a detailed reading of each article. Initial coding categories were derived by comparing each article with all preceding articles. As coding progressed and no new categories emerged, emphasis shifted to a comparison of each article with previously derived categories. Through this procedure, we identified major themes and used them to code articles for all years. As expected, some articles included multiple themes and were more difficult to categorize. In such cases, we listed and kept track of the cothemes, but each article was eventually classified according

to the theme that appeared most prominently, by virtue of its position within the article, the number of lines devoted to it, and/or its mention in the headline. We participated in the data coding. We discussed ambiguous cases and reached a consensus before the final coding of such cases.

Although we agree with Bagdikian (1978, 1990) that images of deviance disseminated by the media are strikingly consistent across markets, we must urge caution in generalizing our findings to other markets and to other news organizations. Because our analysis is restricted to one newspaper in one metropolitan area, we cannot assume that our findings would be replicated in other areas. Moreover, we have no data with which to assess the generalizability of our results to other media, such as television news.

RESULTS

The sheer number of articles referring to the issue of gangs was impressive. The 4,445 articles spread over the 6-year study period represented an average of over two articles per day. Clearly, from 1991 through 1996, gangs and gang crime were a major source of daily news.

MAJOR THEMES IN COVERAGE OF THE GANG PROBLEM

The themes that were presented in stories highlight certain features of the gang problem, often to the exclusion of others. Through content analysis, we identified eight major themes, which are summarized in Table 1.

The first theme, gang crime, which constituted approximately 19 percent of all articles, refers to articles that focused on the criminal activities of gangs. Much like the television news-magazine shows that

TABLE 1: **Typology of Newspaper Articles Dealing with Gangs**

Type	Description
Gang crime	Reports of all criminal gang and gang-related activity
Gang busting	Articles about gang arrests, trials, convictions, and sentences; also includes articles on gang-busting efforts of the police and governmental agencies
Gang accounts	References to gangs and gang activities in order to justify or oppose the creation or suspension of rules/norms not directly or exclusively aimed at gangs or gang activity
Gang resisting	Reports of efforts of and activities sponsored by police, schools, civic organizations, and parents designed to provide kids with alternatives to gangs and efforts to discourage gang activity
Gang references	Single mentions of gang and former gang members, editorial warnings about gangs and references to fictional and historical gangs
Foreign gangs	References to gangs and gang activity in foreign countries
Gang research	Articles primarily devoted to providing information about gangs or reporting the process or results of gang research
Gang rape	Articles in which the primary reference to gangs or gang activity is gang rape

Note. N = 4,445 articles. Source: *Dallas Morning News*, January 1991–December 1996.

Tunnell (1998) studied, the articles we analyzed tended to emphasize serious high-profile crimes such as shootings, stabbings, or robberies. One of the most popular topics of these articles was intergang violence.

> An argument among several teen-agers at a party Saturday morning ended with the gang-related shooting death of a 16-year-old Fort Worth resident, police said. . . . One teen pulled out a semiautomatic handgun and began firing, striking Mr. Pena three times in the chest. Two other teens, whom police would not identify, were hit in their arms or legs and were in fair condition at Harris Methodist-Fort Worth hospital, Detective Sears said.
> "It was a gang-related shooting," he said. "It was a holdover from an argument they had several weeks ago. The guy just pulls a gun out of his pocket and kills him." ("Sixteen-year-old Ft. Worth Boy" 1993:38A)

An image of gang crime that emerged clearly during the years of our study was that no longer could anyone be considered safe from the violence of street gangs. Consider the following example from the summer of 1996.

> It took place at a baseball diamond at Brownwood Park on Walnut Hill Lane just west of Marsh Lane in North Dallas. . . . Mothers and fathers tried to keep cool in the 100-degree heat. Brothers and sisters played behind the metal backstop. In a parking lot just beyond right field, teenagers began to gather. Baggy pants. Caps pulled backward. Suddenly, one began to run, headed in the direction of the game. Then a "pop," like a fire-cracker exploding. The teenagers in the parking lot scattered. The young man who was hit staggered behind the dugout. . . . "Help me. I've been shot. I'm bleeding," he cried, collapsing to the ground, writhing in pain, clutching his left leg. . . . Police say the shooting occurred because a gang leader was angry that his turf had been invaded. (Flourney 1996:1C)

The message that no one is safe from gang crime is conveyed in the first sentence, in which the author fixed the place of the crime in a part of town not normally associated with crime. The protection of gang turf was frequently cited as a precipitator of intergang conflict, and its relatively recent movement into previously safe middle-class neighborhoods made the issue salient to readers who have traditionally felt insulated from the problem. This image was magnified by the fact that the victim was engaged in the kind of conventional activity associated with youth and innocence. In fact, it was consistent with numerous stories of this type in its depiction of innocent victims. Presumably, the victim of this shooting—like many others—was somewhat random and not in any way associated with gangs.

According to newspaper reports, another common situation in which innocent bystanders become the victims of gang violence is the gang initiation.

An 18-year old pregnant woman was killed in a drive-by shooting early Sunday at Mountain Creek park, which is becoming increasingly known as a flashpoint for gang violence. Rebecca Escobedo, who officials said was about five months pregnant, died after she was shot in the back as she stood in a group of about 30 young people at the lakeside park. A second bullet struck another youth, Yolanda Rios, 15, in the upper leg, police reports showed. She was not seriously injured. . . . Detective Navarro said there was no indication that either victim was intentionally shot. . . . A young man who identified himself as Ms. Escobedo's uncle said he thinks his niece may have been an innocent victim of a gang initiation, which requires aspiring members to shoot someone as a prerequisite of membership. (Floyd 1996:13A)

There was also a marked tendency for articles depicting gang crime to stress the youthful age of gang members.

The crimes are awful: the gang rape of a 13-year-old girl and the slaying of a beloved 82-year-old neighborhood woman who walked into the middle of a fight. The prime suspect is even more shocking: a boy just past his 12th birthday, whose alleged acts are so violent that his own mother turned him in after police identified him by name on live television. (Associated Press 1996b:38A)

The image that emerged from these gang crime stories was that of increasingly young gang members who target increasingly young and often innocent victims. Moreover, the message is clear that residents of middle-class and even affluent neighborhoods are no longer safe from the criminal activities of such gangs.

The second theme, gang busting, refers to articles about gang arrests, trials, convictions, and sentences and about anti-gang efforts of the police and other governmental agencies. Gang busting was the primary theme in 12 percent of the articles. These stories tended to fall into one of three categories: those that dealt with police actions, such as arrests of gang members; those that reported the efforts of lawmakers to broaden the discretionary powers of authorities in dealing with gangs; and those that reported the trials and sentencing of celebrated cases. The following is typical of the first type.

When a string of driveby shootings left one teenager dead in west Garland, police gang unit officers turned to their vast database of profiles to find possible suspects. Within days, officers arrested two gang members who now stand accused of the crime. . . . Gang unit officers saw the arrests as another victory for their intelligence network: a computer file that includes personal facts on about 3,300 youths who have been stopped by police. . . . But some civil libertarians and minority activists say the gang unit's policy of stopping youths for even the most minor offenses has gone too far. They say officers stop teens solely for the purpose of gathering information, as opposed to investigating crimes. And they say police indiscriminately stop minority teenagers because they fit the profile of a stereotypical gang member. (Ornstein 1996a:1J).

As with other articles of this type, this one projected an image of the police as highly competent representatives of the social order, who marshal vast resources in an effort to combat criminal forces (Tunnell 1998). However, such efforts are often met with resistance from various civil libertarians who contend that the criminal justice system discriminates against minority groups.

Articles that portrayed the efforts of lawmakers to empower the police also tended to give some print space to groups concerned with civil liberties. Such groups were presented as consistently challenging the creation of regulations and laws that would allow authorities to take a tough stance against gangs. According to news stories, such get-tough approaches appear to be almost universally popular among politicians.

Pledging to once again make juvenile crime a top legislative priority, Gov. George W. Bush on Wednesday proposed a law to allow authorities to randomly frisk paroled youth offenders. . . . The so-called stop-and-frisk proposal would allow law enforcement officials to randomly frisk juvenile offenders as a term of their parole or probation. Mr. Bush said . . . "We need to give our law enforcement officers more tools to tackle tough gangs and tough kids. . . . Stop and frisk will give the police and probation officers another tool to keep offenders on a short leash and help keep guns out of their hands." But one civil rights attorney questioned the constitutionality of such a law, saying it would violate a parolee's right to privacy. (Arrillaga 1996:33A).

Reports of court cases involving gang members revealed a consistently get-tough approach to sentencing. Stories about court cases typically included not only information about the trial and sentencing decision but repeat details of the crime, and they often included comments from interested parties, such as attorneys and members of victims' families. The following is representative of articles dealing with gang-crime trials.

A Houston gang member who participated in the rape and murder of two teenage girls poses a threat to society and must face death by lethal injection, the Texas Court of Criminal Appeals ruled Wednesday. Raul O. Villareal had asked the court to reverse his 1994 death sentence in the 1993 capital murders of 14-year-old Jennifer Ertman and 16-year-old Elizabeth Pena. Mr. Villareal argued that there wasn't enough evidence to find him a future threat to society. Such a finding is required before a criminal can be sentenced to death. The court, the state's highest for criminal appeals, said Miss Ertman's and Miss Pena's murders warranted the death penalty because they were so brutal and Mr. Villareal's actions after the killings were so unremorseful. In June 1993, Miss Ertman and Miss Pena were walking home from a friend's house when they took a shortcut over a railroad trestle in Houston. They stumbled onto a gang gathering where Mr. Villareal was being initiated. He admitted to raping both girls and helping to kill Miss Ertman. (Associated Press 1996d:19A)

According to images that emerge from gang-busting reports, the government, the police, and the judiciary work in concert to defend the public against the criminal activities of gangs. However, such efforts are constantly confronted by challenges from such groups as the American Civil Liberties Union and various minority interest groups. Despite limitations imposed by the appellate process, the courts appear to provide the most solace to those who want to get tough on crime and criminals.

The third theme, gang accounts, constituted 5 percent of the total. This category included articles containing references to gangs or gang activities in order to justify or oppose the creation or suspension of rules that are not directly or exclusively aimed at gangs or gang activity. For example, several articles reported potential gang activity as a reason for opposing no-pass-no-play rules for high school athletes.

Republican gubernatorial candidate George W. Bush on Friday suggested a public discussion over whether the no pass, no play rule is leading to an increase in gang membership. Mr. Bush, who is challenging Democratic Gov. Ann Richards, said he supports no pass, no play. But he said he's open to potential changes if it turns out the regulation causes other problems. . . . "What's beginning to concern me is that gangs are beginning to rival the old team sports . . . and there needs to be a good healthy public debate to determine whether or not team sports may be able to compete with gangs," he said. (Associated Press 1994:16F)

Dress and appearance rules were also justified by reference to gangs, as the following excerpt reveals.

When two male students sported long pony-tails recently, Spence Middle School principal Rina Davis reached for her scissors. Ms. Davis said the students' hairstyles worried her because they resembled the cuts of some gang members. And although the Dallas students had nothing to do with gangs, she didn't want them targeted for recruitment. . . . Although most Dallas-area school officials don't wield shears, many school districts, for the first time since the turbulent 1960s, are tightening student hair codes. But some students and community leaders say many school officials aren't enforcing codes equally. They say administrators often mistakenly presume that all students with long hair are trouble-makers.

And they charge that minority students are often suspended for the way they wear their hair while Anglos are allowed to wear more exotic styles. (Nevins 1990:33A)

As this article illustrates, challenges to gang accounts were typically based on charges of selective and discriminatory enforcement or rules.

Fear of gangs was also used to justify home schooling and alternative schools (Stewart 1996) and to support school uniform policies as a way of eliminating the wearing of gang attire to school (Stahl 1996). Although gang accounts were most often used to justify restrictions on adolescents, such accounts can cut both ways, as shown in a wire-service article picked up by the *Dallas Moving News* in which the interviewee defended skateboarding against attacks by officials and pedestrians. Skateboarding, he argued, "is an outlet that keeps young people from getting involved in gangs and drugs" ("Skateboarders Looking for Room" 1996:17A).

The fourth theme, gang resisting, refers to reports of efforts to discourage gang activity and reports of activities sponsored by police, schools, civic organizations, and parents designed to provide kids with alternatives to gangs. Gang resisting was a prominent theme, accounting for 13 percent of the articles. Although resisting gangs was cited as the primary goal of some programs, it was mentioned as an ancillary goal of a variety of programs. Schools and churches were most frequently mentioned as institutions sponsoring gang-resisting efforts, but private-sector organizations that receive public support were also featured.

A pilot after-school program created by Oak Cliff's Promise House is winning positive reviews at Rosemont Elementary School. . . . Last Wednesday, 10 Rosemont students became the first elementary-age group in Dallas to complete the nonprofit agency's after-school program, which is funded by a $420,000 state grant. "All of these kids are considered at-risk," she said. "This is a prevention program, and these are the kind of kids who can end up in the street and involved in gangs and drugs." (Aubespin 1996:2Y)

This theme also includes success stories of individuals who have overcome gang influences. Many of these articles used a testimonial format. For example, former gang members who had escaped gang life were often allowed to tell their stories in considerable detail. This is the format used in the article "Heavy-weight Sees Boxing as a Way Out of Chicago's Ugly Side" (Diaz 1996). In this article, a young man told the story of a "self-destructive journey" in which, as a former gang member, he stabbed a young woman and was subsequently sent to prison. Now he uses boxing as a way to escape that life and suggested that the sport of boxing is a way out of gang life. Other types of testimonies included those from individuals who are committed to youth and community work, typically as volunteers. For example, one such story focused on the humanitarian efforts of a woman who works with at-risk children in areas referred to as gang havens (Cladwell 1996:1G). She explained her desire to help others by saying, "As a Christian I feel we do have a responsibility to help the less fortunate. . . . the private community has to help" (Cladwell 1996:1G). Many of the stories that used the testimonial format also contained explicit religious references, such as the testimony of a former gang member who declared, "God takes care of my life now. . . . People I used to know don't believe it" (Jacobs 1996:15C). The story went on to say that instead of stealing and selling drugs, this former gang member is now looking for a job (Jacobs 1996:15C). Articles within this category also

tended to focus on forgiveness and rehabilitation rather than retribution, which is a more prominent theme in other categories.

Gang references is the fifth and largest theme and accounted for almost a third of the articles analyzed (33 percent). This category refers to single mentions of and editorial warnings about gang problems as well as references to fictional and historical gangs. Unlike those that constitute our other categories, gang reference articles were not focused on criminal gangs at all. Rather, the term *gang* was used as an oblique reference in the context of a completely different topic, most often to suggest something about the identity of a person, place, or action. For example, perhaps realizing that the term *gang* has become almost synonymous with young criminals, some articles seemed to go out of their way to stipulate that the youths in question were not gang members.

A 13-year-old Lake Highlands boy was charged Sunday with murder in the weekend shooting death of his mother, with whom he had a volatile relationship, police said. . . . "They've always had a volatile relationship and argued," said Lisa Crane, Mrs. McCullough's next-door neighbor. . . . Ms. Crane said the boy is a "clean-cut kid" who loves to play soccer. Earlier this month, he made the Inter 83 boys select soccer team, she said, and did not associate with gangs or display suspicious behavior in the neighborhood. (Ornstein 1996b:1A)

Thus, even when gangs were not involved in crime, the specter of such activity was raised by such disclaimers, thereby reinforcing the underlying assumption that most young criminals are gang members.

In many cases, gang references were used solely to conjure up negative images in the reader's mind. For example, before the 1996 presidential election, one article pronounced, "In the past that Mr. Dole remembers, educating kids was different. But in the aftermath of the atomic age came another blast, the explosion of the nuclear family, vaporizing Wally and Beaver while radiating gangs, drugs and violence" (Reamy 1996:33A)

The sixth theme, foreign gangs (13.5 percent of the total), refers to articles that focused on gangs and gang activity in countries other than the United States. The overwhelming majority of stories about foreign gangs included descriptions of violent criminal activities perpetrated by gang members. In many cases, the crimes reported were presented in the context of an international criminal gang problem, often with explicit references to U.S. gang connections. For example, it was reported in Cape Town, South Africa, that "140 gangs, from the Americans to the Young Heart Breakers, terrorize and plunder the cinder-block slums and working-class towns of the Cape Flats" (Associated Press 1996a:8A). The following was from a report originating in Oslo, Norway.

"Since August 1995, when Bandidos reportedly moved their European headquarters to the Danish village of Stenloese, the conflict has steadily worsened . . . it is unclear what started the feud in the Nordic countries between the Bandidos, based in Corpus Christi, Texas, and the Hells Angels, based in Oakland, California." (Mellgren 1996:1A)

Foreign gang stories reported not only dire social conditions and brutal crimes but also social reactions to gang crimes. One graphic example of this was in a report from Cape Town where police, antigang protestors, and gang members clashed. The article stated that "during an earlier march, masked members of a vigilante group seeking to eradicate drug gangs from impoverished townships, shot to death and burned the body of a notorious gang leader" ("Vigilante Group" 1996:12A)

The message in foreign gang stories seems to be that the gang problem is a global one. Moreover, these articles give the distinct impression that not only are the gang problems that have reached into relatively low crime nations serious, they are essentially American imports. As a result of this encroachment, it seems that no place on earth is impervious to the threats posed by the kind of criminal gangs that have become commonplace in the United States.

The seventh theme, gang research, includes articles devoted to providing information about gangs or reporting the process or results of gang research. Print news does not appear to be an important outlet for disseminating scientific information on gangs. In fact, this was the smallest category, constituting only 2 percent of all articles. When research information on gangs was presented, it was usually in the context of reporting other crime research findings, and these articles often attempted to put gang violence into a less alarmist context. For example, one article titled "Dying Young in Dallas" reported research on child homicides and deaths in Dallas County for the year 1995 (Kessler 1996). It reported that one third of the deaths were gang related. However, in the same article, the executive director of Mothers Against Teen Violence took exception to that statistic, saying that police "too often rely on initial reports linking perpetrators and victims to gangs when later court testimony disproves the connection" (Kessler 1996:1A) This article also lent credence to the idea that the media participate in formulating lines of action and reaffirming certain positions of control by suggesting stricter teen curfews and graduated driver's license programs as ways of dealing with the problem (Kessler 1996). Research articles also differed from other articles in that they often presented critiques of commonly reported information. For example, an article titled "Don't Rush to Judge Victims" (Strickland 1996), brought to light the problem of applying gang labels to teen victims of violent crime. The article stated,

When there is an allegation of gang involvement, empathy for the victim evaporates and eyes glaze over. . . . If we stereotype young victims of gun violence as lawless hardened gang members, we not only do a serious disservice to the innocent victims, but we also minimize the relevance that the problem has for the general population. (Strickland 1996:6J)

The eighth theme, gang rape, includes articles in which the primary reference to gangs or gang activity was gang rape. This relatively small category, which contained 3 percent of the articles, should not be considered a subcategory of gang crime. Rather, it is a unique category because references to gang rape most often do not refer to the activities of actual criminal gangs. In fact, the term *gang rape* is often used to identify any rape committed by multiple offenders, whether or not the rape was gang associated. "Police said the girls had been taking drugs and were drinking during a party at the downtown El Paso motel, passed out and were subsequently gang raped by the five" (Associated Press 1996c:25A)

Although gang members were sometimes involved, it is usually unclear whether the members involved in the rape were from the same gang or whether the rape was in any way gang related. Moreover, these articles frequently contained graphic accounts of gang rapes. "She was gang raped, bludgeoned with a shovel and buried alive in Pine Bluff, Ark., by Mr. Webster, 23, and his co-defendants, according to court testimony" (Payne 1996:8A)

It is important to note that references to women in gang articles most often

portrayed women and girls as victims of gang crime or gang violence. This was particularly true in this category, where the vast majority of the articles focused on women and girls as victims of gang rape and men and boys as the perpetrators of the rape (Thompson and Spugnardi 1999). Although occasional media reports and some qualitative research on female gangs (cf. Molidor 1996) have suggested that young women are sometimes required to have sex with multiple male gang members as part of the initiation into female gangs, we found no newspaper reports of such incidences. In fact, reports of female gang activities in general were rare.

THE POLITICS OF COMMUNITY RESPONSES TO GANGS

Articles presenting the themes gang busting, gang resisting, and gang accounts shared the characteristic of focusing on community responses to gangs. When combined, these community response articles actually outnumbered gang crime articles over the 6-year period (30 percent vs. 19 percent). This finding also holds when comparing the percentages of crime articles to community response articles within years. Perhaps, as Durkheim (1933), Erikson (1966), and others have suggested, crime serves as a catalyst for community organization and response by galvanizing public outrage. Talk about and responses to gang crime are clearly an important part of the gang story, perhaps a bigger part than actual gang activity.

Far from galvanizing public opinion, however, such talk often takes a divisive turn. For example, a major element in many community response stories is the political discourse that surrounds the coverage of gang news. One topic on which such discourse centers is the social control of youth. As numerous gang account articles have shown, the specter of gang crime is a prominent tool used by adults, such as school officials, in their efforts to exert control over various groups of young people. Another focus of such discourse is the politics of race. With the exception of those articles that focused on the gang problem in particular ethnic communities, we found few direct references to the race or ethnicity of gang members. Rather, the issue emerged most prominently in community response articles. As seen in stories dealing with both gang busting and gang accounts, representatives of racial and ethnic minorities are often portrayed as standing in opposition to authorities who attempt to address some aspect of the gang problem. The politics of race became a subtheme running through articles in multiple categories. Thus, although the issue is often dealt with only indirectly, as Charles Silberman (1980:159) noted almost 20 years ago, "in the end, there is no escaping the question of race and crime."

NEWSPAPER COVERAGE AND THE RHETORIC OF THE GANG PROBLEM

The term *motif* has been used to describe "recurrent thematic elements and figures of speech that encapsulate or highlight some aspect of a social problem" and can be applied across a range of "condition-categories" (Ibarra and Kitsuse 1993:43). Best (1996) used this concept to analyze the rhetorical use of gang initiation rites by a variety of sources. By this same definition, our analysis is an investigation of the more general gang problem motif. Several of the articles quoted earlier highlighted different condition categories to which the gang motif was applied in newspaper articles. Among these are what might be described as the problems of (a) crime and delinquency, (b) the failure of public education, (c) adolescent folkway

deviance, (d) the erosion of community, and (e) the erosion of family. We do not suggest that these are the only condition categories to which the gang problem motif could be or has been successfully applied. Rather, this list is illustrative of the ways in which the motif has been woven into newspaper stories.

Obviously, crime and delinquency was the condition most frequently highlighted by the use of the gang problem motif. The majority of what we have classified as gang crime articles is of this sort. Articles that highlight some aspect of the crisis in public education and adolescent folkway deviance are found primarily among those classified as gang accounts. The actors featured in these articles frequently cited the gang problem as a justification for schools to enforce more rigid dress codes and other appearance norms. The politics of educational policy, exemplified by the controversy over the no-pass-no-play policy for high school athletes, also provided a context in which the gang problem motif was frequently used. Accounts of the role of gangs in the erosion of both family and community were woven through several categories of articles but were especially evident in those focusing on gang resistance.

Other important devices used in the production of social problems rhetoric are what Ibarra and Kitsuse (1993:31) called *rhetorical idioms*. These idioms refer to the distinctive ways in which the problematic status of condition categories is elaborated. One of these, the rhetoric of endangerment (Ibarra and Kitsuse 1993:35) is frequently used in discourse about gangs. In many articles, gangs are portrayed as a danger to the health, welfare, and very existence of individuals, families, and communities. At the same time that gangs are implicated as causal factors in a rhetoric of endangerment, they are also implicated in a rhetoric of calamity (Ibarra and Kitsuse 1993:37) both as a symptom and as a consequence of the erosion of community and family.

CONCLUSIONS

In his study of news organizations, Gans (1980) identified two major categories of news: disorder and routine news. He suggested that there are four major types of disorder news: natural, technological, social, and moral. Using this categorization, we found that gang news tended to be primarily social disorder and moral disorder news. Social disorder news stories involve phenomena that present a threat to valued institutions, such as the family, and preferred social patterns, such as public safety. Repeatedly, stories about gangs presented readers with fear-provoking images of families torn apart, schools turned into battle grounds, and communities paralyzed with fear. Gang stories also portrayed threats to the moral order by suggesting that gangs reject commonly held standards of decency and morality. From stories of how gangs constitute a deviant form of family to stories about gang initiations involving sex with HIV-infected partners, gangs are presented as a direct threat to the normative order.

Moral and social disorder news go hand-in-hand with social control news. Social control news tends to emphasize the glamorous and successful side of crime fighting: the capture, trial, and sentencing. Within the category of gang busting, for example, we found stories that focus predominantly on arrests of gang members and the solving of gang crimes. Consistent with research on other types of crime news, gang news gave very little attention to the mundane aspects of the criminal justice process (Tunnell 1998). As expected, most of the gang-busting news emphasized sensational arrests and trials of gang members.

Largely because of their entertainment value, there is a long history of news accounts of crime and crime control within popular newspapers in the United States (Schudson 1978; Sherizan 1978). Some have suggested that news reporting as entertainment is a kind of cultural-mythic storytelling with the presentation of cultural-mythic narratives embedded in stories (Erikson, Baranek, and Chan 1987; Pearce 1973; Thompson 1996; Young 1973). As entertainers, journalists are involved in writing veritable scripts to morality plays, with the moral forces of traditional authority waging war against the evil forces of deviance (Erikson et al. 1987). Stories of evil engage the audience, and the stories of combat and conflict against evil reassure the audience that the prevailing social order is being maintained. Nowhere is this more evident than in gang stories. Articulated through a rhetoric of social problems discourse, stories highlight how gangs undermine the safety and well-being of the community and how the police, courts, and community react. Society combats gang evil through religion, law, and education. The large number of gang response articles relative to gang crime articles found in our data makes sense in this light. Stories of the forces of good reassure the reader and reaffirm the traditional social and moral order. However, to accomplish this reassurance, stories that transform the threat of social and moral disorganization into palpable images (gang attire, gang membership, gang banging, gang turf) must be balanced by those that reaffirm the power and authority of law and order (police patrol, trials, arrests, investigation, task forces). In many ways, the evils of gangs and gang members are more prominently articulated by the drama of community response than by news of actual gang crime.

Perhaps the use of a socially constructed image as a cultural metaphor is the best measure of its power and influence in public discourse. The criminal gang is transformed into a cultural metaphor when the gang-problem motif is used to highlight aspects of other social problems, such as the crisis in public education or the deterioration of community. Nowhere is the power of the gang-as-metaphor more evident than in articles that show how different groups use references to gangs or gang activities to justify or oppose lines of action that are not directly or exclusively aimed at gangs or gang activity. In many gang account articles, gangs are used as a specter to instill fear in order to gain control over resources or the behavior of others. Used in these ways, the gang metaphor becomes a central feature in the rhetoric of social control. Ironically, conformist juveniles are those most often affected by such control strategies, which take the form of curfews, dress codes, and rules of participation. Thus, the symbolic power of the gang metaphor lies in its successful application in settings where gangs are relatively unimportant or inconsequential. Whether it is used to justify or forbid a particular style of dress, defend skateboarding, or enhance a politician's prospects on election day, the gang metaphor is a powerful tool for conjuring up an image that can be exploited by a host of social actors in the quest for power and the negotiation of social influence.

References

Altheide, David. 1985. *Media Power*. Beverly Hills, CA: Sage.

Altheide, David and Robert Snow. 1979. *Media Logic*. Beverly Hills, CA: Sage.

Arrillaga, Pauline. 1996. "Bush Advocates Random Frisking of Youth Parolees." *Dallas Morning News*, September 26, p. 33A.

Associated Press. 1994. "Bush Seeks 'No Pass, No Play' Discussion: Richards says Rule Helps Keep Focus on Academics." *Dallas Morning News*, August 20, p. 16F.

———. 1996a. "Anti-Gang Vigilantes Ignite S. Africa Crisis: Muslim Crime Fighters Stir Fear of Anarchy." *Dallas Morning News*, August 14, p. 8A. DAL1589322.

———. 1996b. "Boy Who Was Tried as an Adult Gets 25-Year Term for Murder." *Dallas Morning News*, December 18, p. 38A.

———. 1996c. "El Paso Men Indicted in Rape of Teens." *Dallas Morning News*, October 12, p. 25A.

———. 1996d. "Gang Member's Appeal Rejected in Rape, Killing." *Dallas Morning News*, November 28, p. 19A.

Aubespin, Eleska. 1996. "After School Program Wins Rosemont's Praise." *Dallas Morning News*, November 26, p. 2Y.

Bagdikian, Ben H. 1978. "The Best News Money Can Buy." *Human Behavior*, October:63–6.

———. 1990. *The Media Monopoly*. Boston: Beacon.

Barak, Greg. 1994. "Media, Society and Criminology." Pp. 1–3 in *Media, Process and the Social Construction of Crime: Studies in Newsmaking Criminology*, edited by Greg Barak. New York: Garland.

Best, Joel. 1993. "But Seriously Folks: The Limitations on the Strict Constructionist Interpretation of Social Problems." Pp. 109–27 in *Constructionist Controversies: Issues in Social Problems Theory*, edited by Gale Miller and James A. Holstein. New York: Aldine de Gruyter.

———. 1996. "The Gang Initiation Rite as a Motif in Contemporary Crime Discourse." *Justice Quarterly* 13:383–404.

Charmaz, Kathy. 1988. "The Grounded Theory Method: An Explication and Interpretation." Pp. 109–26 in *Contemporary Field Research: A Collection of Readings*, edited by Robert M. Emerson. Prospect Heights, IL: Waveland.

Chermak, Steven M. 1995a. "Crime in the News Media: A Refined Understanding of How Crimes Become News." Pp. 95–131 in *Media, Process and the Social Construction of Crime: Studies in Newsmaking Criminology*, edited by Greg Barak. New York: Garland.

———. 1995b. *Victims in the News: Crime and the American News Media*. Boulder, CO: Westview.

Cladwell, Deborah. 1996. "In the Shadow of Plenty." *Dallas Morning News*, September 21, p. 1G.

Cohen, Stanley and Jock Young. 1981. *The Manufacture of News*. Beverly Hills, CA: Sage.

Croteau, David and William Hoynes. 1997. *Industries, Images, and Audiences*. Thousand Oaks, CA: Pine Forge Press.

Diaz, George. 1996. "Heavyweight Sees Boxing as Way Out." *Dallas Morning News*, July 25, p. 18B.

Durkheim, Emile. 1933. *The Division of Labor in Society*. New York: Free Press.

Erikson, Kai T. 1966. *Wayward Puritans: A Study in the Sociology of Deviance*. New York: Wiley.

Erikson, Richard V., Patricia M. Baranek, and Janet B. L. Chan. 1987. *Visualizing Deviance: A Study of News Organizations*. Toronto: University of Toronto Press.

_____. 1991. *Representing Order: Crime, Law, and Justice in the News Media*. Toronto: University of Toronto Press.

Flourney, Craig. 1996. "Terror Comes Too Close to Children." *Dallas Morning News*, July 6, p. 1C.

Floyd, Jacquielynn. 1996. "Pregnant Woman Is Slain." *Dallas Morning News*, October 8, p. 13A.

Gans, Herbert J. 1980. *Deciding What's News: A Study of CBS Evening New, NBC Nightly News, Newsweek and Time*. New York: Pantheon.

Gergen, Kenneth. 1991. *The Saturated Self*. New York, NY: Basic Books.

Glaser, Barney G. and Anselm L. Strauss. 1967. *The Discovery of Grounded Theory: Strategies for Qualitative Research*. Chicago: Aldine.

Graber, Doris A. 1980. *Crime News and the Public*. New York: Praeger.

Ibarra, Peter R. and John I. Kitsuse. 1993. "Vernacular Constituents of Moral Discourse: An Interactionist Proposal for the Study of Social Problems." Pp. 21–54 in *Constructionist Controversies: Issues in Social Problems Theory*, edited by Gale Miller and James A. Holstein. New York: Aldine de Gruyter.

Jacobs, Sally. 1996. "Boston 'Posse' Members Turn From Crime and Gangs to God." *Dallas Morning News*, August 3, p. 15C.

Kessler, Barbara. 1996. "Dying Young in Dallas." *Dallas Morning News*, December 6, p. 1A.

McLuhan, Marshall. 1964. *Understanding Media: Extensions of Man*. New York: Mentor Books.

Media Monitor. 1997. "News of the Nineties: The Top Topics and Trends of the Decade." *Center for Media and Public Affairs: Media Monitor*, XI:3.

Mellgren, Doug. 1996. "Bloody Bikers Shatter Scandinavia's Serenity." *Dallas Morning News*, August 4, p. 1A.

Molidor, Christian. 1996. "Female Gang Members: A Profile of Aggression and Victimization." *Social Work* 41(3):251–57.

Nevins, Annette. 1990. "Tresses Create Stresses." *Dallas Morning News*, December 7, p. 33A.

Ornstein, Charles. 1996a. "Garland Turf War: Some Say Gang Unit Unfairly Targeting Teens, Minorities." *Dallas Morning News*, October 25, p. 1J.

_____. 1996b. "Lake Highlands Boy 13, Charged in Mom's Slaying." *Dallas Morning News*, August 26, p. 1A.

Payne, Chris. 1996. "Life Sentence to Be Sought for Gang Member in Slaying, Prosecutor Says." *Dallas Morning News*, June 27, p. 8A.

Pearce, Frank. 1973. "How to Be Immoral and Ill, Pathetic and Dangerous, All at the Same Time: Mass Media and the Homosexual." Pp. 284–301 in *The Manufacture of News: A Reader*, edited by Stanley Cohen and Jock Young. Beverly Hills, CA: Sage.

Potter, Gary and Victor Kappeler. 1998. *Constructing Crime: Perspectives on Making News and Social Problems*. Prospect Heights, IL: Waveland.

Pritchard, David and Karen D. Hughes. 1997. "Patterns of Deviance in Crime News." *Journal of Communication* 47(3):49–67.

Reamy, George. 1996. "Don't Use Teachers as Scapegoats." *Dallas Morning News*, August 24, p. 33A.

Schudson, Michael. 1978. *Discovering the News*. New York: Basic Books.

Sherizan, Sanford. 1978. "Social Creation of Crime News." Pp. 203–24 in *Deviance and Mass Media*, edited by Charles Winick. Thousand Oaks, CA: Sage.

Silberman, Charles E. 1980. *Criminal Violence, Criminal Justice*. New York: Vintage Books.

"Sixteen-Year-Old Fort Worth Boy Dies in Gang-Related Shooting." 1993. *Dallas Morning News*, June 13, p. 38A.

"Skateboarders Looking for Room to Ride: San Francisco Officials, Pedestrian Cite Problems." 1996. *Dallas Morning News*, August 18, p. 17A. DAL1589914.

Stahl, Lori. 1996. "Arena Financing a Main Topic on Garcia's Austin Agenda." *Dallas Morning News*, December 14, p. 36A.

Stewart, Linda. 1996. "Home-Schooling Fair Finds an Audience." *Dallas Morning News*, August 18, p. 37A.

Strickland, Joyce. 1996. "Don't Rush to Judge Victims." *Dallas Morning News*, December 22, p. 6J.

Surette, Ray. 1992. *Media, Crime and Criminal Justice*. Pacific Grove, CA: Brooks/Cole.

Thompson, Carol Y. 1996. "Women's Crime Concerns and Gun Ownership: Evaluating Media Images." *Journal of Contemporary Criminal Justice* 12:151–72.

Thompson, Carol and Janet Spugnardi. 1999. "Images of Gang Rape in the News." Paper presented at the annual meetings of the Southwestern Social Science Association, March, San Antonio, TX.

Tunnell, Kenneth D. 1998. "Reflections on Crime, Criminals, and Control in News-magazine Television Programs" Pp. 111–22 in *Popular Culture, Crime and Justice*, edited by Frankie Y. Bailey and Donna C. Hale. Belmont, CA: West/Wadsworth.

"Vigilante Group, Police Clash at Cape Town Airport." 1996. *Dallas Morning News*, December 17, p. 12A.

Young, Jock. 1973. "The Myth of the Drug Taker in the Mass Media." Pp. 314–22 in *The Manufacture of News: A Reader*, edited by Stanley Cohen and Jock Young. Beverly Hills, CA: Sage.

Disparities in the Reporting Patterns of Juvenile Homicides in Chicago:

A Map for Social Constructionists

John G. Boulahanis
Martha Heltsley[1]

Juvenile homicide arrests have fallen to their lowest rate in a generation, as the wave of violence that washed through teenage America in the last decade continues to ebb, according to an analysis of FBI crime data. FBI data shows that about 1,400 children ages 10 to 17 were charged with murder in 1999, a 68 percent drop from 1993, and the lowest number since comprehensive national reports on teenage homicide were first pulled together in 1980. It was the nation's fifth consecutive year of declining juvenile crime.

(*Chicago Sun Times* 2000: 52)

It is certainly welcome news that homicides by juveniles are in decline. In fact, serious and violent crime in general is enjoying a decrease according to the FBI (*Chicago Sun Times* 2000). However, due to

---

Reprinted with permission of the authors. Copyright © 2002, John G. Boulahanis and Martha Heltsley. All rights reserved.
[1]We would like to thank Drs. Kathryn Ward, Marc Riedel, and Thomas C. Calhoun for their encouragement and guidance during this project. We are also indebted to Brandyn O'Dell for his assistance in coding, to Dr. Joel Best for "sparking" our love for social construction, and to Dr. Jim LeBeau for teaching us a valuable tool to contribute to the discipline.

the higher rates of juvenile crime in the late 1980s and early 1990s, Mahini (2000) suggests that the perception of the delinquent changed. Previously considered immature and guilty of petty crimes such as joyriding, vandalism, or underage drinking, the delinquent is perceived today as is a serious and motivated perpetrator. Heide (1996: 27) suggests that journalistic reports have portrayed today's delinquent as ". . . more dangerous to society than (his/her) predecessors." In this article, we use Chicago as a test case for examining the accuracy of the media's portrayal of the juvenile who commits homicide. Specifically, we examine the characteristics of juvenile offenders (aged 16 years or younger) arrested for homicide and the characteristics of their victims as reported by the Chicago Police Department (CPD) during 1992 through 1997. This period was chosen because juvenile homicides increased in the early part of the 1990s, peaking in 1994, and decreasing thereafter. Thus, by using this time period, we were able to measure reporting before and after the peak. We then compare the typical characteristics of those cases to the characteristics of juvenile offenders and their victims as reported in two prominent Chicago newspapers (the *Chicago Sun-Times* and the *Chicago Tribune*) during the same years. Additionally, with the use of G.I.S. (Geographic Information System) technology, we map out the spatial distribution of the reporting patterns of juvenile homicide by the media in the city and compare it to the distribution of cases reported to the CPD. Results will indicate any discrepancy between actual crimes reported to the police department and the crimes selected for coverage by the newspapers.

SOCIAL CONSTRUCTION AND THE MEDIA

The media has been called an "image-making industry" (Gusfield 1989: 439). That is, the media can influence or shape reality by providing coverage for some events while ignoring others. Various researchers have explored the role of the media in constructing social problems. These studies include exaggerations concerning strangers abducting children, Halloween sadism (Best 1990), serial murder (Jenkins 1994), drug use (Reinarman 2000), and satanic day care centers (DeYoung 1998). Fishman (1978: 98) argues that on occasion the media creates "crime waves." Fishman (1978) found no evidence supporting an increase in crimes against the elderly, but the overreporting of these atypical crimes perpetuated fear among elderly residents of New York City. Similarly, the media have played a significant role in creating moral panics. An overemphasis on certain crimes promotes a consensus among the public that the threat is real, with inherent consequences (Best 1990; Goode and Ben-Yehuda 1994; Israel 1998). We examine the accuracy in the portrayal of juvenile homicide cases in Chicago

newspapers to investigate the possibility of creating false impressions and unwarranted fear.

MEDIA CONSTRAINTS

News media, in particular, play a significant role in informing individuals about various social issues. Ericson, Baranek, and Chan (1991: 3–4) suggest:

> News perpetually represents order . . . in ways that help people to order their daily lives. As an active *agency* of social control, stability, and change, news representations provide people with perferred versions and visions of social order, on the basis of which they take action. [Italics in original]

Although the media plays a major role in informing society, there are still limitations of resources, space, time, and format. The format shapes the information presented by governing the layout used and the amount of time spent on a particular theme (Altheide 1985; Chermak 1994; Ericson et al. 1991; Gans 1979). Each news medium uses a different format. Television relies heavily on pictures and images, the radio relies on sound, and newspapers are dependent on pictures and text. The content of the news changes on a daily basis, but the format remains relatively stable (Altheide 1985; Gans 1979). In addition to internal constraints, the production of news is also limited by external forces, which include the practice of media hegemony. *Media hegemony* refers to the preference for certain images, symbols, and news that reflect the views of a privileged few (Altheide 1985: 57). Journalists, for example, have the power and authority to shape the news. Ericson et al. (1991: 16) suggest that journalists act as both "selectors" and "formulators." It is ultimately their decisions as to which stories are covered and how they are presented. Journalists do not have sole discretion, as they are governed by "monopoly capitalism"—the news item is a product promoted for audience and sponsor approval (p. 44).

News items are also constrained by the type of information reporters receive. Thus, a mutual dependency often exists between the police and the media. The media is dependent on police for information on crimes and the police are dependent on the media for promoting their claims (Barak 1988; Chermak 1994; Ericson et al. 1991; Fishman 1978). The newsmaking process is by no means random. There are many variables that influence what type of information will be reported to the public. News reports are "neither a pure picture of society nor a fully controlled propaganda message, but is instead an organizational product" controlled by a few key individuals (Surette 1998: 62).

CRIME REPORTING: A PASSION FOR THE "ATYPICAL"

The news media are viewed as "the principle vehicle by which the average person comes to know crime and justice in America" (Barak 1994: 3). Numerous studies have suggested that the media tends to over-report crime—especially murder (Davis 1952; Ericson et al. 1991; Graber 1980; Hubbard, DeFleur and DeFleur 1975;). As Elikann (1999: 55) suggests: "If it bleeds, it leads." However, most researchers have failed to differentiate between adult and juvenile crime. According to Sprott (1996), the reporting patterns of the media as they relate to juvenile delinquency have not been examined to the same extent as the reporting patterns of adult crime. To test whether or not public perceptions about juveniles were based on news-mediated

images, Sprott (1996) conducted a content analysis on cases reported in three Canadian newspapers. Violent crimes were overreported and the articles failed to provide information on the disposition of the case, provided little information about the offender, and seemed to focus primarily on "the impact of crime on others" (p. 280). When queried about estimates of violent juvenile crime on a corresponding survey, almost three-fourths of respondents overestimated the amount of crime and believed homicides involving juvenile offenders had increased (while they had actually decreased). The majority of respondents also indicated that the juvenile court were "too lenient" (p. 280).

Most studies have been conducted on adult crime primarily because it occurs much more often than juvenile crime. Stories depicting youth as violent tend to receive a disproportionate amount of attention. A recent study published in the *American Journal of Public Health* indicated that 55 percent of all stories reported on youth pertained to youth violence (in Elikann 1999: 57). It is also common knowledge that property crimes occur far more frequently than homicide, but numerous studies have concluded that murders are overreported by the media. There are other atypical features of crime that are also overreported by the media. Race, gender, and age are three characteristics that garner the attention of the press.

RACE AS A VARIABLE

Unlike gender and age, race becomes problematic as a variable for use in analyzing newspaper accounts. It is not a standard practice to indicate the race of the offender or victim in articles. There are studies on television news reporting that indicated African Americans are overreported as offenders (Dixon and Linz 2000; Grabe 1999).

However, Sheley and Ashkins (1981), in a New Orleans study, found very little disparity between cases reported to the police and cases that were reported on television and in newspapers.

Race of the victim may also play a role in whether or not a case receives media attention. In examining the victim characteristics of homicides in the *Chicago Sun-Times* and the *Chicago Tribune* to cases reported to the CPD, Johnstone, Hawkins, and Michener (1994) concluded that homicides involving African American and Hispanic victims were underreported in the newspapers. Boulahanis, Esmail, and Heltsley (2000) interviewed reporters from the *Chicago Tribune* and the *Chicago Sun-Times* and found race to be a key variable in determining the value given homicide cases. As one reporter stated:

I'm sorry to say that race influences whether or not to run the story. This is not to say that we are racist, but because we know that the vast majority of homicides are committed by African Americans so they become run-of-the-mill.

Another reporter stated that certain individuals within the CPD take it upon themselves to determine what is newsworthy, and race is often that determinant:

Many desk sergeants in Area headquarters referred to cases that involved African-American offenders and victims as "blue cases" and these cases were usually not reported. Many times I would call the desk sergeant to see if anything interesting had happened to report, and they would respond by saying something to the effect that we just had a couple of blue cases, and that would be the end of it.

These statements suggest that crimes committed by African Americans are so common they lose their appeal in regard to newsworthiness. In regard to race, the sentiments by reporters imply that they are looking for homicides perpetrated by offenders that are "atypical"—not African American. It is very likely that race does play a role in newspaper accounts. However, due to the current formatting of newspaper articles it is sometimes impossible to accurately determine the race of the offender or victim. However, in this study we examine the dates and other characteristics of the homicides as reported in the two newspapers and use this information to find the exact cases reported in CPD data. This method allows us to determine if the news media is guilty of overreporting the atypical cases in regard to race.

GENDER AND AGE OF OFFENDER

Unlike race, gender can easily be noted in newspaper accounts. One of the most consistent findings in criminal justice research has been that most crimes are committed by males. Several studies have suggested that cases involving female offenders tend to be overreported by the news media (c.f., Chermak 1995; Katz 1987; Madriz 1997; Naylor 1995). Cases involving female offenders are rare; thus when they occur, they are perceived to be more newsworthy and receive greater attention. Naylor (1995: 80) argues that although female offenders constitute about 10 percent of the crimes reported to the police, they make up about one-third of the violent cases reported in newspapers. Madriz (1997) warns that the depiction of females may lead others, and particularly females, to be more fearful of women as potential offenders. As one of her research subjects stated: "All you have to do is read the newspapers or watch the news on TV and see how women have become worse than men" (p. 26).

Age of the offender also determines the newsworthiness of the case. According to Chermak (1995), the majority of crimes are committed by individuals aged 17 to 24. However, in conducting a content analysis of two newspapers (*Midwest Tribune* and *Midwest Nightly*), he observed that individuals between the ages of 17 and 24 received disproportionately less attention than cases involving younger and older offenders. Chermak (1995) concluded that the more atypical the case, the greater attention it received in the press. Although individuals between the ages of 17 and 24 commit the majority of crimes and therefore make juvenile homicides somewhat more newsworthy cases, little is known about the role age plays within the group of juveniles.

The definition of a juvenile varies from state to state. In Illinois, a juvenile is defined as any individual who has not reached his/her 17th birthday. Since this research is concerned with juveniles who commit homicides, we decided to break the age division of offenders into aggregates of 14 to 16 year olds, and juveniles younger than 14. If atypical cases are considered more newsworthy, than we should expect to find greater coverage given to homicides committed by females and juveniles under the age of 14.

GENDER AND AGE OF VICTIMS

Gender and age of the victim are two characteristics that greatly influence media coverage. The media consider stories involving children and the elderly more newsworthy because of their rarity and because these two groups are viewed as more defenseless. Chermak (1995) suggests that crimes that would receive little or no attention by the press when an adult is the victim tend to get an exorbitant amount of attention when a child is the victim. To test whether the age of the victim is a determinant in deciding newsworthiness, we di-

vided the victims' ages into the following aggregates: under 14 years, from 14 to 19 years, 20 to 29, 30 to 49, 50 to 64, and 65 and above. Thus we should expect to find the greatest coverage given to victims under the age of 14 and 65 years and older.

Likewise, the gender of the victim plays an important role in the newsworthiness of the case for much the same reason. Chermak (1995: 130) argues: "Society thinks females, like children, are more vulnerable and feels crimes committed against them are more newsworthy." If the atypical is given more coverage, female victims should be disproportionately represented in the media.

The literature thus suggests that the media can distort information by overreporting certain crimes, or by giving attention to certain cases that involve atypical characteristics. Due to their unusual nature, the atypical crimes make better copy. Nelson (1984) argues that the cases that make headlines fit the organizational needs of the media. That is, the cases selected appeal to audience curiosity. The media can therefore overemphasize the frequency of violent crimes and certain characteristics of offenders that create perceptions of fear. If atypical cases are published in news accounts with more frequency than typical cases, then patterns of victimization disappear. We argue that there are patterns concerning juvenile homicide, and we examine the characteristics of the offenders and victims. Data concerning reported cases to the CPD will be compared to the articles that make the news in two Chicago newspapers.

METHODOLOGY

In order to determine the characteristics of juvenile homicides (i.e., homicides involving an offender under the age of 17) reported to the CPD, we used police department data. These data were coded by Carolyn Rebecca Block, Richard Block, and the Illinois Criminal Justice Information Authority.[23] The selection of this data was facilitated by three factors. First, since Chicago is one of the four leading cities with respect to the number of reported annual homicides, it was preconceived that enough cases would be readily available for statistical analysis. Second, the dataset is one of the most complete datasets in existence. Finally, since these data were reported directly by the CPD, they are fairly accurate. According to Marvin Wolfgang (1967), police statistics provide the most accurate data available. He further states that "too many cases are lost through court trials to use court statistics. and to use prison data means a still further reduction of cases that are highly selected to result in incarceration instead of probation or some other form of disposition" (p. 17).

The purpose of analyzing this dataset is to provide some physical characteristics of both juvenile offenders and their victims in Chicago. A content analysis of newspaper articles reported in the *Chicago Sun-Times* and *Chicago Tribune* is conducted. A comparison is made of cases reported to the police and those printed in the papers. In

doing so, variations on the type of weapon, age, gender, and race are examined.

Full-text articles were made available using keyword searches (such as "juvenile murder" and "juvenile homicide") on *WestLaw*, an electronic database. We used 1992 to 1997 as our time frame, thus each story reported during that time period was examined. However, not every story pertained to an actual murder by a juvenile in Chicago—the requirement for this study. Several of the articles were excluded because they either dealt with juveniles who were murdered by adults or discussed juvenile homicide in general terms without focusing on a specific case. Others were omitted because they occurred outside Chicago city limits. Additionally, it is quite possible that some cases were excluded simply because *WestLaw* did not pick up these cases. We minimized this threat by using multiple keyword searches when retrieving the cases. Of all the articles sampled, only 97 stories from the *Sun-Times* and *Tribune* together met the qualifications of this research: actual homicides committed by juvenile perpetrators within the CPD's jurisdiction. These stories were matched to the CPD data using date, age of the victim, and age of the offender as grouping variables. In other words, once we identified which stories received attention, we were able to match them in the data, thus making it possible to differentiate between cases receiving media attention and those that did not receive any attention at all.

The pertinent literature dealing with homicide and the media led us to examine the reporting patterns of age, gender, and race for both offender and victim. We have included type of weapon as an additional variable that we believe may have an impact on the newsworthiness of the story. Weapons were separated into the following categories: guns, knives, and other.

[2]Block, C. R., R. L. Block, & the Illinois Criminal Justice Information Authority. HOMICIDES IN CHICAGO, 1965–1995 [Computer file]. 4th ICPSR version. Chicago, IL: Illinois Criminal Justice Information Authority [producer], 1998. Ann Arbor, MI: Inter-university Consortium for Political and Social Research [distributor], 1998.

[3]Data from 1992 to 1995 came directly from the Chicago Homicide Dataset. Data from 1996 and 1997 was made available by the Chicago Police Department. We are indebted to Superintendent Terry G. Hillard, Lieutenant Lemmer, and Rachel M. Johnston of the Chicago Police Department.

To examine the spatial distribution of reported homicides (both by the news media and by the CPD), data were converted into ArcView, a computer-aided spatial distribution program, and a spatial distribution of juvenile homicides in the city of Chicago was constructed. This mapping procedure takes the geographical district of each reported homicide (which was a variable already provided by the CPD in the reported data and coded in the newspaper data) and matches it using X and Y coordinates, thus plotting it on a map of Chicago. Once plotted, we were able to determine the spatial distribution of the reporting patterns citywide. Ideally, matching street addresses would have provided more detailed information; however, addresses are not included in the dataset although district information was included. Chicago is divided into 25 police districts. The boundaries for each district have remained unchanged since 1982.

FINDINGS

From 1992 to 1997, 383 juvenile homicides were reported to the CPD. Of which, the majority occurred in 1994 and have steadily declined since then.[4] Although newspaper coverage rose steadily from 1992 to 1993, peaked in 1994, declined sharply from 1994 to 1995, increased slightly from 1995 to 1996, and dramatically increased in 1997. Interestingly, coverage of juvenile homicides in 1997 was only slightly less than the coverage given in 1994 when juvenile homicides were at an all time high.

---

[4]Because we deal primarily with reported cases, we selected the first offender and victim in each case. In other words, multiple offenders and multiple victims were excluded from these analyses.

RACE OF OFFENDER

Table 1 examines the race of the offender in cases that receive attention from the press and those that were ignored. The vast majority of juvenile homicides in Chicago involved African-American offenders. This held true for cases that both received news media attention (79.4%) as well as those that received no attention at all (80.1%). Significant differences were noted between Caucasian, Hispanic, and Asian/Other offenders ($2 = 28.058$, $p < .001$, $df = 3$, $= .082$, $p. < .05$). Although less than 2 percent of the cases that received no attention from the media involved Caucasian offenders, more than 10 percent were reported by the media. Similarly, Asian/Other offenders were overrepresented by the media, whereas Latino offenders were underrepresented (18.2% v. 7.2%). As Sheley and Ashkins (1981) found in their study of New Orleans reporting patterns, we found very little disparity in regard to the amount of attention given African-American offenders by the press. Although African Americans clearly made up the majority of offenders, Latinos fell only shortly behind in numbers. However, Latino offenders were underrepresented in the press.

RACE OF VICTIM

Table 2 examines the racial composition of victims that receive attention in the media and those not making the headlines. In examining the race of the victim, significant differences were noted between reported and nonreported cases ($2 = 8.092$, $p < .05$, $df = 3$, $= .145$, $p. < .05$). Caucasian (6.3% v. 12.4%) and Asian/Other offenders (1% v. 3.1%) were overrepresented by the news media, whereas Latinos were underrepresented. African Americans, on the other hand, received a proportionate amount of attention by the papers. Latinos received

TABLE 1:   Race of the Offender

			MEDIA ATTENTION		
			not reported in papers	**reported in papers**	**Total**
Racial, Ethnic Group of Offender	White Non-Latino	Count	5 1.7%	10 10.3%	15 3.9%
	Black Non-Latino	Count	229 80.1%	77 79.4%	306 79.9%
	Latino	Count	52 18.2%	7 7.2%	59 15.4%
	Asian, Other	Count		3 3.1%	3 .8%
	Total	Count	286 100.0%	97 100.0%	383 100.0%

$\chi^2 = 28.058$, $p < .001$, $df = 3$, $\lambda = .082$, $p. < .05$

TABLE 2:   Race of the Victim

			MEDIA ATTENTION		
			not reported in papers	**reported in papers**	**Total**
Racial, Ethnic Group of Victim	White Non-Latino	Count	18 6.3%	12 12.4%	30 7.8%
	Black Non-Latino	Count	217 75.9%	73 75.3%	290 75.7%
	Latino	Count	48 16.8%	9 9.3%	57 14.9%
	Asian, Other	Count	3 1.0%	3 3.1%	6 1.6%
	Total	Count	286 100.0%	97 100.0%	383 100.0%

$\chi^2 = 8.092$, $p < .05$, $df = 3$, $\phi = .145$, $p. < .05$

disproportionately less attention from the media as both offenders and victims.

GENDER OF THE OFFENDER

The vast majority of cases (both reported and nonreported) involved male offenders. No significant gender differences were noted between cases reported (92.7% males) and cases not reported (94.5% males) by the news media.

GENDER OF THE VICTIM

Table 3 examines the gender of the victim in cases receiving and not receiving attention from the Chicago newspaper. Significant differences were observed between the gender of the victim and whether or not the case was reported (2 = 7.220, $p <$ .05, $df = 1$, = .018, $p. < .05$). Female victims received a disproportionate amount of attention by the news media. While they made up only 11.4 percent of the cases that received no attention at all, they represented 26.8 percent of the cases reported by the papers. Compare this to males, who composed 88.6 percent of the unreported cases and 73.2 percent of the cases reported by the media.

AGE OF THE OFFENDER

In general, cases reported in the newspapers tended to involve younger offenders when compared to cases that were not considered newsworthy (14.23 v. 15.21, $t =$ 7.839, $p. < .05$). The age difference is further evident when cases are categorically defined to include offenders under the age of 14 and those between the ages of 14 to 16. As Table 4 indicates, significant differences were found in the age of the offender that garners media attention (2 = 18.675, $p. <$ .001, $df = 1$, = −.221, $p. < .001$). The majority of homicide cases involve offenders between the ages of 14 and 16, but the cases reported by the news media disproportionately involved younger offenders.

AGE OF THE VICTIM

Not unlike age of the offender, the news media tended to overreport cases involving youthful victims. On average, cases receiving media attention tended to involve victims with a mean age of about 20 (19.97), whereas cases that received no attention included significantly older victims (mn = 24.29), a mean difference of about five years. To examine this further,

TABLE 3: Gender of the Victim[1]

| | | | MEDIA ATTENTION | | |
			not reported by media	reported by media	Total
Gender of Victim	Male	Count	226	30	256
		% within Report Status	88.6%	73.2%	86.5%
	Female	Count	29	11	40
		% within Report Status	11.4%	26.8%	13.5%
	Total	Count	255	41	296
		% within Report Status	100.0%	100.0%	100.0%

$\chi^2 = 7.220, p < .05, df = 1, \lambda = .018, p. < .05$

[1]Gender data for 1996 and 1997 not made available by the CPD.

TABLE 4:   Age of the Offender

			MEDIA ATTENTION		
			not reported in papers	**reported in papers**	**Total**
Ofagecat	> 14	Count	18 6.3%	21 21.6%	39 10.2%
	14 to 16	Count	268 93.7%	76 78.4%	344 89.8%
	Total	Count	286 100.0%	97 100.0%	383 100.0%

$\chi^2 = 18.675$, $p < .001$, $df = 1$, $\phi = -.221$, $p. < .001$

we collapsed victim age into various categories to include individuals under 14, 14 to 19, 20 to 29, 30 to 49, 50 to 64, and 65 and older. In doing so, it was discovered that victims under the age of 14 received a disproportionate amount of attention by the newspapers (38.1% v. 5.3%). This finding is consistent with previous research. Chermak

TABLE 5:   Age of Victim

			MEDIA ATTENTION		
			not reported in papers	**reported in papers**	**Total**
Victim age	> 14	Count % within media attention	21 5.3%	37 38.1%	58 11.8%
	14 to 19	Count % within media attention	161 40.7%	27 27.8%	188 38.1%
	20 to 29	Count % within media attention	126 31.8%	16 16.5%	142 28.8%
	30 to 49	Count % within media attention	69 17.4%	10 10.3%	79 16.0%
	50 to 64	Count % within media attention	8 2.0%	4 4.1%	12 2.4%
	65 up	Count % within media attention	11 2.8%	3 3.1%	14 2.8%
	Total	Count % within media attention	396 100.0%	97 100.0%	493 100.0%

$\chi^2 = 85.045$, $p < .001$, $df = 5$, $\phi = .415$, $p. < .001$

(1995) concluded that youthful victims are overreported by the media because society views crimes against children as deplorable. Therefore when it occurs, it elevates the importance of the story, thus causing it to receive a exorbitant amount of attention. However, Chermak (1995) also suggested that the elderly received increased attention as well. Our findings do not support this conclusion. When comparing reported to unreported cases, we find very little variation among the elderly category (65 and older): 3.1 percent (reported) v. 2.8 percent (unreported).

TYPE OF WEAPON

Table 6 provides a cross tabulation between type of weapon and reporting status of the case. As this table suggests, there appears to be a significant association between the type of weapon used in the homicide and whether or not the case received media attention ($2 = 7.057, p. < .05, df = 2, = .136, p. < .05$). Most juvenile homicides involved the use of some type of firearm or gun. However, differences were noted in the "other" category. The "other"

category included cases in which the offender kicked the victim so hard her liver was divided, burned victims, dropped a child from a window, and a variety of unusual methods of killing the victim. The papers tended to overreport cases involving "other" weapons when compared to cases involving more common weapons, which did not receive media attention.

SPATIAL DISTRIBUTION OF CASES

The findings seem to suggest that there are significant differences in the types of stories the news media present to the public. This prompts us to ask whether or not there are geographical differences in the reporting patterns of the news media as well. Figure 1 provides a depiction of the distribution of juvenile homicides reported in the papers to the total number of cases reported to the CPD. Because population varies from district to district, the raw number of homicides reported to the CPD was converted into a rate. As Figure 1 illustrates, homicides reported to the CPD ranged from a low of 0 (Districts 1 and 16) to a high of 43.04 per 100,000 (District 5),

TABLE 6:   Type of Weapon

			MEDIA ATTENTION		
			not reported in papers	**reported in papers**	**Total**
Weapon	gun	Count	251	77	328
			87.8%	79.4%	85.6%
	knife	Count	12	3	15
			4.2%	3.1%	3.9%
	other	Count	23	17	40
			8.0%	17.5%	10.4%
	Total	Count	286	97	383
			100.0%	100.0%	100.0%

$\chi^2 = 7.057, p < .05, df = 2, = .136, p. < .05$

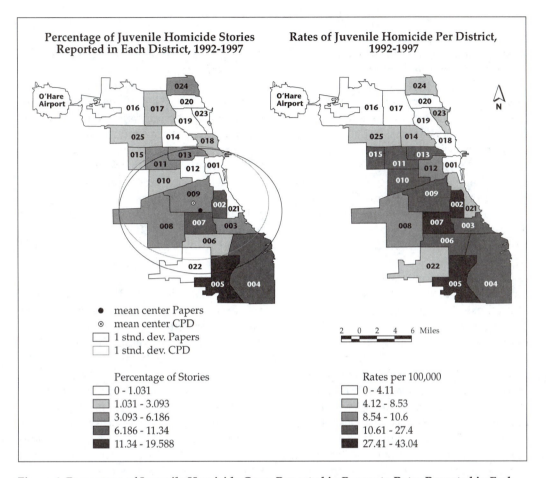

Figure 1. Percentage of Juvenile Homicide Cases Reported in Papers to Rates Reported in Each District

with a mean homicide rate of 14.56 per 100,000 citywide. Newspaper stories in each district ranged from a low of 0 (Districts 1, 19, 21, and 23) to a high of 19 (District 5). With few exceptions, our findings suggest that the reporting patterns of the newspapers correspond with the reported homicide rates in each district. From 1994 to 1997, very few homicides in the northern districts were reported to the CPD. Similarly, these areas were virtually ignored by the newspapers. District 5, on the other hand, suffered the highest rate of reported juvenile homicide in the city (43.04 per 100,000) and received the most cover-

age by the newspapers (almost 20% of all stories reported).

There was some noticeable variation in the spatial distribution of reported juvenile homicides. For example, District 21, which is located in the downtown area, recorded a few homicides, yet was ignored by the news media. This lack in reporting was observed in some of the northern districts as well (Districts 12, 14, and 23). Our findings indicate that the southernmost districts have the highest rates of juvenile homicide and receive the bulk of the media attention. This is surprising in that if newsworthiness were the only variable in the "newsmaking" process, we would expect to see a higher emphasis in the northern districts since they do not normally experience this type of crime. However, this was not found to be the case. In fact, we observed that the majority of attention by the papers was devoted to the southern districts. Overreporting in southern districts was further evident when we mapped out standard deviational ellipses to determine the geographical location of juvenile homicides reported to the CPD and those reported in the newspapers (within one standard deviation). In doing so, we were able to determine the geographical boundaries where most homicides occurred or were reported by the papers. In other words, roughly 68 percent of all cases fall within each ellipse. As Figure 1 illustrates, there is agreement between cases reported by the newspapers and the total number of cases reported to the police. Both ellipses center on District 9 in the central region of the city. However, there is some variation: the distribution of cases reported by the papers is more dispersed, whereas the cases reported to the CPD tended to be more centralized. This suggests that the media tended to slightly overreport incidences from the southern districts of the city.

DISCUSSION

The purpose of this research was to examine the characteristics of juvenile homicide in Chicago from 1992 to 1997, and to explore the accuracy of reporting these characteristics in two Chicago newspapers. In particular, we questioned whether the public was getting a clear perception of the characteristics associated with juvenile offenders and their victims. With the exception of the offender's gender, cases receiving press coverage from the *Chicago Sun-Times* and *Chicago Tribune* were signifi-

cantly different than cases not receiving coverage in terms of the offender's race and age; the race, age, and gender of the victim; and the type of weapon used.

In regard to gender, our findings conflict with Naylor's (1995) study of female offenders receiving a disproportionate amount of media attention. In this study, we found no significant associations between the gender of the offender and amount of media attention. However, the gender of the victim was a significant variable in the reporting of the case, as was found by Chermak (1995). With respect to age, our study yielded mixed results when compared to previous research. Chermak (1995) suggested that both very young children and the elderly receive disproportionate amounts of coverage by the press due to their vulnerability. We found evidence to support that very young children as victims receive greater coverage, but failed to find evidence to support the claim that the elderly receive increased attention as well.

Our findings also suggest that the media are not guilty of overreporting or ignoring all the ordinary aspects of crime. The coverage of African Americans as offenders and as victims were proportional in relation to their appearance in CPD data. Like Sheley and Ashkins (1981), we found almost no disparity in the reporting patterns of African-American offenders. This finding is inconsistent with journalist claims that "blue cases" (or cases involving African-American victims and offenders) were ignored (Boulahanis et al. 2000). In this study, the differences in racial composition of offenders and victims were noted in the disproportionate amount of attention given Caucasians and the underreporting of Latinos. The underreporting of Latinos as offenders and victims is consistent with Johnstone et al. (1994).

One of the limitations to this study is that characteristics of the cases in the article were examined independently. That is, we analyzed the data on race, gender, age, and weapon as distinct properties that we compared to the cases unreported in the media. There are clear patterns noted in juvenile homicide cases in Chicago. Offenders are generally males using guns, and are disproportionately African American. Victims, more often than not, are males over the age of 14 and African American. The majority of the cases reported in this study confirm those statements, but indicate that there are some significant differences found when analyzed separately. Focusing on the atypical features of the news story, without viewing the article as a composite of many separate elements, may exaggerate the importance of these features. In examining the cases receiving press as a composite, we suggest that future researchers may find that most cases have some atypical features. For example, we found one story in which a male African-American offender used a gun to kill an male African-American victim. It sounds rather typical at first glance, but this case involved a "peddle-by" shooting by a juvenile too young to drive a car. Another case involved several African-American teenage males that killed an African-American man by setting him on fire—only the method of murder is unusual. In still another story gang violence broke out and a young female was caught in the crossfire—the innocent victim is the unusual element in this story. Thus cases like these have more typical features than atypical. Only one element is necessary to make a case appear atypical in regard to statistical analysis, and we suggest future researchers should take a more qualitative approach to analyzing this data.

Future researchers may also want to tie this research to perceptions of fear. The basic social constructionist argument concerning the media is that overreporting or underreporting of crimes or certain features of them distort the perceptions of the public. Are the residents less fearful of guns because other methods receive a disproportionate amount of press? Are they more afraid of 10 and 12 year olds because their cases receive a disproportionate amount of attention? Or does the public recognize that these are atypical characteristics and understand that older teenage males using guns are more likely the perpetrators? Life experiences from living in Chicago may override any exaggerations or neglected attention given to homicide cases. We suspect this may likely be the case. It is also impossible to go back in time and measure public perceptions as they relate to juvenile homicide in Chicago. However, a more current comparison of CPD reports and media accounts can include an additional measure of the perceptions of residents. Using this method, the consequences of the atypical characteristics of juvenile homicides will be much clearer. Social constructionism thus has limitations as to its usefulness in this study. This study does suggest that the media find cases with elements of the unusual more newsworthy, but does not provide any evidence supporting a distortion in perceptions. Specifically, it is impossible for us to ascertain if the reporting of atypical cases has an impact on public perceptions.

In examining the spatial distribution of juvenile homicides, we noted much agreement between cases reported to the police and cases reported in the news media. The majority of cases in Chicago occurred in the southern districts and the majority of cases reported in the papers reflect this as well. This causes us to ponder why the area of the city is not one of the elements of a news story that makes it newsworthy. If the media consider atypical cases as more newsworthy, then homicides committed by juveniles in the predominantly white, upper-class areas of the city should fulfill that requirement. We make no argument to suggest that most crimes do not occur in more racially diverse and poorer sections of the city, but do encourage future researchers to explore this phenomenon of neglect more thoroughly. Before stronger claims are made, more advanced geographical analyses need to be conducted.

It is our hope that this research will fill a void in both the constructionist and media studies literature. Although much research has been conducted on the reporting patterns of homicide by the media, very few studies have examined the reporting patterns of cases involving juvenile offenders. The timing for research could not be more perfect for additional research on this subject. Datasets are readily available to examine the increase and decline in juvenile crime, and media accounts are at a more manageable level since the decline in homicide rates. Furthermore, no study, to our knowledge, attempts to use Geographic Information System technology to map out the reporting patterns of homicide, as we have attempted to do. Future studies should consider this technique as a valuable tool to map reporting patterns of the media.

References

Altheide, D. L. 1985. *Media Power*. Beverly Hills, CA: Sage Publishing, Inc.

Barak, G. 1988. "Newsmaking Criminology: Reflections on the Media, Intellectuals, and Crime." In *Media, Process, and the Social Construction of Crime: Studies in Newsmaking Criminology, ed. G. Barak*. New York: Garland Publishing, Inc.

Barak, G. 1994. "Media, Society, and Criminology." In *Media, Process, and the Social Construction of Crime: Studies in Newsmaking Criminology, ed. G. Barak*. New York: Garland Publishing, Inc.

Best, J. 1990. *Threatened Children: Rhetoric and Concern about Child-victims*. Chicago: The University of Chicago Press.

Boulahanis, J. G., A. Esmail, and M. Heltsley., 2000. "An Examination of Juvenile Homicides and Perceptions of Violence in Chicago: A True

Phenomenon or Constructed Reality Caused by the Media." Paper presented at the American Society of Criminology, San Francisco, CA, November 2000.

Chermak, S. 1994. "Crime in the News Media: A Refined Understanding of How Crimes Become News." In *Media, Process, and the Social Construction of Crime: Studies in Newsmaking Criminology, ed. G. Barak*. New York: Garland Publishing, Inc.

Chermak, S. 1995. *Victims in the News: Crime and the American News Media*. Boulder, CO: Westview Press.

Chicago Sun Times 2000. "Juvenile Homicide Arrests at New Low." 15 December, p. 52.

Davis, F. J. 1952. "Crime News in Colorado Newspapers." *American Journal of Sociology* 57: 325–330.

DeYoung, M. 1998. "Moral Panics: The Case for Satanic Day Care Centers." In *Constructions of deviance: Social power, context, and interaction* 3d ed., ed. P. A. Adler and P. Adler. Belmont, CA: Wadsworth Publishing.

Dixon, T. L., and D. Linz. 2000. "Overrepresentation and Underrepresentation of African Americans and Latinos as Lawbreakers on Television News." *Journal of Communication* 50(2): 131–154.

Elikann, P. 1999. *Superpredators: Demoralization of Our Children by the Law*. New York: Plenum Press.

Ericson, R. V., P. M. Baranek and J. B. L. Chan. 1991. *Representing Order: Crime, Law, and Justice in the News Media*. Toronto: University of Toronto Press.

Fishman, M. 1978. "Crime Waves as Ideology." In *The Manufacture of News: Social Problems, Deviance, and the Mass Media, ed. S. Cohen and J. Young*. Beverly Hills, CA: Sage Publications.

Gans, H. J. 1979. *Deciding What's News: A Study of CBS Evening News, NBC Nightly News, Newsweek, and Times*. New York: Pantheon Books.

Goode, E. and N. Ben-Yehuda. 1994. *Moral Panics: Social Construction of Deviance*. Cambridge, MA: Blackwell Publishers.

Grabe, M. E. 1999. "Television News Magazine Crime Stories: A Functionalist Perspective." *Critical Studies in Mass Communication* 16(2): 155–171.

Graber, D. A. 1980. *Crime News and the Public*. New York: Praeger.

Gusfield, J. R. 1989. "Constructing the Ownership of Social Problems: Fun and Profit in the Welfare State." *Social Problems* 36: 431–441.

Heide, K. 1996. "Juvenile Homicide in the United States: Trends and Contributing Factors." In *Lethal Violence: Proceedings of the 1995 Research Working Group, ed. M. Riedel and G. Boulahanis*. Ottawa, Canada.

Hubbard, J. C., L. B. DeFleur and M. L. DeFleur. 1975. "Mass Media Influences on Public Conceptions of Social Problems." *Social Problems* 23: 22–34.

Israel, M. 1998. "Telling Stories of Crime in South Australia." *The Australian and New Zealand Journal of Criminology* 31(3): 213–229.

Jenkins, P. 1994. *Using Murder: Social Construction of Serial Homicide*. New York: Aldine De Gruyter.

Johnstone, J. W. C., D. F. Hawkins, and A. Michener. 1994. "Homicide Reporting in Chicago Dailies. *Journalism Quarterly* 71: 860–872.

Katz, J. 1987. "What Makes Crime 'News'?" *Media Culture and Society* 9: 47–75.

Madriz, E. 1997. *Nothing Bad Happens to Good Girls: Fear of Crime in Women's Lives*. Berkeley: University of California Press.

Mahini, R. B. 2000. "There's No Place Like Home: The Availability of Judicial Review over Certification Decisions Invoking Federal Jurisdiction under the Juvenile Justice and Delinquency Prevention Act." *Vanderbilt Law Review* 53(4): 1311–1354.

Naylor, B. 1995. "Women's Crime and Media Coverage: Making Explanations." In *Gender and Crime, ed. R. E. Dobash, R. P. Dobash, and L. Noaks*. Cardiff, U.K.: The University of Wales.

Nelson, B. J. 1984. *Making an Issue of Child Abuse*. Chicago: University of Chicago.

Reinarman, C. 2000. "The Social Construction of Drug Scares." In *Constructions of Deviance: Social Power, Context, and Interaction* 3d ed., ed. P. A. Adler and P. Adler. California: Wadsworth Publishing.

Sheley, J. F. and C. D. Ashkins. 1981. "Crime, Crime News, and Crime Views." *Public Opinion Quarterly* 45: 492–506.

Sprott, J. B. 1996. "Understanding Public Views of Youth Crime and the Youth Justice System." *Canadian Journal of Criminology*: Vol. 38(3), 271–290.

Surette, R. 1998. *Media, Crime, and Criminal Justice: Images and Realities*. Belmont CA: West/Wadsworth Publishing.

Thomas, W. I. 1923. *The Unadjusted Girl*. Boston: Little, Brown & Company.

Wolfgang, M. E. 1967. "Criminal Homicide and the Subculture of Violence." In *Studies in Homicide, ed. M. E. Wolfgang*. New York: Harper & Row Publishers.

Chapter **6**

Drugs and Delinquency

INTRODUCTION

Goode offers a snapshot of drug use in America in his examination of three national surveys. Predictably, he concluded that legal drug use (alcohol and tobacco) far exceeded illegal drug use. Goode argues that campaigns to discourage illegal drug use have been successful. However, very little attention has been devoted to discouraging legal drug use. If more attention is given to discouraging legal drug use, it too might decrease.

Weaver elaborates on key elements of the complex nexus between drug use and delinquent activity among juveniles. In doing so, he concludes that alcohol and drug use is a "consequence of the process of becoming an adult" for some adolescents. Some juveniles resort to drug use as a mark of independence, a mechanism to achieve autonomy by engaging in inappropriate behavior. However, for other "life-course persistent offenders," drug use carries over into adulthood and may also be an indicator of serious problems. Weaver provides previous research that clearly links drug and alcohol use to delinquency.

Brunelle, Brochu, and Cousineau attempt to reveal various links between drug use and delinquency that exist in the trajectories of youth. To do this, they use a qualitative research approach in examining autobiographical accounts of 38 young drug users (22 boys and 16 girls). Goldstein's tripartite drug-crime model is used as a reference point. This model offers three explanations that link drug use to violence. The psychopharmacological model postulates that the intoxication effects of drug use prompts an individual to violence. The economic compulsive model, on the other hand, suggests that delinquency is a result of the high price tag associated with drug use, whereas the systemic model explains violence as a mechanism that protects the drug markets. Limited support for Goldstein's model was revealed for a psychopharmacological and an economic compulsive model. However, support for the systemic model did not emerge in this study.

Drug Use In America:

An Overview

Erich Goode

The results of drug surveys are media events. Every time the findings of the latest national survey are released, they make the front page. One year, the headline reads "Students Return to Drug Use." The next year, it announces "Illegal Drug Use Declines."

When we read the results of a study on drug use, what's our reaction likely to be? If we are skeptics, we are likely to wonder, *how do they know*? In interviews or with questionnaires, are respondents really completely honest about their consumption of illicit substances? When they are asked questions about the illegal, deviant, or delinquent activities in which they might engage, don't people *lie* a lot? How can we trust the results of studies on illegal drug use?

As it turns out, in studies of deviant behavior, lying is not a major problem—*as long as respondents are convinced that they will remain completely anonymous*. If the people who participate in a study believe their answers will remain confidential, that the researchers will not reveal their names to anyone—that they cannot get into trouble for giving honest answers, no matter what

they say—most of them will give candid and truthful answers. Of course, a great many people have imperfect memories. All of us are sometimes wrong about certain facts, but most respondents give fairly accurate answers in an anonymous survey— *to the best of their ability*. However, this generalization may not apply as well to teenagers as to adults, as we will see.

How do researchers know this? It's really quite simple: the process of *triangulation*. Triangulation entails looking at the same thing using different sources of data. We cross-check something someone says with separate and independent evidence. If people claim not to have used an illegal drug during the past 48 hours, we test their blood, or urine. If respondents tell us they have never been arrested, we check their arrest records. If interviewees say they were enrolled in a particular drug treatment program, we look up the relevant documents in that program's records.

The fact is, every time a study on drug use, deviance, and delinquency makes these kinds of triangular cross-checks, it finds a strong correspondence between what people say they did and what indisputable evidence shows they actually did (Inciardi, 1986, 1992: Johnson et al., 1985). This correspondence is far from perfect, but for our purposes, it is close enough for us to be able to use answers in surveys as an approximation to real-life behavior. As a result, experts believe we can trust the findings from properly conducted surveys on drug use.

TWO MAJOR DRUG SURVEYS

To get an accurate snapshot of patterns of drug use in general, it is very important that a study be nationally representative. This means that a survey's sample of respondents should look like, reflect, or represent the country as a whole with respect to such crucial characteristics as age, sex, race, social class, region of residence, and so on. Otherwise, we will get a very distorted picture of the behavior that takes place in a society in general because we will be drawing conclusions from a sample that is biased, skewed, or unrepresentative—in other words, that looks like part of the whole rather than the whole. For instance, if we want to find out about the drinking patterns of Americans generally, but we draw our sample exclusively from the state of Utah (which has the lowest rate of alcohol consumption in the country), our *findings* may be accurate but our *conclusions* will be inaccurate and extremely misleading.

Researchers who examine national patterns of drug use have the most faith in two surveys: the Monitoring the Future survey and the National Household Survey on Drug Abuse.

The Monitoring the Future survey is conducted every year by a team of researchers at the Institute for Social Research. This survey is based on self-completed questionnaires in selected schools. It began in 1975 as a study of the drug use of high school seniors. In 1980, it added to the sample college students and young adults who were not in college. In 1991, it began studying 8th and 10th graders as well. This

study's sample is huge (between 15,000 and 20,000) and it is representative of the contiguous 48 states. Its response rate is roughly 85 to 90 percent, which is very high. (The nonresponses are made up mainly of absentees.) The Monitoring the Future survey is the best source on adolescent drug use because of the size and representativeness of its sample and because its questionnaires are administered in school rather than at home. Its drawback is that it does not include dropouts and absentees.

A second major data source based on a nationally representative sample is the National Household Survey on Drug Abuse, which has been conducted regularly since 1971. This survey is sponsored and administered by the federal government. Its sample, which is also nationally representative, is drawn from the noninstitutionalized, nonmilitary population older than 12. Interviews are conducted at the respondents place of residence. The 1998 survey (SAMHSA, 1999) drew a sample of 25,000 persons; the 1999 survey was triple that size. For the purposes of analysis, the National Household Survey divides its respondents into four age categories: 12 to 17, 18 to 25, 25 to 34, and 35 and older. Although the National Household Survey on Drug Abuse is the best ongoing study on the consumption of both legal and illegal substances, one of its drawbacks is that adolescents are interviewed at home, which may influence their answers. Obviously, for adults, this is not a problem.

These two surveys provide the foundation for making generalizations about drug use in the American population during the past 40 years. In fact, one of the early National Household Surveys, conducted in 1979, projected patterns of drug use backward in time to 1960 by calculating age of first use (Miller and Cisin, 1980). Also, because we are able to rely on two data sources rather than one, we can apply the principle of triangulation.

These two surveys, therefore, give us an excellent four-decades-long view of patterns of drug use in the United States. They give us a picture of the rate or magnitude of drug use: what percent of the population uses which drugs, which segments of the population use more than others, and what sorts of changes in drug use have taken place over time. There are many issues these surveys do not explore (for instance, the harm that drug use causes or what the drug experience feels like), but for rates, differences in rates by social category, and changes in rates over time, these studies are both unparalleled and absolutely essential. We simply cannot discuss these issues without consulting these two studies. The figures we obtain from these surveys should not be taken as gospel, of course. For one thing, the National Household Survey on Drug Abuse does not locate or interview people who do not live at a fixed address, such as homeless and street people, whose alcohol and drug use is likely to be higher than the population at large. However, along with the Monitoring the Future survey, the National Household Survey gives us a fairly accurate snapshot of the scope of drug use in America.

DRUG USE IN AMERICAN SOCIETY: A CAPSULE SUMMARY

What do these two studies tell us? To begin with, these surveys reveal what is probably a universal rule in the consumption of psychoactive substances and possibly with respect to human behavior in general. It seems to be a universal rule that *legal* drugs are used by more people, and they are used more frequently, than *illegal* drugs. This is as true in other countries as it is in the United States. Our surveys show us that the two legal drugs, alcohol and tobacco, are used by much higher proportions of the population, and with more frequency, than the illegal drugs. The 1998 National Household Survey—the most recent available at this writing—revealed that a majority of Americans age 12 and older (52 percent) had used alcohol at least once during the past month. Just fewer than two-thirds (64 percent) used alcohol during the past year, and eight in ten (81 percent) said that they had had an alcoholic drink at least once during their entire lifetime. (These figures can be found in Table 1.) The figures for tobacco were significantly lower, although still quite substantial: 28 percent of the respondents had smoked during the past month: 31 percent during the past year: and 70 percent at least once during their lives. In comparison, the percentage of Americans who use illegal drugs is much lower than for the legal drugs. In fact, the figure saying that they had used *any* illicit drug using the past month—all illegal drugs added together—was only 6 percent. About one American in ten (11 percent) said that they had used any illegal drug during the last year: and only a third of all Americans (36 percent) had used any illegal drug during their entire lifetime.

Marijuana is by far the most popular illicit drug. It is entirely possible that half of all episodes of use that Americans have with illicit drugs are with marijuana alone. Still, only one American in 20 (5 percent) said that they used marijuana (or hashish) during the past month: one in ten (9 percent) had done so during the past year: and one-third (33 percent) had done so once or more in their lives. The comparable figures for cocaine were: last month. 1 percent; last year, 2 percent: and lifetime, 11 percent. The other illicit drugs were used on a considerably smaller scale than marijuana and cocaine. (Table 18.1 details the rate of drug

TABLE 1:   Use of Selected Drugs, U.S. Population Age 12 and Older, 1998

	PERCENTAGE OF PEOPLE USING DRUGS			
	Lifetime	Past Year	Past Month	Use Ratio
Alcohol	81	64	52	64%
Cigarettes	70	31	28	40%
Marijuana	33	9	5	15%
Cocaine	11	2	1	8%
Crack Cocaine	2	0.4	0.2	10%
LSD	4	1	0.3	4%
Heroin	1	0.1	0.1	5%
Any Illicit Drug	36	11	6	—

Source: Data from Substances Abuse and Mental Health Service Association, *Summary of Findings from the 1998 National Household Survey on Drug Abuse*. (1999, Rockville, MD: Author), pp. 63–67.

use in the United States in 1998 for alcohol, tobacco, and several selected drugs, as well as for the use of any illicit drug.)

The exact magnitude of these figures is not the issue, of course, but it is clear that the legal drugs are used on a vastly greater scale than the illegal drugs. In absolute terms, many people do use harmful, dangerous drugs such as heroin and cocaine, and with alarming frequency, in fact, on the order of hundreds of thousands of people. However, in relative terms, that is, expressed both as a percentage of the population and in comparison with the legal drugs—which are harmful and dangerous as well—their use is at a far lower rate.

Legal drugs are not only used by more people than illegal drugs, they are also used with greater frequency by those who use them. When we compare use during the past month with lifetime use figures, we get a kind of loyalty or continuance ratio. If for a given drug, most of the people who have ever used are still using (that is, have used during the past month), then its users are very loyal; they stick with that drug, they continue using it over time. On the other hand, if with a particular drug, most of the people who used at one time

have discontinued its use (did not use within the past month), its users can be said to be disloyal, that is, they do not stick with that drug. Drugs vary widely with respect to the loyalty of their users.

As a general rule, people are much more loyal to the legal than the illegal drugs; they tend to stick with them longer, they continue using them over a longer period of time. In the United States, slightly fewer than two-thirds (64 percent) of all at least one-time users of alcohol were still using—that is, they had used alcohol at least once during the past month. This is true of only four out of ten (40 percent) consumers of tobacco. In contrast, the loyalty or continuance ratio for marijuana—the "least illegal" of the illegal drugs—is only 15 percent. For cocaine, the continuance or loyalty ratio is 8 percent: for LSD, 4 percent: for heroin, 5 percent: and for crack cocaine, 10 percent. The extent to which users continue using a given drug is the result of a complex mixture of many factors, including the properties of the drug itself—whether it is capable of producing a physical dependency—and the age of its users. Still, a drug's legal status has a great deal to do with user loyalty.

DIFFERENCES IN DRUG USE BETWEEN AGE CATEGORIES

It should come as no surprise that there are extremely large differences in rates of drug use between and among age categories in the population. As a general rule, illicit drug use is low at age 12, rises throughout the adolescent years, reaches a peak in the young adult or 18-to-25-year-old bracket, and then declines throughout the remainder of the life cycle. In contrast, the use of alcohol rises sharply throughout adolescence, but it reaches a plateau in that vast stretch of time between the 18-to-20-year-old bracket and the 40s: in fact, even after the age of 50, its decline is fairly gradual. Clearly, there is something strikingly different about the use of illicit substances; it displays an age-graded pattern that is quite unlike that prevailing for the legal drugs alcohol and tobacco. Deviant or illegal drug use seems to obey a pattern that does not apply to conventional or legal drug use.

The 1998 National Household Survey found an extremely strong relationship between age and illegal drug use. For instance, 10 percent of the 12- to 17-year-olds had used one or more illicit drugs during the past month, 16 percent of the 18- to 25-year-olds, 7 percent of the 26- to 34-year-olds, and only 3 percent of those 35 and older (SAMHSA, 1999, p. 90). Looking at more refined age categories, only 2.9 percent of the respondents who were 12 and 13 years old had used one or more illegal drugs during the previous month, but this figure jumps to 10.8 percent for 14- and 15-year-olds, 16.4 percent for those 16 and 17 years old, and 19.9 percent for the 18- to 20-year-olds. (Let's keep in mind, however, that these interviews were conducted in the respondents' homes, so some teenagers may have kept their use estimates low.) Clearly, between the early to the late teens,

illegal drug use skyrockets, But somewhere in the first half of the 20s, it begins to decline. Only 13.5 percent of the respondents in the 21-to-25-year-old bracket said that they had used at least one illegal drug during the previous month. For persons 26 to 29, this declined again, to 7.4 percent. Drug use declines more or less evenly throughout the 30s and 40s, then drops off fairly sharply after 50; less than 1 percent of the respondents who were older than 50 said that they had used an illegal drug during the past month. Pretty much the same picture is revealed when we look at use during the past year. Clearly, age is massively related to illegal drug use.

Many experts believe that the relationship between age and illegal drug use is an example of the more general relationship between age and deviant behavior. Most young people in their early teens live at home and are monitored and supervised—to a greater or lesser degree—by their parents. Their capacity to engage in deviant behavior such as illicit drugs is limited by the fact that their parents exert a strong influence over their behavior. In contrast, by the late teenage years, most young people have the best of all possible worlds: They have not yet assumed adult responsibilities, but at the same time, parental supervision has slackened. By the early 20s, a sizeable proportion of young people are concerned with college, an occupation, and marriage and family responsibilities, and many deviant activities, including the regular consumption of illegal substances, are seen as threats to these valued enterprises. College, an occupation, marriage, and family roles can be thought of as "investments" that might be lost by one's deviant and criminal behavior. Moreover, young people in the 16-to-20-year-old bracket are extremely strongly attached to their peers, more so than at any other age, and as a general rule, young people are more likely to engage in a larger volume of activities that violate conventional, or at least adult, notions of proper behavior. Finally, teenagers are more likely to think of themselves as invulnerable—they are less likely to think of the consequences of their actions—than adults.

All of this adds up to low levels of drug use in the early teens, a rise in the mid-teenage years, a peak in the late teens, and a decline that begins somewhere between the ages of 20 and 25. However, as we will see, some very recent developments have begun to challenge this model of how illegal drug use specifically, and deviant behavior more generally, operates.

DRUG USE OVER TIME: 1975–1998

A commonly believed myth is that illegal drug use was extremely widespread in the 1960s and declined after that. In fact, exactly the reverse is true. Drug use was extremely low in the early 1960s, it increased during that decade, rose sharply in the 1970s, reached a peak sometime in the late 1970s to early 1980s, and declined during the 1980s. During the decade of the 1990s, *adolescent* drug use increased significantly, but *adult* drug use remained more or less stable. For high school seniors, this up-and-down pattern is especially pronounced when we look at the Monitoring the Future survey, whose findings appear in Table 2.

Looking at the "any illicit drug" category, we see a rise in use between 1975, when 31 percent of the respondents said that they had used one or more illegal drugs during the previous month, and 1979, when this figure reached slightly fewer than four high school seniors in ten (39 percent). However, during the 1980s, illegal drug use declined; by 1991, fewer than half the percentage of 12th graders had used an illegal drug during the previous month (only 16 percent) than was true in 1979. Then, starting in the early 1990s, illicit drug use began to rise once again. In the 1991–1998 period, the percentage of high school seniors who had used at least one illegal drug during the past month rose by ten points, to 26 percent.

In 1991, the Monitoring the Future survey added 8th and 10th graders to its

TABLE 2:   Drug Use in Past Month by High School Seniors (Selected Years, 1975–1998)

	PERCENTAGE OF PEOPLE USING DRUGS						
	1975	**1979**	**1983**	**1987**	**1991**	**1995**	**1998**
Alcohol	68	72	69	66	54	51	52
Cigarettes	37	34	30	30	28	34	35
Marijuana	27	37	27	21	14	21	23
Cocaine	2	6	5	4	1	2	2
LSD	2	2	2	2	2	4	3
Stimulants	9	10	9	5	3	4	5
Heroin	0.4	0.2	0.2	0.2	0.2	0.6	0.5
Any Illicit Drug	31	39	31	25	16	24	26

Source: For data from 1975 to 1995, Lloyd D. Johnston, Patrick O'Malley, and Jerald G. Bachman, *National Survey Results on Drug Use from the Monitoring the Future Study, 1975–1995*, Vol. 1 (1996, Rockville, MD: National Institute on Drug Abuse), p. 88 for 1998, *Monitoring the Future*, 1999, data downloaded from the Internet.

sample. During that year, as with the study's seniors, the percentage of its 8th and 10th graders who used illicit drugs began to rise. In fact, if we look very carefully at this survey's data, something truly remarkable took place during the 1990s. Sociologists refer to a specific age bracket that moves through time as a "cohort." If we follow the Monitoring the Future 1991 8th-grade cohort over time, their rise in drug use is truly astonishing.

In 1991, 5.7 percent of the 8th graders had used at least one illicit drug during the previous month. In 1993, when most of them were in the 10th grade, 14 percent had used one or more illegal drugs. In 1995, when they were seniors, 23.8 percent had used in the previous month, an increase of four times. The comparable figures for marijuana alone are 3.2, 10.9, and 21.2 percent, respectively, which is an increase of six and a half times!

As I pointed out, in the usual pattern, young adults ages 18 to 25 display the highest rates of illegal drugs. In 1991, when 15.4 percent of 18- to 25-year-olds had used an illegal drug during the past month (NIDA, 1991, p. 19), this was also true of 5.7 percent of 8th graders—a ratio of 2.7 times. However, by 1993, the percentages of 18- to 25-year-olds (SAMHSA, 1995, p. 35) and 8th graders who used an illicit drug during the past month were almost identical: 13.5 percent versus 12 percent, almost a ratio of 1:1. By 1994, the use of one or more illicit drugs during the past month by 8th graders (14.3 percent) had actually surpassed that of young adults (13.3 percent). From 1995 to 1998, the young-adult-to-8th-grade 30-day prevalence rate remained more or less stable (Sallett, Goode, and Pooler, 1999). This sudden rise in illicit drug use among very young adolescents to the point that it rivals that of young adults is historically unprecedented.

CHANGES IN HIGH SCHOOL STUDENTS ATTITUDES TOWARD DRUG USE, 1975–1998

The changes in attitudes toward drug use over the past generation or so are at least as interesting as the changes in drug use itself. In fact, attitudes provide a kind of backdrop to a consideration of deviance. To the extent that attitudes are tolerant toward and accepting of any given behavior, then that behavior is not deviant. In contrast, to the extent that attitudes toward a given activity and its participants are negative, condemnatory, and derogatory, then that activity and those participants must be referred to as deviant.

If we were to posit a relationship between attitudes and behavior over time, common sense would predict that the more negative the attitudes about drug use become, the lower that drug use will be; the less negative the attitudes, the higher the drug use. In addition, it makes sense that forms of drug use that are most strongly condemned tend to be those that are least common. In contrast, forms of drug use that are least strongly condemned tend to be more common. It seems that here, common sense prevails: attitudes and behavior are very closely correlated with one another, and in a predictable direction. The behavioral changes we observed—the rise in use in the 1970s, the decline in the 1980s, and the rise once again in the 1990s—are paralleled by a corresponding attitudinal change. The problem is that we run into a chicken-and-egg situation here: It is not clear which one causes the other. However, it is clear that they are strongly related.

The Monitoring the Future survey makes use of three sets of attitudes toward drug use: whether the recreational use of drugs is perceived as harmful, disapproval of persons who use drugs, and attitudes about the legal status of marijuana. Each of these attitudes expresses disapproval (or approval) of drug use. The more harmful drug use is perceived to be, the greater the disapproval of those who use drugs, and the lower the support for marijuana legalization, obviously, the higher the condemnation of drug use. Contrarily, the less harmful drug use is perceived to be, the less that users are disapproved of, and the greater the support for marijuana legalization, the lower the condemnation of drug use. This is as true when we compare attitudes toward one drug versus another, such as when we compare answers given on a year-by-year basis. Attitudes toward drug use and drug use itself follow one another very closely. Attitudes are more condemnatory toward the use of heroin, cocaine, and LSD than toward the use of marijuana. Moreover, the use of these harder drugs is lower than for marijuana. In addition, during those years when condemnation of drug use is highest, use is lowest; when condemnation is lowest, use is highest.

In the 1970s, the proportion of high school seniors who thought that marijuana use was harmful and who disapproved of its use was relatively low. That percentage increased until the early 1990s, after which it declined again. For instance, the Monitoring the Future survey asked the question. "Do you think people risk harming themselves . . . if they smoke marijuana regularly?" In 1978, only 35 percent of the respondents agreed; in 1991, 79 percent, and in 1998, 59 percent. Disapproval of smoking marijuana "once or twice" followed the same pattern. In 1978, it was 33 percent; in 1991, 69 percent; and in 1998, 52 percent (Monitoring the Future, 1999). Much the same up-and-down pattern is revealed in attitudes toward the legality of marijuana as well as the experimental use of the harder drugs, such as LSD and cocaine. (Attitudes toward the regular use and the legality of the harder drugs is strongly opposed across-the-board.) Clearly, in the sweep of time between the 1970s and the 1990s, significant changes were afoot. The huge decline in marijuana use that took place between the late 1970s and the early 1990s was accompanied by a corresponding decline in attitudinal tolerance for the use of the drug. The later increases in use have gone hand in hand with increases in attitudinal tolerance for the recreational use of drugs, especially marijuana. Once again, attitudes toward experimental use of LSD and cocaine follow much the same pattern, but regular use is opposed in all years.

Which one caused the other? Do changes in attitudes toward drugs cause changes in drug use? Or do changes in drug use cause people to change their attitudes toward the activity? It's not clear. Some observers (Bachman, Johnston, and O'Malley, 1998) argue that attitudes change behavior and that individual lifestyle factors such as school performance, religious commitments, and recreational activities outside the home have relatively little impact on drug use. Whatever the causal arrow, it seems clear that both illegal drug use and relatively tolerant attitudes toward illegal drug use among adolescents are likely to continue for the foreseeable future. As today's young people age, their current behavior and attitudes are likely to continue well into adulthood.

References

Bachman, Jerald G., Lloyd D, Johnston, and Patrick M. O'Malley, 1998. "Explaining Recent Increases in Students' Marijuana Use: Impacts of Perceived Risks and Disapproval, 1976 through 1996." *American Journal of Public Health*, 88 (June):887–982.

Inciardi, James A. 1986. *The War on Drugs: Heroin, Cocaine, Crime, and Public Policy*. Palo Alto, CA: Mayfield.

Inciardi, James A. 1992. *The War on Drugs II: The Continuing Epic of Heroin, Cocaine, Crack, Crime, AIDS, and Public Policy.* Mountain View, CA: Mayfield.

Johnson, Bruce D., et al. 1985. *Taking Care of Business: The Economics of Crime by Heroin Abusers.* Lexington, MA: Lexington Books.

Johnston, Lloyd D., Patrick M, O'Malley, and Jerald G. Bachman. 1996. *National Survey Results on Drug Use from the Monitoring the Future Study, 1975–1995,* Vol. 1: *Secondary School Students.* Rockville, MD: National Institute on Drug Abuse.

Miller, Judith Droitcour, and Ira H. Cisin, 1980. *Highlights from the National Survey on Drug Abuse: 1979.* Rockville, MD: National Institute on Drug Abuse.

Monitoring the Future, 1999. Data for 1998 Downloaded from the Internet.

NIDA (National Institute on Drug Abuse). 1991. *National Household Survey on Drug Abuse: Population Estimates 1991.* Rockville, MD: Author.

Sallett, Alphonse, Erich Goode, and William Pooler, 1999. "The Death of a Paradigm?: The Onset and Dynamics of an Adolescent Drug Epidemic." Unpublished paper. Stony Brook, NY: State University of New York.

SAMHSA (Substance Abuse and Mental Health Services Administration). 1995. *National Household Survey on Drug Abuse: Main Findings 1993.* Rockville, MD: Author.

SAMHSA (Substance Abuse and Mental Health Services Administration). 1999. *Summary of Findings from the 1998 National Household Survey on Drug Abuse.* Rockville, MD: Author.

Juvenile Delinquency and Drug Use

Greg S. Weaver

INTRODUCTION

"Drugs are bad . . ." So says Mr. Mackey, the school counselor on the sometimes irreverent and often controversial cartoon *South Park*. The possession and use of various controlled substances by children and teenagers is important in a number of ways. It has been suggested that if a person reaches the age of 21 without abusing alcohol or using drugs, it is very unlikely that he or she will start (National Center on Addiction and Substance Abuse 1997). The relationship between age and substance use receives much attention. Generally speaking, during the teenage years use increases with age (Parker, Calhoun, and Weaver 2000). Age of onset, however, is extremely important as well. Age at first use is a consistent predictor of subsequent use, particularly if use begins before the age of 15. That is, the earlier a person begins to use tobacco, alcohol, or drugs, the likelihood for continued use increases (Schneider Institute for Health Policy 2001). Use of alcohol or drugs may affect the normal development of the adolescent and could influence the occurrence of a number of

problems—some of which may not be observable for years (Hawkins, Catalano, and Miller 1992; Hawkins, Graham, Maguin, Abbott, Hill, and Catalano 1997).

Numerous examples of the relationship between alcohol/drug use and health problems can be identified. For example, among adolescents, sexual activity frequently follows alcohol and/or drug use. One study reports that among persons aged 16–19, 64 and 15 percent of the subjects, respectively, reported alcohol or drug use prior to sexual activity (Kokotailo 1995). Furthermore, alcohol or drug use increases the likelihood of engaging in unprotected sex or other acts that increase the risk of sexually transmitted diseases or trading sexual favors for drugs (Steele 1995). Health concerns are not limited to controlled substances. Inhaling the vapors of commonly available products such as glue or gasoline can have many negative consequences as well, such as damage to the lungs, kidneys, and the brain (CASA 1997).

In the United States, a person 21 years of age and older is, within certain limits, legally permitted to purchase and consume alcohol (Akers 1992). That alcohol use is legal reflects its social acceptance, in spite of the fact that alcohol is a drug. When consumed, the body treats alcohol as a poison and the oxidation or removal phase begins. Dangers associated with alcohol use are well-known. The consequences of alcohol use are pronounced for young persons, a point that has been given much attention in recent years. Alcohol use can result in many negative consequences for an adolescent, including death. It is no surprise then that many of the legal restrictions on alcohol purchase and consumption are based on age.

Alcohol is a prominent factor in motor vehicle accidents. In 1977, 43.2 percent of fatal automobile crashes involving persons aged 16–24 were alcohol-related (Yi, Stinson, Williams, and Dufour 2000). Due in part to concern over deaths of teenagers in motor vehicle crashes in which alcohol was involved, a number of changes occurred. During the decade of the 1980s, the federal government pressured states to again increase the legal drinking age to 21.[1] By 1987, all states had raised the legal drinking age to 21 (Akers 1992). Furthermore, the federal government has also mandated that by 2007, the legal blood alcohol level for operating a motor vehicle (BAL) is to be lowered from .10 to .08. In a measure that affects underage persons directly, a number of states have lowered the legal blood alcohol level for persons younger than 21 to .02, which in effect criminalizes the act of operating a motor vehicle following any alcohol consumption (Schneider Institute for Health Policy 2001).

These legal changes appear to have influenced alcohol use in a number of ways. For example, by 1998 the portion of

fatal, alcohol-related motor vehicle crashes involving persons aged 16–24 had decreased to 29.3 percent. Further evidence for this influence can be observed in the finding that between 1986 (the year prior to all states adopting the legal drinking age of 21) and 1998, the percentage of fatal crashes involving a driver aged 16–20 decreased from 34.3 to 20.2 percent, respectively (Yi et al. 2000). These findings suggest that establishing and enforcing legal controls on alcohol tends to influence consumption patterns (Goode 1999).

A large amount of research also suggests an association between alcohol/drug use and other variables associated with delinquent behavior, such as difficulty in school (e.g., Farrell, Danish, and Howard 1992; Huizinga, Loeber, Thornberry, and Cothern 2000; [Osgood, Johnston, O'Malley, and Bachman 1988]). A number of studies have shown that use of alcohol, marijuana, or other drugs during adolescence is associated with lower academic aspirations lower grades, and increased absenteeism (Brook and Balka 1999; Paulson, Coombs, and Richardson 1990; Sutherland and Shepherd 2001). Among juvenile detainees (discussed in detail in the next section), those juveniles who were attending school were less likely to test positive for any controlled substance than juveniles who were not currently in school (Arrestee Drug Abuse Monitoring Program 2000).

TRENDS IN SUBSTANCE USE AMONG JUVENILES

Drug use levels among juveniles peaked around 1980, and then continued to decline during the remainder of the decade (even before the onset of the "War on Drugs" that began in the mid-1980s) until 1992. From 1992 until 1997, use of alcohol and drugs by

---

[1]Prior to the 1960s, the legal drinking age in all states was 21, but a number of states lowered the age when the legal voting age was lowered to 18. During the 1980s the federal government threatened to deny federal highway funding to states that did not raise the legal drinking age to 21 (Akers 1992).

juveniles increased somewhat, most notice-ably for marijuana (Snyder and Sickmund 1999). By the end of the decade, the general trend had been one of leveling off or de-cline in use (of illicit drugs). With the ex-ception of eighth graders, alcohol use among high school students has not changed significantly in recent years (John-ston, O'Malley, and Bachman 2001).[2]

Of particular interest has been the ap-parent surge in the use of marijuana, which has for the most part been limited to in-creases among persons 20 years of age and younger. A number of studies suggest this phenomenon is related in part to the emer-gence of the "hip-hop" youth subculture, which arguably views use of marijuana as being acceptable (Golub and Johnson 2001). That the increase in marijuana use occurred as cocaine use continued to de-cline has generated quite a bit of interest, particularly because it seems contradictory to the "Gateway" theory of drug abuse, which suggests that use of serious drugs by young persons usually follows use of less harmful substances such as alcohol or marijuana (Kandel 1975).

Another issue receiving increased at-tention of late is the phenomenon of "club drugs," which refers to a variety of sub-stances that, depending on the specific drug, may have stimulant, depressant, or hallucinogenic effects. Of particular impor-tance is the ongoing debate as to the nega-tive consequences of using these substances (See Cloud 2000 for an overview of this controversy). Club drugs are often used with other substances, most frequently al-cohol. These substances are commonly as-sociated with "raves," or dance parties. The *Monitoring the Future* survey and other studies indicate that availability and use of

these drugs is increasing (Drug Abuse Warning Network 2000; Johnston, O'Mal-ley, and Bachman 2001; Office of National Drug Control Policy, 2001).

According to the National Center on Addiction and Substance Abuse (CASA) at Columbia University (2001) in a national survey of teenagers, 28 percent of respon-dents report knowing someone who has used MDMA (Ecstasy). The CASA study further reports that although only 1 in 10 teenagers have ever attended a rave, MDMA could be obtained at 70 percent of these parties. While few deaths are attrib-uted to club drugs, emergency department (ED) mentions have increased signifi-cantly, most notably among juveniles and young adults. For example, while persons aged 6–17 account for only 10 percent of all ED mentions, 57 and 38 percent respec-tively of Rhoypnol and LSD mentions occur among this group (Drug Abuse Warning Network 2000).

Based on early recognition of the connection between drug use and crime, efforts have increased to identify the ex-tent to which substance use may be a fac-tor, as measured by a positive drug test at the time of arrest/detention (Dembo, Williams, Getreu, Genung, Schmeidler, Berry, Wish, and LaVoie, 1991). Not sur-prisingly, results consistently show that a large proportion of arrestees test positive for one or more controlled substances. Un-fortunately, data of this type are collected on a less extensive basis for juvenile detainees.

According to the 1999 survey of the Arrestee Drug Abuse Monitoring Program (ADAM) for juveniles, drug tests were con-ducted on juvenile detainees in nine cities in the United States. According to ADAM (2000) marijuana is by far the drug used most often by juvenile detainees, followed by cocaine and methamphetamine, respec-tively. Sample sizes ranged from 117

---

[2]See Appendix A.

(males only) in Birmingham, Alabama, to 466 in Phoenix, Arizona. In 1999, the percent of male detainees testing positive for any substance ranged from 43.3 percent in Portland, Oregon, to 68.5 percent in Phoenix, Arizona. For female detainees, the percent testing positive ranged from 24.8 percent in San Antonio, Texas, to 47.7 percent in San Diego, California.

DELINQUENCY AND SUBSTANCE USE

Clearly, youths that use alcohol or other drugs are more likely to be involved in other delinquent acts. In that regard, Uihlein (1994) notes that it is often difficult to distinguish delinquent youths from those who are involved in drug use on a number of key constructs such as attachment to parents and/or peers, school achievement, or in terms of having well-defined life plans or goals. Akers (1992) notes the difficulty in conclusively stating that alcohol or drug use *causes* delinquency. Nonetheless, Gottfredson and Hirschi (1990) suggest that much of the activity within the criminal justice system can be attributed to substance use and that drug use trends usually parallel trends in other crime trends as well. Newcomb and McGee (1989) find that among high school students, alcohol use is associated with deviant behavior et al. Similarly, Dembo (1991, p. 271) note that subsequent criminal behavior is positively related to addiction and that arrests for a variety of offenses decrease as drug use subsides.

Of particular importance are those relatively few serious delinquents who are responsible for a disproportionate number of acts (Loeber 1982; VanderWaal, McBride, Terry-McElrath, and VanBuren 2001). It is among these offenders that the relationship between drug use and delinquency is

particularly important. Johnson and Wish (1991), utilizing data from a national, representative sample of persons aged 11–17 show that even among the most serious offenders, drug use is positively related to delinquency.

However, alcohol and drug use by young persons is more complicated than simply acknowledging negative aspects of this behavior. Substance use by juveniles is in some ways a consequence of the transition from childhood to adulthood. A key element of adolescence is the development of independence and becoming involved in activities considered appropriate for adults only, which may include experimentation with alcohol and drugs (Newcomb 1995). No longer a child but not yet an adult, the adolescent seeks to achieve autonomy by engaging in behavior that may be viewed as inappropriate (Bukstein 1995). For example, by the age of 13, most adolescents are biologically capable of reproduction, but for a number of reasons sexual activity is discouraged.

During adolescence, the meaning of the popular axiom "act your age" may be ambiguous. Moffitt (1993, p. 687) refers to this gap between biological and social age as the *maturity gap*. Jessor (1991), acknowledging the negative aspects of marijuana use, notes that it (marijuana use) may have potential positive consequences as well, such as helping one develop a sense of maturity and autonomy. Moffitt (1993) suggests that in comparison to abstainers and abusers, youths that experiment with alcohol and/or drugs may be better adjusted socially than their counterparts. More specifically, adolescent drug users are more likely to be impulsive and have difficulty forming and maintaining relationships with others. Abstainers, on the other hand, tend be emotionally constricted and lack social skills (Shedler and Block 1990).

At the same time, however, although substance use may in some ways accelerate the transition into adulthood, the youth often fails to acquire important requisite skills to facilitate the transition into adulthood and beyond (Newcomb 1995). Furthermore, early use of alcohol or drugs is a strong predictor not only of later use, but also of other potential problems (Hawkins et al. 1997).

In this regard, level of involvement with drugs may be viewed as a continuum of sorts, and the key question becomes at what point does use become problematic for the youth. While not suggesting that alcohol or drug use among juveniles is unimportant, it is possible that aggressive intervention in response to occasional or experimental involvement may do more harm than good (Newcomb 1995). For example, as noted by Peele (1987), a substantial majority of teenagers who have used "hard" drugs such as cocaine do not become abusers. Thus, a number of factors should be taken into account when intervention of the juvenile or adult justice systems occurs.

Much of the previous discussion focuses on two seemingly contradictory findings: first, the consequences of alcohol or drug use by juveniles are many, and, second, that deviant behavior is in some ways the norm for this group. How then, can these points be reconciled? Terrie Moffitt (1993, 1997) offers one perspective that will be the focus of this section. Moffitt concurs with the notion that during adolescence a certain level of delinquent behavior should be expected. This transition stage that precedes adulthood provides a number of opportunities for deviant behavior, which may include sexual activity, delinquent behavior, and alcohol and drug use. During this stage, the influence of parents decreases and the peer group becomes more important. Particularly when the

youth enters high school this influence becomes relevant. At this juncture, "high school" society is dominated by older youths, some of whom are already involved in delinquent activities (Goode 1999; Moffitt 1993).

Moffitt then identifies two different categories of juvenile offenders. Keeping in mind that a certain level of deviant behavior is considered normal for the adolescent, Moffitt characterizes the first category as *adolescence-limited*, meaning that delinquency typically begins in the teenage years. For these offenders, delinquency is often a reflection of the aforementioned desire to engage in "adult" behaviors. For this group, the influence of the peer group is apparent.

The *life-course-persistent* offender refers to those persons who begin committing delinquent acts as children and continue to do so into adulthood and beyond. Moffitt argues that it is necessary to examine not only the early childhood years but the prenatal experience of the mother as well. Citing research showing that factors such as a difficult pregnancy, poor prenatal health care, and alcohol/drug use during pregnancy may influence the normal development of the fetus, Moffitt contends that a number of consequences are a possibility. In brief summary, both the temperment and learning ability of the child may be affected. Generally speaking, children having cognitive and tempermental difficulties are not born into supportive environments. Simply put, a "bad baby" is less likely to receive the attention, nurturing, and patience from parents, which can offset these conditions. Thus, the normal social development of the child is hindered in a number of ways. What happens then, when a child who has problems getting along with others, learning difficulties, and who often exhibits hyperactivity/impulsivity goes to school? The result is in too any cases a series of failed opportunities to correct antisocial behavior. Consequently, these delinquent and criminal patterns are reflected throughout the life course, which Moffitt refers to as *heterotypic continuity* (Akers 2000; Moffitt 1993).

Adolescence-limited offenders, on the other hand are those juveniles that are involved in delinquency primarily during the teenage years. Motivated in part by the "maturity gap" mentioned previously, these individuals in effect explore behaviors and activities associated with adulthood, such as alcohol/drug use, sexual activity, and other delinquent acts. Due to the increased influence of peer group associations during this period, adolescence limited offenders are simply modeling the

behavior of their life-course-persistent counterparts (Moffitt 1993). Think back to your junior/high school experience and recall some of the adjectives used to describe a person who excelled academically, did not use alcohol or drugs, and was not sexually active. However, as the maturity gap ends and pending adult responsibilities become a reality, the motivation for delinquency declines substantially.

CONCLUDING REMARKS

The objective of this chapter has been to elaborate key elements of the complex nexus between drug use and delinquent

---

APPENDIX A: JUVENILE DRUG USE, 1994–2000 (PERCENT REPORTING USE— LIFETIME AND 30 DAYS)

8th Graders

Substance	1994	1995	1996	1997	1998	1999	2000
Any Illicit Drug	25.7	28.5	31.2	29.4	29.0	28.3	26.8
	10.9	12.4	14.6	14.6	12.1	12.2	11.9
Marijuana/Hashish	16.7	19.9	23.1	22.6	22.2	22.0	20.3
	7.8	9.1	11.3	10.2	9.7	9.7	9.1
Cocaine	3.6	4.2	4.5	4.4	4.6	4.7	4.5
	1.0	1.2	1.3	1.1	1.4	1.3	1.2
Crack Cocaine	2.4	2.7	2.9	2.7	3.2	3.1	3.1
	0.7	0.7	0.8	0.7	0.9	0.8	0.8
Alcohol	55.8	54.5	55.3	53.8	52.5	52.1	51.7
	25.5	24.6	26.2	24.5	23.0	24.0	22.4
MDMA (Ecstasy)	-	-	3.4	3.2	2.7	2.7	4.3
	-	-	1.0	1.0	0.9	0.8	1.4

10th Graders

Substance	1994	1995	1996	1997	1998	1999	2000
Any Illicit Drug	37.4	40.9	45.4	47.3	44.9	46.2	45.6
	18.5	20.2	23.2	23.0	21.5	22.1	22.5
Marijuana/Hashish	30.4	34.1	39.8	42.3	39.6	40.9	40.3
	15.8	17.2	20.4	20.5	18.7	19.4	19.7
Cocaine	4.3	5.0	6.5	7.1	7.2	7.7	6.9
	1.2	1.7	1.7	2.0	2.1	1.8	1.8

behavior among juveniles. By placing these activities in the context of adolescence itself, it is clear that for many youths, alcohol and/or drug use and delinquency are in some ways a consequence of the process of becoming an adult. On the other hand, these behaviors may also be indicators of serious problems. Clearly, alcohol and drug use is associated with delinquency, and the accompanying negative consequences should not be ignored.

References

Akers, Ronald L. 1992. *Drugs, Alcohol, and Society: Social Structure, Process, and Policy*. Belmont, CA: Wadsworth.

Akers, Ronald L. 2000. *Criminological Theories: Introduction, Evaluation, and Application*. 3rd ed. Los Angeles: Roxbury.

Arrestee Drug Abuse Monitoring Program. 2000. *1999 Annual Report on Drug Use Among Adult and Juvenile Arrestees*. Washington, DC: USDOJ.

Brook, Judith S., and Elinor B. Balka. 1999. "The Risks for Late Adolescence of Early Adolescent Marijuana Use." *American Journal of Public Health* 89(10): 1549–1555.

Bukstein, Oscar Gary. 1995. *Adolescent Substance Abuse: Assessment, Prevention, and Treatment*. New York: John Wiley & Sons.

Cloud, John. 2000. "The Lure of Ecstasy." *Time* 155(23). 62–68.

Dembo, Richard, Linda Williams, Alan Getreu, Lisa Genung, James Schmeidler, Estrellita Berry, Eric D. Wish, and Lawrence La Voie. 1991. "A Longitudinal Study of the Relationships Among Marijuana/Hashish Use, Cocaine Use and Delinquency in a Cohort of High Risk Youths." *The Journal of Drug Issues* 21(2): 271–312.

Crack Cocaine	2.1	2.8	3.3	3.6	3.9	4.0	3.7
	0.6	0.9	0.8	0.9	1.1	0.8	0.9
Alcohol	71.1	70.5	71.8	72.0	69.8	70.6	71.4
	39.2	38.8	40.4	40.1	38.8	40.0	41.0
MDMA (Ecstasy)	-	-	5.6	5.7	5.1	6.0	7.3
	-	-	1.8	1.3	1.3	1.8	2.6

12th Graders

Substance	1994	1995	1996	1997	1998	1999	2000
Any Illicit Drug	45.6	48.4	50.8	54.3	54.1	54.7	54.0
	21.9	23.8	24.6	26.2	25.6	25.9	24.9
Marijuana/Hashish	38.2	41.7	44.9	49.6	49.1	49.7	48.8
	19.0	21.2	21.9	23.7	22.8	23.1	21.6
Cocaine	5.9	6.0	7.1	8.7	9.3	9.8	8.6
	1.5	1.8	2.0	2.3	2.4	2.6	2.1
Crack Cocaine	3.0	3.0	3.3	3.9	4.4	4.6	3.9
	0.8	1.0	1.0	0.9	1.0	1.1	1.0
Alcohol	80.4	80.7	79.2	81.7	81.4	80.0	80.3
	50.1	51.3	50.8	52.7	52.0	51.0	50.0
MDMA (Ecstasy)	-	-	6.1	6.9	5.8	8.0	11.0
	-	-	2.0	1.6	1.5	2.5	3.6

Source: Johnston, Lloyd D., Patrick M. O'Malley, and Jerald G. Bachman. 2001. *Monitoring the Future: National Results on Adolescent Drug Use, Overview of Key Findings, 2000*. Washington, DC: National Institute on Drug Abuse

Drug Abuse Warning Network. 2000. "Club Drugs." *The DAWN Report* (In Brief). December. Washington, DC: SAMHSA.

Farrell, Albert D., Steven J. Danish, and Catherine W. Howard. 1992. "Relationship Between Drug Use and Other Problem Behaviors in Urban Adolescents." *Journal of Consulting and Clinical Psychology* 60(5): 705–712.

Golub, Andrew, and Bruce D. Johnson. 2001. *The Rise of Marijuana as the Drug of Choice Among Youthful Adult Arrestees.* NIJ Research in Brief (NCJ 187490). Washington, DC: USDOJ.

Goode, Erich. 1999. *Drugs in American Society.* 5th ed. New York: McGraw-Hill.

Gottfredson, Michael R., and Travis Hirschi. 1990. *A General Theory of Crime.* Stanford, CA: Stanford University Press.

Hawkins, J. David, Richard F. Catalano, and Janet Y. Miller. 1992. "Risk and Protective Factors for Alcohol and Other Drug Problems in Adolescence and Early Adulthood: Implications for Substance Abuse Prevention." *Psychological Bulletin* 112(1): 64–105.

Hawkins, J. David, John W. Graham, Eugene Maguin, Robert Abbott, Karl G. Hill, and Richard F. Catalano. 1997. "Exploring the Effects of Age of Alcohol Use Initiation and Psychosocial Risk Factors on Subsequent Alcohol Misuse." *Journal of Studies on Alcohol* 58(3): 280–291.

Huizinga, David, Rolf Loeber, Terence P. Thornberry, and Lynn Cothern. 2000. *Co-occurrence of Delinquency and Other Problem Behaviors.* OJJDP Juvenile Justice Bulletin (NCJ 182211). Washington, DC: USDOJ.

Jessor, Richard. 1991. "Risk Behavior in Adolescence: A Psychosocial Framework for Understanding and Action." *Journal of Adolescent Health* 12: 597–605.

Johnson, Bruce D., Eric D. Wish, James Schmeidler, and David Huizinga. 1991. "Concentration of Delinquent Offending: Serious Drug Involvement and High Delinquency Rates." Journal of Drug Issues 21(2): 205–230.

Johnston, Lloyd D., Patrick M. O'Malley, and Jerald G. Bachman. 2001. *Monitoring the Future: National Results on Adolescent Drug Use, Overview of Key Findings, 2000.* Washington, DC: National Institute on Drug Abuse

Kandel, Denise. 1975. "Stages in Adolescent Involvement in Drug Use." *Science* 190 (November 28): 912–914.

Kokotailo, Patricia. 1995. "Physical Health Problems Associated with Adolescent Substance Abuse. Pp. 112–129 in *Adolescent Drug Abuse: Clinical Assessment and Therapeutic Interventions.* NIDA Research Monograph #156. Washington, DC: USGPO.

Loeber, Rolf. 1982. "The Stability of Antisocial and Delinquent Child Behavior: A Review." *Child Development* 53: 1431–1446.

Moffitt, Terrie E. 1993. "Adolescence-Limited and Life-Course-Persistent Behavior: A Developmental Taxonomy." *Psychological Review* 100(4): 674–701.

Moffitt, Terrie E. 1997. "Adolescence-Limited and Life-Course-Persistent Offending: A Complementary Pair of Developmental Theories." Pp. 11–54 in *Developmental Theories of Crime and Delinquency,* edited by T. P. Thornberry. New Brunswick, NJ: Transaction Publishers.

National Center on Addiction and Substance Abuse (CASA). 1997. *Substance Use and the American Adolescent: A Report by the Commission on Substance Abuse Among America's Adolescents.* New York: Robert Woods Johnson Foundation.

National Center on Addiction and Substance Abuse (CASA). 2001. *National Survey of American Attitudes on Substance Abuse VI: Teens.* New York: Robert Woods Johnson Foundation.

Newcomb, Michael D. 1995. "Identifying High-Risk Youth: Prevalence and Patterns of Adolescent Drug Abuse." Pp. 7–38 in *Adolescent Drug Abuse: Clinical Assessment and Therapeutic Interventions.* NIDA Research Monograph #156. Washington, DC: USGPO.

Newcomb, Michael D., and Linda McGee. 1989. "Adolescent Alcohol Use and Other Delinquent Behaviors: A One-Year Longitudinal Analysis Controlling for Sensation Seeking." *Criminal Justice and Behavior* 16: 345–369.

Office of National Drug Control Policy. 2001. *Pulse Check: Trends in Drug Abuse Mid-Year 2000* (NCJ 186747). Washington, DC: ONDCP.

Osgood, D. Wayne, Lloyd D. Johnston, Patrick M. O'Malley, and Jerald G. Bachman. 1988. "The Generality of Deviance in Late Adolescence and Early Adulthood." *American Sociological Review* 53: 81–93.

Parker, Keith D., Thomas Calhoun, and Greg Weaver. 2000. "Variables Associated with Adolescent Alcohol Use: A Multiethnic Comparison." *Journal of Social Psychology* 140(1): 51–62.

Paulson, Morris J., Robert H. Coombs, and Mark A. Richardson. 1990. "School Performance, Academic Aspirations, and Drug Use Among Children and Adolescents." *Journal of Drug Education* 20(4): 289–303.

Peele, Stanton. 1987. "What Can We Expect from Treatment of Adolescent Drug and Alcohol Abuse?" *Pediatrician* 14: 62–69.

Schneider Institute for Health Policy. 2001. *Substance Abuse: The Nation's Number One Health Problem.* Princeton, NJ: Robert Woods Johnson Foundation.

Shedler, Jonathon, and Jack Block. 1990. "Adolescent Drug Use and Psychological Health." *American Psychologist* 45(5): 612–630.

Snyder, Howard N., and Melissa Sickmund. 1999. *Juvenile Offenders and Victims: 1999 National Report.* Washington, DC: Office of Juvenile Justice and Delinquency Prevention.

Steele, Elizabeth. 1995. "AIDS, Drugs, and the Adolescent." Pp. 130–145 in *Adolescent Drug Abuse: Clinical Assessment and Therapeutic Interventions.* NIDA Research Monograph #156. Washington, DC: USGPO.

Sutherland, I., and JP. Shepherd. 2001. "Social Dimensions of Adolescent Substance Use." *Addiction* 96: 445–458.

Uihlein, Carolyn. 1994. "Drugs and Alcohol." Pp. 149–158 in *The Generality of Deviance*. New Brunswick, NJ: Transaction Press.

VanderWaal, Curtis J., Duane C. McBride, Yvonne M. Terry-McElrath, and Holly VanBuren. 2001. *Breaking the Juvenile Drug-Crime Cycle: A Guide for Practitioners and Policymakers*. Washington, DC: USDOJ.

Yi, Hsiao-ye, Frederick S. Stinson, Gerald D. Williams, and Mary C. Dufour. 2000. *Trends in Alcohol-Related Fatal Traffic Crashes, United States, 1977–98*. National Institute on Alcohol Abuse and Alcoholism Surveillance Report #53. Washington, DC: U.S. Department of Health and Human Services.

Drug–Crime Relations Among Drug-Consuming Juvenile Delinquents:

A Tripartite Model and More

By Natacha Brunelle, Serge Brochu, and Marie-Marthe Cousineau

A feature of the 20th century was the presence of multifaceted problems infringing on an increasingly significant part of the population. This study focuses on the fact that many delinquents are drug users (Lightfoot and Hodgins, 1988; Harlow, 1991; Brochu, 1995) and, inversely, that many regular drug users manifest diverse delinquent behaviors (Hubbard et al., 1989; Covell et al., 1993; Brochu, 1995).

From a phenomenological perceptual stance (Schutz, 1987), we aim in this article at revealing various links between drug use and involvement in crime that exist in the trajectories of youths. To do so, we base our research on youths' own personal perceptions regarding their lived experiences. The emphasis is placed on the subjective logic and meaning associated with events and feelings that they have confronted throughout their lives. To begin, a popular explanatory model of the drug—crime relation is briefly reviewed. This model subsequently serves as the basis or reference throughout the article.

Contemporary Drug Problems, Vol. 27, Issue 4, Winter 2000, pp. 835–866, Federal Legal Publications, Inc., NY

TRIPARTITE MODEL

Goldstein (1985, 1987) uses a tripartite conceptual framework for examining the drug—violence relation. This popular conceptual framework includes the following three possible drug—violence nexuses, which are generalized to overall drug—crime relations over time: psychopharmacological, economic compulsive, and systemic.

PSYCHOPHARMACOLOGICAL MODEL

Originally the psychopharmacological model suggested that the intoxication effects of drugs may cause violence. From this perspective, the intoxicated consumer is impelled toward violence because a drug's criminogenic effect provokes such behavior in him/her. By acting on particular circuits of the user's central nervous system (those circuits that inhibit behavior, for example), the ingestion of certain drugs may trigger violent actions (Blum, 1981; Taylor and Leonard, 1983; Sheard, 1988). This model refers to the desinhibition hypothesis or theory, which stipulates that ingestion of drugs, particularly alcohol, makes people do things they would restrain themselves from doing if they were sober. Goldstein's (1985) psychopharmacological model elaborates further than this original theory. First, psychopharmacological violence may be related to the drug intoxication of the perpetrator, of the victim, or of both. It refers to a possible effect of intoxication on excitability, irritability, and aggressiveness that may lead to violent encounters. It also refers to irritability, associated with withdrawal symptoms from the addictive use of certain drugs such as heroin. Finally, Goldstein et al. (1989) mention that in order to facilitate the commission of the criminal act, persons may use drugs just before perpetrating an offense so as to reduce their nervousness and enhance their courage. In this particular case, some authors would probably argue that the violent act is perhaps more likely linked to the expectations of the user with regard to the effect of the drug than to the drug's psychopharmacological effect per se (Marlatt and Rohsenow, 1980; Peele, 1985; Brochu, 1995).

ECONOMIC COMPULSIVE MODEL

Similarly to Goldstein (1985, 1987), supporters of the popular economic compulsive model (Jarvis and Parker, 1989; Nurco, Hanlon and Kinlock, 1991) explain that regular and abusive use of expensive drugs such as cocaine and heroin sways consumers toward involvement in money-oriented crime (e.g., drug dealing, theft, prostitution).[1] This is explained by the financial disequilibrium that often takes place when legitimate earnings become insufficient to support one's drug habit. Hunt (1991) mentions that many factors influence a drug user's inclination toward money-oriented crime: the frequency of drug use; the price of consumed drugs; insufficient earnings; a criminal record; and an immersion into an addict lifestyle. Moreover, Goldstein et al. (1989) mention that violence

may occur during money-oriented crime and, although unintended, generally results from the circumstances or social context in which the crime is perpetrated (e.g., victim's reaction, presence of a weapon).

SYSTEMIC MODEL

According to Goldstein's (1985, 1987) systemic model, it is within the context of supply and distribution that violence occurs in drug milieus. In fact, violence is argued to be used to ensure the protection and sharing of territories, sales, and stock. It may therefore be seen and understood as an organizational management strategy. Also, violence is used by dealers and traffickers in retrieving debts owed to them. The business of trading illicit drugs is, in this sense, at the root of much of the violence observed within this milieu.

In their analyses of police records regarding New York City homicide events in 1988, Goldstein et al. (1989) showed that systemic violence was associated with the most common drug-related homicides but that alcohol-related homicides were all psychopharmacological in nature. However, reporting results from the DREIM project, in which 268 murderers were interviewed in depth, Goldstein et al. (1992) found the psychopharmacological drug—crime nexus to be more frequent when involving alcohol in particular. Both the 1989 and 1992 articles indicate that cocaine, and specifically crack, was more likely associated with systemic violence.

Goldstein's tripartite model is very enlightening for the understanding of the drug—crime nexus but is more limited in regard to the specific drug—violence nexus. This model is also based on the study of events involving adult criminals and victims rather than juvenile delinquents and victims. Its relevance to the juvenile drug—crime trajectory was never really addressed. Since deviant behaviors generally appear during adolescence, it would be most informative to ask youths about these possible relations.

Furthermore, the methodology used in Goldstein's studies permits us to classify criminal events into three different nexuses between drugs and crime and to evaluate which one is more frequent. It does not, however, allow us to elaborate, nuance, or qualify these types of relations between drugs and crimes. Also, focusing on events does not say much about the more general and evolutionary nature of deviant trajectories. Rather, it gives a somewhat static picture of criminal behavior. Our study is more focused on the actors' standpoint—the actors being juvenile delinquents and drug users.

Guided within a phenomenological perspective (Debuyst, 1989) that assigns a dominant place to the social actor's personal interpretation of real-life situations and events, this article aims at discerning the comprehension that youths acquire of the nature of the drug—crime relation throughout their lives and at showing how this comprehension nuances Goldstein's tripartite drug—crime nexus.

METHODOLOGY

A qualitative research approach was opted for in order to obtain the perceptions of youths in regard to drug—crime nexuses in their trajectory (Pirès, 1997a). Because of its focus on the personal visions that individuals develop when confronted with life-marking events, an autobiographical account (Kohli, 1981; Desmarais and Grell, 1986) was used as the principal data-gathering tool. In addition, the autobiographical account permits one to trace a respondent's pathway or trajectory and

therefore to retrace the chronological processing of experienced events. This approach permits the gathering of more than fact-based information, such as meanings and feelings related to certain situations. By initiating the interviews with an open-ended question, the interviewer permitted respondents to spontaneously tell their stories while at the same time encouraging them to further pursue certain themes with the help of explanatory-type (for precision), reflective-type (to be more profound), and temporal-type (to situate events experienced throughout time) relaunchings. When respondents interrupted their accounts for a considerable lapse of time, the interviewer would help carry on the interview by asking for further elaboration on those themes brought forward only enough to attain the phenomenological insight sought or to discuss themes not yet raised.

SAMPLING

In collecting the youths' perceptions of the process that leads to a deviant lifestyle, and more particularly toward delinquency and/or drug use, we turned for a portion of our study's sample to youths who had been in the custody of judicial institutions or in treatment for drug addiction. This *institutionalized* group, as they are referred to from here on, consisted of adolescents who were in custody in youth detention centers or under treatment in youth-addict centers in Montreal. These respondents were initially solicited between 1995 and 1996. Following this phase, and in order to attain a greater understanding of the process that leads to the adoption of the deviant lifestyle, it also became necessary to meet with youths who had never been taken into custody or admitted into any institution for juvenile delinquents or addict-treatment center. Respondents frequenting youth centers[2] on the island of Montreal—the *non-institutionalized* group—constituted the second part of the study's sample.

To determine the study's sample size, the saturation principle explained by Morse (1994) and Pirès (1997b) was used. So as to attain a sound representation of reality, the data-gathering phase of the study was completed when new themes or ideas were no longer brought forward during the interviews. This was indicated when information became repetitive or redundant, or when the perceived differences were largely anecdotal. The final sample was made up of 38 youths (22 boys and 16 girls 16–18 years old) who were divided into two separate categories: institutionalized youths (n = 28; 18 boys and 10 girls) and non-institutionalized youths (n = 10; 4 boys and 6 girls).

ANALYSES

Content analysis (L'Écuyer, 1987) of the interviews followed two complementary approaches. Thematic analysis (Ghiglione and Matalon, 1978) was the primary mode used in reducing the material throughout the data-collection period and afterwards. A within-case analysis of each interview was conducted through a repetitive reading of transcripts, identification sheets, and preliminary notes. Subsequent cross-case analysis allowed us to center on identifying points of convergence and divergence across the material. Sequential analysis was also conducted in order to account for the flow of events and their repercussions on the youths. This approach permitted the revelation of meaning units, as well as an elaboration and detailing of conceptual categories. It thus became possible to take note of the importance of meanings that youths assigned to different experiences and situations faced throughout their lives, as well as the feelings linked to these events.

RESULTS

Respondents were asked to elaborate on their personal perceptions regarding the possible links between their delinquency and consumption of psychoactive drugs. Goldstein's tripartite model (Goldstein, 1985, 1987) is used as a starting point in the reporting of the respondents' perceptions.

A PSYCHO-PHARMACOLOGICAL RELATION

Thefts, burglaries, and drug dealing clearly represent the majority of crimes committed by the youths in this study. Some respondents, however, also provided accounts involving violent crimes. Assaults were the most common of such crimes, but death threats and robberies were also mentioned throughout the interviews. Some youths attributed a responsibility to drugs when discussing the violence they manifested at various points in their pasts. Others considered that they were more aggressive when they were intoxicated.

David, a regular cannabis consumer and an occasional user of hallucinogens and cocaine, stated that he was more susceptible to fighting when he was intoxicated:

> I'm more likely to get into a fight [when intoxicated] than when I'm straight, that's for sure.

From her point of view, Bérénice felt that her heroin consumption contributed to explaining the death threats she made toward her brother (aggressor):

> In my head, when I was stoned, the easiest way was to kill him [her brother]. . . I was really stoned. I had just taken a hit of heroin. . . . So I grab a big knife. . . . And, right there, I tell my parents: "I'm going to kill him for what he did to me" [he had raped her]. But I was also really fucked up. So then

I went upstairs [to her brother's]. I was going to knock or try and get in, but it would never have worked. I went back downstairs and, at one point, I saw that the cops were arriving. . . .

For Bérénice, the anger felt toward the brother who had raped her was the principal reason for her aggression against him. But she nevertheless felt that her heroin consumption also figured to some point in her reaction at that actual moment in her life. This is so, even though it appears that heroin use is not at all associated with manifestations of violence (Parker and Auerhahn, 1998). It is possible that Bérénice's expectations of the effects of her heroin consumption more likely led her to violent behavior than the heroin in itself (Marlatt and Rohsenow, 1980; Peele, 1985; Brochu, 1995).

In any case, even if youths are intoxicated, this does not necessarily mean that they will commit the criminal act; the context must be propitious to violence (Parker and Auerhahn, 1998). For some, the feeling of being provoked must be present. This was the case with Stéphane, who described how, while under the effects of cannabis, he attacked his school's principal for telling his mother what he had done:

At one point, I got it on with the principal, who told my mother all kinds of things— that I was fighting with everybody, and this and that. So at one point I walked into his office with a baseball bat and I told him: "Now you're going to get it." I was stoned and I was frustrated, so that time I went after him. . . .

Stéphane did not believe his intoxication was the only cause behind this violent episode. He reacted in such a way because he was furious with the school principal for having made his mother

aware of some of his delinquent activities. His anger, above all, was the triggering element in this assault. Also, what the principal had told his mother (that he was fighting with everybody) was never really contested by Stéphane, indicating an aggressive personality.

A youth's personality, beliefs, and feelings and the circumstances surrounding a delinquent act may all lead to the commission of an aggressive act. Usually it is not due simply to intoxication. One must therefore take into consideration various elements that include the product, the individual, and the context (Peele, 1985, Brochu, 1995, 1997) in order to arrive at a better understanding of the drug—crime relation. It is our opinion that one must particularly focus on the meanings that youths attribute to their experiences, which may vary from one adolescent to the next.

This study's respondents did not particularly nor explicitly claim that drugs were responsible for their violent behaviors. In any case, this explanation has been increasingly argued to be inadequate, simplistic, and incomplete (Roth, 1994; Brochu, 1995). Turning to such a psychopharmacological argument very often leads to an unrealistic removal of any responsibility in explaining violent acts (Brochu, 1997).

Consuming to commit crime

Many youths mentioned that at some point during their lives they would consume drugs in order to go on with their crimes. In this sense, drug use plays a utilitarian role. On the one hand, it permits them to acquire courage, to be more relaxed, and to distance themselves from the criminal act, while, on the other hand, it allows for more "fun" during the commission of a crime.

To facilitate the commission of crime:

Some youths, such as Dina, consumed before the commission of a crime in order to gain courage, diminish stress, and control the level of fear:

> With the drugs that I was taking, it would give me the nerve, it gave me more courage. And I always liked challenges. . . .[3]

The taste for challenge seems to be at the root of Dina's explanation for her delinquency. Drugs are therefore a means to taking on such challenges.

More particularly, drug consumption sometimes turns out to be indispensible for activities such as prostitution, because drugs allow prostitutes to be more at ease in this activity (Goldstein, 1979). Thus Isabelle explained that cocaine allowed her to forget the discomfort she usually felt when prostituting herself:

> I'm always stoned when I do that [prostitution]. I did it for a long time without getting stoned and I didn't feel comfortable. You know, you're with a stranger. You don't know who he is.

As Christian relates, drugs may also permit youths to avoid feeling guilty after the commission of a crime and not to worry about the possible consequences:

> I wouldn't think of anything. I wouldn't regret anything. I had money in my pockets. I wouldn't think of anything. I couldn't care less. What's done is done. I wasn't even scared of what could happen after. . . . When I was on that stuff, I wasn't scared of anything.

Forgetting negative feelings such as fear or guilt is a motivation to consume before delinquent activities. However, even though being intoxicated allowed some youths to actually commit their crimes, it remains true that many criminal acts are committed in order to obtain money to acquire drugs. Isabelle, for example, went into prostitution so that she could support her compulsive cocaine consumption, but, at the same time, she had to intoxicate herself so as to be able to overcome the discomforts generally experienced while engaged in this activity. We can therefore observe quite clearly a circular (or reciprocal) link between drugs and delinquency, most particularly present in the case of prostitution.

The psychopharmacological link of Goldstein's tripartite model (1985, 1987) did take into account the intoxication functions of courage and disinhibition necessary to committing crime but did not explicitly highlight its "amnesic" (forgetting or deadening) purpose.

To have more fun when committing crime:

Many youths, such as Oscar, stated that being intoxicated made the commission of a crime more fun:

> I would smoke a joint [hashish] before a crime because it was a lot funnier. . . . If I wouldn't smoke, it would be less fun. . . . It was mainly to party.

This hedonistic aspect of delinquency appears substantially high for some when they are experiencing the effects of drugs. Hence the search for pleasure is at the core of the pre-occupations of these youths (Cusson, 1989; Gottfredson and Hirschi, 1990; Brunelle et al., 1998).

Certain drugs in particular seem to increase the hedonistic pursuit during the commission of a crime. This is especially the case with cannabis. No indications were made along similar lines for other drugs.

This "pleasure link" between drugs and crime was not specifically documented in the traditional psychopharmacological studies, nor was it in Goldstein's tripartite model. Since these studies were concerned with adults rather than youths, this "pleasure link" may be specific to the juvenile drug—crime nexus. Alternatively, it may be that the aims of traditional psychopharmacological studies, as well as their methodology, did not permit such a result to be observed. For example, structured questionnaires used in the majority of quantitative researches do not allow this kind of phenomenological material to emerge. In their study of youths, Carpenter et al. (1988) used a phenomenological perspective similar to ours and also highlighted this hedonistic purpose of drugs during crime commission.

Without denying the drug's capacity to interfere with normal central nervous system action, some authors advise care when assessing psychopharmacological links between drugs and crime (Marlatt and Rohsenow, 1980; Peele, 1985; Brochu, 1995). There is always the possibility that personal beliefs about a drug's effects and the context of intoxication share as much importance in the drug—crime links as intoxication itself.

ECONOMIC COMPULSIVE MODEL OR A QUESTION OF MONEY?

The great majority of our young respondents referred to monetary motivations in their delinquent experiences. Money-oriented crime constitutes, from their personal perceptions, a way to absorb costs and to make a profit. Money-oriented delinquency allows them to obtain the money needed to acquire drugs:

> . . . after a while, drugs become expensive, you know, so you start stealing because you need the money. (Christian)

In analyzing a youth's chronological life account, it is found, as indicated by Brochu (1995), that the economic drug—crime relation is modified throughout the respondent's consumption trajectory. When drug use is occasional, crime is not necessarily the principal source of revenue for youths. For those who are not dependent on drugs, money from crime is sometimes added to revenue from a job, pocket money, or an allowance given by parents:

> My father would give me lots of money, at least $80 (Can.) a day. . . . I also delivered newspapers when I was younger. . . . And I started doing some crimes with my friends—some B&Es [breaking and entries] and stuff. . . . (Sacha)

Moreover, illegally obtained money is not always spent exclusively on drugs. Drugs do not take up all of these youths' lives. Other interests also develop that require some financial resources—clothes, compact discs, recreation, etc.:

> Let's say that I was doing break-ins with some guys, and that we were selling some stuff. . . . So we would be making some cash. Some of that money would go to having a good time [consuming] and some would go to buying cassettes, sweaters, and things like that. (Jonathan)

However, illegal revenues are often spent on drugs to avoid raising any worries or suspicions of parents, who are usually aware of how much money their children should have and are therefore likely to be wary in regard to their children wearing expensive designer clothes:

> Sure, I could have gone to any store and got some new clothes. But like I said, I wouldn't go home with a brand-new wardrobe. (Franco)

For similar reasons, Christian explains why he would not place any of his illegally earned money in the bank:

I didn't have any bank account, I wouldn't put anything in the bank. My parents would have found out about everything. This way, my parents had no idea what was happening.

For some juvenile delinquents, such as Franco and Christian, it would be their criminal endeavors, to some extent, that would lead them into drugs. This was because the clandestine context or secrecy linked to their delinquency was pushing them to quick and ephemeral purchases (e.g., drugs, food, days spent in amusement parks). For those youths who have to hide their profits in order to avoid raising suspicions and to protect themselves if and when they confront the police, consumption seems to become a good way of spending their illicit gains. To a certain extent, physical proximity to their parents hinders adolescents from freely spending their illegal earnings, hence pushing them toward drugs as an alternative spending route. In this sense, these youths consider the consumption of their profits a "safer" expenditure than the purchase of an entirely new wardrobe would be.

From drug dealing to polymorphic money-oriented crime

The economic drug—crime relation does not necessarily present itself for all types of crime. According to the respondents' personal accounts, shoplifting, committed by either institutionalized or non-institutionalized youths, is rarely associated with drug consumption. Drug dealing, on the other hand, is the most likely crime to be directly and most rapidly linked to consumption. Oscar, for example, explains that drug dealing permitted him to cover his regular consumption of hashish and LSD, while any earnings acquired from burglaries were spent elsewhere:

. . . I would make quite a bit of money because I was selling big amounts. So with the dope money I was making, I would buy more drugs. And whatever was left in my pockets, I would spend it [on drugs]. B&Es and stuff like that, that was just for the trip of putting a little bit more money in my pockets . . . that's what I wanted, as much money as possible. In the end, I was spending my money on stuff that was pretty much useless. . . .

Whatever the case, a portion of illegal earnings is spent on drugs, and this even though drugs or money do not initially constitute the principal motivation to commit crimes. As Mathias points out:

I would sell to have some fun on weekends, so that I could pay for my joints with my friends.

As for adults, once youths begin consuming regularly, the increased costs call for additional revenues. Drug-consumption milieus generally supply youths with the contacts and knowledge necessary for getting involved in illegal drug dealing. This generally takes place through regular contacts with one's supplier(s). Nathan clearly explains how a using partner led him to begin frequenting drug dealers, which subsequently led to personal involvement in drug dealing and an eventual personal increase in cocaine (freebase) consumption:

He came over to my place and we smoked and smoked . . . he used to steal bikes from sheds. And he introduced me to a guy who used to steal bikes and who would bring some pretty good hash—anyway, it was top stuff. . . . I started to get to know the guy—he had friends that were good dressers. They were all about 23–24 years old. . . . He started to get interested in me, he used to make lots of money with me. I started to get accepted in his network, to know the right plugs. I knew the crack houses and all the clients personally. . . . It was a crazy business—always money, freebase. I was going through about $200 or $300 to about $500 in a day. . . .

Drug dealing permits an important reduction in the costs of consumption, as well as a more facilitated access to psychoactive substances that may, in turn, lead to increased usage. At the stage of regular consumption, this circular (or reciprocal) pattern between drugs and crime becomes a mutual reinforcement process in these forms of deviance (Faupel, 1991; Brochu, 1995).

To the extent that dependency takes its roots in the lives of some youths, their need for drugs intensifies to the point of becoming their unique and central interest. At this stage of drug dependency, the adolescent consumer does not have the legitimate financial means to meet this compulsive consumption. This therefore leads to involvement in various sorts of money-oriented crimes. This economic-compulsive relation is particularly accentuated among youths who develop a cocaine or heroin dependency, because such illicit drugs are more expensive and more addictive than cannabis, for example. Antoine explains how he became more implicated in crime as he developed a greater cocaine (freebase) dependency:

I started doing more and more. And then I started wanting more and more, and going for more powerful drugs. . . . At 16, I hit rock-bottom [freebase dependency]. I didn't have enough money. I could have worked as much as I wanted, I would borrow and deal drugs, but I never had enough money. I was stuck with this dope problem. That's when I started doing some holdups [armed robberies].

The compulsive need for expensive drugs leads to the accumulation of costs that considerably exceed the legitimate earnings of youths, leading them toward drug dealing, theft, robbery, or prostitution in order to acquire the money needed for their personal consumption habits. Besides, at this stage of the addict's trajectory, the implicated youths state that they committed several types of crimes, including shoplifting, burglary, robbery, drug dealing, and, at times, prostitution. Their crimes become ever more polymorphic in contrast to early stages in the trajectory, when they remained more specialized and limited to drug dealing or burglary, for example. For this reason, Nathan began committing armed robberies during a freebase dependency phase, whereas at the initial stages he would steal bicycles and sell drugs:

I started freebasing. . . . That's when everything went to hell. I became a real crackhead. I wasn't someone to trust, so now, I was out of the network. I really had to steal to get some money. . . . I couldn't let a day go by without doing a hit. I would break into a house or do a holdup everyday . . . I was about 16 years old.

Similarly to adult addicts (Brochu, 1995), initial money-oriented crime increases by several proportions for youths who enter an economic—compulsive stage, as if drug dependency causes some form of catalyzing effect on juvenile delinquency.

An economic link surpassing the habitual economic—compulsive framework

As with adults, one would expect that this economics-based relation between drugs and crime might be observed only when regular consumption involves expensive and addictive drugs such as cocaine and heroin. However, even though the respondents' accounts illustrate that this relation is more accentuated among cocaine addicts, for example, it is also apparent that involvement in money-oriented crime began or was intensified during periods when the respondents were consuming less expensive drugs, and more particularly cannabis, which was the more typical drug for the majority of the sample.

The fragility of youths' economic power:

To understand the situation described above, one must comprehend the fragility of adolescents' economic power. Unemployed adults are generally eligible for government aid (e.g., social welfare, unemployment insurance, rent and housing benefits), while youths are not. Adolescents therefore do not have access to other sources of revenue aside from work (when they reach the eligible working age) or, for some, family allowances. In this sense, youths may get involved in crime in order to support their consumption even for less expensive drugs such as cannabis. It goes without saying that with expensive drugs like cocaine, this assertion becomes even more probable.

Juvenile consumers turn to money-oriented crime more rapidly than adult consumers. The latter generally rely on crime only once they have exhausted the more or less legal options available to them—e.g., selling their possessions or transforming their homes into shooting galleries in exchange for drugs (Faupel, 1991; Taylor, 1998). The situation is rather different for adolescents, who do not have access to such means. For example, selling possessions belonging to one's parents or transforming the family home into a shooting gallery are not conceivable choices. When, for one reason or another, parents cannot provide their children with an allowance or suddenly cease giving an allowance, the youth who does not want to modify his/her consumption habits and does not see any other option commits crimes to support this habit. Antoine's parents, for example, stopped lending him money and threw him out of the house when they discovered that he was using cocaine on a regular basis. Faced with such a situation, Antoine began increasing the number of money-oriented crimes he was involved in to survive and to preserve his consumption habits:

> When my parents found out that I was on dope, they stopped lending me money. They knew what was going on, you know. My parents aren't dumb, they were pretty sure. So things turned pretty bad for me. They threw me out of the house. After that, I had to steal. . . .

In brief, the relation usually made between drugs and crime by the youths interviewed is a purely economic link, stemming from the fact that they have no legitimate financial resources to depend on and support their drug consumption, especially when this consumption reaches the stage of dependency. Arianne clearly summarizes what juvenile addicts experience:

> . . . you have no other choice but crime if you want to get stoned. That's unless you're rich, you know.

Focusing closer attention on Arianne's "if you want to get stoned," the desire to consume appears to overcome the inhibitions that juvenile addicts may have regarding crime. But why do they want to consume to this point to begin with? It has been repeatedly argued that consumption is linked to hedonistic pursuits, but also to a longing to escape personal problems. The latter is particularly the case for the institutionalized youths in our sample (Brunelle et al., 1998). For example, Isabelle says that, in part, she would consume to retreat from the suffering she faced from being beaten by her mother:

. . . can you imagine how I feel, how I was beaten when I was young and how that makes me feel, the sadness that I have inside of me?. . . I thought that I had a much better life on drugs and alcohol. It would make me feel good. Yeah, even with all the sadness I had, I wouldn't even think about it anymore. For me, it was a new life. I was starting a new life and that made me feel good.

The meaning these youths give to their life experiences and the feelings that such experiences provoke become crucial to understanding their commitment to a deviant lifestyle.

Addiction to drugs in itself gradually leads to a state of ill-being or dissatisfaction (Cormier, 1993) that adolescents attempt to escape by consuming on a consistent basis. Drugs offer a temporary and immediate "patch." Money-oriented crime is therefore perceived as a necessary means to attaining their goal, whether that goal is the consumption of a drug to pursue a good feeling or to escape a negative experience.

Youths who are most likely to turn to crime to support their consumption

Must one be initially delinquent or more delinquent before deciding to turn toward money-oriented crime as a means to support a drug habit? The majority of respondents revealed that they had committed crimes before their respective initial experiences with illicit drugs. They were therefore delinquent even before drug use became part of their lifestyles. But this sequence may come in various forms.

Non-institutionalized adolescents are much less likely than institutionalized youths to resort to money-oriented crime to pay for their drugs. This may be explained by a weak initial involvement—preceding their initiation into drugs—in delinquency. Most of the non-institutionalized adolescents admitted to having shoplifted, and,

at times, committed other minor criminal acts (e.g., vandalism) during their childhood or pre-adolescence. This indicates the weak intensity and seriousness of their delinquent experiences. Also, they were generally occasional consumers of cannabis, a relatively inexpensive drug. Furthermore, having little in illegal revenues, they could not have consumed other, more expensive drugs that would have required supplementary earnings (legal or illegal). In the end, the financial needs associated with their consumption are relatively low and, in this sense, do not create any incitement to commit money-oriented crimes.

Moreover, non-institutionalized youths believed they had a lot to lose with regard to their interpersonal and social conditions if they were to get caught. This explains, in large part, the low frequency with which they turned to money-oriented crime to pay for their drug use. In fact, these youths generally expressed more positive perceptions of their lives and more important commitments to their families and schools. They often had very strong relationships with at least one family member that had prosocial values. For example, Samuel identified considerably with his mother, with whom he got along quite well:

You know, I resemble my mom physically and mentally quite a bit. . . . I don't know, but it's like everything I do, I do it the way she would have done it.

According to Samuel, this bond with his **mother** is not independent from his desire to succeed in school:

My mother really wants us to succeed. School is important for her. . . . When I don't do well in school, I know that it'll bother those around me, my family. But it bothers me as well, you know, because I was always educated in that way, to do well in school. It's like I'm used to it. . . .

For Zoé, who aspired to become a probation officer, knowing that a criminal record could compromise or block such a career dissuaded her from getting involved in crime, even though her friends were quite active. Zoé considered that she had too much to lose:

I want be a probation officer. That's why I'm not a delinquent.

As for the institutionalized group of youths, they maintained a quite different perception: that they had nothing to lose by getting involved in crime or drugs:

We went in from the back and we almost emptied the whole house. . . . I really had nothing to lose, so I said: "Go for it." In the end, it was that or being depressed in some corner or always thinking about suicide. . . . (Louis)

In sum, Goldstein's economic—compulsive drug—crime nexus corresponds to the situation of many youths in our study, particularly those who became addicts. For some respondents, however, the economic drug—crime link is widened to more occasional use of less costly drugs than cocaine or heroin. This is due to the fragility of juveniles' economic powers.

ABSENCE OF THE SYSTEMIC-VIOLENCE MODEL

Curiously, youths who engaged in both delinquency and drug use did not highlight Goldstein's systemic-violence model in their accounts. This is odd, considering that Goldstein et al. (1989), in their study of police records on homicide events, came to the conclusion that this model is the most frequent form of drug—violence nexus.

However, it is not so odd considering that in another study using an interview methodology with murderers (Goldstein et al., 1992) they reached a result that emphasized the psychopharmacological model. One may think that the absence of such a systemic link in this study is partially due to the "silent law" surrounding the drug market (Goldstein et al., 1992). In all certainty, we do not think this model does not exist simply because it was not revealed as apparent in our study.

Maybe Goldstein's systemic nexus does not apply to the situation of youths. Goldstein's studies were particularly on drug-related homicides, and the youths under study here were not implicated in such criminal behavior. The majority of our respondents were, at one moment or another, involved in the drug market as sellers. According to the accounts of the youths, their drug-selling activities never led them to homicide or serious assaults. Maybe they did not tell us if they did. Maybe it is a coincidence that these particular youths did not engage in such activities, and others would have. It is also possible that the drug milieu is tougher on adults than on youths. Violence may manifest itself differently for youths than for adults in drug milieus; it could be more of a verbal or psychological nature than of a physical nature. However, these types of violence (verbal and psychological) were not documented in the accounts of youths in this study.

In a certain way, Goldstein's systemic model refers to drug-distribution activities that turn bad and lead to violence (debts, thefts, betrayal). Youths are also involved in drug-selling activities, but they do not seem to lead to as much violence as for adults. Homicides, for example, generally involve adults much more than adolescents (Savoie, 2000). A more general systemic model could refer to all types of crime related to the drug market, particularly drug selling, because many youths engage in this type of criminal behavior. In doing so, the systemic model would be seen more as a general drug—crime nexus than as a drug—violence nexus. The problem with this possible categorization of drug—crime nexus is that, as shown in the previous pages, drug-selling activities are also very linked with economic—compulsive motivations. Thus it would be hard to differentiate the two possible nexuses (economic compulsive and systemic) when drug-selling activities are involved. In any case, our young respondents did not highlight Goldstein's systemic model in their accounts. This is possibly and partially due to their age.

A NONEXISTENT OR INTERMEDIARY RELATION

Independently of Goldstein's tripartite model, some youths asserted that they did not see any link between their delinquency and their drug consumption. Lilianne did not believe that intoxication was ever a reason for the assaults she had committed. She believed she was simply naturally aggressive:

I don't think that drugs caused my fighting, because even in primary school I used to fight. . . . I'm aggressive. . . .

The phenomenon corresponds to the occurrence stage in Brochu's (1995) integrative model. This stage is characterized by occasional consumption and, at times, by a simultaneous, but often independent, presence of criminal Involvement. In this regard, White (1990) believes that the drug—crime nexus among youths is simply due to the synchronic appearance of these deviant behaviors during adolescence. Brochu (1995) refers to White's

model as a correlational model without a common cause.

Another type of correlational drug—crime nexus is called a common cause model by Brochu (1995). Corresponding to this model, some youths asserted that the drug—crime link is related to their peer associations. Associations with peers necessarily implies, from the youths' perspective, involvement in both delinquency and illicit drug consumption, or, in other words, in all prohibited or deviant activities in which the group is involved. Members of the same peer group appear to mutually influence each other in the adoption of deviant behaviors. In this sense, Sacha believes his association with street gangs was in large part responsible for the crimes he had committed:

I think it was because of the gangs [that he had committed those crimes that brought him to a juvenile detention center]. I think that that really influenced me in getting into crime. . . . The others used to tell me: "We're going to do it tonight," and I would go, you know. Maybe sometimes I didn't even feel like going, and they used to bother me and make fun of me, so I used to end up going.

For many youths it is simply a question of not losing face in front of peers. Jocelyn explains that he was not looking for a way to support his consumption of cannabis and hallucinogens. Instead, he did not want to seem scared (to be a "pussy") in front of his "friends":

I wanted to be with my friends, you know, [to steal], so that they wouldn't say that I was a pussy, you know. [*Interviewer: That's an expression. . . .?*] Yeah, scared.

This observation was also made with some girls in our sample. Pamela, for example, explains that she was a user of pot, acid, and, on occasion, cocaine, and that she would participate in criminal activities so she could be like her friends—so they would find her as "cool" as she found them "cool":

I had made some other friends who used to do drugs. I wanted to show them that I was somebody, that I wasn't a simple nobody. I used to do the same things as them . . . they would drink a case of beer, I would drink a case of beer. . . . They stole, I stole. With these guys, I would make some cash. I found them really cool. I wanted to be cool too.

Since adolescence constitutes a period of life in which everyone is in search of their own personal identity, to be accepted and respected in a group is often very important for one's self-perception, as well as for the identity that is formed (Fréchette and LeBlanc, 1987; Beman, 1995). However, among non-institutionalized youths who associated with delinquent gangs, some confirmed their conformist values and considered themselves to be not prone to peer influence. This was the case with Zoé, the girl who aspired to become a probation officer:

I never got involved in anything stupid, you know. It was my friends who used to do those things. I'm not a girl that you can easily influence. If I don't want to do something, I won't do it. If my friends would steal bicycles, I wouldn't. That stuff doesn't interest me.

This demonstrates that the influence of deviant peers is not always a determinant of a youth's trajectory, as the analysis of non-institutionalized youths' life experiences tells us. Why was this influence less a factor with non-institutionalized youths than with youths who were in police custody or in addict treatment centers? Fréchette and LeBlanc (1987) argue that family bonds and commitment to school are important influences on the behaviors of youths who have never been brought into the judicial system. Again, it appears that all of our study's non-institutionalized adolescents have strong positive bonds with at least one family member and that they are less likely than the institutionalized group to abandon school, thus indicating some academic competence and commitment to their studies. In this context, the potential influence of deviant peers is weakened considerably.

In sum, for some youths the drug—crime link seems indirect and at times absent during certain periods in their lives. These periods are characterized by a lifestyle full of strong stimulations, such as the effects of drugs, delinquency, and those associations made with deviant peers. Delinquency and drugs occupy a hedonistic place in their lives. Their respective roles and the link between the two tend to change throughout a youth's trajectory.

A deviant lifestyle

For many of the youths interviewed, the two types of deviance—delinquency and drug consumption—are intertwined to the point where it becomes impossible, or simply irrelevant, to distinguish one from the other. Like many others, Normand explains that he was often under the effects of pot and/or LSD while he was shoplifting, but that he did not necessarily consume in order to commit the crimes. In fact, it seems difficult in his case to know whether one behavior led to another, since, according to his account, he was always intoxicated: "It was more because I was always stoned. I couldn't really say [whether he consumed to commit the crime or whether he was always intoxicated before he decided to commit the crime]." Oscar also illustrates this state of being quite vividly in his account:

I did some B&Es, I did some break-ins with weapons, some robberies, and some assaults. I was never straight during those times, you know. I was always stoned, always on acid. The more it went on, the more I would smoke too.

Clearly one may assume that intoxication may lead to important cognitive distortions that result in youths committing crimes (Taylor, 1983), but other conditions are necessary to explain delinquent behavior. Following Cormier (1993), we believe drugs and delinquency are components of a lifestyle that is more largely deviant. Initial delinquency leads to occasional consumption. The more youths use drugs, the more their lives are organized and structured around getting, consuming, and never lacking one's dose (Cormier, 1993; Macquet, 1994). In this sense, Louis's statement instructs us on the central role of drugs at one time in his life:

It [theft] was always for dope and dope again. Everything [I did] turned around dope.

Nevertheless, not all young users reach the dependence stage of drug use. Hence, for youths who have very limited means to legitimate alternatives, money-oriented crime is often the essential condition for obtaining drugs. It is in this manner that the deviant lifestyle is gradually formed.

CONCLUSION

With the reference point of this article being Goldstein's (1985) tripartite model, our results showed that this framework is useful to the understanding of youths' drug—crime nexus. However, as will be demonstrated, some adjustments are required.

SUPPORT FOR GOLDSTEIN'S TRIPARTITE MODEL

Goldstein's psychopharmacological model is supported by the material provided by the youths in this study. Some respondents did say drug intoxication caused their violent behaviors. However, the psychopharmacological link described by Goldstein (1989) and that is most present throughout the youths' accounts is the use of drugs to facilitate the commission of crime by enhancing courage and reducing nervousness. One could think that without intoxication they would not have gone through with aggression. Nevertheless, the decision to commit violent acts was taken before consuming drugs in many of these cases.

Goldstein's economic—compulsive model was also supported in our findings. Youths who were regular or dependent users of drugs, especially costly drugs like cocaine, did in fact engage in various money-oriented crimes to a greater degree than the other youths in this study.

NUANCES TO THE TRIPARTITE MODEL

In his psychopharmacological model, Goldstein discussed the intoxication functions of courage and disinhibition, but he did not highlight the hedonistic and "amnesic" types of pleasure that were revealed as very important in the drug—crime nexus of youths in this study. Some respondents said they used drugs simply to have more fun when committing crimes. Others talked about how drugs allowed them to avoid or forget negative feelings of guilt, shame, or fear even after their delinquent acts, thus bringing more pleasure to these experiences.

A more nuanced form of Goldstein's economic—compulsive model also appeared in the trajectories of the youths under study. The economic link goes beyond the compulsive needs for expensive drugs for these young boys and girls, who did not necessarily use costly drugs and did not all become addicted drug users. Because youths have weak and limited capacities for generating legitimate revenue, this economic link is present in all phases of their consumption trajectories regardless of which drugs are used. Since the economic resources of adolescents are largely restricted in comparison with those of adults, money-oriented crime rapidly becomes an option for them. The economic link, in terms of financial needs brought on by the consumption of drugs, is more accentuated for youths who become addicts.

Our material allowed us to better understand who is more likely to turn to crime to financially support a drug habit: the institutionalized youths. For the non-institutionalized respondents, the deviant lifestyle appears much less developed, in part because they feel they have much to lose in terms of interpersonal relations and life conditions if they engage in deviant activities. In this sense, our study sheds light not only on reasons why some turn to a deviant lifestyle but also on why others do not, or least do so to a much lesser extent.

Another type of "economic link" emerged from some of the youths accounts. They explained that their illicit revenues were often spent on drugs because such ephemeral purchases permitted the concealment of profits from their delinquent endeavors and, as a result, concealed delinquency itself from parents and police. Thus delinquency can lead to drug use among youths, but the inverse affirmation generally remains more popular.

Regarding Goldstein's systemic model, the results show an absence of this drug—violence nexus in youths' accounts. Many reasons could explain this absence, but we think it is partly due to the respondents' ages. Adults are generally more involved than youths in serious violent offending. Also, it is possible that the drug milieu is "softer" on youths who do in fact engage in drug-selling activities.

Finally, and independently of Goldstein's tripartite model, another type of drug—crime relation emerged from this study. It is a nonexistent or intermediary relation between drugs and crimes. Some youths thought there was no relationship between their drug use and criminal activities, while others believed these deviant behaviors to be indirectly linked to deviant peer associations. For many youths in this study, particularly those institutionalized, committing crimes and using drugs are often simply ways to acquire or preserve a respectable status among peers. Others highlighted the importance of personality in assessing such a drug—crime link. Some think their aggressive natures, as they say, are mostly responsible for their deviant acts. We argue that drugs and crimes are sometimes so tightly linked that it becomes hard, for the youths themselves and for us, to understand the relation between the two, and that we should see these behaviors within the scope of a wider deviant lifestyle.

The portrait of drug—crime relations among this study's youths permits us to understand the commitment of some to a deviant lifestyle. By allowing them to present their own explanations of the various drug—crime links through life history accounts and from a phenomenological perspective, it was possible to gain new and more in-depth insight and to further elaborate on and clarify that knowledge already made available by authors such as Goldstein. The importance of allowing these youths the opportunity to express themselves in regard to their personal trajectories, for both clinical intervention and research objectives aimed at them, therefore remains crucial.

Notes

1. In the present text, money-oriented crime represents all forms of crime that lead to the acquisition of goods or money or to a diminishing of costs. Drug dealing, prostitution, and all forms of theft (i.e., shoplifting, burglary, robbery) are regrouped under this heading.

2. Youth centers are non-profit-making organizations where youths of a neighborhood gather to entertain themselves.

3. Unfortunately we do not know exactly which drug Dina consumed before her crimes. She had tried all drugs except heroin, and she was a regular cannabis consumer.

References

Berman, D.S., "Risk Factors Leading to Adolescent Substance Abuse," *Adolescence*, 30(117): 201–208, 1995.

Blum, R.H., "Violence, Alcohol, and Setting: An Unexplored Nexus," pp. 110–142 in J.J. Collins, ed., *Drinking and Crime*. New York: Guilford Press, 1981.

Brochu, S., *Drogues et criminalité: Une relation complexe.* Collection perspectives criminologiques. Montréal: Presses de l'Université de Montréal, 1995.

Brochu, S., "Drogues et criminalité: Point de vue critique sur les idées véhiculées," *Déviance et société*, 21(3): 303–314, 1997.

Brunelle, N., Brochu, S., Cousineau, M.-M., *Des cheminements vers un style de vie déviant: Adolescents des centres jeunesse et des centres pour toxicomanes.* Université de Montréal Cahier de recherche du CICC (27), 1998.

Carpenter, C., Glassner, B., Johnson, B.D., and Loughlin, J., *Kids, Drugs, and Crime.* Lexington, MA: Lexington Books, 1988.

Cormier, D., *Toxicomanies: Styles de vie.* Montréal: Méridien, 1993.

Covell, R.G., Frisher, M., Taylor, A., Goldberg, D., Green, S., McKeganey, N., Bloor, M., "Prison Experience of Injecting Drug Users in Glasgow," *Drug and Alcohol Dependence*, 32(1): 9–14, 1993.

Cusson, M., *Délinquants pourquoi?* Montréal: Bibliothèque québécoise, 1989.

Debuyst, C., *Acteur social et délinquance.* Bruxelles: Pierre Mardaga, 1989.

Desmarais, D., Grell, P., *Les récits de vie: Théorie, méthode et trajectoires types.* Montréal: Éditions Saint-Martin, 1986.

Faupel, C.E., *Shooting Dope: Career Patterns of Hard-Core Heroin Users.* Gainesville: University of Florida Press, 1991.

Fréchette, M., LeBlanc, M., *Délinquances et délinquants.* Boucherville: Gaëtan Morin, 1987.

Ghiglione, R., Matalon, B., *Les enquêtes sociologiques: Théories et pratiques.* Paris: A. Colin, 1978.

Goldstein, P.J., *Prostitution and Drugs.* Toronto: Lexington, 1979.

Goldstein, P.J., "The Drugs/Violence Nexus: A Tripartite Conceptual Framework," *Journal of Drug Issues*, 14: 493–506, 1985.

Goldstein, P.J., "Impact of Drug-Related Violence," *Public Health Report*, 102: 625–627, 1987.

Goldstein, P.J., Brownstein, H.H., Ryan, P.J., Bellucci, A., "Crack and Homicide in New York City, 1988: A Conceptually Based Event Analysis," *Contemporary Drug Problems*, 16: 651–687, 1989.

Goldstein, P.J., Brownstein, H.H., Spunt, B.J., Fendrich, M., *Drug Relationships in Murder (DREIM) Executive Summary*, NIDA, 1992.

Gottfredson, M.R., Hirschi, T., *A General Theory of Crime.* Standford, CA: Stanford University Press, 1990.

Harlow, C.W., "Drugs and Jail Inmates, 1989," *The Narc Officer*, 37–51, 1991.

Hubbard, R.L., Mardsen, M.E., Rachal, J.V., Harwood, H.J., Cavanaugh, E.R., Ginzburg, E.R., *Drug Abuse Treatment—A National Study of Effectiveness.* Chapel Hill: University of North Carolina Press, 1989.

Hunt, D.E., "Stealing and Dealing: Cocaine and Property Crimes," *NIDA Research Monograph Series, The Epidemiology of Cocaine Use and Abuse*, Rockville, MD: NIDA, 110: 139–150, 1991.

Jarvis, G., Parker, H., "Young Heroin Users and Crime: How Do the 'New Users' Finance Their Habit?" *British Journal of Criminology*, 29: 175–185, 1989.

Kohli, M., "Biography: Account, Text, Method," pp. 29–45 in Daniel Bertaux, ed., *Biography and Society: The Life History Approach in the Social Sciences.* Beverly Hills, CA: Sage, 1981.

L'Écuyer, R. "L'analyse de contenu: Notion et étapes," pp. 49–66 in Jean-Pierre Deslauriers, ed., *Les méthodes de la recherche qualitative.* Québec: Presses de l'Université de Québec, 1987.

Lightfoot, L.O., Hodgins, D., "A Survey of Alcohol and Drug Problems in Incarcerated Offenders," *The International Journal of the Addictions*, 23: 687–706, 1988.

Macquet, C., *Toxicomanies: Aliénation ou styles de vie.* Paris: Éditions l'Harmattan, 1994.

Marlatt, G.A., Rohsenow, D.J., "Cognitive Processes in Alcohol Use: Expectancy and the Balanced Placebo Design," in N.K. Mello (ed.), *Advances in Substance Abuse*, 1, 1980.

Morse, J.M., "Designing Funded Qualitative Research," pp. 220–235 in Norman K. Denzin and Yvonna S. Lincoln, eds., *Handbook of Qualitative Research.* Thousand Oaks, CA: Sage, 1994.

Nurco, D.N., Hanlon, T.E., Kinlock, T.W., "Recent Research on the Relationship Between Illicit Drug Use and Crime," *Behavioral Sciences & the Law*, 9: 221–242, 1991.

Parker, R.N., Auerhahn, K., "Alcohol, Drugs, and Violence," *Annual Review of Sociology*, 24: 291–311, 1998.

Peele, S., *The Meaning of Addiction: Compulsive Experience and Its Interpretation.* Lexington, MA: Lexington Books, 1985.

Pirès, A.P., "De quelques enjeux épistémologiques d'une méthodologie générale pour les sciences sociales," pp. 1–54 in J. Poupart, J.-P. Deslauriers, L.-H. Groulx, A. Laperrière, R. Mayer et A.P. Pirès, eds., *La recherche qualitative: Enjeux épistémologiques et méthodologiques*. Montréal: Gaëtan Morin, 1997a.

Pirès, A.P., "Échantillonnage et recherche qualitative: Essai théorique et méthodologique," pp. 113–169 in J. Poupart, J.-P. Deslauriers, L.-H. Groulx, A. Laperrière, R. Mayer et A.P. Pirès. eds., *La recherche qualitative: Enjeux épistémologiques et méthodologiques*. Montréal: Gaëtan Morin, 1997b.

Roth, J.A., "Psychoactive Substances and Violence," *National Institute of Justice—Research in Brief*. Washington, DC: U.S. Department of Justice, 1994.

Savoie, J., "La criminalité de violence chez les jeunes," *Juristat, Centre canadien de la statistique juridique*, 19(13): 1–15, 2000.

Schutz, A., *Le chercheur et le quotidien: Phénoménologie des sciences sociales*. Paris: Méridiens Klincksieck, 1987.

Sheard, M.H., "Clinical Pharmacology of Aggressive Behavior," *Clinical Neuropharmacology*, 11(6): 483–492, 1988.

Taylor, S.P., "Alcohol and Human Physical Aggression," pp. 280–291 in E. Gottheil, K. Druley, T.E. Skoloda, H.M. Waxman, eds., *Alcohol, Drug Abuse and Aggression*, Springfield, IL: Charles C. Thomas, 1983.

Taylor, A., "Needlework: The Lifestyle of Female Drug Injectors," *Journal of Drug Issues*, 28(1): 77–90, 1998.

Taylor, S., Leonard, K., "Alcohol and Human Physical Aggression," pp. 77–102 in *Aggression: The Theoretical and Empirical Reviews*, 2. New York: Academy Press, 1983.

White, H.R., "The Drug Use-Delinquency Connection in Adolescence," pp. 215–256 in R.A. Weisheit, ed., *Drugs, Crime and the Criminal Justice System*. Cincinnati: Anderson Publishing Co., 1990.

Chapter 7

Peers

INTRODUCTION

Giordano, Cernkovich, and Pugh's classic piece on friendships and delinquency contributed substantially to criminology's understanding of the nature of ties between delinquents. The authors suggest that the peer bond between delinquents is neither strong and enduring as suggested by subculture theory, nor weak and temporary, as suggested by control theory. They find that the bond between delinquent youth is much more complex than previous research has shown.

Esbensen and Huizinga's important research on gangs, drugs, and delinquency sheds light on the nature and activities of gang members. In their survey of youth in "high risk" neighborhoods in Denver, they find strikingly few gang members. Additionally, few gang members report long tenure in the gang, although their criminal offending is particularly high. Their study is an important contribution to our understanding of the transitory yet highly delinquent nature of gang involvement.

In the next piece, Konty and Peek investigate the possibility that for some adolescents, deviance is a positive identity. They propose a label-seeking mechanism in which some adolescents embrace deviance as a way of creating and maintaining status. Konty and Peek find a significant relationship between peer interactions that lead to possible deviance and find interesting gender differences in who is attracted to deviant labels and how the process evolves for boys and girls.

Friendships and Delinquency[1]

Peggy C. Giordano, Stephen A. Cernkovich, and M. D. Pugh

Peer relationships have been central to the logic of most delinquency theories. There is general agreement that delinquency occurs most often within a group context, but there is much less consensus about the nature and quality of the relationships delinquents have with their friends. Early subcultural and differential association theorists emphasized the delinquent group's primary character and relied on such terms as "solidarity" and "esprit de corps" to describe it. This viewpoint is perhaps most firmly anchored in the work of Thrasher, who described the emotional closeness and intimacy of the Chicago gangs he studied. He saw a rapport that was sometimes so complete that one "receives the impression of interpenetration

of personalities, if such a mystical conception is possible" (1963, p. 210). In Shaw's case study, *The Jackroller*, Stanley echoes this view in describing his own relationship with fellow jackrollers: "We were like brothers and would stick by each other through thick and thin. We cheered each other in our troubles and loaned each other dough. A mutual understanding developed, and nothing could break our confidence in each other" (Shaw 1966, p. 66).

Recent investigators have criticized this image of the delinquent group as reflecting "the vicarious gratifications of adult investigators and their own childhood fantasies to a greater extent than they do the perspectives of gang members" (Short and Strodtbeck 1965, p. 231). Perhaps partly in reaction against the earlier rosy imagery, Short and Strodtbeck offered a more complex portrait. While agreeing that the delinquent group "likely offered these youngsters a larger measure of . . . play and interpersonal gratification than any alternative form of association of which they are aware and which is available to them by virtue of preparation and other reality considerations" (p. 233), they stressed the lack of interpersonal skills of many gang boys as part of their more general theory of social disability: "Even within the gang, upon which the boy comes to

[1]This research was supported by PHS Research grant no. MH 29095-03, National Institute of Mental Health, Center for Studies of Antisocial and Violent Behavior. We wish to thank the anonymous reviewers of *AJS* for their helpful comments on an earlier version of this manuscript. Requests for reprints should be sent to Peggy Giordano, Department of Sociology, Bowling Green State University, Bowling Green, Ohio 43403.

be dependent for a large share of interpersonal gratification, interaction in many respects is not rewarding and lacks characteristics essential to the fulfillment of these [interpersonal] needs" (Short 1963, p. xlii). Klein and Crawford (1967) also depicted the gang's cohesion as fragile and as generated more by external forces (e.g., threats from rival gangs) than by personal regard.

But it is control theory that departs more completely from the early subcultural view; indeed, much of its uniqueness as a theoretical position is derived from the way in which it differs from earlier explanations precisely on the peer issue. Hirschi in particular believes that the causal significance of friendships has been overstated, arguing that "since delinquents are less strongly attached to conventional adults than non-delinquents they are less likely to be attached to each other. . . . The idea that delinquents have comparatively warm, intimate social relations with each other (or with anyone) is a romantic myth" (1969, p. 159). Instead, these relationships are described as "cold and brittle" (p. 141). Psychological treatments of delinquency, although differing in etiological emphasis, often describe delinquents' peer relations in a similar fashion. Hartup, in a recent review of research on peer relations, declared unequivocally: "Delinquency among adolescents and young adults can be predicted mainly from one dimension of early peer relations . . . not getting along with others" (1983, p. 165).

The issue of the nature and quality of delinquents' peer relations is thus largely unresolved, but it keeps surfacing because of its theoretical and applied implications. To the degree that delinquents' relationships are found not to be in any real sense primary, cohesive, or solidary, the causal significance of group processes in the etiology of delinquent behavior is believed to be minimized. A well-entrenched finding

in the social psychological/experimental literature is that highly cohesive groups are more able to exact conformity from their members than are more ephemeral or loosely structured ones.[2]

Thrasher not only described the intimacy he believed to be characteristic of the Chicago gang boys but also linked these characteristics to the gang's ability to exert influence on its members: "The individual member of a gang is almost wholly controlled by the force of group opinion. The way everybody in the gang does or thinks is usually sufficient justification or dissuasion for the gang boy. In such cases he is really feeling the pressure of public opinion in that part of his own social world which is most vital to him and in which he wishes to maintain status" (1963, p. 204). Using the same logic, Hirschi reaches opposite conclusions: "It seems reasonable to conclude that persons whose social relations are cold and brittle, whose social skills are severely limited, are incapable of

---

[2]In the real world, it is probable that there is something a little less orderly than a linear relation between intimacy and influence. Glaser (1956) emphasizes situations where individuals may be most influenced by groups of which they are not even members. One's location in the group (whether as a central or marginal actor) can also affect the way in which the group seeks to exert control (Giordano 1983). Ridgeway points out that, under some conditions, cohesiveness, while increasing conformity pressures on members, "at the same time can potentially increase their freedom to rebel against those pressures" (1983, p. 105). Nevertheless, we agree with the basic premise that some amount of intimacy in general enhances the group's ability to exert influence because (1) the more cohesive the group, the higher the level of interaction and communication within it—this maximizes the opportunities for group members to express their views of things—and (2) the more attractive individuals find their membership in a group, the more they may be willing to accede to such influence attempts in order to maintain or enhance their standing.

influencing each other in the manner suggested by those who see the peer group as the decisive factor in delinquency" (Hirschi 1969, p. 141).

In addition to its pivotal role in theories of delinquency causation, the image of the delinquent as socially deficient and lacking close relationships also has implications for treatment. The emphasis on the social maladjustment of delinquents, in at least implicit comparison with other adolescents, sustains the view of intrinsic differences between the two groups (see Matza 1964). While this conception fits well with current juvenile justice treatment strategies that continue to emphasize individual counseling, psychological classification schemes, and so on, it has yet to be demonstrated adequately as an empirical reality.

We agree with Empey, who argued in 1967 and again in 1983 that "definitive research on the precise character of delinquent, as contrasted with conventional, groups is desperately needed" (1982, p. 274). Previous empirical attempts to examine the qualities of friendships of delinquents are less than definitive for several reasons: (1) there has been a kind of cavalier and interchangeable use of potentially very different friendship processes. Psychological studies often equate "peer relations" with sociometric rank (i.e., popularity), usually within the classroom setting. Hirschi (1969) developed the pivotal concept "attachment to peers," but this is variously referred to as "sensitivity to others," "loyalty," "warmth and intimacy," "cohesion," "solidarity," and "dependence on peers." (2) Many of the earlier studies relied primarily on direct observation of delinquent gangs. This methodology allowed a detailed and dynamic analysis of gang behavior. However, in the absence of meaningful control groups, it is impossible to determine

whether the relational qualities observed (positive or negative) would not also be found within other adolescent friendship networks. (3) More recent surveys, while providing a comparison across different levels of self-reported delinquency, have relied on very narrow measurement strategies, usually tapping only one aspect of peer involvement (e.g., time spent with friends) or skirting the friendship relations entirely.[3]

Another typical measurement strategy confounds peer relationships with delinquency involvement itself, focusing on the extent to which the youth is involved with delinquent peers (see, e.g., Short 1957; Jensen 1972; Elliott, Huizinga, and Ageton 1982). A related method has been to compare the subjects' levels of self-reported delinquency directly with the reported levels of their friends' involvements (e.g., Poole and Regoli 1979). These studies are important in that they usually demonstrate high levels of behavioral concordance within friendship networks. We know that delinquents spend considerable time with other delinquents, but the qualities of their relations remain unclear.

While research on the relationship between adolescent male friendship processes and delinquency is, at the least, inadequate, there are almost no data about

---

[3]Hirschi (1969), e.g., based his conclusions about delinquents' lack of attachment to friends primarily on responses to two items (the amount of respect for best friends' opinions and whether respondents would like to be the kind of person that their best friends are). Wiatrowski, Griswold, and Roberts (1981), in another test of control theory, relied on two items about the "importance" of friends and the importance of spending time with friends. Because these items were not predictive of delinquency, they concluded that this reflected "the unimportance of friends to delinquent youth" (p. 535).

females. The few descriptive studies of gangs that include females as members are old (e.g., Bowker, Gross, and Klein's [1980] analysis of unpublished 1964 data) or very narrow, usually centering on females' marginal participation in male gangs or groups (Miller 1973). Nevertheless, the female delinquent is even more likely than her male counterpart to be placed on the socially disabled list: "The need to 'belong' is as great as hunger and thirst. Yet to the youngster who already has problems— either because of belonging to a discriminated racial group or because of inner problems or because of a difficult family relationship—the way to friendship groups is almost totally closed or the hurdles so great she cannot take them" (Konopka 1966, p. 88).

Due to her basic "incapacity for friendship with contemporaries" (p. 123), the delinquent girl will cope with her incredible loneliness by temporarily "losing [herself] in the crowd" (p. 123) or creating a love relationship to fill an interpersonal void. Rittenhouse (1963) provided some empirical support for this view in her finding that "relational strivings" were more characteristic of the delinquent girls she studied, while "status striving" was more typical of delinquent boys. Wattenberg (1956), in an examination of case files of boy and girl "repeaters," found that in their relations with peers, boys "were more often reported to be active in games, members of gangs and getting in trouble with their gangs. More of the girls quarreled with their peers and were 'lone wolves' " (p. 143). Campbell, in a cogent review of existing female delinquency literature, concludes that "there is a complete absence of any theoretical formulations to explain group delinquency among girls. . . . Most writers on the subject have proceeded from the assumption that delinquent girls are isolates and misfits" (1980, p. 380).

CONCEPTUALIZING FRIENDSHIP

Our goal here is to examine characteristics of the friendships of male *and* female adolescents who vary in the extent of their involvement in delinquent behavior. We begin with two assumptions: (1) Friendship relations are complex social bonds that will likely always be described incompletely with reference to a single dimension or construct such as "attachment" or "importance of friends," and (2) attempting to derive a set of comprehensive and meaningful friendship components exclusively from the delinquency literature would probably be misguided intellectual loyalty. This is so because most of our knowledge of how previous delinquency theorists viewed these relationships must be gleaned from bits and pieces of rather evocative imagery (Konopka's [1966] delinquent girls lost in the crowd, the fraternity atmosphere of Thrasher's [1963] gang boys, the excessive dependence of Cohen's [1955] frustrated lower-class boys) instead of from a comprehensive examination of what these friendships were really like.

The developmental and social-psychological literature offer more fully developed analyses of how friendship is actually experienced by adolescents and of similarities and differences in the friendship styles of males and females. Our own interviews with a wide variety of adolescents were also helpful in pointing us away from "our childhood fantasies" or, worse yet, our own middle-aged perspectives on what youthful friendships are or should be like. In addition to these interviews and the developmental literature, exchange theory provided a useful orienting framework. As Burgess and Huston note, "an explicit look at exchange processes sets the stage for considering the relationship itself—rather than the individuals or the larger system as a unit of analysis" (1979, p. 9). A basic characteristic of adolescent friendships is that they are relatively voluntary.[4] Thus, we need first to consider what the participants get out of the relationship, what they enjoy about it—in short, what are its *rewards*?

Exchange theory also underscores the importance of considering *reciprocal effects* in social interaction. Instead of viewing peer influence as a one-directional process (i.e., the monolithic group pressuring the adolescent to dress in a certain way, use drugs, have intercourse, etc.), this theory considers the actor as both recipient and producer of influence in the group (Burgess and Huston 1979).

Finally, exchange theory has also noted a tendency toward *imbalance* in relationships (Chadwick-Jones 1976). Intimacy should not be equated with the absence of problems or conflict in a relationship, nor should perfect reciprocity be a necessary criterion for friendship.[5] As Rubin suggests, "Children's friendships rarely contain only positive sentiments. Because they involve such extensive contact and interdependence, close friendships invariably give rise to negative feelings as well. . . . Among older children, although friends may be expected to be constantly loyal and supportive, to respect each others' rights

and needs, and to agree on just about everything, such expectations cannot be fulfilled in reality" (1980, pp. 73–74). It is important for us to include some of these presumably negative relational qualities because of the assumption that they would be more typical of delinquent than of more conforming friendship groups.

Next we describe the specific elements of friendship that we derived from our general interest in capturing the reward structure of the groups, their characteristic patterns of interaction and influence, and the vicissitudes or the more problematic aspects of these relationships.

REWARDS

McCall and Simmons (1978) outline three kinds of rewards present in intimate relationships: intrinsic rewards (those rewarding in themselves), extrinsic rewards (those having some value independent of the giver), and a third category, the support of role identities.

Intrinsic rewards. —One of the most basic intrinsic rewards of friendship is the opportunity it provides for conversation and the sharing of confidences, or what has been referred to as *self-disclosure*. Chaikan and Derlega (1976) contend that as interpersonal exchange progresses from superficial to intimate levels, the information exchanged is a "barometer of the state of the relationship" (p. 184). According to Jourard, "the amount of personal information that one is willing to disclose to another appears to be an index of the closeness of the affection, love and trust that prevails between two people" (1971, p. 33). In order to fit the image of having cold and brittle relationships delinquents should be less likely than other adolescents to share privacies with one another. Are they?

---

[4]Kimmel (1974) suggests that reward-cost considerations may be most salient in adolescence, where friendship alliances often shift. In middle and old age, commitment and investment in relationships become more critical and may outweigh reward-cost calculations. But it is incorrect to regard peer affiliations as entirely voluntary. Many adolescents whom we interviewed expressed a desire to change or at least expand their friendships, but for a variety of reasons (especially those concerning the feelings of existing friends) they felt unable to do so.

[5]Although Cicero defined friendship as "a complete accord on all subjects human and divine," few relationships we know would qualify.

In addition, research suggests that females disclose more information and more intimate information than males (Pederson and Higbee 1969; Jourard 1971; Marks and Giordano 1978; but see Davidson, Balswick, and Halverson 1980). But do delinquent girls (also consistent with existing literature) evidence a departure from the generally high self-disclosure rates characteristic of other adolescent females?

Basic feelings of *caring and trust* offer a further index of intimacy. Chadwick-Jones (1976) suggests that trust is an essential element in differentiating social from economic exchange. Following Blau's lead, he also notes how "trust tends to build up gradually through cumulative commitment to a relationship." Bell (1981) found support for this in interviews in which respondents indicated that trust was the most important element in their friendships. It is thus important to gauge the extent to which delinquents may differ from other adolescents on what might be called a basic underpinning of intimate friendships.

Extrinsic rewards. —McCall and Simmons define extrinsic rewards as "events and objects [that] are gratifying to the individual simply because they are useful to him in pursuing his various endeavors. Money, labor, information, material goods, privileges, favors, social status, all these elements and more may be helpful to him in carrying out his various enterprises" (1978, p. 147). Our interviews with adolescents suggest a number of ways in which friends "use" one another, even while they protest that this is not a primary basis of their relationships. We include questions about the extrinsic benefits youths may derive from their friendships in order to emphasize that, in addition to their qualitative characteristics, these friendships also have an agenda or content. Sentiments like caring and trust aside,

a friend is also someone to sit with in the cafeteria, to copy a math problem "off of," or to get the car when you cannot. These types of benefits derived from a relationship afford a somewhat less lofty view of adolescents' connectedness, or interrelatedness. Cohen alludes to the intrinsic/extrinsic rewards distinction in noting that "the working class child [and by inference the delinquent boy] is more dependent emotionally and for the satisfaction of many practical needs upon his relationship to his peer groups" (1955, p. 101). But do delinquent youth derive more and/or different kinds of extrinsic or practical benefits from their friendships than their less delinquent counterparts?

Identity support. —McCall and Simmons suggest that a crucial function in any intimate relationship is that of providing identity support. As symbolic beings, we fancy ourselves in a variety of roles, but it is important that others provide us with enough support to keep up these visions of the roles that we rank highly. This addition to the usual intrinsic-extrinsic rewards distinction is attractive, given the important identity work that occurs during adolescence: "The adolescent is about to crystallize an identity and for this needs others of his generation to act as models, mirrors, helpers, testers, foils" (Douvan and Adelson 1966, p. 179; see also Foot, Chapman, and Smith 1980; Seltzer 1982; or even Thrasher, who notes how "the boy sees himself through the gang's eyes" [1963, p. 207]). Thus a group will be rewarding to the extent that it provides a comfortable arena in which to explore identity concerns. One woman interviewed by Bell nicely summarizes the *self-confirmation* role of friendships: "My friends give me a sense of who I am. They do this by letting me express myself and sort of reflect off of them. What I mean is that I can be whoever I want to be and they let me be me" (1981, p. 15).

Are delinquent youths less likely to believe they receive this kind of identity support from friends than adolescents involved in more conforming peer relationships?

PATTERNS OF INTERACTION AND INFLUENCE

It is important to examine more closely the particular nature and extent of the interactions within friendship networks because these can be taken as additional indexes of interdependence and of the degree to which we can legitimately assign the primary group level to them. They also have an advantage (in terms of measurement) in being grounded more in behavior than in sentiment. A basic feature of interaction is the sheer amount of *time* friends spend in each others' company. Although time is in itself a rather qualitatively neutral index of friendship, it is unlikely that youths who have extremely low rates of interaction have the same kinds of opportunities to experience the rewards of friendship, both tangible and intangible, as those who interact more frequently. Do delinquents spend less time with friends than do other adolescents?[6]

A second characteristic that may differentiate friendship styles is how long the relationships last—their *stability*. This appears to relate directly to the "cold and brittle relationships" argument (presumably, what is brittle is more likely to break). Short and Strodtbeck and even Thrasher have commented on the fluidity and instability of many of the gang affiliations they observed. But should delinquents' friendships be characterized as any more ephemeral than those of less delinquent youth? We would caution here against necessarily regarding greater stability as being inherently somehow more positive, especially during adolescence. Bigelow and LaGaipa (1980) note, for example, that children's friendships are not typically characterized by stability until about the age of 16, and they criticize the use of such words as "breakdown" and "instability" in describing children's friendships as implying an unnecessary value judgment.[7]

A third qualitative characteristic of friends' interaction patterns is defined as the degree to which individuals are affected by their friends in making choices about their own behavior—what is usually called *peer pressure* or influence. We have already discussed the presumed link between intimacy and the possibilities for influence, what Thrasher has called "control through rapport" (1963, p. 209). Are delinquents more likely to feel under pressure from friends, and, considering the reciprocal nature of group influence, are they more, or less, likely to believe that they exert social power in these friendship networks themselves?

---

[6]Cohen (1955) suggests that lower-class youths (and, by inference, delinquents) spend *more* time in each other's company than middle-class youths who are often involved in a more formal and varied agenda (such as clubs or athletics). On this dimension, Hirschi appears to be in agreement. In the course of suggesting that if cohesiveness is defined as mutual attraction or respect, delinquent gangs would be characterized by low cohesiveness, he notes that "if cohesiveness is defined by the frequency or duration of interaction among group members, the 'cohesiveness' of the delinquent gang is no doubt often impressive" (1969, p. 160).

---

[7]Sex differences in stability have also been noted. Bell believes that boys' relationships tend to be more stable and lasting, which he hypothesizes may stem from a lower degree of intensity and hence less chance for conflict. Viewed this way, then, stability is produced by a relative lack of intimacy.

THE VICISSITUDES OF FRIENDSHIP[8]

Roll and Millen (1979) have noted the tendency within the existing literature on friendship to see the world of friendship through rose-colored glasses and "were struck by the absence of any attention paid to the everyday travails of friendship" (1979, p. 259). Other writers have alluded to the fragility and vulnerability of children's friendships (Hartup 1975) or characterized them as "tempestuous and changeable" (Douvan and Adelson 1966), but empirical work has been restricted to their more positive aspects. We need to include attention to the strains and imbalances fostered by intimacy as well as to its more obvious satisfactions. We have included three such problem areas. The first is *conflict*, or the extent to which friends have arguments or disagreements with each other. This dimension also figures in the cold and brittle relationships argument. Empey (1967), for example, points to the practice of sounding (trading insults) in delinquent groups and suggests that "primary groups, ideally are supposed to provide warmth and support. With the constant sounding that goes on it is questionable whether lower-class gangs are conducive to close friendships." It is not clear that conflict is necessarily antithetical to intimacy. Indeed, in our own earlier study of friendships of college students, we found that both degree of contact and comfort with friends were associated with higher levels of disagreement (Marks and Giordano 1978; see also Rubin 1980, p. 74). Moreover, it has not been established empirically that the levels of conflict and discord in delinquent groups are any higher than those found within other adolescent friendship networks.

A second problematic aspect of friendship is *imbalance*, which encompasses a lack of equality or reciprocity in the friendship, as well as feelings of jealousy or competition. As with conflict, there is no a priori reason to believe that imbalanced relationships cannot be rewarding or that participants in such relationships will not influence each other. Reisman (1979), for example, makes the distinction between friendships of reciprocity and friendships of receptivity. He contends that the latter are no less important (especially, of course, to the more dependent participant) as a friendship form than are more perfectly reciprocal relations. Thus, the notion of imbalance simply offers another mechanism through which we can better define the contours of these friendships.

A third problematic aspect of friendships we term *loyalty in the face of trouble*. Thrasher (1963) notes that "loyalty is a universal requirement in the gang, and squealing is probably the worst infraction of the code. . . . Most boys prefer to take a beating rather than stool on their associates" (p. 202). Douvan and Adelson (1966) also found that loyalty was a particularly important component of friendship; boys in particular often defined a friend as "one who will support you when trouble comes" (p. 196). (In their view this usually meant trouble with adult authority, parents, teachers, police, etc.) Are there significant differences between delinquents and other adolescents in the salience of this kind of loyalty?

THE NEED FOR COMPARATIVE DATA

Our research strategy here involves an assessment of the differences in the friendship experiences of youths who represent a broad range of delinquency involvement. However, within this general framework, it is particularly important to examine the extent and nature of sex differences.

---

[8]We borrowed this term from Roll and Millen (1979).

Historically, the female offender has been neglected at both the theoretical and empirical levels, but, nevertheless, highly stereotypical images flourish in the literature. These data will allow us to confront directly the image of the female delinquent as a lonely and asocial misfit.

We also see a real need to compare the friendship experiences of black with those of white adolescents, in general and in relation to delinquency involvement. The delinquency literature has not often tackled race differences (as evidenced by the sheer volume of studies that exclude all minorities from the analysis). Studies that do include attention to race have primarily been outcome oriented (more interested in the differences or similarities in *rates* of delinquency involvement by racial category than in the processes leading to those outcomes). The friendship literature is also surprisingly weak in this area. Most of the research studies on adolescent friendships have used samples of whites or, if they have included race, have emphasized the nature and dynamics of cross- versus same-race interactions and friendships, particularly in the school setting (Singleton and Asher 1979). While this interest no doubt stems from concerns about school desegregation and interracial acceptance, the fact that most friendships tend to be intraracial suggests the need for more work on the everyday social networks of black (as well as white) youths and on the ways in which these friendship patterns link up to other behaviors (including but not limited to that of delinquency involvement). (See Kleinman and Lukoff [1978], who also see a need for this kind of analysis.)

THE SAMPLE

The data for this study were derived from personal interviews conducted in 1982 with a sample (*N* = 942) of all youth 12–19 years of age living in private households in a large north central SMSA. A multistage modified probability sampling procedure was employed, in which area segments were selected with known probability. Census data were used to stratify by racial composition and average housing value. Within segments, eligible households and respondents were selected to fill specified sex and race quotas. The respondents were equally divided among males and females, blacks and whites, and lower/middle socioeconomic status respondents. This sampling strategy reflects our interest in simultaneously examining differences in friendship patterns based on ethnicity and gender as well as in delinquency involvement.[9]

THE MEASURES

Our data come from respondents' own perceptions of the nature and characteristics of their relationships instead of from direct observations of friendship networks (the methodological strategy that was more typically employed in much of the early gang research). Either methodology involves "letting go" of potentially important data. Direct observation can most effectively capture the dynamic element of interactions and/or relationships, and it can provide a richer contextual base from which to understand group life. Observational strategies also allow the researcher to check on whether the verbal descriptions youth offer in an interview setting correspond to the reality of their ongoing friendship relations. This discrepancy is perhaps most beautifully illustrated in Liebow's (1967) discussion of friendships on Tally's corner. Although the neighborhood men accorded

---

[9] For further details regarding sampling procedures, see Cernkovich, Giordano, and Pugh (1983).

great importance to their friendships, Liebow observed and documented how certain harsh realities, economic and otherwise, often intruded on their more idealistic perceptions of intimacy.

But the interview approach also has some important advantages. In this research, we are most interested in how youths experience the rewards and vicissitudes of friendship. Some aspects of this must be viewed as subjectively experienced or determined (and to remove all the subjective elements from analysis would represent another kind of distortion). Thus, the adolescents themselves (and not outside observers) are particularly well placed to determine whether they have the trust of their friends, can be themselves in their presence, or sometimes feel left out or marginal.

Some of our other dimensions do have a more objective base. Here we have tried to avoid the global and socially desirable in favor of the specific and, wherever possible, the behavioral (e.g., a question such as "How often do you speak with your friends about the following subjects . . .?" is preferable to "Do you feel that you and your friends can truly communicate with one another?"). Another general strategy has been to include specific attention to the more problematic aspects of relationships—conflicts, jealousy, and the like. The assumption that such problems are common to all relationships should also have the effect of moving respondents off the socially desirable "my friendships are perfect" response set.

Another advantage of this procedure is that it facilitates the kinds of comparisons that are much needed in theory development in criminology. Liebow, for example, observed a small group of lower-class black men living in a particular section of Boston. We do not know very much

about the friendships of the women of Tally's corner, except in relation to each of the men. Neither do we know whether the kind of intimacy that Liebow observed, the levels of conflict, or even the discrepancies (between their ideal and real friendship patterns) would not also be found in more middle-class settings. Our sample size and characteristics allow us to specify the nature of similarities and differences by level of delinquency involvement without bracketing off the possible effects of sex and/or race-ethnicity.

The specific friendship items included in our final interview schedule were developed from unstructured interviews over a 14-year period with a variety of adolescent males and females. Interviews were conducted with youths who ranged in age from sixth graders through high school students, who varied in terms of delinquency involvement, location in the school prestige hierarchy, race, socioeconomic status, and so forth. Interviews were also conducted with institutionalized females and with youths on probation. In addition to these individual interviews, discussions were held with small groups of adolescent friend networks. These small groups served also as consultants throughout the period of developing the more structured interview schedule.

Another source of items was a pool of essays by high school and college students who wrote about things that they liked and disliked about their friends. An earlier study by Marks and Giordano (1978) and the developmental and delinquency literature were also sources for item development. A factor analysis of all the pooled items resulted in 13 distinct dimensions of friendship (see App. A for a complete list of the items that compose each scale). In addition to these qualitative dimensions, youths were asked about the *background characteristics* of their friends. At the beginning of each interview, the respondent provided interviewers with a list of names (first names, nicknames, or initials, to assure anonymity) of the group of friends they usually hang around with.[10] Respondents indicated whether each person listed was male or female and whether most of their friends were either older, about the same age, or younger than themselves. These background variables were included primarily as a check to determine whether there were basic differences in the composition of their friendship groups that might have influenced the qualitative characteristics we have outlined.

Delinquency involvement was measured by a 27-item self-report instrument that is a revised version of that used by Elliott et al. (1982). It contains a broad range of items that include minor as well as major offenses. However, we avoided the use of summated scale scores as the measure of delinquency involvement because of the wide range of seriousness captured by the items (with such a method youths who score in the high-frequency range on status or other nonserious offenses would have been equated with youths who have committed serious felonies). Instead, we developed a categorical offender typology that takes into account the dimensions of both

frequency and seriousness. Five offender categories were defined as follows: (1) *Nonoffenders* are youths who have committed no more than one or two minor offenses and no major offenses during the past year. Minor offenses were defined as behaviors that would usually be treated as a misdemeanor (e.g., running away, petty theft, disorderly conduct), whereas major offenses were defined as those behaviors that would be treated ordinarily as felonies (e.g., grand theft, aggravated assault, breaking and entering). (2) *Low-frequency minor offenders* are youth who scored relatively low (under the median) on the minor offense scale and indicated they had committed no major offenses during the preceding year. (3) *High-frequency minor offenders* have a score above the median on the minor offense scale but admit no involvement in major offenses. (4) *Low-frequency major offenders* had a score below the median on the major offense scale. (5) *High-frequency major offenders* were defined as those who had a score above the median on the major offense scale.

For our purposes here, it is appropriate to consider 1 as the most conforming group, with a gradual increase in level of delinquency involvement to 5, which is the highest level of involvement. For example, although category 5 is defined solely on the basis of participation in serious offenses, we know that the majority of youths in this group have also participated in a wide range of nonserious or status offenses as well. (App. B presents the distribution of offender categories by race and sex.)

FINDINGS

Tables 1–3 present three-way analyses of variance for each of the components of friendship by sex, race, and level of

---

[10]We adopted this strategy instead of focusing on other social units (such as the best friends' dyad or the gang), because we are interested in the context in which most of the respondent's social activity actually takes place. Although restricting attention to the dyad has some methodological advantages (see Kandel 1980), it minimizes the role of the larger group and one's place in it. Also, the gang may be highly visible, but even gang members spend much of their time in smaller networks (see Short and Strodtbeck 1965). Differences between our findings and those of earlier researchers could reflect at least in part the use of this unit of analysis, whose size is essentially determined by the respondent.

delinquency involvement.[11] Because of the potential for age differences even within the period of adolescence (see, e.g., Honess 1979; Bigelow and LaGaipa 1980; Mannarino 1980; Sharabany, Gershoni, and Hofman 1981), age is controlled as a covariate.[12]

THE REWARDS OF FRIENDSHIP

Table 1 presents mean scores as well as *F*-values for the major comparison groups as they relate to the intrinsic, extrinsic, and identity support rewards of friendship.

The two intrinsic rewards scales— self-disclosure and, more particularly, caring and trust—are most relevant to the cold and brittle relationships argument. Contrary to what control theory would predict, there were no significant differences across increasing levels of delinquency involvement in the extent to which respondents believe their relationships contain these elements of caring and trust.

Although there was a significant difference in self-disclosure rates, it reflects a slightly *lower* self-disclosure rate among the least delinquent category, the nonoffenders. Sex differences on these scales are more pronounced. Females are much more likely to self-disclose in intimate ways and to characterize their friendships as consisting of caring and trust than are males.[13] It is important to underscore the lack of interaction between sex and delinquency in

these respects: There were no significant differences among females in rates of caring and trust across the five levels of delinquency, and females at almost every level of delinquency (except black females in the low-frequency minor offender category) are more intimate than are males at a similar level of delinquency involvement.

In addition to these sex differences, a significant main effect for race was obtained: Whites in our sample scored significantly higher on the caring and trust scale than did blacks.

The analysis of covariance of extrinsic rewards revealed, as expected, that youth in the more highly delinquent categories are much more likely to say that they reap certain tangibles from their relationship than are less delinquent youth. (This is one dimension that obviously did not escape our general desire to be independent of delinquency involvement.) What is perhaps more revealing is that there was no significant difference across delinquency levels in the extent to which youths discussed or related to each other on school matters (although the mean scores are somewhat lower for the major offender categories, this difference is not significant). This suggests that, although such youths may not be as school oriented or successful as nondelinquents, youths who do engage in delinquency have not abandoned the concerns of school altogether. Interestingly, more delinquent youth also scored higher on the status-striving scale, which indexed the degree to which they received certain rather adult-oriented benefits from their friendships (e.g., discussions of job plans for the future, help in meeting members of the opposite sex, etc.).[14]

---

[11]Separate analyses of variance revealed no significant differences across levels of delinquency involvement in youths' descriptions of their groups' basic structural features, such as size, age, and sex composition. Thus, any qualitative differences found should represent more than a simple artifact of the structural makeup of these groups.

[12]For a discussion of age differences in friendship processes using the present data, see Kinney (1984).

[13]There is also a race by sex interaction for the self-disclosure scale, produced primarily by the particularly high scores of white females.

---

[14]There is a three-way interaction on the status-striving scale, the result primarily of the higher scores of black male delinquents.

TABLE 1:   Friendship Rewards by Sex, Race, and Level of Delinquency Involvement (Age Controlled)

Independent Variable	Intrinsic Rewards				Extrinsic Rewards						Identity Support	
	Self-Disclosure[a]		Caring and Trust		Tangibles		School		Status Striving[b]		Self-Confirmation[c]	
	Mean	F	Mean	F	Mean	F	Mean	F	Mean	F	Mean	F
Sex:												
Female	3.04	17.15***	4.03	38.00***	1.61	1.85	3.42	32.38***	2.82	8.20**	1.89	
6.60**												
Male	2.82		3.72		1.71		3.09		3.02		2.08	
Race:												
Black	2.90	1.44	3.76	23.80***	1.60	7.28**	3.24	.53	2.94	.61	2.03	1.58
White	2.97		4.02		1.72		3.28		2.89		1.93	
Level of delinquency:												
1. Nonoffender	2.68	3.71**	3.75	1.14	1.27	21.73***	3.34	.59	2.62	5.04***	2.02	.54
2. Low-frequency minor	2.98		3.88		1.51		3.30		2.94		2.04	
3. High-frequency minor	2.97		3.98		1.74		3.29		2.85		1.91	
4. Low-frequency major	2.90		3.85		1.77		3.14		3.04		1.91	
5. High-frequency major	3.08		3.88		2.09		3.18		3.13		2.04	

[a] Sex-by-race interaction ($F = 12.49$).***

[b] Sex-by-race by delinquency interaction ($F = 2.49$).*

[c] Race-by-delinquency interaction ($F = 2.55$).* A higher mean score indicates greater agreement that "they can't be themselves with friends."

* $P < .05$.

** $P < .01$.

*** $P < .001$.

TABLE 2: Patterns of Interaction and Influence by Sex, Race, and Level of Delinquency Involvement (Age Controlled)

| | Level of Contact[a] | | Stability | | PEER INFLUENCE | | | |
| | | | | | (Group → Actor) | | (Actor → Group) | |
Independent Variable	Mean	F	Mean	F	Mean	F	Mean	F
Sex:								
Female	3.21	16.90***	5.09	5.53*	2.54	7.81**	2.42	3.08
Male	3.03		5.66		2.71		2.60	
Race:								
Black	3.08	3.75	5.82	15.80***	2.52	19.80***	2.55	2.50
White	3.18		4.85		2.74		2.46	
Level of delinquency:								
1. Nonoffender	3.00	1.78	4.75	.54	2.43	6.03***	2.15	9.77***
2. Low-frequency minor	3.15		5.54		2.58		2.41	
3. High-frequency minor	3.17		5.42		2.66		2.48	
4. Low-frequency major	3.10		5.52		2.64		2.75	
5. High-frequency major	3.18		5.37		2.83		2.82	

[a]Delinquency-by-sex interaction ($F = 3.10$).*

* $P < .05$.
** $P < .01$.
*** $P < .001$.

TABLE 3: Vicissitudes of Friendship by Sex, Race, and Level of Delinquency Involvement (Age Controlled)

Independent Variable	Conflict		Imbalance		Loyalty in the Face of Trouble[a]	
	Mean	F	Mean	F	Mean	F
Sex:						
Female..........	2.41	5.50*	2.55	10.17***	3.28	4.85*
Male..........	2.73		2.71		3.14	
Race:						
Black..........	2.58	.35	2.62	.46	3.35	42.91***
White..........	2.54		2.64		3.06	
Level of delinquency:						
1. Nonoffender..........	2.10	5.26***	2.50	3.36*	3.58	20.43***
2. Low-frequency minor..........	2.53		2.71		3.35	
3. High-frequency major..........	2.61		2.55		3.13	
4. Low-frequency major..........	2.69		2.64		3.02	
5. High-frequency major..........	2.90		2.72		2.93	

[a]Delinquency-by-race interaction ($F = 5.15$).*** A higher score reflects a greater likelihood that the respondent would drop friends if they were headed for trouble or would be unlikely to lie to protect them (i.e., the higher the score, the less loyal).

* $P < .05$.
** $P < .01$.
*** $P < .001$.

With regard to sex and race differences, the only main effect for race occurred in the area of tangible rewards, where whites were more likely to agree that their friends helped them. Sex differences in the analysis of extrinsic rewards consisted of a much higher score for females in the extent to which they discussed and relied on friends for school-related matters and a significantly higher score by males on the status-striving scale. The lack of any significant difference by gender on the tangibles scale should not be overlooked: females indicated that they are about as likely as males to get drugs or alcohol from friends, to hang out at a friend's house when parents are gone, and so on. Although females as a group are not as delinquent as males, these responses do point to a relatively greater degree of participation by girls and their friends in what are usually considered "hedonistic/youth culture activities" than is generally assumed.

In the extent to which respondents felt a lack of identity support (felt that they couldn't be themselves within their friendship groups) there were no significant differences across levels of delinquency involvement. That is, more delinquent youths believe that they enjoy the rewards of self-confirmation within friendships about as much as less delinquent adolescents do. Similarly, there were no main effects for race; however, as a subgroup, males were significantly more likely to believe that they couldn't be themselves while with their group.[15]

PATTERNS OF INTERACTION AND INFLUENCE

As table 2 suggests, there were no significant differences across delinquency levels in the frequency of reported interaction with friends. Females do report higher levels of contact; however, this difference is in large part attributable to their much higher rates of "talking on the phone with friends."[16] Although the relationships of delinquents have often been described as tenuous and unstable, we find no significant differences across delinquency levels in the length of time respondents reported being friends. On the other hand, main effects were found for both race and sex. Consistent with Bell's (1981) research, males reported that they had been friends for somewhat longer average times. In addition, the friendships of blacks were found to be significantly more stable than those of white youths.

In general, the findings reported above suggest a lack of significant differences across many qualitative indexes in the ways in which youths who vary significantly in delinquency involvement describe the levels of intimacy and interaction within their friendship groups. However, delinquent youth did report higher levels of susceptibility to peer influence than did their less delinquent counterparts (See table 2). A higher level of susceptibility was also reported by whites and males in our sample.

In addition to reporting a significantly greater level of susceptibility to peer influence, we also obtained an interesting main effect for the reciprocal peer influence measure. Delinquents were significantly more

---

[15]A significant delinquency-by-race interaction is produced by the somewhat higher agreement of blacks with a higher delinquency score.

[16]There is also a significant sex-by-delinquency interaction, which is produced by the relatively low contact scores of nonoffender males.

likely to believe that they "often pressured their friends to behave in certain ways" than were the less delinquent youths. Males were also slightly more likely to believe that they exerted social power, as were blacks, but these differences were not significant.

THE VICISSITUDES OF FRIENDSHIP

Regarding the extent to which disagreement or conflicts were found in these friendships (see table 3), there was a significant main effect for delinquency: delinquent youths reported higher levels of disagreement than did less delinquent adolescents. Males also reported significantly higher levels of conflict, whereas there were no differences in conflict levels reported by black in contrast to those reported by white adolescents.

In addition, there was a significant difference by delinquency in the scale indexing feelings of imbalance (as well as jealousy and competition in the group), but the means do not form a simple linear pattern. There were no main effects for race, but males were more likely as a group to experience these feelings.

Finally, the more delinquent youths, not unexpectedly, believed that they would be more loyal to their friends in the face of trouble. (This is another scale in which the findings should not be altogether surprising, given the likelihood that delinquents may have had more previous experience with trouble, lying to police, etc.). On the other hand, blacks, as well as females, scored somewhat lower on these items; indicating they would be less likely either to stick by friends heading for trouble or lie to protect them.[17]

---

[17]A significant delinquency-by-race interaction is the result of the higher loyalty scores of white delinquents.

DISCUSSION AND CONCLUSION

In this article, we have developed several dimensions along which to make basic comparisons of the qualities and behaviors that characterize adolescents' friendships. The factor analysis of all the pooled friendship items corroborated our suspicion that it is impossible to capture the essence of these relationships using a single attached-unattached, or positive-negative, dimension. Nevertheless, these friendship components have allowed us to examine the validity of many of the images about delinquents' relationships that have emerged from our major delinquency theories.

The data present a picture more complex than that provided by control theorists, who have depicted the friendships of delinquents as "exploitive rather than warm and supportive" (Empey 1982, p. 273) or, alternatively, by earlier subcultural theorists who may have idealized the gang as a noble fraternity characterized only by camaraderie and we-feeling. Overall, we find that youths who are very different in their levels of involvement in delinquency are nevertheless quite similar in the ways in which they view their friendship relations. There were no differences in the average length of time respondents reported being friends (stability) or in the ongoing frequency of their interactions (contact). Delinquents were somewhat more likely than their less delinquent counterparts to share privacies with one another (self-disclosure) and were about as likely to believe that they can "be themselves" while in the company of these friends (self-confirmation). Contrary to the central assertion of the cold and brittle relationships argument, delinquents were no less likely than others to believe that they have the trust of friends and that these friends "really care about them and what happens to them."

At the same time, delinquents did report significantly higher levels of disagreements (conflict) with friends. This finding is important in a methodological sense, in that it demonstrates that the delinquent respondents (as well as other subgroups, including males, who score higher on conflict) are capable of perceiving and describing their relationships in a relatively complicated way instead of adapting a uniformly positive or negative response set. That these adolescents are willing to talk about some negative aspects of their relationships gives added weight to the validity of their more positive responses. But beyond this methodological note, what meaning should be attached to these conflict scores? One interpretation is that these responses represent at least partial support for the control theory conception of delinquent friendships. But there is an alternative explanation. Viewed in the contexts of the levels of contact, self-disclosure, and caring and trust already reported, the somewhat higher conflict levels may be taken as additional indicators of intimacy and the importance of the friendships to these youths. A more neutral conclusion is that these results simply reflect a different friendship style that should not be viewed as either positive (attached) or negative (cold and brittle). Another difference in style is reflected in the greater emphasis on loyalty in responses of the more delinquent youths. A stronger belief in such values as lying to protect friends may be based more on their greater familiarity with such situations than on a particularly deep fraternal bond or code (à la Thrasher).

An examination of what we might call the interactive content of the friendships also reveals a mixed pattern. Delinquents indicated that they were more likely to reap certain tangible as well as social (status-striving) extrinsic benefits from their friends, but there were no significant differences found for the extrinsic rewards scale measuring school concerns. The higher scores on two extrinsic rewards scales do not indicate that delinquents' relations are inherently more important (or extrinsic) than are those of less delinquent youth. We obviously did not exhaust the list of all the extrinsic rewards youth might derive from friends. But taken together, the scores of delinquent youth on *both* intrinsic and extrinsic factors suggest that delinquents, at least as much as other adolescents, derive a variety of significant benefits from their friendship relations.

On the basis of these findings, we would reverse Hirschi's previously quoted statement concerning the link between attachment and influence. It is reasonable to conclude that when adolescent friendships are relatively warm and intimate and provide some combination of intrinsic, extrinsic, and identity support functions for the participants, actors are likely to exert considerable influence upon each other. An examination of the pattern of responses of group 1 (the nonoffenders) is illustrative. On almost every dimension, members of this most conforming group are least attached to friends. Generally, they have the lowest levels of interaction, the lowest levels of caring and trust, the lowest rates of self-disclosure; also, they are the least likely to admit to the group's influence on their own behavior. In contrast, the more delinquent groups are more likely to believe that they may be influenced by friends and that they exert considerable influence on the group. This finding is important, in that it suggests a pattern of mutual reinforcement within these groups rather than a one-way influence process. The control theory conception of peer attachment may have emerged largely as a reaction against the earlier image of the delinquent group as being all powerful in its effects. The individual actor seemed to be a passive agent who, on entering the group, took on its attitudes and values.

The findings presented here are consistent with the contention of control theory that individuals may bring certain delinquent values to the group at the outset. This would explain youths' responding that they often pressure their friends, as well as the reverse. Although we have not dealt directly with the important issue of what causes the initial attraction to the delinquent or any group, most of the developmental/friendship literature favors the concept of a similarity in values (value homophily) preceding entrance into the friendship. But we believe with Kandel (1980) that there are important processes that continue to work once the individuals have been drawn together; elements of mutual reinforcement and influence that strengthen delinquent patterns beyond what would be expected from their initial values. As Hirschi himself concludes, "there are group processes important in the causation of delinquency whose automatic operation cannot be predicted from the characteristics of persons" (1969, p. 230). This attempt to modify his earlier position about the role of peers is not linked to control theory or quoted as often as are his data that empirically demonstrated a lack of attachment in delinquent friendships. The data presented here seriously contradict the lack-of-attachment thesis. Other contributions of control theory (namely, the view that important processes such as family attachment precede the group's influence) might be integrated with the somewhat more complicated images of the delinquent and his friends that emerge from this study.

SEX DIFFERENCES

It is important to view even the significant differences across delinquency categories against the often more dramatic variations in friendship style and influence attributable to the basic demographic variable of sex. The experiences associated with gender in our society appear to frame the style and content of friendships. *Females, regardless* of their level of involvement in *delinquency*, are likely to be involved in *more intimate* relationships. In addition to casting doubt generally on the cold and brittle relationships argument, these data also question the image of the female delinquent as a lonely and asocial misfit, unable to establish adequate peer relations. The similar or generally higher scores of females on these friendship dimensions also call into question a popular explanation for the overall gender differences in criminality, namely, that females are not as peer oriented as are their male counterparts: "Sutherland maintains that most criminal behavior is learned within intimate personal groups. . . . The family has traditionally been the group with which females are most intimately connected, even during adolescence. They are also likely to be more carefully supervised within the family. If crime is learned within intimate personal groups, and for most females the crucial primary group is a restrictive family, they are much less likely to learn criminal behavior" (Leonard 1982, p. 107).

The data here (and in other developmental studies) would lead us to suggest that the statement above somewhat oversimplifies the importance of peer friendships to adolescent girls. Females spend as much (if not more, counting phone conversations) time in the company of their friends as do males. They reap many rewards, both intrinsic and extrinsic, from these friendships. Therefore, rather than discount their peer involvements, we must discover more about the differential dynamics within these networks that seem to amplify delinquency in the case of boys but generally inhibit it among girls (but not always, because some girls do develop delinquent patterns). These data offer some clues. It will be recalled that males as a group were more likely to believe that friends exerted a variety of pressures on them; their conflict scores were also higher. If we conceive of delinquent acts as a set of behaviors requiring some risk taking or daring—that is, some sort of push (Short and Strodtbeck 1965)—it may be that the friendship styles of males are most conducive to the kind of group processes that move individual members to the point of collective action. In contrast, females are less likely to indicate that these overt pressures and conflicts characterize their relationships. These differences in the norms governing appropriate friendship style may serve to inhibit delinquency among females even in the presence of other factors that might otherwise promote it (e.g., poor family relations, economic marginality, contact with delinquent opportunities, and the like). Females who do become involved in delinquent acts, then, would have to adopt both a set of attitudes in which they saw delinquency as appropriate, possible, or desirable behavior (Harris 1977; Giordano 1978) and a friendship style in which they would encourage each other as a group to act on these orientations.

RACE DIFFERENCES

Variations in the friendship patterns of black and white respondents also suggest the possibility of ethnic differences in the role of group processes in the etiology of delinquent behavior. At the risk of oversimplification, we would describe the responses of *blacks* as being *similar* in many ways to those of *whites* but also as reflecting a *less intense friendship style*. That is, blacks were less likely to believe that their friends pressured them to behave in certain ways, they were less likely to believe that they would lie to protect friends, and they scored significantly lower on the caring and trust scale. At the same time, their friendships had greater average stability than those of whites. As noted previously, there is very little literature examining the friendship patterns of black adolescents, but what we have found appears consistent with these findings. Berg and Medrich (1977) observed friendship patterns in a predominantly black low-income neighborhood and in an affluent white neighborhood. They found friendships in the former to be less exclusive and more spontaneous than those of the white youths. Iscoe and Harvey (1964) found that black youths were less likely to respond (in an experimental setting) to peer pressure on a task that involved counting a metronome click than were whites. They also found that the peak age at conformity occurred almost three years earlier for black than for white subjects. Finally, Billy and Udry (1983), in a study of factors affecting sexual behavior, found that among whites there was a more direct relationship between the sexual intercourse behavior of same-sex friends and respondents than for blacks in their sample. These few findings suggest the need to develop more refined theories that take into account differences in the salience of friendships and in the style of being friends for black in contrast to white youth. Our speculation is that, even though delinquent acts might be equally likely to occur within a group context, peer pressure will play a more direct role in the delinquency of white than in that of black adolescents. However, more interview-observational data on the specific situational and social contingencies that produce delinquent action among blacks, in comparison with whites or other ethnic groups (as well as for males in contrast to females), is obviously needed.

TOWARD A SOCIOLOGY OF NERDS

Another line of research suggested by the present study is a more systematic follow-up of the adolescents who really can be classified as loners and misfits within the adolescent stratification system. We have shown here that delinquents appear to be fairly successful in negotiating and maintaining a set of social relationships (even if, as Sherif and Sherif [1964] note, it makes some people uncomfortable to think that "antisocial" people can actually be quite social). However, more research needs to be focused on those youths who score very low on these or similar friendship dimensions. We need to know a great deal more about the social (as opposed to purely clinical or psychological) factors that give rise to being considered marginal or, worse, being ignored entirely. Following from this, we need to assess the consequences of this lack of peer support particularly as it may be connected with emotional distress or illness. We would hypothesize that these outcomes are more likely results of poor peer adjustment than is delinquency involvement.[18]

APPENDIX A

DIMENSIONS OF FRIENDSHIP

The factor analysis of all the pooled items yielded the following dimensions, each with a simple factorial complexity.

1. Intrinsic rewards
   (a) Self-disclosure: How often do you talk to your friends about the following things? Questions or problems about sex; how your parents treat you; whether your parents understand you; things you have done about which you feel guilty (a revised version of West and Zingle's [1969] self-disclosure scale, for use with adolescent samples).
   (b) Caring/trust: "I feel comfortable calling my friends when I have a problem; I can trust them—I can tell them private things and know they won't tell other people; they care about me and what happens to me; they're easy to talk to."

2. Extrinsic rewards

   Because extrinsic rewards, almost by definition, have a content and are not value free, we attempted in the original extrinsic rewards scale to include a wide range—from the more pro-social ("They help me with my school work") to the more antisocial ("They get drugs for me"). Other items were

---

[18]Terms used by adolescents to refer to these marginal youth, along with their own descriptions of who belongs in these categories offer a glimpse into the potentially devastating consequences for individuals so labeled. Terms include: wastes or waste products, glugs, grimers, dirt balls ("didn't do drugs or alcohol but should have"), scum, trashheads, grubbers, nobodies ("they stay out of everyone's way"); speds ("the special education students—they can be found helping the janitor in the cafeteria"); queers ("nonathletic males with wimpy bodies who are not into partying"); the bores ("they make high grades, go to school dances, wear drab clothes, are usually ugly

and just kind of there"); nerds ("don't dress in style, scummy looking, no one knows who they are, they don't know what alcohol and drugs are"); loners ("people who don't have any friends at all, just faces"); losers ("they just don't fit in anywhere. But people don't physically abuse them. Mostly they like to intimidate them and make fun of them while kiddingly trying to be their friend to impress other students"); "we never bothered to give them a name; they were just left completely alone" (these descriptions were taken from diagrams made by undergraduates who were asked to depict the stratification systems within their high schools).

more neutral in that both delinquent and nondelinquent youth might, e.g., "talk about problems at school." The factor analysis resulted in three distinct clusters of rewards:

(a) Tangibles: "They get a car for us to use; they get booze for me; they get drugs for me; when their parents go out, we hang out at their house."

(b) Help with school: This includes how often respondent talks with friends about how well he or she gets along with his or her teachers; how often respondent talks with friends about problems he or she has at school, and how often friends help with schoolwork.

(c) Status striving: This includes how often respondent talks with friends about job plans for the future, gets their help in meeting people to date, feels that people look up to him more because of his

3. Identity support
   (a) Self-confirmation: "I can't really be myself if I want to stay friends with these people."

4. Patterns of Interaction
   (a) Contact: How often during the week do you spend time with your friends other than at school? How often during the week do you speak to your friends on the telephone?
   (b) Stability: In general, how many years have you been friends with most of these people?
   (c) Peer influence (group ? actor): Sometimes people are influenced by their friends as to how they act and think about things. Please tell me the number on this card that indicates how much you agree or disagree with each of these statements: I sometimes do things because my close friends are doing them; I

sometimes do things because that's what the popular kids in school are into; I sometimes do things so my friends won't think I'm chicken; I sometimes do things because my friends give me a hard time or hassle me until I do them; I sometimes do things so my friends won't think I'm immature; I don't like being different or sticking out in a crowd so I sometimes go along with things for that reason; I sometimes do things not because my friends pressure me but just because I think it will impress them; I sometimes do things because I don't want to lose the respect of my friends.

(d) Peer influence (actor ? group): "I probably pressure my friends to do things more than they pressure me; I sometimes talk my friends into doing things they really don't want to do."

5. The vicissitudes of friendship
   (a) Conflict: How often do you have disagreements or arguments with your friends? How often do you purposely not talk to your friends because you are mad at them?
   (b) Imbalance: "Sometimes they just won't listen to me or my opinion." "I think I like most of the people in my group more than they like me." "Some people in the group are always trying to impress people outside our group." "There is too much competition in the group." "There is too much jealousy in the group."
   (c) Loyalty/trouble: If you found that your group of friends was leading you into trouble, would you still hang around with them? If your friends got into trouble with the police, would you be willing to lie to protect them? (Minor, n.d.)

TABLE 1: Distribution of Offender Categories by Race and Sex (*N* = 884)

	Nonoffender (1)	Low-Frequency Status Offender (2)	High-Frequency Status Offender (3)	Low-Frequency Major Offender (4)	High-Frequency Major Offender (5)	Total (6)
Males:						
White..............	20	47	39	54	36	196
Nonwhite..........	28	74	49	41	41	233
Females:						
White..............	34	67	70	30	16	217
Nonwhite..........	48	78	48	38	26	238
Total..............	130	266	206	163	119	884

Note.—Because of their relatively small number, minorities other than blacks have been excluded from the present analysis.

References

Bell, Robert R. 1981. *Worlds of Friendship*. Beverly Hills, Calif.: Sage.

Berg, Mary, and Elliott A. Medrich. 1977. "Children in Five Neighborhoods." Report by the Children's Time Study, School of Law, University of California, Berkeley.

Bigelow, Brian J., and John J. LaGaipa. 1980. "The Development of Friendship Values and Choices." Pp. 15–44 in Foot, Chapman, and Smith, eds.

Billy, O.J., and Richard Udry. 1983. "Patterns of Adolescent Friendship and Effects on Sexual Behavior." Paper presented at the annual meeting of the American Sociological Association, Detroit.

Bowker, Lee H., H. S. Gross, and Malcolm W. Klein. 1980. "Female Participation in Delinquent Gang Activities." *Adolescence* 15 (59): 509–19.

Burgess, R. L., and T. L. Huston, eds. 1979. *Social Exchange in Developing Relationships*. New York: Academic Press.

Campbell, Anne C. 1980. "Friendship as a Factor in Male and Female Delinquency." Pp. 365–89 in Foot, Chapman, and Smith, eds.

Cernkovich, Stephen A., Peggy C. Giordano, and Meredith D. Pugh. 1983. "Serious Chronic Offenders: The Missing Cases in Self-Report Measures of Delinquency." Paper presented at the annual meeting of the American Society of Criminology, Denver.

Chadwick-Jones, J. K. 1976. *Social Exchange Theory: Its Structure and Influence in Social Psychology*. New York: Academic Press.

Chaikan, Alan L., and Valerian Derlega. 1976. "Self-Disclosure." In *Contemporary Topics in Social Psychology*, edited by John H. Thibaut, Janet Spencer, and Robert Carson. Englewood Cliffs, N.J.: General Learning Press.

Cohen, Albert K. 1955. *Delinquent Boys*. New York: Free Press.

Davidson, Bernard, Jack O. Balswick, and Charles F. Halverson. 1980. "Factor Analysis of Self-Disclosure for Adolescents." *Adolescence* 15 (60): 947–57.

Douvan, Elizabeth, and Joseph Adelson. 1966. *The Adolescent Experience*. New York: Wiley.

Elliott, Delbert S., David Huizinga, and Suzanne S. Ageton. 1982. "Explaining Delinquency and Drug Use." National Youth Survey Project Report no. 21. Boulder, Colo.: Behavioral Research Institute.

Empey, LaMar T. 1967. "Delinquency Theory and Recent Research." *Journal of Research in Crime and Delinquency* 4:28–42.

———. 1982. *American Delinquency: Its Meaning and Construction*. Homewood, Ill.: Dorsey.

Foot, Hugh C., Antony J. Chapman, and Jean R. Smith, eds. 1980. *Friendship and Social Relations in Children*. New York: Wiley.

Giordano, Peggy C. 1978. "Girls, Guys and Gangs: The Changing Social Context of Female Delinquency." *Journal of Criminal Law and Criminology* 69 (1): 126–32.

———. 1983. "Sanctioning the High Status Deviant: An Attributional Analysis." *Social Psychology Quarterly* 46 (4): 329–42.

Glaser, Daniel. 1956. "Criminality Theories and Behavioral Images." *American Journal of Sociology* 61 (March): 433–44.

Harris, Anthony. 1977. "Sex and Theories of Deviance: Toward a Functional Theory of Deviant Type-Scripts." *American Sociological Review* 42:3–15.

Hartup, W. W. 1975. "The Origins of Friendship." In *Friendship and Peer Relations*, edited by M. Lewis and L. A. Rosenblum. New York: Wiley.

———. 1983. "Peer Relations." Pp. 1–282 in *Carmichael's Manual of Child Psychology*, 4th ed., vol. 4. Edited by P. H. Mussen and E. M. Hetherington. New York: Wiley.

Hirschi, Travis. 1969. *Causes of Delinquency*. Berkeley: University of California Press.

Honess, Terry. 1979. "Children's Implicit Theories of Their Peers: A Developmental Analysis." *British Journal of Psychology* 70:417–24.

Iscoe, I., M. Williams, and J. Harvey. 1964. "Age, Intelligence, and Sex as Variables in the Conformity Behavior of Negro and White Children." *Child Development* 35:451–60.

Jensen, Gary F. 1972. "Parents, Peers, and Delinquent Action: A Test of the Differential Association Perspective." *American Journal of Sociology* 78:562–75.

Jourard, Sidney M. 1971. *Self-Disclosure: An Experimental Analysis of the Transparent Self*. New York: Wiley Interscience.

Kandel, Denise. 1980. "Drug and Drinking Behavior among Youth." *Annual Review of Sociology* 6:235–85.

Kimmel, D. C. 1974. *Adulthood and Aging: An Interdisciplinary, Developmental View*. New York: Wiley.

Kinney, David. 1984. "Adolescent Peer Influence: A Multidimensional Approach." M.A. thesis, Bowling Green State University, Bowling Green, Ohio.

Klein, Malcolm W., and Lois Y. Crawford. 1967. "Groups, Gangs and Cohesiveness." *Journal of Research in Crime and Delinquency* 4:63–75.

Kleinman, Paul H., and Irving F. Lukoff. 1978. "Ethnic Differences in Factors Related to Drug Use." *Journal of Health and Social Behavior* 19:190–99.

Konopka, Gisela. 1966. *The Adolescent Girl in Conflict*. Englewood Cliffs, N.J.: Prentice-Hall.

Leonard, Eileen. 1982. *Women, Crime and Society: A Critique of Theoretical Criminology*. New York: Longman.

Liebow, Elliot. 1967. *Tally's Corner: A Study of Negro Street Cornerman*. Boston: Little, Brown.

McCall, George, and J. L. Simmons. 1978. *Identities and Interactions*. New York: Free Press.

Mannarino, Anthony P. 1980. "The Development of Children's Friendships." Pp. 45–63 in Foot, Chapman, and Smith, eds.

Marks, J., and Peggy Giordano. 1978. "A Qualitative Analysis of Cross-Sex Friendship." Paper presented at the annual meeting of the Midwest Sociological Society.

Matza, David. 1964. *Delinquency and Drift*. New York: Wiley.

Miller, Walter B. 1973. "Race, Sex and Gangs." *Society* 11:32–35.

Minor, William. n.d. "Maryland Youth Survey." College Park: University of Maryland, Institute of Criminal Justice and Criminology.

Pedersen, Darhl, and Kenneth L. Higbee. 1969. "Personality Correlates of Self-Disclosure." *Journal of Social Psychology* 78:81–89.

Poole, Eric D., and Robert M. Regoli. 1979. "Parental Suport, Delinquent Friends, and Delinquency: A Test of Interaction Effects." *Journal of Criminal Law and Criminology* 70 (2): 188–93.

Reisman, John M. 1979. *Anatomy of Friendship*. Lexington, Mass.: Lewis.

Ridgeway, Cecilia. 1983. *The Dynamics of Small Groups*. New York: St. Martin's.

Rittenhouse, Ruth. 1963. "A Theory and Comparison of Male and Female Delinquency." Ph.D. dissertation, University of Michigan, Ann Arbor.

Roll, Samuel, and Levenett Millen. 1979. "The Friend as Represented in the Dreams of Late Adolescents: Friendship without Rose-colored Glasses." *Adolescence* 24 (54): 255–75.

Rubin, Zick. 1980. *Children's Friendships*. Cambridge, Mass.: Harvard University Press.

Seltzer, Vivian Center. 1982. *Adolescent Social Development: Dynamic Functional Interaction*. Lexington, Mass.: Heath.

Sharabany, Ruth, Ruth Gershoni, and John E. Hofman. 1981. "Girlfriend, Boyfriend: Age and Sex Differences in Intimate Friendship." *Developmental Psychology* 17 (6): 800–808.

Shaw, Clifford. 1966. *The Jackroller*. Chicago: University of Chicago Press.

Sherif, Muzafer, and Carolyn W. Sherif. 1964. *Reference Groups: Exploration $$$int Conformity and Deviation of Adolescents*. New York: Harper & Row.

Short, James F. 1957. "Differential Association and Delinquency." *Social Problems* 4 (3) 233–39.

—. 1963. *The Gang*. Chicago: University of Chicago Press.

Short, James F., Jr., and Fred L. Strodtbeck. 1965. *Group Process and Gang Delinquency*. Chicago: University of Chicago Press.

Singleton, L. C., and S. R. Asher. 1979. "Racial Integration and Children's Peer Preferences: An Investigation of Developmental and Cohort Differences." *Child Development* 50:936–41.

Thrasher, Frederick M. 1963. *The Gang*. Chicago: University of Chicago Press.

Wattenberg, William. 1956. "Differences between Girl and Boy Repeaters." *Journal of Educational Psychology* 47 (3): 137–46.

West, Lloyd, and Harvey W. Zingle. 1969. "A Self-Disclosure Inventory for Adolescents." *Psychological Reports* 24:439–45.

Wiatrowski, M. D., D. B. Griswold, and M. K. Roberts. 1981. "Social Control Theory and Delinquency." *American Sociological Review* 46 (5): 525–41.

Gangs, Drugs, and Delinquency in a Survey of Urban Youth*

Finn-Aage Esbensen
David Huizinga

Gang-related research can be traced back to the early part of this century (e.g., Asbury, 1927; Puffer, 1912; Thrasher, 1927) and has been closely associated with the development of criminological theory. During the 1950s, coinciding with the media coverage of gangs, social science researchers and theorists such as Cohen (1955), Miller (1958), and Cloward and Ohlin (1960) paved the way for subsequent researchers in the scientific study of gangs (e.g., Klein, 1971; Moore, 1978; Short and Strodbeck, 1965; Spergel, 1966). These research efforts were either generally grounded in prior theory or interested in testing new theoretical explanations of gang delinquency. By the 1970s, however, interest in gangs had become passe and some wondered if gangs had met their demise (Bookin-Weiner and Horowitz, 1983).

It was not until the urban gang violence of the early and mid-1980s that academic and media attention once again focused on the gang problem. As with most of the early gang studies, the majority of recent gang research has relied on observational methods and has produced a wealth of information about specific gangs and their members (e.g., Campbell, 1991;

Hagedorn, 1988; MacLeod, 1987; Sullivan, 1989; Vigil, 1988). Relatively few gang research projects have used survey methods, however. Notable examples of survey research on gangs include Bowker and Klein (1983), Esbensen et al. (1993), Fagan (1989), Klein (1971), Morash (1983), Thornberry et al. (1993), and Winfree et al. (1991). With the exception of Fagan's (1989) reliance on a snowball sample of gang members, the other studies cited relied on more representative samples of youths.

In addition to observational and survey methods, other gang researchers have relied on law enforcement records to examine gang offenses and to describe gang members. Klein and Maxson (1989) and Spergel (1990) discussed the extent to which official data provide rather subjective assessments of gang behavior.[1]

While research design and methods of data collection have been varied and the generalizability of results has been questioned, concern has also been raised with regard to the applicability of the old gang knowledge to the new gang situation. Hagedorn (1988), for instance, noted the changing nature of the ethnic-racial composition of inner cities and the lack of contemporary research to address the current status of gangs. While being rather critical

Criminology, Vol. 31, No. 4, 1993, pp. 565–590. American Society of Criminology Publishers of prior gang research, he noted that "the theories of the fifties and sixties were rigorously examined by sociologists and for the most part failed to stand the test of empirical verification" (p. 27). A number of other gang commentators have echoed the need for further theoretical and empirical examination of gang formation and behavior. Interestingly, one point of consensus in the voluminous gang literature is the high rate of criminal activity among gang members. Regardless of methodology and design, the consensus is that gang members commit all kinds of crimes at a greater rate than do nongang members.

The call for more empirical analysis of gangs in conjunction with the consistent finding of high rates of offending by gang members provided the impetus for conducting the analyses reported here. Despite almost a century of gang research, an important question (and the one guiding this research) remains; Are gang members more delinquent because of their gang affiliation or were they predisposed to delinquent activity prior to their gang initiation? That is, is the gang unit a criminogenic peer group, do delinquent youths seek out gangs, or do both processes occur? Using longitudinal

data from the first four years (1988–1991) of the ongoing Denver Youth Survey (DYS),[2] we examine the temporal ordering of gang membership and involvement in delinquent activity.

STUDY DESCRIPTION

SAMPLE AND ECOLOGICAL AREAS

In order to ensure sufficient numbers of serious or chronic juvenile offenders in a household sample of Denver, we identified "high-risk" neighborhoods from which to select prospective respondents.[3] Based on the results of earlier studies, we selected 35 variables from the 1980 census data representing seven conceptual areas: family structure, ethnicity, socioeconomic status (SES), housing, mobility, marital status, and age composition. Using a factor analysis of variables within each of these seven conceptual domains, we identified 11 distinct factors. Four of the theoretically derived concepts identified above produced two distinct factors. The socioeconomic domain, for example, resulted in the identification of an upper SES (e.g., high education, household income over $40,000, and professional and managerial occupations) and a lower SES factor (e.g., families in poverty, incomes under $10,000, and laborer occupations).

---

[1]One common problem, for example, is whether any crime committed by a gang member should be labeled a *gang crime* regardless of the circumstances surrounding the offense. Using law enforcement data from Chicago and Los Angeles, Maxson and Klein (1990) examined gang homicide rates by applying the different definitions of "gang-related" criminal activity used in those two cities. Using the more narrow definition of gang-related homicides employed by the Chicago police (i.e., "a killing is considered gang-related only if it occurs in the course of an explicitly defined collective encounter between two or more gangs"; Maxson and Klein, 1990:77) would reduce the gang homicide rate in Los Angeles by about half. The fact that such discrepancies in prevalence rates can be derived simply by different definitional criteria should cause researchers, theorists, and policymakers substantial discomfort.

[2]This research is part of the Program of Research on the Causes and Correlates of Delinquency, with companion projects at the University at Albany-SUNY and the University of Pittsburgh.

[3]An apparently recent development in American gang structure or organization is that gangs are no longer confined to "chronic" gang cities but are making an appearance in "emerging" gang cities, often small and medium-sized cities with no history of gang activity (Spergel, 1990:182). According to Lou Lopez, former commander of the Denver Police Department Gang Intervention Program, "the gang influence can be traced back to the late 1970s when Denver Police officers started to notice young Hispanic youth dressed in 'chollo' attire" (Lopez, 1989:i).

We subsequently ran a cluster analysis to identify and combine similar block groups of the city. Seven distinct clusters emerged, three of which we very loosely identified as being "socially disorganized." The first cluster or grouping of block groups was economically disadvantaged; it had high rates of poverty and unemployment and high numbers of unemployed school-dropout youths. It also had a high racial mix (white, African–American, and Hispanic), and high rates of single-parent households and persons per room (density). The second cluster was also economically disadvantaged, although not as severely as the first: it had a highly mobile population, many unmarried persons and few intact families, and many multiple-unit dwellings. The third cluster was a predominantly minority cluster (African–American) with higher than average rates of single-parent and unmarried-person households and a high rate of persons per room.

The geographic areas covered by these clusters include areas identified by arrest data from the Denver Police Department as having high crime rates. Using arrest data, we identified those neighborhoods within the socially disorganized areas that were in the upper one-third of the crime distribution.[4] These socially disorganized, high-crime areas became the neighborhoods for inclusion in the study sample. Although this sample selection precludes generalizations to the total disorganized areas, it ensures that youths living in these areas are likely to be in highly criminogenic environments as well, and it

is to these disorganized, high-crime areas that findings apply. A more detailed description of the sampling design and the social ecology analysis is provided in Esbensen and Huizinga (1990).

SELECTION OF RESPONDENTS

The overall design of the ongoing research project is based on a prospective, sequential longitudinal survey. The longitudinal survey involves a sequence of annual personal interviews with a probability sample of five birth cohorts. At the point of the first annual survey, the birth cohorts were 7, 9, 11, 13, and 15 years of age. Assuming the period effects between adjacent cohorts are not too large, the use of these birth cohorts (samples) results in overlapping age ranges during the first four years of the study, which allows examination of developmental sequences across the full span from age 7 to 18.

To identify study participants, a stratified probability sample of 20,300 households was selected from the 48,000 in the targeted households. Then, a screening questionnaire was used to identify those households that contained an appropriately aged respondent (i.e., 7, 9, 11, 13, or 15 years old). This sampling procedure resulted in 1,527 completed interviews in the first year (a completion rate of 85% among identified eligible youths); the youths were distributed across the five cohorts. Fifty-two percent of the sample are male, 48% female; 33% are African–American, 45% Hispanic, 10% Anglo, and 12% "other" (primarily Asian and native American).

Annual retention rates for the first four annual in-person interviews have been high by prevailing standards, 91% to 93%,[5] and complete data covering all four years are available for 85% of the original sample (some youths not interviewed in a given year are located and interviewed in

---

[4]A number of block groups defined as socially disorganized did not have high crime rates, and, therefore, were excluded from the sample. Conversely, block groups that had high crime rates but were not socially disorganized according to our analysis also were excluded from the high-risk sample.

later years). In this paper, only data from the three oldest cohorts are used for the full analyses because of the distinctly different developmental stages represented by the two youngest cohorts (aged seven and nine during the first annual data collection), for whom gang involvement was not a major factor. Data for the nine-year-old cohort, however, were included in the specific analyses for years three and four, when these youths were aged 11 and 12.[6]

METHODS

DEFINITION OF GANGS AND GANG MEMBERSHIP

Arriving at a definition of the term *gang* is no simple task; considerable debate exists regarding an appropriate definition (see Covey et al., 1992). We have adopted the position espoused by Miller (1974) and Klein and Maxson (1989), that is, in order to be considered a gang, the group must be involved in illegal activity.

Considerable data about gang membership were collected during the survey's 90-minute, in-person interviews. One early finding from this line of questioning was that approximately 5% of youths in the

------

[5]Given that the survey was conducted in "high-risk" neighborhoods with high rates of mobility, these high retention rates are a testament to the diligence and expertise of the field staff involved in tracking respondents thoughout the survey.

[6]Some concern may be raised by the relatively young age range included in this sample (i.e., ages 11 through 18). We acknowledge that others have documented the recent trend of youths remaining in gangs well into their twenties and even thirties. Clearly, the DYS sample is an adolescent sample and may not be representative of gangs in general. As a result of the sampling frame, this sample may contain more "transient" members than would an older sample. Analyses of transient and stable members, however, did not produce different results. This age issue will be addressed as subsequent data waves become available.

DYS indicated that they were gang members in any given year (39 in wave 1, 37 in wave 2, 41 in wave 3, and 76 in wave 4). Respondents were asked early in the interview if they were "members of a street or youth gang." All those responding affirmatively were later asked a series of questions about their gangs. Examination of this follow-up information indicated that what some of the youths described as gangs could best be defined as informal youth groups, or in some instances, church groups, that did not necessarily include involvement in delinquent behavior. As mentioned above, to be considered a gang member, the youth had to indicate that the gang was involved in illegal activity. An affirmative response to either of two follow-up questions (i.e., perceived gang involvement in fights with other gangs and participation in illegal activities) was used to exclude nondelinquent gangs from the analysis. While the exclusion of respondents who indicated their gang was not involved in these activities reduced the number of potential gang members to 27 in wave 1, 33 in wave 2, 32 in wave 3, and 68 in wave 4, this process permits a more stringent and, arguably, more accurate description of juvenile *delinquent* gang membership and activity. The 32 gang members in wave 3 represent 2.7% of the general sample of youths aged 11 to 17, and the 68 gang members in wave 4 represent 6.7% of the youths when they were 12 to 18 years of age. From this, one might conclude that gang membership is a relatively infrequent phenomenon in Denver, even among this "high-risk" sample of urban youths.

What are these gangs like? Descriptive data provided by respondents paint a picture of what Yablonsky (1959:109) referred to as "near groups"—groups characterized by limited cohesion, impermanence, shifting membership, and diffuse role definition, but at the same time that had some level of identification as a gang, as evidenced by having a gang name and use of gang colors and initiation rites. Year 4 data are representative of the descriptive information provided across the four years of data collection: 97% of the members indicated their gangs had a formal name (37 gangs were identified by the 68 gang members); 86% indicated their gang had initiation rites; and 97% reported that their gang had symbols or colors. With regard to shifting membership and impermanence, when asked what role they would like to have or what role they expect to have in the gang someday, over 60% of year 4 gang members indicated that they would like to *not* be a member and expected *not* to be a member sometime in the future.

Self-reported delinquency data were also collected from all respondents. The measures are improved versions of our earlier work (e.g., Huizinga and Elliott, 1986) and avoid some of the problems of even earlier self-report inventories. The measures exclude traditional trivial offenses, such as defying parental authority, and include serious offenses often excluded from early self-report inventories (e.g., rape, robbery, and aggravated assault). Additionally, follow-up questions were included as integral parts of the measures. These follow-up questions allow for determination of the seriousness and appropriateness of initial responses. If, for example, a respondent indicated that he or she had committed an aggravated assault during the prior year but follow-up information revealed that it was accidental and that the victim truly was not injured, the original response would be changed to zero.

For analysis purposes, our delinquency and drug use measures focus on those behaviors often considered to be of greatest concern. To this end, we developed four levels of delinquency: (1) street offending, (2) other serious offending, (3) minor offending, and (4) nonoffending. We used a subset of

the street offenses to create a measure of drug sales[7] in order to address the concern that gangs are disproportionately involved in drug distribution (e.g., Fagan, 1989). One gang expert has even suggested that youth gangs of the 1990s have established a national network of drug distribution similar to the "mafia's" alcohol distribution network during prohibition (Taylor, 1990).

Street offenses focus on serious crimes that occur on the street and are often of concern to citizens and policymakers, alike. *Other serious offenses* includes behaviors that, while not in the street crime category, are nevertheless considered as serious delinquency. *Minor offenses* refers primarily to status offenses and other public nuisance type behaviors. These categories of delinquent behavior generally reflect the seriousness weighting used by Wolfgang et al. (1985). We dichotomized *drug use* into alcohol use and "other drug use," including marijuana and other illicit drugs. For the analyses reported below, all youths were categorized based on their most serious level of involvement in delinquency and drug use. Thus, if an individual reported committing a minor, a serious, and a street offense in a given year, that individual was classified as a street offender. Appendix A provides a listing of the items included in the self-reported delinquency and drug use classifications.

RESULTS

GANG MEMBER DEMOGRAPHICS

Gangs have traditionally been thought of as being a predominantly male phenomenon, and relatively few studies have

---

[7]The drug sale measure consists of two items from the street offending scale. We ran specific analyses to verify that these drug sale items were not "driving" the street offender results.

concentrated on female gang members (exceptions include Bowker and Klein, 1983; Campbell, 1990, 1991; Giordano, 1978; Harris, 1988; Morash, 1983; Quicker, 1983). This has resulted in considerable ignorance concerning not only the role of female gang members, but also the number of females involved in gang activity. Campbell (1991) reports a long and rich history of female gangs and female members in male gangs; she suggests that at one point approximately 10% of New York City gang members were female, and that female membership might have been as high as 33% in one gang. Fagan (1990) reported female gang membership to be approximately 33% in his survey.

The demographic characteristics of both gang and nongang members are presented in Table 1. As seen there, the DYS data confirm that a significant proportion of all gang members are female—a fact not generally acknowledged in media presentations of gangs. Cross-sectional analysis of DYS gang data reveals that females constituted from 20% to 46% of gang members during the four-year study period. Thus, while there is evidence that gang members are primarily males, there is reason to believe that females are more involved in gangs than is generally acknowledged. One caveat, however, is that while female gang membership may well be greater than that presented in the popular press, female gang members are less likely to report high levels of involvement in delinquent activity. In wave 3, for example, female gang members reported an average individual offending rate of 14.0 on the general delinquency scale, and male gang members reported an average offending rate of 36.9 offenses on that scale.

As with gender, it is often assumed that gang members are youths from ethnic-racial minority backgrounds (e.g., Fagan, 1989; Spergel, 1990). A 1989 survey of law enforcement officials in 45 cities across the nation found that African–American and Hispanics made up 87% of gang membership (cited in Gurule, 1991). Due to the nature of the DYS sample (78% of the sample is African–American or Hispanic), it is not possible to address the ethnic distribution of gang membership, although it does appear that African–American and Hispanic youths tend to be overrepresented in the DYS gang subsample (ranging from 85% to 94% of gang members in the various years). Given the disproportionate number of minority youths in the sample, however, it should be expected that the majority of gang members would also be African–American or Hispanic.

Gang membership does appear to be somewhat associated with age. In year 4, for example, 27% of gang members were 18 years old, 31% were 16, 36% were 14 years old, and 7% were 12. Given this age distribution, at what age do youths join gangs? Gang members were asked when they joined their gang. Analysis of these responses for year 4 revealed that most did not join until their teenaged years, although a few respondents did indicate that they joined the gang before the age of 12.

GANG DELINQUENCY

Are gang members more involved in delinquency than nongang members? Examination of Table 2 results in a firm yes for males and a qualified yes for female gang members.[8] Both prevalence and individual offending rates for gang members

---

[8]Throughout the analyses reported in this paper, we truncated the self-reported frequency of offending at 99 in order to minimize the effect of "outliers." We also limited the frequency analysis to active offenders and thus use the terms individual offending rates and lambda interchangeably throughout the text to refer to the average offending rate among active offenders. For a discussion of lambda, consult Blumstein et al. (1988).

TABLE 1: Demographic Characteristics of the Denver Youth Survey Sample

	Year 1		Year 2		Year 3		Year 4	
	Gang	Nongang	Gang	Nongang	Gang	Nongang	Gang	Nongang
Sex								
Male, N	15	441	27	397	24	555	53	511
Column %	54%	52%	80%	52%	74%	52%	80%	50%
Female, N	12	400	7	390	8	514	13	516
Column %	46%	48%	20%	48%	25%	48%	20%	50%
Total N	27	841	33	801	32	1102	68	1027
Race								
Af.-Am., N	7	320	14	283	15	385	28	371
Column %	26%	38%	42%	37%	48%	36%	42%	36%
Hisp., N	16	374	14	352	14	470	35	443
Column %	60%	45%	43%	46%	42%	44%	52%	43%
White, N	0	71	2	65	0	104	2	103
Column %	0%	9%	7%	8%	0%	10%	3%	10%
Other, N	4	75	1	67	2	110	2	110
Column %	14%	9%	8%	9%	7%	10%	3%	11%
Total N	27	830	33	801	32	1102	68	1026
Age, Birthyear								
1972, N	14	256	11	226	11	228	18	227
Column %	52%	30%	33%	30%	35%	22%	27%	22%
1974, N	10	291	17	268	11	275	20	257
Column %	38%	35%	52%	35%	33%	26%	31%	25%
1976, N	3	294	5	273	10	276	24	257
Column %	10%	35%	16%	36%	32%	26%	36%	25%
1978, N	—	—	—	—	0	291	5	285
Column %	—	—	—	—	0%	27%	7%	28%
Total N	27	830	33	801	32	1102	68	1027

NOTE: These data are weighted to represent the stratified sample. As a result, the integral values are approximates and do not always provide the exact percentage.

TABLE 2: Year 4 Prevalence and Individual Offending Rates (IOR) of Gang and Nongang Members Controlling for Sex

	MALES						FEMALES					
	Gang			Nongang			Gang			Nongang		
Offense Type	N	Prev.	IOR	N	Prev.	IOR	N	Prev.	IOR	N	Prev.	IOR
Street	53	.85*	22.3**	511	.18	8.3	13	.76*	5.9	515	.07	2.7
Drug Sales	53	.29*	22.8**	511	.03	30.5	13	.18*	10.5	515	.01	6.8
Serious	53	.83*	31.8**	510	.32	10.0	13	.61*	5.1	516	.18	10.0
Minor	49	.87*	29.0**	500	.56	11.6	13	.93*	18.7	499	.54	10.1
Alcohol Use	53	.71*	48.4**	510	.35	24.1	13	.85*	36.9	516	.32	16.7
Other Drug Use	52	.52*	46.8**	491	.13	20.0	13	.69*	11.9	516	.13	23.6

* *p* < .05 (chi-square).
** *p* < .05 (*T* test, separate variance estimate of *t*).

and nongang members are reported for four types of delinquent behavior and two types of drug use during year 4. It is important to examine prevalence rates first in that this identifies the number of active offenders involved in each specific behavior.

The prevalence rates for male and female gang members are significantly greater than those for their nongang counterparts. Gang membership is almost synonymous with involvement in all types of delinquency. Male gang members, for example, reported a prevalence rate of .85 for street offenses and .83 for other serious offenses. This is substantially higher than the prevalence rates of .18 and .32, respectively, for nongang males. The difference in prevalence rates is even more pronounced for females; .76 of female gang members reported involvement in street offending compared with .07 for nongang females. For each type of behavior, the prevalence rate for female gang members is consistently greater than that for male nongang members. Gang members during year 4 report being involved in a variety of delinquent activities; with male prevalence rates ranging between .29 for drug sales and .93 for minor offending, these youths clearly do not specialize in any one type of activity. Nongang members had much lower rates of involvement in all types of delinquent activities and drug use than did the gang members, as evidenced by prevalence rates of .01 and .03 for females and males, respectively, involved in drug sales, and nongang prevalence rates of .07 and .18 for female and male involvement, respectively, in street-level offending (compared with .76 and .85 for female and male gang members).

As with gender, it is often assumed that gang members are youths from ethnic-racial minority backgrounds (e.g., Fagan, 1989; Spergel, 1990). A 1989 survey of law enforcement officials in 45 cities across the nation found that African-American and Hispanics made up 87% of gang membership activity. Nongang members had much lower rates of involvement in all types of delinquent activities and drug use than did the gang members, as evidenced by prevalence rates of .01 and .03 for females and males, respectively, involved in drug sales, and nongang prevalence rates of .07 and .18 for female and male involvement, respectively, in street-level offending (compared with .76 and .85 for female and male gang members).

With respect to the individual offending rates, however, there are no statistically significant differences between female gang and nongang members. Nongang females who were involved in delinquent activity, whether assault, theft, or drug use, reported nearly the same level of activity. Male gang members, however, had individual offending rates, that were two to three times greater than those of nongang males involved in each specific activity, with the exception of drug sales. To illustrate the value of examining both prevalence and individual offending rates, we interpret the street-level offending data for males. While there were only 53 male gang members, 85% of them (45 members) reported involvement in street offenses. Those 45 gang members reported committing an average of 22.3 offenses per person. This translates into 1,003 ($45 \times 22.3 = 1,003.5$) offenses.[9] For the nongang members, only 18% of the 511, or

---

[9]Given what is known about the extent of co-offending among juveniles, it is exceedingly difficult, if not impossible, to make a reasonable transition from offender-specific data to offense data. For example, the fact that 20 youths reported committing an aggravated assault does not necessarily mean that 20 assaults were committed. For discussion of this co-offending issue, consult, for example, Elliott et al. (1985), Fagan (1990), Johnson (1979), and Krohn (1986).

92 males, reported committing street crimes. And, they reported committing only 8.3 offenses per person, for a total of 764 offenses. Thus, while male gang members accounted for only 33% of street offenders in year 4, they reported committing 57% of street offenses.

Additional analyses were conducted to determine if the level of gang involvement was associated with levels of offending. Gang members were categorized as core or peripheral members based on their responses to the question, How would you describe your position in the gang? All those indicating that they were leaders or one of the top persons were classified as core members. All others were considered as peripheral members. No age or sex differences were found between the core and peripheral members. More important, and perhaps somewhat surprising, introduction of this control did not result in any statistically significant differences between the two levels of gang involvement and self-reported delinquency. That is, the peripheral members reported the same level of delinquent activity as did the core members.

With respect to gang activity, gang members were asked a series of questions about the kinds of activities in which the gang was involved. Given our definition of gangs and desire to describe *delinquent* gangs, the responses listed below confirm that in addition to being delinquent gangs, the *perception* of gang members is that members of their gangs are involved in a wide range of illegal activity. While fights with other gangs is the most frequently mentioned form of illegal activity, approximately three-fourths of the gang members reported that their gang was involved in the following: robberies, joyriding, assaults of other people, thefts of more than $50, and drug sales. Clearly, illegal activities are a prominent part of the *perceived*

gang experience, and these descriptions coincide with the self-reported levels of delinquency discussed above. It is interesting, however, that only 30% of male and 18% of female gang members indicated in the self-report inventory that they themselves were involved in drug sales during the preceding year.

LONGITUDINAL ANALYSES

With four years of longitudinal data available for 85% of the original sample, it becomes possible to examine the stability of gang membership. Consistent with the research literature (e.g., Hagedorn, 1988; Klein, 1971; Short and Strodbeck, 1965; Thornberry et al., 1993; Vigil, 1988; Yablonsky, 1959, 1963), we found gang membership to lack stability.[10] Of the 90 gang youths for whom we have complete data for all four years, 67% were members in only one year, 24% belonged for two years, 6% belonged for three years, and only 3% belonged for all four years.

A major purpose of this paper is to address the temporal ordering of delinquency and gang membership. That is, are gang members more delinquent prior to becoming gang members or is the heightened level of delinquent activity contemporaneous with gang membership? And, perhaps equally important, what is the delinquency level of gang members in years following their departure from the gang? Answers to these questions help identify gang influences on behavior and address the often-debated theoretical issue of "feathering versus flocking." Table 3 summarizes the relationship between gang membership and

[10]In their study of high-risk youth in Rochester, for example, Thornberry et al. (1993) found that 55% of gang members were members for only one year.

TABLE 3: Prevalence of Street Offending Among Gang and Nongang Members Controlling for Year of Membership (N = 730)

Year of Gang Membership[a]	N[b]	PREVALENCE OF STREET OFFENDING			
		Year 1	Year 2	Year 3	Year 4
Nongang	640	70	72	94	80
		.11	.11	.15	.13
Year 1 Only	10	7	1	2	3
		.72	.09	.20	.28
Year 2 Only	9	2	6	3	3
		.23	.65	.32	.35
Year 3 Only	10	1	2	8	5
		.09	.21	.77	.53
Year 4 Only	31	3	8	12	23
		.10	.25	.39	.74
Years 3 and 4	10	4	7	9	9
		.44	.73	.91	.88
Years 2, 3, and 4[c]	5	3	3	5	5
Years 1, 2, 3, and 4[c]	3	2	3	3	2

NOTE: These data are weighted to represent the stratified sample. As a result, the integral values are approximates and do not always provide the exact percentage.

[a]These refer to consecutive years of membership. An additional 12 youths reported gang membership during 2 nonconsecutive years.

[b]The N reflects those cases for which four years of complete data are available. For gang members, complete four-year data are available for 90 of 112 (80%) youths. For nongang youths, complete four-year data are available for 640 of 729 (88%) youths.

[c]Samples are too small to allow calculation of reliable prevalence estimates.

street-level offending during the four years examined. This particular analysis is restricted to those youths in the three oldest cohorts for whom complete longitudinal data were available (N = 730).]

Annual prevalence data illustrate that, overall, gang members were particularly likely to be involved in street offenses during the year in which they were gang members, with lower levels of involvement both before and after their time in the gang. However, the indication is that regardless of their year of membership, youths who have been gang members at some point in time, have higher prevalence rates for street offending than do youths who have never belonged to a gang. Among year 1 gang members, 72% were classified as street offenders. By years 2, 3, and 4, when these youth were no longer in a gang, the percentage of those youths who were street offenders had decreased substantially and was only slightly higher than the prevalence rate for non-gang youths. For year 2 gang members, 23% were classified as street offenders in year 1, 65 in year 2 (when they were gang members), and then 32% and 35%, respectively, in the two subsequent years when they were no longer in the gang. For youths who were gang members during year 3 or year 4, a gradual increase in the number of street offenders can be seen prior to their joining the gang, and then a sharp increase in the prevalence rate over the year immediately preceding gang membership (from 21% to 77% for year 3 gang members and from 39% to 74% for year 4 members). The prevalence rates of street offending for stable gang members, that is, those reporting gang membership for two or more consecutive years, exceed those of the transient, one-year only members.

In Table 3 we controlled for the actual years of gang membership and the prevalence of street offending, which permitted examination of stable and transient members. Due to the low number of stable gang members and interest in other delinquency measures, in Table 4 we report differences in the prevalence rate between gang members and nongang youths for two types of delinquency (street-level offending and other serious offenses) and illicit drug use. In this table, the behavior of gang members in a specific year is tracked for the four-year study period. This means that the stable gang members are included in multiple years, which inflates the overall pattern. However, we thought it inappropriate to exclude stable members from the analysis.

In Table 4, *year of gang membership* refers to all those individuals who reported belonging to a gang that year. *Prevalence*

TABLE 4: Prevalence of Street Offending, Serious Offending, and Illegal Drug Use Among Gang and Nongang Members

Year of Gang Membership	Sample Size		Street Offenses		Serious Offenses		Illicit Drug Use	
	Gang	Nongang	Gang	Nongang	Gang	Nongang	Gang	Nongang
Year 1 Membership								
Year 1 Behavior	25	835	.85*	.15	.93*	.36	.42*	.13
Year 2 Behavior	25	766	.41*	.15	.61*	.32	.52*	.15
Year 3 Behavior	21	782	.39*	.20	.51	.36	.36*	.14
Year 4 Behavior	22	779	.40*	.19	.48	.30	.27	.19
Year 2 Membership								
Year 1 Behavior	32	757	.50*	.13	.66*	.37	.29*	.13
Year 2 Behavior	33	764	.69*	.13	.89*	.30	.47*	.13
Year 3 Behavior	30	737	.59*	.18	.68*	.35	.44*	.14
Year 4 Behavior	30	729	.63*	.18	.70*	.28	.39*	.18
Year 3 Membership								
Year 1 Behavior	31	768	.43*	.13	.53	.37	.23	.13
Year 2 Behavior	29	736	.55*	.14	.67*	.32	.42*	.13
Year 3 Behavior	32	1059	.90*	.15	.75*	.32	.60*	.10
Year 4 Behavior	30	1026	.77*	.15	.66*	.27	.42	.15
Year 4 Membership								
Year 1 Behavior	61	733	.33*	13	.54*	.35	.13	.13
Year 2 Behavior	60	695	.51*	.12	.73*	.29	.34*	.14
Year 3 Behavior	65	983	.58*	.14	.65*	.31	.37*	.10
Year 4 Behavior	67	1026	.83*	.12	.79*	.25	.56*	.13

* $p < .05$ (chi-square).

of offending refers to whether these individuals reported engaging in any of the specified behaviors in each year. Consistent with the detailed findings for street offending reported in Table 3, prevalence rates for each type of behavior are highest during the gang member's year of actual gang membership. For example, among the year 3 gang members, 43% committed street offenses in year 1, 55% in year 2, 90% in year 3, and 77% in year 4. Each of these prevalence rates is substantially greater than the comparable annual rate for those youths who were not gang members in year 3, all of which were between .13 and .15. In separate analyses controlling for gang membership status (i.e., transient and stable), similar differences between gang and nongang youths were found, although the differences between transient members and nongang youth were less pronounced.

Examination of these prevalence rates across years permits an assessment of the temporal relationship between gang membership and delinquency. While some people believe that "birds of a feather flock together," others believe in a socialization explanation (e.g., Elliott and Menard, in press). In Table 4 there is some evidence to support the selection or "birds of a feather" explanation. Gang members have higher prevalence rates of involvement in delinquency in years preceding their gang membership. Year 3 gang members, for example, have a higher rate of participation in street offending (.43 compared with .13), but not other serious offenses or illicit drug use, in year 1 than do nongang members. By year 2, the prevalence rates for

year 3 gang members are higher than those of the nongang members for all three behaviors, and in year 3, the largest discrepancy is noted.

While rates of participation are, in fact, higher in years preceding and during gang membership, Table 4 also reveals that these rates of delinquent activity decline in years subsequent to gang membership.[11] By year 4, the year 1 gang members are more similar to those youths who reported never having belonged to a gang, although they still report statistically significant higher rates of participation in street offending (40% compared with 19%).

The preceding discussion focused on the prevalence of street offending and other types of delinquency among gang and nongang members. Of equal importance, and essential to the understanding of the level of delinquent behavior, is examination of individual offending rates, or lambda (i.e., average number of offenses per active offender) for these two groups (Table 5). As with prevalence rates, the individual offending rates of gang members are substantially greater than those of nongang members.[12] As with prevalence rates, gang members clearly have higher offending rates than do nongang members, but this is especially pronounced during the year in which the youths reported being a gang member (e.g., in year 2, gang members categorized as street offenders committed an average of 31.2 street offenses each, compared with 7.6 such offenses for nongang members.

---

[11]Analyses in which the sample was disaggregated by gender produced similar results for males. Female gang members, however, only had higher prevalence rates than female nonmembers during the actual year of membership.

[12]Once again, analyses disaggregated by gender reveal that these differences are more pronounced for male gang members than female gang members. While males seem to be on a trajectory of increasingly higher rates of offending in years prior to gang initiation, as with prevalence rates, females appear to have higher rates of offending primarily only during their actual year of gang membership.

TABLE 5: Individual Offending Rates of Street Offending, Serious Offending, and Illegal Drug Use Among Gang and Nongang Members

| | INDIVIDUAL OFFENDING RATES | | | | | |
| Year of Gang Membership | Street Offenses | | Serious Offenses | | Illicit Drug Use | |
	Gang	Nongang	Gang	Nongang	Gang	Nongang
Year 1 Membership						
Year 1 Behavior	29.2*	6.8	31.4*	8.8	47.4*	15.8
Year 2 Behavior	12.9	6.8	15.0	7.9	34.1	14.9
Year 3 Behavior	7.2	5.9	9.7	5.9	13.1	14.8
Year 4 Behavior	10.7	5.2	17.6*	5.6	26.4	10.9
Year 2 Membership						
Year 1 Behavior	19.7*	4.5	17.3*	7.1	13.0	12.2
Year 2 Behavior	31.2*	7.6	32.2*	11.1	38.2*	17.4
Year 3 Behavior	9.2	8.5	15.3*	6.3	21.0	17.3
Year 4 Behavior	10.8	9.2	11.4	8.1	19.6	14.9
Year 3 Membership						
Year 1 Behavior	13.9*	2.0	12.7*	5.1	10.6	7.1
Year 2 Behavior	20.9*	2.0	24.8*	7.2	22.3*	8.0
Year 3 Behavior	34.5*	5.7	29.8*	8.3	56.8*	23.3
Year 4 Behavior	22.9*	4.2	29.4*	6.6	38.8	20.1
Year 4 Membership						
Year 1 Behavior	8.8*	1.8	9.1*	3.8	3.6	6.2
Year 2 Behavior	13.4*	1.7	22.1*	4.0	11.2	9.2
Year 3 Behavior	14.4*	2.8	13.3*	5.6	27.0*	11.6
Year 4 Behavior	19.7*	6.7	28.1*	10.0	39.5*	21.7

* $p < .05$ (*T* test, separate variance estimate of *t*).

Table 5 also reveals that the mean number of street offenses committed by gang members in years preceding their joining the gang is significantly higher than that of nongang members, but that in the years following their departure, there is a dramatic reduction, although they remain more delinquent than their nongang counterparts. By year 2, for example, there were no statistically significant differences between the year 1 gang members and those who were not gang members in year 1. Similarly, by year 3, there were no statistically significant differences for street offending and illicit drug use between the year 2 gang and nongang members.

A popular perception is that gang members are frequent drug users. During their year of membership, gang members reported significantly higher rates of marijuana and other illegal drug use. However, unlike the delinquency measures, drug use prior to and subsequent to gang membership, generally, was not found to be statistically different from the drug use of nongang youths.

In sum, while gang members had higher rates of involvement than nongang members in street offending and other serious offending not only during the year in which they were gang members but also in the years preceding membership, the rate is particularly high and pronounced during the gang years. These higher rates of individual offending, however, decrease substantially once the youths leave the gang. In analyses not presented, this trend is especially pronounced for males in the sample. Illegal drug use fits the same pattern—it is highest during the gang year. However, drug use by gang members is not significantly different from that of nongang members in years when they are not affiliated with a gang.

SUMMARY AND DISCUSSION

In the preceding analyses, we addressed three issues: (1) the prevalence and demographic characteristics of gang members in a general survey of urban youths; (2) the relationship between delinquency and drug use among gang youths; and (3) the temporal relationship between offending and gang membership. With regard to the number of urban youths who belong to gangs, two observations should be made. First, even in a sample of high-risk urban youths, gang membership is a statistically infrequent phenomenon. Second, depending on the definition of gang used, different estimates of gang membership are obtained. Prior to controlling for the criminal conduct of gangs, estimates of gang membership were in excess of 5% during each study year. However, when the analysis was restricted to youths who belonged to *delinquent* gangs, slightly less than 3% of the total sample during years 1 through 3 could then be classified as gang members. By year 4, when the cohorts were aged 12 to 18 years, the number of youths reporting to be members of delinquent gangs had increased to almost 7%. Such definitionally induced discrepancies in prevalence of gang membership highlight the need to establish consensus on an operational definition of gangs.

As has been repeatedly argued by Klein and Maxson (1989) and more recently by Spergel and Chance (1991), there is considerable need for a uniform definition of gang and gang behavior. Whether from a research or policy perspective, it is important that a common consensus be reached. While the earlier calls for a uniform definition emphasized jurisdictional differences among law enforcement agencies, our research suggests that a common definition should be employed by survey researchers. A uniform definition of gangs and gang behavior would be a point of departure for a better understanding of a phenomenon that may well be substantially distorted because of a lack of a common means for studying, describing, and regulating gang behavior.

The importance of general surveys is highlighted by examination of the demographic characteristics of gang members. Contrary to much prior research on gangs, females were found to be quite active in gangs (approximately 25% of gang members during the four-year study period were female). While this is higher than the prevailing stereotype, it is consistent with Fagan's (1990) and Campbell's (1991) estimates. Why is it that so many studies fail to report any substantial involvement of females in gangs? It may be, as Campbell (1991:vii) suggests, that writings about gangs, as well as other social science topics, historically have been written by men about men. Thus, female gang membership may well have been systematically underreported in prior research endeavors. A casual examination of early gang research provides some evidence for this argument. Cohen (1955) and Cloward and Ohlin (1960), for example, excluded females from their research and conceptualizations.

A second possibility is that the reliance on official data or purposive samples of gang members has resulted in a biased representation of not only gang member-ship, but gang behavior as well. Yet another possible explanation may be associated with the sampling or site selection in the DYS and other general surveys. In any lo-calized survey project, it is possible that a particular site or sample is atypical and nonrepresentative of other populations or sites. However, given the similarity of find-ings between Fagan's (1990) three-city study and the DYS, the high percentage of female gang members may be an accurate accounting of gang membership in the late 1980s. A fourth possibility is that there has been a historical change in female delin-quency or in the role of females in gangs. With respect to this issue, Huizinga and Esbensen (1991) reported no change in self-reported levels of offending among two samples of urban females, one from 1978 and the other from 1989.

Another characteristic of gang mem-bership found to be contrary to widely held, media-promoted stereotypes is the notion that youths become gang members for life. While media accounts generally portray gangs as surrogate families for dis-enfranchised youths, this view is not sup-ported by our research nor by the majority of gang research of the past three decades (e.g., Fagan, 1989; Hagedorn, 1988; Klein, 1971; Short and Strodbeck, 1965; Thorn-berry et al., 1993; Vigil, 1988; Yablonsky, 1959, 1963). Very few of the youths in the DYS survey reported being in a gang for more than one year. And, many of those youths in a gang indicated that they would like *not* to be a gang member and expected to leave the gang in the future. It appears that the majority of gang members are pe-ripheral or transitory members who drift in and out of the gang.

With regard to involvement in delin-quent activity, gang members were found to be considerably more active in all types of delinquency, including drug sales and

drug use, than were nongang members. It is important, however, to provide a caveat concerning gang involvement in drug sales. As concluded by Klein et al. (1991), while drug sales/distribution is an activity engaged in by individual gang members, we did not find evidence that drug sales was an organized gang activity involving all gang members. That is, although 80% of the year 4 gang members indicated that the gang was involved in drug sales, only 28% of these very gang members reported that they sold drugs. Further, drug sales is only one of a variety of illegal activities in which the gang is involved. As reported by Fagan (1989), we found that all of the gangs were involved in what Klein (1984) has called "cafeteria-style" delinquency.

The temporal relationship between offending and gang membership is impor-tant, and one that can best be examined with longitudinal data of a general popula-tion. Participant observation of existing gang members relies on selective retro-spective information and generally ex-cludes comparison groups. Cross-sectional surveys cannot examine the developmen-tal sequences that we believe are necessary to explain the process of gang recruitment.

The longitudinal analyses reported here indicate that involvement of gang members in delinquency and drug use is rather strongly patterned. While gang members had higher rates of involvement than nongang members in street crime and other serious forms of offending even be-fore joining the gang, their prevalence and individual offending rates were substan-tially higher during the actual year of membership. Similar results were also re-ported in a study of high-risk youths in Rochester, New York (Thornberry et al., 1993). Their findings for "stable" gang members mirrored those reported here. Their "transient" gang members, however, did not appear to have significantly higher rates of offending than nongang members in years prior to or following gang membership. Our findings, in conjunction with those from the Rochester study, lead us to conclude that it is not solely individual characteristics that are associated with higher levels of involvement in street crime. Rather, there may well be factors within the gang milieu that contribute to the criminal behavior of gang members.

Thus, while the high prevalence and individual offending rates prior to gang membership may lead one to espouse the view that they are supportive of a social control perspective, which maintains that people select others of similar values as friends (e.g., Hirschi, 1969), that may be premature. Given that the highest rates of offending occurred during gang years, these data may be more supportive of a learning perspective, which maintains behavior is learned within particular groups and settings (e.g., Burgess and Akers, 1966; Elliott and Menard, in press; Sutherland and Cressey, 1970). A third possibility is what Thornberry et al. (1993:59) have referred to as an "enhancement" model, in which both processes are operative. Without a test of theoretically relevant variables, such conclusions are mere projection. The temporal ordering of such key factors as peer group norms and values and respondent behavior must be examined prior to going beyond the mere speculation stage. Elliott and Menard (in press) have documented with National Youth Survey data that the acquisition of delinquent friends generally precedes the onset of delinquency. The data we have presented suggest that delinquent involvement precedes gang membership. It is here that we do not want to make the tempting juxtaposition and equate gang membership with delinquent friends, for it may well be that gang membership is but a more formalized form of co-offending that was initiated within a delinquent peer group in prior years. Answers to such theoretically important issues should be tested fully, and we hope that our research provides a basis for subsequent work on this issue.

From a policy standpoint, our findings suggest, at least tentatively, that gang intervention strategies should focus not only on decreasing the influence of gangs on individual gang member behavior, but also on the conditions that foster gang development. Although gang members are more highly delinquent than their nongang peers, the trend toward increasing delinquency is prevalent at least two years prior to gang initiation. An important aim should thus be to retard this initial escalation of delinquent activity and disrupt gang effects before peer group behavior becomes formalized within the gang environment.

References

Asbury, Herbert 1927 The Gangs of New York. New York: Capricorn.

Blumstein, Alfred, Jacqueline Cohen, and David Farrington 1988 Criminal career research: Its value for criminology. Criminology 26:1–35.

Bookin—Weiner, Hedy and Ruth Horowitz 1983 The end of the gang: Fact or fad? Criminology 21:585–602.

Bowker, Lee H. and Malcolm W. Klein 1983 The etiology of female juvenile delinquency and gang membership: A test of psychological and social structural explanations. Adolescence 18:740–751.

Burgess, Robert L., and Ronald L. Akers 1966 A differential association-reinforcement theory of criminal behavior. Social Problems 14:128–147.

Campbell, Anne 1990 Female participation in gangs. In C. Ronald Huff (ed.), Gangs in America. Newbury Park, Calif.: Sage.

1991 The Girls in the Gang. 2d. ed. Cambridge, Mass.: Basil Blackwell.

Cloward, Richard A. and Lloyd E. Ohlin 1960 Delinquency and Opportunity: A Theory of Delinquent Gangs. New York: Free Press.

Cohen, Albert 1955 Delinquent Boys: The Culture of the Gang. Glencoe, Ill.: Free Press.

Covey, Herbert C., Scott Menard, and Robert J. Franzese 1992 Juvenile Gangs. Springfield, Ill.: Charles C Thomas.

Elliott, Delbert S. and Scott Menard In press Delinquent friends and delinquent behavior: Temporal and developmental patterns. In David Hawkins (ed.), Current Theories of Crime and Deviance. New York: Springer-Verlag.

Elliott, Delbert S., David Huizinga, and Suzanne S. Ageton 1985 Explaining Deinquency and Drug Use. Beverly Hills, Calif.: Sage.

Esbensen, Finn—Aage and David Huizinga 1990 Community structure and drug use: From a social disorganization perspective. Justice Quarterly 7:691–709.

Esbensen, Finn—Aage. David Huizinga, and Anne W. Weiher 1993 Gang and non-gang youth: Differences in explanatory variables. Journal of Contemporary Criminal Justice 9:94–116.

Fagan, Jeffrey 1989 The social organization of drug use and drug dealing among urban gangs. Criminology 27:633–669.

1990 Social processes of delinquency and drug use among urban gangs. In C. Ronald Huff (ed.), Gangs in America. Newbury Park, Calif.: Sage.

Giordano, Peggy C. 1978 Girls, guys, and gangs: The changing social context of female delinquency. Journal of Criminal Law and Criminology 69:126–132.

Gurule, Jimmy 1991 The OJP initiative on gangs: Drugs and violence in America. NIJ Reports 224:4–5.

Hagedorn, John M. 1988 People and Folks: Gangs, Crime and the Underclass in a Rustbelt City. Chicago: Lakeview Press.

Harris, Mary G. 1988 Cholas: Latino Girls and Gangs. New York: AMS.

Hirschi, Travis 1969 Causes of Delinquency. Berkeley: University of California Press.

Huizinga, David and Delbert S. Elliott 1986 Reassessing the reliability and validity of self-report delinquency measures. Journal of Quantitative Criminology 2:293–327.

Huizinga, David and Finn—Aage Esbensen 1991 Are there changes in female delinquency and are there changes in underlying explanatory factors? Paper presented at the Annual Meeting of the American Society of Criminology, San Francisco.

Johnson, Richard E. 1979 Juvenile Delinquency and Its Origins. Cambridge: Cambridge University Press.

Klein, Malcolm W. 1971 Street Gangs and Street Workers. Englewood Cliffs, N.J.: Prentice–Hall.

1984 Offense specialization and versatility among juveniles. British Journal of Criminology 24:185–194.

Klein, Malcolm W. and Cheryl L. Maxson 1989 Street gang violence. In Neil A. Weiner and Marvin E. Wolfgang (eds.), Violent Crime, Violent Criminals. Newbury Park, Calif.: Sage.

Klein, Malcolm W., Cheryl L. Maxson, and Lea C. Cunningham 1991 "Crack," street gangs, and violence. Criminology 29:623–650.

Krohn, Marvin D. 1986 The web of conformity: A network approach of the explanation of delinquent behavior. Social Problems 33:s81–s93.

Lopez, Lou 1989 Gangs in Denver. Denver: Denver Public Schools.

MacLeod, Jay 1987 Ain't No Makin' It: Leveled Aspirations in a Low-Income Neighborhood. Boulder, Colo.: Westview Press.

Maxson, Cheryl L. and Malcolm W. Klein 1990 Street gang violence: Twice as great or half as great? In C. Ronald Huff (ed.), Gangs in America. Newbury Park. Calif.: Sage.

Miller, Walter B. 1958 Lower class culture as a generating milieu for gang delinquency. Journal of Social Issues 14:5–19.

1974 American youth gangs: Past and present. In Alfred Blumberg (ed.). Current Perspectives on Criminal Behavior. New York: Knopf.

Moore, Joan W. 1978 Homeboys: Gangs, Drugs, and Prison in the Barrios of Los Angeles. Philadelphia: Temple University Press.

Morash, Merry 1983 Gangs, groups, and delinquency. British Journal of Criminology 23:309–331.

Puffer, J. Adams 1912 The Boy and His Gang. Boston: Houghton Mifflin.

Quicker, John C. 1983 Homegirls: Characterizing Chicano Gangs. San Pedro, Calif.: International University Press.

Short, James F. and Fred L. Strodbeck 1965 Group Processes and Gang Delinquency. Chicago: University of Chicago Press.

Spergel, Irving A. 1966 Street Gang Work: Theory and Practice. Reading, Mass.: Addison-Wesley.

1990 Youth gangs: Continuity and change. In Norval Morris and Michael Tonry (eds.), Crime and Justice: An Annual Review of Research. Chicago: University of Chicago Press.

Spergel, Irving A. and Ronald L. Chance 1991 National youth gang suppression and intervention program. NIJ Reports 224:21–24.

Sullivan, Mercer L. 1989 Getting Paid: Youth Crime and Work in the Inner City. Ithaca, N.Y.: Cornell University Press.

Sutherland, Edwin H. and Donald R. Cressey 1970 Criminology. New York: J.B. Lippincott.

Taylor, Carl S. 1990 Gang imperialism. In C. Ronald Huff (ed.), Gangs in America. Newbury Park, Calif.: Sage.

Thornberry, Terence, Marvin D. Krohn, Alan J. Lizotte, and Deborah Chard-Wierschem 1993 The role of juvenile gangs in facilitating delinquent behavior. Journal of Research in Crime and Delinquency 30:55–87.

Thrasher, Frederick M. 1927 The Gang: A Study of One Thousand Three Hundred Thirteen Gangs in Chicago. Chicago: University of Chicago Press.

Vigil, James D. 1988 Barrio Gangs: Street Life and Identity in Southern California. Austin: University of Texas Press.

Winfree, L. Thomas, Teresa Vigil, and G. Larry Mays 1991 Social learning theory and youth gangs: A comparison of high school students and adjudicated delinquents. Paper presented at the Annual Meeting of the American Society of Criminology, San Francisco.

Wolfgang, Marvin, Robert M. Figlio, Paul E. Tracy, and Simon I. Singer 1985 The National Survey of Crime Severity. Washington, D.C.: Government Printing Office.

Yabionsky, Lewis 1959 The delinquent gang as a near group. Social Problems 7:108–117. 1963 The Violent Gang. New York: Macmillan.

APPENDIX A:
Self-report Delinquency and Drug Use Scales

Street Delinquency

1. Stolen or tried to steal money or things worth more than $50 but less than $100.
2. Stolen or tried to steal money or things worth more than $100.
3. Stolen or tried to steal a motor vehicle.
4. Gone into or tried to go into a building to steal something.
5. Attacked someone with a weapon or with the idea of seriously hurting or killing them.
6. Used a weapon, force, or strongarm methods to get money or things from people.
7. Physically hurt or threatened to hurt someone to get them to have sex with you.
8. Been involved in gang fights.
9. Snatched someone's purse or wallet or picked someone's pocket.
10. Stolen something from a car.
11. Sold marijuana.
12. Sold hard drugs.
13. Knowingly bought, sold, or held stolen goods or tried to do any of these things.

Other Serious Delinquency

1. Stolen or tried to steal money or things worth more than $5 but less then $50.
2. Stolen or tried to steal money or things worth less than $5.
3. Gone joyriding.
4. Hit someone with the idea of hurting them.
5. Thrown objects such as rocks or bottles at people.
6. Had or tried to have sexual relations with someone against their will.
7. Carried a hidden weapon.
8. Purposely damaged or destroyed property that did not belong to you.
9. Purposely set fire to a house, building, car, or other property or tried to do so.
10. Used checks illegally or used a slug or fake money to pay for something.
11. Used or tried to use credit or bank cards without the owner's permission.

Minor Delinquency

1. Avoided paying for things such as movies, bus or subway rides, food, or computer services.
2. Lied about your age to get into someplace or to buy something.
3. Run away from home.
4. Skipped classes without an excuse.
5. Hitchhiked where it was illegal to do so.
6. Been loud, rowdy, or unruly in a public place.
7. Begged for money or things from strangers.
8. Been drunk in a public place.
9. Been paid for having sexual relations with someone.

Alcohol Use
1. Drunk beer.
2. Drunk wine.
3. Drunk hard liquor.

Marijuana
1. Used marijuana or hashish.

Other Drugs
1. Used tranquilizers such as valium, librium, thorazine, miltown, equanil, meprobamate.
2. Used barbiturates, downers, reds, yellows, blues.
3. Used amphetamines, uppers, ups, speed, pep pills, or bennies.
4. Used hallucinogens, LSD, acid, peyote, escaline, psilocybin.
5. Used cocaine, or coke other than crack.
6. Used crack.
7. Used heroin.
8. Used angel dust or PCP.

Label-Seeking for Status:
Peers, Identities, and Domains of Deviance

Mark A. Konty
Charles W. Peek

ADOLESCENT DEVIANT BEHAVIOR: THREE FINDINGS

THE GENERALITY OF DEVIANCE

People who break into houses also tend to use drugs. People who get into fights also tend to steal. Those who drive too fast also tend to drink and drive. In general, people who are willing to commit one type of illegal act are inclined to commit other types of illegal acts.[1]

At one time criminologists assumed that most delinquents are "specialists." That is, they specialize in one or two similar types of illegal activity. For example, burglars specialize in the skills of breaking and entering, the school bully is a specialist at fighting, and the drug dealer is a capable capitalist. Criminals were thought to specialize for two reasons. First, it was assumed that most illegal acts required specialized skills. Thus, many criminologists

believed that breaking into a car or home required different skills than winning a fight or rolling a joint. The second reason for the specialist assumption was theoretical. The motivation to rob a liquor store should be different than the motivation to beat up a classmate or snort a line of cocaine. In part, this focus on specialized motivations occurred because many early criminologists studied only one type of crime. These early theorists therefore tended to offer unique explanations for the phenomenon they studied. For example, Edwin Sutherland, a highly influential criminologist, conducted a case study of a thief and, later, white-collar criminals.[2] Sutherland developed his theory of differential association to explain the criminal life of a thief and later extended the scope of his theory to explain white-collar crime and other types of criminal behavior.

Empirical research, however, has clearly demonstrated that most criminals are not specialists, but rather generalists. People who break into houses also tend to drink too much, use illegal drugs, get into fights with others, or maybe rob a liquor store. This is not to say that every criminal commits every type of criminal act. Rather, there is a tendency among people willing to break one law to break other laws. There is a strong and positive correlation between different types of illegal acts. This empirical fact has come to be called the generality of deviance, even though the evidence primarily focuses on the generality of criminal behavior.

Since correlations are simply indicators of trends or relationships between variables, there are exceptions to the generality of deviance. Some juveniles will only break a few minor laws in their youth, others will break many. Some adolescents will smoke pot and binge drink but never rob a convenience store. Some adolescents may get into a lot of fights but never kill anyone. But *generally*, those who break one law are likely to break others.

If deviance and not just crime is indeed general, then we would expect other types of deviance to be related to criminal behavior. In almost any social situation there are rules that govern behavior. Families, for example, have a variety of rules governing the conduct of the children. These rules or norms may vary from family to family, but most families have some kind of normative regulations in place, including a system for punishing offenses. These acts of deviance may be as simple as eating cookies before dinner or watching television before homework is completed. Family deviance can also be more serious, beating up a younger sibling or stealing money from Mom's purse, for example.

Families are not the only source of noncriminal rules and norm enforcement. Schools have lengthy "codes of conduct" designed to regulate the behavior of students. Although some of these rules may also be prohibited by criminal statute (truancy, drug use), most are not. Cheating on an exam and talking back to a teacher are acts prohibited by school policy and punishable

by school officials, but they are not subject to criminal penalty. Similarly, public spaces are usually governed by a set of rules. People are generally required to remain quiet during movies or to stand in line at Burger King. The management may ask a person to leave the premises if these rules are violated.

The fact that adolescents are exposed to many noncriminal rules and sources of norm enforcement suggests that adolescent deviance is much broader than law breaking. If all deviance—criminal and noncriminal—is general, then we would expect that there would be no adolescent deviance specialists. Youths who fight with their parents and cheat on tests may also be more likely to shoplift and use drugs. However, it may also be the case that adolescents who are willing to argue with their parents, pass notes in class, and make loud noises in the movie theater are not willing to break the law. This remains an open empirical question.

PEERS AND DEVIANCE

The relationship between deviant peers and deviant behavior is as robust as the relationship among different criminal acts. Reams of research data demonstrate that most delinquents have delinquent friends. In pop psychology this effect is sometimes called "peer pressure." Anecdotal evidence tells us that Johnny threw the rock at the window because Billy called him a chicken, or that Jenny skipped school because Susan told her it was the cool thing to do. It is easy for us to believe that adolescents misbehave because a peer pressures them into doing so. Anecdotal evidence, however, frequently fails to pass scientific muster, and hence there remains considerable debate about the explanation for the relationship between delinquent peers and delinquency.

Most of the debate centers on the causal ordering. Some explanations argue that peers directly influence delinquency by teaching each other how and why to commit deviant acts. The association with deviant peers and the subsequent learning of procriminal beliefs cause the deviant behavior. Other theories argue that "birds of a feather, flock together"—essentially that delinquents are deviant first, and then seek out other delinquents. The delinquent's deviant behavior precedes the association with deviant peers, and hence the deviant behavior causes the association with deviant peers. These are distinctly different explanations, each one offering a different causal ordering.

So which comes first, the chicken or egg? Research has shown that both of these causal orders happen and neither the association with delinquent peers nor the onset of delinquency comes first all of the time. Sometimes adolescents become deviant then seek out deviant peers, sometimes relationships with deviant peers precede delinquency.[3]

How can deviant associations be both cause and effect? Some research suggests that association with deviant peers provides a status opportunity,[4] and status is a highly important goal for most adolescents.[5] Perhaps what is happening with the peer/delinquency relationship is simply that adolescent deviance provides an opportunity for juveniles to acquire peer status. Juveniles perform deviant acts to gain access to a deviant peer group, then continue with deviant behavior to maintain that status.

GENDER AND DEVIANCE

The relationship between gender and deviance, measured almost exclusively by the association between gender and criminal delinquency, is perhaps the most consistent criminological finding. Males commit more crime, more types of crime, more serious crimes, and continue to commit crimes later into the life-course than females. Most explanations for this gender disparity either refer to differences in social control between boys and girls or to different types of gender socialization. Some even suggest that biases in the criminal justice system may account for some of the variation.

Given the substantial differences between male and female social experiences, many scholars have suggested that explanations for male deviance may not apply to female deviance. Indeed, a vast majority of the studies on delinquency are about male delinquency and ignore or trivialize female delinquency. Historically, many scholars dismissed female deviance as something pathological, caused by mental defect. It has only been in recent years that feminist scholars began to focus on the unique qualities of female social experience.[6] Much attention has been given to this insight in recent years, but the debate over different or similar explanations for male and female deviance remains.

SYMBOLIC INTERACTION THEORY[7]

Symbolic interactionism is a broad theoretical paradigm with many branches and schools of thought. These various approaches share several theoretical principles. The social situation is considered to be one of, if not the, most powerful causal influence on behavior. People define situations and tailor their behavior accordingly from one situation to the next. Each successive situation one encounters carries a new set of definitions or meanings as well as a new set of relationships. For example, young people may behave very differently in their peer groups than they do around adults. Among teenagers the meaning of a tattoo or piercing may be very different than for their parents. Social norms regarding fighting, drinking, or cheating may be different for adolescents and adults. Relationships between peers are often very different than relationships between children and their parents.

Symbolic interactionists also recognize that there is a reciprocal relationship between actors and situations. Not only are people shaped by the situation, but they can also act to shape the situation. Individuals may bring new definitions to situations. For example, tattoos and piercings were once considered to be a sign of a lower working class status, but young people in the middle class began to define tattoos and piercings as something desirable or "cool."[8] Music and clothing tastes also change in this manner as do definitions of what type of behavior is right or wrong in a situation (social norms).

People are also capable of choosing new situations with new definitions. There is often a limited set of choices available and symbolic interactionists make no assumptions about "rational" actors choosing the situations with the most benefits and least costs. Many choices are simply not available to us. It is exceedingly difficult for a homeless man to obtain entrance to a Republican Party dinner. Some choices are quite difficult to realize. Very few people have ever experienced the thrill of outer space. Nonetheless, we do have choices. An adolescent may join the band or the basketball team, thus being exposed to a new situation. Similarly, a teenager may seek out a new set of friends, perhaps deviant peers, and in doing so encounter new situations with new

definitions. Symbolic interactionist theory, however, makes no assumptions about these choices being "rational" in the sense that they maximize benefits and minimize costs.[9]

The situation represents the social component in symbolic interactionism. There is also an individual component. Most symbolic interaction theorists views the individual as a set of socially-constructed identities. According to the symbolic interactionist perspective, who and what we think we are is a product of our social experience. One of the primary assumptions of symbolic interactionism is that people will act on the identities they have for themselves. People are motivated to confirm their identities, acting in ways that reinforce their beliefs about themselves. With identities come expectations for behavior, and most of the time people act according to these expectations.

Situations and identities are inexorably connected. What it means to be a woman in Afghanistan is different than what it means on the streets of Paris. Conversely, how a woman acts among her friends is different than how she acts with her spouse. The definition of the situation provides the context within which an identity is enacted. Thus, identities can change or be chosen much as situations are. For example, students acquire new meanings, norms, and relationships as they progress from primary to secondary education. In first grade, being a student means coloring, standing in line for lunch, and disliking members of the opposite sex. In high school, being a student means homework, going out for lunch, and not being able to get the opposite sex out of your mind. Across situations, or over time, identities can change. People can also, to a limited extent, choose their identities. A teenager may decide she no longer likes the relatively low status of playing in the high school band and instead decides to join a deviant peer group with a reputation for fighting and partying.

APPLYING SYMBOLIC INTERATION THEORY TO ADOLESCENT DEVIANCE

SYMBOLIC INTERACTION AND THE GENERALITY OF DEVIANCE

The principles of symbolic interactionism easily address the issue of the generality of deviance. Criminal behavior is behavior that is defined as criminal by legal statute. Across situations, the same behavior is defined as illegal. Presumably everyone knows that killing another person is illegal, just as they know that it is illegal to rob a liquor store or shoot heroin. Breaking a law is somewhat risky as society defines the act as illegal and proscribes punishment for performing the act. Engaging in criminal activity, therefore, constitutes an act with similar meaning in the eyes of the criminal justice system and most of society.

Other types of deviance, however, are not restricted by law. Noncriminal deviance is behavior that runs counter to a situational norm but may not be restricted in other situations. The situational nature of most social norms is a well-established fact. We all know, for example, that talking out loud is deviant in a movie theater but is encouraged at a sporting event. However, it is quite normative to talk during the *Rocky Horror Picture Show*, but it is considered deviant to talk while a golfer is putting. Noncriminal deviance does not have the same transsituational properties that criminal deviance does. Break a law and you are labeled a criminal by general society and you may be punished with severe sanctions. Have sex without a condom and you may

be considered "stupid" or "risky" but the only punishment is perhaps a disease or unwanted pregnancy. Argue with your parents and you may be labeled a "bad kid," and maybe your parents will ground you. The difference between criminal and noncriminal deviance is a very different definition of the situation.

The definition and regulation of deviant behavior within situations gives rise to *domains of deviance*. Depending on the situation, different norms may apply and different persons interact in defining deviant behavior and enforcing norms. The criminal law constitutes the most general and organized domain. Rules are codified and the criminal justice system exists for the sole purpose of enforcing these rules. Smaller and less formal domains include specific situations where we enact our daily interactions. The family is the first domain that we come into contact with. Our parents define appropriate behavior, monitor that behavior, and provide sanctions when necessary. The school is another domain that most everyone interacts within. Schools have a slightly more formalized rule structure and policy regarding punishment, but nowhere near the scale of the criminal domain. Even our daily lifestyle choices could be said to constitute a domain. Wearing purple hair and torn jeans to a nice restaurant is sure to draw a few stares. Viewing pornography is legal but there are doubtless many women who would rather not date a man with a huge porn collection. The lifestyle domain is even less formal than the family domain and can only be defined in terms of public appearances and behaviors. Done privately, many lifestyle choices pass without notice, but ask someone to urinate on you in public and see what reaction you get. Churches and work places also constitute domains of deviance as each has its own set of rules and enforcers.

Rephrasing the issue concerning the generality of deviance of noncriminal with criminal deviance in terms of domains raises our first set of research questions: *Is deviance general across criminal and noncriminal domains?* For that matter, given the specificity of deviance to interaction situations, *how general is deviance among noncriminal domains?*

SYMBOLIC INTERACTION AND THE PEER/DEVIANCE RELATIONSHIP

Principles of symbolic interaction can also be brought to bear in explaining the peer/deviance relationship. The inexorable link of individual identities to interaction in situations, witnessed in youths' efforts to shape and maintain their identities in these situations, provides an explanation for why deviance sometimes precedes associations with deviant peers when, at others, deviance follows these associations. Deviance precedes associations with deviant peers when adolescents seeking deviant identities act accordingly, and then link up with deviant peers as a source for maintaining these identities. Deviance follows associations with deviant peers when adolescents enact deviant identities with these peers in order to maintain and support such identities. Deviant behavior and deviant peers are not viewed in the typical cause-and-effect manner. Instead, deviant behavior and deviant peers are related because both result from youths' pursuit of deviant identities.

But why seek deviant identities? Labeling theory argues that juveniles become more delinquent after acquiring a negative, pejorative label from official rule enforcers.[10] Typically, the effects of deviant labeling are thought to be negative. The person's public presentation is tainted and the spoiled identity has negative consequences for the person. Labeling theory has always considered the acquisition of deviant identities to be a negative outcome, something to be avoided. Yet sometimes it seems that adolescents go out of their way to acquire a negative or deviant evaluation from adults. Adults often view adolescent life as characterized by bizarre fashions and strange musical tastes, but many young people seem to relish this negative attention.

Adolescents may hold a different definition of the situation. They see deviant identities as frequently conferring greater status and more self-efficacy in an age bracket where these valued attributes are in short supply. We know that people will act in ways to present themselves as they wish others to see them.[11] If adolescents wish to acquire status by adopting a deviant identity, then they seek a deviant label. Noncriminal deviance is a relatively easy type of behavior that can accomplish this identity confirmation.

The importance of deviant identities to understanding the peer/delinquency relationship, as well as adolescents seeking these identities by trying to acquire deviant labels, generates our second set of research questions. First, *how well is the desire to seek deviant labels correlated with adolescent deviant activity compared to other standard explanations of this behavior?* Further, *will a desire to seek negative labels be more associated with noncriminal than criminal deviance?*

SYMBOLIC INTERACTION, GENDER, AND DEVIANCE

Symbolic interaction theory points to gender differences in identities and situations as the primary forces behind the rather extensive male-female variation in delinquent conduct. Through both socialization and interaction, boys and girls learn, create, and maintain very different identities. For example, young females incorporate nurturance into their identities through socialization, whereas young males are learning to be tough, an image that contradicts the feelings expressed by nurturance. Girls and boys attempt to promote and reaffirm these respective elements of their identities by "doing gender"—practicing these identities when interacting with others.[12] Since girls and boys are often segregated in social situations, either by choice or custom, it is very likely that they experience different situations. When boys and girls are in the same situation they may experience that situation differently. For example, young males and females are frequently held to different sets of norms in interactional settings, such as norms pertaining to physical aggressiveness (more permissible for males) and norms concerning the display of personal emotions other than anger (more permissible for females).

These gender differences in identities and situations may lie at the heart of gender variations in deviant conduct. The male identity of toughness provokes risky male behavior in some circumstances because such behavior promotes this element of the male identity. The more risky the consequences, the better it supports a tough male identity. Because toughness is not an image that most young females try to exhibit, they may not engage as much in seriously risky behavior. Instead, girls may display a tendency toward conformity that also displays the nurturing character of the female identity.[13]

Because young females and males generally experience situations differently, they are also likely not to have the same experiences within specific domains of deviance. There is considerable evidence that boys and girls have different experiences with the criminal justice system, within families, at school, at work, and in public.[14]

Use of gender differences in identities and situations to explain male-female variations in deviant conduct leads to our third set of research questions. First, *will the generality of deviance vary by gender*? Second, *will label-seeking be the same for boys and girls*?

RESEARCH

This research is part of a preliminary project that sought to address the issues and questions outlined above. The data for this project comes from 141 self-report surveys administered to adolescents living in a mid-size (200,000) Texas city. Eighty-one subjects (28 females) were recruited from a local coffee shop that served as a hangout for the local punk rock subculture. The coffee shop routinely hosted concerts by punk bands, and these subjects were recruited with a free ticket to a concert. Sixty subjects (16 female) were recruited from the local juvenile detention facility. The self-described punk rockers and the incarcerated delinquent youth can be described as a sample of "deviant" adolescents.

The deviant behavior of these adolescents was measured with a self-report survey. Each subject was given a list of behaviors and instructions to "Please indicate the number of times you have done this behavior in the last 12 months." The list of behaviors was designed to encompass the criminal, family, and school domains of deviance. The criminal domain was divided into three factors: a "serious offenses" factor that measured more serious crimes; a "status offenses" factor that measured law breaking that only applies to juveniles; and a "substance abuse" factor that measured law breaking with regard to alcohol and marijuana (see Appendix A for a list of the behaviors from each domain and their means). Each response was converted into a standard z score to assure all responses were measured on the same scale. The scores were averaged together to provide an indicator of the respondent's deviance within that domain.

In order to examine possible influences on the deviant behaviors, we measured subjects' attitudes that, according to various theories, may predict the deviant behavior. Our label-seeking hypothesis was measured with attitudes toward negative, deviant labels. The subject's responses to a list of statements eliciting opinions about these labels (on a Likery-type scale from "strongly agree" to "strongly disagree") measure desire to seek a deviant label. These responses were averaged to provide a scale indicating the subject's preference for negative labels (see Appendix B for a list of label-seeking statements).

Since many other theories seek to explain the empirical issues we are exploring here, we decided to conduct a rough test of three of these theories to determine if label-seeking is a better predictor of noncriminal deviance than more traditional criminological approaches. We use measures derived from social learning theory, self-control theory, and strain theory to compare with our measures of label-seeking.

Social learning theories argue that people become deviant when they learn definitions that are favorable toward deviant behavior.[15] We measured the subjects' attitudes toward family, school, and conformity (see Appendix B). We reasoned that negative attitudes toward the family and school should be associated with deviance in the family or school domains, whereas negative attitudes toward conformity may be a better correlate of deviance in general. This theory predicts that attitudes favorable to deviance should be domain specific. Thus, negative attitudes toward the family should be correlated with family deviance, negative attitudes toward the school should be correlated with school deviance, and so on.

Self-control theories argue that people are deviant because they lack the capacity to control their impulses and delay gratification.[16] These impulses tell the person to acquire whatever they desire without delay. This theory claims that deviance is general because the inability to control the impulse to steal is the same as the inability to control the impulse to fight with one's parents. Similar types of analogous behavior are all caused by the same lack of self-control. Risky endeavors are considered to be analogous to criminal behavior. We measure attitudes toward risk taking as an indicator of low self-control (see Appendix B). Low self-control, according to the theory, should explain all types of rule breaking and hence all types of deviance.

Social strain theory argues that people are deviant because they experience a negative affective state.[17] That is, people experience strain from social and group life that generates negative feelings and emotions. When negative affect is not dealt with by conventional means, deviant behavior results. We measured negative affect with attitudes about how society as a whole treats the subject (see Appendix B). If the subject believes that society is treating them unfairly, negative affect should result. Deviant behavior in response to experiencing negative affect should theoretically manifest itself in any of the domains.

FINDINGS

For background purposes, Table 1 presents the means for all variables, for the total sample and separately for boys and girls. Unexpectedly, probability levels for the gender differences in means among the five domains of deviance show only one not due to chance. Greater substance abuse (criminal domain) among boys is very likely a real difference, because there is

TABLE 1:   Mean, Standard Deviations, and Means Comparison Total Sample and Gender

	Sample Means (standard deviation)	Boys' Means (standard deviation)	Girls' Means (standard deviation)	Probability[a] (*t*)
Serious Offenses (criminal domain)	.00 (.81)	.0209 (.854)	−.0465 (.706)[b]	.649 (.456)
Status Offenses (criminal domain)	.00 (.80)	−.0530 (.754)	.1169 (.899)	.246 (1.091)
Substance Abuse (criminal domain)	.00 (.78)	.0926 (.814)	−.2081 (.673)	.034 (2.138)
School Deviance (school domain)	.00 (.79)	−.0419 (.787)	.0889 (.817)	.184 (1.335)
Family Deviance (family domain)	.00 (.65)	−.0535 (.609)	.1208 (.739)	.368 (.903)
Label-Seeking Attitudes	2.79 (.89)	2.75 (.84)	2.88 (1.01)	.440 (.775)
School Attitudes	2.31 (1.22)	2.57 (.93)	3.10 (1.14)	.004 (2.291)
Family Attitudes	2.73 (1.03)	2.05 (1.01)	2.89 (1.46)	.001 (3.969)
Conformity Attitudes	2.30 (1.11)	2.49 (1.16)	1.89 (.89)	.003 (3.071)
Negative Attitudes	3.16 (.96)	3.15 (.96)	3.17 (.98)	.901 (.124)
Risk-Taking Attitudes	3.22 (.96)	3.18 (.93)	3.32 (1.03)	.425 (.800)

[a]probability that the difference between the boys' mean and the girls' mean was due to chance.
[b]these are the means of the averaged *z* scores, and a negative number simply means that the value was below the sample mean, which is 0.

only about a three-percent likelihood that this difference is due to random data fluctuation. Unlike most other sets of findings, in this sample boys do not exhibit more deviant conduct than girls in any domain except substance abuse. In addition, no statistically significant gender differences (differences which have at least a 5-percent likelihood or less of being chance occurrences) in means occur on any of the sets of attitudes, surprisingly not even in risk-taking attitudes.

Tables 2 and 3 present Pearson correlation coefficients between the domains of deviance for males and females respectively (the higher the coefficient, the more the deviance in each pair overlaps). These results speak to our first set of research questions concerning the generality of deviance within in the two noncriminal domains, among the three criminal domains, and between the noncriminal and criminal domains.

These tables indicate generality of deviance between the two noncriminal domains: both adolescent males (Table 2) and adolescent females (Table 3) who break family rules are also likely to violate school norms. However, this overlap is far more substantial among girls than boys, since the correlation coefficient measuring this overlap is more than twice as large among females than among males. Deviance is also general for both genders among the three criminal domains, with the lone exception being the lack of an association between females' serious offenses and substance abuse. The generality of the criminal domains is stronger for males than females. The average correlation coefficient between male criminal domains (.52) is nearly double the

TABLE 2:   Pearson Correlations between Domains of Deviance Male Sample

	Serious Offenses (criminal domain)	Status Offenses (criminal domain)	Substance Abuse (criminal domain)	Family Deviance (family domain)
School Deviance (school domain)	.473 (*p* < .001)	.468 (*p* < .001)	.543 (*p* < .001)	.338 (*p* = .001)
Family Deviance (family domain)	.037 (*p* = .723)	.103 (*p* = .315)	.181 (*p* = .076)	
Substance Abuse (criminal domain)	.637 (*p* < .001)	.430 (*p* < .001)		
Status Offense (criminal domain)	.497 (*p* < .001)			

TABLE 3:   Pearson Correlations between Domains of Deviance Female Sample

	Serious Offenses (criminal domain)	Status Offenses (criminal domain)	Substance Abuse (criminal domain)	Family Deviance (family domain)
School Deviance (school domain)	.099 (*p* = .525)	.362 (*p* = .016)	.646 (*p* < .001)	.791 (*p* < .001)
Family Deviance (family domain)	.053 (*p* = .735)	.399 (*p* = .007)	.620 (*p* < .001)	
Substance Abuse (criminal domain)	.010 (*p* = .949)	.431 (*p* = .003)		
Status Offense (criminal domain)	.355 (*p* = .018)			

average coefficient between female criminal domains (.27), showing a greater generality of criminal deviance among these males.

These data also show some generality between deviance in noncriminal and criminal domains, but not nearly as much as the generality among criminal domains. Girls who report more family or school deviance are also more involved in status offenses and substance abuse, whereas boys with greater school deviance are also higher in all three types of criminal deviance. But family deviance among boys does not correlate with rule breaking in any of the three criminal domains, and neither school nor family deviance among girls is connected to serious criminal offenses. Compared to the nearly complete generality of deviance among all criminal domains (with the exception noted above), deviance in noncriminal domains is far less general than deviance in these criminal domains.

Our attitude measures of theoretical forces derived from label seeking, control, learning, and strain theories were used to address a second set of research questions. One issue is how label seeking compares to the other three theories as explanations of adolescent deviant activity. Tables 4 and 5 show that seeking deviant labels to promote and sustain deviant identities correlates with adolescent deviance at least as well as indicators of social learning theory and better than measures of strain and control theories. After control-

ling for the effects of all other indicators with the use of partial correlation estimates, label seeking provides two of the four significant associations with boys' deviant conduct in Figure 1. Boys who seek deviant identities through deviant labels report more status offenses and more serious offenses, while nonconventional definitions of family (one indicator of social learning theory) are related to greater family and school deviance. None of the other indices of social learning theory (school attitudes, conformity attitudes) or the measures of strain (negative attitudes) and self-control (risk-taking attitudes) display

TABLE 4:   Relationships Between Causal Attitudes and Domains of Deviance Partial Correlation Coefficient Male Sample

	School Deviance	Family Deviance	Substance Abuse	Status Offenses	Serious Offenses
Label-Seeking Attitudes	.1203	.0384	.1081	.3298	.2377
Family Attitudes	.2262*	.2813*	.1280	.1616	.1313
School Attitudes	−.1122	−.1034	−.0413	.1653	.0452
Conformity Attitudes	−.0500	−.1805	−.0566	.0497	.0788
Negative Attitudes	−.0252	.1240	.0046	−.1470	.0209
Risk-Taking Attitudes	.0876	.2307*	−.0002	−.0096	−.0063

* $p \le .05$

TABLE 5:   Relationships Between Causal Attitudes and Domains of Deviance Partial Correlation Coefficient Female Sample

	School Deviance	Family Deviance	Substance Abuse	Status Offenses	Serious Offenses
Label-Seeking Attitudes	.3452*	.2325	.3166*	.2299	−.1041
Family Attitudes	.0059	.0985	−.0219	.0887	.1052
School Attitudes	−.1093	−.1837	.1116	−.1997	.1191
Conformity Attitudes	.0233	.0556	.2174	.3505*	−.0349
Negative Attitudes	.1660	.2476	−.0276	.1434	.2910*
Risk-Taking Attitudes	.0626	.0851	.1614	−.1939	−.0467

* $p \le .10$

any significant association with deviance in any of the five domains.

In Figure 2, label seeking also produces two of the four significant associations with deviance among girls. Net of the effects of all other attitudes, adolescent females who favor pursuing deviant labels reveal higher levels of deviance in both the school and substance abuse domains. Girls with more negative attitudes toward conformity (another indicator of social learning theory) and who have negative societal attitudes (the measure of strain theory) report more deviance in the status offense and serious offense domains respectively. Again, none of the other two indicators of social learning theory (family attitudes, school attitudes) or risk-taking attitudes (an index of self-control theory) exhibit any association with deviance in any domain.

The other issue in this set of research questions concerns whether a desire to seek deviant labels is more associated with noncriminal than criminal deviance. For male youth the answer is no, since we've just seen that both associations of label-seeking attitudes with male deviance are with deviance in criminal domains. Although label seeking is associated with noncriminal school deviance among female youth. it is also related to deviance in the criminal domain of substance abuse; so it is not associated *more* with noncriminal than criminal deviance.

Our third set of research questions explore whether girls are more likely than boys to specialize in less risky noncriminal deviance, if the generality of deviance both within and between criminal and noncriminal domains varies by gender, and whether intentional label seeking is differently connected to the deviance of boys versus girls. Data pertaining to these issues have already been presented. Recall that in Table 1 girls did not exhibit a statistically significant greater participation than boys

in either noncriminal school or family deviance, nor for that matter did male/female differences emerge in any criminal domain of deviance except substance abuse. So, these adolescent females do not perform more or less of any type of deviance except for substance abuse.

Gender differences did emerge in Tables 2m and 2f concerning the generality of deviance. Recall that adolescent females displayed more generality of deviance than males between the two noncriminal domains, whereas more overlap existed for males than females in deviance among the three criminal domains. Gender variation in patterns of sharing deviance between noncriminal and criminal domains also occurred: family deviance did not overlap with any criminal domain for boys, whereas neither school nor family deviance connected to deviance in the serious offense criminal domain among girls.

Intentional label seeking is also related in different ways to the deviance of boys versus girls. Recall from Tables 1 and 2 that boys with more positive attitudes toward seeking deviant labels and identities report more deviance in two criminal domains of status offense and serious offense. On the other hand, girls with more desire to seek deviant labels show greater deviant involvement in the criminal substance abuse and in the noncriminal school domain.

DISCUSSION

Each set of findings heralds the promise of symbolic interaction theory in explaining adolescent deviance. The symbolic interaction principle that identities drive behavior helps to understand the surprising results in the first set of findings from Table 1: females reporting similar levels of deviance as males in all domains except substance abuse, and no gender differences on attitudes toward risk taking or other attitudes. Consider that our respondents were not taken from a cross-section of all youth in which males tend to acquire more deviant identities than females. Instead, both male *and female* respondents were already participating in deviant groups (punk rockers or incarcerated youth) and likely already possessed and were maintaining—or in the process of constructing—deviant self-images. Roughly equal gender distribution of these identities and efforts to sustain them through deviant interaction with others argues for few gender differences in either deviant conduct or attitudes toward risky behavior in this set of youth. If representative samples demonstrate that there is greater concentration of deviant male identities in the general population, this would also account for the typical finding that males are more deviant and more often approve of risky behavior.

Symbolic interaction theory also informs findings on our first set of research questions. Because noncriminal deviance domains represent different situations—different norms and punishments for norm violations—than criminal domains, less overlapping deviance should occur between criminal and noncriminal domains than among domains in either category. This is precisely what the second set of findings demonstrates. Apparently, symbols, meanings, and situations vary enough between noncriminal and criminal contexts to reduce the generality between noncriminal and criminal deviance.

The symbolic interactionist position that the process of creating and sustaining identities underlies social behavior ties deviant behavior to the promotion and maintenance of deviant identities. This position suggests deviant label seeking—the effort to create or sustain deviant identities in the eyes of others—as a key force that generates deviant conduct. Results on our second set

of research questions support this position. After controls for other attitudes, the desire to seek deviant labels was linked to deviance in more domains for both adolescent males and females than were measures of any of the other three standard theories of deviance.

Findings from our third set of research questions illustrate the importance of both identities and situations to understanding gender differences in deviance. Because there is likely little gender variation in the distribution of deviant identities in our selective sample of punkers and incarcerated youth (nearly everyone probably has some kind of deviant identity), these girls are no more likely than boys to perform noncriminal or criminal deviance. However, gender differences are likely in boys' and girls' definitions of various situations as they experience domains differently. If boys and girls have divergent "takes" on various domains of deviance, then these differences should result in gender differences between these domains. Indeed, this is what we found. More overlap exists among females between the two noncriminal domains; deviance is more general for males among the three criminal domains, and patterns of connections between noncriminal and criminal domains vary by gender.

Finally, the interest of symbolic interaction theory in both identities and situations merge to predict that the intentional seeking of deviant labels will vary by gender. The same deviant identity (e.g., "punker," "incarcerated delinquent") may have different meanings to females than males because these identities are constructed in social situations (domains of deviance) that apply differently to males and females, and because these boys and girls already possess a gender identity that directs all further identity construction. Thus, a girl punk rocker could maintain a deviant identity by performing simple noncriminal acts of deviance or, in the case of our findings, less serious acts of delinquency such as substance abuse. For males it may be necessary to perform more serious acts of delinquency to achieve the same deviant identity.

Two problems with this sample warrant a cautious approach to these findings. First, the sample size is relatively small in the world of social science. This increases the probability of sampling error and makes it more difficult to detect significant differences and correlations. Second, this is a selective sample and not a random probability sample, which means that our findings cannot be generalized to any population, including punk rock or juvenile delinquent populations. So, these results can't be considered definitive answers to any of our research questions. What they do demonstrate is the sizeable potential of symbolic interaction theory for understanding adolescent deviance, a potential we think subsequent research in this area should note.

Notes

1. For more on this topic see *The Generality of Deviance*, edited by Travis Hirschi and Michael Gottfredson, 1994, Transaction Publications.

2. See Edwin Sutherland's interesting works on *The Professional Thief*, 1937, University of Chicago Press; and *White Collar Crime*, 1949, Dryden.

3. To see longitudinal evidence of this reciprocal relationship, see "Gangs, Drugs, and Delinquency in a Survey of Urban Youth" by Finn.-Aage Esbense and David Huizinga in *Criminology*, 1993, V. 4., pp. 565–587.

4. For more on status attainment through deviant identities, see *Renegade Kids, Suburban Outlaws*, by Wayne S. Wooden and Randy Blazak, 2001, Wadsworth.

5. For more on the importance of peer status among adolescents, see *Peer Power: Preadolescent Culture and Identity*, by Patricia A. Adler and Peter Adler, 1998, Rutgers University Press.

6. For more on the relationship between gender and juvenile delinquency as well as the double standard applied to boys and girls behavior, see *Girls, Delinquency, and Juvenile Justice*, by Meda Chesney-Lind and Randall S. Sheldon, 1998, Wadsworth.

7. For more on the various approaches to symbolic interaction, see *Symbolic Interactionism: A Structural Perspective*, by Sheldon Stryker, 1980, Benjamin Cummings, *Symbolic Interactionism: An Introduction, An Interpretation, An Integration*, by Joel Charon, 1998, Prentice Hall; *Symbolic Interactionism as Affect Control*, by Neil MacKinnon, 1994, SUNY Press.

8. For more on the co-option of tattooing and piercing by middle class youths, see *Renegade Kids, Suburban Outlaws*, by Wayne S. Wooden and Randy Blazak, 2001, Wadsworth.

9. In fact, some theories employing symbolic interactionist principles argue that people's choices reflect a motivation to maintain fundamental sentiments rather than a motivation to maximize benefits and minimize costs. For example, see *Symbolic Interaction as Affect Control*, by Neil J. MacKinnon, 1994, State University of New York Press.

10. For more on labeling theory, see *Labeling Deviant Behavior, Its Sociological Implications*, by Edwin M. Schur, 1971, Harper and Row.

11. For more on people's self-presentation, see *The Presentation of Self in Everyday Life*, by Erving Goffman, 1959, Doubleday.

12. For more on the process of doing gender, see "Doing Gender" by Candace West and Don H. Zimmerman, in *The Social Construction of Gender* edited by J. Lorber and S.A. Farrell, 1991, Sage Publications.

13. For more information on the role of gender identity in the production of deviance, see *Crime as Structured Action: Gender, Race, Class and Crime in the Making*, by James W. Messerschmidt, 1997, Sage Publications.

14. For an excellent discussion of the gendered double standard in defining deviant behavior, see *Labeling Women Deviant: Gender, Stigma, and Social Control*, by Edwin Schur, 1984, Random House Publishing.

15. For more on this theory, see *Deviant Behavior: A Social Learning Approach*, by Ronald Akers, 1977, Wadsworth.

16. For more on this theory, see *A General Theory of Crime* by Michael Gottfredson and Travis Hirschi, 1990, Stanford University Press.

17. For more on this theory, see "Foundation for a General Strain Theory of Crime and Delinquency," in *Criminology v. 30*, by Robert Agnew, 1992.

APPENDIX A
SELF-REPORT QUESTIONS: MEANS DOMAINS OF DEVIANCE

"Below are some ways people frequently behave. For each behavior, please estimate the number of times you have acted this way *DURING the last 12* months."

SERIOUS OFFENSES (= .8365)

Taken something from a store without paying for it: 7.69

Intentionally hurt someone bad enough to need bandages or medical treatment: 1.82

Intentionally damaged property: 5.01

Threatened someone with a weapon: 1.43

Broken into a vehicle or building: 2.66

STATUS OFFENSES (= .4489)
Run away from home: .78
Skipped school: 12.18

SUBSTANCE ABUSE (= .6861)
Drunk alcohol to get drunk: 33.29
Driven while intoxicated: 3.2
Used marijuana: 34.43

FAMILY DEVIANCE (= .8268)
Ignored chores or family responsibilities: 25.22

Argued or had a nonviolent fight with your parents: 25.61

Lied to your parents about where you were or your actions: 26.22

Made bad grades despite your parents' warnings: 9.27

Lied to your family about how you were doing in school: 5.74

Watched television or movies your parents disapproved of: 11.59

Listened to music your parents disapproved of: 27.14

Worn a hairstyle your parents disapproved of: 8.60

Worn clothing your parents disapproved of: 25.26

SCHOOL DEVIANCE (= .8102)
Not studied for a test when you knew you needed to: 23.11

Argued or had a nonviolent fight with teachers or school administrators: 6.12

Lied to teachers or school administrators: 15.32

Cheated on a test: 10.76

APPENDIX B
CAUSAL ATTITUDES

LABEL-SEEKING ATTITUDES (= .5584)
I am pleased when my parents don't like my music:

I don't want other people to think I'm a punk with no motivation or future: (reversed)

I want other people to think I'm a crazy teenager:

I don't care if my parents think me and my friends look funny:

EDUCATION ATTITUDES (= .7035)
Education is important in leading a happy life: (reversed)

Going to school is a waste of time:

FAMILY ATTITUDES (= .5113)
My family is important to me: (reversed)

I look forward to getting married and having children: (reversed)

It is okay for anyone 14 years old to have sex:

CONFORMITY ATTITUDES (= .5108)
Dress and appearance should be considered a sign of success: (reversed)

Conforming to society's rules is very important:

NEGATIVE ATTITUDES (= .6595)
It is hard for someone like me to find a job:

I am angry because society won't let me look and behave like an individual:

Society tries to keep people like me from being successful:

Authority figures seem to single me out for harsh or unfair treatment:

RISK-TAKING ATTITUDES (= .5701)

I like the feeling of standing next to the ledge of a high place:

I don't understand people who enjoy climbing dangerous mountains: (reversed)

I would not like to try any drug which might produce strange or dangerous effects on me: (reversed)

A sensible person avoids activities that are dangerous: (reversed)

Chapter **8**

Girls and Delinquency

INTRODUCTION

The differential causes of girls' and boys' delinquency have been debated among criminologists for years. Past research on girls and delinquency has suggested that stress in interpersonal situations affect delinquency. Using Agnew's General Strain Theory, Robert Agnew and Timothy Brezina investigate such a relationship with multiple measures of stress in interpersonal relationships. They shed light on the potentially crime-producing situations that success with the opposite sex and dating has for both boys and girls.

Delinquency research has long concerned itself with the "gender gap" in offending. Mears, Ploeger, and Warr investigate possible explanations for the large gap in boys' and girls' rates of delinquency. Drawing from Carol Gilligan's groundbreaking work that suggests that girls and boys differ on how they are socialized toward moral evaluations, Mears et al. suggest that moral evaluations of behavior and associations with delinquent peers interact to increase or decrease the likelihood of delinquency.

Until recently, little was known about girls' offending and victimization in gangs. Jody Miller, in her interview study of 20 female gang members in a Midwestern town, chronicles the victimization risks experienced by girls in mixed-sex gangs. Paradoxically, the girls in her sample often reported that they joined gangs to feel a sense of protection, yet the gang membership effected their victimization risk. She argues that girls face unique victimization risks due to their gender and their gang affiliation.

Relational Problems with Peers, Gender, and Delinquency

Robert Agnew
Timothy Brezina

There has been much debate over whether mainstream theories of delinquency are able to explain female delinquency (e.g., Box, 1983; Daly & Chesney-Lind, 1988; Leonard, 1982; Morris, 1987; Smith, 1979; Smith & Paternoster, 1987). Much attention, in particular, has focused on individual-level versions of classic strain theory (CST). CST contends that delinquency is more likely when individuals are unable to achieve their goals. According to CST, the dominant goal in the United States is monetary success or middle-class status. Large segments of the population are said to be prevented from achieving this goal through legitimate channels. Certain of these individuals *may* turn to delinquency; employing illegitimate means to achieve their goals (e.g., theft), striking out at others in their anger, or retreating into drug use[1] (Cloward & Ohlin, 1960; Cohen, 1955; Merton, 1938). Some criminologists claim that this theory is applicable to both males and females (Adler, 1975; Simons, Miller, & Aigner, 1980), whereas others claim that a distinct version of strain theory may be

Robert Agnew, Youth & Society, Vol. 29, No. 1, pp. 84–111, copyright © 1997 by Sage Publications, Inc. Reprinted by permission of Sage Publications, Inc.

necessary to explain female crime and delinquency (see Cernkovich & Giordano, 1979; Leonard, 1982; Naffine, 1987). In particular, researchers such as Morris (1964) have argued that females are concerned with the quality of their interpersonal ties to others rather than with economic success (see Cohen, 1955; Leonard, 1982). Female delinquency, then, is said to be a function of interpersonal rather than economic strain—requiring the application of a theoretical explanation that addresses the criminogenic role of negative interpersonal relations as opposed to structures of blocked opportunity (cf. Agnew, 1992).

Most tests of strain theory have ignored this latter argument, and have instead examined the impact of economic strain on males and, occasionally, females. Results in this area are mixed. Some studies suggest that economic strain has a weak to moderate effect on delinquency among both males and females; other studies suggest that economic strain is unimportant among both males and females (e.g., Cernkovich & Giordano, 1979; Datesman, Scarpitti, & Stephenson, 1975; Elliott, Huizinga, & Ageton, 1985; Hill & Crawford, 1990; Johnson, 1979; Rankin, 1980; Simons et al., 1980; Simpson & Elis, 1995). Only two studies have focused specifically on interpersonal strain as a cause of female crime (Morris, 1964; Sandhu & Allen, 1969). These studies have produced contradictory results, although both suffer from serious methodological problems. This study attempts to fill a gap in the literature by examining the effect of interpersonal strain on male and female delinquency. The focus, in particular, is on relational problems with peers among a nationally representative group of high school sophomores. Data suggest that peer relations assume paramount importance during the high school period (see Agnew, 1997; Warr, 1993). Further, certain data suggest that peer problems may constitute perhaps the dominant source of strain among adolescents (Ambert, 1994). If the arguments of researchers such as Morris have any merit, we would expect that (a) relational problems with peers will be positively related to female delinquency and (b) such problems will be more strongly related to female than male delinquency—suggesting that somewhat distinctive versions of strain theory may be necessary for females and males. Before testing these arguments, however, we discuss the relevance of interpersonal strain to male and female delinquency.

INTERPERSONAL STRAIN, GENDER, AND DELINQUENCY

Although the relevance of economic strain to females (and males) is questionable, several theorists have argued that females are especially concerned about the quality of their interpersonal relations with others and are therefore more vulnerable to what might be called interpersonal or relational strain. Cohen (1955) was one of the first to make this argument when he stated that "people do not simply want to excel, they want to excel *as a man* or *as a woman*" (p. 138; emphases in original). Males were

said to be concerned with monetary success or middle-class status, whereas females were said to be concerned with relational goals—particularly relations with the opposite sex and marriage (also see the discussion in Cernkovich & Giordano, 1979). Leonard (1982) echoed this argument:

> The goal women have traditionally been taught to seek is marriage and children. A women might legitimately achieve tremendous financial success in the business world and still find people curious to know if she is married and has a family. If the answer is no, her success is tained. (pp. 57–58)

Ruth Morris (1964) defined relational goals more broadly, claiming that females are interested not only in males and finding a husband but in "positive affective relationships" in general (see Naffine, 1987, p. 16). Allison Morris (1987) likewise broadened the definition of relational goals. In a critique of Leonard, she argued that females are not only concerned with forming close relationships to others; they are also concerned about the quality of those relationships. She pointed out, for example, that abused women are under great strain even though they are married and have families. These arguments suggest that the relational goals of females encompass both romantic and nonromantic relationships. Further, such goals have two primary components: the establishment of close ties to others (e.g., having close friends, being married) and the maintenance of good relationships with these others. Numerous researchers outside of criminology have made essentially the same argument, claiming that females are more concerned than males with the establishment and maintenance of close ties to others. This argument, in fact, is at the core of much recent work on the psychology of gender (e.g., Brown & Gilligan, 1992; Gilligan, 1982; Gilligan, Lyons, & Hanmer, 1989; Jordan, 1995; J. Miller, 1986).

The relational goals of females are usually said to be a function of the socialization process and women's structural position in society (Box, 1983; Danzinger, 1983; Klein, 1973; Smart, 1977; Steffensmeier & Allan, 1995). In contrast to males, females are socialized to be other oriented, to "feel as the other feels," and to be attuned to other's needs and concerns (Miller, 1991, p. 14). As a result, females' "sense of self becomes very much organized around being able to make and then to maintain affiliations and relationships. Eventually, for many women the threat of disruption of connections is perceived not just as a loss of a relationship but as something closer to a total loss of self" (J. Miller, 1986, p. 83). Finally, females *are* more often in subordinate and dependent positions—positions in which they depend on others for material, psychological, and other types of support (Smart, 1977, p. 65). Occupancy in these positions is said to provide an additional incentive for females to attach greater importance to the establishment and maintenance of positive relationships with others.

Consistent with these arguments, numerous studies indicate that females tend to have friendships that are more intimate and affectionate than those of males (e.g., Aukett, Ritchie, & Mill, 1988; Bell, 1981; Davidson & Duberman, 1982; Williams, 1985). Bell (1981) interpreted these findings to mean that females, in comparison to males, do indeed attach greater importance and significance to interpersonal relationships. Although more direct evidence is sparse, some research seems to confirm Bell's interpretation. Based on extended interviews with men and women, Rubin (1985) found that women place a higher intrinsic value on friendships: "Among

women, for whom relationships are never far from center stage, friends are necessary even when work life is important and gratifying. Among men, for whom work lies at the heart of life, even their very identity, relationships are of secondary concern" (p. 142).

Mazur (1989) reached a very similar conclusion from her analysis of survey data. She too found that females tend to place more value on interpersonal relationships than males, with females scoring higher on scales of "affiliation motivation" (also see Beutel & Marini, 1995; Chesney-Lind & Shelden, 1992; Gilligan, 1982; Norman, Murphy, Gilligan, & Vasudev, 1981–1982; Rokeach, 1973; Rosenberg, 1965).

Moreover, it appears that females find their more intimate relationships to be of important therapeutic value. Females, for instance, report that they often turn to their relationships for emotional support, being more willing than males to share their problems and confidences with others (Aukett et al., 1988; Rubin, 1985). The flip side of female relationships, however, is the possibility that females may experience greater distress when interpersonal difficulties arise. Because females tend to attach greater importance to their relationships, and because they seek to derive more from them, relational problems (or losses) may be more disruptive to females than to males. Indeed, the stress literature suggests that females are more distressed by interpersonal problems than are males (see Frost & Averill, 1982).

This is not to say that females necessarily experience more interpersonal problems than males. Data suggest that females may experience some types of interpersonal problems, like sexual abuse, more often than males (see Chesney-Lind & Shelden, 1992); but that males may experience other types of problems, like conflicts with friends, more often than females (Campbell,

1993; Eagly & Steffen, 1986; Frodi, Macaulay, & Thome, 1977; Frost & Averill, 1982; Giordano, Cernkovich, & Pugh, 1986; Lempers & Clark-Lempers, 1992). Rather, females experience more subjective strain or distress in response to interpersonal problems.

Further, the developmental literature suggests that such strain or distress may be especially strong during the adolescent period. There are several reasons for this. First, adolescent females are said to develop a relatively strong desire to fit in with others (Brown & Gilligan, 1992; Gilligan et al., 1989). Second, adolescent females are often under a great deal of stress, which may exacerbate the negative impact of interpersonal problems. In addition to the stressors they share with males, like the transition to high school and major biological changes, adolescent females are subject to certain unique stressors. Most notably, adolescent females often discover that fitting in with others means conforming to a very restrictive set of gender norms (Agnew, 1995b, 1997; Brown & Gilligan, 1992; Gove & Herb, 1974). Adolescent females, then, attach increased importance to relationships at the very time that relationships are becoming more difficult to successfully manage. Third, adolescent females and males often lack the social supports, coping skills, and coping resources that are available to adults (Agnew, 1997; Brown & Gilligan, 1992). As a consequence of all these factors, females surpass males in depression and certain other psychological difficulties during the adolescent period (Brown & Gilligan, 1992; Gilligan et al., 1989; Gove & Herb, 1974).

In sum, much theoretical argument and some empirical data suggest that females may be more concerned with interpersonal goals than males. And, given this argument, several theorists have argued that interpersonal or relational problems will be more likely to lead to deviance among females—particularly delinquency among adolescent females. Initially, theorists suggested that interpersonal strain among females would lead to sexual deviance (Cohen, 1955; Leonard, 1982; Morris, 1964). That is, females who could not establish close ties to others through "legitimate" channels—such as physical attractiveness—might attempt to establish such ties through "illegitimate" channels involving sex. This argument, however, was based on the mistaken assumptions that females are only concerned with romantic relationships and that most female delinquency is sexual in nature (for a discussion, see Leonard, 1982, p. 133; Morris, 1987, pp. 59–62). More contemporary theorists have noted that relational problems may lead to a range of different offenses. In fact, it is possible to argue that such problems might lead to virtually any type of delinquency. Relational problems, in particular, might lead to (a) escape behaviors like running away, truancy, and cutting classes (see Chesney-Lind, 1989; Chesney-Lind & Shelden, 1992); (b) aggressive behaviors directed against the source of the relational problems and perhaps others (see Agnew, 1992); (c) property offenses, including the theft of items thought to make one more attractive or popular (Chesney-Lind & Shelden, 1992, p. 43; Morris, 1987); and (d) drug use, as one attempts to cope with the negative emotions generated by relational problems (see Agnew, 1992).

Relational problems, then, might bear a special relationship to several types of delinquency. Only two studies, however, have focused specifically on gender, relational problems, and delinquency. The best known is that of Ruth Morris (1964). She examined 56 matched quartets from Flint, Michigan. Each quartet consisted of a delinquent boy and girl (two or more police contacts) and a nondelinquent boy and girl. The members of each quartet were matched in terms of social class, intelligence, age, and school grade. There were three measures of relational problems: coming from a broken home, self-reports of "family tension," and interviewer ratings of personal appearance and grooming. She found that broken homes predicted delinquency among the girls in her sample but not the boys, and that family tension had a bigger effect on girls' delinquency than on boys' delinquency. Further, grooming had a stronger effect on delinquency among girls. There were no differences between the delinquents and nondelinquents in appearance, however, and the delinquents reported dating more often. Morris interpreted these findings to mean that relational problems are more consequential for girls than boys.

There are, however, certain problems with her study. She examined a nonrepresentative sample from a single city. Her matching procedure did not control for certain potentially important variables that might be correlated with both relational problems and delinquency—like level of social control. Two of her three measures of relational problems are indirect. That is, she was assuming that those from broken homes and those with poor grooming/appearance have more relational problems (the more frequent dating of the delinquents, rated lower in grooming, raises questions about this assumption). Further, the grooming measure was of questionable validity and reliability, being based on the rating of an adult interviewer (see Morris, 1987, p. 61). An official measure of delinquency was employed (it is not unreasonable to assume that official processing may be influenced by appearance and family status—thus biasing the results; see Morris, 1987, p. 61). And when examining peer relations, the focus was on the "dating relationship" (Morris, 1964, p. 83). Friendship relations were not considered, even though

much data suggest that friendships play a major role in the lives of adolescents. Given such problems, it is no surprise that the Morris study is viewed with suspicion by many researchers—although it was a pioneering study for its time.

The second attempt to examine relational problems was conducted by Sandhu and Allen (1969). They focused on a sample of 110 delinquent girls at a Florida training school and a control group of 135 girls at two Florida high schools. The girls in each group were similar in terms of age, race, and marital status, although they differed in terms of broken home status and social class (social class was statistically controlled in the analysis). Sandhu and Allen focused on the disjunction between marital goals and the legitimate means to reach such goals. They predicted that the delinquent girls would place just as much emphasis on marriage as the nondelinquent girls but would report more obstacles to marriage. They found, instead, that the delinquent girls were less committed to marital goals and perceived fewer obstacles to the fulfillment of their marital goals. Sandhu and Allen, however, stated that their prediction was not necessarily wrong. They suggested that due to psychological problems, the delinquent girls may not have been able to consciously admit that they faced obstacles to marriage.

The Sandhu and Allen study suffers from many of the same problems as the Morris (1964) study (see Naffine, 1987, p. 17). It was a small sample of questionable representativeness. Relevant variables were not controlled for in the analysis. Official measures of delinquency were employed. Sandhu and Allen questioned the validity of their measure of relational problems (obstacles to marriage). And the focus was once again on romantic problems. In addition, they did not examine the impact of romantic problems on males.

Although Morris (1964) and Sandhu and Allen (1969) are the only researchers to specifically examine interpersonal strain, Giordano et al. (1986) conducted a study of peer relations and delinquency of some relevance. They surveyed 942 adolescents from a single city and focused on a number of dimensions of friendship that are related to relational problems—such as conflict and the lack of reciprocity. They found that certain of these dimensions, like conflict, were related to delinquency. They did examine gender differences in the dimensions of friendship, but did not always report whether the dimensions of friendship had a similar relationship to delinquency for males and females. Also, their study focused on nonromantic relationships. Nevertheless, their study is the most comprehensive examination of friendship and delinquency so far conducted, and certain of their relevant findings are mentioned below.

Other studies have examined the impact of relational problems with parents on male and female delinquency. Such studies usually find that family conflict has similar effects on males and females or stronger effects on females (e.g., Cernkovich & Giordano, 1987; Dornfeld & Kruttschnitt, 1992; Simons et al., 1980). Many researchers, however, have argued that one of the distinguishing features of adolescence is a reduced concern with family and an increased concern with peers (see Agnew, 1997; Chesney-Lind & Shelden, 1992, p. 82). And data suggest that relational problems with peers are the most distressing problems faced by adolescents (Ambert, 1994). Given these arguments, it is perhaps most appropriate to examine interpersonal strain among adolescents by focusing on peer relations.

This study attempts to overcome the problems of previous research in several ways. First, a nationally representative sample of several thousand high school students—both male and female—is employed. Second, the focus is on peer relational problems of both a romantic and nonromantic nature. Further, this study examines both the existence of close ties to peers (i.e., one's level of popularity) *and* the quality of relations with peers. Third, self-report measures of deviance/delinquency are employed. And fourth, this study controls for a range of variables that may be correlated with both peer relational problems and delinquency.

It is predicted that peer relational problems of both a romantic and nonromantic nature will be significantly related to delinquency among the females in this study, and that such problems will bear a stronger relationship to female than male delinquency.

DATA AND METHOD

Data are from the first follow-up survey of the National Education Longitudinal Study of 1988 (NELS:88), sponsored by the National Center for Education Statistics, U.S. Department of Education (Ingels et al., 1992). Beginning in 1988, data were collected on a cohort of 25,000 eighth graders attending 1,000 public and private schools across the United States. NELS:88 was designed to provide data about various educational processes and outcomes experienced by youth as they progressed through their educational careers. In the spring of 1990, a follow-up survey was conducted of the initial cohort. Data from this first follow-up survey include a number of items relevant to interpersonal relations and delinquent behavior.

The first follow-up employed a two-stage probability design—sampling high schools at the first stage and 10th-grade students within schools at the second stage. A total of 17,754 students were surveyed, with these students constituting a representative sample of all 10th-grade students in public and private schools in the United States. All analyses in this article are based on an approximately 20% random subsample (N = 3,595) of this sample of 17,754.[2]

This data set was chosen because it contains several questions regarding relations with same- and opposite-sex peers. The major focus on the data set, however, is on schooling. This is reflected in several of the measures reported below.

MEASURES

Peer Relations

Questions regarding peer relations are shown in Table 1 and deal with one's popularity with peers and how well one gets along with peers. These questions are rather general in nature, with respondents being asked to make global assessments regarding their popularity and the quality of their relationships. These global assessments have the advantage of summarizing the respondent's impressions across a range of domains and simplifying the data analysis. At the same time, future research should attempt to obtain more detailed information regarding peer relations. Respondents, in particular, may report that they have poor relations with peers for a number of reasons—ranging from disagreements over social and political issues to the experience of physical and sexual abuse. Certain of these reasons may be associated with delinquency, whereas others may not (see Giordano et al., 1986).

Table 1 shows the means and standard deviations of males and females on each item. The mean scores for males and females are quite similar for most items. The males are slightly more likely to state that they do not get along with boys and girls,

although not all of the gender differences on these items are statistically significant.

The 10 items in Table 1 were factor analyzed to create a smaller set of scales. An oblique method of rotation was used, and items that loaded at least .50 on one and only one factor were taken as indicators of that factor. Separate factor analyses were conducted for males and females, since certain of the items may have different meanings for males and females (e.g., "I do not get along very well with girls").

Three scales emerged for both males and females, with the scales being similar in content. Table 1 shows the items in each scale for males and females, along with the factor loadings for each item. The first scale is Poor Peer Relations. High scorers on this scale state that they do not get along very well with boys and girls and that it is difficult to make friends with members of their own sex. In addition, high scorers on the female version of this scale state that they do not make friends easily with girls. High scorers, in short, do not get along with and are not popular with their peers. This scale refers primarily to peer relations of a nonromantic nature.

High scorers on the second scale, Positive Relations With the Opposite Sex, state that they are very popular with the opposite sex, get a lot of attention from members of the opposite sex, and make friends easily with boys (in the case of females) or girls (in the case of males).

Finally, high scorers on the Peer Problems When Entering High School scale state that it was more difficult to make friends in high school and that they felt more alone in high school. In addition, the males state that they often feel "put down" by other students. This item did not load on any of the scales for the females, so it was treated separately in all analyses involving females. The "make friends easily with boys" item did not load on any of the

TABLE 1:   Question Wordings, Descriptive Statistics, and Factor Loadings for Items Measuring Peer Relations, by Gender

	FEMALES		MALES		FACTOR LOADINGS: FEMALES			FACTOR LOADINGS: MALES		
	M	SD	M	SD	I	II	III	I	II	III
1. I do not get along very well with girls	1.66	1.19	1.85*	1.35	.91			.85		
2. I do not get along very well with boys	1.62	1.18	1.91*	1.35	.74			.93		
3. It is difficult to make friends with members of my own sex	1.71	1.23	1.85*	1.21	.74			.73		
4. I make friends easily with girls[a]	5.03	1.18	4.77	1.31	.61				.90	
5. I get a lot of attention from members of the opposite sex	4.35	1.35	4.31	1.42		.86			.91	
6. I'm not very popular with members of the opposite sex[b]	4.65	1.42	4.54*	1.50		.74			.58	
7. I make friends easily with boys	4.96	1.22	4.93	1.11		.74				
8. It was more difficult to make friends in high school	2.03	0.77	2.03	0.69			.89			.83
9. I felt more alone in high school	1.94	0.80	1.95	0.74			.89			.84
10. In school, I often feel put down by other students	2.00	0.77	2.01	0.69						.58

NOTE: The first nine items are statements that respondents can describe as "false," "mostly false," "more false than true," "more true than false," "mostly true," and "true." The last statement is one with which respondents can "strongly agree," "agree," "disagree," or "strongly disagree." Factor I = Poor Peer Relations, Factor II = Positive Relations With the Opposite Sex, Factor III = Peer Problems Entering High School.

[a]The scoring of responses for this item was reversed for females in the regression analysis.
[b]The scoring of responses for this item was reversed for both males and females in all analyses.
*Differences between male and female means significant, $p < .05$ (two-tailed).

scales for males, so it was treated separately in all analyses involving males.

Control Variables: Social Control Measures

Someone might argue that any association between relational problems and delinquency is spurious, both being caused by low social control. Low social control may lead to delinquency for all of the reasons listed by Hirschi (1969) and others. Likewise, it may lead to relational problems. Individuals low in social control may not possess the social skills for effective interaction, since they were not as well socialized as others. They have fewer restraints on their behavior, so they may be more likely to act in ways that antagonize others. And they may possess fewer of the resources that contribute to popularity. It is therefore important to control for measures of social control in all analyses.

Twenty-four items related to social control were factor analyzed using the procedure described above. Four measures of social control were created based on this analysis, with the measures being identical for males and females. High scorers on the three-item Parental Attachment scale state that they like their parents, get along well with their parents, and feel that their parents understand them. High scorers on the five-item Parental Supervision scale state that their parents try to find out who their friends are, where they go at night, how they spend their money, what they do with their free time, and where they are after school. High scorers on the five-item Teacher Attachment scale state that the teaching is good at their school, the teachers are interested in the students, the teachers praise them for hard work, the teachers seldom put down students, and the teachers listen to them. High scorers on the three-item Commitment to Education scale

state that they have high grades in English and mathematics and that they expect to obtain an advanced degree.

Unfortunately, there was no measure of peer attachment or how much the respondent likes his or her friends. Hirschi (1969) described peer attachment as a form of social control, arguing that it prevents delinquency because delinquency might jeopardize valued relationships with peers. Peer attachment, however, might also be viewed as one dimension of relational problems. Individuals who do not like their friends presumably are higher in relational problems than those who do like their friends. Peer attachment is undoubtedly related to the above two dimensions of relational problems: popularity with friends and the quality of relationships with friends. To some extent, peer attachment might be viewed as an outcome of these variables. We are most likely to be attached to friends if they like us and get along well with us. At the same time, peer attachment is somewhat distinct from these variables. Giordano et al. (1986) found that measures of peer attachment such as caring and trust loaded on a distinct factor from various measures of peer interaction such as conflict. The absence of a peer attachment measure is therefore a problem, although Giordano et al. (1986) found that their measure of caring and trust in friends—which is quite similar to most measures of peer attachment—was unrelated to delinquency in males and friends. Further, peer attachment has not emerged as a consistent predictor of delinquency in most prior research (see Agnew, 1991).

Control Variables: Differential Association

It may also be the case that relational problems and delinquency are caused by the beliefs of the adolescent regarding delinquency and the nature of the adolescent's friends. Adolescents with deviant beliefs may be more likely to antagonize friends and engage in delinquency. Likewise, adolescents with deviant friends may be more likely to have conflicts with friends and engage in delinquency (see Giordano et al., 1986).

Twenty-six items related to deviant beliefs and peers were factor analyzed using the procedures described above. Four scales were derived from the analysis, and they are identical for males and females. High scorers on the six-item School Deviance Is Okay scale state that they often feel it is okay to cut a couple of classes, skip school a whole day, cheat on tests, copy someone's homework, talk back to teachers, and disobey school rules. High scorers on the seven-item School Delinquency Is Okay scale state that they feel it is often okay to belong to gangs, steal things from school, destroy school property, drink alcohol and use drugs at school, bring weapons to school, and abuse teachers.

Unfortunately, there were no measures of the amount of deviance committed by friends. Several questions, however, asked about the values of friends. High scorers on the four-item Friends Value Education scale state that their friends feel it is very important to study, get good grades, finish high school, and continue one's education past high school. High scorers on the four-item Friends Value Popularity scale state that their friends feel it is very important to play sports, be popular with students, have a steady boy/girlfriend, and be willing to party (copies of all scales and factor results are available from the first author).

These measures of differential association, along with the above social control measures, are among the leading independent variables in microlevel delinquency research. As Agnew (1995c) pointed out,

these variables are closely related to one another. Low social control may lead to the adoption of deviant beliefs and association with deviant peers, whereas deviant beliefs and peer associations may reduce social control. Further, one can also argue that our strain measures are reciprocally related to the social control and differential association measures (see Agnew, 1995a, 1995c). Such interrelationships, however, are not a serious concern, since our focus is not on testing the relative importance of the leading crime theories. Rather, we simply want to explore whether a neglected variable in delinquency research—interpersonal strain—has an effect on male and female delinquency after other major variables are controlled for.

Delinquency

The data set was somewhat limited in its measurement of self-reported delinquency, with many of the measures focusing on school-related delinquency. High scorers on a six-item measure of Delinquency stated that they frequently (a) get into physical fights at school, (b) are late for school, (c) cut or skip classes, (d) have five or more drinks in a row, (e) use marijuana, and (f) use cocaine. The fighting, lateness, and skipping class measures focus on behavior during the first half of the current school year. Approximately 25% of the males and 8% of the females reported fighting at least once. Approximately 74% of the males and 75% of the females were late at least once (7.2% of the males and 6.7% of the females were late more than 10 times). Approximately 39% of the males and 34% of the females skipped or cut class at least once (5.4% of the males and 3.3% of the females skipped or cut class more than 10 times). The drinking measure focuses on behavior during the last 2 weeks, whereas the marijuana and cocaine measures focus on use during the last 30 days. Approximately 24% of the males and 17% of the females reported having five or more drinks in a row at least once in the last 2 weeks. Approximately 9% of the males used marijuana and 2% used cocaine at least once in the last 30 days. The corresponding figures for females are 4% and 0.3%. Variation in the delinquency scale, then, is more heavily influenced by the items dealing with escape attempts from school (lateness, cutting class).

Although it would of course be desirable to have additional measures of delinquency, interpersonal strain has been linked to aggression, escape attempts from school, and drug use in theoretical accounts. Also, these measures have the advantage of dealing with externalizing and internalizing behaviors. It is often claimed that females are more likely to respond to problems by engaging in internalizing behaviors like drug use and escape attempts, whereas males are more likely to engage in externalizing behaviors like aggression (e.g., Campbell, 1993; Cloward & Piven, 1979). Given these claims, separate analyses were performed for fighting, escape attempts from school, and drug use. Results from these separate analyses are reported when they differ substantially from the main analysis. Future research should build on this study by focusing on additional types of deviance, including property crimes.

It should be noted that the recall period for the above delinquency measures is rather short—ranging from the last 2 weeks to the previous school term. This increases the accuracy of recall, and also partially alleviates a serious problem in cross-sectional research dealing with the temporal ordering between the independent variables and the delinquency measures. In virtually all cross-sectional research, the recall period for the delinquency measures is a year or more. The

measures for most of the independent variables, however, refer to the respondent's current situation. The temporal ordering among the variables, then, is such that the delinquency measures precede most of the independent variables in time. Because of this, one can easily argue that any association between delinquency and the independent variables is due to the fact that delinquency causes the independent variables (see Thornberry, 1987). This study does not solve this problem; however, it reduces it, since *both* the delinquency measures and the measures for the independent variables refer to current behavior.

RESULTS

The Delinquency measure was regressed on the measures of peer relations, social control, and differential association. Separate regressions were performed for males and females.[3] The correlation matrices for these regressions are shown in the appendix. The regression results are shown in Table 2.

It was predicted that problems with peers would affect female delinquency and would have a larger effect on female than male delinquency. The data provide little support for these predictions. The only peer variable to be significantly associated with female delinquency is Positive Relations With the Opposite Sex. And contrary to predictions, we find that females who report positive relations are *more* rather than less delinquent. This might be explained in terms of learning and opportunity theories; females who are popular with and spend a lot of time with boys are more exposed to the higher deviance of boys and may find that they have more opportunities to engage in types of delinquency like drug and alcohol use. Related to this, certain studies find a positive association between dating and delinquency (e.g., Hirschi, 1969).

TABLE 2:   The Effects of Peer Relations Variables on Female and Male Delinquency,
            Controlling for Other Variables

	DELINQUENCY	
	Females	Males
Poor Peer Relations	.06(.05)	.10(.18)**
Positive Relations With Opposite Sex	.08(.08)*	.15(.25)**
Peer Problems Entering High School	.04(.09)	.10(.35)**
Feel Put Down by Students	−.03(−.12)	
Make Friends Easily With Boys		.08(.42)*
Control variables		
Parental Attachment	.02(.02)	−.05(−.09)
Parental Supervision	−.01(−.01)	−.04(−.06)
Teacher Attachment	−.04(−.05)	−.03(−.07)
Commitment to Education	−.13(−.11)**	−.11(−.15)**
School Deviance Is Okay	.21(.22)	.18(.44)**
School Delinquency Is Okay	.22(.58)**	.27(.42)**
Friends Value Education	−.09(−.19)**	.01(.03)
Friends Value Popularity	.03(.05)	−.01(−.04)
R^2 (adjusted)	.22	.24
N	1,398	1,217

NOTE: Standardized effects shown, with unstandardized effects in parentheses.
*$p < .05$ (two-tailed). **$p < .01$ (two-tailed).

In addition, females who are popular with the opposite sex may face considerable pressure from their male peers to exploit such opportunities to engage in deviance. Recent writings on female sexual development suggest that adolescent females must often struggle with potentially conflicting desires in the context of opposite-sex relationships—desires that may eventuate in higher levels of deviant behavior. On one hand, they have a desire to engage themselves as active participants in peer relationships, whereas on the other hand, they wish to contribute to the development of harmonious peer relations. In the context of opposite-sex relations, females often feel that they must sacrifice the former desire for the latter. Males tend to discourage personal agency on the part of females, having "picked up

the idea" that females should adapt to them (Gilligan, 1982; Miller, 1991).[4] Thus, to maintain harmonious relations with the opposite sex, females may face pressure to conform to males' needs, demands, and activities. This may also mean that popular females are likely to face pressures to adapt to the higher levels of deviance demonstrated by males—an observation consistent with our finding that Positive Relations With the Opposite Sex is related to higher levels of female delinquency.

Separate analyses of the specific types of delinquency support the above results, with one minor and one major exception. The minor exception involves Peer Problems When Entering High School, which has a standardized effect of .08 ($p <$ .05) on escape attempts from school among females. The major exception involves

Poor Peer Relations, which has a standardized effect of .16 ($p < .01$) on fighting among females. Poor Peer Relations, in fact, is the best predictor of fighting among females. This finding challenges the assertion that females respond to problems by engaging in internalizing rather than externalizing behaviors (see Dornfeld & Kruttschnitt, 1992; Hoffman & Su, 1994). It is important to emphasize, however, that this finding may not generalize to other types of problems. Interpersonal problems may bear a special relationship to aggression. Violent acts, in particular, typically emerge out of interpersonal disputes with others (Felson, 1994; Luckenbill, 1977).

In sum, the peer relation variables have little effect on female delinquency—with the notable exception of the effect of Poor Peer Relations on fighting.

The second part of our prediction was that peer relations would be more strongly associated with delinquency among females than males. There are certain dangers in comparing the effect of the peer relation measures between males and females, since the content of these measures differs slightly between males and females. Nevertheless, the data in Table 2 suggest that peer relations may be more important for males than females. In particular, the Poor Peer Relations and the Peer Problems When Entering High School measures each have a positive association with delinquency among males. As was the case with the females, we find that Positive Relations With the Opposite Sex is associated with *higher* delinquency. Also, boys who say that they make friends easily with other boys are slightly higher in delinquency.

These data suggest that having same and opposite sex friends does *not* reduce delinquency among males; if anything, it may lead to a slight increase in delinquency. Any reduction in strain that results from having friends is probably offset by the increased opportunities for delinquency and the increased exposure to delinquent others that friends sometimes provide. These data, then, suggest that the absence of close ties to peers is not a significant source of delinquency in males. Likewise, it is not a significant source of delinquency in females. However, the quality of relationships with peers is a significant source of delinquency in males (and to a lesser extent, females), with poor-quality relationships being associated with higher levels of delinquency. Separate analyses of the specific types of delinquency generally support these findings, although Poor Peer Relations and Peer Problems When Entering High School have a somewhat weaker effect on escape attempts from school.

There remains the question of why peer problems have perhaps a larger effect on males than females. Two related explanations may be advanced in this area. We earlier argued that interpersonal relations are more important to females than to males, but perhaps that is not the case among the 10th graders in this recent sample. Two questions in the survey allow us to measure the importance attached to interpersonal relations. One question asks respondents how important it is to have strong friendships, whereas the other asks about the importance of finding the right person to marry. These are rather gross measures of the importance of interpersonal relations, but the males and females in this survey give similar responses. Among the males, 70.8% state that it is "very important" to find the right person to marry and 76.3% state it is "very important" to have strong friendships. The corresponding figures for females are 82.8% and 78.6%. The large majority of males and females, then, rate interpersonal relations as important. It may be that males and females rate interpersonal relations as important for different reasons. Drawing on the psychology of gender literature, we might argue that females are more likely to value interpersonal ties for the intrinsic satisfactions they provide. Adolescent males, however, may value interpersonal ties because such ties function as indicators of their achievements and because others provide an audience for the recognition of their achievements. In any event, gender differences in the importance attached to interpersonal relations appear slight among the 10th graders in this sample. Perhaps sharper gender differences will emerge as the respondents age—leaving the peer-dominated world of adolescence and entering adulthood, where occupational and other concerns loom larger.

Second, not only may peer problems be important to both male and female adolescents (albeit for different reasons), but males may be more likely to respond to such problems with delinquency. As the psychology of gender literature argues, there may be gender differences in the types of relational problems that elicit concern and in the response to those problems. Males are said to be more concerned with unfair treatment, whereas females are said to be more concerned with fractured relationships and helping others in need. And females are said to be more likely to respond to relational problems by making an effort to restore or maintain harmonious relations with others—even though this often means self-sacrifice on their part (see Gilligan & Attanucci, 1988; Gilligan et al., 1989; J. Miller, 1986). Related to this, the psychological reaction to relational problems is said to differ among males and females. Although both males and females may experience anger in response to relational problems, the anger of females is more often accompanied by emotions such as guilt, shame, and depression (see Agnew, 1995b; Brown &

Gilligan, 1992; Campbell, 1993; Jordan, 1995; J. Miller, 1986). There are a variety of reasons for this, including the greater need of females for connectedness with others, their greater concern with the plight of others, and their increased tendency toward self-blame when interpersonal problems arise. Males are less likely to experience such accompanying emotions; their anger is more likely to take the form of moral outrage. The depression and guilt of females may reduce the likelihood of most forms of delinquency, whereas the moral outrage of males may often propel them into delinquency. In addition, a range of other reasons has been offered for the greater tendency of males to respond to problems with delinquency. Such reasons have to do with gender differences in social control, opportunities for delinquency, and the disposition to delinquency (see Agnew, 1995b).

CONCLUSION

Interpersonal strain has been largely neglected in quantitative delinquency research, despite theoretical arguments that such strain is related to delinquency—at least among females. The connection of interpersonal strain with female delinquency, in fact, probably explains much of the neglect for this variable, since most empirical research has focused on male delinquency. The data in this article, although tentative, suggest that interpersonal strain may have a role to play in the explanation of delinquency. These data, however, also challenge many of the theoretical arguments made regarding interpersonal strain and delinquency.

Contrary to theoretical predictions, interpersonal strain is perhaps more important among males than among females. Further, to the extent that interpersonal strain is important among females, it seems to lead to externalizing behavior such as fighting rather than internalizing behavior such as drug use. Once again, however, it should be noted that this finding may not generalize to other types of strain or stress (however, see Dornfeld & Kruttschnitt, 1992; Hoffman & Su, 1994).

These data also begin to shed light on the types of interpersonal strain related to delinquency. The absence of close ties to peers does not increase delinquency. If anything, the *presence* of close ties to peers is associated with slightly higher levels of delinquency. This is especially true of romantic ties. Males and females who report that they are very popular with the opposite sex are somewhat more likely to engage in delinquency. This is likely due to the fact that they have more opportunities for delinquency, since they are probably more often involved in unsupervised activities with other peers. This finding, then, is more consistent with the assumptions and expectations of social control and social learning theories of delinquency. In contrast to individual-level strain theories (e.g., Agnew, 1992), these perspectives highlight the fact that the presence of peer ties may contribute to (instead of reduce) delinquency to the extent that they result in lower levels of social control (e.g., reduced time spent on homework and family activities) and deviant learning (e.g., rewards and praise from peers for drug and alcohol use).

Yet, although the absence of close ties to peers may not increase delinquency, *poor relations with peers* may lead to higher delinquency. The Poor Peer Relations and Peer Problems When Entering High School measures were positively associated with delinquency among males. The association was less strong among females, although the Poor Peer Relations measure was the strongest correlate of fighting among females. Thus, apart from the sheer presence

of peer ties, the *quality* of existing ties does appear to be important with respect to the development of delinquent behavior—an observation that *is* consistent with the assumptions of individual-level strain theory (Agnew, 1992).

Further research should build on this study by more precisely examining the different types of interpersonal strain that individuals experience. As indicated, this study employed rather general measures of interpersonal strain. Respondents, for example, were simply asked whether they "get along very well" with others. Future research should attempt to develop a typology of interpersonal problems ranging from mild disagreements over unimportant issues to serious physical and sexual assaults. We may find gender differences in the specific types of interpersonal strain experienced, as well as differences in the relationship of these types of strain to delinquency. In this connection, a broad range of delinquent acts should be examined, since particular types of strain might be more relevant to some types of delinquency than others.

Future research should also include measures of peer attachment and the delinquency of one's peers. In particular, it would be interesting to determine whether poor relations with both conventional and delinquent peers are associated with higher delinquency. Poor relations with delinquent peers may lead to an increase in strain, but this increase may be offset by a reduction in the influence of these peers. Agnew (1991), for example, found that delinquent peers have a larger effect on delinquency when attachment to these peers is high. Poor peer relations, then, might undermine the influence of delinquent peers. We attempted to provide a rough test of this idea by determining whether the Poor Peer Relations measure interacted with the Friends Value

Education measure in its effect on delinquency (i.e., do poor peer relations have a smaller effect on delinquency when friends do *not* value education). The evidence for such an interaction was mixed, but there was some suggestion that Poor Peer Relations might actually have a *larger* positive effect on delinquency when friends do not value education. Poor relations with *delinquent* peers, then, might increase rather than decrease the likelihood of delinquency. The Friends Value Education measure, however, is obviously not the best measure of peer delinquency.

Finally, future research should employ longitudinal data. One might claim that delinquency has a causal effect on poor peer relations and thereby accounts for the association between these variables. This is a problem with all cross-sectional research. As Thornberry (1987) and others have pointed out, one can argue that delinquency causes virtually every independent variable typically examined in delinquency research. Certain data from qualitative research and experimental studies suggest that the quality of peer relations does have a causal effect on deviance (Daly, 1992; Frost & Averill, 1982; Gilfus, 1992; E. Miller, 1986), but this needs to be verified with longitudinal research involving representative samples from larger populations. The data in this study suggest that such research is worthwhile. The quality of peer relations is associated with delinquency and is the strongest correlate of fighting among females.

NOTES

1. The focus of this article is on individual-level interpretations of strain (or anomie) theory. Unlike macrosocial versions of strain theory (see Bernard, 1987), these interpretations focus on the individual-level consequences of structural and environmental conditions as they pertain to the development of deviant behavior, such as the frustration and anger generated by blocked opportunities or aversive environments (for a justification of individual-level interpretations, see Agnew, 1987; Menard, 1995). In contrast to macrosocial versions, individual-level interpretations of strain theory are most relevant to, and more frequently invoked in, the debate that is addressed in this article regarding the relevance of classic strain theory to female delinquency.

2. The NELS:88 is based on a complex sampling procedure that makes use of a stratified cluster design. As a result, certain weighting procedures are required to account for the oversampling of various populations. In addition, standard errors produced by conventional analyses need to be adjusted to account for design effects. Following the procedures suggested by Ingels et al. (1992), our analyses were weighted by the relative weight (final survey weight divided by the average of the weight), and standard errors were adjusted with the overall design effect of the first follow-up study.

3. Separate regressions were also performed by sex and racial group: White males, White females, Black males, Black females, Hispanic males, and Hispanic females. These analyses generally support the major conclusion of this study: Peer relations are more important for males than females. Peer relations, however, appear to be more consequential for Blacks than for other racial groups. We plan to explore this difference further in a subsequent study.

4. Michelle Fine's (1993) work on the suppression of female desire, agency, and sense of entitlement suggests that females who internalize traditional notions of "femininity" may be especially susceptible to the influence of opposite-sex peers. Such females "are the least likely to feel entitled or in control of their lives," and as a result, "they may feel more vulnerable to male pressure" (Fine, 1993, p. 97). Females who adopt traditional notions of femininity, then, may also be highly vulnerable to the deviant influences of male peers. Ironically, conventional institutions such as the family and school may actually contribute to such vulnerability to the extent that these institutions endorse traditional conceptions of females as passive and self-sacrificing creatures (as opposed to the idea that females are capable and rightfully entitled to make their own social and sexual demands within opposite-sex relations).

REFERENCES

Adler, F. (1975). *Sisters in crime*. New York: McGraw-Hill.

Agnew, R. (1987). On testing structural strain theories. *Journal of Research in Crime and Delinquency, 24,* 281–286.

Agnew, R. (1991). The interactive effect of peer variables on delinquency. *Criminology, 29,* 47–72.

Agnew, R. (1992). Foundation for a general strain theory of crime and delinquency. *Criminology, 30,* 47–87.

Agnew, R. (1995a). The contribution of social-psychological strain theory to the explanation of crime and

APPENDIX
CORRELATION MATRIX BETWEEN DELINQUENCY, THE PEER VARIABLES, AND THE CONTROL VARIABLES

	1	2	3	4	5	6	7	8	9	10	11	12	13
Female sample													
1. Delinquency	1.0												
2. Poor Peer Relations	.14	1.0											
3. Positive Relations With Opposite Sex	.05	-.19	1.0										
4. Peer Problems Entering High School	.06	.37	-.21	1.0									
5. Feel Put Down by Students	.04	.13	-.22	.22	1.0								
6. Parental Attachment	-.15	-.32	.05	-.19	-.14	1.0							
7. Parental Supervision	-.05	-.04	.15	.08	.01	.01	1.0						
8. Teacher Attachment	-.20	-.12	.11	-.09	-.28	.21	.09	1.0					
9. Commitment to Education	-.24	-.14	.10	-.11	-.11	.07	.17	.24	1.0				
10. School Deviance Is Okay	.37	.12	.01	-.02	.12	-.27	-.06	-.37	-.17	1.0			
11. School Delinquency Is Okay	.37	.18	.02	.08	.03	-.30	-.02	-.17	-.19	.46	1.0		
12. Friends Value Education	-.24	-.13	.10	-.03	-.17	.18	.14	.24	.26	-.33	-.19	1.0	
13. Friends Value Popularity	.04	-.08	.20	-.10	-.03	-.03	.06	-.07	.10	.14	.01	.13	1.0
Male sample													
1. Delinquency	1.0												
2. Poor Peer Relations	.09	1.0											
3. Positive Relations With Opposite Sex	.08	-.42	1.0										
4. Peer Problems Entering High School	.05	.33	-.37	1.0									
5. Make Friends Easily With Boys	.01	-.44	.47	-.39	1.0								
6. Parental Attachment	-.16	-.26	.22	-.24	.31	1.0							
7. Parental Supervision	-.11	-.12	.17	-.10	.22	.09	1.0						
8. Teacher Attachment	-.22	-.09	.10	-.16	.12	.22	.14	1.0					
9. Commitment to Education	-.19	-.12	.10	-.06	.11	.13	.15	.18	1.0				
10. School Deviance Is Okay	.42	.02	.03	-.09	-.03	-.22	-.15	-.39	-.15	1.0			
11. School Delinquency Is Okay	.38	.09	-.02	-.03	-.05	.20	-.13	-.27	-.15	.59	1.0		
12. Friends Value Education	-.19	-.15	.08	-.09	.13	.22	.21	.21	.25	-.34	-.28	1.0	
13. Friends Value Popularity	.07	-.07	.26	-.15	.18	-.04	.11	-.08	.02	.16	.06	.15	1.0

delinquency. In F. Adler & W. S. Laufer (Eds.), *The legacy of anomie theory: Advances in criminological theory, Volume 6*. New Brunswick, NJ: Transaction.

Agnew, R. (1995b, November). *Gender and crime: A general strain theory perspective*. Paper presented at the annual meeting of the American Society of Criminology, Boston.

Agnew, R. (1995c). Testing the leading crime theories: An alternative strategy focusing on motivational processes. *Journal of Research in Crime and Delinquency, 32*, 363–398.

Agnew, R. (1997). Stability and change in crime over the life course: A strain theory explanation. In T. P. Thornberry (Ed.), *Developmental theories of crime and delinquency: Advances in criminological theory, Volume 7*. New Brunswick, NJ: Transaction.

Ambert, A.-M. (1994). A qualitative study of peer abuse and its effects: Theoretical and empirical implications. *Journal of Marriage and the Family, 56*, 119–130.

Aukett, R., Ritchie, J., & Mill, K. (1988). Gender differences in friendship patterns. *Sex Roles, 19*, 57–66.

Bell, R. R. (1981). Friendships of women and of men. *Psychology of Women Quarterly, 5*, 402–417.

Bernard, T. J. (1987). Testing structural strain theories. *Journal of Research in Crime and Delinquency, 24*, 262–280.

Beutel, A. M., & Marini, M. M. (1995). Gender and values. *American Sociological Review, 60*, 436–448.

Box, S. (1983). *Power, crime, and mystification*. London: Tavistock.

Brown, L. M., & Gilligan, C. (1992). *Meeting at the crossroads*. Cambridge, MA: Harvard University Press.

Campbell, A. (1993). *Men, women, and aggression*. New York: Basic Books.

Cernkovich, S. A., & Giordano, P. C. (1979). Delinquency, opportunity, and gender. *Journal of Criminal Law and Criminology, 70*, 145–151.

Cernkovich, S. A., & Giordano, P. C. (1987). Family relationships and delinquency. *Criminology, 25*, 295–321.

Chesney-Lind, M. (1989). Girls' crime and woman's place: Toward a feminist model of female delinquency. *Crime & Delinquency, 35*, 5–29.

Chesney-Lind, M., & Shelden, R. G. (1992). *Girls, delinquency, and juvenile justice*. Pacific Grove, CA: Brooks/Cole.

Cloward, R. A., & Ohlin, L. E. (1960). *Delinquency and opportunity*. New York: Free Press.

Cloward, R. A., & Piven, F. F. (1979). Hidden protest: The channeling of female innovation and resistance. *Signs: Journal of Women in Culture and Society, 4*, 651–669.

Cohen, A. K. (1955). *Delinquent boys*. New York: Free Press.

Daly, K. (1992). Women's pathways to felony court: Feminist theories of lawbreaking and problems of representation. *Review of Law and Women's Studies, 2*, 11–52.

Daly, K., & Chesney-Lind, M. (1988). Feminism and criminology. *Justice Quarterly, 5*, 497–538.

Danzinger, N. (1983). Sex-related differences in the aspirations of high school students. *Sex Roles, 9*, 683–695.

Datesman, S. K., Scarpitti, F. R., & Stephenson, R. M. (1975). Female delinquency: An application of self and opportunity theories. *Journal of Research in Crime and Delinquency, 12*, 107–123.

Davidson, L. R., & Duberman, L. (1982). Friendship: Communication and interactional patterns in same-sex dyads. *Sex Roles, 8*, 809–822.

Dornfeld, M., & Kruttschnitt, C. (1992). Do the stereotypes fit? Mapping offender-specific outcomes and risk factors. *Criminology, 30*, 397–419.

Eagly, A. H., & Steffen, V. J. (1986). Gender and aggressive behavior: A meta-analytical review of the social psychological literature. *Psychological Bulletin, 100*, 309–328.

Elliott, D. S., Huizinga, D., & Ageton, S. S. (1985). *Explaining delinquency and drug use*. Beverly Hills, CA: Sage.

Felson, M. (1994). *Crime and everyday life*. Thousand Oaks, CA: Pine Forge.

Fine, M. (1993). Sexuality, schooling, and adolescent females: The missing discourse of desire. In L. Weis & M. Fine (Eds.), *Beyond silenced voices: Class, race, and gender in United States schools*. Albany: State University of New York Press.

Frodi, A., Macaulay, J., & Thome, P. R. (1977). Are women always less aggressive than men? A review of the experimental literature. *Psychological Bulletin, 84*, 634–660.

Frost, W. D., & Averill, J. R. (1982). Differences between men and women in the everyday experience of anger. In J. R. Averill (Ed.), *Anger and aggression*. New York: Springer-Verlag.

Gilfus, M. E. (1992). From victims to survivors to offenders: Women's routes of entry and immersion into street crime. *Women and Criminal Justice, 4*, 63–89.

Gilligan, C. (1982). *In a different voice: Psychological theory and women's development*. Cambridge, MA: Harvard University Press.

Gilligan, C., & Attanucci, J. (1988). Two moral orientations: Gender differences and similarities. *Merrill-Palmer Quarterly, 34*, 223–237.

Gilligan, C., Lyons, N. P., & Hanmer, T. J. (1989). *Making connections*. Troy, NY: Emma Willard School.

Giordano, P. C., Cernkovich, S. A., & Pugh, M. D. (1986). Friendships and delinquency. *American Journal of Sociology, 91*, 1170–1292.

Gove, W. R., & Herb, T. R. (1974). Stress and mental illness among the young: A comparison of the sexes. *Social Forces, 53*, 256–265.

Hill, G. D., & Crawford, E. M. (1990). Women, race, and crime. *Criminology, 28*, 601–626.

Hirschi, T. (1969). *Causes of delinquency*. Berkeley: University of California Press.

Hoffman, J. P., & Su, S. S. (1994, November). *The conditional effects of negative life events on delinquency and drug use: A strain theory assessment of gender differences.* Paper presented at the 1994 annual meeting of the American Society of Criminology, Miami.

Ingels, S. J., Scott, L. A., Lindmark, J. A., Frankel, M. R., Myers, S. L., & Wu, S. C. (1992). *National Educational Longitudinal Study of 1988. First follow-up: Student component data file, user's manual* (National Center for Education Statistics). Washington, DC: Government Printing Office.

Johnson, R. E. (1979). *Juvenile delinquency and its origins.* Cambridge: Cambridge University Press.

Jordan, J. V. (1995). A relational approach to psychotherapy. *Women and Therapy, 16*, 51–61.

Klein, D. (1973). The etiology of female crime: A review of the literature. *Issues in Criminology, 8*, 3–30.

Lempers, J. D., & Clark-Lempers, D. S. (1992). Young, middle, and late adolescents' comparisons of the functional importance of five significant relationships. *Journal of Youth and Adolescence, 21*, 53–96.

Leonard, E. B. (1982). *Women, crime and society: A critique of theoretical criminology.* New York: Longman.

Luckenbill, D. F. (1977). Criminal homicide as a situated transaction. *Social Problems, 25*, 176–186.

Mazur, E. (1989). Predicting gender differences in same-sex friendships from affiliation motive and value. *Psychology of Women Quarterly, 13*, 277–291.

Menard, S. (1995). A developmental test of Mertonian anomie theory. *Journal of Research in Crime and Delinquency, 32*, 136–174.

Merton, R. (1938). Social structure and anomie. *American Sociological Review, 3*, 672–682.

Miller, E. M. (1986). *Street woman.* Philadelphia: Temple University Press.

Miller, J. B. (1986). *Toward a new psychology of women.* Boston: Beacon.

Miller, J. B. (1991). The development of women's sense of self. In J. V. Jordan et al. (Eds.), *Women's growth in connection: Writings from the Stone Center.* New York: Guilford.

Morris, A. (1987). *Women, crime and criminal justice.* Oxford, UK: Basil Blackwell.

Morris, R. R. (1964). Female delinquency and relational problems. *Social Forces, 43*, 82–89.

Naffine, N. (1987). *Female crime: The construction of women in criminology.* Sydney: Allen and Unwin.

Norman, D. K., Murphy, J. M., Gilligan, C., & Vasudev, J. (1981–1982). Sex differences and interpersonal relationships: A cross-sectional sample in the U.S. and India. *International Journal of Aging and Human Development, 14*, 291–306.

Rankin, J. H. (1980). School factors and delinquency: Interactions by age and sex. *Sociology and Social Research, 64*, 420–434.

Rokeach, M. (1973). *The nature of human values.* New York: Free Press.

Rosenberg, M. (1965). *Society and the adolescent self-image.* Princeton, NJ: Princeton University Press.

Rubin, L. B. (1985). *Just friends: The role of friendship in our lives.* New York: Harper & Row.

Sandhu, H. S., & Allen, D. E. (1969). Female delinquency: Goal obstruction and anomie. *Review of Canadian Sociology and Anthropology, 6*, 107–110.

Simons, R. L., Miller, M. G., & Aigner, S. M. (1980). Contemporary theories of deviance and female delinquency: An empirical test. *Journal of Research in Crime and Delinquency, 17*, 42–53.

Simpson, S. S. (1991). Caste, class, and violent crime: Explaining differences in female offending. *Criminology, 29*, 115–135.

Simpson, S. S., & Elis, L. (1995). Doing gender: Sorting out the cast and crime conundrum. *Journal of Criminology, 33*, 37–81.

Smart, C. (1977). *Women, crime and criminology: A feminist critique.* London: Routledge & Kegan Paul.

Smith, D. A. (1979). Sex and deviance: An assessment of major sociological variables. *Sociological Quarterly, 20*, 183–195.

Smith, D. A., & Paternoster, R. (1987). The gender gap in theories of deviance: Issues and evidence. *Journal of Research in Crime and Delinquency, 24*, 140–172.

Steffensmeier, D., & Allan, E. (1995). Criminal behavior: Gender and age. In J. F. Sheley (Ed.), *Criminology: A contemporary handbook.* Belmont, CA: Wadsworth.

Thornberry, T. P. (1987). Towards an interactional theory of delinquency. *Criminology, 25*, 863–891.

Warr, M. (1993). Age, peers, and delinquency. *Criminology, 31*, 17–40.

Williams, D. G. (1985). Gender, masculinity-femininity, and emotional intimacy in same-sex friendship. *Sex Roles, 12*, 587–600.

Robert Agnew received a Ph.D in sociology from the University of North Carolina at Chapel Hill. He is professor of sociology at Emory University. His research interests focus on the causes of delinquency, particularly strain theories of delinquency.

Timothy Brezina received a Ph.D in sociology from Emory University. He is an assistant professor of sociology at Washington State University, Vancouver. His research interests include criminological theory, especially strain theories of juvenile delinquency. His current research addresses the adaptive functions of delinquent behavior, including the consequences of delinquent acts as experienced by the offender.

Explaining the Gender Gap in Delinquency:

Peer Influence and Moral Evaluations of Behavior

Daniel P. Mears
Matthew Ploeger
Mark Warr

Gender is one of the strongest and most frequently documented correlates of delinquent behavior. Males commit more offenses than females at every age, within all racial or ethnic groups examined to date, and for all but a handful of offense types that are peculiarly female (Steffensmeier and Allan 1995; Wilson and Herrnstein 1985). Unlike some putative features of delinquency that are method-dependent (e.g., social class differences), sex differences in delinquency are independently corroborated by self-report, victimization, and police data, and they appear to hold cross-culturally as well as historically (Hindelang 1979; Hindelang, Hirschi, and Weis 1979; Steffensmeier and Allan 1995; Wilson and Herrnstein 1985). So tenacious are sex differences in delinquency, in fact,

The authors express their thanks to Christopher G. Ellison. Jack P. Gibbs, Arthur Sakamoto, Mark C. Stafford, Daniel A. Powers, and Thomas W. Pullum for their comments and suggestions. Direct correspondence to Daniel Mears at the Department of Sociology, University of Texas at Austin, Austin, TX 78712-1088.

Daniel P. Mears, Matthew Ploeger, and Mark Warr, Journal of Research in Crime and Delinquency, Vol. 35, No. 3, pp. 251–257, copyright © 1998 by Sage Publications, Inc. Reprinted by permission of Sage Publications, Inc.

that it is difficult to argue with Wilson and Herrnstein's (1985) conclusion that "gender demands attention in the search for the origins of crime" (p. 104).

Explanations for gender differences in offending have been promulgated at least since the time of Lombroso, who opined that the female criminal is "of less typical aspect than the male because she is less essentially criminal" (Lombroso and Ferrero [1895] 1958:111). Lombroso's observations notwithstanding, efforts to explain the gender/crime relation have not fared well, and some sharp philosophical and methodological differences have arisen as to how investigators ought to proceed. Some analysts argue that conventional theories of delinquency were largely designed to explain male delinquency and that separate theories are required to account for male and female delinquency. Smith and Paternoster (1987), however, strongly warn against premature rejection of existing theories: "Since most empirical tests of deviance theories have been conducted with male samples, the applicability of these theories to females is largely unknown. Moreover, the fact that most theories of deviance were constructed to account for male deviance does not mean that they *cannot* account for female deviance" (p. 142).

Rather than postulating separate etiological theories for males and females, Smith and Paternoster (1987) join a number of investigators (cf. Simons, Miller, and Aigner 1980) in suggesting that males and females differ in their rates of delinquency because they are *differentially exposed* to the *same* criminogenic conditions. In a close variant of this position, other investigators (e.g., Johnson 1979) have suggested that males and females are *differentially affected* by exposure to the same criminogenic conditions. If such arguments are correct, then it is pointless to construct entirely separate theories to explain the delinquent behavior of males and females.

One traditional theory of delinquency that holds promise for a unified explanation of gender differences in offending is Sutherland's (1947) theory of differential association. In this classic sociological theory, Sutherland argued that delinquency is learned behavior and that it is learned in intimate social groups through face-to-face interaction. When individuals are selectively or differentially exposed to delinquent companions, Sutherland (1947:7) argued, they are likely to acquire "an excess of definitions favorable to violation of law over definitions unfavorable to violation of law" and consequently engage in delinquent conduct. Sutherland's theory was subsequently recast in modern social learning terms (Burgess and Akers 1966) and enjoys considerable empirical support today (Akers 1994). Although Sutherland did not limit his theory to peer influence, tests of the theory have generally concentrated on peers, and association with delinquent peers remains the single strongest predictor of delinquent behavior known today (Empey and Stafford 1991; Warr 1993).

Several studies suggest that differential association may be a critical factor in explaining gender differences in delinquency. Using self-report data from a sample of Iowa teenagers, Simons et al. (1980) found that males and females experienced substantially different levels of exposure to delinquent peer attitudes in their everyday lives. "Males were much more likely than females to have friends who were supportive of delinquent behavior" (p. 51). But although these investigators were able to establish sex-linked differences in exposure to delinquent friends, they did not isolate and quantify the effect of such exposure on sex-specific rates of delinquency.

Other studies illustrate the variant approach described earlier. Johnson (1979) tested an integrated model of delinquency containing family, school, socioeconomic, deterrence, and peer variables. Among both sexes, the effect of delinquent associates outweighed all other variables in the model. But the effect of delinquent peers on self-reported delinquency was substantially stronger among males than females. Smith and Paternoster (1987) examined the ability of strain theory, differential association, control theory, and deterrence theory to explain sex differences in adolescent marijuana use. They, too, found that association with deviant peers had the largest effect on marijuana use among both males and females, but the effect was once again stronger for males than females. Despite the strikingly similar findings of these two studies, not all investigators have obtained similar results (see Smith and Paternoster 1987). Most, however, have failed to employ appropriate interaction terms or tests of significance in making gender comparisons, or have used widely divergent measures of peer influence.

This article draws on Sutherland's theory of differential association with a view to explaining gender differences in delinquency. Following the logic of Sutherland's theory, the analysis is organized around three general questions: Do male and female adolescents differ in their exposure to peers, and, more specifically, in their exposure to delinquent peers? Are males and females who are exposed to delinquent peers differentially affected by those peers? And if males and females are affected differently by exposure to delinquent peers, why is this true?

The third question is the most fundamental, and it requires elaboration. Some analysts have speculated that same-sex friendships among male and female adolescents are qualitatively different, with male culture placing greater emphasis on daring or risk-taking (Giordano, Cernkovich, and Pugh 1986; Johnson 1979). Without denying that possibility, the present analysis stems from a rather different premise. That is, we suspect that females ordinarily possess something that acts as a barrier to inhibit or block the influence of delinquent peers.

What might that barrier be? One possible answer lies with moral evaluations of conduct. The notion that individuals refrain from conduct because they morally disapprove of it has a long history in criminology, but it appears in a wide variety of theoretical guises (e.g., subcultural theory, religiosity and crime, deterrence theory), and research on the issue, although promising, is not systematic, comparable, or cumulative (Burkett and Ward 1993; Erickson, Gibbs, and Jensen 1977; Grasmick and Bursik 1990; Hindelang 1974; Tittle 1980; Wilson and Herrnstein 1985).

Nevertheless, if moral evaluations do affect conduct, how does that bear on gender differences in offending? Gilligan (1982) has suggested that females are socialized in such a way that they are more constrained by moral evaluations of behavior than are males. In her influential book, Gilligan argued that moral development in females is guided by the primacy of human relationships and by an overriding obligation to care for and to avoid harming others. This

other-oriented quality of female moral development, she added, contrasts sharply with the moral socialization of males. If the moral imperative of women is "an injunction to care" (p. 100), Gilligan argued, men tend to construe morality in more utilitarian terms, that is, as a set of mutually acknowledged rights that protect them from *interference* from others. Thus, the driving principle of male morality is not responsibility to others, but the freedom to pursue self-interest. These gender-linked differences in socialization described by Gilligan imply that females will be more reluctant than males to engage in conduct that harms others, including criminal conduct.

Gilligan did not present direct empirical evidence for her thesis, but research on moral development in children and adolescents provides support for her argument. Although males and females evidently do not differ in the complexity of moral reasoning (Cohn 1991; Walker 1984), there appear to be qualitative differences in such reasoning. In longitudinal and cross-sectional studies of children and adolescents, Eisenberg, Fabes, and Shea (1989) have observed that from the age of about 11 or 12, girls "are more other-oriented in their prosocial moral reasoning than are boys" (p. 139). Similarly, Gibbs, Arnold, and Burkhart (1984) report that moral judgments among females rely on a greater degree of "empathic role-taking" (p. 1042), and Bebeau and Brabek (1989) found that females display a higher degree of "ethical sensitivity" to others than do males.

If moral evaluations of conduct do function as a barrier to peer influence, and if that barrier is higher for females than for males, then we ought to observe a strong difference in the effect of delinquent peers on males and females, a difference that is itself conditioned by sex-linked differences in moral evaluations. Putting the matter more formally, we would expect to find a significant three-way interaction between gender, moral evaluations, and the number of delinquent friends an adolescent has. The model to be estimated can thus be stated as

$$\hat{D} = a + b_1 S + b_2 F + b_3 M + b_4 (S \times F) + b_5 (S \times M) + b_6 (F \times M) + b_7 (S \times F \times M),$$

where D = the incidence of delinquent behavior, S = sex, F = number of delinquent friends, and M = moral evaluations. The model permits the effect of delinquent peers to vary according to both gender and moral evaluations and thereby provides a direct test of the hypothesis that moral evaluations have a greater restraining effect on peer influence among females than among males. We turn now to a discussion of the data and measures used to estimate the model.

DATA AND MEASURES

Data for this study come from the National Youth Survey (NYS), a continuing longitudinal study of delinquent behavior among a national probability sample of 1,725 persons aged 11 to 17 in 1976. The NYS sample was obtained through a multistage probability sampling of households in the continental United States (Elliott, Huizinga, and Ageton 1985). In each wave of the study, respondents were asked a series of questions about events and behavior that occurred during the preceding year. Although the first wave of interviews was conducted in 1976, data for the present analysis come from Wave III of the NYS ($N = 1,626$), which captured respondents during the period of adolescence (ages 13 to 19).

The NYS collects self-report data on a wide range of delinquent behaviors, using the general question, "How many times in the last year have you [act]?" In addition to their own behavior, respondents are asked questions about the friends who they "ran around with," friends who they are asked to identify by name and who they are requested to think of whenever answering questions about peers. For our purposes, the crucial variable of interest is the number of delinquent friends reported by the respondent, measured by the question, "Think of your friends. During the last year how many of them have [act]?" (1 = *none of them*, 2 = *very few of them*, 3 = *some of them*, 4 = *most of them*, 5 = *all of them*). Respondents' moral evaluations of each act were measured by responses to the following question: "How wrong do you think it is for someone your age to [act]?" (1 = *not wrong at all*, 2 = *a little bit wrong*, 3 = *wrong*, 4 = *very wrong*).

Although the NYS collects data on a large number of offenses, questions concerning peer delinquency, respondents' delinquency, and moral evaluations are asked about different sets of offenses, sets that only partially overlap. Precisely comparable data on all three of these dimensions are available for only a small number of offenses. Three of these marijuana use, alcohol use, and cheating exhibit only minimal sex differences (the smallest, in fact, of any offenses measured in the NYS). Another three burglary, grand theft, and selling hard drugs are among the most highly sex-differentiated offenses, but they are so rare among females that virtually none of the females in the sample committed the offenses. Fortunately, there is one offense theft of property worth less than 5—that exhibits a large sex difference (a male/female ratio of 2.0) and is sufficiently common among both sexes to afford statistical analysis. The analysis will therefore concentrate on this offense, but we have taken care to include data on other offenses in the analysis whenever possible.

FINDINGS

The first aim of the analysis is to describe sex differences in delinquent behavior using data from the NYS. Table 1 reports the percentage of males and females who committed each of 11 NYS offenses during the year preceding the survey.[1] The patterns evident in these data are consistent with those reported by previous investigators (e.g., Wilson and Herrnstein 1985). Gender differences in delinquency are quite pervasive, but they vary a good deal from one offense to the next. The largest differences are found among the most serious offenses, where the ratio of male to female offenders exceeds 5:1 (grand theft) and even 8:1 (burglary). By contrast, drug offenses (alcohol and marijuana use), as noted earlier, exhibit little or no sex difference in prevalence, as does cheating on school tests. These patterns are evident regardless of whether one considers the prevalence of offenders (as in Table 1) or the mean incidence of offending (not shown).

The next three tables all bear on the first research question: Are males and females differentially exposed to delinquent peers? The data presented in Table 2 show that, compared to females, males spend more time on average with their friends (delinquent or not) on weekday afternoons and evenings, but not on weekends. The differences are not large, however, amounting to less than half an afternoon or evening per week. A much more stark contrast between the sexes, however, is evident in Table 3. That table displays the percentage of male and female respondents who reported that at least some of their friends had committed each offense. The differences are once again minimal for cheating and for drug and alcohol use. Among the remaining offenses, however, the proportion of males who have delinquent friends exceeds that of females by factors of approximately 1.5 to 2.5, or by differences in the range of about 10 to 25 percent. The most general or inclusive item, simply "break the law," has a male/female ratio of roughly 2:1.

Males, it seems, are substantially more likely than females to be exposed to delinquent friends. Table 4 provides evidence on

TABLE 1: Percentage of Males and Females Reporting Delinquent Acts

Offense	MALES		FEMALES		Ratio	Difference
	Percentage	N	Percentage	N		
Alcohol use	69.2	481	61.3	450	1.1	7.9*
Burglary	4.2	863	.5	763	8.4	3.7***
Cheating	42.6	863	40.8	763	1.0	1.8
Destroying property	32.8	862	14.4	763	2.3	18.4***
Drunkenness	31.9	862	20.6	763	1.5	11.3***
Hitting someone	48.3	863	21.4	763	2.3	26.9***
Marijuana use	38.4	862	33.0	763	1.2	5.4*
Prescription drug use	10.1	863	6.2	763	1.6	3.9**
Selling hard drugs	2.4	863	.5	763	4.8	1.9**
Theft over $50	4.2	863	.8	762	5.3	3.4***
Theft under $5	18.9	862	9.6	762	2.0	9.3***

*$p \leq .05$, **$p \leq .01$, ***$p \leq .001$ (two-tailed tests).

TABLE 2:   Mean Time Spent with Friends by Sex

	MALES		FEMALES		
Time	*Mean*	N	*Mean*	N	t
Weekday afternoons[a]	2.76	788	2.50	722	3.04**
Weekday evenings[b]	2.42	788	2.03	722	4.69***
Weekends[c]	3.64	786	3.64	720	.02

[a]"On the average, how many afternoons during the school week, from the end of school or work to dinner, have you spent with your friends?" (0–5).
[b]"On the average, how many evenings during the school week, from dinnertime to bedtime, have you spent with your friends?" (0–5).
[c]"On the weekends, how much time have you generally spent with your friends?" (1 = *very little*, 2 = *not too much*, 3 = *some*, 4 = *quite a bit*, 5 = *a great deal*).
**$p \leq .01$, ***$p \leq .001$ (two-tailed tests).

TABLE 3:   Percentage of Males and Females with Delinquent Peers

	MALES		FEMALES			
Offense	Percentage	N	Percentage	N	Ratio	Difference
Alcohol use	77.7	860	72.7	759	1.1	5.0*
Burglary	18.5	856	7.3	757	2.5	11.2***
Cheating	85.2	838	79.9	746	1.1	5.3**
Destroying property	52.3	857	27.3	757	1.9	25.0***
Drunkenness	76.2	858	72.3	759	1.1	3.9
Give or sell alcohol	39.3	854	28.5	758	1.4	10.8***
Hitting someone	54.5	857	32.0	757	1.7	22.5***
Marijuana use	58.5	857	54.7	759	1.1	3.8
Prescription drug use	22.8	855	15.6	754	1.5	7.2***
Selling hard drugs	12.2	860	8.6	758	1.4	3.6*
Suggest you break the law	38.0	860	20.4	759	1.9	17.6***
Theft over $50	14.9	854	7.9	758	1.9	7.0***
Theft under $5	57.4	848	37.8	751	1.5	19.6***

*$p \leq .05$, **$p \leq .01$, ***$p \leq .001$ (two-tailed tests).

the effect of this differential exposure. The table presents three OLS (ordinary least-squared) regression models for petty theft, with self-reported incidence the dependent variable in each model.[2] The first model incorporates a dummy variable representing respondent's sex (1 = male, 0 = female), and the second model includes both sex and the proportion of delinquent friends reported by the respondent. If sex differences in delinquency are in fact attributable to differential exposure to delinquent friends, then the coefficient for sex in model 1, which is highly significant, should be substantially reduced or eliminated in model 2.

TABLE 4:   OLS Coefficients for the Regression of Self-Reported Theft on Sex and Delinquent Peers

	Sex	Delinquent Peers	Sex × DP	Intercept	R2	N
Model 1	.275***			.206***	.02	1,624
	(.051)			(.037)		
Model 2	.117*	.522***		−.619***	.23	1,598
	(.047)	(.025)		(.051)		
Model 3	−.189	.419***	.178***	−.455***	.24	1,598
	(.097)	(.038)	(.050)	(.069)		

NOTE: Numbers in parentheses are standard errors. OLS = ordinary least squares.
*$p \leq .05$, ***$p \leq .001$ (two-tailed tests).

A comparison of models 1 and 2 in Table 4 shows that the coefficient for sex does indeed diminish once delinquent friends is held constant. In fact, the coefficient drops to less than one half of its initial value. Despite this reduction, however, the coefficient for sex remains statistically significant. Differential exposure to delinquent peers, therefore, does seem to partially account for sex differences in delinquency, but it is clearly not a sufficient explanation.

Now recall the second major question: Are males and females *affected* differently by delinquent friends? Evidence bearing on that question is presented in model 3 of Table 4. In that model, an interaction term (sex × delinquent friends) has been included to allow for differences in slopes for males and females. Examination of the model shows that the interaction term is positive and highly significant, indicating that the effect of delinquent peers is in fact greater among males than among females.

The evidence from Table 4 points to an initial conclusion: males are more strongly affected by delinquent friends than are females. Why is this true? As we

postulated earlier, the answer may lie in the constraining effect of moral evaluations. Before turning to a direct test of that hypothesis, let us first consider some preliminary evidence. Table 5 shows the percentage of male and female respondents who rated each offense in the NYS as "very wrong." The difference between the sexes in these ratings is statistically significant in every case, with females more apt than males to rate the offenses as very wrong. But consistent though these differences may be, models 1 and 2 in Table 6 show that sex differences in moral evaluations are not in themselves sufficient to explain sex differences in delinquency. The sex effect in model 1 remains strong and statistically significant even after controlling for differences in moral evaluations of the offense (model 2).

Much more critical is the role of moral evaluations in regulating or conditioning the effect of delinquent peers. Model 3 in Table 6 includes an interaction between moral evaluations and delinquent friends, and Figure 1 shows a plot of the model. Inspection of model 3 shows that the interaction term is highly significant, and a close look at the plot in Figure 1

TABLE 5: Percentage of Males and Females Who Perceive Each Act as "Very Wrong"

	MALES		FEMALES			
Offense	Percentage	N	Percentage	N	Ratio	Difference
Alcohol use	22.4	863	28.3	763	.8	−5.9**
Burglary	58.9	861	76.9	763	.8	−18.0***
Cheating	25.1	862	30.8	763	.8	−5.7**
Destroying property	56.1	863	73.0	763	.8	−16.9***
Drunkenness	19.1	863	25.7	763	.7	−6.6**
Giving or selling alcohol	40.5	861	56.0	763	.7	−15.5***
Hitting someone	33.5	863	50.6	763	.7	−17.1***
Marijuana use	38.4	863	45.5	763	.8	−7.1**
Prescription drug use	55.5	863	70.1	763	.8	−14.6***
Selling hard drugs	70.6	863	80.3	763	.9	−9.7***
Theft over $50	63.4	863	78.6	763	.8	−15.2***
Theft under $5	30.9	863	41.7	763	.7	−10.8***

$**p \leq .01$, $***p \leq .001$ (two-tailed tests).

TABLE 6: OLS Coefficients for the Regression of Self-Reported Theft on Sex, Delinquent Peers, Moral Evaluations, and All Interactions

	Sex	DP	ME	DP	Sex × ME	Sex × ME	DP × DP × ME	Sex × Intercept	R^2	N
Model 1	.275*** (.051)							.206*** (.037)	.02	1,624
Model 2	.191*** (.049)		−.469*** (.035)					1.758*** (.123)	.11	1,624
Model 3		1.282*** (.094)	.295*** (.068)			−.277*** (.031)		−1.352*** (.229)	.29	1,598
Model 4	.434 (.346)	1.184*** (.118)	.487*** (.106)	−.196 (.150)	−.257 (.145)	−.396*** (.054)	.159* (.070)	−1.419*** (.254)	.29	1,598

NOTE: Numbers in parentheses are standard errors. DP = delinquent peers; ME = moral evaluations.
$*p \leq .05$, $***p \leq .001$ (two-tailed tests).

reveals that the effect of delinquent peers diminishes very rapidly as moral disapproval increases. Moral evaluations, then, do appear to mitigate or counteract the influence of delinquent peers.

Having laid the necessary foundation, we may now turn to the central hypothesis of this study: Do moral evaluations of conduct provide a stronger barrier to peer influence among females than among males? As noted earlier, the hypothesis implies a three-way interaction between sex, moral evaluations, and delinquent peers. Because such higher order interactions spread

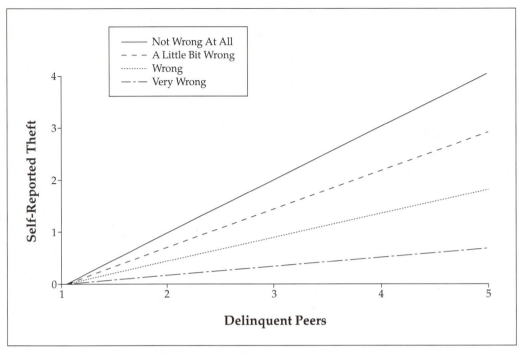

Figure 1. Plotted Equation from Table 6 (Model 3)

the data rather thinly (2 sexes × 5 categories of peers × 4 levels of moral evaluation), the moral evaluation scale was collapsed to produce a scale scored as 1 = *not wrong at all/a little bit wrong*, 2 = *wrong*, and 3 = *very wrong*. The fitted three-way interaction model (including the implied lower order terms) is given as model 4 in Table 6.

It is immediately evident from the table that the three-way interaction term is statistically significant. Because three-way interactions are difficult to visualize, Figure 2 displays a plot of model 4. The plot contains six regression lines, three for males who report strong, moderate, and little or no disapproval of the offense, and three for females in those same categories. Looking at the regression lines, observe that several features stand out. Among

both males and females, moral evaluations act to regulate or restrain the effect of delinquent peers (compare the regression lines within each sex). But the impact of those evaluations is different for the two sexes. Among males and females who show little or no disapproval of the act (the uppermost two lines), the effect of delinquent peers is very similar; both groups exhibit strong sensitivity to peers. As moral disapproval increases, however, males and females diverge from one another, with females showing less susceptibility than males to peer influence. In fact, among females who strongly disapprove of the offense (the lowermost line), the effect of delinquent friends is effectively *eliminated* (i.e., the slope is not significantly different from zero), meaning that females in this category are essentially immune to peer

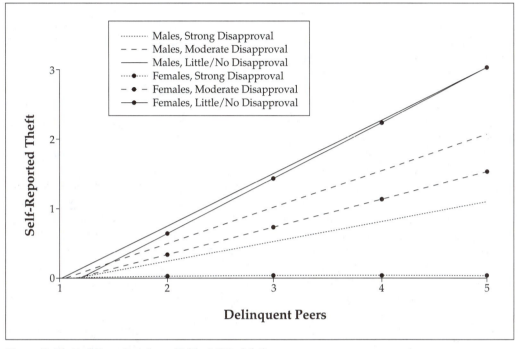

Figure 2. Plotted Equation from Table 6 (Model 4)

influence. But the same cannot be said of males, for whom peers continue to have a statistically significant effect even when moral disapproval is strong.

CONCLUSION

The findings of this study point to several tentative conclusions. Males and females differ in exposure to delinquent peers, with males substantially more likely than females to have delinquent friends. This differential exposure contributes to sex differences in delinquency, but it is not the sole source of those differences. Quite aside from differences in exposure to peers, males appear to be more strongly affected by delinquent peers than are females. This fact, in turn, evidently reflects the greater effect of moral evaluations in

counteracting peer influence among females. Although the number of delinquent peers an adolescent has is the strongest known predictor of delinquent behavior, the moral judgments of females are apparently sufficient to reduce and even eliminate the impact of delinquent peers.

Why are moral evaluations of behavior so effective in combating peer influence among females? Given the results of our analysis, it would be difficult to reject the argument by Gilligan and others that the primary socialization of women instills moral values that strongly discourage behavior that hurts or harms others. To be sure, our analysis is not a direct test of Gilligan's thesis, if only because it focused on the intensity rather than the quality of moral evaluations and did not examine the socialization process itself. Nevertheless, the results of this analysis clearly attest to the power of moral evaluations among females, and they demonstrate that the consequence of those evaluations is to reduce the frequency of antisocial behavior among females.

Our analysis also suggests that it is fruitless to construct utterly different theories to explain the delinquency of males and females. As we have seen, both males and females are affected—though to different degrees—by a common factor: association with delinquent friends. What differs between the sexes, it seems, are not the *generative* factors that give rise to delinquency, but rather the *inhibitory* factors that prevent or counteract it (see Gibbs 1975). Although we have focused on peer influence in this analysis, it may be the case that, among females, moral evaluations counteract a variety of criminogenic conditions, from economic deprivation to dysfunctional family organization. If the present analysis is any indicator, there may be few, if any, generative factors that can overcome the moral constraints of most females. Viewed that way, the enormous sex ratios in offending observed in these and other data seem less startling or inexplicable.

There is at least one factor, however, that may neutralize the moral evaluations of females, one that bears directly on the phenomenon of peer influence. Several studies conducted during the past two decades suggest that, for some females, delinquency is a consequence of exposure to delinquent males. Giordano (1978), for example, reported that girls who spend time in mixed-sex groups are significantly more likely to engage in delinquency than are girls who participate in same-sex groups. Warr (1996) found that females were much more likely than males to report that the instigator in their delinquent group was of the opposite sex. Stattin and

Magnusson (1990) discovered that elevated levels of delinquency among females who experience early menarche is attributable to their tendency to associate with older males, and Caspi et al. (1993) observed that New Zealand girls in all-female schools were significantly less likely to engage in delinquency than were girls in mixed-sex schools.

Despite this evidence, it remains unclear just how often males contribute to the delinquency of females, and it is equally unclear whether the relations that link male and female offenders are ordinarily romantic in nature or similar to those of same-sex offenders. Nevertheless, there remains the intriguing possibility that relations with males are one of the few generative factors capable of overcoming the strong moral objections that females commonly hold toward illegal behavior.

One final theoretical issue deserves attention. Although the conceptualization of delinquency employed here borrows heavily from Sutherland's theory of differential association, it nonetheless differs from that theory in at least one respect. According to Sutherland's theory, delinquency is a consequence of attitudes or "definitions" acquired from others, attitudes that ostensibly include moral evaluations of behavior. Individuals, in short, become delinquent by adopting the attitudes of significant others. Tests of differential association, however, consistently indicate that attitude transference among peers is not the primary mechanism by which delinquency is transmitted (Warr and Stafford 1991), implying that other, more direct, mechanisms of social learning (e.g., imitation, direct and vicarious reinforcement) may be at work (see Akers 1985). Our findings, too, cast doubt on the notion of attitude transference that undergirds Sutherland's theory. It appears from our analysis that the moral evaluations of adolescents—especially females—are frequently a barrier that restrains peer influence rather than a conduit that transmits it. If that interpretation is correct, then Sutherland's theory may require modification.

Notes

1. The figures for "destroying property" in Table 1 are a composite of several items (destroying property belonging to parents, other family members, a school, or other persons). The figures for "hitting someone" are a composite of three items (hitting a teacher, parent, or student). In both cases, respondents were coded as offenders if they reported committing any of the constituent offenses. The NYS collects self-report data on more than fifty offenses, including detailed information on drug use (hallucinogens, heroin, cocaine, barbiturates, amphetamines, etc.). However, only those offenses for which there were identical or analogous data on other relevant variables (i.e., peer delinquency and moral evaluations) are included in Table 1.

2. The dependent variable is coded as a simple integer count truncated at 5+ to eliminate extreme scores. Only 2.1 percent of the cases had scores exceeding 5.

References

Akers, Ronald L. 1985. *Deviant Behavior: A Social Learning Approach*. Belmont, CA: Wadsworth.

———. 1994. *Criminological Theories: Introduction and Evaluation*. Los Angeles: Roxbury.

Bebeau, Muriel J, and Mary M. Brabeck. 1989. "Ethical Sensitivity and Moral Reasoning among Men and Women in the Professions." Pp. 144–63 in *Who Cares? Theory, Research, and Educational Implications of the Ethic of Care*, edited by Mary M. Brabeck. New York: Praeger.

Burgess, Robert L, and Ronald L. Akers. 1966. "A Differential Association-Reinforcement Theory of Criminal Behavior." *Social Problems* 14:128–47.

Burkett, Steven R. and David A. Ward. 1993. "A Note on Perceptual Deterrence, Religiously Based Moral Condemnation, and Social Control." *Criminology* 31:119–34.

Caspi, Avshalom, Donald Lynam, Terrie E. Moffitt, and Phil A. Silva. 1993. "Unraveling Girls' Delinquency: Biological, Dispositional, and Contextual Contributions to Adolescent Misbehavior." *Developmental Psychology* 29:19–30.

Cohn, Lawrence D. 1991. "Sex Differences in the Course of Personality Development: A Meta-Analysis." *Psychological Bulletin* 109:252–66.

Eisenberg, Nancy, Richard Fabes, and Cindy Shea. 1989. "Gender Differences in Empathy and Prosocial Moral Reasoning: Empirical Investigations." Pp. 127–43 in *Who Cares? Theory, Research, and Educational Implications of the Ethic of Care*, edited by Mary M. Brabeck. New York: Praeger.

Elliott, Delbert S., David Huizinga, and Suzanne Ageton. 1985. *Explaining Deliquency and Drug Use*. Beverly Hills, CA: Sage.

Empey, LaMar T. and Mark C. Stafford. 1991. *American Delinquency: Its Meaning and Construction*. 3d ed. Belmont, CA: Wadsworth.

Erickson, Maynard, Jack P. Gibbs, and Gary Jensen. 1977. "The Deterrence Doctrine and the Perceived Certainty of Legal Punishments." *American Sociological Review* 42:305–17.

Gibbs, Jack P. 1975. *Crime, Punishment, and Deterrence*. New York: Elsevier North-Holland.

Gibbs, John C., Kevin D. Arnold, and Jennifer E. Burkhart. 1984. "Sex Differences in the Expression of Moral Judgment." *Child Development* 55:1040–3.

Gilligan, Carol. 1982. *In a Different Voice: Psychological Theory and Women's Development*. Cambridge, MA: Harvard University Press.

Giordano, Peggy C. 1978. "Girls, Guys and Gangs: The Changing Social Context of Female Delinquency." *Journal of Criminal Law and Criminology* 69:126–32.

Giordano, Peggy C., Stephen A. cernkovich, and M. D. Pugh. 1986. "Friendships and Delinquency." *American Journal of Sociology* 91:1170–202.

Grasmick, Harold and Robert J. Bursik. 1990. "Conscience. Significant Others, and Rational Choice: Extending the Deterrence Model." *Law and Society Review* 24:837–61.

Hindelang, Michael. 1974. "Moral Evaluations of Illegal Behavior." *Social Problems* 21:370–85.

———. 1979. "Sex Differences in Criminal Activity." *Social Problems* 27:143–56.

Hindelang, Michael J., Travis Hirschi, and J. Weis. 1979. "Correlates of Delinquency: The Illusion of Discrepancy between Self-Report and Official Measures." *American Sociological Review* 44:995–1014.

Johnson, Richard. 1979. *Juvenile Delinquency and Its Origins*. Cambridge: Cambridge University Press.

Lombroso, Caesar and William Ferrero. [1895] 1958. *Female Offender*. Reprint, New York: Philosophical Library.

Simons, Ronald L., Martin G. Miller, and Stephen M. Aigner. 1980. "Contemporary Theories of Deviance and Female Delinquency: An Empirical Test." *Journal of Research in Crime and Delinquency* 17:42–53.

Smith, Douglas A, and Raymond Patermoster, 1987. "The Gender Gap in Theories of Deviance: Issues and Evidence." *Journal of Research in Crime and Delinquency* 24:140–72.

Stattin, H. and D. Magnusson. 1990, *Pubertal Matura-tion in Female Development*. Hillsdale, NJ: Lawrence Erlbaum.

Steffensmeier, Darrell J. and Emilie Allan. 1995. "Criminal Behavior: Gender and Age." Pp. 83–113 in *Criminology: A Contemporary Handbook*. 2d ed. Edited by Joseph F. Sheley. Belmont, CA: Wadsworth.

Sutherland, Edwin H. 1947. *Criminology*. 4th ed. Philadelphia: Lippincott.

Tittle, Charles R. 1980. *Sanctions and Social Deviance: The Question of Deterrence*. New York: Praeger.

Walker, Lawrence J. 1984. "Sex Differences in the De-velopment of Moral Reasoning: A Critical Review." *Child Development* 55:677–91.

Warr, Mark. 1993. "Age, Peers, and Delinquency." *Criminology* 31:17–40.

———. 1996. "Organization and Instigation in Delin-quent Groups." *Criminology* 34:11–37.

Warr, Mark and Mark C. Stafford. 1991. "The Influ-ence of Delinquent Peers: What They Think or What They Do?" *Criminology* 29:851–66.

Wilson, James Q. and William Herrnstein. 1985. *Crime and Human Nature*. New York: Simon & Schuster.

Gender and Victimization Risk Among Young Women in Gangs

Jody Miller

An underdeveloped area in the gang literature is the relationship between gang
participation and victimization risk.
There are notable reasons to consider the
issue significant. We now have strong evidence that delinquent lifestyles are associated with increased risk of victimization
(Lauritsen, Sampson, and Laub 1991).
Gangs are social groups that are organized around delinquency (see Klein 1995),
and participation in gangs has been
shown to escalate youths' involvement in
crime, including violent crime (Esbensen
and Huizinga 1993; Esbensen, Huizinga,
and Weiher 1993; Fagan 1989, 1990;
Thornberry et al. 1993). Moreover, research on gang violence indicates that the
primary targets of this violence are other
gang members (Block and Block 1993;
Decker 1996; Klein and Maxson 1989;
Sanders 1993). As such, gang participation
can be recognized as a delinquent lifestyle
that is likely to involve high risks of victimization (see Huff 1996:97). Although
research on female gang involvement has

expanded in recent years and includes the
examination of issues such as violence
and victimization, the oversight regarding the relationship between gang participation and violent victimization extends
to this work as well.

The coalescence of attention to the
proliferation of gangs and gang violence
(Block and Block 1993; Curry, Ball, and
Decker 1996; Decker 1996; Klein 1995;
Klein and Maxson 1989; Sanders 1993), and
a possible disproportionate rise in female
participation in violent crimes more generally (Baskin, Sommers, and Fagan 1993;
but see Chesney-Lind, Shelden, and Joe
1996), has led to a specific concern with examining female gang members' violent activities. As a result, some recent research
on girls in gangs has examined these
young women's participation in violence
and other crimes as offenders (Bjerregaard
and Smith 1993; Brotherton 1996; Fagan
1990; Lauderback, Hansen, and Waldorf
1992; Taylor, 1993). However, an additional
question worth investigation is what relationships exist between young women's
gang involvement and their experiences
and risk of victimization. Based on in-
depth interviews with female gang members, this article examines the ways in
which gender shapes victimization risk
within street gangs.

Jody Miller, Journal of Research in Crime and Delinquency, Vol. 35, No. 4, pp. 429–453, copyright © 1998
by Sage Publications, Inc. Reprinted by permission of
Sage Publications, Inc.

GENDER, VIOLENCE, AND VICTIMIZATION

Feminist scholars have played a significant role in bringing attention to the overlapping nature of women's criminal offending and patterns of victimization, emphasizing the relationships of gender inequality and sexual exploitation to women's participation in crime (Arnold 1990; Campbell 1984; Chesney-Lind and Rodriguez 1983; Daly 1992; Gilfus 1992). In regard to female gang involvement, recent research suggests that young women in gangs have disproportionate histories of victimization before gang involvement as compared with non-gang females (Miller 1996) and gang males (Joe and Chesney-Lind 1995; Moore 1991). Moreover, there is evidence that young women turn to gangs, in part, as a means of protecting themselves from violence and other problems in their families and from mistreatment at the hands of men in their lives (Joe and Chesney-Lind 1995; Lauderback et al. 1992).

This is not surprising, given the social contexts these young women face. Many young women in gangs are living in impoverished urban "underclass" communities where violence is both extensive and a "sanctioned response to [the] oppressive material conditions" associated with inequality, segregation, and isolation (Simpson 1991:129; see also Sampson and Wilson 1995; Wilson 1996). Moreover, violence against *women* is heightened by the nature of the urban street world, where gendered power relations are played out (Connell 1987), crack markets have intensified the degradation of women (Bourgois and Dunlap 1993; Maher and Curtis 1992), and structural changes may have increased cultural support for violence against women (Wilson 1996).

The social world of adolescence is highly gendered as well (Eder 1995; Lees 1993; Thorne 1993). It is a period in which peer relationships increase in significance for youths, and this is magnified, especially for girls, with increased self-consciousness and sensitivity to others' perceptions of them (Pesce and Harding 1986). In addition, it is characterized by a "shift from the relatively asexual gender system of childhood to the overtly sexualized gender systems of adolescence and adulthood" (Thorne 1993:135). Young women find themselves in a contradictory position. Increasingly, they receive status from their peers via their association with, and attractiveness to, young men, but they are denigrated for their sexual activity and threatened with the labels *slut* and *ho* (Eder 1995; Lees 1993). The contexts of adolescence and the urban street world, then, have unique features likely to make young women particularly vulnerable to victimization. Thus, for some young women, gang involvement may appear to be a useful means of negotiating within these environments.

However, as Bourgois (1995) notes, actions taken to resist oppression can ultimately result in increased harm. Among young women in gangs, an important question to examine is how participation in gangs itself shapes young women's risk of victimization, including the question of whether gang involvement places girls at higher risks of victimization because of a potential increased involvement in crime. Lauritsen et al. (1991) found that "adolescent involvement in delinquent lifestyles strongly increases the risk of both personal and property victimization" (p. 265). Moreover, gender as a predictor of victimization risk among adolescents decreases when participation in delinquent lifestyles is controlled for (Lauritsen et al. 1991). That is, much of young men's greater victimization risk can be accounted for by their greater participation in offending behaviors.

Among gang members, then, involvement in crime is likely associated with increased risk for victimization. Gang girls' participation in crime is thus an important consideration if we hope to understand the relationship between their gang membership and victimization risk.

GIRLS, GANGS, AND CRIME

Research comparing gang and nongang youths has consistently found that serious criminal involvement is a feature that distinguishes gangs from other groups of youths (Bjerregaard and Smith 1993; Esbensen and Huizinga 1993; Esbensen et al. 1993; Fagan 1989, 1990; Klein 1995; Thornberry et al. 1993; Winfree et al. 1992). Until recently, however, little attention was paid to young women's participation in serious and violent gang-related crime. Most traditional gang research emphasized the auxiliary and peripheral nature of girls' gang involvement and often resulted in an almost exclusive emphasis on girls' sexuality and sexual activities with male gang members, downplaying their participation in delinquency (for critiques of gender bias in gang research, see Campbell 1984, 1990; Taylor 1993).

However, recent estimates of female gang involvement have caused researchers to pay greater attention to gang girls' activities. This evidence suggests that young women approximate anywhere from 10 to 38 percent of gang members (Campbell 1984; Chesney-Lind 1993; Esbensen 1996; Fagan 1990; Moore 1991), that female gang participation may be increasing (Fagan 1990; Spergel and Curry 1993; Taylor 1993), and that in some urban areas, upward of one-fifth of girls report gang affiliations (Bjerregaard and Smith 1993; Winfree et al. 1992). As female gang members have become recognized as a group worthy of criminologists' attention, we have garnered new information regarding their involvement in delinquency in general, and violence in particular.

Recent research on female gang involvement indicates that the pattern of higher rates of criminal involvement for gang members holds for girls as well as their male counterparts (Bjerregaard and Smith 1993; Esbensen and Winfree forthcoming; Thornberry et al. 1993). The enhancement effect of gang membership is most noticeable for serious delinquency and marijuana use (Thornberry et al. 1993). Bjerregaard and Smith (1993) summarize:

> The traditional gang literature has generally suggested that gang membership enhances delinquent activity, and particularly serious delinquent activity for males, but not for females. In contrast, our study suggests that for females also, gangs are consistently associated with a greater prevalence and with higher rates of delinquency and substance use. Furthermore, the results suggest that for both sexes, gangs membership has an approximately equal impact on a variety of measures of delinquent behavior. (P. 346)

An interesting counterpart is provided by Bowker, Gross, and Klein (1980), who suggest there is evidence of "the structural exclusion of young women from male delinquent activities" within gangs (p. 516). Their (male) respondents suggested that not only were girls excluded from the planning of delinquent acts, but when girls inadvertently showed up at the location of a planned incident, it was frequently postponed or terminated. Likewise, Fagan (1990) reports greater gender differences in delinquency between gang members than between nongang youths (pp. 196–97). Male gang members were significantly more involved in the most serious forms of delinquency, whereas for alcohol use, drug sales, extortion, and property damage, gender differences were not significant.

However, Fagan also reports that "prevalence rates for female gang members exceeded the rates for non-gang males" for all the categories of delinquency he measured (see also Esbensen and Winfree 1998). Fagan (1990) summarizes his findings in relation to girls as follows:

> More than 40% of the female gang members were classified in the least serious category, a substantial difference from their male counterparts [15.5 percent]. Among female gang members, there was a bimodal distribution, with nearly as many multiple index offenders as petty delinquents. Evidently, female gang members avoid more serious delinquent involvement than their male counterparts. *Yet their extensive involvement in serious delinquent behaviors well exceeds that of non-gang males or females.* (P. 201, my emphasis)

Few would dispute that when it comes to serious delinquency, male gang members are involved more frequently than their female counterparts. However, this evidence does suggest that young women in gangs are more involved in serious criminal activities than was previously believed and also tend to be more involved than nongang youths—male or female. As such, they likely are exposed to greater victimization risk than nongang youths as well.

In addition, given the social contexts described above, it is reasonable to assume that young women's victimization risk within gangs is also shaped by gender. Gang activities (such as fighting for status and retaliation) create a particular set of factors that increase gang members' victimization risk and repeat victimization risk—constructions of gender identity may shape these risks in particular ways for girls. For instance, young women's adoption of masculine attributes may provide a means of participating and gaining status

within gangs but may also lead to increased risk of victimization as a result of deeper immersion in delinquent activities. On the other hand, experiences of victimization may contribute to girls' denigration and thus increase their risk for repeat victimization through gendered responses and labeling—for example, when sexual victimization leads to perceptions of sexual availability or when victimization leads an individual to be viewed as weak. In addition, femaleness is an individual attribute that has the capacity to mark young women as "safe" crime victims (e.g., easy targets) or, conversely, to deem them "off limits." My goal here is to examine the gendered nature of violence within gangs, with a specific focus on how gender shapes young women's victimization risk.

METHODOLOGY

Data presented in this article come from survey and semistructured in-depth interviews with 20 female members of mixed-gender gangs in Columbus, Ohio. The interviewees ranged in age from 12 to 17; just over three-quarters were African American or multiracial (16 of 20), and the rest (4 of 20) were White. The sample was drawn primarily from several local agencies in Columbus working with at-risk youths, including the county juvenile detention center, a shelter care facility for adolescent girls, a day school within the same institution, and a local community agency.[1] The project was structured as a gang/nongang comparison, and I interviewed a total of 46 girls. Gang membership was determined during the survey interview by self-definition: About one-quarter of the way through the 50+ page interview, young women were asked a series of questions about the friends they spent time with. They then were asked whether these friends were gang involved and whether they themselves were gang members. Of the 46 girls interviewed, 21 reported that they were gang members,[2] and an additional 3 reported being gang involved (hanging out primarily with gangs or gang members) but not gang members. The rest reported no gang involvement.

A great deal of recent research suggests that self-report data provide comparatively reliable and valid measures of youths' gang membership (see Bjerregaard and Smith 1993; Fagan 1990; Thornberry et al. 1993; Winfree et al. 1992). This research suggests that using more restrictive measures (such as initiation rituals, a gang name, symbolic systems such as colors or signs) does not change substantive conclusions concerning gang members' behaviors when comparing self-defined gang members to those members who meet these more restrictive definitions. Although most researchers agree that the group should be involved in illegal activities in order for the youth to be classified as a gang member (see Esbensen et al. 1993; Esbensen and Huizinga 1993; Fagan 1989), other research that has used self-nomination without specifying crime as a defining feature has nonetheless consistently found serious criminal involvement as a feature that distinguishes gangs from other groups of youths (Fagan 1990; Thornberry et al. 1993; Winfree et al. 1992). All the gang members in my sample were members of groups they described as delinquent.

Cooperation from agency personnel generally proves successful for accessing gang members (see Bowker et al. 1980; Fagan 1989; Short and Strodtbeck 1965). However, these referrals pose the problem of targeting only officially labeled gang youth. I took several steps to temper this problem. First, I did not choose agencies that dealt specifically with gang members, and I did not rely on agency rosters of

"known" gang members for my sample. As a result of the gang/nongang comparative research design, I was able to avoid oversampling girls who were labeled as gang members by asking agency personnel to refer me not just to girls believed to be gang involved but also any other girls living in areas in Columbus where they might have contact with gangs. Second, although I was only moderately successful, throughout the project I attempted to expand my sample on the basis of snowball techniques (see Fagan 1989; Hagedorn 1988). I only generated one successful referral outside of the agency contexts. However, I was successful at snowballing *within* agencies. Several girls I interviewed were gang involved but without staff knowledge, and they were referred to me by other girls I interviewed within the facilities. Thus, in a limited capacity, I was able to interview gang members who had not been detected by officials. Nonetheless, my sample is still limited to youths who have experienced intervention in some capacity, whether formal or informal, and thus it may not be representative of gang-involved girls in the community at large.

The survey interview was a variation of several instruments currently being used in research in a number of cities across the United States and included a broad range of questions and scales measuring factors that may be related to gang membership.[3] On issues related to violence, it included questions about peer activities and delinquency, individual delinquent involvement, family violence and abuse, and victimization. When young women responded affirmatively to being gang members, I followed with a series of questions about the nature of their gang, including its size, leadership, activities, symbols, and so on. Girls who admitted gang involvement during the survey participated in a follow-up interview to talk in more depth about their gangs and gang activities. The goal of the in-depth interview was to gain a greater understanding of the nature and meanings of gang life from the point of view of its female members. A strength of qualitative interviewing is its ability to shed light on this aspect of the social world, highlighting the meanings individuals attribute to their experiences (Adler and Adler 1987; Glassner and Loughlin 1987; Miller and Glassner 1997). In addition, using multiple methods, including follow-up interviews, provided me with a means of detecting inconsistencies in young women's accounts of their experiences. Fortunately, no serious contradictions arose. However, a limitation of the data is that only young women were interviewed. Thus, I make inferences about gender dynamics, and young men's behavior, based only on young women's perspectives.

The in-depth interviews were open-ended and all but one were audiotaped. They were structured around several groupings of questions. We began by discussing girls' entry into their gangs—when and how they became involved, and what other things were going on in their lives at the time. Then, we discussed the structure of the gang—its history, size, leadership, and organization, and their place in the group. The next series of questions concerned gender within the gang; for example, how girls get involved, what activities they engage in and whether these are the same as the young men's activities, and what kind of males and females have the most influence in the gang and why. The next series of questions explored gang involvement more generally—what being in the gang means, what kinds of things they do together, and so on. Then, I asked how safe or dangerous they feel gang membership is and how they deal with risk. I concluded by asking them to speculate about

why people their age join gangs, what things they like, what they dislike and have learned by being in the gang, and what they like best about themselves. This basic guideline was followed for each interview subject, although when additional topics arose in the context of the interview, we often deviated from the interview guide to pursue them. Throughout the interviews, issues related to violence emerged; these issues form the core of the discussion that follows.

SETTING

Columbus is a particular type of gang city. Gangs are a relatively new phenomenon there, with their emergence dated around 1985 (Maxson, Woods, and Klein 1995). In addition, it is thriving economically, experiencing both population and economic growth over the last decade (Rusk 1995). As such, it is representative of a recent pattern of gang proliferation into numerous cities, suburbs, and towns that do not have many of the long-standing problems associated with traditional gang cities, such as deindustrialization, population loss, and the deterioration of social support networks (see Curry et al. 1996; Hagedorn 1988; Klein 1995; Maxson et al. 1995; Spergel and Curry 1993). Even as Columbus has prospered, however, its racial disparities have grown (Columbus Metropolitan Human Services Commission 1995:17). In fact, in relative terms (comparing the gap between African Americans and Whites), racial disparities in measures such as income and percentage poverty in Columbus are equal to or even greater than in many cities experiencing economic and population declines.[4]

According to recent police estimates, Columbus has about 30 active gangs, with 400 to 1,000 members (LaLonde 1995). Most of these groups are small in size (20 or fewer members) and are either African American or racially mixed with a majority of African American members (Mayhood and LaLonde 1995). Gangs in Columbus have adopted "big-city" gang names such as Crips, Bloods, and Folks, along with the dress styles, signs, and graffiti of these groups, although gangs are and have been primarily a "homegrown" problem in Columbus rather than a result of organized gang migration (Huff 1989). Local police view these groups as criminally oriented, but not especially sophisticated. On the whole, gangs in Columbus seem to match those described in other cities with emergent gang problems—best characterized as "relatively autonomous, smaller, independent groups, poorly organized and less territorial" than in older gang cities (Klein 1995:36).

The young women I interviewed described their gangs in ways that are very much in keeping with these findings. All 20 are members of Folks, Crips, or Bloods sets.[5] All but 3 described gangs with fewer than 30 members, and most reported relatively narrow age ranges between members. Half were in gangs with members who were 21 or over, but almost without exception, their gangs were made up primarily of teenagers, with either one adult who was considered the OG ("Original Gangster," leader) or just a handful of young adults. The majority (14 of 20) reported that their gangs did not include members under the age of 13.

Although the gangs these young women were members of were composed of both female and male members, they varied in their gender composition, with the vast majority being predominantly male. Six girls reported that girls were one-fifth or fewer of the members of their gang; 8 were in gangs in which girls were between a quarter and a third of the overall membership; 4 said girls were between 44

and 50 percent of the members; and 1 girl reported that her gang was two-thirds female and one-third male. Overall, girls were typically a minority within these groups numerically, with 11 girls reporting that there were 5 or fewer girls in their set.

This structure—male-dominated, integrated mixed-gender gangs—likely shapes gender dynamics in particular ways. Much past gang research has assumed that female members of gangs are in auxiliary subgroups of male gangs, but there is increasing evidence—including from the young women I spoke with—that many gangs can be characterized as integrated, mixed-gender groups. For example, from interviews with 110 female gang members in three sites (Boston, Seattle, and Pueblo, Colorado), Curry (1997) found integrated mixed-gender gangs to be the predominant gang structure of female gang members, with 57.3 percent of girls describing their gangs as mixed-gender.[6] It is likely that gang structure shapes both status orientations and criminal involvement among gang members (Brotherton 1996), and that these differences may also be mediated by ethnicity (Brotherton 1996; Joe and Chesney-Lind 1995; Moore and Hagedorn, 1996). Generalizability beyond mixed-gender, predominantly African American gangs in emergent gang cities, then, is questionable.

GENDER, GANGS, AND VIOLENCE

GANGS AS PROTECTION AND RISK

An irony of gang involvement is that although many members suggest one thing they get out of the gang is a sense of protection (see also Decker 1996; Joe and Chesney-Lind 1995; Lauderback et al. 1992), gang membership itself means exposure to victimization risk and even a willingness to be victimized. These contradictions are apparent when girls talk about what they get out of the gang, and what being in the gang means in terms of other members' expectations of their behavior. In general, a number of girls suggested that being a gang member is a source of protection around the neighborhood. Erica,[7] a 17-year-old African American, explained, "It's like people look at us and that's exactly what they think, there's a gang, and they respect us for that. They won't bother us. . . . It's like you put that intimidation in somebody." Likewise, Lisa, a 14-year-old White girl, described being in the gang as empowering: "You just feel like, oh my God, you know, they got my back. I don't need to worry about it." Given the violence endemic in many inner-city communities, these beliefs are understandable, and to a certain extent, accurate.

In addition, some young women articulated a specifically gendered sense of protection that they felt as a result of being a member of a group that was predominantly male. Gangs operate within larger social milieus that are characterized by gender inequality and sexual exploitation. Being in a gang with young men means at least the semblance of protection from, and retaliation against, predatory men in the social environment. Heather, a 15-year-old White girl, noted, "You feel more secure when, you know, a guy's around protectin' you, you know, than you would a girl." She explained that as a gang member, because "you get protected by guys . . . not as many people mess with you." Other young women concurred and also described that male gang members could retaliate against specific acts of violence against girls in the gang. Nikkie, a 13-year-old African American girl, had a friend who was raped by a rival gang member, and she said, "It was a Crab [Crip] that raped my girl in Miller Ales, and um, they was ready to kill him." Keisha, an African American 14-year-old,

explained, "If I got beat up by a guy, all I gotta do is go tell one of the niggers, you know what I'm sayin'? Or one of the guys, they'd take care of it."

At the same time, members recognized that they may be targets of rival gang members and were expected to "be down" for their gang at those times even when it meant being physically hurt. In addition, initiation rites and internal rules were structured in ways that required individuals to submit to, and be exposed to, violence. For example, young women's descriptions of the qualities they valued in members revealed the extent to which exposure to violence was an expected element of gang involvement. Potential members, they explained, should be tough, able to fight and to engage in criminal activities, and also should be loyal to the group and willing to put themselves at risk for it. Erica explained that they didn't want "punks" in her gang: "When you join something like that, you might as well expect that there's gonna be fights. . . . And, if you're a punk, or if you're scared of stuff like that, then don't join." Likewise, the following dialogue with Cathy, a White 16-year-old, reveals similar themes. I asked her what her gang expected out of members and she responded, "to be true to our gang and to have our backs." When I asked her to elaborate, she explained,

Cathy: Like, uh, if you say you're a Blood, you be a Blood. You wear your rag even when you're by yourself. You know, don't let anybody intimidate you and be like, "Take that rag off." You know, "you better get with our set." Or something like that.

JM: Ok. Anything else that being true to the set means?

Cathy: Um. Yeah, I mean, just, just, you know, I mean it's, you got a whole bunch of people comin'

up in your face and if you're by yourself they ask you what's your claimin', you tell 'em. Don't say "nothin'."

JM: Even if it means getting beat up or something?

Cathy: Mmhmm.

One measure of these qualities came through the initiation process, which involved the individual submitting to victimization at the hands of the gang's members. Typically this entailed either taking a fixed number of "blows" to the head and/or chest or being "beaten in" by members for a given duration (e.g., 60 seconds). Heather described the initiation as an important event for determining whether someone would make a good member:

When you get beat in if you don't fight back and if you just like stop and you start cryin' or somethin' or beggin' 'em to stop and stuff like that, then, they ain't gonna, they'll just stop and they'll say that you're not gang material because you gotta be hard, gotta be able to fight, take punches.

In addition to the initiation, and threats from rival gangs, members were expected to adhere to the gang's internal rules (which included such things as not fighting with one another, being "true" to the gang, respecting the leader, not spreading gang business outside the gang, and not dating members of rival gangs). Breaking the rules was grounds for physical punishment, either in the form of a spontaneous assault or a formal "violation," which involved taking a specified number of blows to the head. For example, Keisha reported that she talked back to the leader of her set and "got slapped pretty hard" for doing so. Likewise, Veronica, an African American 15-year-old, described her leader as "crazy, but we gotta listen to 'im. He's just

the type that if you don't listen to 'im, he gonna blow your head off. He's just crazy."

It is clear that regardless of members' perceptions of the gang as a form of "protection," being a gang member also involves a willingness to open oneself up to the possibility of victimization. Gang victimization is governed by rules and expectations, however, and thus does not involve the random vulnerability that being out on the streets without a gang might entail in high-crime neighborhoods. Because of its structured nature, this victimization risk may be perceived as more palatable by gang members. For young women in particular, the gendered nature of the streets may make the empowerment available through gang involvement an appealing alternative to the individualized vulnerability they otherwise would face. However, as the next sections highlight, girls' victimization risks continue to be shaped by gender, even within their gangs, because these groups are structured around gender hierarchies as well.

GENDER AND STATUS, CRIME AND VICTIMIZATION

Status hierarchies within Columbus gangs, like elsewhere, were male dominated (Bowker et al. 1980; Campbell 1990). Again, it is important to highlight that the structure of the gangs these young women belonged to—that is, male-dominated, integrated mixed-gender gangs—likely shaped the particular ways in which gender dynamics played themselves out. Autonomous female gangs, as well as gangs in which girls are in auxiliary subgroups, may be shaped by different gender relations, as well as differences in orientations toward status, and criminal involvement.

All the young women reported having established leaders in their gang, and this leadership was almost exclusively male. While LaShawna, a 17-year-old African American, reported being the leader of her set (which had a membership that is two-thirds girls, many of whom resided in the same residential facility as her), all the other girls in mixed-gender gangs reported that their OG was male. In fact, a number of young women stated explicitly that only male gang members could be leaders. Leadership qualities, and qualities attributed to high-status members of the gang—being tough, able to fight, and willing to "do dirt" (e.g., commit crime, engage in violence) for the gang—were perceived as characteristically masculine. Keisha noted, "The guys, they just harder." She explained, "Guys is more rougher. We have our G's back but, it ain't gonna be like the guys, they just don't give a fuck. They gonna shoot you in a minute." For the most part, status in the gang was related to traits such as the willingness to use serious violence and commit dangerous crimes and, though not exclusively, these traits were viewed primarily as qualities more likely and more intensely located among male gang members.

Because these respected traits were characterized specifically as masculine, young women actually may have had greater flexibility in their gang involvement than young men. Young women had fewer expectations placed on them—by both their male and female peers—in regard to involvement in criminal activities such as fighting, using weapons, and committing other crimes. This tended to decrease girls' exposure to victimization risk comparable to male members, because they were able to avoid activities likely to place them in danger. Girls *could* gain status in the gang by being particularly hard and true to the set. Heather, for example, described the most influential girl in her set as "the hardest girl, the one that don't take no crap, will stand up to anybody."

Likewise, Diane, a White 15-year-old, described a highly respected female member in her set as follows:

> People look up to Janeen just 'cause she's so crazy. People just look up to her 'cause she don't care about nothin'. She don't even care about makin' money. Her, her thing is, "Oh, you're a Slob [Blood]? You're a Slob? You talkin' to me? You talkin' shit to me?" Pow, pow! And that's it. That's it.

However, young women also had a second route to status that was less available to young men. This came via their connections—as sisters, girlfriends, cousins—to influential, high-status young men.[8] In Veronica's set, for example, the girl with the most power was the OG's "sister or his cousin, one of 'em." His girlfriend also had status, although Veronica noted that "most of us just look up to our OG." Monica, a 16-year-old African American, and Tamika, a 15-year-old African American, both had older brothers in their gangs, and both reported getting respect, recognition, and protection because of this connection. This route to status and the masculinization of high-status traits functioned to maintain gender inequality within gangs, but they also could put young women at less risk of victimization than young men. This was both because young women were perceived as less threatening and thus were less likely to be targeted by rivals, and because they were not expected to prove themselves in the ways that young men were, thus decreasing their participation in those delinquent activities likely to increase exposure to violence. Thus, gender inequality could have a protective edge for young women.

Young men's perceptions of girls as lesser members typically functioned to keep girls from being targets of serious violence at the hands of rival young men, who instead left routine confrontations with rival female gang members to the girls in their own gang. Diane said that young men in her gang "don't wanna waste their time hittin' on some little girls. They're gonna go get their little cats [females] to go get 'em." Lisa remarked,

Girls don't face much violence as [guys]. They see a girl, they say, "we'll just smack her and send her on." They see a guy—'cause guys are like a lot more into it than girls are, I've noticed that—and they like, well, "we'll shoot him."

In addition, the girls I interviewed suggested that, in comparison with young men, young women were less likely to resort to serious violence, such as that involving a weapon, when confronting rivals. Thus, when girls' routine confrontations were more likely to be female on female than male on female, girls' risk of serious victimization was lessened further.

Also, because participation in serious and violent crime was defined primarily as a masculine endeavor, young women could use gender as a means of avoiding participation in those aspects of gang life they found risky, threatening, or morally troubling. Of the young women I interviewed, about one-fifth were involved in serious gang violence: A few had been involved in aggravated assaults on rival gang members, and one admitted to having killed a rival gang member, but they were by far the exception. Most girls tended not to be involved in serious gang crime, and some reported that they chose to exclude themselves because they felt ambivalent about this aspect of gang life. Angie, an African American 15-year-old, explained,

I don't get involved like that, be out there goin' and just beat up people like that or go stealin', things like that. That's not me. The boys, mostly the boys do all that, the girls we just sit back and chill, you know.

Likewise, Diane noted,

For maybe a drive-by they might wanna have a bunch of dudes. They might not put the females in that. Maybe the females might be weak inside, not strong enough to do something like that, just on the insides. . . . If a female wants to go forward and doin' that, and she wants to risk her whole life for doin' that, then she can. But the majority of the time, that job is given to a man.

Diane was not just alluding to the idea that young men were stronger than young women. She also inferred that young women were able to get out of committing serious crime, more so than young men, because a girl shouldn't have to "risk her whole life" for the gang. In accepting that young men were more central members of the gang, young women could more easily participate in gangs without putting themselves in jeopardy—they could engage in the more routine, everyday activities of the gang, like hanging out, listening to music, and smoking bud (marijuana). These male-dominated mixed-gender gangs thus appeared to provide young women with flexibility in their involvement in gang activities. As a result, it is likely that their risk of victimization at the hands of rivals was less than that of young men in gangs who were engaged in greater amounts of crime.

GIRLS' DEVALUATION AND VICTIMIZATION

In addition to girls choosing not to participate in serious gang crimes, they also faced exclusion at the hands of young men or the gang as a whole (see also Bowker et al. 1980). In particular, the two types of crime mentioned most frequently as "off-limits" for girls were drug sales and drive-by shootings. LaShawna explained, "We don't really let our females [sell drugs] unless they really wanna and they know how to do it and not to get caught and everything." Veronica described a drive-by that her gang participated in and said, "They wouldn't let us [females] go. But we wanted to go, but they wouldn't let us." Often, the exclusion was couched in terms of protection. When I asked Veronica why the girls couldn't go, she said, "so we won't go to jail if they was to get caught. Or if one of 'em was to get shot, they wouldn't want it to happen to us." Likewise, Sonita, a 13-year-old African American, noted, "If they gonna do somethin' bad and they think one of the females gonna get hurt they don't let 'em do it with them. . . . Like if they involved with shooting or whatever, [girls] can't go."

Although girls' exclusion from some gang crime may be framed as protective (and may reduce their victimization risk vis-à-vis rival gangs), it also served to perpetuate the devaluation of female members as less significant to the gang—not as tough, true, or "down" for the gang as male members. When LaShawna said her gang blocked girls' involvement in serious crime, I pointed out that she was actively involved herself. She explained, "Yeah, I do a lot of stuff 'cause I'm tough. I likes, I likes messin' with boys. I fight boys. Girls ain't nothin' to me." Similarly, Tamika said, "girls, they little peons."

Some young women found the perception of them as weak a frustrating one. Brandi, an African American 13-year-old, explained, "Sometimes I dislike that the boys, sometimes, always gotta take charge and they think, sometimes, that the girls don't know how to take charge 'cause we're like girls, we're females, and like that." And Chantell, an African American 14-year-old, noted that rival gang members "think that you're more of a punk." Beliefs that girls were weaker than boys meant that young women had a harder time proving that they

were serious about their commitment to the gang. Diane explained,

> A female has to show that she's tough. A guy can just, you can just look at him. But a female, she's gotta show. She's gotta go out and do some dirt. She's gotta go whip some girl's ass, shoot somebody, rob somebody or something. To show that she is tough.

In terms of gender-specific victimization risk, the devaluation of young women suggests several things. It could lead to the mistreatment and victimization of girls by members of their own gang when they didn't have specific male protection (i.e., a brother, boyfriend) in the gang or when they weren't able to stand up for themselves to male members. This was exacerbated by activities that led young women to be viewed as sexually available. In addition, because young women typically were not seen as a threat by young men, when they did pose one, they could be punished even more harshly than young men, not only for having challenged a rival gang or gang member but also for having overstepped "appropriate" gender boundaries.

Monica had status and respect in her gang, both because she had proven herself through fights and criminal activities, and because her older brothers were members of her set. She contrasted her own treatment with that of other young women in the gang:

> They just be puttin' the other girls off. Like Andrea, man. Oh my God, they dog Andrea so bad. They like, "Bitch, go to the store." She like, "All right, I be right back." She will go to the store and go and get them whatever they want and come back with it. If she don't get it right, they be like, "Why you do that bitch?" I mean, and one dude even smacked her. And, I mean, and, I don't, I told my brother once. I was like, "Man, it ain't even like that. If you ever see someone tryin'

to disrespect me like that or hit me, if you do not hit them or at least say somethin' to them. . . ." So my brothers, they kinda watch out for me.

However, Monica put the responsibility for Andrea's treatment squarely on the young woman: "I put that on her. They ain't gotta do her like that, but she don't gotta let them do her like that either." Andrea was seen as "weak" because she did not stand up to the male members in the gang; thus, her mistreatment was framed as partially deserved because she did not exhibit the valued traits of toughness and willingness to fight that would allow her to defend herself.

An additional but related problem was when the devaluation of young women within gangs was sexual in nature. Girls, but not boys, could be initiated into the gang by being "sexed in"—having sexual relations with multiple male members of the gang. Other members viewed the young women initiated in this way as sexually available and promiscuous, thus increasing their subsequent mistreatment. In addition, the stigma could extend to female members in general, creating a sexual devaluation that all girls had to contend with.

The dynamics of "sexing in" as a form of gang initiation placed young women in a position that increased their risk of ongoing mistreatment at the hands of their gang peers. According to Keisha, "If you get sexed in, you have no respect. That means you gotta go ho'in' for 'em; when they say you give 'em the pussy, you gotta give it to 'em. If you don't, you gonna get your ass beat. I ain't down for that." One girl in her set was sexed in and Keisha said the girl "just do everything they tell her to do, like a dummy." Nikkie reported that two girls who were sexed into her set eventually quit hanging around with the gang because they were harassed so much. In fact, Veronica said the young men in her set purposely tricked girls into believing they were being sexed into the gang and targeted girls they did not like:

> If some girls wanted to get in, if they don't like the girl they have sex with 'em. They run trains on 'em or either have the girl suck their thang. And then they used to, the girls used to think they was in. So, then the girls used to just come try to hang around us and all this little bull, just 'cause, 'cause they thinkin' they in.

Young women who were sexed into the gang were viewed as sexually promiscuous, weak, and not "true" members. They were subject to revictimization and mistreatment, and were viewed as deserving of abuse by other members, both male and female. Veronica continued, "They [girls who are sexed in] gotta do whatever, whatever the boys tell 'em to do when they want 'em to do it, right then and there, in front of whoever. And, I think, that's just sick. That's nasty, that's dumb." Keisha concurred, "She brought that on herself, by bein' the fact, bein' sexed in." There was evidence, however, that girls could overcome the stigma of having been sexed in through their subsequent behavior, by challenging members that disrespect them and being willing to fight. Tamika described a girl in her set who was sexed in, and stigmatized as a result, but successfully fought to rebuild her reputation:

> Some people, at first, they call her "little ho" and all that. But then, now she startin' to get bold. . . . Like, Like, they be like, "Ooh, look at the little ho. She fucked me and my boy." She be like, "Man, forget y'all. Man, what? What?" She be ready to squat [fight] with 'em. I be like, "Ah, look at her!" Uh huh. . . . At first we looked at her like, "Ooh, man, she a ho, man." But now we look at her like she just our kickin' it partner. You know, however she got in that's her business.

The fact that there was such an option as "sexing in" served to keep girls disempowered, because they always faced the question of how they got in and of whether they were "true" members. In addition, it contributed to a milieu in which young women's sexuality was seen as exploitable. This may help explain why young women were so harshly judgmental of those girls who were sexed in. Young women who were privy to male gang members' conversations reported that male members routinely disrespect girls in the gang by disparaging them sexually. Monica explained,

I mean the guys, they have their little comments about 'em [girls in the gang] because, I hear more because my brothers are all up there with the guys and everything and I hear more just sittin' around, just listenin'. And they'll have their little jokes about "Well, ha I had her," and then and everybody else will jump in and say, "Well, I had her, too." And then they'll laugh about it.

In general, because gender constructions defined young women as weaker than young men, young women were often seen as lesser members of the gang. In addition to the mistreatment these perceptions entailed, young women also faced particularly harsh sanctions for crossing gender boundaries—causing harm to rival male members when they had been viewed as nonthreatening. One young woman[9] participated in the assault of a rival female gang member, who had set up a member of the girl's gang. She explained, "The female was supposingly goin' out with one of ours, went back and told a bunch of [rivals] what was goin' on and got the [rivals] to jump my boy. And he ended up in the hospital." The story she told was unique but nonetheless significant for what it indicates about the gendered nature of gang violence and

victimization. Several young men in her set saw the girl walking down the street, kidnapped her, then brought her to a member's house. The young woman I interviewed, along with several other girls in her set, viciously beat the girl, then to their surprise the young men took over the beating, ripped off the girl's clothes, brutally gang-raped her, then dumped her in a park. The interviewee noted, "I don't know what happened to her. Maybe she died. Maybe, maybe someone came and helped her. I mean, I don't know." The experience scared the young woman who told me about it. She explained,

I don't never want anythin' like that to happen to me. And I pray to God that it doesn't. 'Cause God said that whatever you sow you're gonna reap. And like, you know, beatin' a girl up and then sittin' there watchin' somethin' like that happen, well, Jesus that could come back on me. I mean, I felt, I really did feel sorry for her even though my boy was in the hospital and was really hurt. I mean, we coulda just shot her. You know, and it coulda been just over. We coulda just taken her life. But they went farther than that.

This young woman described the gang rape she witnessed as "the most brutal thing I've ever seen in my life." While the gang rape itself was an unusual event, it remained a specifically gendered act that could take place precisely because young women were not perceived as equals. Had the victim been an "equal," the attack would have remained a physical one. As the interviewee herself noted, "we coulda just shot her." Instead, the young men who gang-raped the girl were not just enacting revenge on a rival but on a *young woman* who had dared to treat a young man in this way. The issue is not the question of which is worse—to be shot and killed, or gang-raped and left for dead. Rather, this particular act sheds light on how gender may function to structure victimization risk within gangs.

DISCUSSION

Gender dynamics in mixed-gender gangs are complex and thus may have multiple and contradictory effects on young women's risk of victimization and repeat victimization. My findings suggest that participation in the delinquent lifestyles associated with gangs clearly places young women at risk for victimization. The act of joining a gang involves the initiate's submission to victimization at the hands of her gang peers. In addition, the rules governing gang members' activities place them in situations in which they are vulnerable able to assaults that are specifically gang related. Many acts of violence that girls described would not have occurred had they not been in gangs.

It seems, though, that young women in gangs believed they have traded unknown risks for known ones—that victimization at the hands of friends, or at least under specified conditions, was an alternative preferable to the potential of random, unknown victimization by strangers. Moreover, the gang offered both a semblance of protection from others on the streets, especially young men, and a means of achieving retaliation when victimization did occur.

Lauritsen and Quinet (1995) suggest that both individual-specific heterogeneity (unchanging attributes of individuals that contribute to a propensity for victimization, such as physical size or temperament) and state-dependent factors (factors that can alter individuals' victimization risks over time, such as labeling or behavior changes that are a consequence of victimization) are related to youths' victimization and repeat victimization risk. My findings

here suggest that, within gangs, gender can function in both capacities to shape girls' risks of victimization.

Girls' gender, as an individual attribute, can function to lessen their exposure to victimization risk by defining them as inappropriate targets of rival male gang members' assaults. The young women I interviewed repeatedly commented that young men were typically not as violent in their routine confrontations with rival young women as with rival young men. On the other hand, when young women are targets of serious assault, they may face brutality that is particularly harsh and sexual in nature because they are female—thus, particular types of assault, such as rape, are deemed more appropriate when young women are the victims.

Gender can also function as a state-dependent factor, because constructions of gender and the enactment of gender identities are fluid. On the one hand, young women can call upon gender as a means of avoiding exposure to activities they find risky, threatening, or morally troubling. Doing so does not expose them to the sanctions likely faced by male gang members who attempt to avoid participation in violence. Although these choices may insulate young women from the risk of assault at the hands of rival gang members, perceptions of female gang members—and of women in general—as weak may contribute to more routinized victimization at the hands of the male members of their gangs. Moreover, sexual exploitation in the form of "sexing in" as an initiation ritual may define young women as sexually available, contributing to a likelihood of repeat victimization unless the young woman can stand up for herself and fight to gain other members' respect.

Finally, given constructions of gender that define young women as nonthreatening, when young women do pose a threat to male gang members, the sanctions they face may be particularly harsh because they not only have caused harm to rival gang members but also have crossed appropriate gender boundaries in doing so. In sum, my findings suggest that gender may function to insulate young women from some types of physical assault and lessen their exposure to risks from rival gang members, but also to make them vulnerable to particular types of violence, including routine victimization by their male peers, sexual exploitation, and sexual assault.

This article has offered preliminary evidence of how gender may shape victimization risk for female gang members. A great deal more work needs to be done in this area. Specifically, gang scholars need to address more systematically the relationships between gang involvement and victimization risk rather than focusing exclusively on gang members' participation in violence as offenders. My research suggests two questions to be examined further, for both female and male gang members. First, are gang members more likely to be victimized than nongang members living in the same areas? Second, how does victimization risk fluctuate for gang members before, during, and after their gang involvement? Information about these questions will allow us to address whether and how gang involvement has an enhancement effect on youths' *victimization*, as well as their delinquency.

With the growing interest in masculinities and crime (see Messerschmidt 1993; Newburn and Stanko 1994), an important corollary question to be examined is how masculinities shape victimization risk among male gang members. The young women I interviewed clearly associated serious gang violence with the enactment of masculinity and used gender constructions to avoid involvement in those activities they perceived as threatening.

Young men thus may be at greater risk of serious physical assaults, because of their greater involvement in serious gang crime and violence, and because gender constructions within the gang make these activities more imperative for young men than for young women.

Notes

1. I contacted numerous additional agency personnel in an effort to draw the sample from a larger population base, but many efforts remained unsuccessful despite repeated attempts and promises of assistance. These included persons at the probation department, a shelter and outreach agency for runaways, police personnel, a private residential facility for juveniles, and three additional community agencies. None of the agencies I contacted openly denied me permission to interview young women; they simply chose not to follow up. I do not believe that much bias resulted from the nonparticipation of these agencies. Each has a client base of "at-risk" youths, and the young women I interviewed report overlap with some of these same agencies. For example, a number had been or were on probation, and several reported staying at the shelter for runaways.

2. One young woman was a member of an all-female gang. Because the focus of this article is gender dynamics in mixed-gender gangs, her interview is not included in the analysis.

3. These include the Gang Membership Resistance Surveys in Long Beach and San Diego, the Denver Youth Survey, and the Rochester Youth Development Study.

4. For example, Cleveland, Ohio provides a striking contrast with Columbus on social and economic indicators, including a poverty rate double that found in Columbus. But the poverty rate for African Americans in Cleveland is just over twice that for Whites, and it is more than three times higher in Columbus.

5. The term *set* was used by the gang members I interviewed to refer to their gangs. Because they adopted nationally recognized gang names (e.g., Crips, Bloods, Folks), they saw themselves as loosely aligned with other groups of the same name. This term was used to distinguish their particular gang (which has its own distinct name, e.g., Rolling 60s Crips) from other gangs that adopted the broader gang name. I will use the terms *set* and *gang* interchangeably.

6. This was compared to 36.4 percent who described their gangs as female auxiliaries of male gangs, and only 6.4 percent who described being in independent female gangs (Curry 1997; see also Decker and Van Winkle 1996).

7. All names are fictitious.

8. This is not to suggest that male members cannot gain status via their connections to high-status men, but that to maintain status, they will have to

successfully exhibit masculine traits such as tough-ness. Young women appear to be held to more flexi-ble standards.

9. Because this excerpt provides a detailed de-scription of a specific serious crime, and because de-mographic information on respondents is available, I have chosen to conceal both the pseudonym and gang affiliation of the young woman who told me the story.

References

Adler, Patricia A, and Peter Adler. 1987. *Membership Roles in Field Research*. Newbury Park, CA: Sage.

Arnold, Regina. 1990. "Processes of Victimization and Criminalization of Black Women." *Social Justice* 17 (3): 153–66.

Baskin, Deborah. Ira Sommers, and Jeffrey Fagan. 1993. "The Political Economy of Violent Female Street Crime." *Fordham Urban Law Journal* 20:401–17.

Bjerregaard, Beth and Carolyn Smith. 1993. "Gender Differences in Gang Participation, Delinquency, and Substance Use." *Journal of Quantitative Crimi-nology* 4:329–55.

Block, Carolyn Rebecca and Richard Block. 1993. "Street Gang Crime in Chicago." Research in Brief. Washington, DC: National Institute of Justice.

Bourgois, Philippe. 1995. *In Search of Respect: Selling Crack in El Barrio*, Cambridge, UK: Cambridge Uni-versity Press.

Bourgois, Philippe and Eloise Dunlap. 1993. "Exorcis-ing Sex-for-Crack: An Ethnographic Perspective from Harlem." Pp. 97–132 in *Crack Pipe as Pimp: An Ethnographic Investigation of Sex-for-Crack Exchanges*, edited by Mitchell S. Ratner. New York: Lexington Books.

Bowker, Lee H., Helen Shimota Gross, and Malcolm W. Klein. 1980. "Female Participation in Delinquent Gang Activities." *Adolescence* 15 (59): 509–19.

Brotherton, David C. 1996. " 'Smartness,' 'Toughness,' and 'Autonomy': Drug Use in the Context of Gang Female Delinquency." *Journal of Drug Issues* 26 (1): 261–77.

Campbell, Anne. 1984. *The Girls in the Gang*. New York: Basil Blackwell.

———. 1990. "Female Participation in Gangs." Pp. 163–82 in *Gangs in America*, edited by C. Ronald Huff. Beverly Hills, CA: Sage.

Chesney-Lind, Meda. 1993. "Girls, Gangs and Vio-lence: Anatomy of a Backlash." *Humanity & Society* 17 (3): 321–44.

Chesney-Lind, Meda and Noelie Rodriguez. 1983. "Women under Lock and Key: A View from the In-side." *The Prison Journal* 63 (2): 47–65.

Chesney-Lind, Meda, Randall G. Shelden, and Karen A. Joe. 1996. "Girls, Delinquency, and Gang Mem-bership." Pp. 185–204 in *Gangs in America*, 2d ed., edited by C. Ronald Huff. Thousand Oaks, CA: Sage.

Columbus Metropolitan Human Services Commis-sion. 1995. *State of Human Services Report—1995*. Columbus, OH: Columbus Metropolitan Human Services Commission. March, Orlando, FL.

Connell, R. W. 1987. *Gender and Power*. Stanford, CA: Stanford University Press.

Curry, G. David. 1997. "Selected Statistics on Female Gang Involvement." Paper presented at the Fifth Joint National Conference on Gangs, Schools, and Community, March, Orlando, FL.

Curry, G. David, Richard A. Ball, and Scott H. Decker. 1996. Estimating the National Scope of Gang Crime from Law Enforcement Data. Research in Brief. Washington, DC: National Institute of Justice.

Daly, Kathleen. 1992. "Women's Pathways to Felony Court: Feminist Theories of Lawbreaking and Prob-lems of Representation." *Review of Law and Women's Studies* 2 (1): 11–52.

Decker, Scott H. 1996. "Collective and Normative Fea-tures of Gang Violence." *Justice Quarterly* 13 (2): 243–64.

Decker, Scott H, and Barrik Van Winkle. 1996. *Life in the Gang*. Cambridge, UK: Cambridge University Press.

Eder, Donna. 1995. *School Talk: Gender and Adolescent Culture*. New Brunswick, NJ: Rutgers University Press.

Esbensen, Finn-Aage. 1996. Comments presented at the National Institute of Justice/Office of Juvenile Justice and Delinquency Prevention Cluster Meet-ings, June, Dallas, TX.

Esbensen, Finn-Aage and David Huizinga. 1993. "Gangs, Drugs, and Delinquency in a Survey of Urban Youth." *Criminology* 31 (4) 565–89.

Esbensen, Finn-Aage, David Huizinga, and Anne W. Weiher. 1993. "Gang and Non-Gang Youth: Differ-ences in Explanatory Factors." *Journal of Contempo-rary Criminal Justice* 9 (2): 94–116.

Esbensen, Finn-Aage and L. Thomas Winfree. 1998. "Race and Gender Differences between Gang and Non-Gang Youth: Results from a Multi-Site Sur-vey." *Justice Quarterly* 15(3):505–25.

Fagan, Jeffrey. 1989. "The Social Organization of Drug Use and Drug Dealing among Urban Gangs." *Criminology* 27(4): 633–67.

———. 1990. "Social Processes of Delinquency and Drug Use among Urban Gangs." Pp. 183–219 in *Gangs in America*, edited by C. Ronald Huff. New-bury Park, CA: Sage.

Gilfus, Mary E. 1992. "From Victims to Survivors to Offenders: Women's Routes of Entry and Immer-sion into Street Crime." *Women and Criminal Justice* 4 (1): 63–89.

Glassner, Barry and Julia Loughlin. 1987. *Drugs in Adolescent Worlds: Burnouts to Straights*. New York: St. Martin's.

Hagedorn, John M. 1988. *People and Folks: Gangs, Crime and the Underclass in a Rustbelt City*. Chicago: Lake View Press.

Huff, C. Ronald. 1989. "Youth Gangs and Public Policy." *Crime and Delinquency* 35 (4): 524–37.

————. 1996. "The Criminal Behavior of Gang Members and Nongang At-Risk Youth." Pp. 75–102 in *Gangs in America*, 2d ed., edited by C. Ronald Huff. Thousand Oaks, CA: Sage.

Joe, Karen A. and Meda Chesney-Lind. 1995. "Just Every Mother's Angel: An Analysis of Gender and Ethnic Variations in Youth Gang Membership." *Gender & Society* 9(4): 408–30.

Klein, Malcolm W. 1995. *The American Street Gang: Its Nature, Prevalence and Control*. New York: Oxford University Press.

Klein, Malcolm W. and Cheryl L. Maxson. 1989. "Street Gang Violence." Pp. 198–231 in *Violent Crime, Violent Criminals*, edited by Neil Weiner and Marvin Wolfgang. Newbury Park, CA: Sage.

LaLonde, Brent. 1995. "Police Trying to Contain Gang Problem." *The Columbus Dispatch*, September 3, p. 2A.

Lauderback, David, Joy Hansen, and Dan Waldorf. 1992. " 'Sisters Are Doin' It for Themselves': A Black Female Gang in San Francisco." *The Gang Journal* 1 (1): 57–70.

Lauritsen, Janet L. and Kenna F. Davis Quinet. 1995. "Repeat Victimization among Adolescents and Young Adults." *Journal of Quantitative Criminology* 11 (2): 143–66.

Lauritsen, Janet L., Robert J. Sampson, and John H. Laub. 1991. "The Link between Offending and Victimization among Adolescents." *Criminology* 29 (2): 265–92.

Lees, Sue. 1993. *Sugar and Spice: Sexuality and Adolescent Girls*. New York: Penguin.

Maher, Lisa and Richard Curtis. 1992. "Women on the Edge of Crime: Crack Cocaine and the Changing Contexts of Street-Level Sex Work in New York City." *Crime, Law and Social Change* 18:221–58.

Maxson, Cheryl L., Kristi Woods, and Malcolm W. Klein. 1995. Street Gang Migration in the United States. Final Report to the National Institute of Justice.

Mayhood, Kevin and Brent LaLonde. 1995. "A Show of Colors: A Local Look." *The Columbus Dispatch*, September 3, pp. 1–2A.

Messerschmidt, James W. 1993. *Masculinities and Crime: Critique and Reconceptualization of Theory*. Lanham, MD: Rowman and Littlefield.

Miller, Jody. 1996. "The Dynamics of Female Gang Involvement in Columbus, Ohio." Paper presented at the National Youth Gang Symposium, June, Dallas, TX.

Miller, Jody and Barry Glassner. 1997. "The 'Inside' and the 'Outside': Finding Realities in Interviews." Pp. 99–112 in *Qualitative Research*, edited by David Silverman. London: Sage.

Moore, Joan. 1991. *Going Down to the Barrio: Homeboys and Homegirls in Change*. Philadelphia: Temple University Press.

Moore, Joan and John M. Hagedorn. 1996. "What Happens to Girls in the Gang?" Pp. 205–18 in *Gangs in America*, 2d ed., edited by C. Ronald Huff. Thousand Oaks, CA: Sage.

Newburn, Tim and Elizabeth Stanko. 1994. *Just Boys Doing Business?: Men, Masculinities and Crime*. New York: Routledge.

Pesce, Rosario C. and Carol Gibb Harding. 1986. "Imaginary Audience Behavior and Its Relationship to Operational Thought and Social Experience." *Journal of Early Adolescence* 6 (1): 83–94.

Rusk, David. 1995. *Cities without Suburbs*. 2d ed. Washington, DC: The Woodrow Wilson Center Press.

Sampson, Robert J. and William Julius Wilson. 1995. "Toward a Theory of Race, Crime, and Urban Inequality." Pp. 37–54 in *Crime and Inequality*, edited by John Hagan and Ruth D. Peterson. Stanford, CA: Stanford University Press.

Sanders, William. 1993. *Drive-Bys and Gang Bangs: Gangs and Grounded Culture*. Chicago: Aldine.

Short, James F. and Fred L. Strodtbeck. 1965. *Group Process and Gang Delinquency*. Chicago: University of Chicago Press.

Simpson, Sally. 1991. "Caste, Class and Violent Crime: Explaining Differences in Female Offending." *Criminology* 29 (1): 115–35.

Spergel, Irving A. and G. David Curry. 1993. "The National Youth Gang Survey: A Research and Development Process." Pp. 359–400 in *The Gang Intervention Handbook*, edited by Arnold P. Goldstein and C. Ronald Huff. Champaign, IL: Research Press.

Taylor, Carl. 1993. *Girls, Gangs, Women and Drugs*. East Lansing: Michigan State University Press.

Thornberry, Terence P., Marvin D. Krohn, Alan J. Lizotte, and Deborah Chard-Wierschem. 1993. "The Role of Juvenile Gangs in Facilitating Delinquent Behavior." *Journal of Research in Crime and Delinquency* 30 (1): 75–85.

Thorne, Barrie. 1993. *Gender Play: Girls and Boys in School*. New Brunswick, NJ: Rutgers University Press.

Wilson, William Julius. 1996. *When Work Disappears: The World of the New Urban Poor*. New York: Knopf.

Winfree, L. Thomas, Jr., Kathy Fuller, Teresa Vigil, and G. Larry Mays. 1992. "The Definition and Measurement of 'Gang Status': Policy Implications for Juvenile Justice." *Juvenile and Family Court Journal* 43:29–37.

Chapter **9**

Policy and Crime

INTRODUCTION

Previous research has suggested that within the last few decades, the rehabilitation model has been replaced by a "just dessert" model, which argues
that the punishment should be proportional to the seriousness of the
crime. In doing so, juvenile waivers to adult courts have become more
common than ever before. In his article Champion examines recent trends
in juvenile waiver or transfer hearings in four states (Tennessee, Virginia,
Mississippi, and Geogia) by examining monthly court reports and official
records from 1980 to 1988. During this time period, the number of hearings increased from 228 (1980) to 466 (1988), and the number of waivers
more than doubled from 163 (1980) to 466 (1988). In examining the types
of cases involved in these waivers, Champion discovered that the increase
in waivers is due to property offenses rather than violent offenses. In addition, after examining the disposition of waived cases, Champion concludes
that waivers to the adult court did not necessarily translate into more
severe penalties. For example, although waivers increased from 1980 to
1988, the number of juveniles receiving probation increased as well, from
40 percent (1980) to 62 percent (1988).

Although extensive research has been conducted on public attitudes
of the death penalty, very little attention has been devoted toward examining perceptions when the offender is a juvenile. Skovron, Scott, and
Cullen address this issue by examining public perceptions of juvenile
homicide by conducting a telephone survey of adult residents in two major

midwestern cities—Cincinnati and Columbus, Ohio—in February and March, 1986. Their findings indicate that whereas recent opinion polls suggest that an overwhelming majority of the public favors capital punishment when the offender is an adult, support for the execution of juvenile offenders was much smaller. The majority of respondents opposed capital punishment when the offender is a juvenile (69% in Cincinnati and 65.3% in Columbus). Additionally, for both the Cincinnati and Columbus samples, an inverse relationship was observed between belief in the effectiveness of rehabiltation and support for the juvenile death penalty. In other words, individuals who favored rehabilitation were less likely to favor the death penalty. In the Columbus sample, significant differences were also noted between religion (more religious respondents tended to favor juvenile capital punishment) and gender (males were more supportive of capital punishment than females).

The study by Rosenbaum and Hanson examines both short- and long-term effects of the Drug Abuse Resistance Education Program (D.A.R.E.) on students' attitudes, beliefs, social skills, and drug use behavior. To measure this, they examined longitudinal trends in student and teacher responses in elementary schools in Illinois with D.A.R.E. programs to schools without these programs on a yearly basis for six years. Each school that received D.A.R.E. was paired with a similar school in the area (rural, urban, suburban) which was not offered the program, thus acting as a control group. The findings revealed that the D.A.R.E. program had short-term effects on resistance skills and attitudes about drugs, however, these effects did not carry over into the junior high and high school years. In comparing community interactions, the findings indicated that urban and rural youth tended to fare better (i.e., reduced drug use) after D.A.R.E., whereas suburban students experienced significant increases in drug use after participation.

Teenage Felons and Waiver Hearings:
Some Recent Trends, 1980–1988

Dean J. Champion

INTRODUCTION

In 1985, thirty-two boys and nine girls in Tennessee ranging in age from 12 to 17 were charged with murder or manslaughter. An additional 417 boys and girls were accused of robbery with a deadly weapon and robbery; 83 were taken into custody for assault to murder; 2,704 were charged with assault, 164 with rape, 1,878 with burglary, and 108 with arson (Green 1987). Most of these serious juvenile offenders were processed entirely by the juvenile justice system and were not transferred to the jurisdiction of an adult criminal court. However, the proportion of waiver hearings for the most serious offenders was considerably higher in 1985 than in earlier years.

In the last few decades, the public has become increasingly concerned with the apparent leniency of the courts in dealing with criminals (Metchik 1987, Harris 1986). The rehabilitation model of corrections has gradually been replaced by a more punitive, "just-desserts" rationale that seeks to adjust the punishment to fit the crime committed. One result of this philosophical shift has been the implementation of large-scale sentencing reforms at the state and federal levels. These reforms have indirectly affected the juvenile justice system.

As the amount of violent crime committed by juveniles has escalated systematically, public disenchantment with the processing of juvenile cases has also increased. The results have been a noticeable shift toward adult court processing of juveniles and adoption of a more punitive philosophy on juvenile sanctions in general (Miller 1986, Greenwood 1986).

Although juveniles are now entitled to waiver or transfer hearings and have the right to legal representation as well as the right to present evidence in their own behalf for defeating waivers, the discretion to transfer a juvenile to adult criminal court rests exclusively with the juvenile judge. Proportionately few transfer hearings result in favorable rulings for the juveniles involved (Rubin 1985). Although some states, such as Minnesota, have attempted to introduce an element of objectivity in juvenile waiver hearings by establishing more systematic guidelines and classification schemes for judges to follow, these changes have not had the desired or predicted results. For instance, in Minnesota, ironically, the percentage of waivers granted after the statute was implemented was substantially greater than the percentage granted under presumably more subjective circumstances in earlier years (Osbun and Rode 1984).

Dean J. Champion, Crime & Delinquency, Vol. 35, No. 4, pp. 577–585, copyright © 1989 by Sage Publications, Inc. Reprinted by permission of Sage Publications, Inc.

Historically, juvenile courts have sought to insulate juvenile offenders from the trappings of adult courts in an effort to minimize the possible criminogenic effects of labeling resulting from exposure to criminal-like case processing. Informal handling of juvenile cases has been common, and diversion has been used extensively to decrease juveniles' contact with the justice system. The use of probation has been considerable, even when serious offenses have been committed or alleged.

For instance, in 1985, 14,435 adjudication hearings were conducted in Tennessee. Of these, 7,597, or 53%, resulted in adjudications as delinquent where serious person and property offenses were involved. Over 90% of these adjudications resulted in probation, warnings, or counseling, while only 450, or 6%, resulted in commitment to secure state juvenile facilities.

Some experts claim that a majority of juveniles who commit serious offenses are well-aware of the small likelihood of being detained in secure facilities if they are arrested and adjudicated delinquent. Thus, it is suggested that they use their status as

juveniles to great advantage of waivers in Tennessee, Virginia, Mississipi, and Georgia. In addition, it identified and charted the punishments imposed when transferred juveniles were convicted in criminal courts. Are waiver hearings in these states being conducted for more juveniles more frequently? Are more severe punishments being imposed on those who are waived?

Information about the frequency of waiver hearings was supplied by juvenile services agencies and personnel in each state. Data were obtained from monthly court reports and other official records for the years 1980 through 1988. The aggregate numbers of waiver hearings in these four states in the years 1980–88 are shown in Table 1.

Table 1 shows that between 1980 and 1988, the number of juvenile waiver hearings in these four states rose from 228 in 1980 to 466 in 1988, an increase of over 100%. Interestingly, the percentage of waiver hearings resulting in successful waivers to adult court jurisdiction rose also from 71.5% to 86.2% during these years. Thus, not only was there a significant

TABLE 1:   Aggregate Numbers of Waiver Hearings and Transfers to Adult Courts in Virginia, Tennessee, Mississippi, and Georgia, 1980–1988

Year	Number of Hearings	Waivers	Percentage
1980	228	163	71.5
1981	249	179	71.9
1982	301	226	75.1
1983	356	294	82.6
1984	451	385	85.3
1985	416	337	81.0
1986	485	419	86.1
1987	472	413	87.6
1988	466	402	86.2
Totals	3,424	2,818	82.3

1980–1988 increase: 238 cases (104.3%)

increase in waiver hearings during the 1980–88 period, there was also a significant increase in the number of successful waiver hearings (i.e., those resulting in criminal court jurisdiction).

Using the FBI's index offenses as a guide and allowing for "other" offense categories, a profile was devised for the types of offenses involved in waiver hearings during the 1980–88 period. The offense profiles upon which successful waiver hearings were based are shown in Table 2.

An examination of the percentage distributions of index offenses shown in Table 2 discloses some interesting patterns for the five-year period. For example, the proportion of homicide offenses declined systematically from 42% in 1980 to 31% in 1988. Likewise, declines were observed for rape and robbery. However, property offense categories such as vehicular theft, burglary, and larceny increased during the same time period. Thus, collectively, burglary, larceny,

and vehicular theft accounted for 19% of the offenses alleged in successful waivers in 1980, but for 50% of the crimes in successful waivers in 1988. These figures suggest a fairly consistent increase in the proportionate representation of property offenses in waiver hearings during the 1980–88 period.

Numerically, 68 successful waiver hearings involved homicide in 1980, whereas 124 of the cases involved homicide in 1988. Thus, nearly twice as many juveniles charged with homicide were the subject of successful transfer hearings in 1988 as in 1980, but there was a proportionate decrease in homicide cases among the waived cases during the same time period. There were 31 property offenses involved in successful waiver hearings in 1980 compared with 221 property offenses, almost seven times as many, in 1988. This finding is consistent with the work of Nimick, Szymanski, and Snyder (1986) and others

TABLE 2: Offense Categories for Successful Waiver Hearings, 1980–1988

	YEAR								
	(PERCENT ROUNDED TO NEAREST WHOLE NUMBER)								
Offenses	1980	1981	1982	1983	1984	1985	1986	1987	1988
Homicide	42	39	38	36	35	34	35	32	31
Vehicular Theft	6	7	7	8	9	11	15	16	17
Arson	NA	NA	NA	2	3	4	4	3	5
Aggravated Assault	4	5	5	2	2	2	2	5	4
Burglary	4	7	8	16	17	16	14	16	17
Larceny	9	12	14	16	17	20	15	15	16
Robbery	20	17	13	11	8	7	6	5	8
Rape	14	12	11	8	7	4	4	3	3
Other	1	1	4	1	2	2	5	5	3
Total Percent	100	100	100	100	100	100	100	100	100
Number	163	179	226	294	385	337	419	413	402
Grand Total = 2,818 waivers									

showing significant increases in property offenses as the subject matter of waivers in several states in recent years.

An inspection of juvenile crime patterns in these states for the period 1980–88 shows a fairly stable offense distribution, with slight variations in violent and property crime categories upward and downward respectively. Yet property offenses are increasingly represented proportionately in waiver hearings. This suggests that waivers are used increasingly as alternatives to juvenile court case processing for offenses that are not necessarily physically harmful to others.

The present findings suggest a trend toward the increased use of waivers for less serious property offenses and a proportionate decrease in the use of waivers for violent offenses such as rape, robbery, and homicide. However, an inspection of the numerical incidence of rape, robbery, and homicide indicates similar or slightly increased numbers of these offenses from one year to the next. Furthermore, the use of waivers in these jurisdictions has more than doubled during the 1980–88 period.

WAIVED OFFENDER DISPOSITIONS

An analysis was made of the dispositions of all 2,818 waivers to criminal courts during the 1980–88 period. Table 3 shows these dispositions by year.

An inspection of Table 3 shows that between 1980 and 1988, the relative number of dismissals or acquittals of waived cases dropped from 38% to 22%, although there was a systematic increase in the actual number of cases each year. By the same token, the relative number of cases resulting in convictions with probation rose from 40% in 1980 to 62% in 1988. No particular pattern was apparent involving incarceration in jails, although the number of convicted offenders sentenced to prison or intermediate punishments increased slightly across years.

DISCUSSION

The trend in the juvenile jurisdictions examined here is toward use of the waiver for increasing numbers of juvenile offenders.

TABLE 3:   Criminal Court Dispositions of 2,818 Waivers, 1980–1988 (Percentages Rounded)

Year	Dismissed Acquitted	Probation	Jail	Prison	Other[a]
1980	62 (38%)	66 (40%)	11 (7%)	8 (5%)	16 (10%)
1981	65 (36%)	82 (46%)	17 (9%)	7 (4%)	8 (4%)
1982	74 (33%)	107 (47%)	18 (8%)	14 (6%)	13 (6%)
1983	79 (27%)	156 (53%)	28 (9%)	14 (5%)	17 (6%)
1984	92 (24%)	221 (57%)	19 (5%)	17 (4%)	36 (10%)
1985	84 (25%)	195 (58%)	20 (6%)	17 (5%)	21 (6%)
1986	101 (24%)	234 (56%)	25 (6%)	17 (4%)	42 (10%)
1987	87 (21%)	248 (60%)	25 (8%)	21 (5%)	32 (8%)
1988	88 (22%)	249 (62%)	16 (4%)	20 (5%)	29 (7%)
Total	732 (26%)	1,558 (55%)	179 (6%)	135 (5%)	214 (8%)
	Grand Total = 2.818 (100%)				

[a]Split sentences, home incarceration, electronic monitoring, community-based supervision, etc.

Diversion of cases to the jurisdiction of criminal courts may be interpreted as a "get-tough" policy toward more serious juvenile offenders, although, as has been shown for the jurisdictions examined here, the types of offenses alleged in these waivers are increasingly property offenses rather than more serious violent crimes. If the primary objective of transfers is to subject juvenile offenders to more stringent penalties in criminal courts for committing more serious crimes, then the wrong offender population is being targeted for waivers here.

It has been suggested by several prosecutors in the juvenile jurisdictions examined that many of those juveniles subject to waiver motions are recidivists or chronic delinquents who have histories of previous minor offenses. Thus, the waiver appears to be used more as a means of dealing with recidivists than with violent juveniles. At least in these jurisdictions, the general class of waived offenders is increasingly made up of nonviolent juvenile recidivists.

Although four different states were involved in this analysis, there are no particular differences in offense profiles that might indicate, for instance, that Georgia is punishing its juveniles more than is Tennessee. On the average, 55% of all waivers during the 1980–88 period resulted in probation. In 26% of all cases, charges were dismissed or offenders were acquitted. Only 11% of all waivers resulted in incarceration in either jail or prison, with jail accounting for the preponderance of incarcerations. When we consider other dispositions such as intensive supervised probation in community-based facilities, the figures for juveniles being acquitted, having their cases dismissed, or being sentenced to probation or a probation alternative rise to over 89%. This can hardly be viewed as "getting tough" on juvenile crime. In fact, according to several juvenile

court prosecutors, it is likely that many of those juveniles who received probation or had their cases dismissed in criminal courts would have been adjudicated as delinquent by juvenile judges and sentenced to secure confinement in one of several secure state detention facilities.

If waivers are not resulting in more severe penalties for juveniles, what are they accomplishing? These findings suggest that their use in the present jurisdictions is primarily cosmetic. In defense of juvenile court prosecutors, however, it should be noted that several of them are consistently disappointed about how juveniles are treated after being waived to criminal courts. It is clear that their intentions are to make it possible for transferred juveniles to receive more severe penalties than they otherwise could. However, criminal courts seem inclined to treat less seriously those cases waived to their jurisdiction by juvenile courts. One important explanation for this extensive leniency toward youthful offenders transferred to criminal courts is that their age becomes a mitigating circumstance. Furthermore, offenses considered serious by juvenile courts may be considered less serious by criminal court judges. When transferred to criminal courts, youthful burglars and thieves become part of a large adult aggregate that is often extended probation as a means of alleviating jail overcrowding and allocating scarce prison space for more dangerous offenders.

An examination of cases resulting in jail or prison incarcerations shows that most of these involve violent offenders convicted of homicide, robbery, and rape. It is suggested that juvenile authorities in the jurisdictions examined can increase the likelihood of obtaining more severe penalties for serious offenders if they restrict the use of waivers to only the most serious violent offenses. But if they let juvenile recidivism involving petty offenses override the fact of crime seriousness, criminal courts are unlikely to impose on these offenders.

Significant juvenile justice policy decisions need to be made in these jurisdictions if the manifest "just-desserts" objective of waivers is to be realized. Presently, however, these hearings are, as Ted Rubin (1985, p. 26) says, public-placating "escape valves" used to rid juvenile courts of chronic recidivists, regardless of the insignificance of their offenses.

References

Green, Judy 1987, *1985 Tennessee Annual Juvenile Court Statistical Report*. Nashville, TN: Tennessee Children's Commission, Tennessee Council of Juvenile and Family Court Judges, Tennessee Juvenile Justice Commission.

Greenwood, Peter W. 1986. *Intervention Strategies for Chronic Juvenile Offenders: Some New Perspectives*. Westport, CT: Greenwood Press.

Harris, Patricia M. 1986. "Is the Juvenile Justice System 'Lenient'?" *Criminal Justice Abstracts* 18: 104–18.

Metchlk, Eric. 1987. "Predicting Pre-Trial Behavior of Juvenile Offenders in Adult Court." Paper presented at the American Society of Criminology Meeting, Montreal.

Miller, Frank W., Robert O. Dawson, George E. Dix and Raymond I. Parnas. 1985. *The Juvenile Justice Process*. Mineola, NY: Foundation Press.

Miller, Marc. 1986. "Changing Legal Paradigms in Juvenile Justice." In *Intervention Strategies for Chronic Juvenile Offenders: Some New Perspectives*, edited by Peter W. Greenwood. Westport, CT: Greenwood Press.

New Jersey Division of Criminal Justice. 1985. *Juvenile Waivers to Adult Court: A Report to the New Jersey State Legislature*. Trenton, NJ.

Nimick, Ellen, Linda Szymanski, and Howard Snyder. 1986. *Juvenile Court Waiver: A Study of Juvenile Court Cases Transferred to Criminal Court*. Pittsburgh: National Center for Juvenile Justice.

Osbun, Lee Ann and Peter A. Rode. 1984. "Prosecuting Juveniles as Adults: The Quest for 'Objective' Decisions." *Criminology* 22:187–202.

Reed, David. 1983. *Needed: Serious Solutions for Serious Juvenile Crime*. Chicago: Chicago Law Enforcement Study Group.

Rubin, H. Ted. 1985. *Behind the Black Robes: Juvenile Court Judges and the Court*. Beverly Hills, CA: Sage.

Sagatun, Inger, Loretta L. McCollum, and Leonard P. Edwards. 1985. "The Effect of Transfers from Juvenile to Criminal Court: A Loglinear Analysis." *Journal of Crime and Justice* 8:65–92.

Schack, Elizabeth T. and Hermine Nessen. 1984. *The Experiment That Failed: The New York Juvenile Offender Law—A Study Report*. New York: Citizen's Committee for Children of New York, Inc.

Singer, Simon I. 1985. *Relocating Juvenile Crime: The Shift from Juvenile to Criminal Justice*. Albany, NY: Nelson A. Rockefeller Institute of Government, State University of New York.

Streib, Victor L. 1983. "Death Penalty for Children: The American Experience with Capital Punishment for Crimes Committed While Under Age Eighteen." *Oklahoma Law Review* 36:613–41.

The Death Penalty for Juveniles:

An Assessment of Public Support

Sandra Evans Skovron
Joseph E. Scott
Francis T. Cullen

Recently the issue of the death penalty for juveniles has received considerable media and public attention.[1] The executions of Charles Rumbaugh in September 1985, Terry Roach in January 1986, and J. Kelly Pinkerton in May 1986 focused attention on the issue of executing criminals for murders they committed while under the age of 18. Rumbaugh's execution by the state of Texas was the first such execution in over twenty years. More recently, the death sentence imposed by the state of Indiana on Paula Cooper for a murder she committed at the age of 15 focused international attention and condemnation on the American policy of permitting the death penalty to be applied to juveniles (Hackett, King, and Stanger 1987).

Several trends are reflected in the re-emergence of executions for offenses committed while the offenders are juveniles. Generally there has been a resurgence of capital punishment in the United States; executions of youthful offenders reflect this increased reliance on capital punishment and the increase in executions

throughout the system. In addition, the trend toward harsher penalties for serious juvenile criminals and the increased tendency to transfer them to adult court where they are subject to adult penalties have created a context conducive to the use of execution as a sanction for juvenile murderers.

Statutes in 37 states provide for capital punishment. Eighteen of these states have established minimum ages for its imposition: Eleven state legislatures have set 18 as the minimum age, while the remaining seven require the offender to be at least 16 or 17. Nineteen other states have established no minimum age for execution (*Thompson v. Oklahoma* 1988, pp. 2693–96).[2] In jurisdictions permitting the execution of juvenile offenders, the death penalty may not be imposed by the juvenile courts. A youth must be waived to the jurisdiction of the adult court; then, if convicted, he or she may face the death penalty.

The United States has a long history of executions for crimes committed by persons under the age of 18. The first such execution occurred in the Massachusetts Bay Colony in 1642. Since that time, 281 juvenile offenders have been executed in 36 jurisdictions throughout the United States (Streib 1986). As of January 1986,

Sandra Evans Skovron, Joseph E. Scott, and Francis T. Cullen, Crime & Delinquency, Vol. 35, No. 4, pp. 546–561, copyright © 1989 by Sage Publications, Inc. Reprinted by permission of Sage Publications, Inc.

33 inmates were on death row for crimes they committed while under the age of 18.

The juvenile death penalty is almost unique to the United States. All European countries and the vast majority of other nations prohibit it (Wilson 1983, p. 345). Amnesty International reports that this is the case even among totalitarian regimes. In 1976 the United Nations adopted a resolution providing that the minimum age for execution should be 18.[3]

A great deal of controversy exists over the juvenile death penalty within the United States. Not only has this penalty been rejected by such organizations as Amnesty International and the United Nations, but at its annual meeting in 1983, the American Bar Association adopted a resolution opposing it (Streib 1983, p. 614). The juvenile death penalty also was rejected in the Model Penal Code.[4]

Considerable research has been conducted on public support for the death penalty. Since 1966 such support has increased steadily in the United States (Vidmar and Ellsworth 1974). Recent polls conducted by Gallup and by the National Opinion Research Center found that well over 70% of the American public favored capital punishment (*Public Opinion* 1985, p. 38). These findings were consistent with other recent surveys (Warr and Stafford 1984, p. 104).

In addition to assessing levels of support for capital punishment, researchers have shown a great deal of interest in understanding this support. They have examined the relationships between personality characteristics, such as conservatism and authoritarianism, and advocacy of the death penalty. Attempts have been made to explain support for the death penalty by examining the demographic, background, and occupational characteristics of individuals.[5] In addition, researchers have tried to explain changes in levels of support as results of changes in social conditions, such as increases in crime rates or in the risk or fear of criminal victimization (Rankin 1979; Taylor, Scheppele, and Stinchcombe 1979; Thomas and Foster 1975; Vidmar 1974).

The resurgence of the death penalty in this country may reflect the increasingly punitive attitudes of the public and the desire to get tough with serious offenders (Finckenauer 1988). Indicators show that the public holds punitive attitudes: not only are there high levels of support for capital punishment as noted above, but polls reveal that a substantial majority of the population believes that the "courts are not harsh enough with criminals" (*Public Opinion* 1982, p. 36). It is risky to assume, however, that citizens embrace uniformly punitive views on crime policy. As Flanagan and Caulfield (1984, p. 41) observed, "The mood of the public in regard to correctional reform is diverse, multidimensional, and complex."

Further, we cannot assume that because citizens support capital punishment overwhelmingly, they also support its imposition on juvenile offenders. Despite the extensive research on public attitudes toward capital punishment, little effort has been made to examine attitudes toward the juvenile death penalty. The little research that exists seems to indicate that public opinion on the juvenile death penalty differs markedly from opinion on capital punishment in general. A 1965 Gallup Poll revealed that although 45% of the respondents favored the death penalty, only 23% favored it for those under 21 years of age (Vidmar and Ellsworth 1982, p. 69). More recent research conducted in Nashville, Tennessee, and in Macon, Georgia, in 1985 indicated overwhelming public opposition to the execution of offenders for crimes they committed while under the age of 18. In both cities the juvenile death penalty was opposed by a margin of more than two to one (Southern Coalition on Jails and Prisons 1986, p.1)

Obtaining more thorough information on public attitudes toward the juvenile death penalty is particularly important because the courts have evaluated public opinion in deciding death penalty cases.[6] For example, the Maryland Court of Appeals upheld the constitutionality of imposing the death penalty for offenses committed by persons under the age of 18 (*Trimble v. Maryland* 1984).[7] The court explicitly considered public opinion in its ruling, inferring the support of contemporary society for the juvenile death penalty from the existence of laws permitting the execution of murderers below the age of 18 in 60% of the states at that time (Klein 1985).

More recently, the United States Supreme Court held that the Eighth and Fourteenth Amendments prohibited the execution of William Wayne Thompson for a murder committed at the age of 15 (*Thompson v. Oklahoma* 1988). A plurality of four justices, relying on a review of legislative statutes and jury behavior, reached the conclusion that "the imposition of the death penalty on a 15-year-old offender is now generally abhorrent to the conscience of the community" (*Thompson v. Oklahoma*, p. 2697). As evidence for this conclusion, Justice Stevens stated:

> Most state legislatures have not expressly confronted the question of establishing a minimum age for imposition of the death penalty . . . the 18 states that have expressly established a minimum age in their death penalty statutes all . . . require that the defendant have attained at least the age of 16 at the time of the capital offense. (*Thompson v. Oklahoma*, p. 2693–94, 2695–96)

Further, the plurality of justices stated that the last execution of an offender for a crime committed while under age 16 occurred in 1948. Statistics on jury behavior

revealed that from 1982 through 1986, only 5 out of 1,393 offenders sentenced to death were less than 16 years old at the time of the offense (*Thompson v. Oklahoma*, p. 2697).

Justices O'Connor and Scalia questioned the data used by the plurality to reach the conclusion "that the Eighth and Fourteenth Amendments prohibit the execution of a person who was under 16 years of age at the time of his or her offense" (*Thompson v. Oklahoma*, p. 2700). In a concurring opinion, Justice O'Connor stated that there is "danger in inferring a settled societal consensus from statistics like those relied on in this case" (*Thompson v. Oklahoma*, p. 2709).[8] Justice Scalia's dissent suggested that the plurality "utterly failed in justifying its holding on the basis of 'evolving standards of decency' evidenced by the work product of state legislatures and sentencing juries" (*Thompson v. Oklahoma*, p. 2718).

This article examines and provides a more thorough understanding of public attitudes on the death penalty for juvenile offenders. Rather than inferring citizens' attitudes from statutes and jury behavior, this study assessed public support for the juvenile death penalty through surveys of two communities. The study also examined the demographic and attitudinal characteristics of respondents related to support for this penalty.

METHODOLOGY

The data were collected through a telephone survey of adult residents of two major midwestern cities—Cincinnati and Columbus, Ohio—in February and March 1986. Random digit dialing was used; telephone prefixes were weighted as to the number assigned in order to give each household an equal opportunity to be included. Business and government agency numbers were eliminated from the sample.

Six hundred adults were surveyed, three hundred in each of the two communities.

The demographic characteristics of the samples appear in Table 1. The survey respondents from the two communities were comparable with regard to age, education, income, race, and sex. This finding was expected; census data showed that the cities were similar in population size and composition. The Columbus and Cincinnati respondents differed in religious affiliation, however, the Columbus sample had more Protestant respondents and fewer Catholic respondents than the Cincinnati sample. These figures reflected differences in the population compositions of the two cities; comparison of the characteristics of the two samples with data from the U.S. Census showed that the samples were comparable to the larger populations from which they were drawn (Bureau of the Census 1983a, 1983b).

Respondents were contacted and told that the purpose of the survey was to determine public attitudes toward issues of current interest in their community. They were then asked a number of demographic questions, and questions regarding their

TABLE 1:   Demographic Characteristics of Respondents

	CINCINNATI		COLUMBUS	
	Percent	**Number**	**Percent**	**Number**
Age				
Under 30	28.0	84	35.0	105
30–44	36.3	109	32.3	97
45 and over	35.7	107	32.7	98
Education				
Some High School	14.4	43	9.4	27
High School Graduate	26.4	79	31.5	90
Some College	28.8	86	28.7	82
College Graduate	30.4	91	30.4	87
Income				
Under $20,000	30.4	77	32.2	84
$20,000–29,999	22.1	56	27.7	72
$30,000–49,999	32.8	83	25.4	66
$50,000 or more	14.6	37	14.6	14
Race				
White	85.0	250	87.2	258
Black	14.3	42	10.1	30
Other	0.7	2	2.7	8
Religious Affiliation				
Protestant	42.3	126	50.5	143
Jewish	3.7	11	2.8	8
Catholic	33.9	101	20.8	59
Other	16.1	48	20.8	59
None	4.0	12	4.9	14
Sex				
Male	47.3	142	50.0	150
Female	52.7	158	50.0	150

attitudes toward a variety of criminal justice issues and policies. Among the latter questions was one assessing attitudes toward the death penalty for juvenile offenders. Information was also obtained on the respondents' support for the death penalty for adults.

FINDINGS

OVERALL LEVEL OF SUPPORT FOR THE JUVENILE DEATH PENALTY

To assess support for the imposition of the death penalty on juveniles, the following question was asked:

Ohio presently has the death penalty for adults convicted of murder. Would you favor or oppose the state passing a law to allow the death penalty for juveniles over 14 years of age convicted of murder?

This research is limited inasmuch as the survey included only one item concerning the juvenile death penalty. This question assessed attitudes toward the execution of offenders for capital offenses committed when they were over 14 and under 18 years of age. As the Supreme Court noted, however, in *Thompson v. Oklahoma*, public support may differ regarding the execution of older and younger juvenile murderers. The question excluded the youngest juveniles (under 14) from consideration. Even so, had it asked specifically about older youths (e.g., 16- or 17-year old juveniles), different levels of support for

and opposition to the juvenile death penalty might have been found.

The data reflecting the respondents' attitudes toward the juvenile death penalty appear in Table 2. Public attitudes in the two cities were very similar. In Cincinnati, 25% of respondents favored passage of such legislation and 69% opposed it. In Columbus, 30% favored the juvenile death penalty and 65.3% opposed it. Overall, about two-thirds of the respondents were opposed to the passage of a law allowing the execution of juveniles over the age of 14 who commit murder. This finding was similar to the results of previous research on public attitudes conducted in Georgia and Tennessee (Southern Coalition on Jails and Prisons 1986, p. 1).

Notably, the support found for the juvenile death penalty was considerably smaller than that generally found for the adult death penalty: as noted, recent opinion polls have indicated that well over 70% of the public favors capital punishment (*Public Opinion* 1985, p. 38). This research shed additional light on that issue. The survey included the following question:

If you were serving on a jury for a trial of an adult guilty of murder, would it be *extremely difficult, difficult, somewhat difficult*, or *not difficult at all* for you to vote to have the offender put to death?

In contrast to the findings with regard to the death penalty for juveniles, 50.3% of the Cincinnati sample and 47.8% of the Columbus sample said they would

TABLE 2:   Respondent Attitudes Toward the Death Penalty for Juveniles. Support of a State law allowing the death penalty for juveniles over the age of 14 convicted of murder

	Favor	Oppose	Don't know
Cincinnati	25.0% (75)	69.0% (207)	6.0% (18)
Columbus	30.0% (90)	65.3% (196)	4.7% (14)

experience little or no difficulty in voting to impose the death penalty on an adult offender convicted of murder. Only 31.8% of Cincinnati residents and 28.5% of Columbus residents said they would find this task extremely difficult.[9]

SOURCES OF SUPPORT FOR THE JUVENILE DEATH PENALTY

Probit regression analysis of the relationship between respondents' demographic and attitudinal characteristics and support for the juvenile death penalty was conducted. Probit analysis was chosen because many of the assumptions of ordinary

least-squares regression are violated when the dependent variable is dichotomous.[10] The independent variables included in the analysis appear in Table 3. Two scales, a rehabilitation effectiveness scale and a rehabilitation policy scale, were constructed from the rehabilitation items on the survey and were included as independent variables. A principal component factor analysis with varimax rotation of the rehabilitation items revealed two dimensions of attitudes toward rehabilitation.[11] The rehabilitation effectiveness scale had a coefficient of reliability of alpha equal to .711 for the Cincinnati sample and .773 for the Columbus sample. Scale scores ranged from 4 to

TABLE 3:   Description of Variables

Variable	Description
Age (in years)	Cincinnati: x = 41.96, sd = 17.00; Columbus: x = 39.20, sd = 16.88
Education	0–8 years = 1; 9–11 years = 2; 12 years = 3; 13–15 years = 4; 16 years = 5; 17 + years = 6. Cincinnati: x = 3.83, sd = 1.33; Columbus: x = 3.85, sd = 1.18
Income	$10,000 = 1; $10,000–19,999 = 2; $20,000–29,999 = 3; $30,000–39,999 = 4; $40,000–49,999 = 5; $50,000 or more = 6. Cincinnati: x = 3.47, sd = 1.54; Columbus: x = 3.34, sd = 1.54
Race	Nonwhite = 0; White = 1. Cincinnati: x = 0.85, sd = 0.35; Columbus: x = 0.87, sd = 0.33
Religiosity	Very religious = 1; Somewhat religious = 2; Not very religious = 3; Not religious at all = 4. Cincinnati: x = 1.91, sd = 0.68; Columbus: x = 2.14, sd = 0.82
Sex	Female = 0; Male = 1. Cincinnati: x = 0.47, sd = 0.50; Columbus: x = 0.50, sd = 0.50
Effectiveness of Rehabilitation	Ranges from 4 to 16; higher scores indicate greater belief in effectiveness. Cincinnati: x = 10.86, sd = 2.00; Columbus: x = 10.65, sd = 2.35
Support of Rehabilitation as Penal Policy	Ranges from 3 to 9; higher scores indicate greater support. Cincinnati: x = 7.53, sd = 1.19; Columbus: x = 7.46, sd = 1.31

16; higher scores indicated greater belief in the efficacy of rehabilitation. The coefficient of reliability of alpha for the rehabilitation policy scale was .792 for the Cincinnati sample and .751 for the Columbus sample. Scale scores ranged from three to nine; higher scores indicated greater support for rehabilitation as penal policy.

The results of the probit analysis appear in Table 4. An examination of the "pseudo R^2s" (Aldrich and Nelson 1984, p. 57) revealed that the probit models, predicting support for the juvenile death penalty, were weak.

Examination of the coefficients and the standard errors for the statistically significant variables revealed no substantial effects. For the Cincinnati sample, only one statistically significant relationship was found—an inverse relationship between belief in the effectiveness of rehabilitation programs and support for the juvenile death penalty. Respondents who expressed greater belief in the effectiveness of rehabilitation programs were less likely to support the juvenile death penalty. The same relationship was found for the Columbus sample, but additional statistically significant relationships also were found for that

TABLE 4: Probit Parameter Estimates for Predictions of Support for the Juvenile Death Penalty

	Cincinnati	Columbus
Constant	−0.365	1.751*
	(.662)[a]	(.638)
Age	0.001	−0.005
	(.005)	(.005)
Education	0.100	−0.109
	(.066)	(.073)
Income	0.015	−0.003
	(.048)	(.050)
Race	0.279	−0.104
	(.194)	(.196)
Sex	0.126	0.623*
	(.168)	(.171)
Religiosity	0.135	−0.231*
	(.123)	(.102)
Effectiveness of Rehabilitation	−0.101*	−0.088*
	(.043)	(.035)
Support of Rehabilitation as Penal Policy	−0.042	−0.071*
	(.032)	(.031)
Pseudo R2[b]	.075**	.102**

[a]The numbers in parentheses are the standard errors of the coefficients.
[b]The Pseudo R2 is calculated according to the formula presented by Aldrich and Nelson (1984, p. 57); Pseudo R^2 = C + (N + C), where C = chi-square and N = sample size.
*Significant at p < .05
**Chi-square significant at p < 0.5

sample. Citizens who were more supportive of rehabilitation as penal policy and those who rated themselves as less religious were less supportive of the juvenile death penalty. In addition, male respondents in the Columbus sample were more likely than female respondents to support the juvenile death penalty.

Like previous research on attitudes toward criminal justice issues (Langworthy and Whitehead 1986; Skovron, Scott, and Cullen 1988), this research found that attitudinal variables were related more significantly and more consistently to public attitudes toward the juvenile death penalty than were demographic variables. Among the demographic characteristics analyzed, only gender was related significantly to attitudes toward the death penalty for juveniles, and this relationship was significant only for the Columbus sample. Attitudes toward the juvenile death penalty were related significantly to respondents' religiosity, philosophies of punishment, and attitudes toward the effectiveness of rehabilitation programs. Citizens who rated themselves as more religious, who favored more punitive policies, and who thought that rehabilitation programs were ineffective were more likely to support the juvenile death penalty than those who were less religious, who favored rehabilitation programs for offenders, and who believed in the effectiveness of those programs. These findings were consistent with previous death penalty research results (Warr and Stafford 1984).

DISCUSSION

Consistent with the opinion expressed in *Thompson v. Oklahoma*, the majority of the citizens surveyed disapproved of the execution of young juvenile offenders. Public opposition to the death penalty for young offenders may reflect many of the same beliefs that led to creation of the juvenile justice system. As Empey (1982) has noted, the creation of the juvenile court was linked to the rise of the belief that children possess distinct differences from adults and therefore should be treated differently by the justice system. By the turn of the twentieth century, children were viewed as less responsible, more malleable, and more amenable to rehabilitation than adults (Platt 1969).

Despite recent trends toward increased punitiveness in the juvenile justice system, it appears that citizens have not totally relinquished these beliefs. When Cullen, Golden, and Cullen (1983) surveyed a sample of the Illinois public and various groups of Illinois criminal justice practitioners and policymakers, they found a high degree of support for juvenile rehabilitation; over 80% of those surveyed stated that it would be "irresponsible to stop trying to rehabilitate juveniles." Further, that study revealed higher levels of support and optimism regarding rehabilitation of juvenile offenders than adult offenders. The authors concluded that the research revealed "attitudes supportive of the 'differentness' of the juvenile offender, a differentness which offers optimistic possibilities for salvation and rehabilitation" (Cullen et al. 1983, p.7).

More recent research, based on the same survey data used in the present study, further corroborated the findings of high levels of public support for rehabilitation of juvenile criminals and greater belief in the effectiveness of rehabilitation programs for juveniles than for adults. The survey of adult residents of Cincinnati and Columbus, Ohio revealed that 85% of the Cincinnati sample and 74% of the Columbus sample thought that rehabilitation programs were "very helpful" or "helpful" for juvenile offenders. In comparison, only

60% of the Cincinnati residents and 57% of the Columbus residents thought that rehabilitation programs were similarly helpful for adults (Cullen et al., forthcoming).

Similar views were expressed by the plurality in *Thompson v. Oklahoma* in ruling unconstitutional the imposition of the death penalty on a youth who was 15 at the time of the crime. Although the Court did not specifically address rehabilitation as a correctional goal, Justice Stevens's comments appeared to support rehabilitation as the focus of corrections for juvenile murderers:

> This Court has already endorsed the proposition that less culpability should attach to a crime committed by a juvenile than to a comparable crime committed by an adult since inexperience, less education, and less intelligence make the teenager less able to evaluate the consequences of his or her conduct while at the same time he or she is much more apt to be motivated by mere emotion or peer pressure than is an adult. Given this lesser culpability, as well as the teenager's capacity for growth and society's fiduciary obligations to its children, the retributive purpose underlying the death penalty is simply inapplicable to the execution of a 15 year old offender. (*Thompson v. Oklahoma*, p. 2688)

Only four justices held that imposition of the death penalty on offenders 15 years of age and younger is unconstitutional. A fifth justice—O'Connor—held that the imposition of this sanction is unconstitutional if the legislature has not specifically established a minimum age for execution. Three additional justices—Scalia, Rehnquist, and White—dissented from the decision of the Court. Justice Kennedy was appointed to the Court subsequent to the consideration of this case and did not participate in the decision.[12]

The research described above was limited inasmuch as it relied on only one item assessing support for the juvenile death penalty; that item assessed attitudes only toward the execution of persons 14 years of age and older. More research on public attitudes toward capital punishment for juveniles is needed. Such research is particularly relevant because the Supreme Court relies on an assessment of "evolving standards of decency that mark the progress of a maturing society" in determining whether the Eighth Amendment's prohibition against cruel and unusual punishment applies (*Trop v. Dulles* 1958, p. 101). As noted above, the Supreme Court reviews relevant state statutes to assess the will of the public. Research demonstrates, however, that legislators and policymakers have overestimated the degree to which citizens favor harsh policies (Gottfredson and Taylor 1983, Riley and Rose 1980). Although seven states have established minimum ages for execution below the age of 18, this fact may not be a valid measure of public support for the juvenile death penalty in these states.

Future research should be directed toward attaining greater understanding of societal attitudes toward the juvenile death penalty. It seems reasonable to anticipate greater support for executing older juvenile offenders than younger ones. Still, important questions remain: At what point does a majority of the public cease to consider age a mitigating factor in capital cases? To what extent does age weigh against other elements in a capital offense (e.g., victim's race, aggravating conditions) in determining public attitudes? How do citizens view the punishment of defendants who commit murders while juveniles, but are tried and convicted after they pass into adulthood? Direct assessments of public opinion on the execution of juvenile offenders would provide valuable information for assessing societal attitudes toward acceptable sanctions.

Notes

1. Throughout this article, "the juvenile death penalty" refers to the policy of permitting the execution of offenders for murders they committed while under the age of 18. The executions themselves may take place after the offenders turn 18.

2. The Bureau of Justice Statistics (1988) reported that at the end of 1987, 15 states specified minimum ages for execution below 18, and 9 of these states provided for minimum ages below 16. However, the Bureau failed to distinguish between states that specify minimum ages for execution in capital punishment statutes and those that determine minimum age by statutory provisions setting the age at which juveniles may be transferred to criminal court to be tried as adults.

3. International Covenant on Civil and Political Rights, art. 6.5, G.A. Res. 2200A, 21 U.N. GAOR Supp. (No. 16) at 49, 52, U.N. Doc. A/63/6 (1976) (entered into force March 23, 1976).

4. Model Penal Code 210.6 (1) (d) (1980).

5. For more extensive reviews, see Finckenauer (1988), Gelles and Straus (1975), Vidmar and Ellsworth (1982), and Vidmar and Miller (1980).

6. See *Furman v. Georgia* (1972) 408 U.S. 238, *Woodson v. North Carolina* (1976) 428 U.S. 280, *Gregg v. Georgia* (1976) 428 U.S. 153, and *Coker v. Georgia (1977) 433 U.S. 584* for examples of the use of information on public attitudes in death penalty cases.

7. See Klein (1985) for a more thorough discussion of this case.

8. Justice O'Connor concurred in the judgment of the Court, stating that the "petitioner and others who were below the age of 16 at the time of their offense may not be executed under the authority of a capital punishment statute that specifies no minimum age at which the commission of capital crime can lead to the offender's execution" (*Thompson v. Oklahoma* 1988, p. 2711).

9. It also should be noted that when respondents were asked to rate the difficulty they would experience in recommending the death penalty, substantial percentages (49.3% of Cincinnati residents and 52.2% of Columbus residents) said that they would experience difficulty in recommending that penalty. This finding may indicate that when respondents are asked about behavioral aspects of support for the death penalty, different results are found than when they are asked only whether they favor or oppose a policy.

10. See Aldrich and Nelson (1984) for a discussion of the violated assumptions and their impacts.

11. Attitudes toward the effectiveness of rehabilitation were measured by the following items:

Do you think that rehabilitation programs are very helpful (= 4), helpful (= 3), slightly helpful (= 2), or not helpful at all (= 1), for violent offenders?

Do you think that rehabilitation programs are very helpful (= 4), helpful (= 3), slightly helpful (= 2), or not helpful at all (= 1), for nonviolent offenders?

Do you think that rehabilitation programs are very helpful (= 4), helpful (= 3), slightly helpful (= 2), or not helpful at all (= 1), for juvenile offenders?

Do you think that rehabilitation programs are very helpful (= 4), helpful (= 3), slightly helpful (= 2), or not helpful at all (= 1), for adult offenders?

Attitudes toward support for rehabilitation as penal policy were assessed by the following items:

Do you favor (= 2) or oppose (= 1) expanding the rehabilitation programs now being undertaken in prison?

Which of the following is the best policy for dealing with inmates in your opinion?

- —Psychological counseling (= 4)
- —Educational and vocational training (= 3)
- —Keeping inmates locked in their cells (= 2)
- —Hard labor (= 1)

What do you think should be the main emphasis in most prisons?

- —Trying to rehabilitate the individual so that he might return to society as a productive citizen (= 3)
- —Protecting society from future crimes the offender might commit (= 2)
- —Punishing the individual convicted of a crime (= 1)

The factor loadings for the Columbus sample appear below.

Variable	Factor 1	Factor 2
Expand rehabilitation programs	−.040	.654
Best policy for prisoners	−.067	.683
Main emphasis for prisoners	.108	.615
Effective for violent offenders	.610	−.023
Effective for nonviolent offenders	.716	.019
Effective for juvenile offenders	.694	−.017
Effective for adult offenders	.750	.021

The inclusion of two scales to measure different aspects of attitudes toward rehabilitation in the probit regression could have led to problems of multicollinearity. Multicollinearity was not a problem, however, because the correlation between the scales was only .381 for the Cincinnati sample and .324 for the Columbus sample.

12. While this article was in press, the Court ruled (June 26, 1989) by 5-4 votes in two separate cases—*Wilkins v. Missouri* and *Stanford v. Kentucky*—that it was constitutional to execute convicted murderers who were 16 or 17 when they committed the crime.

Cases

Coker v. Georgia. (1977) 433 U.S. 584

Furman v. Georgia. (1972) 408 U.S. 238

Gregg v. Georgia. (1976) 428 U.S. 153

Thompson v. Oklahoma. (1988) 108 S.Ct. 2687

Trimble v. Maryland. (1984) 300 Md. 387, 478 A.2d 1143

Trop v. Dulles. (1958) 356 U.S. 86

Woodson v. North Carolina. (1976) 428 U.S. 280

References

Aldrich, John H. and Forrest D. Nelson. 1984. *Linear Probability, Logit, and Probit Models*. Beverly Hills: Sage.

Bureau of the Census. 1983a. *1980 Census of Population and Housing: Cincinnati, Ohio-Ky.-Ind. Standard Metropolitan Statistical Area*. Washington, DC: U.S. Government Printing Office.

___.1983b. *1980 Census of Population and Housing: Columbus, Ohio Standard Metropolitan Area*. Washington, DC: U.S. Government Printing Office.

Bureau of Justice Statistics. 1988. *Capital Punishment 1987*. Washington, DC: U.S. Department of Justice.

Cullen, Francis T., Kathryn M. Golden, and John B. Cullen. 1983. "Is Child Saving Dead? Attitudes Toward Juvenile Rehabilitation in Illinois." *Journal of Criminal Justice* 11: 1-13.

Cullen, Francis T., Sandra Evans Skovron, Joseph E. Scott, and Velmer S. Burton. Forthcoming. "Public Support for Correctional Treatment: The Tenacity of Rehabilitative Ideology." *Criminal Justice and Behavior*.

Empey, LaMar T. 1982. *American Delinquency: Its Meaning and Construction*. Homewood, IL: Dorsey.

Finckenauer, James O. 1988. "Public Support for the Death Penalty: Retribution as Just Desserts or Retribution as Revenge?" *Justice Quarterly* 5:81–100.

Flanagan, Timothy J. and Susan L. Caulfield. 1984. "Public Opinion and Prison Policy: A Review." *The Prison Journal* 64:31–46.

Gelles, Richard J. and Murray A. Straus. 1975. "Family Experience and Public Support of the Death Penalty." *American Journal of Orthopsychiatry* 45:596–613.

Goltfredson, Stephen D. and Ralph B. Taylor. 1983. *The Correctional Crisis: Prison Populations and Public Policy*. Washington, DC: U.S. Department of Justice.

Hackett, George, Patricia King, and Theodore Stanger. 1987. "Indiana Killer, Italian Martyr: A Death Row Cause." *Newsweek*, Sept. 21, 37.

Just, Rona L. 1984. "Executing Youthful Offenders: The Unanswered Question in Eddings v. Oklahoma." *Fordham Urban Law Journal* 13:471–510.

Klein, Robert Anthony. 1985. "Juvenile Criminals and the Death Penalty: Resurrection of the Question Left Unanswered in Eddings v. Oklahoma." *New England Journal of Criminal and Civil Confinement* 11:437–87.

Langworthy, Robert H. and John T. Whitehead. 1986. "Liberalism and Fear as Explanations of Punitiveness." *Criminology* 24:575–91.

Platt, Anthony. 1970. *The Child Savers*. Chicago: University of Chicago Press.

Public Opinion. 1982. "Opinion Roundup: Crime—The Public Gets Tough." *Public Opinion* 5:36.

___.1985. "Opinion Roundup: Death Penalty Considered." *Public Opinion* 8:38–39.

Rankin, Joseph. 1979. "Changing Attitudes Toward Capital Punishment." *Social Forces* 58:194–211.

Riley, Pamela Johnson and Vicki McNickle Rose. 1980. "Public and Elite Opinion Concerning Correctional Reform: Implications for Social Policy." *Journal of Criminal Justice* 8:345–56.

Skovron, Sandra Evans, Joseph E. Scott, and Francis T. Cullen. 1988. "Prison Crowding: Public Attitudes Toward Strategies of Population Control." *Journal of Research in Crime and Delinquency* 25:150–69.

Southern Coalition on Jails and Prisons. 1986. "SCJP Poll Results: Don't Execute Juveniles." *Southern Coalition Report on Jails & Prisons* 13:1.

Streib, Victor L. 1983. "Death Penalty for Children: The American Experience with Capital Punishment for Crimes Committed while under Age Eighteen." *Oklahoma Law Review* 36:613–41.

___.1986. "Persons Executed for Crimes Committed while under Age Eighteen." *Augustus* 9:20–25.

Taylor, Douglas C., Kim Lane Scheppele, and Arthur L. Stinchcombe. 1979. "Salience of Crime and Support for Harsher Criminal Sanctions." *Social Problems* 26:413–24.

Thomas, Charles W. and Samuel C. Foster. 1975. "A Sociological Perspective on Public Support for Capital Punishment." *American Journal of Orthopsychiatry* 45:641–57.

Tyler, Tom R. and Rence Weber. 1982. "Support for the Death Penalty: Instrumental Response to Crime, or Symbolic Attitude?" *Law and Society Review* 17:21–45.

Vidmar, Neil. 1974. "Retributive and Utilitarian Motives and other Correlates of Canadian Attitudes toward the Death Penalty." *Canadian Psychologist* 15:337–56.

Vidmar, Neil and Phoebe C. Ellsworth. 1974. "Public Opinion and the Death Penalty." *Stanford Law Review* 26:1245–70.

___.1982. "Research on Attitudes toward Capital Punishment." Pp. 68–92 in *The Death Penalty in America*, edited by H.A. Bedau. Oxford: Oxford University Press.

Vidmar, Neil and Dale T. Miller. 1980. "Social Psychological Processes Underlying Attitudes toward Legal Punishment." *Law and Society Review* 14:565–602.

Warr, Mark and Mark Stafford. 1984. "Public Goals of Punishment and Support for the Death Penalty." *Journal of Research in Crime and Delinquency* 21:95–111.

Wilson, William. 1983. "Juvenile Offenders and the Electric Chair: Cruel and Unusual Punishment or Firm Discipline for the Hopelessly Delinquent?" *University of Florida Law Review* 35:344–71.

Assessing the Effects of School-Based Drug Education:

A Six-Year Multilevel Analysis of Project D.A.R.E.

Dennis P. Rosenbaum
Gordon S. Hanson

Drug Abuse Resistance Education (D.A.R.E.) is the most popular school-based drug education program in the United States. It is administered in about 70 percent of the nation's school districts, reaching 25 million students in 1996, and has been adopted in 44 foreign countries (Law Enforcement News 1996). Its effectiveness in combating drug usage, however, has been a matter of bitter controversy, and this debate is taking place in the context of rising drug use among our nation's youths. After large declines in drug use in the 1980s, the national trend began to reverse in the early 1990s: The percentage of high school seniors who reported using illegal drugs "during the past year" increased from 22 percent in 1992 to 35 percent in 1995—a 59 percent increase (Johnston, O'Malley, and Bachman 1996). Marijuana is one drug for which dramatic increases were observed. The number of eighth graders who reported using marijuana

during their lifetime jumped from 10.2 percent in 1991 to 19.9 percent in 1995—a 92 percent increase. Reports from the Office of National Drug Control Policy (1997) reflect a growing concern about recent trends in drug use attitudes and behaviors among America's youths, and call upon the nation to act swiftly to prevent a future drug epidemic.

This growing drug problem has caused a flurry of media coverage and political finger-pointing, all leading to closer scrutiny of our nation's efforts to control and prevent drug abuse. The spotlight has been especially strong on America's most popular and visible program—D.A.R.E. Whether or not D.A.R.E. has been an effective preventive program has been the subject of considerable debate and research. The publication of a national study that questioned the effectiveness of D.A.R.E. in preventing drug use (Ringwalt et al. 1994) opened the door to an avalanche of criticism in the popular press and canceled endorsements by some police executives (e.g., NBC Dateline 1997). Of course, the problem of demonstrating effectiveness in drug prevention is not unique to D.A.R.E. Several literature reviews and meta-analyses of school-based drug prevention

Dennis P. Rosenbaum, and Gordon S. Hanson, Journal of Research in Crime and Delinquency, Vol. 35, No. 4, pp. 381–412, copyright © 1998 by Sage Publications, Inc. Reprinted by permission of Sage Publications, Inc.

programs have concluded that most are ineffective in preventing drug use (see Bangert-Drowns 1988; Battjes 1985; Botvin 1990; Bruvold and Rundall 1988; Ennett et al. 1994; Hansen 1992; Ringwalt et al. 1994; Tobler 1986).

The latest pressure on school-based drug education programs comes from federal legislation. Congress enacted the *Drug-Free Schools and Communities Act* in 1987 (and many subsequent amendments) to beef up our nation's drug education and prevention programs. Effective July 1, 1998, local school districts will be expected, for the first time, to provide evidence of program effectiveness in order to receive federal Title IV funds. Funding will only be available for "research-based" strategies that are consistent with the new "Principles of Effectiveness." One of the core principles is that "grant recipients shall . . . select and implement programs that have demonstrated that they can be effective in preventing or reducing drug use, violence, or disruptive behavior."[1] The new *Safe and Drug-Free Schools and Communities Act* (SDFSCA) language will force many states, school districts, and schools to give more attention to drug education goals, processes, and evaluation results. If proposed school-based programs are taken at face value, their main goal is clear—to prevent drug use among the target population. Whether programs can achieve this goal is an empirical question that should be answered, in part, through rigorous evaluation research.

The present article reports on a comprehensive longitudinal evaluation of D.A.R.E. that occurred between 1989 and 1996 in the state of Illinois. This article includes the final analyses of the full data set collected as part of the Illinois D.A.R.E. study, which tracked students from fifth and sixth grades through their junior and senior years of high school.

THE D.A.R.E. PROGRAM

D.A.R.E. is a series of school-based drug and violence prevention programs for kids in kindergarten through 12th grade. It is a cooperative venture between law enforcement agencies, schools, and the local community, and it involves the use of trained, uniformed police officers in the classroom to teach a carefully planned drug prevention curriculum. Created in 1983 as a collaborative venture between the Los Angeles Police Department and the Los Angeles Unified School District, D.A.R.E. has expanded to become the largest drug education initiative in the world. The core D.A.R.E. curriculum, which is the subject of this research, focuses on children in their last year of elementary school (5th or 6th grade). It is based on the assumption that students at this age are the most receptive to antidrug messages as they approach the age of drug experimentation.

THEORETICAL FRAMEWORK

Evaluations of D.A.R.E.'s effectiveness as a public policy can also be viewed as a test of its theoretical underpinnings. Although some researchers have referred to D.A.R.E. as "atheoretical" (Winfree, Esbensen, and Osgood 1996), this is far from accurate. Unlike the earlier generation of drug education programs in the 1970s, D.A.R.E. is solidly grounded in a body of theory and research that laid the foundation for a second generation of school-based prevention initiatives. The program is primarily rooted in the social skills and social influence model of drug education. As Botvin (1990) notes, a variety of strategies can be characterized as part of this "psychosocial" approach to drug prevention, but three general categories of programs can be identified: psychological inoculation, resistance skills training, and personal and social skills training. D.A.R.E. has elements of each approach in its curriculum.

Botvin (1990) compares psychological inoculation to "traditional preventive medicine" in that individuals are exposed to weak doses of "infection" so that "antibodies" may be developed. (D.A.R.E.'s "vaccine" takes the form of simulated temptations and pressures to use drugs.) The resistance skills training approach places emphasis on teaching specific skills for evading or resisting these "negative social influences," including subtle media influences (D.A.R.E. students engage in role-playing scenarios to resist peer offers of drug use). The personal and social skills training approach is not problem specific but more broadly oriented to the "acquisition of generic personal and social skills." These will have the incidental effect of preventing the development of socially learned behaviors and attitudes that are believed to be associated with substance use. Recent applications of the personal and social skills approach were modeled after earlier interventions shown to be effective in preventing cigarette smoking (Flay et al. 1983). Some successful applications of this model to drug abuse have been reported in the literature (Botvin 1990; Clayton, Cattarello, Day, and Walden 1991; Flay 1985; Hansen 1992; Tobler 1986). Particular attention is given to helping youths develop the social skills to recognize and respond appropriately to peer pressure.

From the outline of the curriculum (see Table 1), it is apparent that D.A.R.E. also includes what Botvin (1990) calls "information dissemination" and "affective education." The former is designed to provide students with enough knowledge to make informed cost-benefit decisions about drug use (e.g., D.A.R.E. includes information on drug use, misuse, and consequences; media influences; and drug use

alternatives). The latter is similar to the personal-and-social-skills approach but is focused on a strategy of "social enrichment." D.A.R.E. attempts to do this by focusing the curriculum on self-esteem building, managing stress, decision-making, role modeling, and forming support systems. The general hypothesis implicit in the D.A.R.E. model is that classroom instruction by trained police officers will result in enhanced self-esteem, self-understanding, and assertiveness; a clearer sense of values; and more responsible decision-making habits, which, in turn, should make students less vulnerable to the enticements and pressures to use drugs and alcohol.

PREVIOUS D.A.R.E. EVALUATIONS

There have been many outcome evaluations of the core D.A.R.E. curriculum, but the methodological rigor of these assessments varies considerably. Most of these studies are of limited scientific value because of their weak research designs, poor sampling and data collection procedures, inadequate measurement, and analysis problems. Indeed, the boldest claims of D.A.R.E.'s success are especially vulnerable to such criticism given rampant problems with internal validity. Most evaluations have been posttest-only designs; that is, the survey instrument is administered for the first time after students have participated in the program. Some of these ex post facto evaluations did not include any type of control group (Aniskiewicz and Wysong 1987; Carstens, Pecchia, and Rohach 1989; Correll 1990; McMahon and Wuorenma 1992; Netburn 1989; Silva 1995). Other studies required the respondents to recall, retrospectively, whether or not they had received D.A.R.E. (DeJong 1987; Donnermeyer forthcoming; Dukes, Stein, and Ullman 1996, 1997; Fife 1994; Wysong, Aniskiewicz, and Wright 1994), or

TABLE 1: Original D.A.R.E. Curriculum

Session	Topic	Description
1.	First visit/personal safety	Introduction of D.A.R.E. and law enforcement officer safety practices; discussion of personal rights
2.	Drug use and misuse	Harmful effects from misuse of drugs
3.	Consequences	Consequences of using and choosing not to use alcohol, marijuana, and other drugs
4.	Resisting pressures	Sources of pressure, types of pressure to use drugs
5.	Resistance techniques	Refusal strategies for different types of peer pressure
6.	Building self-esteem	Identifying positive qualities in oneself; giving/receiving compliments; importance of self-image
7.	Assertiveness	Personal rights/responsibilities discussion; situations calling for assertiveness skills
8.	Managing stress without drugs	Identification of sources of stress; when stress can be helpful or harmful; ways to manage stress; deep-breathing exercise
9.	Media influences	Media influences on behavior; advertising techniques
10.	Decision-making and risk-taking	Risk-taking behaviors; reasonable and harmful risks; consequences of various choices; influences on decisions
11.	Drug use alternatives	Reasons for using drugs; alternative activities
12.	Role modeling	Meet older student leaders/role models who do not use drugs
13.	Forming support system	Types of support groups; barriers to friendships; suggestions to overcoming barriers to forming friendships
14.	Ways to deal with gang pressures	Types of gang pressure; how gangs differ from groups; consequences of gang activity
15.	D.A.R.E. summary	D.A.R.E. review
16.	Taking a stand	Taking appropriate stand when pressured to use drugs
17.	D.A.R.E. culmination	Award assembly: recognition of participants

NOTE: D.A.R.E. = Drug Abuse Resistance Education.

they used a nonequivalent control group (McDonald, Towberman, and Hague 1990). Many of these evaluations reached conclusions that were favorable to D.A.R.E.,[2] some on the basis of responses to as few as five survey items. The limitations of these studies are too numerous to be listed here, but clearly, the observed differences may be the result of self-selection processes (or other preexisting differences) rather than the D.A.R.E. program (see Cook and Campbell 1979:98).[3]

There have been several D.A.R.E. evaluations that could be classified as "quasi-experimental." Three used pretest-posttest designs without a control group

(Anonymous 1987; Kethineni, Leamy, and Guyon 1991; Wiegand 1991), and two of those were also flawed by survey instruments of the type used in the weakest of the ex post facto evaluations. A larger number of quasi-experimental evaluations (Becker, Agopian, and Yeh 1992; Clayton 1987; Etheridge and Hicks 1989; Faine and Bohlander 1988, 1989; Harmon 1993; Lindstrom 1996; Manos, Kameoka, and Tanji 1986; McCormick and McCormick 1992; Walker 1990) have sufficient scientific integrity to allow estimates of causal effects. These quasi-experimental studies produced more modest assessments of D.A.R.E. than the weaker evaluations. They uncovered fairly consistent short-term effects of D.A.R.E. on mediating variables such as knowledge, attitudes, and social skills (Becker et al. 1992; Clayton 1987; Faine and Bohlander 1989) but provided little evidence of D.A.R.E.'s impact on drug use behaviors.

The strongest design used to assess D.A.R.E. (with the fewest threats to validity) is the randomized experiment. Only a few evaluations have used experimental designs with sufficiently large sample sizes and repeated measurement over one or more years (Clayton, Cattarello, Day, and Walden 1991; Clayton, Cattarello, and Johnstone 1996; Clayton, Cattarello, and Walden 1991; Ennett et al. 1994; Ringwalt, Curtin, and Rosenbaum 1990; Ringwalt, Ennett, and Holt 1991; Rosenbaum et al. 1994). These studies clearly indicate that D.A.R.E.'s positive effects on students tend to dissipate over time. D.A.R.E. has its largest short-term benefits on students' knowledge about drugs, but statistically significant positive effects have also been observed for social skills, drug-related attitudes, attitudes toward the police, and, less, frequently, self-esteem. The effects on drug use behaviors are often small and nonsignificant, although significant short-term reductions in tobacco use have been noted on more than one occasion (see meta-analysis by Ennett et al. 1994). The literature of D.A.R.E.'s effectiveness as a drug prevention strategy can be summarized in this way: The stronger the research design is, the less impact researchers have reported on drug use measures.

One of the major limitations of even the best D.A.R.E. evaluations is the short lag between pretest and posttests. Despite the growth in the number of D.A.R.E. studies, surprisingly few are longitudinal in nature. Most of the stronger studies have examined program effects immediately after students participated in D.A.R.E.

(Becker et al. 1992; Faine and Bohlander 1988; Harmon 1993; Kethineni et al. 1991; Lindstrom 1996; Manos et al. 1986; Ringwalt et al. 1990, 1991; Walker 1990); a few have looked at one-year and two-year outcomes (Clayton, Cattarello, Day, and Walden 1991; Clayton, Cattarello, and Walden 1991; Ennett et al. 1994; Rosenbaum et al. 1994). Given the relatively low base rates for drug use at the ages of 11 or 12 (when D.A.R.E. is introduced), short time lags between pretest and posttest measurement can severely restrict the opportunity to detect preventive effects.

Most of the students in the present study entered high school at wave 5 of the survey. This is the point at which marijuana use within the past 30 days, for example, begins to rise dramatically, from 2.5 percent of those surveyed at wave 4 to more than 25 percent at wave 8. D.A.R.E. is typically administered in sixth grade, well in advance of the steep rise in usage patterns common to most substances. Thus, a real test of program effectiveness must extend to the age-group where opportunities for drug use are substantial; otherwise, there will be a ceiling or upper limit on the dependent variable.

Prior D.A.R.E. research has virtually ignored the possible effects of supplemental (i.e., post-D.A.R.E.) drug education during the middle school and high school years. School-based drug prevention is now mandatory in many states, including Illinois, where this study was conducted. This post-D.A.R.E. instruction could have the effect of contaminating the control group and confounding the effects of the treatment. Also, D.A.R.E. may be more or less effective in combination with other drug education initiatives.

The national study by Silvia and Thorne (1997) found that students were exposed to a wide range of drug prevention programs at all grade levels and that these programs were delivered inconsistently with wide variability. One statewide study (Donnermeyer forthcoming) reports evidence of a cumulative "booster effect"; that is, students who participated in multiple drug use prevention activities reported less drug use than students who reported less exposure to school-based activities. Unfortunately, this study is a one-shot cross-sectional design[4] that suffers from numerous threats to validity, including self-selection at the individual and school levels. Rather than rely on students' recall, which is vulnerable to considerable memory decay, the present study measures their exposure to supplemental drug education by interviewing their teachers on an annual basis.

Finally, previous D.A.R.E. evaluations have been plagued by a variety of data-analytic problems, ranging from improper use of statistical tests to a failure to use covariates or control variables in the analysis. Even the strongest D.A.R.E. evaluations typically suffer from the problem of treating individuals as the only unit of analysis when, in fact, students are "nested" within specific schools. Statistically minded critics have argued that evaluations of school-based programs fail to consider school-level effects in the analysis of data collected from individual students, a mistake that can lead to overly liberal estimates of program effects (Murray and Hannan, 1990). The current study corrects this problem through the use of multilevel analyses.

EARLIER FINDINGS FROM THIS LONGITUDINAL STUDY

In both published and unpublished technical reports, we have reported the effectiveness of this program at various measurement points. Given that the literature contains only one other long-term study of D.A.R.E., we believe it is important to summarize the earlier findings here.

Drug use outcomes. Immediately after graduation from the D.A.R.E. program, students in the experimental group reported a significant decline in recent (30-day) use of cigarettes relative to the control group, but no other changes were observed on a wide range of drug and alcohol behavior measures. Follow-up studies conducted one, two, and three years after the program found that D.A.R.E. had no main effects on any of the drug and alcohol measures.[5] After four years, some new drug use measures were added (considered inappropriate for younger students), and we found that D.A.R.E. students were significantly older when they "first got drunk" and when they started drinking "at least once a month." These delayed-onset effects, however, were not sustained at the five-year measurement point. In fact, after five years, the program was associated with unexpected adverse effects on the primary drug outcomes; that is, D.A.R.E. students, relative to controls, reported significantly higher scores on the Total Drug Use and Total Alcohol Use indexes, as well as the severity of drinking.

Mediating variables. The presence of D.A.R.E. was associated with a number of hypothesized changes in attitudes, beliefs, and social skills. At the immediate posttest, significant gains were observed on seven outcome measures. Students exposed to D.A.R.E. (in comparison with those in the control group) were more likely to report negative attitudes toward drugs in general, negative peer attitudes toward drugs, greater awareness of media influences concerning beer (and cigarettes), positive changes in self-esteem, greater assertiveness in social situations, and positive attitudes toward the police.

Over time, however, the effects of D.A.R.E. on attitudinal and psychological variables declined. After one year, the effects on self-esteem, assertiveness, and attitudes toward the police had dissipated. Four attitudinal effects continued after two years, but after three years, all such effects were gone with one exception: D.A.R.E. students continued to feel more confident in their ability to resist peer pressure. After four years, however, all effects relevant to attitudes, beliefs, and social skills were gone.

Academic and school behavior. Overall, with a few subgroup exceptions, D.A.R.E. had no effect on self-reported grades, the number of times students were in trouble with teachers, the number of times they skipped class, or the frequency of their involvement in delinquent or criminal activities.

The present article uses the entire six-year data set to estimate the effects of D.A.R.E. on students' attitudes, beliefs, social skills, and behaviors. To date, the results of this longitudinal study suggest that the effects of D.A.R.E. have waned over time. Some conflicting findings across the years may be due to interactions between program and maturational effects or may be due to slight improvements in the measurement and analytic procedures that were introduced by the researchers. Hence, the complete data set is used here to test the fundamental hypothesis that D.A.R.E. had a significant overall effect on theory-based and program-based outcomes. This study is not a wave-by-wave analysis (as previously completed) but rather addresses the basic question of whether, in the final analysis, students who participated in D.A.R.E. are different from students in the control group when all posttest data are analyzed.

METHODOLOGY

The Illinois D.A.R.E. evaluation was conducted as a randomized field experiment with one pretest and multiple planned posttests. The researchers identified 18 pairs of elementary schools representing urban, suburban, and rural areas in Illinois.[6] Schools were matched in each pair by type, ethnic composition, number of students with limited English proficiency, and the percentage of students from low-income families.[7] None of these schools had previously received D.A.R.E. For the 12 pairs of schools located in urban and suburban areas, one school in each pair was randomly assigned to receive D.A.R.E. in the spring of 1990; the remaining schools were placed in the control group. For each of the remaining 6 pairs, all in rural communities, a nonrandom assignment process was necessary due to logistic considerations that affect the availability of D.A.R.E. officers. The remaining six "treatment" schools were selected from rural areas in which D.A.R.E. officers were already assigned, and six more control schools were then selected from nearby counties or in the same county. The same matching variables were used for all schools in the study.

Two types of surveys were administered each year over the six years of data collection: one for students and one for specific teachers. The purpose of the student survey was to determine D.A.R.E.'s overall effects on students' beliefs, attitudes, and behaviors related to drug use. The student survey data are the primary focus of this longitudinal evaluation. The teacher survey provided additional information to assess the extent of students' exposure to post-D.A.R.E. drug prevention programs during each current academic year.

RECRUITMENT OF SCHOOLS AND STUDENTS

Two waves of data (pre-post) were collected from the 36 schools in the first year (1989–1990). In the second year (wave 3, 1991), when students left these elementary schools and entered middle school, the recruitment process was repeated with about 150 schools. In the third year and beyond, as students continued to move, transfer, and graduate, the number of schools in the sample fluctuated between 150 and 300. For the 1992–1993 academic year, most students of the evaluation sample entered high school for the first time, which required the research team to develop relationships with an entirely new group of school officials.

Similar to the initial procedure, letters were mailed to all high school superintendents and principals from the existing sample of schools, informing them of students' prior participation in the study, seeking their cooperation, requesting verification of enrollment, and explaining the research procedures. With all the transience in the sample, the research staff was continually making contacts with representatives from new schools. A financial inducement to participate in the study was offered to major schools, depending on the number of students participating from their school and the level of cooperation obtained.

In each school, eligible students were those who had participated in the wave 1 survey in 1989. Passive consent procedures (to obtain parental permission) were approved by the Institutional Review Board of the University of Illinois at Chicago. Consent forms were mailed to parents in January 1990 requesting their child's participation for three academic years. The letter informed parents of the purpose and

content of the project, stressed the confidentiality of the information to be collected,[8] and invited parents to return the form in a stamped envelope if they did not wish their child to participate. During the fall of 1993, a new consent letter was distributed to parents by mail or through the school, requesting their consent for the final three years of the study.

CHANGES IN THE EVALUATION

Two issues emerged in the drug education literature during the course of this evaluation. First, there was the possible "contaminating" influence of students being exposed to additional drug education programs in the years following their participation in D.A.R.E. Evaluators inevitably face "multiple treatment interference" (Cook and Campbell 1979) as they attempt to estimate the effects of D.A.R.E. in the context of subjects' exposure to other types of drug education.[9] With the rapid growth of drug education in recent years (including the enactment of legislation *requiring* that schools teach drug education), students in *both* the experimental (D.A.R.E.) group and the control group were frequently given some additional drug prevention education in subsequent years. To the extent that these supplemental programs had some favorable impact on students, they may have equalized the two groups on drug-related outcomes and therefore biased the evaluation findings in favor of the null hypothesis (i.e., increase the likelihood of finding no difference between the experimental and control groups). The reverse outcome is also possible. Researchers have lamented this problem in the literature but have rarely taken steps to measure or control for the effects of this "contamination." With additional survey work, we were able to develop a cumulative index of a student's exposure to supplemental drug education programs over *several* years. This measure also allowed us to test the "booster" hypothesis, namely, that additional drug education programs at the middle school and high school levels will boost or reinforce the antidrug messages and skills received in the D.A.R.E. program, and that this consistent reinforcement will make a difference in drug use behaviors during the years of greatest opportunity and pressure.

A second issue concerns the proper approach to data analysis. As noted earlier, statisticians now recommend that school-level effects be assessed when analyzing data collected from students representing multiple school settings. There is now considerable support for this argument among statisticians and other methodologists, who have developed new statistical programs for conducting multilevel analysis (e.g., Hedeker and Gibbons 1993). Furthermore, a time frame that carries well beyond the "nesting" of students in their original elementary schools, and involves a multiwave posttest analysis, is more likely to need some means of controlling for the difference between students who have been surveyed at all waves and those who dropped out or were absent at one or more waves.

Multilevel analysis software such as Hedeker's MIXOR and MIXREG has been developed in part to control for the attrition-related effects of being in the experimental or control group. Differential attrition may inflate or deflate estimates of program effectiveness. The results of logistic regression analysis indicate that attrition in the present data set was more likely among students in the control group, students from single-parent families, African Americans, Hispanics, urban students, and male students. However, an analysis of variance (ANOVA) found no support for the hypothesis that the participants' experimental

condition (0, 1) interacted with attrition status (0, 1) to influence any of the four major drug use measures (defined below). More important, we used a mixed-level analysis strategy that controls for violations of the assumption of random variance and accounts for both individual differences and clustering within schools (see details in Results section). This strategy incorporates the above-named variables as covariates in the regression equation.

DESCRIPTION OF STUDENT INSTRUMENT

The effects of D.A.R.E. were assessed with multiple mediating and outcome measures. The reliability and validity of these measures have been established in previous research and only slight modifications were made in the present investigation. The following measures were used:

- *Drug use behaviors*. Students were asked two sets of questions about their use of various drugs, including tobacco, alcohol, and other substances. The format for these questions was originally devised by Moskowitz and his colleagues (1981) for their Drug and Alcohol Survey and has been used in many studies. Students indicated whether they had used these substances in "their whole life" and "during the last month (30 days)." Students were instructed not to count the legitimate use of substances, either for religious services (i.e., wine) or because they were prescribed by a doctor (e.g., Librium™, codeine). A composite Alcohol Use Index was constructed from measures of four different types of alcohol: beer, wine, wine coolers, and hard liquor. For the 30-day Alcohol Use Index, a value of 1 indicated that the student had used one of four different types of alcoholic beverage during the past 30 days; a value of 2 indicated use of two or more. A 30-day Total Drug Use Index was a combination of students' responses to 11 different types of drugs and alcohol questions. (In addition to the four alcohol measures, this index included smokeless tobacco, marijuana, inhalants, hallucinogens, cocaine, "other drugs," and "alcohol to get drunk".) For the 30-day Total indexes, a value of 1 indicated that the student had admitted to one or two types of drug use during the past month, whereas 2 indicated three or more. Similarly, the lifetime measures were scored as continuous variables with ranges from 1 to 4 for Alcohol Use and 1 to 11 for Total Drug Use.

- *Onset of alcohol use.* To measure the onset of alcohol use, students were asked to indicate how old they were when they "first got drunk or very high using alcohol." They also reported how old they were when they began to drink "at least one drink at least once a month."

- *General attitudes toward drugs.* Students indicated their level of agreement with eight statements about drug use, which Moskowitz et al. (1981) originally developed for the Drug and Alcohol Survey. After reversing the scores of positively worded items, a scale was computed by summing student responses so that a high score represented a positive attitude toward drugs (alpha range = .78–.89).

- *Attitudes toward the use of specific drugs.* These questions, also extracted from the Drug and Alcohol Survey, assess specific attitudes toward those substances that youths are most likely to use. We grouped together (i.e., summed) student responses to questions about their attitudes toward beer, wine coolers, and wine. A higher score on this scale indicates a more positive attitude toward alcohol use (alpha range = .82–.90).

- *Perceived benefits and costs of using drugs.* Students were asked eight questions about their perceptions concerning the benefits and five questions about the costs of smoking cigarettes and drinking beer and wine coolers (Moskowitz et al. 1981). By adding student responses, four indexes were created to assess the perceived costs and benefits of using cigarettes and alcohol. A higher score indicates the undesired outcome of lower

perceived costs and higher perceived benefits of drug use (alpha range = .82–.86, .86–.90, .81–.86, .86–.90).

- *Perceptions of the media's influences on smoking and beer drinking.* These two constructs were measured by totaling student responses to questions about media influences on beer drinking and cigarette smoking (Bauman 1985). Students indicated what they thought (1) television and (2) newspapers and magazines made beer drinking and cigarette smoking "look like." Students who responded that the media made substance use look like "both a good and a bad thing to do" or "neither a good nor a bad thing to do" were scored as a neutral intermediate category between those who thought it was a "good" and a "bad" thing to do. A higher score indicates less student recognition of media attempts to make drugs look attractive (alpha range = .79–.82, .79–.85).

- *Self-esteem.* This construct was measured by adding six items extracted from the Rosenberg (1965) Self-Esteem Scale, which was developed for use with adolescents. Questions were modified slightly to make the language more appropriate for contemporary students. A higher score indicates higher self-esteem (alpha range = .80–.88).

- *Attitudes toward police.* Students rated five items extracted from the Attitudes Toward Police Scale developed by Faine and Bohlander (1989). The items were then summed, with a higher score indicating more favorable attitudes toward the police (alpha range = .84–.90).

- *Peer resistance skills.* Students responded to four hypothetical situations in which either their best friend or an acquaintance offered them either cigarettes or alcohol (Hansen 1989). They then rated their ability to "say no" on a 4-point scale ranging from *not sure at all* to *very sure.* The four items were summed, with a higher score indicating a greater confidence in one's ability to resist peer pressure to use substances (alpha range = .86–.90).

- *School performance.* Self-reported grades were used as a measure of school performance. The range was from 1 to 8, from less than D's (coded as 1) to mostly A's (coded as 8). A separate component of this study conducted at wave 4 revealed that self-reported grades were a good reflection of official grades (i.e., the correlation coefficient between the two was .60).

- *Delinquent and violent behavior.* A multi-item index was created to measure students' involvement in delinquent behaviors. Several of these items are derived from the High School Senior Survey conducted by the University of Michigan (Johnston, O'Malley, and Bachman 1988). Behaviors include group violence, theft of property under $50, theft of property over $50, shoplifting, and damage to school property. Participation in a group fight (involving one group or gang against another) was also treated as a separate measure of violence.

RESULTS

CHARACTERISTICS OF THE STUDENT SAMPLE

The results reported here are based on the combined sample of students surveyed at all waves. The wave-by-wave characteristics are shown in Table 2.

About two-thirds of the students were in sixth grade at the time of wave 1 data collection (with the remainder in fifth grade). Roughly 6 of 10 students indicated that they were living with both parents in the same household at all waves. Slightly more than half (52 percent) were exposed to D.A.R.E. in the spring of 1990, whereas the remaining students were assigned to

TABLE 2:   Characteristics of Students[a]—All Waves

	1	2	3	4	5	6	7	8
Gender								
Male	51.1	50.7	50.4	50.4	51.1	48.5	48.2	49.1
Female	48.9	49.3	49.6	49.6	48.9	51.5	51.8	50.9
Race/ethnicity								
White	51.1	51.5	50.4	52.1	54.6	58.6	60.2	62.8
African American	29.8	25.9	29.1	28.6	26.7	25.3	22.9	21.0
Hispanic	10.8	9.8	10.8	10.7	10.7	11.5	8.7	10.6
Other	8.4	12.9	8.8	8.7	7.2	7.4	6.7	5.6
Wave 1 Grade								
Fifth	34.4	35.4	33.6	33.2	35.9	30.5	30.1	31.0
Sixth	65.6	64.6	66.4	66.8	64.1	69.5	69.9	69.0
Intact family								
Yes	63.8	59.9	59.1	60.0	60.6	62.4	61.3	61.7
No	36.2	40.1	40.9	40.0	39.4	37.6	38.7	38.3
Area								
Urban	41.0	38.9	39.2	38.0	36.0	29.9	28.8	27.1
Suburban	35.7	36.6	35.8	36.8	37.4	41.5	40.4	41.6
Rural	23.2	24.5	25.0	25.2	26.5	28.5	30.8	31.4
Group								
D.A.R.E.[b]	54.2	51.6	53.8	53.2	53.1	53.0	52.4	52.2
Control	45.8	48.4	46.2	46.8	46.9	47.0	47.6	47.8

[a]Figures are percentages.

[b]D.A.R.E. = Drug Abuse Resistance Education.

the control group. Attrition over the six years was most noticeable among the urban and African American samples.

ANALYSIS STRATEGY

We used a random-effects ordinal regression model that allowed us to examine the relationship between D.A.R.E. and individual-level outcomes while controlling for random effects. We used the MIXOR and MIXREG programs, developed at the University of Illinois at Chicago by Donald Hedeker and his colleagues. The program uses a maximum marginal likelihood solution and is applicable to both probit and logistic response functions (see Hedeker and Gibbons 1993; Hedeker, Gibbons, and Davis 1991). Maximum marginal likelihood regression was used within the framework of multilevel analysis. Each substantive model included an indicator for whether the student had received D.A.R.E., plus a set of binary-coded control variables that included race/ethnicity, gender, family structure (intact vs. nonintact), and metropolitan status (urban, suburban, or rural).

Merging waves. Data from the seven posttest surveys were merged. The analysis strategy involved a level and trend comparison of the D.A.R.E. and control groups across all posttest waves. Cases were sorted by student identification number so that there would be up to seven observations per student, with each observation representing a different wave of posttest data.

Before adding each wave to the composite data set, a "time" variable was created, with all the observations for a particular wave receiving the same time value. After merging the seven posttest waves, the time variable was recoded so that wave 2 was time 0, wave 3 was time 1,

and so on up to wave 8, or time 6. The time variable was the basis for determining the existence of significant changes in attitudes or drug usage over time, and of controlling for this trend in the comparison of D.A.R.E. group and control group responses. The basic model for all attitude measures, and for the delinquency index, can be simply expressed as

$$Y = b_0 + b_1 \text{ Time} + b_2 \text{ D.A.R.E.} + b_3 \text{ (D.A.R.E.)} * \text{(Time)} + \text{demographic and area covariates,}$$

where Y is the scale mean for the dependent variable or outcome measure, b_0 is the wave 2 or time 0 mean, controlling for the demographic and area covariates, b_1 is the rate of change per wave or year, b_2 is the effect of D.A.R.E. on the wave 2 or time 0 mean, and b_3 is the effect of D.A.R.E. on the rate of change per wave or year. D.A.R.E. is equal to 0 or 1, where 0 = control group and 1 = D.A.R.E. group. When D.A.R.E. is 0, all terms in the equation containing D.A.R.E. become 0.

For analyses where the dependent variable was some type of alcohol and total substance use, a binary variable for high school years (grades 9 through 12) was added and interacted with time in the same manner as the D.A.R.E. variable. The high school variable was added to control for the dramatic increases in drug usage during those years.

To test for differential effects on female, African American, and Hispanic students, these demographic covariates were interacted with D.A.R.E. and added to a second model. The area covariates were interacted with D.A.R.E. in a third model to test for D.A.R.E. effect (b2) differences in rural, urban, and suburban areas.

Exposure to supplemental drug education. At each wave, beginning with wave 3 (one year after exposure to D.A.R.E.), a survey of the "most knowledgeable" local school teacher was conducted to determine the number of hours of additional drug education that students received at their current schools: The number of hours per week was multiplied by the number of weeks of drug education. The cumulative supplemental drug education variable was computed by adding the number of hours at that wave to the number of hours at each preceding wave. To correct for skewness, these figures were then grouped into five dosage levels at intervals of 36 cumulative hours, with the exception that the highest level included all students with more than 144 cumulative hours. In separate models, this variable was also interacted with D.A.R.E. to estimate the effect of D.A.R.E. plus supplemental drug education in relation to the effect of supplemental drug education only.[10]

Recoding. Several attitudinal and drug use scales were skewed and therefore necessitated recoding before the regression analysis. The Delinquency Index and Peer Resistance scales were recoded into 3-point scales (1–3) with roughly equal numbers of cases in each group. Four-point scales were created for Perceived Benefits of Alcohol and Cigarettes, General Attitude toward Drugs, and Self-Esteem. Again, the groups were of similar size.

Clustering and random variance. A variable representing the 36 original schools was retained to estimate the effect of students being "nested" within particular schools at the time of exposure or non-exposure to D.A.R.E. (see Hedeker and Gibbons 1993; Murray and Hannan 1990 for a detailed discussion of this issue). It was expected that this "clustering" effect would have eroded over time and that the principal violation of the assumption of

constant variance would be subject specific rather than school specific. The results of regression analysis at specific time points largely confirmed this expectation. The other time points and all other scales and usage measurements had intracluster correlations below .05, and most were well below that level.[11]

This made a three-level analysis unnecessary, but student identification numbers were used for bilevel analysis. With continuous outcome measures, regressor effects were estimated while controlling for the effect of subject-level variance in the constant term and over time.[12] The random effects were statistically significant in all models. Hence, controlling for subject-level variance differences across waves was an important analytic contribution to all models used to estimate program effects.

EFFECTS ON HYPOTHESIZED MEDIATING VARIABLES

We tested the hypothesis that D.A.R.E. would have a sustained effect on the variables that are assumed to mediate the relationship between drug education and drug use, namely, students' attitudes, beliefs, and social skills pertaining to drug use. On the whole, the results did not support this hypothesis (see Table 3). When controlling for changes in these variables over time and for changes in cumulative exposure to supplemental drug education, only one significant D.A.R.E. effect remained. Specifically, students who participated in D.A.R.E. were more likely than students in the control group to report awareness of media efforts to make beer appear attractive. Even here, the D.A.R.E. interaction with time (.01**) was significant in the opposite direction, suggesting that the sophistication of the control group would eventually catch up to the D.A.R.E. group. All other D.A.R.E. effects were small and nonsignificant.

TABLE 3:   **Main Effects of D.A.R.E.[a] and Supplemental Drug Education (SDE) on Attitudes, Beliefs, and Social Skills[b]**

Outcome Scale	Adjusted Mean Wave 2	Slope (TIME)	D.A.R.E., D.A.R.E. by Time	SDE
Attitudes toward Police	3.23	−.10**	−.02, .01	−.03**
Toward Specific Drugs[c]	1.52	.11**	−.00, −.00	.03*
Benefits of Alcohol	1.72	.08**	.05, −.01	.04*
Benefits of Cigarettes	1.86	−.04**	.05, −.00	.02
Cost of Alcohol	1.47	.08**	.01, .00	.00
Cost of Cigarettes	1.68	.11**	.05, −.00	.03**
Delinquency Index	1.92	−.04**	−.03, −.01	.04**
General Attitude	1.55	.12**	.04, −.02	.02
Media Influence on				
Beer	1.39	−.03**	−.07**, .01**	−.01**
Cigarettes	1.39	−.02**	−.03, .00	−.01**
Self-Eastern	2.74	.02	−.04, .03	.01
Peer Resistance Skills	2.27	.05**	.02, −.01	−.00

NOTE: Slope indicates direction and significance of change per wave. Level 2 observations = 1,254 for most analyses.

[a]D.A.R.E. = Drug Abuse Resistance Education.
[b]Regression analysis controls for gender (female), African American, Hispanic, intact family, and rural and suburban schools.
[c]Current scale includes only beer, wine, and wine coolers.

*p < .05
**p < .01.

Although not posited as a mediating variable, we also examined the impact of D.A.R.E. on violence and delinquency prevention. Our Delinquency Index, which measures incidents of theft, vandalism, and/or participation in group violence, showed change over time in the desired direction, but not as a result of D.A.R.E. Also, a separate analysis of individual and group violence revealed no D.A.R.E. effects. Previous evidence that African American students reported less group violence after D.A.R.E was no longer statistically significant.

In addition, we examined the hypothesis that D.A.R.E. would be able to improve academic performance. Self-reported grades, on a scale of 1 (*below D*) to 8 (*mostly A's*),

were used to measure academic performance. Although the trend was favorable, the overall results did not support this hypothesis. In the face of a significant drop in grades over time (.07 per wave), the D.A.R.E. effect was positive (.09 per wave) but was only significantly higher for rural students (.29*).

A test of the booster hypothesis revealed that exposure to supplemental drug education appears to have been largely counterproductive: Every additional 36 hours of cumulative drug education; were associated with significantly more negative attitudes toward police; more positive attitudes toward drugs, alcohol, and cigarettes; and more delinquency (see Table 3). The only favorable outcome was that students with more supplemental drug education reported greater awareness of attempted media influences on drug use.

Whether supplemental drug education is causing the adverse change in drug-related attitudes or whether these pro-drug attitudes (and perhaps behaviors) are driving some schools to introduce more supplemental drug education is unclear. In any event, these findings transform the "booster" hypothesis into a question of whether D.A.R.E. is able to neutralize the undesirable perceptions and behaviors associated with follow-up booster programs. The analysis of D.A.R.E.'s interaction with supplemental drug education suggests that the core program may be having this effect (see Table 4). The interaction model separates the joint effects of D.A.R.E. and supplemental drug education from the independent cumulative effect of supplemental drug education alone. The result is that the negative and positive coefficients, respectively, tend to cancel each other out. The Perceived Benefits of Alcohol index, for example, is higher by .08 for each dosage level of supplemental drug education without D.A.R.E., but only .01 higher (.08** minus .07*) for students who participated in D.A.R.E. However, D.A.R.E.'s significant interaction effects with supplemental drug education were accompanied by adverse changes in D.A.R.E.'s interaction with the time variable. This will be discussed further in the analysis of the drug use outcomes.

D.A.R.E. also appears to have differential subgroup effects. Curiously, D.A.R.E. has been less effective in communicating the costs associated with alcohol and cigarette use to African American participants

TABLE 4: D.A.R.E.[a]-by-Supplemental Drug Education (SDE) Interaction Effects on Attitudes, Beliefs, and Social Skills[b]

Outcome Scale	Adjusted Mean Wave 2	D.A.R.E., D.A.R.E. by Time		SDE	D.A.R.E., and SDE
Attitudes toward Police	3.22	−.01,	.00	−.04**	.02
Toward Specific Drugs[c]	1.53	−.02,	.02	.06**	−.05**
Benefits of Alcohol	1.73	.03,	.02	.08**	−.07*
Benefits of Cigarettes	1.88	.03,	.03	.05**	−.06**
Cost of Alcohol	1.48	−.00,	.02	.03*	−.05**
Cost of Cigarettes	1.70	.03,	.03*	.06**	−.07**
Delinquency Index	1.91	−.03,	−.01	.03*	.01
General Attitude	1.55	.04,	−.01	.02	−.02
Media Influence on					
Beer	1.39	−.07**	.01*	−.01**	.00
Cigarettes	1.39	−.03,	.00	−.01*	.00
Self-Esteem	2.73	−.02,	.01	−.00	.04
Peer Resistance Skills	2.26	.04,	−.02	−.02	.04*

NOTE: Level 2 observations = 1,254 for most analyses.

[a]D.A.R.E. = Drug Abuse Resistance Education.

[b]Regression analysis controls for time, D.A.R.E. by time, gender (female), African American, Hispanic, intact family, and rural and suburban schools.

[c]Current scale includes only beer, wine, and wine coolers.

*p < .05. ** p < .01.

yet more effective in helping this group recognize media attempts to promote beer and cigarettes. Hispanic D.A.R.E. graduates had a significantly lower delinquency score than the reference group. D.A.R.E. appears to have had the desired effect of enhancing self-esteem and one's perceived ability to resist peer pressure in urban and rural areas but appears to have had negligible or counterproductive effects in suburban areas. Suburban D.A.R.E. graduates also had a significantly higher delinquency score than non-D.A.R.E. suburban students.

EFFECTS ON DRUG USE

We tested the hypothesis that D.A.R.E. would have a sustained preventive effect on drug use behaviors. All analyses of drug use activity had to control for the reality of increased usage over time, as well as for dramatic shifts in level and rate of increase during the high school years (grades 9–12). Students moving into and through the high school years provided the most powerful explanation for the increases in drug use beginning at wave 5, or what was grade 9 for most students. As noted earlier, two composite Alcohol Use indexes were constructed to measure the use of four types of alcohol in the past 30 days and

during the participant's lifetime. In addition, two composite Total Drug Use indexes were developed to measure usage of 11 types of drugs and alcohol in the past 30 days and during the participant's lifetime.

The results provide no support for the drug prevention hypothesis (see Table 5). After controlling for the effect of the high school years (grades 9–12) and supplemental drug education, we found that D.A.R.E. had no significant impact on any of the four primary drug use scales. That is, students who participated in D.A.R.E. were no different from students in the control group with regard to their recent and lifetime use of drugs and alcohol.

The ineffectiveness of supplemental drug education was apparent once again, as cumulative exposure to these activities is associated with significantly higher levels of composite drug use. The apparent neutralizing effect of D.A.R.E. is again evident. As shown in Table 6, students whose supplemental drug education was preceded by D.A.R.E. were less likely to use drugs than students in the control group who were exposed to additional drug education. However, the reader should be cautioned that the result of combining D.A.R.E and supplemental drug education is to return students to the level of drug

TABLE 5: Main Effects of D.A.R.E.[a] and Supplemental Drug Education (SDE) on Drug Use[b]

Outcome Scale	Adjusted Mean Wave 2	Slope (TIME)	D.A.R.E., D.A.R.E. by Time	SDE
30-Day Alcohol Use	0.33	.02	.07, −.01	.03**
Lifetime Alcohol Use	1.07	.13**	.11, −.02	.09**
30-Day Total Drug Use	0.34	.03	.06, −.01	.04**
Lifetime Total Drug Use	1.51	.22**	.15, −.04	.15**

NOTE: Level 2 observations = 1,254 for most analyses.

[a]D.A.R.E. = Drug Abuse Resistance Education.

[b]Regression analysis controls for gender (female), African American, Hispanic, intact family, rural and suburban schools, high school grades, and high school grades by time.

*$p < .05$. ** $p < .01$.

TABLE 6:   D.A.R.E.[a]-by-Supplemental Drug Education (SDE) Interaction Effects on Drug Use[b]

Outcome Scale	Adjusted Mean Wave 2	D.A.R.E., D.A.R.E. by Time		SDE	D.A.R.E. and SDE
30-Day Alcohol Use	0.34	.05,	.01	.05**	−.04
Lifetime Alcohol Use	1.09	.07,	.03	.14**	−.10**
30-Day Total Use	0.36	.04,	.02	.07**	−.06**
Lifetime Total Use	1.55	.07,	.07	.25**	−.22**

NOTE: Level 2 observations = 1,254 for most analyses.

[a]D.A.R.E. = Drug Abuse Resistance Education.

[b]Regression analysis controls for time, gender (female), African American, Hispanic, intact family, rural and suburban schools, high school grades, and high school grades by time.

**p < .01.

use that would be expected without any drug education. Also, the interaction of D.A.R.E. with the time variable is negative when D.A.R.E. and supplemental drug education effects are estimated separately, but it shows adverse effects when D.A.R.E. and supplemental drug education are interacted (see Table 6).

This peculiarity suggested that wave-by-wave regression estimates and means comparisons should be made. When this was done for estimates of total lifetime drug use, it was found that D.A.R.E.'s interaction with supplemental drug education was only statistically significant at wave 4 and dissipated to the point of being positive (i.e., adverse) at wave 8. Wave-by-wave means comparisons revealed that higher

levels of supplemental drug education were not necessarily associated with greater drug use *within* waves, and the apparent adverse effect may be due to the *overall* correlation of supplemental drug education with increased drug use over time.

There were few differences in D.A.R.E.'s impact on drug use across different communities. The only significant subgroup effect occurred with suburban D.A.R.E. students. As shown in Table 7, suburban students who participated in D.A.R.E. reported significantly higher rates of drug use on all four composite indexes than suburban students who did not participate in the program.[13] Controlling for cumulative exposure to supplemental drug education reduced the probability

TABLE 7:   D.A.R.E.[a]-by-Area Interaction Effects on Drug Use[b]

30-Day Alcohol Use	0.45	.01	−.03	.09*
Lifetime Alcohol Use	1.25	.09	−.04	.18*
30-Day Total Drug Use	0.48	−.01	−.05	.09*
Lifetime Total Drug Use	1.82	.06	−.17	.28*

NOTE: Level 2 observations = 1,767 for most analyses.

[a]D.A.R.E. = Drug Abuse Resistance Education.

[b]Regression analysis controls for time, D.A.R.E. by time, gender (female), African American, Hispanic, intact family, area, D.A.R.E. by area, high school grades, and high school grades by time.

*p < .05.

value to marginally significant ($p < .10$) for three of the four measures, leaving untouched the apparent adverse effect on the Lifetime Total Drug Use index. We should emphasize that the effect sizes are small. Suburban participation in D.A.R.E. is associated with an increased level of drug use of 3 to 5 percentage points on average, depending on the type of drug.

To rule out the possibility that D.A.R.E. might be having beneficial effects on specific types of drugs or alcohol (e.g., cigarette smoking), but not on composite indicators, we conducted a series of statistical tests on individual drug use items. Given the distribution of responses, these items were appropriate for treatment as dichotomous variables and hence were subjected to multilevel logistic regression using the MIXOR program (Hedeker and Gibbons 1993). As shown in Table 8, the results are consistent with the previous analyses and provide no support for the hypothesis that D.A.R.E. would have a sustained preventive impact on specific types of drug use. Controlling for the powerful effect of the high school years (grades 9 through 12), supplemental drug education was associated with significantly higher usage likelihoods. The *net* effect of interacting D.A.R.E. and supplemental drug education were odds ratios close to 1.00 (i.e., no different from the control group) for all 10 measures. Only three of these interactions differed significantly from the effect of supplemental drug education alone, and they were accompanied by significant adverse shifts in the interaction of D.A.R.E. and time.

TABLE 8:   D.A.R.E.[a]-by-Supplemental Drug Education (SDE) Interaction Effects on Drug Use Likelihoods[b]

Outcome Measure	High School Grades	D.A.R.E.	SDE	D.A.R.E. and SDE
Last 30 days				
Beer	1.96**	1.07	1.21**	1.05
Cigarettes	2.54**	0.92	1.25**	1.04
Drinking to get drunk	4.09**	1.16	1.16*	1.00
Marijuana	1.83	0.84	1.67	1.11
Smokeless tobacco	1.36	0.73[c]	1.46**	0.89**
Lifetime				
Beer	1.50[d]	1.08	1.25**	1.11
Cigarettes	2.35**	1.14[c]	1.48**	1.03**
Drinking to get drunk	3.53**	1.44	1.12	0.98
Marijuana	1.21	0.72	1.14	1.10
Smokeless tobacco	0.65**[d]	1.01[c]	1.42**	0.89**

NOTE: Level 2 observations = 1,254 for most analyses.

[a]D.A.R.E. = Drug Abuse Resistance Education.

[b]Logistic regression analysis controls for time, gender (female), African American, Hispanic, intact family, rural and suburban schools, high school grades by time, and D.A.R.E. by time.

[c]Interaction of D.A.R.E. with time is positive and statistically significant.

[d]Interaction of high school grades with time is positive and statistically significant.

*$p < .05$. **$p < .01$.

Finally, we tested the hypothesis that D.A.R.E. could delay the onset of drinking alcohol—measures believed to be important as students reached high school. The study measured the age at which students first "got drunk" and started having "at least one drink at least once a month." Students in the control group first got drunk and started drinking regularly between the ages of 14 and 15. The effect of D.A.R.E. on these two measures was not statistically significant. These small changes were in the positive direction for delaying the onset of getting drunk (.11) and in the negative direction for delaying regular drinking (–.05).

SUMMARY AND CONCLUSIONS

We believe the findings from this study are especially important given the centrality of D.A.R.E. to the national drug control policies of the United States and dozens of other countries. These results are also noteworthy because of the paucity of controlled longitudinal studies that can answer the most fundamental question: Can this popular school-based program prevent drug use at the stage in adolescent development when drugs become available and are widely used, namely, during the high school years? Unfortunately, the answer to this question is "No." Specifically, the main finding is that levels of drug use (using a variety of measures and analyses) did not differ as a function of whether students participated in D.A.R.E. This outcome confirms the results of previous controlled evaluations and goes further to provide an extended test of the D.A.R.E. hypothesis. Across many settings and research projects, D.A.R.E. has been unable to show consistent preventive effects on drug use, and the observed effects have been small in size and short-lived.

We can only speculate about the reasons for not finding larger and more persistent effects from this program. First, there may be some degree of theory failure with respect to curriculum content or instructional methods. Ennett and her colleagues (1994) argue that the D.A.R.E. curriculum uses less interactive methods (e.g., peer discussions) than programs that have been shown to be more effective in preventing drug use. Hansen and McNeal (1997) argue that the components of the curriculum should be revisited because "D.A.R.E. is either targeting inappropriate mediating processes or insufficiently impacting appropriate mediating constructs." On the basis of an empirical analysis, they argue that several mediating variables should be given more attention because of their established ability to affect substance use onset, including the participant's personal commitment to avoid drug use, erroneous perceptions about the prevalence and acceptability of drug use, and the belief that drug use would be incongruent with one's values and lifestyle.

In the present study, we found that D.A.R.E. was able to have both immediate and short-term effects (up to two years) on several mediating variables (e.g., resistance skills, attitudes about drugs), but nearly all these effects dissipated with the passage of time and did not survive into the critical high school years. Unfortunately, the absence of good booster programs creates a "catch-22" for the elementary school D.A.R.E. program, as researchers attempt to link mediating variables to drug use. In fifth and sixth grades, the base rates for drug use are generally too low to detect program effects, but by the time drug use levels reach measurable variability (two to three years later), the likelihood of sustained effects from the original program has been dramatically reduced in the absence of sound reinforcement programs.

D.A.R.E. advocates argue that the null findings from this research provide evidence that *more* D.A.R.E. programming (not less) is needed at the junior high and high school levels to reinforce the lessons of the not-so-effective core program. Whether police officers can be effective with older students, who show considerably less respect for authority, is uncertain. Hence, there is a compelling need to evaluate these D.A.R.E. and other booster programs before widespread implementation. Unfortunately, the practice of school-based drug education at these higher grade levels is dismal (despite the availability of promising prototype programs), which may partially account for the observed positive correlation between supplemental drug education and drug use. However, self-selection is a simpler and more plausible explanation for this finding, suggesting that schools experiencing larger drug problems are more likely to initiate drug education programs. In any event, our data suggest that these cumulative prevention efforts are, at best, ineffective at combating the dramatic rise in drug use as youths become older.[14]

Despite some correlations in the data, it would be a mistake to conclude that D.A.R.E. either neutralizes the possible adverse effects of supplemental drug education or (depending on your choice of explanations) has beneficial effects on schools where the worst drug problems have led administrators to select additional booster programs. A closer inspection of the data revealed that the interactions of D.A.R.E. and supplemental drug education are likely due to the nonrandom application of dosage levels across different subgroups.[15] Because levels of exposure to supplemental drug education were not controlled in the research design, we are unable to draw any strong conclusions about their impact in the same way that we can about D.A.R.E. On this note, we should emphasize that D.A.R.E. did not prevent drug use *regardless* of whether the analysis controlled for students' exposure to supplemental drug education.[16]

One of the limitations of the current study is that it focuses on the effectiveness of a D.A.R.E. curriculum that has since been modified by D.A.R.E. America. Changes introduced in 1994 were arguably small, but additional research is needed to determine whether the new curriculum and the accompanying modifications to officer training were sufficient to enhance the effectiveness of the elementary school program.

The present study found that D.A.R.E. had the most beneficial effects on urban children and the fewest beneficial effects on suburban children. In fact, we found some evidence of a possible boomerang effect among suburban kids. That is, suburban students who were D.A.R.E. graduates scored higher than suburban students in the control group on all four major drug use measures. Because schools were carefully matched and then randomly assigned within the same suburban communities, we are doubtful that these effects can be explained by factors such as sampling or other design issues. Furthermore, because this set of findings was replicated in a separate study (to be published), with completely different samples of students, we believe it should not be ignored in future research.

Members of our research team conducted classroom observations in several schools in an attempt to understand and explain the observed differences between urban and suburban schools. In this preliminary study, blind observers looked for possible differences in instructor teaching styles, student responses, and school environments. Although we did not find striking differences in classroom instruction or teacher-student interaction, other differences were noteworthy: (1) At urban schools, D.A.R.E. officers tended to spend more time on the school grounds and typically interacted more with students outside the classroom, including the playground setting. In contrast, D.A.R.E. officers in suburban schools were quick to move on to another school. In essence, students in urban schools had more opportunity to "connect" or "bond" with the D.A.R.E. officer than did their suburban counterparts and to see them as part of the school environment. (2) At urban schools, D.A.R.E. was typically offered to students at the fifth-grade level, whereas in suburban schools, it was offered at the sixth-grade level. Given the well-documented differences in student academic achievement and teaching resources (favoring the suburban schools), one would expect to see the standardized D.A.R.E. curriculum administered at the fifth-grade level in the suburbs. Under the current arrangement, our informal interviews suggest that suburban students are less impressed with the D.A.R.E. officers, perhaps because students' expectations for teaching performance and their own academic progress are substantially higher than in the typical inner-city school. Other unconfirmed hypotheses offered to explain the suburban boomerang effect include the possibility of (1) more negative attitudes about police in the suburbs, which would undermine the instructor's credibility; (2) a greater need to rebel against authority figures and the "Say No to Drugs" message; and/or (3) less knowledge about drugs and, therefore, a greater fascination with drug paraphernalia and drug information introduced by the D.A.R.E. officer.

If these urban-suburban differences are replicated in future research, one policy implication is that a standardized curriculum and training package may need to be modified or tailored in response to community differences. Although standardization is one of D.A.R.E.'s greatest strengths, too much uniformity may limit its effectiveness. Given the stark reality of very large differences between communities in their cultural/ethnic composition, income levels, family problems, and quality of local education, the idea that "one size fits all" may need to be reexamined in this particular field. At this point in time, the best available evidence suggests that D.A.R.E. may have different effects in different communities and may need to be adjusted accordingly.

Collectively, these findings suggest that it may be time to reexamine our drug prevention policies and practices. Our society, searching for a silver bullet or a panacea to the drug problem, has expected far too much from a single program. Compounding the problem, parents, educators, and police officers have confused program popularity with program effectiveness. Drug prevention experts, both researchers and practitioners, have worked closely with the federal government to outline many of the key components of effective prevention strategies (e.g., Sloboda and David 1997), and this dialogue is continuing. Whether these research-based prototypes can be implemented and sustained on a large scale, producing consistently favorable results under real-world conditions, remains an empirical question. The D.A.R.E. organization has demonstrated that it can create a viable delivery system, supported by a strong marketing package. One important question is whether police officers can deliver a more effective drug prevention program if the best available knowledge and curricula are used. Thus, a logical next step is for the federal government to fund a large randomized field trial in diverse settings, testing various prototype curriculum elements with alternative delivery systems. In the meantime, concerned communities, armed with the best available knowledge about effective program practices, can develop their own prevention plans, keeping in mind that there are no simple solutions to complex social problems.

Notes

1. This legislative requirement seems directly responsive to a major Department of Education study that recommended that

> [t]he Safe and Drug-Free Schools and Communities Act (SDFSCA) program at the national level should consider supporting and encouraging more use of approaches that the research has found to be effective and less use of approaches that do not have strong evidence of effectiveness. (Silvia and Thorne 1997:E-27).

2. The study of Wysong, Aniskiewicz, and Wright (1994) was a notable exception, suggesting a possible "boomerang" effect with regard to use of hallucinogens. Also, Donnermeyer (forthcoming) was not specifically evaluating the Drug Abuse Resistance Education (D.A.R.E.) program, but some portion of his sample was exposed to the program.

3. In one evaluation, the sample was supplemented via "random replacement" after high attrition between pretest and posttest (Nyre, Rose, and Bolus 1990).

4. Students in the 11th grade were asked to recall their exposure to drug education classes over the previous six years.

5. After three years, we reported that the presence of D.A.R.E. was associated with favorable changes on the Total Drug Use and Total Alcohol Use indexes *after controlling for* students' exposure to subsequent drug education. A note of caution: This was our first attempt to measure post-D.A.R.E. drug education, and we used a dichotomous indicator of educational activity in the current year only. After four years, a multiyear composite index was constructed to capture *cumulative* exposure to drug education, and the D.A.R.E. effects reported the previous year were not replicated under these conditions.

6. Using the definitions employed by the Metropolitan Statistical Area (MSA) method of the Office of Management and Budget, two "large central cities" (i.e., population greater than 400,000) were selected as urban test sites, Chicago and East St. Louis. The eligible suburban communities were defined as those areas surrounding Chicago and within the Chicago MSA, which has a population of 8 million. Two of the four suburban areas selected could be considered "central cities" (i.e., population greater than 50,000),

but they were included because of their primary status as suburbs of Chicago. For all urban and suburban communities in the sample, schools were matched with other schools in the same community/city. Using the MSA method, "rural" was defined as any non-MSA. Rural schools were selected from non-MSA communities in eight northern and central Illinois counties where a D.A.R.E. officer was within driving distance.

7. Aggregate family income, by school, was determined by the percentage of students in that school who were eligible for the free or reduced-price lunch program of the United States Department of Agriculture.

8. We requested and received a Certificate of Confidentiality from the National Institute on Drug Abuse (NIDA), which provides broad legal protections against any efforts to breach the confidentiality of our records.

9. The only other longitudinal study to track students for more than two years discovered that students in the control group received drug education as part of their health science curriculum in the first year (Clayton, Cattarello, and Walden 1991).

10. Because supplemental drug education data were not gathered at wave 2, models with supplemental drug education effects included had about 500 fewer level 2 observations.

11. Only two attitude scales, Attitudes toward Police and Attitude toward Specific Drugs, had intra-cluster correlations as high as .05 (.055 and .052, respectively, at time 0, wave 2).

12. The sole exception was for estimates of the age at which the student had "at least one drink at least once a month." The random effect over time for this outcome measure—and for all dichotomous outcome measures—was too small to be estimated.13. Table 7 actually contains the results of three different models. Each area was used, in turn, as the reference category, controlling for the D.A.R.E. interaction with each of the other two areas. Urban was the reference category for the adjusted mean at wave 2.

14. For most students, we are fairly certain that their supplemental drug education did not include a D.A.R.E. curriculum or any of the prototype programs that are being recommended as alternatives to D.A.R.E. Rather, most of these activities were local efforts that, in our opinion, were not well conceived (i.e., not based on scientific research and lacking important content) or were poorly implemented.

15. Specifically, there was some evidence that levels of supplemental drug education were uneven across experimental conditions, metropolitan status, and time, leaving permanent effects on cumulative exposure measures across waves. A cumulative index can only increase consistent with trends in drug use.

16. We reported primarily models that controlled for supplemental drug education (because of the importance of the booster hypothesis), but the analyses performed without it produced very similar results.

References

Aniskiewicz, R. E. and E. E. Wysong. 1987. *Project DARE Evaluation Report: Kokomo Schools Spring, 1987.* Kokomo: Indiana University at Kokomo, Department of Sociology.

Anonymous. 1987. *Project DARE Evaluation, Spring, 1987.* Pittsburgh, PA.

Bangert-Drowns, R. L. 1988. "The Effects of School-Based Substance Abuse Education: A Meta-Analysis." *Journal of Drug Education* 18:243–65.

Battjes, R. J. 1985. "Prevention of Adolescent Drug Abuse." *The International Journal of the Addictions* 20:1113–24.

Bauman, K. 1985. *A Study of Cigarette Smoking Behavior among Youth: Adolescent Questionnaire.* Chapel Hill: University of North Carolina, School of Public Health, Department of Maternal and Child Health.

Becker, H. R., M. E. Agopian, and S. Yeh. 1992. "Impact Evaluation of Drug Abuse Resistance Education (DARE)." *Journal of Drug Education* 22:283–91.

Botvin, G. J. 1990. "Substance Abuse Prevention: Theory, Practice, and Effectiveness." Pp. 461–519 in *Drugs and Crime*, edited by M. Tonry and J. Q. Wilson. Chicago: University of Chicago Press.

Bruvold, W. H. and T. G. Rundall. 1988. "A Meta-Analysis and Theoretical Review of School Based Tobacco and Alcohol Intervention Programs." *Psychology and Health* 2:53–78.

Carstens, S. J., D. J. Pecchia, and L. R. Rohach. 1989. *DARE-Drug Abuse Resistance Education—Is It Working?* Crystal, MN: Robinsdale Area Schools, Independent School District 281.

Clayton, R. R., A. Cattarello, L. E. Day, and K. P. Walden. 1991. "Persuasive Communication and Drug Prevention: An Evaluation of the DARE Program." Pp. 295–313 in *Persuasive Communication and Drug Abuse Prevention*, edited by L. Donoher, H. Sypher, and W. Bukoski. Hillsdale, NJ: Lawrence Erlbaum.

Clayton, R. R. 1987. "Project DARE in Lexington: Evaluation of the Pilot Phase." Department of Sociology, University of Kentucky, Lexington. Unpublished report.

Clayton, R. R., A. M. Cattarello, and P. Walden. 1991. "Sensation Seeking as a Potential Mediating Variable for School-Based Prevention Intervention: A Two-Year Follow-up of D.A.R.E." *Health Communications* 29:229–39.

Clayton, R. R., A. M. Cattarello, and B. M. Johnstone. 1996. "The Effectiveness of Drug Abuse Resistance Education (Project D.A.R.E.): Five-Year Follow-up Results. *Preventive Medicine* 25:307–18.

Cook, T. D. and D. T. Campbell. 1979. *Quasi-Experimentation: Design and Analysis Issues for Field Settings.* Chicago: Rand McNally.

Correll, J. K. 1990. "Drug Abuse Resistance Education D.A.R.E." Department of Defense Dependents-M Evaluation Report, Washington, DC.

DeJong, W. 1987. "A Short-Term Evaluation of Project D.A.R.E. (Drug Abuse Resistance Education): Preliminary Indications of Effectiveness." *Journal of Drug Education* 17:279–94.

Donnermeyer, J. F. Forthcoming. "Prevention Education and Substance Use." *Journal of School Health* 68.

Dukes, R., J. Stein, and J. Ullman. 1996. "The Long Term Effects of DARE. *Evaluation Review* 20:49–66.

_. 1997. "The Long Term Effects of DARE. *Evaluation Review* 21:473–500.

Ennett, S. T., N. S. Tobler, C. L. Ringwalt, and R. L. Flewelling. 1994. "How Effective Is Drug Abuse Resistance Education? A Meta-Analysis of Project D.A.R.E. Outcome Evaluations." *American Journal of Public Health* 84:1394–1401.

Etheridge, B. and S. L. Hicks. 1989. "An Evaluation of the North Carolina DARE Program." Department of Public Instruction, Raleigh, NC, Unpublished report.

Faine, J. R. and E. Bohlander. 1988. *Drug Abuse Resistance Education: An Assessment of the 1987–88 Kentucky State Police D.A.R.E. Program.* Bowling Green: Western Kentucky University, the Social Research Laboratory.

_. 1989. *D.A.R.E. in Kentucky Schools 1988–1989: An Evaluation of the Drug Abuse Resistance Education Program.* Bowling Green: Western Kentucky University, the Social Research Laboratory.

Fife, B. L. 1994. *An Assessment of the D.A.R.E. Program in Fort Wayne, Indiana.* Muncie, IN: Ball State University, Department of Political Science.

Flay, B. R. 1985. "Psychosocial Approaches to Smoking Prevention: A Review of Findings." *Health Psychology* 4:449–88.

Flay, B. R., J. R. D' Avernas, J. A. Best, M. W. Kersall, and K. B. Ryan. 1983. "Cigarette Smoking: Why Young People Do It and Ways of Preventing It." Pp. 132–83 in *Pediatric and Adolescent Behavioral Medicine*, edited by P. McGrath and P. Firestone. New York: Springer-Verlag.

Hansen, W. B. 1989. *Prevention Program Guide: A Manual for the Uniform Evaluation of School-Based Drug and Alcohol Prevention Programs.* Winston-Salem, NC: Bowman-Gray School of Medicine.

_. 1992. "School-Based Substance Abuse Prevention: A Review of the State of the Art in Curriculum, 1980–1990." *Health Education Research* 7:403–30.

Hansen, W. B. and R. B. McNeal. 1997. "How D.A.R.E. Works: An Examination of Program Effects on Mediating Variables." *Health Education & Behavior* 24:165–76.

Harmon, M. A. 1993. "Reducing the Risk of Drug Involvement among Early Adolescents: An Evaluation of Drug Abuse Resistance Education (DARE)." *Evaluation Review* 17:221–39.

Hedeker, D. and R. D. Gibbons. 1993. "A Random-Effects Ordinal Regression Model for Multilevel Analysis." *Biometrics* 50:933–44.

Hedeker, D., R. D. Gibbons, and J. M. Davis. 1991. "Random Regression Models for Multicenter

Clinical Trials Data." *Psychopharmacology Bulletin* 27:73–77.

Johnston, L. D., P. M. O'Malley, and J. G. Bachman. 1988. *Illicit Drug Use, Smoking, and Drinking by America's High School Students, College Students, and Young Adults.* DHHS Publication No. ADM89–1602. Washington, DC: Government Printing Office.

_. 1996. "Monitoring the Future Survey (Summary of Findings through 1995)." University of Michigan, Ann Arbor. Press release.

Kethineni, S., D. A. Leamy, and L. Guyon. 1991. "Evaluation of the Drug Abuse Resistance Education Program in Illinois: Preliminary Report." Illinois State University, Normal.

Law Enforcement News. 1996. "When It Comes to the Young, Anti-Drug Efforts Are Going to Pot." *Law Enforcement News* 22:441–47.

Lindstrom, P. 1996. "Partnership in Crime Prevention: Police-School Cooperation." Presented at the annual convention of the American Society of Criminology, November 20–23, Chicago.

Manos, M. J., K. Y. Kameoka, and J. H. Tanji. 1986. *Evaluation of Honolulu Police Department's Drug Abuse Resistance Education Program.* Manoa: University of Hawaii, School of Social Work, the Youth Development and Research Center.

McCormick, F. C. and E. R. McCormick. 1992. *An Evaluation of the Third Year Drug Abuse Resistance Education (D.A.R.E.) Program in St. Paul.* St. Paul, MN: Educational Concepts.

McDonald, R. M., D. B. Towberman, and J. L. Hague. 1990. *Volume II: 1989 Impact Assessment of Drug Abuse Resistance Education in the Commonwealth of Virginia.* Richmond: Virginia Commonwealth University, Institute for Research in Justice and Risk Administration.

McMahon, S., and R. J. Wuorenma. 1992. *D.A.R.E. Evaluation for September-January 1991/1992.* Bellevue, WA: Bellevue Police Department.

Moskowitz, J. M., G. A. Schaeffer, J. W. Condon, E. Schaps, and J. Malvin. 1981. *Psychometric Properties of the "Drug and Alcohol Survey."* Rockville, MD: National Institute of Drug Abuse.

Murray, D. M. and P. J. Hannan. 1990. "Planning for the Appropriate Analysis in School-Based Drug-Use Prevention Studies." *Journal of Consulting and Clinical Psychology* 58:458–68.

NBC Dateline. 1997. "Truth or D.A.R.E.?" Producer Debbie Schoolie, February 21, 1997.

Netburn, A. N. 1989. "Drug Abuse Resistance Program D.A.R.E." Department of Defense Dependents-A Evaluation Report, Washington, DC.

Nyre, G. F., C. Rose, and R. E. Bolus. 1990. *DARE Evaluation Report for 1985–1989.* Los Angeles; Evaluation and Training Institute.

Office of National Drug Control Policy. 1997. *The National Drug Control Strategy, 1997.* Washington, DC: Executive Office of the President. Document NCJ163915.

Ringwalt, C. R., T. R. Curtin, and D. P. Rosenbaum. 1990. *A First Year Evaluation of D.A.R.E. in Illinois.* Chicago: University of Illinois at Chicago, Center for Research in Law and Justice.

Ringwalt, C. R, S. T. Ennett, and K. D. Holt. 1991. "An Outcome Evaluation of Project D.A.R.E. (Drug Abuse Resistance Education)." *Health Education Research* 6:327–37.

Ringwalt, C. R., J. M. Greene, S. T. Salt, R. Iachan, and R. R. Clayton. 1994. *Past and Future Directions of the D.A.R.E. Program: An Evaluation Review.* Draft Final Report to the National Institute of Justice. Research Triangle Park, NC: Research Triangle Institute.

Rosenbaum, D. P., R. L. Flewelling, S. L. Bailey, C. L. Ringwalt, and D. L. Wilkinson. 1994. "Cops in the Classroom: A Longitudinal Evaluation of Drug Abuse Resistance Education (DARE)." *Journal of Research in Crime and Delinquency* 31:3–31.

Rosenberg, M. 1965. *Society and Adolescent Self-Image.* Princeton, NJ: Princeton University Press.

Silva, R. K. 1995. *Evaluation of Idaho's DARE "Drug Abuse Resistance Education Projects."* Meridian: Idaho State Department of Law Enforcement.

Silvia, E. S. and J. Thorne. 1997. *School-Based Drug Prevention Programs: A Longitudinal Study in Selected School Districts.* Research Triangle Park, NC: Research Triangle Institute. Prepared for U.S. Department of Education under contract LC9007001.

Sloboda, Z. and S. L. David. 1997. *Preventing Drug Use among Children and Adolescents: A Research-Based Guide.* Washington, DC: U.S. Department of Health and Human Services, National Institutes of Health, National Institute of Drug Abuse. NIH Publication No. 97–4212.

Tobler, N. 1986. "Meta-Analysis of 143 Adolescent Drug Prevention Programs: Quantitative Outcome Results of Program Participants Compared to a Control or Comparison Group." *Journal of Drug Issues* 16:537–67.

Walker, S. 1990. *The Victoria Police Department Drug Abuse Resistance Education Programme (D.A.R.E.) Programme Evaluation Report #2.* Victoria, British Columbia: Federal Government of Canada, the Ministry of the Solicitor-General.

Wiegand, B. 1991. *D.A.R.E.: School Year 1991 Evaluation Report.* Washington, DC: Department of Defense Dependents Schools-Pacific.

Winfree, L. T., Jr., F. Esbensen, and D. W. Osgood. 1996. "Evaluating a School-Based Gang-Prevention Program." *Evaluation Review* 20:181–203.

Wysong, F., R. Aniskiewicz, and R. Wright. 1994. "Truth in DARE." *Social Problems* 41:448–72.